PROPERTY OF:

MARY BORGEN

TORRANCE HALL
DULUTH
STATE
COLLEGE
DULUTH MINNESOTA

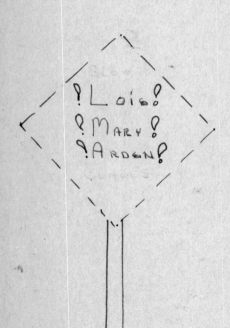

?LOIS?
?MARY?
?ARDEN?

A College Book of Prose

By

SELMA W. SCHNEIDER
Duluth Junior College

and

JOHN ALBERT SANFORD
University of Minnesota

GINN AND COMPANY

BOSTON · NEW YORK · CHICAGO

LONDON · ATLANTA · DALLAS · COLUMBUS · SAN FRANCISCO

The Athenæum Press

GINN AND COMPANY · PRO-
PRIETORS · BOSTON · U.S.A.

PREFACE

"WHENCE comes it, this universal big black Democracy? ... On this side of the Atlantic and on that, Democracy, we apprehend, is forever impossible! ... Alas, that there should be human beings requiring to have these things argued of, at this late time of day! I say, it is the everlasting privilege of the foolish to be governed by the wise; to be guided in the right path by those who know it better than they."

This is not a quotation from a speech by Adolf Hitler, but part of an essay written by Thomas Carlyle in 1850 and included in this volume. Caustic challenges were hurled at democracy long before our time. As the student of this book will soon discover, very few of today's problems are exclusively modern. Jonathan Swift's bitter denunciation of militarism in *Gulliver's Travels*, published in 1726, is an equally brilliant indictment of modern fascism. Francis Bacon's vision of an ideal world of science in *The New Atlantis* (1626) contains an accurate account of our complex civilization. Thomas Paine, the great champion of the American Revolution, was a far more skillful propagandist than his modern imitators.

To provide the student with a reasonable amount of historical perspective in approaching today's problems is the aim of this book. Its method is to permit the student to see in literature a record of the continuity of human experience. The basic ideas of the great prose writers of the past are reflected in the conclusions reached by the essayists of our own time. Assembled here are ideas and opinions from four and a half centuries on the problems which personally concern every student today: on dictatorships and democracies, on warfare and propaganda, on education and science, on art and literature, and on such purely personal problems, too, as friendship and marriage. The material is presented not with the purpose of showing any evolutionary process but rather with the purpose of enabling the student to connect the ideas of the present with the standards of the past. Such historical perspective not only provides a logical approach to today's problems; it should also encourage balance of judgment.

The contemporary selections have been chosen for their clarity and variety of style as well as for their content. We have striven to meet realistically the student's need for models in his own writing. Since many instructors alternate short theme assignments with papers requiring more sustained effort, long as well as short selections are reprinted, in order to provide examples of the structural organization demanded by these two types of composition. Particular attention has been given to the choice of autobiographies, biographies, and book reviews, since experience has shown that these are forms with which the student commonly needs help.

The editorial apparatus has been made, it is hoped, both helpful and unobtrusive. The brief biographical notes will aid the student in placing the selections in their proper historical perspective as well as in estimating the author's position in English literature. Whenever a selection has special historical interest, as, for example, Croker's notorious review of Keats's *Endymion*, an outline of the essential facts is given. These notes, together with suggested theme topics and study helps on the essays, are printed in a separate section at the close of the volume.

S. W. S.
J. A. S.

CONTENTS

Autobiography

Biography

College

Vocations and Professions

Government

CONTENTS

Propaganda

War

Art of Living

CONTENTS

Fine Arts

Science

Research Papers

Reviews

CONTENTS

Literature

Science

Research Papers

Review

BIOGRAPHICAL NOTES

STUDENT HELPS AND THEME SUGGESTIONS

INDEX

A
College Book of Prose

Autobiography

AUTOBIOGRAPHY[1]

Thomas Henry Huxley

And when I consider, in one view, the many things . . . which I have upon my hands, I feel the burlesque of being employed in this manner at my time of life. But, in another view, and taking in all circumstances, these things, as trifling as they may appear, no less than things of greater importance, seem to be put upon me to do.—Bishop Butler to the Duchess of Somerset

THE "many things" to which the Duchess's correspondent here refers are the repairs and improvements of the episcopal seat at Auckland. I doubt if the great apologist, greater in nothing than in the simple dignity of his character, would have considered the writing an account of himself as a thing which could be put upon him to do whatever circumstances might be taken in. But the good bishop lived in an age when a man might write books and yet be permitted to keep his private existence to himself; in the pre-Boswellian epoch, when the germ of the photographer lay concealed in the distant future, and the interviewer who pervades our age was an unforeseen, indeed unimaginable, birth of time.

At present, the most convinced believer in the aphorism *Bene qui latuit, bene vixit,* is not always able to act up to it. An importunate person informs him that his portrait is about to be published and will be accompanied by a biography which the importunate person proposes to write. The sufferer knows what that means; either he undertakes to revise the "biography" or he does not. In the former case, he makes himself responsible; in the latter, he allows the publication of a mass of more or less fulsome inaccuracies for which he will be held responsible by those who are familiar with the prevalent art of self-advertisement. On the whole, it may be better to get over the "burlesque of being employed in this manner" and do the thing himself.

It was by reflections of this kind that, some years ago, I was led to write and permit the publication of the subjoined sketch.

I was born about eight o'clock in the morning on the 4th of May, 1825, at Ealing, which was, at that time, as quiet a little country village as could be found within a half-a-dozen miles of Hyde Park Corner. Now it is a suburb of London, with, I believe, 30,000 inhabitants. My father was one of the masters in a large semi-public school which at one time had a high reputation. I am not aware that any portents preceded my arrival in this world, but, in my childhood, I remember hearing a traditional account of the manner in which I lost the chance of an endowment of great practical value. The win-

[1]Written in 1889.

dows of my mother's room were open, in consequence of the unusual warmth of the weather. For the same reason, probably, a neighbouring beehive had swarmed, and the new colony, pitching on the window-sill, was making its way into the room when the horrified nurse shut down the sash. If that well-meaning woman had only abstained from her ill-timed interference, the swarm might have settled on my lips, and I should have been endowed with that mellifluous eloquence which, in this country, leads far more surely than worth, capacity, or honest work, to the highest places in Church and State. But the opportunity was lost, and I have been obliged to content myself through life with saying what I mean in the plainest of plain language, than which, I suppose, there is no habit more ruinous to a man's prospects of advancement.

Why I was christened Thomas Henry I do not know; but it is a curious chance that my parents should have fixed for my usual denomination upon the name of that particular Apostle with whom I have always felt most sympathy. Physically and mentally I am the son of my mother so completely—even down to peculiar movements of the hands, which made their appearance in me as I reached the age she had when I noticed them—that I can hardly find any trace of my father in myself, except an inborn faculty for drawing, which unfortunately, in my case, has never been cultivated, a hot temper, and that amount of tenacity of purpose which unfriendly observers sometimes call obstinacy.

My mother was a slender brunette, of an emotional and energetic temperament, and possessed of the most piercing black eyes I ever saw in a woman's head. With no more education than other women of the middle classes in her day, she had an excellent mental capacity. Her most distinguishing characteristic, however, was rapidity of thought. If one ventured to suggest she had not taken much time to arrive at any conclusion, she would say, "I cannot help it, things flash across me." That peculiarity has been passed on to me in full strength; it has often stood me in good stead; it has sometimes played me sad tricks, and it has always been a danger. But, after all, if my time were to come over again, there is nothing I would less willingly part with than my inheritance of mother wit.

I have next to nothing to say about my childhood. In later years my mother, looking at me almost reproachfully, would sometimes say, "Ah! you were such a pretty boy!" whence I had no difficulty in concluding that I had not fulfilled my early promise in the matter of looks. In fact, I have a distinct recollection of certain curls of which I was vain, and of a conviction that I closely resembled that handsome, courtly gentleman, Sir Herbert Oakley, who was vicar of our parish, and who was as a god to us country folk, because he was occasionally visited by the then Prince George of Cambridge. I remember turning my pinafore wrong side forwards in order to represent a surplice, and preaching to my mother's maids in the kitchen as nearly as possible in Sir Herbert's manner one Sunday morning when the rest of the family were at church. That is the earliest indication I can call to mind of the strong clerical affinities which my friend Mr. Herbert Spencer has always ascribed to me, though I fancy they have for the most part remained in a latent state.

My regular school training was of the briefest, perhaps fortunately, for though my way of life has made me acquainted with all sorts and conditions of men, from the highest to the lowest, I deliberately affirm that the society I fell into at school was the worst I have ever known. We boys were average lads, with much the same inherent capacity for good and evil as any others; but the people who were set over us cared about as much for our intellectual and moral welfare as if they were baby-farmers. We were left to the operation of the struggle for existence among ourselves, and bullying was the least of the ill practices current among us. Almost the only cheerful reminiscence in connection with the place which arises in my mind is that of a battle I had with one of my classmates, who had bullied me until I could stand it no longer. I was a very slight lad, but there was a wild-cat element in me which, when roused, made up for lack of weight, and I licked my adversary effectually. However, one of my first experiences of the extremely rough-and-ready nature of justice, as exhibited by the course of things in general, arose out of the fact that I—the victor—had a black eye, while he—the vanquished—had none, so that I got into disgrace and he did not. We made it up, and thereafter I was unmolested. One of the greatest shocks I ever received in my life was to be told a dozen years afterwards by the groom who brought me my horse in a stable-yard in Sydney that he was my quondam antagonist. He had a long story of family misfortune to account for his position, but at that time it was necessary to deal very cautiously with mysterious strangers in New South Wales, and on inquiry I found that the unfortunate young man had not only been "sent out," but had undergone more than one colonial conviction.

As I grew older, my great desire was to be a mechanical engineer, but the fates were against this and, while very young, I commenced the study of medicine under a medical brother-in-law. But, though the Institute of Mechanical Engineers would certainly not own me, I am not sure that I have not all along been a sort of mechanical engineer *in partibus infidelium*. I am now occasionally horrified to think how very little I ever knew or cared about medicine as the art of healing. The only part of my professional course which really and deeply interested me was physiology, which is the mechanical engineering of living machines; and, notwithstanding that natural science has been my proper business, I am afraid there is very little of the genuine naturalist in me.

I never collected anything, and species work was always a burden to me; what I cared for was the architectural and engineering part of the business, the working out of the wonderful unity of plan in the thousands and thousands of diverse living constructions, and the modifications of similar apparatuses to serve diverse ends. The extraordinary attraction I felt towards the study of the intricacies of living structure nearly proved fatal to me at the outset. I was a mere boy—I think between thirteen and fourteen years of age—when I was taken by some older student friends of mine to the first *post-mortem* examination I ever attended. All my life I have been most unfortunately sensitive to the disagreeables which attend anatomical pursuits, but on this occasion my curiosity overpowered all other feelings, and I spent two or three hours in gratifying it. I did not cut myself, and none of the ordinary symptoms of dissection-poison supervened, but poisoned I was somehow, and I remember sinking into a strange state of apathy. By way of a last chance, I was sent to the care of some good, kind people, friends of my father's, who lived in a farmhouse in the heart of Warwickshire. I remember staggering from my bed to the window on the bright spring morning after my arrival, and throwing open the casement. Life seemed to come back on the wings of the breeze, and to this day the faint odor of wood-smoke, like that which floated across the farm-yard in the early morning, is as good to me as the "sweet south upon a bed of violets." I soon recovered, but for years I suffered from occasional paroxysms of internal pain, and from that time my constant friend, hypochondriacal dyspepsia, commenced his half century of co-tenancy of my fleshly tabernacle.

Looking back on my *Lehrjahre*, I am sorry to say that I do not think that any account of my doings as a student would tend to edification. In fact, I should distinctly warn ingenuous youth to avoid imitating my example. I worked extremely hard when it pleased me, and when it did not—which was a very frequent case—I was extremely idle (unless making caricatures of one's pastors and masters is to be called a branch of industry), or else wasted my energies in wrong directions. I read everything I could lay hands upon, including novels, and took up all sorts of pursuits to drop them again quite as speedily. No doubt it was very largely my own fault, but the only instruction from which I ever obtained the proper effect of education was that which I received from Mr. Wharton Jones, who was the lecturer on physiology at the Charing Cross School of Medicine. The extent and precision of his knowledge impressed me greatly, and the severe exactness of his method of lecturing was quite to my taste. I do not know that I have ever felt so much respect for anybody as a teacher before or since. I worked hard to obtain his approbation, and he was extremely kind and helpful to the youngster who, I am afraid, took up more of his time than he had any right to do. It was he who suggested the publication of my first scientific paper—a very little one—in the *Medical Gazette* of 1845, and most kindly corrected the literary faults which abounded in it, short as it was; for at that time, and for many years afterwards, I detested the trouble of writing, and would take no pains over it.

It was in the early spring of 1846, that, having finished my obligatory medical studies and passed the first M.D. examination at the London University,—though I was still too young to qualify at the College of Surgeons—I was talking to a fellow-student (the present eminent physician, Sir Joseph Fayrer), and wondering what I should do to meet the imperative necessity for earning my own bread, when my friend suggested that I should write to Sir William Burnett, at that time Director-General for the Medical Service of the Navy, for an appointment. I thought this rather a strong thing to do, as Sir William was personally unknown to me, but my cheery friend would not listen to my scruples, so I went to my lodgings and wrote the best letter I could devise. A few days afterwards I received the usual official circular acknowledgment, but at the bottom there was written an instruction to call at Somerset House on such a day. I thought that looked like business, so at the appointed time I called and sent in my card, while I waited in Sir William's ante-room. He was a tall, shrewd-looking old gentleman, with a broad Scotch accent—and I think I see him now as he entered with my card in his hand. The first thing he did was to return it, with the frugal reminder that I should probably find it useful on some other occasion. The second was to ask whether I was an Irishman. I suppose the air of modesty about my appeal must have struck him. I satisfied the Director-General that I was English to the backbone, and he made some inquiries as to my student career, finally desiring me to hold myself ready for examination. Having passed this, I was in Her Majesty's Service, and entered on the books of Nelson's old ship, the *Victory*, for duty at Haslar Hospital, about a couple of months after I made my application.

My official chief at Haslar was a very remarkable person, the late Sir John Richardson, an excellent naturalist, and far-famed as an indomitable Arctic traveller. He was a silent, reserved man, outside the circle of his family and intimates; and, having a full share of youthful vanity, I was extremely disgusted to find that "Old John," as we irreverent youngsters called him, took not the slightest notice of my worshipful self either the first time I attended him, as it was my duty to do, or for some weeks afterwards. I am afraid to think of the lengths to which my tongue may have run on the subject of the churlishness of the chief, who was, in truth, one of the kindest-hearted and most considerate of men. But one day, as I was crossing the hospital square, Sir John stopped me, and heaped coals of fire on my head by telling me that he had tried to get me one of the resident appointments, much coveted by the assistant surgeons, but that the Admiralty had put in another man. "However," said he, "I mean to keep you here till I can get you something you will like," and turned upon his heel without waiting for the thanks I stammered out. That explained how it was I had not been packed off to the West Coast of Africa like some of my juniors, and why, eventually, I remained altogether seven months at Haslar.

After a long interval, during which "Old John" ignored my existence almost as completely as before, he stopped me again as we met in a casual way, and describing the service on which the *Rattlesnake* was likely to be employed, said that Captain Owen Stanley, who was to command the ship, had asked him to recommend an assistant surgeon who knew something of science; would I like that? Of course I jumped at the offer. "Very well, I give you leave; go to London at once and see Captain Stanley." I went, saw my future commander, who was very civil to me, and promised to ask that I should be appointed to his ship, as in due time I was. It is a singular thing that, during the few months of my stay at Haslar, I had among my messmates two future Directors-General of the Medical Service of the Navy (Sir Alexander Armstrong and Sir John Watt-Reid), with the present President of the College of Physicians and my kindest of doctors, Sir Andrew Clark.

Life on board Her Majesty's ship in those days was a very different affair from what it is now, and ours was exceptionally rough, as we were often many months without receiving letters or seeing any civilised people but ourselves. In exchange, we had the interest of being about the last voyagers, I suppose, to whom it could be possible to meet with people who knew nothing of fire-arms—as we did on the south coast of new Guinea—and of making acquaintance with a variety of interesting savage and semi-civilised people. But, apart from experience of this kind and the opportunities offered for scientific work, to me, personally, the cruise was extremely valuable. It was good for me to live under sharp discipline; to be down on the realities of existence by living on bare necessaries; to find out how extremely well worth living life seemed to be when one woke up from a night's rest on a soft plank, with the sky for canopy and cocoa and weevilly biscuit the sole prospect for breakfast; and, more especially, to learn to work for the sake of what I got for myself out of it, even if it all went to the bottom and I along with it. My brother officers were as good fellows as sailors ought to be and generally are, but, naturally, they neither knew nor cared anything about my pursuits, nor understood why I should be so zealous in pursuit of the objects which my friends, the middies, christened "Buffons," after the title conspicuous on a volume of the *Suites à Buffon*, which stood on my shelf in the chart room.

During the four years of our absence, I sent home communication after communication to the "Linnean Society," with the same result as that obtained by Noah when he sent the raven out of his ark. Tired at last of hearing nothing about them, I determined to do or die, and in 1849 I drew up a more elaborate paper and forwarded it to the Royal Society. This was my dove, if I had only known it. But owing to the movements of the ship, I heard nothing of that either until my return to England in the latter end of the year 1850, when I found that it was printed and published, and that a huge packet of separate copies awaited me. When I hear some of my young friends complain of want of sympathy and encouragement, I am inclined to think that my naval life was not the least valuable part of my education.

Three years after my return were occupied by a battle between my scientific friends on the one hand and the Admiralty on the other, as to whether the latter ought, or ought not, to act up to the spirit of a pledge they had given to encourage officers who had done scientific work by contributing to the expense of publishing mine. At last the Admiralty, getting tired, I suppose, cut short the discussion by ordering me to join a ship, which thing I declined to do, and as Rastignac, in the *Père Goriot* says to Paris, I said to London "*à nous deux.*" I desired to obtain a Professorship of either Physiology or Comparative Anatomy, and as vacancies occurred I applied, but in vain. My friend, Professor Tyndall, and I were candidates at the same time, he for the Chair of Physics and I for that of Natural History in the University of Toronto, which, fortunately, as it turned out, would not look at either of us. I say fortunately, not from any lack of respect for Toronto, but because I soon made up my mind that London was the place for me, and hence I have steadily declined the inducements to leave it, which have at various times been offered. At last, in 1854, on the translation of my warm friend Edward Forbes, to Edinburgh, Sir Henry de la Beche, the Director-General of the Geological Survey, offered me the post Forbes vacated of Paleontologist and Lecturer on Natural History. I refused the former point blank, and accepted the latter only provisionally, telling Sir Henry that I did not care for fossils, and that I should give up Natural History as soon as I could get a physiological post. But I held the office for thirty-one years, and a large part of my work has been paleontological.

At that time I disliked public speaking, and had a firm conviction that I should break down every time I opened my mouth. I believe I had every fault a speaker could have (except talking at random or indulging in rhetoric), when I spoke to the first important audience I ever addressed, on a Friday evening at the Royal Institution, in 1852. Yet, I must confess to having been guilty, *malgré moi*, of as much public speaking as most of my contemporaries, and for the last ten years it ceased to be so much of a bugbear to me. I used to pity myself for having to go through this training, but I am now more disposed to compassionate the unfortunate audiences, especially my ever friendly hearers at the Royal Institution, who were the subjects of my oratorical experiments.

The last thing that it would be proper for me to do would be to speak of the work of my life, or to say at the end of the day whether I think I have earned my wages or not. Men are said to be partial judges of themselves. Young men may be, I doubt if old men are. Life seems terribly foreshortened as they look back and the mountain they set themselves to climb in youth turns out to be a mere spur of immeasurably higher ranges when, by failing breath, they reach the top. But if I may speak of the objects I have had more or less definitely in view since I began the ascent of my hillock, they are briefly these: To promote the increase of natural knowledge and to forward the application of scientific methods of investigation to all the problems of life to the best of my ability, in the conviction which has grown with my growth and strengthened with my strength, that there is no alleviation for the sufferings of mankind except veracity of thought and of action, and the resolute facing of the world as it is when the garment of make-believe by which pious hands have hidden its uglier features is stripped off.

It is with this intent that I have subordinated any reasonable, or unreasonable, ambition for scientific fame which I may have permitted myself to entertain to other ends; to the popularization of science; to the development and organisation of scientific education; to the endless series of battles and skirmishes over evolution; and to untiring opposition to that ecclesiastical spirit, that clericalism, which in England, as everywhere else, and to whatever denomination it may belong, is the deadly enemy of science.

In striving for the attainment of these objects, I have been but one among many, and I shall be well content to be remembered, or even not remembered, as such. Circumstances, among which I am proud to reckon the devoted kindness of many friends, have led to my occupation of various prominent positions, among which the Presidency of the Royal Society is the highest. It would be mock modesty on my part, with these and other scientific honours which have been bestowed upon me, to pretend that I have not succeeded in the career which I have followed, rather because I was driven into it than of my own free will; but I am afraid I should not count even these things as marks of success if I could not hope that I had somewhat helped that movement of opinion which has been called the New Reformation.

EARLY DAYS[1]

Mark Twain

MY PARENTS removed to Missouri in the early 'thirties; I do not remember just when, for I was not born then and cared nothing for such things. It was a long journey in those days, and must have been a rough and tiresome one. The home was made in the wee village of Florida, in Monroe County, and I was born there in 1835. The village contained a hundred people and I increased the population by 1 per cent. It is more than many of the best men in history could have done for a town. It may not be modest in me to refer to this, but it is true. There is no record of a person doing as much—not even Shakespeare. But I did it for Florida, and it shows that I could have done it for any place—even London, I suppose.

Recently some one in Missouri has sent me a picture of the house I was born in. Heretofore I have always stated that it was a palace, but I shall be more guarded now.

I used to remember my brother Henry walking into a fire outdoors when he was a week old. It was remarkable in me to remember a thing like that, and it was still more remarkable that I should cling to the delusion, for thirty years, that I *did* remember it—for of course it never happened; he would not have been able to walk at that age. If I had stopped to reflect, I should not have burdened my memory with that impossible rubbish so long. It is believed by many people that an impression deposited in a child's memory within the first two years of its life cannot remain there five years, but that is an error. The incident of Benvenuto Cellini and the salamander must be accepted as authentic and trustworthy; and then that remarkable and indisputable instance in the experience of Helen Keller— However, I will speak of that at another time. For many years I believed that I remembered helping my grandfather drink his whisky toddy when I was six weeks old, but I do not tell about that any more, now; I am grown old and my memory is not as active as it used to be. When I was younger I could remember anything, whether it had happened or not; but my faculties are decaying now, and soon I shall be so I cannot remember any but the things that never happened. It is sad to go to pieces like this, but we all have to do it.

My uncle, John A. Quarles, was a farmer, and his place was in the country four miles from Florida. He had eight children and fifteen or twenty negroes, and was also fortunate in other ways, particularly in his character. I have not come across a better man than he was. I was his guest for two or three months

[1]From *Mark Twain's Autobiography* by Samuel Langhorne Clemens. Published in 1924, fourteen years after the death of Mark Twain. Harper & Brothers, publishers.

every year, from the fourth year after we removed to Hannibal till I was eleven or twelve years old. I have never consciously used him or his wife in a book, but his farm has come very handy to me in literature once or twice. In *Huck Finn* and in *Tom Sawyer, Detective* I moved it down to Arkansas. It was all of six hundred miles, but it was no trouble; it was not a very large farm—five hundred acres, perhaps—but I could have done it if it had been twice as large. And as for the morality of it, I cared nothing for that; I would move a state if the exigencies of literature required it.

It was a heavenly place for a boy, that farm of my uncle John's. The house was a double log one, with a spacious floor (roofed in) connecting it with the kitchen. In the summer the table was set in the middle of that shady and breezy floor, and the sumptuous meals—well, it makes me cry to think of them. Fried chicken, roast pig; wild and tame turkeys, ducks, and geese, venison just killed; squirrels, rabbits, pheasants, partridges, prairie-chickens; biscuits, hot batter cakes, hot buckwheat cakes, hot "wheat bread," hot rolls, hot corn pone; fresh corn boiled on the ear, succotash, butter-beans, stringbeans, tomatoes, peas, Irish potatoes, sweet potatoes; buttermilk, sweet milk, "clabber"; watermelons, muskmelons, cantaloupes—all fresh from the garden; apple pie, peach pie, pumpkin pie, apple dumplings, peach cobbler—I can't remember the rest. The way that the things were cooked was perhaps the main splendor—particularly a certain few of the dishes. For instance, the corn bread, the hot biscuits and wheat bread, and the fried chicken. These things have never been properly cooked in the North—in fact, no one there is able to learn the art, so far as my experience goes. The North thinks it knows how to make corn bread, but this is mere superstition. Perhaps no bread in the world is quite so good as Southern corn bread, and perhaps no bread in the world is quite so bad as the Northern imitation of it. The North seldom tries to fry chicken, and this is well; the art cannot be learned north of the line of Mason and Dixon, nor anywhere in Europe. This is not hearsay; it is experience that is speaking. In Europe it is imagined that the custom of serving various kinds of bread blazing hot is "American," but that is too broad a spread; it is custom in the South, but is much less than that in the North. In the North and in Europe hot bread is considered unhealthy. This is probably another fussy superstition, like the European superstition that ice-water is unhealthy. Europe does not need ice-water and does not drink it; and yet, notwithstanding this, its word for it is better than ours, because it describes it, whereas ours doesn't. Europe calls it "iced" water. Our word describes water made from melted ice—a drink which has a characterless taste and which we have but little acquaintance with.

It seems a pity that the world should throw away so many good things merely because they are unwholesome. I doubt if God has given us any refreshment which, taken in moderation, is unwholesome, except microbes. Yet there are people who strictly deprive themselves of each and every eatable, drinkable, and smokable which has in any way acquired a shady reputation. They pay this price for health. And health is all they get for it. How strange it is! It is like paying out your whole fortune for a cow that has gone dry.

The farmhouse stood in the middle of a very large yard, and the yard was fenced on three sides with rails and on the rear side with high palings; against these stood the smoke-house; beyond the palings was the orchard; beyond the orchard were the negro quarters and the tobacco fields. The front yard was entered over a stile made of sawed-off logs of graduated heights; I do not remember any gate. In a corner of the front yard were a dozen lofty hickory trees and a dozen black walnuts, and in the nutting season riches were to be gathered there.

Down a piece, abreast the house, stood a little log cabin against the rail fence; and there the woody hill fell sharply away, past the barns, the corn-crib, the stables, and the tobacco-curing house, to a limpid brook which sang along over its gravelly bed and curved and frisked in and out and here and there and yonder in the deep shade of overhanging foliage and vines—a divine place for wading, and it had swimming pools, too, which were forbidden to us and therefore much frequented by us. For we were little Christian children and had early been taught the value of forbidden fruit.

In the little log cabin lived a bedridden whiteheaded slave woman whom we visited daily and looked upon with awe, for we believed she was upward of a thousand years old and had talked with Moses. The younger negroes credited these statistics and had furnished them to us in good faith. We accommodated all the details which came to us about her; and so we believed that she had lost her health in the long desert trip coming out of Egypt, and had never been able to get it back again. She had a round bald place on the crown of her head, and we used to creep around and gaze at it in reverent silence, and reflect that it was caused by fright through seeing Pharaoh drowned. We called her "Aunt" Hannah, Southern fashion. She was superstitious, like the other negroes; also, like them, she was deeply religious. Like them, she had great faith in prayer and employed it in all ordinary exigencies, but not in cases where a dead certainty of result was urgent. Whenever witches were around she tied up the remnant of her wool in little tufts, with white thread, and this promptly made the witches impotent.

All the negroes were friends of ours, and with those of our own age we were in effect comrades. I say in effect, using the phrase as a modification. We were comrades, and yet not comrades; color and condition interposed a subtle line which both parties were conscious of and which rendered complete fusion impossible. We had a faithful and affectionate good friend, ally, and adviser in "Uncle Dan'l," a middle-aged slave whose head was the best one in the negro quarter, whose sympathies were wide and warm, and whose heart was honest and simple and knew no guile. He has served me well these many, many years. I have not seen him for more than half a century, and yet spiritually I have had his welcome company a good part of that time, and have staged him in books under his own name and as "Jim," and carted him all around—to Hannibal, down the Mississippi on a raft, and even across the Desert of Sahara in a balloon—and he has endured it all with the patience and friendliness and loyalty which were his birthright. It was on the farm that I got my strong liking for his race and my appreciation of certain of its fine qualities. This feeling and this estimate have stood the test of sixty years and more, and have suffered no impairment. The black face is as welcome to me now as it was then.

In my schoolboy days I had no aversion to slavery. I was not aware that there was anything wrong about it. No one arraigned it in my hearing; the local papers said nothing against it; the local pulpit taught us that God approved it; that it was a holy thing, and that the doubter need only look in the Bible if he wished to settle his mind—and then the texts were read aloud to us to make the matter sure; if the slaves themselves had an aversion to slavery, they were wise and said nothing. In Hannibal we seldom saw a slave misused; on the farm, never.

There was, however, one small incident of my boyhood days which touched this matter, and it must have meant a good deal to me or it would not have stayed in my memory, clear and sharp, vivid and shadowless, all these slow-drifting years. We had a little slave boy whom we had hired from some one, there in Hannibal. He was from the eastern shore of Maryland, and had been brought away from his family and his friends, halfway across the American continent, and sold. He was a cheery spirit, innocent and gentle, and the noisiest creature that ever was, perhaps. All day long he was singing, whistling, yelling, whooping, laughing—it was maddening, devastating, unendurable. At last, one day, I lost all my temper, and went raging to my mother and said Sandy had been singing for an hour without a single break, and I couldn't stand it, and *wouldn't* she please shut him up. The tears came into her eyes and her lip trembled, and she said something like this:

"Poor thing, when he sings it shows that he is not remembering, and that comforts me; but when he is still I am afraid he is thinking, and I cannot bear it. He will never see his mother again; if he can sing, I must not hinder it, but be thankful for it. If you were older, you would understand me; then that friendless child's noise would make you glad."

It was a simple speech and made up of small words, but it went home, and Sandy's noise was not a trouble to me any more. She never used large words, but she had a natural gift for making small ones do effective work. She lived to reach the neighborhood of ninety years and was capable with her tongue to the last—especially when a meanness or an injustice roused her spirit. She has come handy to me several times in my books, where she figures as Tom Sawyer's Aunt Polly. I fitted her out with a dialect and tried to think up other improvements for her, but did not find any. I used Sandy once, also; it was in *Tom Sawyer*. I tried to get him to whitewash the fence, but it did not work. I do not remember what name I called him by in the book.

I can see the farm yet, with perfect clearness. I can see all its belongings, all its details; the family room of the house, with a "trundle" bed in one corner and a spinning-wheel in another—a wheel whose rising and falling wail, heard from a distance, was the mournfulest of all sounds to me, and made me home-sick and low spirited, and filled my atmosphere with the wandering spirits of the dead; the vast fireplace, piled high, on winter nights, with flaming hickory logs from whose ends a sugary sap bubbled out, but did not go to waste, for we scraped it off and ate it; the lazy cat spread out on the rough hearthstones; the drowsy dogs braced against the jambs and blinking; my aunt in one chimney corner, knitting; my uncle in the other, smoking his corn-cob pipe; the slick and carpetless oak floor faintly mirroring the dancing flame tongues and freckled with black indentations where fire coals had popped out and died a leisurely death; half a dozen children romping in the background twilight; "split"-bottomed chairs here and there, some with rockers; a cradle—out of service, but waiting, with confidence; in the early cold mornings a snuggle of children, in shirts and chemises, occupying the hearthstone and procrastinat-ing—they could not bear to leave that comfortable place and go out on the windswept floor space between the house and kitchen where the general tin basin stood, and wash.

Along outside of the front fence ran the country road, dusty in the summer-time, and a good place for snakes—they liked to lie in it and sun themselves; when they were rattlesnakes or puff adders, we killed them; when they were black snakes, or racers, or belonged to the fabled "hoop" breed, we fled, without shame; when they were "house snakes," or "garters," we carried them home and put them in Aunt Patsy's work basket for a surprise; for she was prejudiced against snakes, and always when she took the basket in her lap and they began to climb out of it it disordered her mind. She never could seem to get used to them; her opportunities went for nothing. And she was always cold toward bats, too, and could not bear them; and yet I think a bat is as friendly a bird as there is. My mother was Aunt Patsy's sister and had the same wild superstitions. A bat is beautifully soft and silky; I do not know any creature that is pleasanter to the touch or is more grateful for caressings, if offered in the right spirit. I know all about these coleoptera, because our great cave, three miles below Hannibal, was multitudinously stocked with them, and often I brought them home to amuse my mother with. It was easy to manage if it was a school day, because then I had ostensibly been to school and hadn't any bats. She was not a suspicious person, but full of trust and confidence; and when I said, "There's something in my coat pocket for you," she would put her hand in. But she always took it out again, herself; I didn't have to tell her. It was remarkable, the way she couldn't learn to like private bats. The more experience she had, the more she could not change her views.

Down the forest slopes to the left were the swings. They were made of bark stripped from hickory saplings. When they became dry they were dangerous. They usually broke when a child was forty feet in the air, and this was why so many bones had to be mended every year. I had no ill luck myself, but none of my cousins escaped. There were eight of them, and at one time and another they broke fourteen arms among them. But it cost next to nothing, for the doctor worked by the year—twenty-five dollars for the whole family. I remember two of the Florida doctors, Chowning and Meredith. They not only tended an entire family for twenty-five dollars a year, but furnished the medicines themselves. Good measure, too. Only the largest persons could hold a whole dose. Castor oil was the principal beverage. The dose was half a dipperful, with half a dipperful of New Orleans molasses added to help it down and make it taste good, which it never did. The next standby was calomel; the next, rhubarb; and the next, jalap. Then they bled the patient, and put mustard plasters on him. It was a dreadful system, and yet the death rate was not heavy. The calomel was nearly sure to salivate the patient and cost him some of his teeth. There were no dentists. When teeth became touched with decay or were otherwise ailing, the doctor knew of but one thing to do—he fetched his tongs and dragged them out. If the jaw remained, it was not his fault. Doctors were not called in cases of ordinary illness; the family grandmother attended to those. Every old woman was a doctor, and gathered her own medicines in the woods, and knew how to compound doses that would stir the vitals of a cast-iron dog. And then there was the "Indian doctor"; a grave savage, remnant of his tribe, deeply read in the mysteries of nature and the secret properties of herbs; and most backwoodsmen had high faith in his powers and could tell of wonderful cures achieved by him. In Mauritius, away off yonder in the solitudes of the Indian Ocean, there is a person who answers to our Indian doctor of the old times. He is a negro, and has had no teaching as a doctor, yet there is one disease which he is master of and can cure and the doctors can't. They send for him when they have a case. It is a child's disease of a strange and deadly sort, and the negro cures it with a herb medicine which he makes, himself, from a prescription which has come down to him from his father and grandfather. He will not let anyone see it. He keeps the secret of its components to himself, and it is feared that he will die without divulging it; then there will be consternation in Mauritius. I was told these things by the people there, in 1896.

We had the "faith doctor," too, in those early days—a woman. Her specialty was toothache. She was a farmer's old wife and lived five miles from Hannibal. She would lay her hand on the patient's jaw and say, "Believe!" and the cure was prompt. Mrs. Utterback. I remember her very well. Twice I rode out there behind my mother, horseback, and saw the cure performed. My mother was the patient.

Doctor Meredith removed to Hannibal, by and by, and was our family physician there, and saved my life several times. Still, he was a good man and meant well. Let it go.

I was always told that I was a sickly and precarious and tiresome and uncertain child, and lived mainly on allopathic medicines during the first seven years of my life. I asked my mother about this, in her old age—she was in her eighty-eighth year—and said:

"I suppose that during all that time you were uneasy about me?"

"Yes, the whole time."

"Afraid I wouldn't live?"

After a reflective pause—ostensibly to think out the facts—"No—afraid you would."

THESE CRUDE YOUNG MEN[1]

Bliss Perry

HALF the advantage of going to college lies in going away to college. Your mother packs your trunk, your father gives you his blessing and some money, and you are off, like the hero of a picaresque novel, to make your own way in the world. To my sister Grace, who left for Wellesley just as I was entering Williams, college was a romantic adventure. "Pioneers, O Pioneers!"

For me it meant loading a little furniture into the lumber wagon and driving across the field where the Thompson Laboratories now stand to the

[1]From *And Gladly Teach*, by Bliss Perry. Houghton Mifflin Company, publishers, 1935.

south entry of West College, on whose fourth floor I was to room for the next four years, taking my meals at home. It was the only sensible thing to do, for an old law of Williams allowed free tuition to the sons of professors. Father, with five boys to educate, and Professor Safford, with four, were the most obvious beneficiaries of this ancient statute. I admired Father's pioneering energy in seeking out Mark Hopkins's college for himself, instead of following his own father's example and going to Harvard. I still like to meet men who tell me that they went to Amherst because Garman taught there, or to Bowdoin for Hyde, or to Yale for "Billy" Sumner, or Stanford for David Starr Jordan. It makes education seem real. In my student days in Germany, men were constantly migrating from one university to another in order to get the benefit of some particular course offered that year by a famous scholar. For men mature enough to know what they want, all this is admirable; but it is fairly certain that not one out of ten American freshmen knows what he wants or where he can find it.

So all the Perry and Safford boys, aware that the paternal salary never exceeded twenty-five hundred dollars, went cheerfully to Williams; and there was one period of fourteen years when either a Safford or a Perry, or both, ornamented the college nine. But we could scarcely feel that romantic glamour about Williams which many of our classmates experienced. We had been born and bred in that briar bush. Still, we thought it as good as any other, and indeed it was, for most of us; though we were informed occasionally that a gifted and ambitious boy might be better off at Harvard, where the youthful President Eliot was introducing some very radical ideas. . . .

The studies of our freshman year . . . were the immemorial Latin, Greek, and mathematics. The fifty or more boys in our class recited in each of these subjects every day. There were no sections; good, bad, and indifferent students had precisely the same assignments and were called up in turn. We were doing, literally, what our fathers had done before us. My first Latin lesson, in the preface to Livy, was, as I discovered later in Father's diary, exactly the same assignment which he had had in 1848; and it was also precisely what my son had at Williams as a freshman in 1916. For sixty-eight years at least, and probably much longer, it was the same squirrel in the same cage! One would think that some Professor of Latin, at some time, in an access of emotional insanity might have altered the assignment, even if he kept the dreadful secret to himself.

The theory was, of course, that what freshmen needed was grammatical drill, and that certain Latin and Greek texts were convenient, not to say hallowed implements for this purpose. The irony of the situation was that some of us actually liked Latin and Greek, loved to turn those splendid periods into the best English which we could command, and were ready to be interested in whatever the Greeks and Romans had to say. But we fared less well in the classroom than some boy with an accurate verbal memory for the list of rules and exceptions as set down in the grammars of Goodwin and Allen and Greenough. I had been captivated in school by the poetry of Virgil. That meant to me the six books of the *Aeneid* that were then required, but I cannot recall that any teacher informed me that Virgil had ever written anything but those six books. What Virgil's real place was in Roman literature and in world literature was never mentioned. I liked to read Horace, and a knowledge of the scansion certainly increased my sense of his cleverness, but in the college classroom his wit and wisdom seemed to evaporate, and there was only the grammar and scansion left. The extracts which we read from Thucydides and Herodotus were interesting, but we were warned never to use "ponies," and no one hinted to us that we would do well to read in an English translation the entire work of these or any other Greek authors. Professor Fernald was an admirable drillmaster in the rudiments of the Greek language, but his conscientious interpretation of his duty as a teacher left him no time to initiate us into the wonders of Greek literature—even in an English dress.

I obeyed strictly that rule forbidding the use of translations. When we came to read Cicero's *Letters*—for which no "pony" was available—many of my friends were in sore trouble. I have lived long enough to hear Cicero described today as a "stuffed shirt," but I found his *Letters* amusing and eloquent, and I wish that as an undergraduate I could have had Gaston Boissier's *Cicéron et ses Amis*, which I remember reading with my children one winter in Rome. But I had four classmates who could not read a sentence of the *Letters* without a translation, though they knew their Latin grammar well enough. We were then reciting to Professor E. H. Griffin at five in the afternoon. I used to come up from baseball practice about four, and having then a knack for fluent though somewhat inaccurate reading of Latin at sight, I would translate Cicero's *Letters* to my four grammatical classmates. I do not doubt that my Latinity was much like David Garrick's. "He has not Latin enough," declared Samuel Johnson, who had once taught "Davy." "He finds out the Latin by the meaning rather than the meaning by the Latin." At any rate, that was what Professor Griffin evidently thought of me, for at the end of the term all of my four friends received a better grade in Latin than I did....

Enough, however, of Greek and Latin! Our third subject was mathematics, in which we were instructed, in a gloomy basement room of the old gymnasium, by Professor Dodd. "In his younger days," as I have written elsewhere, "he had been a Latinist, until the loss, by fire, of his manuscript Latin grammar disheartened him, and he accepted a chair of elementary mathematics, which he kept till his death. He fulfilled his duties as instructor with perfect gravity and fidelity, but cared wholly for other things: for his collections of Phaedrus and black-letter Chaucers; for Scott's novels, which he used to read through once each year; for the elder dramatists; for Montaigne and Lamb. Weather permitting, he drove from twenty to forty miles a day in his rusty, mud-covered buggy; he knew every wild flower, every lovely or bold view, within reach of Williamstown. To be his companion upon one of these drives was to touch the very essence of fine, whimsical, irresponsible scholarship."

But to us freshmen he appeared to be simply a taskmaster. The system by which, irrespective of our training and aptitudes, we were all herded together in one classroom, was not of his devising. He was himself performing an uncongenial duty, and he did not see why we should not perform ours. We had a few brilliant mathematicians who used to annoy him purposely by substituting original demonstrations in place of those given in Loomis. We had one man, at least, who had no conception whatever of the meaning of geometry, but whose verbal memory was so remarkable that he could recite every proposition by heart. Dodd gave him a high mark and he ultimately became a bishop.

Yet one adventure of my own in his classroom may serve to illustrate Professor Dodd's wisdom and patience in handling a sulky boy. I disliked mathematics intensely, and aimed to do just enough work to secure a passing grade. One day, in our study of trigonometry, he told us to be ready to box the compass. It did not involve ten minutes of work, but I balked at it, holding that boxing the compass was a sheer mechanical exercise, beneath the dignity of a college classroom. Dodd called us up by lot—or at least pretended to so do—for we were never certain that the name written on a piece of paper and drawn from his pasteboard box was the name which he actually announced. At any rate, "Perry" was the first name called to box the compass. I rose decorously, shook my head firmly, and sat down. It meant a "zero." For six days running, this little ceremony was repeated, to the delight of the class. Then I consulted the oracle of the coal-closet, for on the inside of that closet door in No. 32 West College I kept a careful record of my "zeros" and "x's" under Dodd. Those six "zeros" in a row looked as big as the national debt, and a very few minutes of applied mathematics proved to me that I could not afford to take another one if I wished to pass the course. Accordingly on the seventh day, when the Professor began the hour by inquiring mildly, in his queer throaty voice: "Perry, are you ready to box the compass for us today?" I boxed it, amid great applause. Dodd twinkled, but said nothing; he knew all along that he held the winning card.

Our life in West College, as in the other dormitories of that period, was

22

primitive enough to have satisfied Rousseau. In fact, we may almost be said to have lived like the beasts that perish. There was no water except what we carried up in pitchers from an outside pump. It may be imagined that we carried as little as possible. Even in the gymnasium, which I frequented for four winters to keep in training for baseball, there were only three or four hand-basins for washing. "Showers" had not been invented, and there was neither water nor money for tubs. We had to provide ourselves with coal stoves, as no dormitory was heated. There was no service of any kind, except that ash-cans and slop-pails were placed in the hallway of each floor, to be emptied whenever the college janitor got around to it. If we chose to sweep our rooms occasionally and make up our beds, we did so; but this was a matter of individual taste rather than prescription. Carpets were a rare luxury: I had an oilcloth to cover the middle of the room, a table with a kerosene "student-lamp," two or three chairs, a bookcase, and a few prints.

But happiness, as many an unwashed philosopher has pointed out, does not depend upon furnishings. We had youth and health and high spirits. I fear we kicked too many ash-cans and pails downstairs; and since our fathers were charged two dollars a term for any windows we might break and we considered this charge an economic outrage, we took pains to smash, each term, two dollars' worth of glass, very roughly calculated. Carpenter Clark, in deep gloom, described a student as "a window-breaking animal." That was also the opinion of Dr. Chadbourne, who lived in the beautiful President's House opposite West College. The favorite sport of the denizens of the north entry of West College was to smash a few panes of glass, start the ash-cans rolling, blow a tin horn, and yell "Chad!" Instantly, at any hour of the day or night, the President would jump out of his front door like a "jack-in-the-box," gold-headed cane in hand, his eyes blazing behind his gold-rimmed glasses, and his beard and coat-tails flying all abroad. If he caught a student he would expel him on the spot, though he usually took him back, with the kindliest admonitions, the next morning. I used to wonder that it never seemed to occur to so bright a man that, if he simply stayed in his study, our whole game would be spoiled. He thought himself, however, a masterful disciplinarian, and that the secret of discipline was in threats. He was the first President of Williams to take any interest in the beauty of the college grounds, but his method of persuading undergraduates to share his desire for better lawns was simply to post notices: "Keep off the Grass." We had never heard of such a thing, and those words became, alas, the unofficial motto of his administration! Professors were expected to act as policemen. A few years later, at Princeton, when the same question arose of protecting the lawns against the ball-playing and short-cut propensities of undergraduates, I heard President

23

Patton drawl out indolently but with finality: "Are not pleasant relations between students and faculty more important than a little grass?"

It was fortunate that most of our surplus energy went into athletics rather than mischief. Williams had given up intercollegiate rowing, and organized football was still a thing of the future, but everyone played baseball after a fashion, and it is impossible to convey to a present-day undergraduate the enthusiasm which we felt for it. The annual "horn-game" between freshmen and sophomores, when tin horns and monstrous "devil's fiddles" were used by each class to rattle the opposing team, was the chief athletic event of the year—more important, in fact, than the "college" nine's games with Amherst. I happened to be captain of our class team, and caught. The mask, invented by Thayer of Harvard, was just coming into use, but the first models had brittle wire and were likely to be broken by a foul tip. Otherwise the catcher had no protection whatever: neither chest pad nor shin-guards nor even a regulation glove, though many catchers bought a pair of farmers' buckskin gloves, cutting off the fingers of the left-hand glove, and padding the palm with a handkerchief. This helped a little, but not much. Fielders' gloves were unknown, and most of us carried bone-bruises from one end of the season to the other. Pitchers were beginning to work the curve ball, though still compelled to throw underhand, at a distance of only forty-five feet from the plate. There was no coaching except what the captain ventured to offer, and he had to be tactful about that; and there was no medical or other supervision. If we were hurt, we were hurt. I still carry the scar of a left finger badly broken by a foul tip; I remember pushing the bone back under the skin, wrapping a handkerchief around it and playing the game out, since we had no other catcher. It was boyish folly, of course, but any one of us would have preferred to lose a finger rather than lose a ball game.

We formed our own social groups with entire freedom. There was of course, among the freshmen, a "West College crowd," a "South College crowd," and so on; but these associations were spontaneous and flexible. The Greek letter fraternities, which since our time have assumed great prominence in the social life of Williams, were then a minor matter. There was no organized "rushing season," and though a few freshmen were pledged in advance, not more than a third of each class—and those mainly the wealthier men—joined the fraternities. The rest of us were called "neutrals," and though we indulged in occasional satire upon what we considered the snobbishness of awarding a claim for social distinction upon a cash basis, there was little heart-burning over it, and no apparent effect upon class politics or individual popularity. The question of remaining a "neutral" was simplified for me by

Father's attitude. As an undergraduate he had been a charter member of Alpha Delta Phi, but twenty-five years of observation had convinced him, rightly or wrongly, that the fraternities did more harm than good, and he directed his sons not to accept an invitation. By the time his youngest boy entered college, Father had retired from teaching and relaxed his rule; so that Lewis, who had already been excused from learning to milk (the only real blot upon his career, in the opinion of his older brothers!), was allowed the additional indulgence of joining a fraternity.

There were, however, two other undergraduate organizations (both of them now extinct) which I joined early and greatly enjoyed: the Lyceum of Natural History, and the Philologian Literary Society. The "L.N.H." had had an honorable history, had sent out the first scientific expedition ever attempted by an American college, and had helped to train many distinguished naturalists. . . . As Professor Tenney's chair had not been filled, we were obliged to work without any supervision, but we had rooms in Jackson Hall, and free access to the zoological collections. We organized our own field work, wrote reports, and tried our hand at dissections. I spent a good deal of time trying to learn to mount birds, but I had no real instruction in that art, and finally, after removing the skin from a great blue heron—a rank feeder on frogs and fish, and quite too "high" when it was brought in—I abandoned the effort in disgust.

The rivalry between the Philologian and Philotechnian literary societies had once been intense, and freshmen had been pledged to one or the other before entering college. I "went" Philologian, like my father. Each society had pleasant rooms in South College, with excellent libraries, which were then more used by undergraduates than the college library. At the weekly meetings there were essays, orations, and debates. We elected an undergraduate "critic," who was usually merciless. I debated with zeal throughout my college course, and was thought by my classmates to have uncanny luck in being on the winning side. As a matter of fact I had a "system," whose secret I guarded as closely as I had once guarded old Hadsell's "side-holt." It was very simple. In a small college you knew rather accurately the mental habits of each of your opponents in debate. If the other boy was likely to spend two hours in preparation, I spent four; if he spent ten, I would spend twenty. It worked. Not long ago, I explained this "system" to a group of Harvard intercollegiate debaters, but it did not seem to impress them. They had hoped I would talk about the "strategy" and "tactics" of debating—which are indeed interesting enough; but if you have mastered a particular subject twice as well as the other fellow, you may not need any strategy in order to smash him. Alas, how fluent and cocksure I was in those old debating days, and when we Philologians man-

25

handled the Philotechnians in joint debates—the smiling Mark Hopkins acting as judge, as he did in my father's time—how ineffably proud we were! It seemed almost as important, though perhaps not quite, as banging out a base-hit when a hit was needed.

At the end of freshman year, I was promoted to the "college" or varsity nine, and usually played third base thereafter. Bowdoin, Union, and Amherst were about the only colleges we played, though some of our keenest games were with semi-professional teams from manufacturing towns near-by, like Hoosac Falls, Blackinton, North Adams, and Renfrew. We had both a spring and a fall season, and toward the end of my senior year I discovered that baseball was taking a great deal of time. For four years I had scarcely gone trout-fishing or mountain-climbing except in vacations, and now I had developed a sudden passion for archery. I explained this to Captain Fred Fox at the close of a Saturday game, and resigned from the team. The Amherst game was only two or three weeks away. Fox was a taciturn fellow, and one of my best friends, but when I mentioned the claims of archery, he found plenty of words for once, and on Monday I was the first man to report for practice. I think I have wanted few things in life more ardently than to make a hit the last time I came to bat in college. I got it—and then an extra game was scheduled, and I had to get it all over again. Even now, after more than half a century, I have vivid dreams of those old strains and chances and mis-chances of the game. When the Boston Symphony Orchestra played *Till Eulenspiegel* for the first time in Cambridge, a very musical lady declared that there were only two men in Sanders Theatre who smiled at the right moments, Professor Münsterberg and myself. I did not dare to confess to her that I was really one hundred and forty miles distant from the music, playing over again a ball game against Renfrew, where I came in very fast from third base to field a bunt and missed it altogether! What Münsterberg may have been thinking of, I cannot say.

Our classroom work in the sophomore and junior years gained somewhat in interest and variety. The elective system had not then been introduced, except that a few choices were offered, as for instance between French and German. . . .

I chose German rather than French. Professor Gilson, a lame man with a dark, silky beard, was a Romantic by temperament and had been confirmed in it by long sojourns in Germany. He was an intimate in our household, and had given me as a small boy Kingsley's *Water Babies*, a book full of the strangest natural history, and containing what I thought was a wonderful sentence spoken by Mother Carey (*natura naturans*) in her Peacepool: "I am not going to trouble myself to make things. I sit here and make them make themselves." That seemed to me to explain Darwinism. I tried hard to please Gilson now, and he was a patient and enthusiastic teacher. I can never read the wonderful quatrain of the Harper's song in *Wilhelm Meister*, beginning

> *Wer nie sein Brot mit Tränen ass,*

—lines that reveal the very essence of Gilson's own personality—without remembering how he asked us once to bring an English translation of that quatrain to the next recitation. I toiled all the evening over a metrical translation, quite unaware that thousands of men had attempted that task without much success. As we were going into the classroom the next day, I was accosted by "Fatty" Smith, the best poker-player in our class, but notably weak in German. "Bliss," he said, "lend me your translation. Gilson called you up yesterday, and he won't call you today; but he is sure to call me!" It seemed priggish to refuse, for "Fatty" was in a tight place; and I parted with my carefully wrought jewel. Smith was the first man called, and obediently wrote that translation upon the blackboard. Gilson read it, looked quizzically at "Fatty" Smith, and then his eye roamed over the class and rested upon me. "Perry," he said blandly, "will you write *your* translation upon the blackboard?" I had to think fast, but by dint of using phrases which I had rejected the night before, I managed to produce a second version. Gilson shook his head as if in deep depression. "Bliss," he remarked sadly, addressing me by my first name, "your poetical style reminds me of Ossian." I suppose none of us knew who Ossian was, but I found Macpherson's poems in the college library that afternoon, and decided that Professor Gilson had not intended to compliment me. Charming, lonely, sorrow-stricken Gilson, with his inner life so completely hidden from that group of happy-go-lucky boys!

> *Wer nie sein Brot mit Tränen ass,*
> *Wer nie die kummervollen Nächte*
> *Auf seinem Bette weinend sass,*
> *Der kennt euch nicht, ihr himmlischen Mächte!*

Under the system of required courses then in vogue, we all studied three subjects under my father: the Constitution of the United States, English history, and political economy. His public reputation, then at its height, had been won in the latter field, but it often happens that a teacher with wide-ranging intellectual interests is known to the academic public mainly by one of his courses, while his best teaching may actually be done in courses that do not catch the public eye. I think that my father's lectures on the Constitution were admirable, although we were not mature enough to grasp all of their implications. We could not appreciate, for instance, the significance of many of those Supreme Court decisions which he analyzed with such zest. As Grandfather Smedley once said of John Bascom's sermons in a little church in Pownal, "He put the fodder too high for the calves." On the other hand, his course in the history of England has been criticized as being too elementary —"practically a memoriter exercise." I cannot agree with this verdict. It is true that we were required to familiarize ourselves, for each recitation, with a few pages of J. R. Green's *Short History of the English People*, then a new and—to me at least—a fascinating book. But this was only the beginning: we had to rise and state the substance of each of Green's paragraphs in our own words, and then discuss the facts and judgments involved, amid constant questioning and illustrations offered by the Professor and the class. To me it was an immensely stimulating course, and in view of my subsequent studies, quite the most valuable one which I had at Williams, although there were some moments in Mark Hopkins's recitation room which made a deeper impression upon me at the time.

In the famous course on political economy I was self-conscious, and often alarmed lest Father, in the intensity of his convictions, should become too excited. He had just turned fifty in our junior year, and seemed in robust health and splendid vitality; but he had toiled and thought and felt too passionately, and ten years later he was a broken man. On many aspects of his subject he was content with clear and dispassionate exposition. Production and exchange, labor and capital, land and currency and credit, he could discuss with scientific precision and poise. But when he came to foreign trade and American tariffs, he smelled the battle like a war-horse. His very bones cried out against "Protection, falsely so called." I had heard all this at home since I had heard anything, and I had no doubt that Father, like his friends W. G. Sumner and David A. Wells, was on the right side of the tariff reform argument. I think so still. But I hated to have my classmates egg him on, by their questions, to more and more dogmatic and extravagant utterance. There was no help for it. His absolute frankness, his devotion to truth as he saw it, his ethical conviction that tariffs drawn in favor of privileged groups were simply a question of Right and Wrong, made him a formidable advocate, and his wit and humor were weapons that often made the class howl with delight, even though these weapons were turned against their own arguments. "Peri's" classroom was alive—everyone admitted that; but I wondered whether it were not too controversial, too much of a spectacle. A generation later, at Harvard, one might have seen much the same intermittent intolerance in a very different man, Irving Babbitt. Babbitt had naturally a finely critical intelligence, but when he touched Rousseau and Romanticism he threw dispassionate criticism to the winds and became a stark, uncompromising dogmatist, a Peter the Hermit, leading a Crusade. A delightful passage in Logan Pearsall Smith's *More Trivia* may serve to illustrate the point:

"I expressed my conviction briefly; but the time-honored word I made use of seemed unfamiliar to [these youngsters];—they looked at each other and began whispering together. Then one of them asked in a hushed voice, 'It's *what*, did you say?'

"I repeated my monosyllable loudly. Again they whispered together, and again their spokesman came forward.

" 'Do you mind telling us how you spell it?'

" 'I spell it, I spell it with a *W*!' I shouted. 'W-R-O-N-G—*Wrong*!' "

Arthur Latham Perry and Irving Babbitt had scarcely a trait in common except this: they respected the unfashionable word "Wrong" and were not afraid to shout it.

In view of my undergraduate interest in speaking, writing, and miscellaneous reading, it is curious that I can recall so little about our class work in English. I remember that we studied D. J. Hill's *Rhetoric* and were informed that the distinction between "synecdoche" and "metonymy" was important. We had a *Manual of English Literature*, and must, I suppose, have recited from it. My brother Carroll, whose class also used a *Manual*, avers that he learned just one thing about English literature in college, namely, that "The lyrics of Edmund Waller can never die." I did not carry away from the classroom even as much as that.

We were obliged to write and deliver "orations" once or twice a year under the supervision of the Professor of Rhetoric, Llewellyn Pratt. He was a courteous, cultivated gentleman, and a master of public speech; and no doubt he gave our productions as much attention as they deserved. It was very little. We had also, during part of each year, the services of a friendly and enthusiastic Professor of Oratory, George L. Raymond, author of many volumes of verse and a series of books on Esthetics. We used his *Orator's Manual*, containing an ingenious and elaborate system of voice-production, stress, gesticulation, posture, etc. We called him "Bulldozer," because he was nervous in the classroom and easily overawed; his nickname when he taught at Princeton was "Mary"—for the same reason. But no one could be kinder to me, or more encouraging. Up to my senior year, the "gloomy shine" of my oratorical efforts had not impressed the judges of our contests, but now, under "Bulldozer's" direction, I toiled away, in the big empty Museum room of Jackson Hall, at his "vocal exercises," and learned the trick of deep-breathing and the proper "placing" of the voice. Even the moth-eaten stuffed moose behind the glass cases must have thought the performances of this young Demosthenes absurd, and I let no one, except Raymond, know what I was doing. But I was bent, grimly and ferociously, upon mastering every secret of *The Orator's Manual*, in order to win the Graves Prize speaking contest at Commencement. And there was really more than that at stake, though I did not then suspect it.

Whatever the defects of the curriculum were in our day, we had the inestimable advantage of plenty of time to ourselves. In our senior year, for example, we recited in ethics or philosophy, at nine in the morning and five in the afternoon. Dr. Chadbourne and Dr. Hopkins were supposed to divide these courses, but Dr. Chadbourne spent the fall term stumping the country for Garfield, and as he was retiring from office at the end of the year (and was also trying to run two cotton mills!) he left most of the senior instruction to Dr. Hopkins. We had textbook assignments, but a half-hour of preparation was all that most of us gave. The theory was that seniors should have ample time for reading, writing and general reflection upon man's place in the universe! This suited me exactly and the winter nights in Williamstown were long.

I had been elected an editor of the college paper, *The Athenaeum*, in my sophomore year, and was greatly flattered until I discovered that the youngest editor was expected to read all the proof and write whatever verses were needed for "fillers." I kept at it, however, and learned to write my share of those smart and caustic editorials which long have been the curse of Williams journalism. I wrote about new books, hailing Swinburne's latest volume, for instance, with all the rapture with which undergraduates of today have welcomed D. H. Lawrence and Ernest Hemingway. Robert Louis Stevenson was just beginning to print short stories. Any day might bring a new book by Browning or Tennyson, Darwin or Huxley, Hardy or Arnold. Emerson and Carlyle were living, though they had ceased to write. But Whitman, Whittier, Holmes, Longfellow, and Lowell were still productive. Melville was alive, though we did not know it, and Mark Twain was very much alive indeed. And so were Victor Hugo and Ibsen, Turgeniev and Tolstoi and Karl Marx.

"Here is God's plenty," and enough to turn any boy's head. No one was aware of the deep and subtle change about to take place in the spirit of English literature. We had already had the best that the Victorians could offer, and after 1880 there was to be less of that "quality of nobleness" which had been the distinctive trait of English writing since 1830. But we boys in a rural New England college knew nothing about literary tendencies or literary labels: it never occurred to us that we were "Victorians" or "Puritans" or even New Englanders. There were the books if we wanted to read them, and whether the authors were American or English, Romantics or Realists, mattered little to us.

I read without any plan or purpose except to gratify an appetite for books. Unluckily, none of us, I think, read in college any Latin and Greek except what was required. That was the tragedy of the system: we broke with the classics just when they might have served us most. I read no French as an undergraduate and only a little more German than was demanded. I was still reading Emerson, and began now to dip into some of the authors whom he praised, like Montaigne and Rabelais and old Burton of the *Anatomy of Melancholy*. I had read Milton and Wordsworth and Whittier since childhood, and can no more recall my first reading of *The Scarlet Letter* than my first reading of *Hamlet*. But now I began to make some discoveries: Keats and Byron (though neither Shelley nor Coleridge as yet), Carlyle (to whom I was introduced by a "village atheist," a Welsh cobbler who trained his dog to bark whenever the Methodist Church bell rang!) and Browning and Walt Whitman. What happiness in picking such "finds" as these from the upper shelves of the college library, and carrying them off to 32 West College! I was warned that Mark Hopkins had declared that *he* could not understand Browning, but secretly I believed that the old gentleman had not made much of an effort. I was sure that there was "gold in them hills," and I mined them for a score of years. There was no one to share my enthusiasm for Browning and Whitman, but Fred Bard and I used to wander over the hills spouting Swinburne and *The Earthly Paradise* and *Sigurd the Volsung* to each other, and when Fred reported that his barber in New York (or it may have been a barkeeper) could declaim more pages of *Sigurd the Volsung* than either of us, our cup of delight was full.

Yet I think that for the majority of our class the chief intellectual adventure of the senior year was the morning or evening hour with Mark Hopkins. He was then seventy-eight, but his powerful frame and noble features showed little or no trace of the burden of years, and there was never, up to the time of his death at eighty-five, any apparent diminution of his mental vigor. This exceptional endowment played its part in the spell which he cast upon his contemporaries. No one can furnish an adequate definition of greatness, but Mark Hopkins, like Gladstone and Bismarck, gave the beholder the instant impression of being in the presence of a great man. He had already become in his lifetime a legend, a symbol of teaching power: "Mark Hopkins on one end of a log, and a student on the other."

Four of his pupils and colleagues, Professors Bascom, A. L. Perry, Carter, and Spring, have made painstaking analyses of the Doctor's personality and methods. They all agree that he was not, in the strict academic sense, a "scholar"; the source of his power was not in his knowledge of books. But that is an old story in the history of the world: "He taught them as one having

31

authority, and not as the scribes." Any teacher can study books, but books do not necessarily bring wisdom, nor that human insight essential to consummate teaching skill. I think that the peculiar gift of Mark Hopkins has rarely been better described than by a single phrase from my old friend Professor Dodd. I was driving with him over Mason's Hill, a year or two after my graduation, and I was telling him about attending the brilliant lectures on the history of philosophy which Stanley Hall was then giving to Williams seniors.

"After all," I said—captivated by the new horizons which Stanley Hall was opening for us—"Dr. Hopkins taught us nothing about the history of philosophy." "No," said Dodd slowly, "he taught you nothing *about* philosophy, but he taught you *to philosophize*." This is essentially what my father wrote, in pointing out that the Doctor's favorite question—"What do *you* think about it?"—was the key to his success as a teacher. After beginning by asking the pupil what the textbook stated upon this and that topic, the Doctor would almost invariably inquire: "*What do you think about it?*" "It stole the hearts of crude young men to hear such a man as he was plumping down upon them from his desk, as if it were a matter of much importance, such a question as that! It suddenly increased their own self-respect."

To discover that you had a mind—narrow, commonplace, or ill-trained, perhaps, but a mind of your own, was a thrilling experience. You rose when your name was called, and sometimes the Doctor's initial questions, like those of Socrates, seemed remote from the matter in hand. The fascination lay partly in the effort to guess what the Doctor was driving at. He knew, and we did not, but the game gradually revealed itself as one bland question succeeded another. He always had an objective and sometimes the class perceived it more quickly than the boy who was on his feet, trying to keep his wits and to avoid foolish answers. But often the objective was remote: we were like a party of mountain-climbers, conscious that we were well above the timberline, but ignorant of the particular peak for which the guide was headed. We were having a good climb and were made to feel that we could keep up the pace and get some grand views, even though the Doctor did not seem to care whether we reached any particular hut by nightfall. To some men in each class, no doubt, he seemed a philosopher without a system, a moralist indifferent to definitions. He was in truth a builder of character who could lay a stone wall without ever looking at a blue-print.

All of use recognized his immense latent power. "Half his strength he put not forth." Yet this apparently indolent wrestler with ideas—never dogmatic, never over-earnest, never seeming to desire converts to any creed or platform—was ceaselessly active in studying the members of each class and in directing, however subtly, the questions by which he sought to develop and test their individual capacity. "Also he knew men at once," it was said of Cosimo de' Medici, "when he looked into their eyes."

I must limit myself to a single illustration of this wise handling of one of his "crude young men." In our senior year the mutterings of the famous Andover controversy in theology began to be heard throughout New England. Was "everlasting" punishment the same thing as "eternal" punishment? What was really at issue was not the exact meaning of some Greek words, but the whole Calvinistic conception of the actuality of a fire and brimstone hell. I had been brought up in a very liberal and deeply religious household, and I knew that on this question of a material hell my father and his friend John Bascom thought very differently from Grandfather Smedley. Being now twenty and fond of debating, I was wholly on the side of the "new theology," as it was then called. Nobody knew where Dr. Hopkins really stood, although he was supposed to be a pillar of Orthodoxy. He was an old man and a wise one, and refused to be drawn into controversy.

One Saturday morning, in reviewing some passage from a textbook, he called me up and put this question: "Perry, do you think that the fear of future punishment is a proper motive for human action?" I fear the light of battle gleamed in my eyes, for I saw the whole of the New Theology at stake in the Doctor's apparently abstract and innocent inquiry. And the textbook had said "Yes"; which was only an additional reason why a self-confident youth should take the other side. So I straightened my shoulders and answered "No, sir."

The Doctor looked me over. "I will repeat the question," he said slowly. "Do you think that the fear of future punishment is a proper motive for human action?"

"No, sir, I do not." I was ready to debate against a whole Bench of Bishops; *Athanasius contra mundum*; Luther at the Diet of Worms, etc., etc.

To my disappointment, the Doctor straightway called up "Turk" Parsons, a missionary's son, who recited the textbook position with fluent precision. But by that time the Doctor seemed to have lost all interest in the question, and went on to something else. The fight was evidently off, and I sulked for the rest of the hour. When the class was dismissed, I had to pass directly in front of the Doctor's desk. He leaned over toward me, bowing his magnificent shoulders and superb head. It was as if an old lion had turned in his cage to look at you, only that all the bars were magically down.

"Bliss," he said gravely, "did I understand you to say that you thought the fear of future punishment was not a proper motive for human action?"

I was still obstinate, "Yes, sir, that is what I think."

The leonine features relaxed into a captivating smile. "Well, now, Bliss," he remarked confidentially, as if to a very intimate friend: *"a great many young men have felt about that question exactly as you do."*

All the anger and conceit went out of me. I saw myself, not as a lonely rebel, but as one of the great company of the immature. With one sentence Mark Hopkins had put me in my place, and had nevertheless managed to let me feel that he liked me. I hope I had manners enough to thank him, for no teacher had ever rendered me a greater service.

The class of 1881 was the last to be graduated under President Chadbourne. We represented, although we were not aware of it, the end of an era. President Carter's administration was to bring in new professors, new methods of instruction, new buildings and endowments, and a large increase in the number of undergraduates. The rural isolation of Williamstown began to be less marked, though it was still to be a score of years before telephones and motor cars began to herald vaster changes still. I do not pretend to hold a brief for the old order of things, either at Williams or at the other Eastern colleges of our time, but before the old order is quite forgotten, it is fair to say that with all of its obvious defects, it bred some very good men. William Howard Taft (Yale, 1878), Woodrow Wilson (Princeton, 1879), and Theodore Roosevelt (Harvard, 1880) all belonged to our undergraduate generation. Their children, and now their grandchildren, have enjoyed far richer academic opportunities than those three men. Whether the second and third generations have worked as hard or felt as keen a prompting of ambition for leadership is perhaps an idle question; but the educational conditions that obtained in the late eighteen-seventies were not quite so unfruitful as they might easily be made to appear.

At Williams, at least, it must be admitted that during the eighteen-seventies there were more teachers of national reputation, in proportion to the total number of the faculty, than there have been in any subsequent period. The multiplication of courses and instructors, made necessary by the sudden increase of students, has resulted, as probably in all American colleges, in a lowering of the proportion of teachers of exceptional ability. There is less extreme poverty, and no physical hardship whatever, for Williams undergraduates today; but whether luxurious surroundings are really any stimulus to scholarship—even in the "houses" of Harvard and the "colleges" of Yale—remains to be proved.

Our social life, like our esthetic life, was undeniably barren. We had practically no contact with our professors outside of the classroom, and it did not occur to us that this might be desirable. When one thinks of the tutors and preceptors and advisers and deans of today, it is curious to remember that we had no one to "hold our hand" in time of trouble, and that—precisely like the university students of France and Germany both then and now—we had not the slightest desire to have our hands held. We wanted to be let alone. We chafed very little over the rigid requirements of attendance: chapel twice a day, and no allowance whatever of classroom "cuts" except for illness. Discipline, swift and simple, was administered by the professors who served as "class officers," for deans had not been invented.

About half the men in our class confessed to taking an occasional drink, although I do not remember seeing a single drunken undergraduate in the four years. Nevertheless, of the ten men who were photographed for the varsity nine in our senior year, four were hopelessly ruined by drink before they reached middle life. My own impression is that at Williams, Princeton, and Harvard—the colleges that I have known best—there has been a fairly steady improvement in undergraduate morals for the past fifty years. (My son says that I know nothing about it!) There is certainly less attention given to formal religious exercises, such as the class and college prayer meetings of half a century ago, and the rôle of religious leadership of the college, once taken by such professors as Albert Hopkins, is now left to chaplains and pastors. It is probably true that the informal and inevitable ethical discussions by undergraduates avoid just now the unfashionable words "right" and "wrong." The boys use other synonyms in their restless search for originality in expression. But to affirm that they are no longer interested in what was once called right and wrong seems to me a complete misunderstanding of the undergraduate mind. "Not interested in right or wrong?" said one of my ablest colleagues once, as we were walking home from a lecture on Goethe's *Faust*; "why, at bottom, young fellows aren't interested in anything else!"

Whatever the gains or losses which the subsequent years have brought to American colleges, our undergraduate days were now over. Trained or un- trained, wise or foolish, we had had our chance. Our Commencement was saddened by the assassination of President Garfield, just as he was leaving Washington on the way to his twenty-fifth reunion at Williamstown. He was one of the most popular of the alumni, and his election to the Presidency had been one of the excitements of our senior year. Only a few hours after the tragic news reached us (Saturday, July 2) came the first of the Commence- ment festivities: the Graves Prize contest in the public delivery of the six best essays written by seniors. No one pays much attention to such contests now, but in our day crowds attended them. I remember how "Bulldozer" Raymond rushed up to us six boys—who were quite excited enough already—to tell us that all subsequent Commencement exercises would probably be canceled, as

Garfield's death was momentarily expected; and that we must do our best before the great audience that had gathered. My speech was on Russian Nihilism, and I had toiled as hard over it as the Boy Orator of the Platte did upon his "cross of gold" masterpiece. And I doubt if even Bryan ever declaimed with fiercer conviction that he was right! For once my "gloomy shine" seemed to dazzle the eyes of the judges, and I had my reward for all the lonely months of practice in the cold and empty Jackson Hall.

On Sunday President Chadbourne preached his last Baccalaureate. The news from Washington seemed more encouraging. On Monday we beat Amherst in baseball. In the evening we listened to Senator J. J. Ingalls's oration before the Adelphic Union of the literary societies. I had to preside, but recall the orator's eloquence less vividly than my own struggle to decide whether I ought to wear my new (and first) swallow-tail or blue suit. Luckily I put on the latter, for the famous Senator from Kansas strolled down to the church ten minutes late, smoking a long cigar, and clad in a checked suit of a very loud pattern. He explained that the trunk containing his evening clothes had been lost in New York. Privately I believed that that trunk was, as the Senator once said of purity in politics, "an iridescent dream." On Tuesday I read a long and solemn Class Poem inspired by George Eliot; Mr. T. B. Aldrich showed me a great kindness in rejecting it for the *Atlantic Monthly*. In the blazing noonday of Wednesday, clad now like most of my classmates in a swallow-tail, I delivered a graduating oration on "The People's Poet"; probably a plea for more men like Burns. But I remember nothing whatever about it except Professor Pratt's candid remark upon the manuscript: "Page after page, Bliss, you seem just on the point of saying something, but you never quite reach that point!" However, I forgave this undoubtedly just criticism, for I collected the Van Vechten Prize for extemporaneous speaking, and had more money in my pocket than I had ever had in my life.

Of course, in those final days I was trying to do too many things. Even now, and many times each year, I have a recurrent dream that I am about to be summoned to the platform to deliver a graduating speech; but alas, it is unwritten, and there are only a few minutes left. Oddly enough, there is always a double consciousness about this dream, for I invariably say to myself, in my distress: "You have been making all kinds of addresses, for half a century. You could easily make a better speech than these youthful classmates of yours, if only there were five minutes in which to collect your thoughts." But there are no five minutes:—that is the agony of this hallucination. There is not even one minute! And then I wake up, roll over, and thank Heaven that I have retired and need never make another speech.

A HOLIDAY WITH FATHER[1]

Clarence Day

ONCE in a long while, as a great treat, Father took me down to his office. This could happen only on a Saturday morning, when there was no school. I felt very important and grown-up on the days I went to "The Office"—not after I got there, to be sure, but as I was leaving the house, with Mother and my three little brothers respectfully seeing me off.

If it was a rainy day, Father would prepare for rough weather by wearing a derby hat and a black rubber mackintosh over his usual tailed coat. (He seldom was informal enough to wear a sack suit in town except on warm days, or when he left New York to go to the country, in summer.) If the sun was out, he wore a silk hat and carried a cane, like his friends. When he and they passed each other on the street, they raised their canes and touched the brims of their hats with them, in formal salute.

I admired this rich and splendid gesture, and wished I could imitate it, but I was too young for a cane. I was soberly dressed in a pepper-and-salt sack suit with short pants and the usual broad flat white Eton collar that boys wore in the eighties—a collar that started out very stiff and immaculate every morning and was done for by dinner time. Black laced or buttoned shoes and black stockings. We only wore brown in the country in summer.

On one of these Saturdays, although it was sunny, Father put on his derby. I didn't know why until later. I hopped along by his side as he walked through the long rows of comfortable-looking brownstone houses from Madison Avenue over to Sixth, climbed the stairs of the Elevated, and stood on the platform, chatting with one of his friends, while we waited for the next train.

Soon a stubby little steam engine, with its open coal car piled full of anthracite, and its three or four passenger cars swinging along behind, appeared round the curve. White smoke poured from the smokestack. The engineer leaned out from his window. "Too-oot, too-too-toot!" whistled the engine as it came puffing in. We got on board and walked leisurely through the cars till Father found a seat that he liked.

During the journey downtown, except when the smoke from the engine was too thick for me to see out, I stared fascinatedly into the windows of cheap red brick tenements, or at the even more interesting interiors of lodging houses for tramps. The second-floor rooms of the lodging houses were

[1]Reprinted from *Life With Father* by Clarence Day, by permission of and special arrangement with Alfred A. Knopf, Inc., authorized publishers. Copyright 1935 by Clarence Day.

crowded, but I envied the tramps in them. They looked so easy-going. Not a thing to do; just tilt their chairs back against the wall, in comfortable old clothes, and smoke. If I were a tramp, I wouldn't have to scrub every last bit of grime out of my knuckles each Friday, and put on tight white kid gloves, and pull some unwieldy little girl around a waxed floor at dancing school. It wouldn't cost so very much, either. The lodging-house sign said in big letters, "Ten Cents a Night."

I never had a chance to see such sights except when I went downtown with Father, for Mother kept away from the Elevated. It was comparatively new, and she felt that the horsecars were better. Besides, Sixth Avenue was so cindery and sooty that ladies disliked it. They did go that far west sometimes, to shop, and they went as far east as Lexington, but in general they lived and walked in the long narrow strip between those two boundaries.

When Father and I left the train at the end of our journey, I found myself in a tangle of little streets full of men and boys but no women. If some lonely bonnet chanced to be bobbing along in the crowd, we all stared at it. Most of the business buildings were old and many of them were dirty, with steep, well-worn wooden stairways, and dark, busy basements. Exchange Place and Broad Street were full of these warrens, and there were some even on Wall Street. The southern corner of Wall Street and Broadway was one of the dingiest. Father raised his cane and said as we passed, "That's where Great-Aunt Lavinia was born."

A few doors beyond the Assay Office we came to a neat but narrow five-story building and walked up the front stoop. This was No. 38 Wall Street. Father's office occupied the ground floor, at the top of the stoop, and on the back part of the second floor he had a small storeroom.

The office was busy in what seemed to me a mysterious way. The cashier, who never would let me go inside his cage, sat in there on a stool, with a cash drawer, a safe full of books, another safe for securities, and a tin box full of postage stamps, which he doled out as needed. One or two bookkeepers were making beautifully written entries in enormous leather-bound ledgers. They had taken the stiff white detachable cuffs off their shirtsleeves and stacked them in a corner, and they had exchanged their regular jackets for black alpaca coats. Future bookkeepers or brokers who now were little office boys ran in and out. Western Union messengers rushed in with telegrams. In the front room there was a long table full of the printed reports issued by railroads about their earnings and traffic. Only twenty or thirty industrial stocks were traded in on the Exchange in those days, and Father's office ignored them. On or around the table were the *Commercial & Financial Chronicle*, the *Journal of Commerce*, a blackboard, a ticker, and four or five whiskery men. Two were arguing heatedly about Henry Ward Beecher, and the others were shaking their heads over some crazy proposal by the "Knights of Labor" to have an eight-hour day.

Father went into his private office, where a little coal fire was burning, hung his hat on a rack, and unlocked and sat down at his desk. While he opened his mail, I proudly brought in two stone jugs of ink, one of greenish black made in England, and one to use when he wrote letters of which he wished to keep copies, because with this ink impressions could be taken to put in his files. I cleaned and filled all Father's inkwells, and put fresh steel pens in his penholders. He had quill pens at home, but he used only steel pens at the office, and as he had no stenographer he wrote a good share of the firm's letters in longhand, himself.

There were lots of things to do in the office besides filling inkwells. It was fun to scamper around the streets carrying all the messages (which are telephoned nowadays), or to roll colored pencils down the clerks' slanting desks, or try to ring the bell on the typewriter. The latter was a new contraption which seldom was used except on important occasions, when the bookkeeper or one of the office boys had to stop work and pick at it.

All of a sudden it was noon. The customers left. The ticker came to a stop. At half past twelve Father called to me and we went out for lunch.

"Will you be back, Mr. Day?" the cashier asked respectfully, but eagerly too. On days when Father said yes, all the clerks looked disappointed. They bent over their desks, saying nothing, till Father went out of the door, but if I lingered behind for a moment I heard them slamming their ledgers about. Not only did they and the office boys all have to stay, but the rule was that they couldn't even smoke until Father had gone home for the day.

Today he said no, however. I saw them getting out their sulphur matches as he was crossing the threshold, and the instant he stepped into the hall they struck them on the seats of their pants.

I trotted along at Father's side down to Beaver Street, where there stood a mellow old building. It had the look of a friendly, hospitable country hotel. There were green blinds and little outside balconies on its upper floors, and windows with looped lacy curtains; and white pillars stood at the entrance, at the top of a low flight of steps.

This was Delmonico's, and the food was so good there that even I had heard it talked of, uptown. It was one of the places that just suited people like Father.

Delmonico's stood upon a triangular-shaped plot of ground, with the front doors at the apex, and when we arrived we met a bottlenecked jam at the entrance. Silk-hatted men, who had been lunching in a lingering way, had suddenly remembered apparently that they were due back in Wall Street, and they were shoving each other, politely but urgently, to force their way out.

As Father and I went in the long crowded room, the head waiter led us with a flourish to a table for two. The air was fragrant with cigar smoke and the appetizing smell of rich, greasy cooking. A stately-looking foreigner who was standing at the side of the room caught Father's eye and bowed to him in a dignified way.

"Lorenzo," Father said to him, as he approached us, "This is my son."

I bobbed my head at him, rather embarrassed, and Mr. Lorenzo Crist Delmonico bowed and said he was happy to meet me.

As he left us, old François, Father's regular waiter, hurried up to our table, and he and Father had a talk, in French, about the best dish to order. They spoke so rapidly that I couldn't understand a word of it, except that François kept assuring Father that we could rely on the sauce. "*Parfaitement.*" It seemed that the last time that Father had relied on this sauce, an admittedly difficult kind, he had had a severe disappointment.

When anything of this sort occurred, I had noted, François had a healing way of dealing with such a catastrophe. He seemed even more shocked and perturbed at a failure than Father, and he would snatch the offending dish away and come racing back with a substitute. Usually he was accompanied at such moments by one of the Delmonico family—Lorenzo or Charles—who bent over the table to examine the new dish as it was placed before Father, murmuring most sympathetically about the unhappy misfortune.

Today the sauce and everything else was not only successful but perfect, and Father and François smiled and nodded in a congratulatory way to each other. I used to wonder why Father never got into rages at Delmonico's as he did at home, but I see now that he may have felt lonely at home, where there were no brother experts.

Father was fond of French cooking and of being served by French waiters. At home he had to put up with an Irish waitress who was changed every few months, and with cooking which, though excellent of its kind, after all wasn't French. He ate it with relish and gusto, when it came up to his standards, but he did so like a city man in the country, enjoying good, simple fare.

I didn't always appreciate French cooking myself. It tasted all right, but it was dainty and there wasn't much of it. It seemed to me that Father got along with a very light lunch. When he was having his demi-tasse, however, and saw a hungry look on my face, he smiled understandingly and beckoned to François, who smiled too and presently came running back with a large chocolate éclair. The richness of its soft, thick yellow interior and the melting-ness of its chocolate outside were so delicious that time stood still as I happily ate it, and I almost forgot where I was.

After lunch, instead of taking me back uptown, Father walked down to the Battery, and to my surprise we got on the boat at South Ferry. We had never done this before. I now saw why he was wearing his derby. We were going out to the country. Off we steamed across the sweet-smelling bay filled with sail-boats and four-masted schooners and tugboats and barges, and when we landed on Staten Island Father told me that we were going to see Buffalo Bill.

We got seats in a flimsy wooden stand full of splintery benches, and there was the Wild West spread out before us—dust, horses, and all. The wonderful marksmanship of riders who hit glass balls with their rifles—balls tossed into the air and shot at with careless ease as the horsemen dashed by; the herds of cattle, the lariats, the brass band, the old Deadwood Stage Coach, the thrilling attack on it by Indians, the last-minute rescue. Father dragged me out just before the rescue so that we could get seats on the ferryboat, but I caught a glimpse of it anyway as I was being hauled through the exit.

I wanted to be a cowboy, I told Father on the way home. He chuckled and said no I didn't. He said I might as well be a tramp.

I wondered if I'd better tell him that this idea, too, had occurred to me, no further back than that very morning. I decided that upon the whole it mightn't be a good day to mention it, just after Father had taken me to lunch at Delmonico's. I did venture to ask him, however, what was the matter with cowboys.

Father briefly explained that their lives, their food, and their sleeping accommodations were outlandish and "slummy." They lived in the wilds, he informed me, and they had practically gone wild themselves. "Put your cap on straight," he added. "I am trying to bring you up to be a civilized man."

I adjusted my cap and walked on, thinking over this future. The more I thought about it, the less I wanted to be a civilized man. After all, I had had a very light lunch, and I was tired and hungry. What with fingernails and improving books and dancing school, and sermons on Sundays, the few chocolate éclairs that a civilized man got to eat were not worth it.

SEA CHANGE[1]

Bertha Damon

T WELVE miles from North Stonefield on Long Island Sound was Pine Beach—"the Sea" we always called it. Before the gentle water was spread a wide beach of smooth white sand, backed for two miles by a low bluff, green with wiry grass and darkened with pine trees, beyond which stretched wide salt marshes and fresh meadows, where wild beach-plum bushes straggled, fringed polygala brightened the cart tracks, and pink-and-white marshmallows blew in the sea wind. All through, serpentine creeks crept coiling to the sea; they were full of crabs that rather asked to be caught on bits of pork tied to a string. On the low bluff Grandma built herself a summer cottage, a retreat as she thought, for the place was quite unsettled. Later on it was to be still more unsettled, because her sister-in-law Charity got her to build a double cottage with her—but of that, by and by.

Early in May each year, Grandma and her family, and our few simple needments in some inherited carpetbags, made exodus from North Stonefield in a carryall, with Juno the cow hitched protesting to the rear, bound for "the Sea." In the Bible it said men went "down to the sea in ships," but we could never make out how to do that. Caleb Whipple's horse, who always dragged us, was annually elected to this job because he was considered by Grandma as "so safe," a virtue not commonly to be found in horses, and menfolks. During our safe slow progress I used to try to pass the time by wondering whether if Grandma with her superior purposefulness should be made to change places with the lackadaisical horse, she could not drag both him and us faster; or if the wilful and sinewy Juno, her energies worse than wasted pulling backwards in the rear of the carryall, given opportunity, would not sweep us onward, rushing as the chariot of the Lord. But sooner or later— no, always later, we got to "the Sea" and Caleb's horse crawled back to North Stonefield with him. Having been hired by the day—it took just a day to complete the round trip of twenty-four miles—the horse and Caleb had nothing to regret.

"The Sea" was in Grandma's eyes a perfect place for summer life, for there Thoreau's "simplify, simplify" could be reduced to the lowest common denominator. Something like camping, not housekeeping, was the ideal, and clothes were minimum. The cottage itself Thoreau would have approved. It was merely a shelter, one board thick. As Caleb was wont to say in admiration of its airiness, "You could spit through it anywheres." And the

[1]Reprinted from *Grandma Called It Carnal* by Bertha Damon. Simon and Schuster, publishers, 1938.

boards were warped in the singularly clear sunlight and drenched with big rains that blew up from the south sometimes, across the billows. There were five cozy rooms; there was a porch in back looking at the little seashore garden, the beds full of brighter colored flowers than those at home, edged with stones and shells. A porch in front, draped with white honeysuckle, looked pleasantly at the Sea.

In Grandma's house in North Stonefield the furnishings were chiefly inherited from the past; few, antique, simple; Grandma did not allow them to be changed. But in the sea cottage she permitted Martha to follow what was then the fashion in such lighthearted places; to go modern, as it were. The cottage sitting room was consistently marine. Nothing we found on the beach but must suffer (suffer is the word) a sea change into something rich and strange for household adornment. The sitting-room walls, like those of all the other rooms in the cottage, were of plain vertical boards. There plainness ended. At frequent intervals they were hung with "pictures" created from pressed sea moss of various colors mounted on white paper and framed in seashell frames, made by pressing into putty in patterns "gold," "silver," and "pearl" shells and those of razor clams and snails. Tufts of dried sea moss dangled tastefully about, and on all horizontal surfaces, whether of stringers, shelves, or furniture tops, sea-polished stones were arranged.

In the middle of the room stood the world's most ingenious "parlor table." It had been covered all over with putty in which were inlaid shells of every sort, in rosettes, scrolls, and borders. Aunt Martha herself had made it: it was her masterpiece. Some estheticians hold that the perfectly utile is always beautiful. This table was not even imperfectly utile; draw your own conclusions as to its esthetic value. It could not be written upon; it must not have books or magazines laid on it; it was only to be looked at. You could look at it as long as you wanted to. The "mantelpiece" over nothing in particular—the fireplace was in the next room—was draped with a "lambrequin" made of pinked black felt tabs, on each of which was appliquéd a recognizable though not realistic starfish, horseshoe crab, anchor or such like. The hooked rugs, too, had gone marine under Aunt Martha's hand in patterns of gray-sailed ships (Great-Uncle Aaron's trousers) on navy-blue seas (Mrs. Tuttle's husband's jumpers), but the braided and crocheted rugs had to be content to coil round and round in circles. Over against the west wall, under the windows, was the home-built couch covered with a bright velvet and satin "crazy quilt."

"If expense was no object," said our neighbor Mrs. Sparkes, "you could of had window drapes of fish net hanging from crossed oars."

But expense was decidedly an object, so the windows fell short of that suggested glory. In one corner was the exquisite little melodeon Aunt Charity and Uncle Matthew had taken to China to show the heathen, shown, and brought back again. Its shining rosewood top was hidden by a white cotton scarf embroidered with tufts of milkweed "silk." Tall bunches of dried salt-marsh grasses and cattails, stuck in large bottles and vases on the floor in unlikely places, served further to remind us, sometimes unexpectedly, that we were indeed living marinishly.

In those days we had not heard that being sanitary has anything to do with interior decoration; we did not dream of avoiding moldings, details, and what have you, so that a room must look as it does to the patient in a hospital, "easy to clean up just as soon as you die." Nor had we cause to crave in our domestic setting the peace that comes from blankness; we had enough peace elsewhere. Outdoors for days on end the biggest event was low tide. We did not take the newspaper. As soon as the waves had well receded, we ran out to read the scraps of news the sea had left along the beach. There were always pools of glittering water with little fish or crabs temporarily landlocked, wet shells for the delight of the discovering eye or the adornment of the cottage, and tufts of beautiful colored sea moss; and, for the more practical there were tufts of homely gelatinous sea moss to be collected and dried for future blanc mange, rocks, robbed of their protecting waters, from which clustering blue-black mussels and gray oysters could be gathered, and muddy flats which, struck with a hoe, emitted geysers from the latent clams waiting to be dug and cooked. Indoors, often about the only excitement to be had was from looking at our household goods and gear. And anyhow, though it may seem as if we should have been distracted, we got so used to our magpie scheme of decoration that generally we were scarcely aware of what was going on in our rooms.

All over our sea house the scrubbed pine floors, with islands of rugs, were always a little gritty with sand. The victuals fell just short of grittiness. And someone had said that meals in the Griswold cottage were like the tides—"two every twenty-four hours and an hour later each day." But they were glamorous. At "the Sea" in the field of victuals as in others one could with fewer means achieve greater ends than ever. There Grandma abrogated her law of strictly vegetarian diet, and though we were never allowed fish elsewhere, there we became delightfully piscivorous. Perhaps the edible creatures which came as it were direct to us from God, no sinful middleman intervening, seemed to her purer. And certainly they were cheaper.

Driftwood burned in the fireplace; over the green and rosy flames lobsters, or clams, or mussels boiled in an iron pot of sea water; oysters we roasted in their shells on a grate over the embers. Many an excellent feast we made on the great horseshoe crabs, those queer survivals of a prehistoric age, whose shells, edged with satin, we hung up for wall pockets, which became traps for old letters and all kinds of flotsam. There were strange poetic desserts: beach plums cooked with sugar, purple in deep cerise-colored juice, and sea-moss blanc mange of an unearthly color and texture.

Grandma herself had a great love for her daily dip. Grandma did not swim, of course; no lady did, or could, I believe, in the costume Modesty dictated. Not "go swimming" but "go in bathing" was the specific term. And as Grandma's approach to the Sea was therefore that of a lady about to take a bath and in public, she was naturally abashed. But how else could she have a real salt-water bath? The Sea could be had only outdoors. In the interests of morality Grandma went in as early in the morning as possible, when fewer people were about, even though that was less comfortable than later when the water and air had warmed up.

Grandma managed to outgarb even the garb of other lady bathers. What Grandma wore under that which met the eye I can only guess, and my guess is a full quota of underclothes. Most good women wore corsets when they suffered the Sea's embrace, but Grandma did not believe in corsets in or out of water. What Grandma had on outside—and what a lot of outside there did seem to be—were long full trousers of a somber gray flannel, gathered at the ankle and falling in a large ruffle, like that on the foot of a cocker spaniel, to conceal any possible seductions of the instep. Over these a long tunic, gathered obscuringly above the bosom in a yoke and at the waist into a belt, fell in voluminous folds half-way below the knee. That this was a sports model was indicated by four rows of white tape stitched on whatever horizontal or vertical edges were available. Accessories are important. On Grandma's head she wore a large shade hat, tied under the chin by a scarf that came down from across the top and bent the brim so that the effect was that of a double-ender coal scuttle. Long stockings and rubbers tied on with tape finished the costume.

Still feeling too naked, Grandma wore from house porch to first sea ripple a vast black mantle, concealing all these concealments. Grandma's idea was always to "keep the body under," and in her bathing costume to keep it under deeper than usual. When she went into the Sea dry, not even a satyr ship-wrecked on a desert island would have looked twice, and when she came out of the Sea wet—well, he would have turned away. It was Grandma's firm purpose to conceal physical charms so as not to arouse voluptuous suggestion. In this she was completely successful.

Yet Grandma did not look funny. She came out from the cottage porch in such a dignified way, and walked down across the beach as gravely as if she were going to church. At the edge of the first wave she laid aside her mantle. Gradually she waded into the sparkling water till up to the waist. Then slowly she bent her knees and immersed herself to the armpits. She rose; again she immersed, this time to the neck, almost as seriously as if it were a baptism. She repeated this process with satisfaction a few times and then came out, still calm, still self-composed, resumed her vast mantle and returned to her cottage with gentle unbroken dignity. No one would have dreamed of laughing.

At the Sea, even Aunt Martha came near having a good time. There were croquet tournaments, in which Aunt Martha, in a shirtwaist and a sailor hat, was specially good in knocking her opponent's ball off the mowed piece, conclusively. She and all of us, in order to have good times, had to dodge Great-Aunt Charity pretty constantly. She had just come back from being a missionary to the "heathen" in China, and, I suppose, just to keep her hand in, kept using on us the technique she had perfected among them. How I wished I could talk with just one heathen and learn from him, firsthand, exactly what impression Great-Aunt Charity had made on him and his, and see if it at all resembled that made on me, a Christian child. I wondered if being without the Gospel would make Great-Aunt Charity easier to take. She used to go about organizing prayer meetings to be held in her cottage at the very best times of day for doing more worldly things. She made you feel you had to go or seem to neglect God socially. Aunt Charity was quite a force at the Sea. She had one of those frequent, but not spontaneous smiles that did for her face what artificial flowers do for some rooms. Smiles, somehow, were more *used* in those days; they were instruments, weapons, what not. Aunt Charity's smile always met its match, however, when it came up against Aunt Martha's.

Every evening we read aloud to Grandma and heard the Sea accompanying. We went early to bed; the bedticks were filled with salt-marsh hay that had the disconcerting habit of emitting inexplicable squeaks, but we slept peacefully, and all night breathed sea and honeysuckle mingled.

And so our delightful life in salty Eden went on. When first, aged five, I saw the Sea, I said "Grandma's pond," and it was just that for two or three years. Then a sister or so of Grandma's and several neighbors built themselves cottages and we were a community.

And then, and then—how it came about I was never able to fathom. Grandma and her sister-in-law, Great-Aunt Charity, were involved in building a double cottage together. Whether the structure went up to the sound of hymns or not, as soon as it was finished, at least, trouble began.

For one thing, Charity was always twitting Grandma that Grandma's half of the cottage was six inches over on Charity's land. My young mind was so full of its own preoccupations that it had little room for details of the bitter game my elders and betters chose to spend their time playing. But one incident, dramatic, shocking, remains. For a long time Grandma was not convinced of this geoarchitectural error on her part. That period was bad enough. Then came a period when she was, and that to Grandma was unbearable. Finally rationalizing did its perfect work. Grandma said Charity had complained; she said Charity was in the right of it; she said justice should be done. Whenever Grandma said justice, something was likely to happen.

When autumn came and Charity went, and Grandma was once more alone by her Sea, she hired an innocent carpenter from another village. She got him to saw her half of the cottage from Charity's half, clean from ridge to mudsill. She then had this half of hers set exactly six and one-half inches to the east, on her own indisputable land. For some reason perfectly good in Grandma's mind, she took along with her own half of the cottage the middle partition, leaving Charity's half-cottage open to all outdoors. I was always fascinated by the thought that if only I had been there I could for once have played dollhouse perfectly, moving Aunt Charity's sacred furniture about, even in the two upstairs bedrooms, if I could have stood outside with my head in the pinetops like Gulliver in Lilliput . . . or maybe, lacking a miracle, I might have had a ladder.

Now Grandma was proud and sure that justice had been done—or she let on she was: Charity had not liked Grandma's part of the cottage to be over on her side of the property line, and Grandma had fixed it so that it was not there any more. But Grandma didn't tell anyone yet.

When in the spring Aunt Charity came back to her seashore property, sure enough, she found out by herself that it was unencumbered. There was a great deal of talk all around, between Aunt Charity and her friends, between Grandma and her friends, and, most of all, between Grandma and Aunt Charity. Grandma, of course, being more in the wrong than Charity, had to talk louder and faster at the time and a great many years longer, always justifying herself for sawing the cottage in two and most of all for that delicate little detail of carrying off the partition. I believe her claim was that Charity's having required her to move her part of the cottage over onto her own land entailed the expense of a carpenter and some rollers and a horse, which the value of the partition didn't begin to offset—something like that. Grandma could be relied upon to have a good strong reason that seemed watertight, but somehow wasn't.

Almost all her life Grandma justified herself in stout dialectic. But in her latter years she gave signs of beginning to think that while her act was no longer a modern instance, it had never even been a wise saw. One day when Charity had long since gone to her reward, whatever it was, and Grandma was timidly drawing nearer to hers, she said to me, "Bertha, this may be heresy and I don't want to shake your faith—"

"Don't worry, Grandma."

"But I have almost, almost come to believe that God will in the last judgment have mercy on the heathen."

"Why, Grandma, Grandma!" I said, not surprised about God but about Grandma.

"Yes," Grandma affirmed, "those who believe in God are saved not by Works but by Grace. Yet God is a just God. Now it has come to seem clear to me that if His justice stands, His Grace will surely have to extend to take in the heathen who are in darkness if he takes in Charity and me, for we"— "we," said Grandma though Charity had never sawed a board, "we did what we did in the full light of Gospel."

Biography

MINUTES OF THE LIFE OF
MR. JOHN MILTON[1]

John Aubrey (1681)

[His parentage]

MR. JOHN MILTON was of an Oxfordshire family. His mother was a Bradshaw.

His grandfather, . . ., (a Roman Catholic), of Holton, in Oxfordshire, near Shotover.

His father was brought up in the University of Oxon, at Christ Church, and his grandfather disinherited him because he kept not to the Catholic religion. He found a Bible in English in his chamber. So thereupon he came to London, and became a scrivener (brought up by a friend of his; was not an apprentice), and got a plentiful estate by it, and left it off many years before he died. He was an ingenious man; delighted in music; composed many songs now in print, especially that of *Oriana*.

I have been told that the father composed a song of fourscore parts for the Landgrave of Hesse, for which [his] highness sent a medal of gold, or a noble present. He died about 1647; buried in Cripplegate church, from his house in the Barbican.

[His birth]

His son John was born in Bread Street, in London, at the Spread Eagle, which was his house (he had also in that street another house, the Rose; and other houses in other places).

He was born Anno Domini . . . the . . . day of . . ., about . . . o'clock, in the . . .

(John Milton was born the 9th of December, 1608, die Veneris, half an hour after 6 in the morning.)

[His precocity]

Anno Domini 1619, he was ten years old, as by his picture; and was then a poet.

[School, college and travel]

His school-master then was a Puritan, in Essex, who cut his hair short.

He went to school to old Mr. Gill, at Paul's school. Went, at his own charge only, to Christ's College in Cambridge at fifteen, where he stayed eight years at least. Then he travelled into France and Italy (had Sir H. Wotton's commendatory letters). At Geneva he contracted a great friendship with the learned Dr. Diodati of Geneva (vide his poems). He was acquainted with

[1]From *The Student's Milton* by F. A. Patterson. F. S. Crofts & Co., publishers.

Sir Henry Wotton, Ambassador at Venice, who delighted in his company. He was several years [Quaere, how many? Resp., two years.] beyond sea, and returned to England just upon the breaking out of the civil wars.

From his brother, Christopher Milton: When he went to school, when he was very young, he studied very hard, and sat up very late, commonly till twelve or one o'clock at night, and his father ordered the maid to sit up for him; and in those years (10) composed many copies of verses which might well become a riper age. And was a very hard student in the University, and performed all his exercises there with very good applause. His first tutor there was Mr. Chapell; from whom receiving some unkindness [whipped him], he was afterwards (though it seemed contrary to the rules of the college) transferred to the tuition of one Mr. Tovell, who died parson of Lutterworth.

He went to travel about the year 1638 and was abroad about a year's space, chiefly in Italy.

[Return to England]

Immediately after his return he took a lodging at Mr. Russell's, a tailor, in St. Bride's churchyard, and took into his tuition his sister's two sons, Edward and John Phillips, the first 10, the other 9 years of age; and in a year's time made them capable of interpreting a Latin author at sight, etc., and within three years they went through the best of Latin and Greek poets.—Lucretius and Manilius [and with him the use of the globes and some rudiments of arithmetic and geometry] of the Latins, Hesiod, Aratus, Dionysius Afer, Oppian, Apollonii *Argonautica*, and Quintus Calaber. Cato, Varro, and Columella *De re rustica* were the very first authors they learned. As he was severe on one hand, so he was most familiar and free in his conversation to those to whom most sour in his way of education. N.B. He made his nephews songsters, and sing, from the time they were with him.

[First wife and children]

He married his first wife, . . . Powell, of . . . Fosthill, in Oxfordshire, Anno Domini . . ., by whom he had 4 children. Hath two daughters living: Deborah was his amanuensis; he taught her Latin, and to read Greek to him when he had lost his eyesight, which was Anno Domini . . .

[Separation from his first wife]

(She went from him to her mother at . . . the King's quarters, near Oxford), Anno Domini . . . and [he] wrote the *Triplechord*, about divorce.

Two opinions do not well on the same bolster. She was a . . . Royalist and went to her mother, near Oxford (the King's quarters). I have so much charity for her that she might not wrong his bed: but what man, especially contemplative, would like to have a young wife environed and stormed by the sons of Mars, and those of the enemy party?

His first wife (Mrs. Powell, a Royalist) was brought up and lived where there was a great deal of company and merriment (dancing, etc.). And when she came to live with her husband, at Mr. Russell's in St. Bride's churchyard, she found it very solitary: no company came to her; oftentimes heard his nephews beaten and cry. This life was irksome to her, and so she went to her parents at Fosthill. He sent for her, after some time; and I think his servant was evilly entreated: but as for the matter of wronging his bed, I never heard the least suspicions; nor had he, of that, any jealousy.

[Second wife]

He had a middle wife, whose name was (he thinks Katherine) Woodcock. No child living by her.

[Third wife]

He married his second wife, Mrs. Elizabeth Minshull, Anno . . . (the year before the sickness): a gentle person, a peaceful and agreeable humour.

[His public employment]

He was Latin secretary to the Parliament.

[His blindness]

His sight began to fail him at first upon his writing against Salmasius, and before it was fully completed one eye absolutely failed. Upon the writing of other books, after that, his other eye decayed.

His eyesight was decaying about 20 years before his death. His father read without spectacles at 84. His mother had very weak eyes, and used spectacles presently after she was thirty years old.

[Writing after his blindness]

After he was blind he wrote these following books, viz: *Paradise Lost, Paradise Regained, Grammar, Dictionary* (imperfect).

I heard that after he was blind that he was writing a Latin dictionary. [In the hands of Moses Pitt.] Vidua affirmat she gave all his papers (among which this dictionary, imperfect) to his nephew that he brought up, a sister's son, . . . Phillips, who lives near the Maypole in the Strand. She has a great many letters by her from learned men, his acquaintance, both of England and beyond the sea.

[His later residences]

He lived in several places, e.g. Holburn near Kingsgate. He died in Bunhill, opposite to the Artillery-garden wall.

[His death and burial]

He died of the gout struck in, the 9th or 10th of November, 1674, as appears by his apothecary's book.

He lies buried in St. Gile's Cripplegate, upper end of chancel at the right hand (vide his gravestone). Memorandum: his stone is now removed; for, about two years since (now 1681), the two steps to the communion table were raised. I guess John Speed and he lie together.

[Personal characteristics]

His harmonical and ingenious soul did lodge in a beautiful and well-proportioned body.

In toto nusquam corpore menda fuit.
—Ovid.

He was a spare man. He was scarce so tall as I am. [Quaere, quot feet I am high. Resp., of middle stature.]

He had auburn hair. His complexion exceeding fair—he was so fair that they called him *the lady of Christ's College*. Oval face. His eye a dark gray.

He had a delicate tuneable voice, and had good skill. His father instructed him. He had an organ in his house: he played on that most.

Of a very cheerful humour: he would be cheerful even in his gout fits, and sing.

He was very healthy and free from all diseases (seldom took any physic, only sometimes he took manna); only toward his latter end he was visited with the gout, spring and fall.

He had a very good memory; but I believe that his excellent method of thinking and disposing did much to help his memory.

He pronounced the letter R (littera canina) very hard. ("A certain sign of a satirical wit"—from John Dryden.)

[Portraits of him]

His widow has his picture, drawn very well and like, when a Cambridge scholar.

She has his picture when a Cambridge scholar, which ought to be engraven; for the pictures before his books are not *at all* like him.

[His habits]

His exercise was chiefly walking.

He was an early riser (scil. at 4 o'clock manè); yea, after he lost his sight. He had a man read to him. The first thing he read was the Hebrew Bible, and that was at 4h. manè, ½h. +. Then he contemplated.

At 7 his man came to him again, and then read to him again, and wrote till dinner: the writing was as much as the reading. His (2nd) daughter, Deborah (married in Dublin to one Mr. Clarke (sells silk, etc.); very like her father), could read to him Latin, Italian and French, and Greek. The other (1st) sister is Mary, more like her mother.

After dinner he used to walk 3 or 4 hours at a time (he always had a garden where he lived); went to bed about 9.

Temperate, rarely drank between meals.

Extreme pleasant in his conversation, and at dinner, supper, etc.; but satirical.

[His acquaintance]

He was visited much by learned [men], more than he did desire.

He was mightily importuned to go into France and Italy. Foreigners came much to see him and much admired him, and offered to him great preferments to come over to them: and the only inducement of several foreigners that came over into England was chiefly to see Oliver Protector and Mr. John Milton; and would see the house and chamber where he was born. He was much more admired abroad than at home.

His familiar learned acquaintance were:

Mr. Andrew Marvell, Mr. Skinner, Dr. Paget, M.D.

Mr. . . . Skinner, who was his disciple.

John Dryden, Esq., Poet Laureate, who very much admires him, and went to him to have leave to put his *Paradise Lost* into a drama in rhyme. Mr. Milton received him civilly and told him he would give him leave to tag his verses.

His widow assures me that Mr. Hobbes was not one of his acquaintance, that her husband did not like him at all; but he would acknowledge him to be a man of great parts and a learned man. Their interest and tenets did run counter to each other—vide Mr. Hobbes' *Behemoth*.

IN THE LABORATORY WITH AGASSIZ[1]

Samuel H. Scudder

I_T WAS_ more than fifteen years ago [from 1874] that I entered the laboratory of Professor Agassiz, and told him I had enrolled my name in the Scientific School as a student of natural history. He asked me a few questions about my object in coming, my antecedents generally, the mode in which I afterwards proposed to use the knowledge I might acquire, and, finally, whether I wished to study any special branch. To the latter I replied that, while I wished to be well grounded in all departments of zoology, I purposed to devote myself specially to insects.

"When do you wish to begin?" he asked.

"Now," I replied.

This seemed to please him, and with an energetic "Very well!" he reached from a shelf a huge jar of specimens in yellow alcohol.

"Take this fish," said he, "and look at it; we call it a haemulon; by and by I will ask what you have seen."

With that he left me, but in a moment returned with explicit instructions as to the care of the object entrusted to me.

"No man is fit to be a naturalist," said he, "who does not know how to take care of specimens."

I was to keep the fish before me in a tin tray, and occasionally moisten the surface with alcohol from the jar, always taking care to replace the stopper tightly. Those were not the days of ground-glass stoppers and elegantly shaped exhibition jars; all the old students will recall the huge neckless glass bottles with their leaky, wax-besmeared corks, half eaten by insects, and begrimed with cellar dust. Entomology was a cleaner science than ichthyology, but the example of the Professor, who had unhesitatingly plunged to the bottom of the jar to produce the fish, was infectious; and though this alcohol had a "very ancient and fishlike smell," I really dared not show any aversion within these sacred precincts, and treated the alcohol as though it were pure water. Still I was conscious of a passing feeling of disappointment, for gazing at a fish did not commend itself to an ardent entomologist. My friends at home, too, were annoyed when they discovered that no amount of eau-de-Cologne would drown the perfume which haunted me like a shadow.

In ten minutes I had seen all that could be seen in that fish, and started in search of the Professor—who had, however, left the Museum; and when I returned, after lingering over some of the odd animals stored in the upper apartment, my specimen was dry all over. I dashed the fluid over the fish as

[1]From *Every Saturday* (April 4, 1874) 16, 369–370.

if to resuscitate the beast from a fainting-fit, and looked with anxiety for a return of the normal sloppy appearance. This little excitement over, nothing was to be done but to return to a steadfast gaze at my mute companion. Half an hour passed—an hour—another hour; the fish began to look loathsome. I turned it over and around; looked it in the face—ghastly; from behind, beneath, above, sideways, at a three-quarters' view—just as ghastly. I was in despair; at an early hour I concluded that lunch was necessary; so, with infinite relief, the fish was carefully replaced in the jar, and for an hour I was free.

On my return, I learned that Professor Agassiz had been at the Museum, but had gone, and would not return for several hours. My fellow-students were too busy to be disturbed by continued conversation. Slowly I drew forth that hideous fish, and with a feeling of desperation again looked at it. I might not use a magnifying-glass; instruments of all kinds were interdicted. My two hands, my two eyes, and the fish: it seemed a most limited field. I pushed my finger down its throat to feel how sharp the teeth were. I began to count the scales in the different rows, until I was convinced that that was nonsense. At last a happy thought struck me—I would draw the fish; and now with surprise I began to discover new features in the creature. Just then the Professor returned.

"That is right," said he; "a pencil is one of the best of eyes. I am glad to notice, too, that you keep your specimen wet, and your bottle corked."

With these encouraging words, he added:

"Well, what is it like?"

He listened attentively to my brief rehearsal of the structure of parts whose names were still unknown to me: the fringed gill-arches and movable operculum; the pores of the head, fleshy lips and lidless eyes; the lateral line, the spinous fins and forked tail; the compressed and arched body. When I had finished, he waited as if expecting more, and then, with an air of disappointment:

"You have not looked very carefully; why," he continued more earnestly, "you haven't even seen one of the most conspicuous features of the animal, which is as plainly before your eyes as the fish itself; look again, look again!" and he left me to my misery.

I was piqued; I was mortified. Still more of that wretched fish! But now I set myself to my task with a will, and discovered one new thing after another, until I saw how just the Professor's criticism had been. The afternoon passed quickly; and when, toward its close, the Professor inquired:

"Do you see it yet?"

"No," I replied, "I am certain I do not, but I see how little I saw before."

"That is next best," said he, earnestly, "but I won't hear you now; put away your fish and go home; perhaps you will be ready with a better answer in the morning. I will examine you before you look at the fish."

This was disconcerting. Not only must I think of my fish all night, studying, without the object before me, what this unknown but most visible feature might be; but also, without reviewing my discoveries, I must give an exact account of them the next day. I had a bad memory; so I walked home by Charles River in a distracted state, with my two perplexities.

The cordial greeting from the Professor the next morning was reassuring; here was a man who seemed to be quite as anxious as I that I should see for myself what he saw.

"Do you perhaps mean," I asked, "that the fish has symmetrical sides with paired organs?"

His thoroughly pleased "Of course! of course!" repaid the wakeful hours of the previous night. After he had discoursed most happily and enthusiastically—as he always did—upon the importance of this point, I ventured to ask what I should do next.

"Oh, look at your fish!" he said, and left me again to my own devices. In a little more than an hour he returned, and heard my new catalogue.

"That is good, that is good!" he repeated; "but that is not all; go on"; and so for three long days he placed that fish before my eyes, forbidding me to look at anything else, or to use any artificial aid. "Look, look, look," was his repeated injunction.

This was the best entomological lesson I ever had—a lesson whose influence has extended to the details of every subsequent study; a legacy the Professor has left to me, as he has left it to many others, of inestimable value, which we could not buy, with which we cannot part.

A year afterward, some of us were amusing ourselves with chalking outlandish beasts on the Museum blackboard. We drew prancing starfishes; frogs in mortal combat; hydra-headed worms; stately crawfishes, standing on their tails, bearing aloft umbrellas; and grotesque fishes with gaping mouths and staring eyes. The Professor came in shortly after, and was as amused as any at our experiments. He looked at the fishes.

"Haemulons, every one of them," he said; "Mr. —— drew them."

True; and to this day, if I attempt a fish, I can draw nothing but haemulons.

The fourth day, a second fish of the same group was placed beside the first, and I was bidden to point out the resemblances and differences between the two; another and another followed, until the entire family lay before me, and a whole legion of jars covered the table and surrounding shelves; the odor had become a pleasant perfume; and even now, the sight of an old, six-inch, worm-eaten cork brings fragrant memories.

The whole group of haemulons was thus brought in review; and, whether engaged upon the dissection of the internal organs, the preparation and examination of the bony framework, or the description of the various parts, Agassiz's training in the method of observing facts and their orderly arrangement was ever accompanied by the urgent exhortation not to be content with them.

"Facts are stupid things," he would say, "until brought into connection with some general law."

At the end of eight months, it was almost with reluctance that I left these friends and turned to insects; but what I had gained by this outside experience has been of greater value than years of later investigation in my favorite groups.

TOSCANINI[1]

Stefan Zweig

I love him who yearns for the impossible.

Second part of *Faust*

ANY attempt to detach the figure of Arturo Toscanini from the fugitive element of the music re-created under the magical spell of his baton, and to incorporate it in the more enduring substance of the written word, must, willy-nilly, become something more than the mere biography of a conductor. He who tries to describe Toscanini's services to the Spirit of Music and his wizard's influence over his audiences is describing, above all, an ethical deed. For Toscanini is one of the sincerest men of our time, devoting himself to the service of art with such fidelity, ardour, and humility as we are rarely privileged to admire in any other sphere of creative activity. He bows his head before the higher will of the master he interprets, so that he combines the mediating function of the priest with the fervour of the disciple, combines the strictness of the teacher with the unresting diligence and veneration of the pupil. This guardian of the hallowed and primal forms of music is always concerned with an integral effect rather than with detail, with faithful representation rather than with outward success. Since he invariably puts into his work his personal genius and the whole of his peculiar moral and spiritual energy, what he does sets an example, not in the realm of music alone, but for all artists in every domain. His individual triumphs transcend the boundaries of music to become the supra-personal victory of creative will

[1]From *Toscanini* by Paul Stefan. Copyright 1936 by The Viking Press, Inc., New York.

over the inertia of matter—a splendid proof that, even in a disintegrated and shattered age like ours, now and again it is possible for the gifted few to achieve the miracle of perfection.

For the fulfilment of his colossal task Toscanini has, year after year, steeled his soul with unparalleled inflexibility. Nothing but perfection will satisfy him. Thus he shoulders his burden, and manifests his moral grandeur. The fairly good, the nearly perfect, the approximate, he cannot endure. Toscanini detests compromise in all its forms, abominates an easy-going satisfaction. In vain will you remind him that the perfect, the absolute, are rarely attainable in this world; that, even to the sublimest will, no more is possible than an approach to perfection, since perfection is God's attribute, not man's. His glorious unwisdom makes it impossible for him to recognize this wise dispensation. For him the idea of the absolute is supreme in art; and like one of Balzac's heroes, he devotes his whole life to "la recherche de l'absolu." Now, the will of one who persistently endeavours to attain the unattainable has irresistible power both in art and in life.

When Toscanini wills, all must will; when he commands, all must obey. Every musician who has been guided by the movements of his wonder-working baton will testify that, within the range of the elemental energy that radiates from it, lassitude and inaccuracy are dispelled. By a mysterious induction some of his own electrical energy passes from him into every muscle and nerve, not only of the members of the orchestra, but also of all those who come to hear and to enjoy Toscanini's will; for as soon as he addresses himself to his task, each individual is inspired with the power of a divine terror, with a communicable strength which, after an initial phase of palsied alarm, induces in those affected by it a might which greatly transcends the ordinary. The discharge of his own tensions increases the capacity for musical appreciation of those who happen to be in his neighbourhood, expanding the faculties of every musician and, one might even say, of the lifeless instruments as well. As out of every score he extracts its most deeply hidden mysteries, so, with his unceasing demands, does he extract from every performer in the orchestra the utmost of which each is capable, imposing a fanatical zeal, a tenseness of will and execution, which the individual, unstimulated by Toscanini, has never before known and may never again experience.

This forcible stimulation of the will is no easy or comfortable matter. Perfectionment must be fought for sternly, savagely, indefatigably. One of the most marvelous spectacles of our day, one of the most glorious revelations to every creative or interpretative artist, an hour never to be forgotten is the privilege of watching Toscanini when engaged in his struggle for perfection, in his contest for the maximum effect. The onlooker is enthralled, breathless, almost terrified, as he beholds. In general an artist's fight for supreme achievement takes place in privacy. The poet, the novelist, the painter, the composer, works alone.

From sketches and from much-corrected manuscripts one must guess the ardours of creation. But whoever witnesses a rehearsal conducted by Toscanini sees and hears Jacob wrestling with the angel—sights and sounds no less alarming and splendid than a thunderstorm.

In whatever medium an artist works, the study of Toscanini will help to keep him faithful to his ideals, that he may resemble the conductor who, with sublime patience and sublime impatience, constrains to fit into the scheme of a flawless vision so much that, but for him, would remain rough-hewn and indistinct. For—and this is Toscanini's most salient characteristic—his interpretation of a work does not come into being at rehearsal. A symphony he is to conduct will have been thoroughly worked over in his mind from the score, and the finest shades of its tonal reproduction will have been settled for him long before he takes his place at the desk. A rehearsal, for him, is no more than an instrumental adaptation to what he has already heard again and again with the mind's ear. His extraordinary frame needs only three or four hours' sleep in the twenty-four. Night after night he sits up, the composer's text close to his near-sighted eyes, scanning it bar by bar, note by note. He weighs every modulation, scrupulously ponders every tone, mentally rehearses the rhythmic combinations.

Since he is a man of unrivalled memory, the whole and the parts become incorporated into his being, and the written score is henceforward little more than waste paper. Just as in a Rembrandt etching the lightest line has made its peculiar, its personal contribution to the copper plate, so in Toscanini's most musical of brains has every phrase been indelibly registered before he begins to conduct the first rehearsal. All that remains for him to do is to impose on others the clarity of his own will; to transform his Platonic idea, his perfected vision, into orchestrated sound; to ensure the concerted outward reproduction of the music that exists in his mind; to make a multiplicity of instrumentalists obey the law which for him has already been formulated in imagined perfection.

This is an enterprise bordering on the impossible. An assemblage of persons having different temperaments and talents is to work as a unit, fulfilling and realizing, with photographic and phonographic accuracy, the inspired vision of one individual. A thousand times Toscanini has made a success of this undertaking, which is at once his torment and his delight. To have watched the process of unceasing assimilation whereby he transforms multiplicity into unity, energetically clarifying the vague, is a memorable lesson for

61

anyone who reverences art in its highest form as symbolical of morality. It is thus that during rehearsal observer and auditor come to understand that Toscanini's work is ethical as well as artistic.

Public performance discloses to connoisseurs, to artists, to virtuosi, Toscanini as a leader of men, Toscanini celebrating one of his triumphs. This is the victorious march into the conquered realm of perfection. At rehearsal, on the other hand, we witness the struggle for perfection. There alone can be discerned the obscure but genuine and tragical image of the fighter; there alone are we enabled to understand the courage of Toscanini the warrior. Like battlefields, his rehearsals are full of the tumult and the fever of fluctuating successes. In them, and only in them, are the depths of Toscanini's soul revealed.

Every time he begins a rehearsal, it is, in very truth, as if he were a general opening a campaign; his outward aspect changes as he enters the hall. At ordinary times, when one is alone with him, or with him among a circle of intimates, though his hearing is extraordinarily acute, one is inclined to fancy him rather deaf. Walking or sitting he has his eyes fixed on vacancy, in a brown study, his arms folded, his brows knitted, a man aloof from the world. Though the fact is shown by no outward signs, something is at work within him; he is listening to inner voices, is in a reverie, with all his senses directed inward. If you come close to him and speak to him, he starts; half a minute or more may elapse before his deep-set dark eyes light up to recognize even a familiar friend, so profoundly has he been shut away, spiritually deaf to everything but the inner music. A day-dreamer, in the isolation and concentration of the creative and interpretative artist—such is Toscanini when not "on the battlefield."

Yet the instant he raises his baton to undertake the mission he is to fulfill, his isolation is transformed into intimate communion with his fellows, his introspection is replaced by the alertness of the man of action. His figure stiffens and straightens; he squares his shoulders in martial fashion; he is now the commandant, the governor, the dictator. His eyes sparkle beneath their bushy brows; his mouth is firmly set; his movements are brisk, those of one ready for all emergencies, as he steps up to the conductor's desk and, with Napoleonic glance, faces his adversaries. For that is what the waiting crowd of instrumentalists has become to him at this supreme instant—adversaries to be subjugated, persons with conflicting wills, who have to be mastered, disciplined, and brought under the reign of law. Encouragingly he greets his fellow-musicians, lifts his baton, and therewith, like lightning into a lightning-rod, the whole power of his will is concentrated into this slender staff.

A wave of the magic wand, and elemental forces are unchained; rhythmically the orchestra is guided by his clear-cut and virile movements. On, on, on; we feel, we breathe, in unison. Suddenly (the sudden cessation hurts, and one shrinks as from the thrust of a rapier), the performance, which to us, less sensitive than the conductor, has seemed to be going flawlessly, is stopped by a sharp tap on the desk. Silence fills the hall, till the startling stillness is startlingly broken by Toscanini's tired and irritable "Ma no! Ma no!" This abrupt negative, this pained exclamation, is like a sigh of reproach. Something has disturbed him. The sound of the instruments, plain to us all, has been discordant with the music of Toscanini's vision, audible to him alone.

Quietly, civilly, speaking very much to the point, the conductor now tries to make the orchestra understand how he feels the music ought to be rendered. He raises his baton once more, and the faulty phrase is repeated, less faultily indeed; but the orchestral reproduction is not yet in full harmony with the master's inward audition. Again he stops the performance with a tap. This time the explanation that ensues is less patient, more irritable. Eager to make his meaning perfectly plain, he uses all his powers of persuasion, and so great is his faculty for expression that in him the gesticulative talent proper to an Italian rises to the pitch of genius. Even the most unmusical of persons cannot fail to grasp, from his gestures, what he wants, what he demands, when he demonstrates the rhythm, when he imploringly throws his arms wide, and then fervently clasps them at his breast, to stress the need for a more lively interpretation; or when, setting his whole body plastically to work, he gives a visual image of the tone-sequences in his mind. More and more passionately does he employ the arts of persuasion, imploring, miming, counting, singing; becoming, so to say, each instrument in turn as he wishes to stimulate the performer who plays it; one sees him making the movements of a violinist, a flautist, a kettledrummer. If the reader will glance at the rehearsal-photographs in this book, he will see that a sculptor who should wish to represent desire and impatience, yearning, tension, and urgency, could find no more satisfactory model than Toscanini gesticulating to the orchestra.

But if, despite this fiery incitation, despite this urgent exemplification, the orchestra still fails to grasp and to fulfil the conductor's wishes, Toscanini's suffering at their non-success and their mortal fallibility becomes intense. Distressed by the discordancy between the orchestral performance and the inward audition, he groans like a sorely wounded man, and seems beside himself because he cannot get on properly with his work. Forgetting the restraints of politeness, losing control, in his wrath against the stupidity of material obstacles, he rages, curses, and delivers volleys of abuse. It is easy to understand why none but his intimates are allowed to attend these rehearsals, at which he knows he will be overcome by his insatiable passion for perfection.

More and more alarming grows the spectacle of the struggle, as Toscanini strives to wring from the instrumentalists the visioned masterpiece which has to be fashioned in the sphere of universally audible reality. His body quivers with excitement, his voice becomes hoarse, his brow is beaded with sweat; he looks exhausted and aged by these immeasurable hours of strenuous toil; but never will he stop an inch short of the perfection of his dream. With unceasingly renewed energy, he pushes onward and onward until the orchestra has at length been subjected to his will and can interpret the composer's music exactly as it has presented itself to the great conductor's mind.

Only he who has been privileged to witness this struggle for perfection hour after hour, day after day can grasp the heroism of a Toscanini; he alone can estimate the cost of the super-excellence which the public has come to expect as a matter of course. In truth the highest levels of art are never attained until what is enormously difficult seems to have been attained with consummate ease, until perfection appears self-evident. If you see Toscanini of an evening in a crowded concert-hall, the magician who holds sway over the dutiful instrumentalists, guiding them as if they were hypnotized by the movements of his baton, you might think his triumph won without effort— himself, the acme of security, the supreme expression of victory. In reality Toscanini never regards a task as definitively performed. What the public admires as completion has for him already become once more a problem. After fifty years' study of a composition, this man who is now verging upon seventy is never wholly satisfied with the results; he can in no case get beyond the stimulating uncertainty of the artist who is perpetually making new trials. Not for him a futile comfort; he never attains what Nietzsche calls the "brown happiness" of relaxation, of self-content. No other living man perhaps suffers so much as does this superlatively successful conductor from the imperfection of all the instrumental reproduction as compared with the music of his dreams.

Other inspired conductors are at least vouchsafed fleeting moments of rapture. Bruno Walter, for example, Toscanini's Apollonian brother in the realm of music, has them (one feels) from time to time. When he is playing or conducting Mozart, his face is now and again irradiated by the reflection of ecstasy. He is upborne on the waves of his own creation; he smiles unwittingly; he dreams as he is dandled in the arms of music.

But Toscanini, the insatiable, the captive of his longing for perfection, is never granted the grace of self-forgetfulness. He is consumed, as with undying fires, by the craving for ever-new forms of perfection. The man is absolutely sincere, incapable of pose. There is nothing studied about his behaviour when, at the close of every concert, during the salvos of applause, he looks embarrassed and ashamed as he retires, coming back reluctantly and only through politeness when forced to respond to the acclamations of the audience. For him all achievement is mysteriously mournful. He knows that what he has so heroically wrested from fate is pre-eminently perishable; he feels, like Keats, that his name is "writ in water." The work of an interpretative artist cannot endure; it exists only for the moment, and leaves nothing that the senses of coming generations will be able to delight in. Thus his successes, magnificent though they are, can neither delude nor intoxicate him. He knows that in the sphere of orchestral reproduction there is nothing perdurable; that whatever is achieved must be re-achieved from performance to performance, from hour to hour. Who can be better aware than this man, to whom peace and full fruition are denied because he is insatiable, that art is unending warfare, not a conclusion but a perpetual recommencement?

Such moral strictness of conception and character is a signal phenomenon in art and in life. Let us not repine, however, that so pure and so disciplined a manifestation as Toscanini is a rarity, and that only on a few days each year can we enjoy the delight of having works so admirably presented to us by this master of his craft. Nothing can detract more from the dignity and the ethical value of art than the undue facility and triteness of its presentation thanks to the marvels of modern technique, whereby wireless and gramophone offer the sublime at any moment to the most indifferent; for thanks to this ease of presentation, most people forget the labour of creation, consuming the treasures of art as thoughtlessly and irreverently as if they were swilling beer or munching bread.

It is therefore, in such days as ours, a benefaction and a spiritual joy to behold one who so forcibly reminds us that art is sacramental labour, is apostolical devotion to the perpetually elusive and divine elements in our world; that it is not a chance gift of luck, but a hard-earned grace; is more than tepid pleasure, being likewise, and before all, creative need. In virtue of his genius and in virtue of his steadfastness of character, Toscanini has wrought the miracle of compelling millions to accept our glorious patrimony of music as a constituent part of the living present. This interpretative wonder bears fruit far beyond its obvious frontiers; for what is achieved within the domain of any one art is an acquirement for art in general. Only an exceptional man imposes order upon others, and nothing arouses profounder veneration for this outstanding apostle of faithfulness in work than his success in teaching a chaotic and incredulous epoch to feel fresh reverence for its most hallowed heritage.

FORTY RUBLES A MONTH[1]

Eve Curie

Yes, Marie's existence had still further to be despoiled and made bare. The few months she had lived in the Rue d'Allemagne had been a stage in acclimatization. Now the girl sank slowly into solitude. The beings she rubbed elbows with existed for her no more than the walls she touched in passing, and conversation hardly cut in upon the silence in which she enveloped her hours. For more than three solid years she was to lead a life devoted to study alone: a life in conformity with her dreams, a "perfect" life in the sense in which that of the monk or the missionary is perfect.

Her life had to be of monastic simplicity in any case: for since Marie had voluntarily deprived herself of the board and lodging she had had at the Dluskis', she had to meet her expenses herself. And her income—made up by her own savings, divided in slices, and the small sums her father could send her—resolved itself into forty rubles a month.

How could a woman, a foreigner, live decently in Paris in 1892 with forty rubles a month, *three francs* a day, paying for her own room, meals, clothes, paper and books, as well as her fees at the university? Such was the problem the young student had urgently to solve. But Marie never failed to find the solution of a problem.

Manya to her brother Joseph, March 17, 1892:

You have no doubt learned from Father that I decided to live nearer to the schools, as it had become necessary for several reasons, above all for the present quarter. The plan is now realized: I am writing to you, in fact, from my new lodging, 3 Rue Flatters. It is a little room, very suitable, and nevertheless very cheap. In a quarter of an hour I can be in the chemistry laboratory, in twenty minutes at the Sorbonne. Naturally, without the Dluskis' help I should never have been able to arrange things like this.

I am working a thousand times as hard as at the beginning of my stay: in the Rue d'Allemagne my little brother-in-law had the habit of disturbing me endlessly. He absolutely could not endure having me do anything but engage in agreeable chatter with him when I was at home. I had to declare war on him on this subject. After a few days Bronya and he began to feel badly about me, and they came to see me. We drank tea, bachelor fashion, and then we went downstairs to see the S.'s, who also live here.

Is your wife taking care of Father, as she promised me? Let her take care, just the same, not to cut me out altogether at home! Father is beginning to speak of her a little too tenderly, and I am afraid that he will be forgetting me soon. . . .

[1] From *Madame Curie: A Biography*, by Eve Curie, copyright, 1937, by Doubleday, Doran & Company, Inc.

Marie was not the only student who lived on a hundred francs a month in the Latin Quarter: most of her Polish comrades were as poor as she was. Some lived by threes or fours in the same lodging and took their meals together; others, who lived alone, devoted several hours a day to housekeeping, cooking and sewing, and by sheer ingenuity ate as much as they wanted, shod and clothed themselves in greater or lesser elegance. This was the method adopted earlier by Bronya, whose talents as a prize cook had been celebrated among her comrades.

Marie disdained to follow such wise examples. She was too fond of her tranquility to share her lodging with a friend or two. She was too haunted by work to bother about her own comfort. Even if she had wished to do so, for that matter, she would have been incapable of it: the girl who had been a governess in strange families at seventeen, giving seven or eight hours of lessons a day, had never found time or occasion for learning how to keep house. Everything that Bronya had learned when she was mistress of her father's house was unknown to Marie. And the report had it, in the Polish colony, that "Mademoiselle Sklodovska doesn't know what you use to make soup."

She did not know, and she did not want to know. Why should she pass a morning initiating herself into the mysteries of a broth, when she might have been learning several pages of physics, or making an interesting analysis in the laboratory?

By deliberate intention she had suppressed diversions from her schedule, as well as friendly meetings and contact with human beings. In the same way she decided that material life had no importance; that it did not exist. And, fortified by this principle, she made for herself a Spartan existence, strange and inhuman.

Rue Flatters, Boulevard Port-Royal, Rue des Feuillantines. . . . All the rooms Marie was to inhabit were alike in discomfort and cheapness of rent. The first was situated in a poorly furnished house where students, doctors and officers of the neighboring garrison lived. Later on the girl, in search of absolute calm, was to take an attic like a servant's room at the top of a middle-class house. For fifteen or twenty francs a month she found a tiny nook which obtained light from a loophole giving directly on the slope of the roof. Through this skylight appeared a small square of the sky. There was no heat, no lighting, no water.

Marie furnished this place with all the objects she possessed: an iron folding bed, the mattress she had brought from Poland, a stove, a white wooden table, a kitchen chair, a washbasin; a petroleum oil lamp, covered by a two-penny shade; a pitcher which she had to fill at the tap on the landing; an alcohol heater about as big as a saucer, which was to cook her meals for the next three years; two plates, a knife, a fork, a spoon, a cup, a stewpan; and finally a kettle and three glasses into which, according to Polish custom, the student would pour tea when the Dluskis came to see her. On the occasions—very rare at present—when Marie received visitors, the rights of hospitality were asserted: the girl lighted the little stove, whose zigzag pipe described complicated angles in the room. And for a seat she pulled out of its corner the bulging brown trunk which served her as wardrobe and chest of drawers.

No service, of course: even one hour of cleaning a day would have over-weighted the expense side of the budget. Transportation costs were suppressed: Marie went to the Sorbonne on foot in all weathers. Coal was kept down to a minimum: one or two sacks of "lumps" for the winter, which the girl bought from the merchant on the corner and hoisted up the steep stairs herself to the sixth floor, bucketful by bucketful, stopping at each floor to breathe. Lights were at a minimum: as soon as night fell, the student took refuge in that blessed asylum called the Library of Sainte-Geneviève, where the gas was lighted and it was warm. Seated at one of the big rectangular tables with her head in her hands, a poor Polish girl could work until they closed the doors at ten o'clock. From then on all that was needed was enough petroleum to keep the light going in her room until two in the morning. Then, with her eyes reddened by fatigue, Marie left her books and threw herself on the bed.

The only thing she knew how to do, in the humble practical domain, was to sew—a memory of the "manual training" at the Sikorski boarding school, and of the long days in Szczuki when the governess, as she supervised the children's study, took up her sewing. . . . It would be rash to conclude from this that the exile ever, by chance, bought a bit of stuff at a low price and made herself a new blouse. She seems to have sworn, on the contrary, never to give up her Warsaw dresses, and wore them, shiny, old-fashioned and threadbare, forever. But she took great care of her clothes, cleaned them and mended them. She also condescended to wash her linen in a basin when she was too tired to work and needed relaxation.

Marie did not admit that she could be cold or hungry. In order not to buy coal—and through sheer carelessness too—she often neglected to light the little stove with the twisted pipe, and she wrote figures and equations without noticing that her fingers were getting numb and her shoulders shaking. A hot soup or a bit of meat would have comforted her; but Marie did not know how to make soup. Marie could not spend a franc and lose a half hour to cook herself a chop. She hardly ever entered the butcher's shop, and even less the restaurant: it was too dear. For weeks at a time she ate nothing but buttered bread and tea. When she wanted a feast, she went into a creamery in the Latin

Quarter and ate two eggs, or else bought herself a piece of chocolate or some fruit.

On this diet the fresh, solid girl who had left Warsaw a few months before rapidly grew anaemic. Often, as she was getting up from her table, her head would go round. She had just time to get to her bed when she would lose consciousness. Coming back to herself, she would ask why she had fainted; she would think herself ill and disdain her illness as she did everything else. It never occurred to her that she was dropping with weakness and that her only disease was that of starvation.

Naturally, she did not boast of this superb organization of existence to the Dluskis. Every time she went to see them she replied in monosyllables to their questions on her progress as a cook, or on her daily menus. If her brother-in-law said she did not look well, she affirmed that she was overworked—which was, in fact, in her eyes, the only reason for her fatigue. And then, dismissing such worries with a gesture of indifference, she would begin to play with her niece, Bronya's baby, for whom she had great affection.

But one day when Marie fainted in front of one of her comrades, the latter hurried to the Rue d'Allemagne to warn the pair of young doctors. Two hours later Casimir was leaping up the six flights of stairs to the attic where the girl, a little pale, was already studying tomorrow's lesson. He examined his sister-in-law. He examined even more carefully the clean plates, the empty stewpan, and the whole room, in which he could discover only one comestible, a packet of tea. All at once he understood—and the questioning began.

"What did you eat today?"

"Today? I don't know. I lunched a while ago."

"What did you eat?" Casimir's voice took her up implacably.

"Some cherries and . . . and all sorts of things."

In the end Marie was obliged to confess: since the evening before she had nibbled at a bundle of radishes and half a pound of cherries. She had worked until three that morning and had slept four hours. Then she had gone to the Sorbonne. On her return she had finished the radishes. Then she had fainted.

The doctor made no long speeches. He was furious. Furious against Marie, whose ash-gray eyes looked at him with profound fatigue and innocent mirth. Furious at himself, for he accused himself of not watching attentively enough over "the little one" who had been confided to him by M. Sklodovski. Without listening to his sister-in-law's protests he handed her her hat and coat, and ordered her to take the books and papers she would need for the coming week. Then, silent, dissatisfied, unhappy, he carried her off to La Villette; from the threshold of the flat he hailed Bronya, who dashed for the kitchen.

Twenty minutes passed, and Marie swallowed, mouthful by mouthful, the medicines ordered for her by Casimir: an enormous underdone beefsteak and a plateful of crackling fried potatoes. As if by a miracle, the color came back to her cheeks. On the same evening Bronya herself came at eleven o'clock to put the light out in the narrow room where she had set up a bed for her sister. For several days Marie, well fed and cared for, "took the cure" and regained her strength. Then, obsessed by the approaching examinations, she returned to her attic, promising to be reasonable in the future.

And the next day she began again to live on air.

Work! . . . Work! Plunged altogether into study, intoxicated by her progress, Marie felt herself equal to learning everything mankind had ever discovered. She attended courses in mathematics, physics and chemistry. Manual technique and the minute precision of scientific experiment became familiar to her, little by little; soon she was to have the joy of being charged by Professor Lippmann with researches of no great importance, which nevertheless permitted her to show her deftness and the originality of her mind. In the physics laboratory of the Sorbonne, a high and wide room queerly ornamented by two little staircases which led to an interior gallery, Marie Sklodovska timidly tried her strength.

She had a passionate love for that atmosphere of attention and silence, the "climate" of the laboratory, which she was to prefer to any other up to her last day. She was on her feet, always on her feet, in front of an oak table supporting precision instruments, or else in front of the chemical hood where some material in fusion bubbled away, worried at by the fierce blowpipe. She was hardly to be distinguished, in her big smock of wrinkled linen, from the thoughtful young men who bent beside her over other blowpipes and other instruments. Like them, she respected the concentration of the place. She made no noise, she pronounced no useless word.

One master's degree was not enough; Marie decided to obtain two: one in physics and one in mathematics. Her plans, once so humble, increased and grew richer so rapidly that she had not the time—and above all not the audacity—to confide them to M. Sklodovski, who, as she knew, impatiently awaited her return to Poland. As usual, the excellent man offered his help. But it could be felt that he was vaguely worried at having hatched this independent creature who had taken to flying with her own wings after so many years of submission and sacrifice.

M. Sklodovski to Bronya, March 5, 1893:

. . . Your last letter mentions for the first time that Manya intends to take her examinations for the master's. She has never spoken to me about it in her letters, even though I have questioned her on the subject. Write me exactly when these examinations will take place, at what date Manya can hope to pass them, what are the fees for them and how much the diploma will cost. I must think of all this in advance so as to be able to send some money to Manya, and on this my personal plans will depend.

. . . I intend to keep the lodging I now occupy for next year: for myself and for Manya—if she comes back—it is perfectly suitable.

. . . Little by little Manya will work up a list of pupils, and in any case I am ready to share what I have with her. We shall manage without trouble. . . .

Marie, however shy she might be, could not avoid meeting human beings every day. Some of the students were cordial and friendly with her. Foreign women were highly regarded at the Sorbonne. These poor girls, generally gifted, coming from far away to the university which the Goncourts called "the nursing mother of study," inspired sympathy among young Frenchmen. The Polish girl was tamed. She discovered that her companions, who were "grinds" for the most part, esteemed her and wished to show her kindness. This kindness sometimes would have liked to become extremely kind indeed. Marie must have been very pretty: her friend, Mlle Dydynska, a charming and somewhat over-excited young woman who had appointed herself as bodyguard, one day threatened to beat off a group of too-eager admirers with her umbrella.

Allowing Mlle Dydynska to repel advances which left her indifferent, the girl drew nearer to men who did not pay court to her and with whom she could talk about her work. Between a physics lesson and a laboratory hour she would chatter with Paul Painlevé, who was already a professor; with Charles Maurain or Jean Perrin—future leaders of French science. These were distant comradeships. Marie had no time to give to friendship or to love. She loved mathematics and physics.

Her brain was so precise, her intelligence so marvelously clear, that no "Slavic" disorder intruded to corrupt her effort. She was supported by a will of iron, by a maniacal taste for perfection, and by an incredible stubbornness. Systematically, patiently, she attained each of the ends she had set for herself: she passed first in the master's examination in physics in 1893,[2] and second in the master's in mathematics in 1894[3].

She had decided to know the French language perfectly, as it was indispensable to her; and instead of cooing incorrect, sing-song sentences for years, as many Poles do, she learned her spelling and syntax with infallible sureness, and hounded down the very last traces of her accent. Only a very slight rolling

[2]Licence ès Sciences Physiques.   [3]Licence ès Sciences Mathématiques.

of the "r" was to remain ever afterward as one of the graces of her rather muted voice, so sweet and charming.

With her forty rubles a month she succeeded in living, and even, by depriving herself of the indispensable, achieved sometimes a certain amount of luxury: an evening at the theater, a journey to the suburbs, whence she brought back flowers picked in the woods to glow for several days on her table. The little peasant of other days was not dead; lost in the great city, she lay in wait for the birth of the leaves, and as soon as she had a little time and money she hurried to the woods.

Marie to M. Sklodovski, April 16, 1893:

The other Sunday I went to Le Raincy, near Paris, in a pretty and agreeable neighborhood. The lilacs and the fruit trees, even the apples, were in full bloom and the air was filled with the scent of flowers.

In Paris the trees get green as early as the beginning of April. Now the leaves have sprung out and the chestnuts are blooming. It is as hot as in summer: everything is green. In my room it is beginning to be torrid. Luckily in July, when I shall be working for my examinations, I shall not be here any more, for I have taken the lodging only to the eighth of July.

The nearer the examinations come, the more I am afraid of not being ready. At the worst, I shall wait until November, but that will make me lose my summer, which doesn't appeal to me. For that matter, we must wait and see. . . .

July. Fever, haste, agonizing trials, crushing mornings when, shut in with thirty students in the examination hall, Marie was so nervous that the letters danced before her eyes and she could not even read the fateful paper for several minutes, with its statement of the problem and the "questions on the course." When the composition was turned in, there came days of waiting until the solemn moment of publication of the results. Marie slipped in among the contestants and their families, crowded into the amphitheater where the names of the elect would be read aloud, in order of merit. Pushed and shoved about as she was, she waited for the entrance of the examiner. And in a sudden silence she heard him pronounce first of all her own name: *Marie Sklodovska.*

Nobody was to guess her emotion. She tore herself away from the congratulations of her comrades, escaped from the crowd and made off. The time for holidays had come now—for the departure to Poland and home.

Such homecomings among the poor Poles had their rites, which Marie scrupulously observed. She moved her furniture—bed, stove and utensils—into safety with a compatriot rich enough to keep her Paris lodging during the summer months. She took leave of her garret: before quitting it forever, she cleaned it thoroughly. She said good-by to the portress, whom she would not see again, and bought some provisions for her journey. Having counted up what she had left, she went into a big shop and did what she had not done for a year: she looked for trinkets, for scarves. . . .

It was accounted a shame to return to one's native land with money in the pocket. Grand style, supreme elegance, the law, required one to spend literally everything on presents for one's family and get into the train at the Gare du Nord without a sou. Was this not a wise course? Two thousand kilometers away, at the other end of the rails, there were M. Sklodovski and Joseph and Hela, a familiar roof to sleep under, as much food as one could eat, and a seamstress who, for a few *groszy*, could cut out and sew linen and big woollen dresses: the dresses which Marie would wear when she came back to the Sorbonne again in November.

She was to reappear there cheerful and a bit too fat, having been stuffed with food for three months in all the houses of all the Sklodovskis in Poland, indignant as they were at her thinness. And again she faced a scholastic year in which she would work, learn, prepare an examination, grow thin.

But each time the autumn returned the same anxiety assailed Marie: how could she go back to Paris? Where was she to find money? Forty rubles at a time, her savings were being exhausted; and she thought with shame of the little pleasures her father deprived himself of to come to her help. In 1893 the situation seemed desperate and the girl was on the point of giving up the journey when a miracle took place. That same Mlle Dydynska who had defended her with an umbrella the year before now extended even more opportune protection. Certain that Marie was destined to a great future, she moved heaven and earth in Warsaw to have the "Alexandrovitch Scholarship" assigned to her—a scholarship for students of merit who wished to pursue their efforts abroad.

Six hundred rubles! Enough to live on for fifteen months! Marie, who knew so well how to ask favors for other people, would never have thought of soliciting this help, and above all could never have had the boldness to make the necessary approaches. Dazzled and enchanted, she took flight for France.

Marie to her brother Joseph, September 15, 1893:

. . . I have already rented my room, on the sixth floor, in a clean and decent street which suits me very well. Tell Father that in that place where I was going to take a room there was nothing free, and that I am very satisfied with this room: it has a window that shuts tight, and when I have arranged it properly it should not be cold here, especially as the floor is of wood and not tiles. Compared to my last year's room it is a veritable palace. It costs one hundred and eighty francs a year, and is therefore sixty francs cheaper than the one Father spoke to me about.

I hardly need say that I am delighted to be back in Paris. It was very hard for me to separate again from Father, but I could see that he was well, very lively, and that he could do without me—especially as you are living in Warsaw. And as for me, it is my whole life that is at stake. It seemed to me, therefore, that I could stay on here without having remorse on my conscience.

Just now I am studying mathematics unceasingly, so as to be up to date when the courses begin. I have three mornings a week taken by lessons with one of my French comrades who is preparing for the examination I have just passed. Tell Father that I am getting used to this work, that it does not tire me as much as before, and that I do not intend to abandon it.

Today I begin the installation of my little corner for this year—very poorly, but what am I to do? I have to do everything myself; otherwise it's all too dear. I must get my furniture into shape—or rather what I pompously call my furniture, for the whole thing isn't worth more than twenty francs.

I shall write soon to Joseph Boguski and ask him for information about his laboratory. My future occupation depends on this.

Marie to her brother, March 18, 1894:

. . . It is difficult for me to tell you about my life in detail; it is so monotonous and, in fact, so uninteresting. Nevertheless I have no feeling of uniformity and I regret only one thing, which is that the days are so short and that they pass so quickly. One never notices what has been done; one can only see what remains to be done, and if one didn't like the work it would be very discouraging.

I want you to pass your doctor's thesis. . . . It seems that life is not easy for any of us. But what of that? We must have perseverance and above all confidence in ourselves. We must believe that we are gifted for something, and that this thing, at whatever cost, must be attained. Perhaps everything will turn out very well, at the moment when we least expect it. . . .

The Alexandrovitch Scholarship was providential. With passionate avarice Marie tried to string out her six hundred rubles, so as to remain a little longer in the paradise of lecture halls and laboratories. Some years later, with the same passionate avarice, she was to save six hundred rubles out of her first earnings—a technical study ordered from her by the Society for the Encouragement of National Industry—and was to take them to the secretary of the Alexandrovitch Foundation, stupefied though he was at a restitution without precedent in the annals of the committee. Marie had accepted this scholarship as testimony of confidence in her, a debt of honor. In her uncompromising soul she would have adjudged herself dishonest if she had kept for one unnecessary moment the money which now could serve as life buoy to another poor young girl.

Rereading a little poem of my mother's, written in Polish, on this time of her life, and remembering the accounts of it that she sometimes gave me, with many a smile and humorous remark, looking at the only portrait of herself which she dearly cherished: the small photograph of a student girl with daring eyes and determined chin, I have felt that she never ceased to prefer these hard, fervent days to all others.

Ah! how harshly the youth of the student passes,
While all around her, with passions ever fresh,
Other youths search eagerly for easy pleasures!
And yet in solitude
She lives, obscure and blessed,
For in her cell she finds the ardor
That makes her heart immense.

But the blessed time is effaced.
She must leave the land of Science
To go out and struggle for her bread
On the grey roads of life.
Often and often then, her weary spirit
Returns beneath the roofs
To the corner ever dear to her heart
Where silent labor swelled
And where a world of memory has rested.

No doubt Marie knew other joys later. But even in her hours of infinite tenderness, even in the hour of triumph and fame, the eternal student was never so content with herself, so proud, as in the poverty and fire of this integral effort. She was proud of her poverty; proud of living alone and independent in a foreign city. Working in the evening beneath the lamp in her poor room she felt that her destiny, still insignificant, mysteriously related itself to the high existences she most admired, and that she became the humble unknown companion of those great scientists of the past, who were, like her, shut into their ill-lighted cells, like her detached from their time, and, like her, spurred their minds to pass beyond the sum of acquired knowledge.

Yes, these four heroic years were, not the happiest of Marie Curie's life, but the most perfect in her eyes, the nearest to those summits of the human mission toward which her gaze had been trained. When one is young and solitary and swallowed up in study, one can "not have enough to live on"—and yet live to the fullest. An immense enthusiasm gave this girl of twenty-six the power to ignore the trials and privations she endured; to magnify her sordid existence into magic. Later on, love, maternity, the worries of a wife and mother, the complexities of crushingly hard work, were to restore the visionary to real life. But in the enchanted moment when she was poorer than she was ever to be again, she was as reckless as a child. She floated lightly in another world, that which her thought was to regard always as the only pure and true one.

Each day could not be altogether excellent in an adventure like this. There were unforeseen accidents which suddenly upset everything and seemed irremediable: a fatigue impossible to surmount, a short illness requiring care. Still other, and terrifying catastrophes: the one pair of shoes, with leaky soles, gave out finally, and the purchase of new shoes became necessary. This meant a budget upside down for weeks, and the enormous expense had to be made up at all costs, on meals or on petroleum for the lamp.

Or else the winter was longer than usual and the sixth-floor garret was icy. It was so cold that Marie could no longer sleep; she shivered and chattered with it. Her supply of coal was exhausted. . . . But what of that? Could a Polish girl be conquered by a Parisian winter? Marie lighted her lamp again and looked about her. She opened the fat trunk and gathered together all the garments she possessed. She put on all she could, then, having slipped into bed, she piled the rest, her other dress, her linen, on top of the single coverlet. But it was still too cold. Marie stretched out her arm, pulled the one chair over to her, raised it and piled it, too, on top of the amassed garments, giving herself some sort of illusion of weight and heat.

All she had to do now was to wait for sleep, without moving, so as to preserve the scaffolding of which she was the living base. Meanwhile, a layer of ice was slowly forming in the water pitcher.

E. B. W.[1]

James Thurber

THREE—no, six years ago (how the time flies!) a gentleman came to the offices of *The New Yorker* and asked for E. B. White. He was shown into the reception room and Mr. White was told that someone was waiting for him there. White's customary practice in those days, if he couldn't place a caller's name, was to slip moodily out of the building by way of the fire escape and hide in the coolness of Schrafft's until the visitor went away. He is not afraid of process servers, blackmailers, borrowers, or cranks; he is afraid

[1]From *The Saturday Review of Literature*, October 15, 1938.

of the smiling stranger who tramples the inviolable flowers of your privacy bearing a letter of introduction from an old Phi Gam brother now in the real estate game in Duluth. White knows that the Man in the Reception Room may not be so easy to get rid of as a process server—or even a blackmailer: he may grab great handfuls of your fairest hours, he may even appropriate a sizeable chunk of your life, for no better reason than that he was anchor man on your brother's high school relay team, or married the sister of your old girl, or met an aunt of yours on a West Indies cruise. Most of us, out of a politeness made up of faint curiosity and profound resignation, go out to meet the smiling stranger with a gesture of surrender and a fixed grin, but White has always taken to the fire escape. He has avoided the Man in the Reception Room as he has avoided the interviewer, the photographer, the microphone, the rostrum, the literary tea, and the Stork Club. His life is his own. He is the only writer of prominence I know of who could walk through the Algonquin lobby or between the tables at Jack and Charlie's and be recognized only by his friends.

But to get back to the particular caller of six years ago whom we left waiting in the reception room. On that occasion, out of some obscure compulsion, White decided to go out and confront the man and see what he wanted. "I'm White," he told the stranger he found sitting alone in the room. The man rose, stared for a long moment at the audacious fellow in front of him, and then said, with grim certainty, "You are not E. B. White." White admits that his hair leaped up but it is my fond contention that his heart did, too. I like to think that he was a little disappointed when he realized, as he was bound to, that the man was wrong. I like to insist that he resumed his burden of identity with a small sigh. (Where the remarkable interview got to from the tense point to which I have brought it here I shall leave it to my memoirs to tell.)

In the early days of *The New Yorker* the object of this searching examination signed his first few stories and poems with his full name: Elwyn (as God is my judge) Brooks White. I cannot imagine what spark of abandon, what youthful spirit of devil-may-care prompted a poet who loves to live half-hidden from the eye to come out thus boldly into the open. He didn't keep it up long; he couldn't stand the fierce glare of polysyllabic self-acknowledgment. For the past twelve years he has signed his casuals and his verses merely with his initials, E. B. W. To his friends he is Andy. It was a lucky break that saved him from Elly or Wynnie or whatever one might make out of Elwyn in the diminutive. He went to Cornell and it seems that every White who goes there is nicknamed Andy for the simple if rather faraway reason that the first president of the University was named Andrew White.

It used to be (indeed I believe it still is) a wonder and a worry to White's boss, Mr. Harold Ross, the mystic and wonderful editor of *The New Yorker*, that his favorite and most invaluable assistant avoided people, lived along the untrodden ways, hid by mossy stones, and behaved generally in what Ross was pleased to call an anti-social manner. For a restlessly gregarious man who consorts with ten thousand people from Groucho Marx to Lord Dalhousie it is difficult to comprehend the spirit of Walden Pond. As long ago as the late nineteen twenties there were hundreds of people who implored Ross to introduce them to the man who wrote, on the already famous first page of *The New Yorker*, those silver and crystal sentences which have a ring like the ring of nobody else's sentences in the world. White declined to be taken to literary parties, or to any other kind of parties, but one day Ross lured him to the house of a certain literary lady who, White was persuaded to believe, would be found alone. When the door of her house was opened to them, Ross pushed White into a hallway loud with the chatter of voices proceeding from a crowded living room, the unmistakably assertive voices of writers and artists. Ross made the serious mistake of entering the living room first. When he looked around for White, that shy young man had quietly disappeared. He had proceeded deviously through the house, to the disciplined dismay of the servants, out the back door, and over trees and fences, or whatever else may have been in his way, to the freedom he so greatly cherishes, leaving the curtsy, the compliment, and the booksy chat to writers who go in for that sort of thing.

"Isn't there," Ross demanded of him one time, "*any*body you would like to meet?" White gave this difficult question his grave consideration and said, at what Alexander Woollcott would call long last, "Yes. Willie Stevens and Helen Hayes." It is a proof of the reckless zeal and the devoted energy of Harold Ross that he instantly set about trying to get hold of Willie Stevens for the purpose of inviting him to a dinner in New York at which White and Miss Hayes were to be the only other guests. I am desolated to report that this little coming together could not be accomplished: Willie apparently knew too many people the way it was and declined the invitation with that gentle old world courtesy of which he was so consummate a master. Ross did manage finally to bring White face to face with Helen Hayes. Our hero, I am informed, was discontented and tongue-tied during their brief, jumpy conversation and was glad when it was all over. I suppose Miss Hayes was, too.

E. B. W. was born in Mount Vernon, N. Y., and will be forty next year. He had an ordinary, normal childhood, monkeying with an old Oliver typewriter, shooting with an air gun at the weathervane on his father's barn. At Cornell he charmed and astonished his English professors with a prose style so far above Cayuga's ordinary run of literary talent as to be considered something of a miracle. The *Cornell Sun* under White's editorship must have been the best written college newspaper in the country. After Cornell he drove a model T Ford across the country with a friend named Howard Cushman. When they ran out of money, they played for their supper—and their gasoline —on a fascinating musical instrument that White had made out of some pieces of wire and an old shoe or something. In Seattle the young explorer got a job as reporter on the *Times*, the kind of newspaper that did not allow you to use the verb "to mangle." Accurately reporting, one day, the anguished cry of a poor husband who found the body of his wife in the municipal morgue, White wrote "My God, it's her!" and when the city editor changed this to "My God, it is she!" our wanderer moved sadly on to where they had a better understanding of people and a proper feeling for the finer usages of the English tongue. He became mess boy on a ship bound for Alaska, commanded by an old whaling captain, and manned by a crew who knew that a man says it's her when he finds her dead.

Shortly after *The New Yorker* was founded, its editors began to get occasionally manuscripts from an unknown young man named E. B. White who was a production assistant in an advertising agency. Harold Ross and Katharine Angell, his literary editor, were not slow to perceive that here were the perfect eye and ear, the authentic voice and accent for their struggling magazine. It took months, however, to trap the elusive writer into a conference and weeks to persuade him to come to work in the office; he finally agreed to give them his Thursdays. It is not too much to say that Andy White was the most valuable person on the magazine. His delicate tinkering with the works of *The New Yorker* caused it to move with a new ease and grace. His tag lines for those little newsbreaks which the magazine uses at the bottom of columns were soon being read joyfully aloud around town. His contributions to the Talk of the Town, particularly his Notes and Comment on the first page, struck the shining note that Ross had dreamed of striking. He has written a great many of the memorable picture captions, including the famous one that has passed (usually misquoted) into song and legend, editorial and, I daresay, sermon: "I say it's spinach and I say the hell with it." He had a hand in everything: he even painted a cover and wrote a few advertisements. One day nine years ago he decided that some pencil drawings I had absently made and thrown on the floor should be published in *The New Yorker*, so he picked them up, inked in the lines, and, to the surprise of us all, including Ross, got them published in *The New Yorker*.

Andy White understands begonias and children, canaries and goldfish, dachshunds and Scottish terriers, men and motives. His ear not only notes the louder cosmic rhythms but catches the faintest ticking sounds. He plays a fair ping pong, a good piano, and a terrible poker (once, holding four natural jacks, he dropped out of the betting under the delusion that there were eight jacks in the deck and all he had was half of them.) He has steadfastly refused to learn to play bridge or to take out life insurance. Once he offered an airplane pilot a thousand dollars to take him through a stormy dawn from Roosevelt Field to Chicago because a mysterious phone call had made him believe a friend was in great distress. The pilot had to make a forced landing in Pittsburgh, so that all White had to pay to see for himself that all was quiet along Lake Michigan was eight hundred dollars and his railroad fare from Pittsburgh. When a band of desperadoes stole his Buick sedan out of a quiet Turtle Bay garage and used it in the robbery of an upstate bank, White was suspected by the New York police of being the "brain guy" who devised the operations of a large and dangerous mob. For days detectives shrewdly infested his office, peering under tables, asking questions, staring in suspicious bewilderment at the preposterous array of scrawls, dentist's dates, symbols, phone numbers, photographs, and maps that littered his walls. Eventually they went shrewdly away but every time I hear the sirens scream, I think they are coming for White. The former suspect is a good man with ax, rifle, and canoe (for several years he was part owner of a boys' camp in darkest Canada), and he sails a thirty-foot boat expertly. Two of his favorite books are Van Zanten's "Happy Days" and Alain-Fournier's "The Wanderer." In the country he is afflicted with hay fever and in the city with a dizziness that resembles ordinary dizziness only as the mist resembles the rain. He expects every day of his life that something will kill him: a bit of mould, a small bug, a piece of huckleberry pie.

Some years ago White bought a farm in Maine and he now lives there the year around with his wife, who was Katharine Angell, and their son. He spends most of his time delousing turkeys, gathering bantam eggs, building mice-proof closets, and ripping out old fireplaces and putting in new ones. There is in him not a little of the spirit of Thoreau who believed "that the world crowds round the individual, leaving him no vista, and shuts out the beauty of the earth; and that the wholesome wants of man are few." Now and then, between sunup and milking time, Andy White manages to write a casual or a poem for *The New Yorker*, and he does a monthly department for *Harper's Magazine*. Many of the things he writes seem to me as lovely as a tree— say a maple after the first frost, or the cherry hung with snow. What he will go on to do in his forties and fifties I have no idea. If he simply continues to do what he has always done, it will be all right with me.

College

OF EDUCATION

John Milton

To Master Samuel Hartlib[1]

Master Hartlib:

I am long since persuaded that to say or do aught worth memory and imitation, no purpose or respect should sooner move us than simply the love of God and of mankind. Nevertheless to write now the reforming of education, though it be one of the greatest and noblest designs that can be thought on, and for the want whereof this nation perishes, I had not yet at this time been induced but by your earnest entreaties and serious conjurements; as having my mind for the present half diverted in the pursuance of some other assertions, the knowledge and the use of which cannot but be a great furtherance both to the enlargement of truth, and honest living, with much more peace. Nor should the laws of any private friendship have prevailed with me to divide thus or transpose my former thoughts, but that I see those aims, those actions which have won you with me the esteem of a person sent hither by some good providence from a far country to be the occasion and the incitement of great good to this island.

And, as I hear, you have obtained the same repute with men of most approved wisdom, and some of highest authority among us; not to mention the learned correspondence which you hold in foreign parts, and the extraordinary pains and diligence which you have used in this matter, both here and beyond the seas; either by the definite will of God so ruling, or the peculiar sway of nature, which also is God's working. Neither can I think that, so reputed and so valued as you are, you would, to the forfeit of your own discerning ability, impose upon me an unfit and overponderous argument; but that the satisfaction which you profess to have received from those incidental discourses which we have wandered into, hath pressed and almost constrained you into a persuasion that what you require from me in this point, I neither ought, nor can in conscience, defer beyond this time both of so much need at once, and so much opportunity to try what God hath determined.

I will not resist, therefore, whatever it is either of divine or human obligement, that you lay upon me; but will forthwith set down in writing, as you request me, that voluntary idea, which hath long in silence presented itself to me, of a better education, in extent and comprehension far more large, and yet of time far shorter and of attainment far more certain than hath been yet in practice. Brief I shall endeavor to be; for that which I have to say, assuredly

---

[1]Written in 1644.

this nation hath extreme need should be done sooner than spoken. To tell you, therefore, what I have benefited herein among old renowned authors, I shall spare; and to search what many modern Januas and Didactics, more than ever I shall read, have projected, my inclination leads me not. But if you can accept of these few observations which have flowered off, and are as it were the burnishing of many studious and contemplative years altogether spent in the search of religious and civil knowledge, and such as pleased you so well in the relating, I here give you them to dispose of.

The end, then, of learning is to repair the ruins of our first parents by regaining to know God aright, and out of that knowledge to love him, to imitate him, to be like him, as we may the nearest by possessing our souls of true virtue, which, being united to the heavenly grace of faith, makes up the highest perfection. But because understanding cannot in this body found itself but on sensible things, nor arrive so clearly to the knowledge of God and things invisible, as by orderly conning over the visible and inferior creature, the same method is necessarily to be followed in all discreet teaching. And seeing every nation affords not experience and tradition enough for all kind of learning, therefore we are chiefly taught the languages of those people who have at any time been most industrious after wisdom; so that language is but the instrument conveying to us things useful to be known. And though a linguist should pride himself to have all the tongues that Babel cleft the world into, yet if he have not studied the solid things in them, as well as the words and lexicons, he were nothing so much to be esteemed a learned man as any yeoman or tradesman competently wise in his mother-dialect only.

Hence appear the many mistakes which have made learning generally so unpleasing and so unsuccessful; first, we do amiss to spend seven or eight years merely in scraping together so much miserable Latin and Greek as might be learned otherwise easily and delightfully in one year. And that which casts our proficiency therein so much behind is our time lost partly in too oft idle vacancies given both to schools and universities; partly in a preposterous exaction, forcing the empty wits of children to compose themes, verses, and orations, which are the acts of ripest judgment, and the final work of a head filled by long reading and observing with elegant maxims and copious invention. These are not matters to be wrung from poor striplings, like blood out of the nose, or the plucking of untimely fruit. Besides the ill habit which they get of wretched barbarizing against the Latin and Greek idiom with their untutored Anglicisms, odious to be read, yet not to be avoided without a well-continued and judicious conversing among pure authors, digested, which they scarce taste. Whereas, if after some preparatory grounds of speech by their certain forms got into memory, they were led to the praxis thereof in some chosen short book lessoned thoroughly to them, they might then forthwith proceed to learn the substance of good things, and arts in due order, which would bring the whole language quickly into their power. This I take to be the most rational and most profitable way of learning languages, and whereby we may best hope to give account to God of our youth spent herein.

And for the usual method of teaching arts, I deem it to be an old error of universities, not yet well recovered from the scholastic grossness of barbarous ages, that instead of beginning with arts most easy (and those be such as are most obvious to the sense), they present their young unmatriculated novices at first coming with the most intellective abstractions of logic and metaphysics; so that they having but newly left those grammatic flats and shallows, where they stuck unreasonably to learn a few words with lamentable construction, and now on the sudden transported under another climate, to be tossed and turmoiled with their unballasted wits in fathomless and unquiet deeps of controversy, do for the most part grow into hatred and contempt of learning, mocked and deluded all this while with ragged notions and babblements, while they expected worthy and delightful knowledge; till poverty or youthful years call them importunately their several ways, and hasten them, with the sway of friends, either to an ambitious and mercenary, or ignorantly zealous divinity: some allured to the trade of law, grounding their purposes not on the prudent and heavenly contemplation of justice and equity, which was never taught them, but on the promising and pleasing thoughts of litigious terms, fat contentions, and flowing fees; others betake them to state affairs, with souls so unprincipled in virtue and true generous breeding that flattery, and court shifts, and tyrannous aphorisms appear to them the highest points of wisdom, instilling their barren hearts with a conscientious slavery, if, as I rather think, it be not feigned. Others, lastly, of a more delicious and airy spirit, retire themselves (knowing no better) to the enjoyments of ease and luxury, living out their days in feast and jollity; which, indeed, is the wisest and the safest course of all these, unless they were with more integrity undertaken. And these are the errors, and these are the fruits of misspending our prime youth at the schools and universities as we do, either in learning mere words, or such things chiefly as were better unlearned.

I shall detain you now no longer in the demonstration of what we should not do, but straight conduct ye to a hillside, where I will point ye out the right path of a virtuous and noble education; laborious indeed at the first ascent, but else so smooth, so green, so full of goodly prospect and melodious sounds on every side that the harp of Orpheus was not more charming. I doubt not but ye shall have more ado to drive our dullest and laziest youth, our stocks and stubs, from the infinite desire of such a happy nurture, than we have now to hale and drag our choicest and hopefullest wits to that asinine feast of sow-thistles and brambles which is commonly set before them as all the food and entertainment of their tenderest and most docible age. I call, therefore, a complete and generous education, that which fits a man to perform justly, skillfully, and magnanimously all the offices, both private and public, of peace and war. And how all this may be done between twelve and one-and-twenty, less time than is now bestowed in pure trifling at grammar and sophistry, is to be thus ordered:

First, to find out a spacious house and ground about it fit for an academy, and big enough to lodge a hundred and fifty persons, whereof twenty or thereabout may be attendants, all under the government of one who shall be thought of desert sufficient, ability either to do all, or wisely to direct and oversee it done. This place should be at once both school and university, not needing a remove to any other house of scholarship, except it be some peculiar college of law, or physic, where they mean to be practitioners; but as for those general studies which take up all our time from Lily to the commencing, as they term it, master of art, it should be absolute. After this pattern, as many edifices may be converted to this use as shall be needful in every city throughout this land, which would tend much to the increase of learning and civility everywhere. This number, less or more, thus collected, to the convenience of a foot-company, or interchangeably two troops of cavalry, should divide their day's work into three parts as it lies orderly: their studies, their exercise, and their diet.

For their studies: first, they should begin with the chief and necessary rules of some good grammar, either that now used, or any better; and while this is doing, their speech is to be fashioned to a distinct and clear pronunciation, as near as may be to the Italian, especially in the vowels. For we Englishmen, being far northerly, do not open our mouths in the cold air wide enough to grace a southern tongue; but are observed by all other nations to speak exceedingly close and inward, so that to smatter Latin with an English mouth is as ill a hearing as law French. Next, to make them expert in the usefullest points of grammar, and withal to season them and win them early to the love of virtue and true labor, ere any flattering seducement or vain principle seize them wandering, some easy and delightful book of education would be read to them, whereof the Greeks have store, as Cebes, Plutarch, and other Socratic discourses. But in Latin we have none of classic authority extant, except the two or three first books of Quintilian, and some select pieces elsewhere.

But here the main skill and groundwork will be to temper them such lectures and explanations, upon every opportunity, as may lead and draw them in willing obedience, inflamed with the study of learning and the admiration of virtue; stirred up with high hopes of living to be brave men and worthy patriots, dear to God, and famous to all ages: that they may despise and scorn all their childish and ill-taught qualities, to delight in manly and liberal exercises, which he who hath the art and proper eloquence to catch them with, what with mild and effectual persuasions, and what with the intimation of some fear, if need be, but chiefly by his own example, might in a short space gain them to an incredible diligence and courage, infusing into their young breasts such an ingenuous and noble ardor as would not fail to make any of them renowned and matchless men. At the same time, some other hour of the day, might be taught them the rules of arithmetic; and soon after the elements of geometry, even playing, as the old manner was. After evening repast, till bedtime, their thoughts will be best taken up in the easy ground of religion, and the story of Scripture.

The next step would be to the authors of agriculture, Cato, Varro, and Columella, for the matter is most easy; and if the language be difficult, so much the better; it is not a difficulty above their years. And here will be an occasion of inciting and enabling them hereafter to improve the tillage of their country, to recover the bad soil, and to remedy the waste that is made of good; for this was one of Hercules' praises. Ere half these authors be read (which will soon be with plying hard and daily), they cannot choose but be masters of any ordinary prose: so that it will be then seasonable for them to learn in any modern author the use of the globes, and all the maps, first with the old names, and then with the new; or they might be then capable to read any compendious method of natural philosophy;—and at the same time might be entering into the Greek tongue, after the same manner as was before prescribed in the Latin; whereby the difficulties of grammar being soon overcome, all the historical physiology of Aristotle and Theophrastus are open before them, and, as I may say, under contribution. The like access will be to Vitruvius, to Seneca's *Natural Questions*, to Mela, Celsus, Pliny, or Solinus. And having thus passed the principles of arithmetic, geometry, astronomy, and geography, with a general compact of physics, they may descend in mathematics to the instrumental science of trigonometry, and from thence to fortification, architecture, enginery, or navigation. And in natural philosophy they may proceed leisurely from the history of meteors, minerals, plants, and living creatures, as far as anatomy.

Then also in course might be read to them, out of some not tedious writer, the institution of physic,[2] that may know the tempers, the humors, the seasons, and how to manage a crudity,[3] which he who can wisely and timely do, is not only a great physician to himself and to his friends, but also may, at some time

2Of medicine.   3Indigestion.

or other, save an army by this frugal and expenseless means only; and not let the healthy and stout bodies of young men rot away under him for want of this discipline, which is a great pity, and no less a shame to the commander. To set forward all these proceedings in nature and mathematics, what hinders but that they may procure, as oft as shall be needful, the helpful experiences of hunters, fowlers, fishermen, shepherds, gardeners, apothecaries; and in the other sciences, architects, engineers, mariners, anatomists; who doubtless would be ready, some for reward, and some to favor such a hopeful seminary. And this will give them such a real tincture of natural knowledge as they shall never forget, but daily augment with delight. Then also those poets which are now counted most hard will be both facile and pleasant, Orpheus, Hesiod, Theocritus, Aratus, Nicander, Oppian, Dionysius; and in Latin, Lucretius, Manilius, and the rural part of Virgil.

By this time, years and good general precepts will have furnished them more distinctly with that act of reason which in ethics is called proairesis,[4] that they may with some judgment contemplate upon moral good and evil. Then will be required a special reinforcement of constant and sound indoctrinating, to set them right and firm, instructing them more amply in the knowledge of virtue and the hatred of vice; while their young and pliant affections are led through all the moral works of Plato, Xenophon, Cicero, Plutarch, Laertius, and those Locrian remnants; but still to be reduced in their nightward studies wherewith they close the day's work, under the determinate sentence of David or Solomon, or the evangels and apostolic Scriptures. Being perfect in the knowledge of personal duty, they may then begin the study of economics. And either now or before this they may have easily learned, at any odd hour, the Italian tongue. And soon after, but with wariness and good antidote, it would be wholesome enough to let them taste some choice comedies, Greek, Latin, or Italian; those tragedies also that treat of household matters, as *Trachiniae*, *Alcestis*, and the like.

The next remove must be to the study of politics; to know the beginning, end, and reasons of political societies, that they may not, in a dangerous fit of the commonwealth, be such poor, shaken, uncertain reeds, of such a tottering conscience, as many of our great counselors have lately shown themselves, but steadfast pillars of the state. After this, they are to dive into the grounds of law, and legal justice; delivered first and with best warrant by Moses; and, as far as human prudence can be trusted, in those extolled remains of Grecian lawgivers, Lycurgus, Solon, Zaleucus, Charondas, and thence to all the Roman edicts and tables, with their Justinian; and so down to the Saxon and common laws of England, and the statutes.

[4]Choice between good and evil.

Sundays also and every evening may be now understandingly spent in the highest matters of theology, and church history, ancient and modern; and ere this time the Hebrew tongue at a set hour might have been gained, that the Scriptures may be now read in their own original; whereto it would be no impossibility to add the Chaldee and the Syrian dialect. When all these employments are well conquered, then will the choice histories, heroic poems, and Attic tragedies of stateliest and most regal argument, with all the famous political orations, offer themselves; which, if they were not only read, but some of them got by memory, and solemnly pronounced with right accent and grace, as might be taught, would endue them even with the spirit and vigor of Demosthenes or Cicero, Euripides or Sophocles.

And now, lastly, will be the time to read with them those organic arts which enable men to discourse and write perspicuously, elegantly, and according to the fitted style of lofty, mean,[5] or lowly. Logic, therefore, so much as is useful, is to be referred to this due place with all her well-couched heads and topics, until it be time to open her contracted palm into a graceful and ornate rhetoric, taught out of the rule of Plato, Aristotle, Phalereus, Cicero, Hermogenes, Longinus. To which poetry would be made subsequent, or indeed rather precedent, as being less subtle and fine, but more simple, sensuous, and passionate. I mean not here the prosody of a verse, which they could not but have hit on before among the rudiments of grammar; but that sublime art which in Aristotle's *Poetics*, in Horace, and the Italian commentaries of Castelvetro, Tasso, Mazzoni, and others, teaches what the laws are of a true epic poem, what of a dramatic, what of a lyric, what decorum is, which is the grand masterpiece to observe. This would make them soon perceive what despicable creatures our common rimers and play-writers be; and show them what religious, what glorious and magnificent use, might be made of poetry, both in divine and human things.

From hence, and not till now, will be the right season of forming them to be able writers and composers in every excellent matter, when they shall be thus fraught with an universal insight into things. Or whether they be to speak in parliament or council, honor and attention would be waiting on their lips. There would then also appear in pulpits other visages, other gestures, and stuff otherwise wrought than what we now sit under, oft-times to as great trial of our patience as any other that they preach to us. These are the studies wherein our noble and our gentle youth ought to bestow their time in a disciplinary way from twelve to one-and-twenty, unless they rely more upon their ancestors dead than upon themselves living. In which methodical course it is so supposed they must proceed by the steady pace of learning onward, as

[5]Intermediate.

at convenient times, for memory's sake, to retire back into the middle ward, and sometimes into the rear of what they have been taught, until they have confirmed and solidly united the whole body of their perfected knowledge, like the last embattling of a Roman legion. Now will be worth the seeing what exercises and what recreations may best agree and become these studies.

The course of study hitherto briefly described is, what I can guess by reading, likest to those ancient and famous schools of Pythagoras, Plato, Isocrates, Aristotle, and such others, out of which were bred up such a number of renowned philosophers, orators, historians, poets, and princes all over Greece, Italy, and Asia, besides the flourishing studies of Cyrene and Alexandria. But herein it shall exceed them, and supply a defect as great as that which Plato noted in the commonwealth of Sparta. Whereas that city trained up their youth most for war, and these in their academies and Lyceum all for the gown, this institution of breeding which I here delineate shall be equally good both for peace and war. Therefore about an hour and a half ere they eat at noon should be allowed them for exercise, and due rest afterwards; but the time for this may be enlarged at pleasure according as their rising in the morning shall be early.

The exercise which I commend first is the exact use of their weapon, to guard, and to strike safely with edge or point. This will keep them healthy, nimble, strong, and well in breath; is also the likeliest means to make them grow large and tall, and to inspire them with a gallant and fearless courage, which being tempered with seasonable lectures and precepts to them of true fortitude and patience, will turn into a native and heroic valor and make them hate the cowardice of doing wrong. They must be also practiced in all the locks and gripes of wrestling, wherein Englishmen were wont to excel, as need may often be in fight to tug, to grapple, and to close. And this perhaps will be enough, wherein to prove and heat their single strength.

The interim of unsweating themselves regularly, and convenient rest before meat, may both with profit and delight, be taken up in recreating and composing their travailed spirits with the solemn and divine harmonies of music, heard or learned; either while the skillful organist plies his grave and fancied descant in lofty fugues, or the whole symphony with artful and unimaginable touches adorn and grace the well-studied chords of some choice composer; sometimes the lute or soft organ-stop waiting on elegant voices, either to religious, martial, or civil ditties; which, if wise men and prophets be not extremely out, have a great power over dispositions and manners, to smooth and make them gentle from rustic harshness and distempered passions. The like also would not be unexpedient after meat, to assist and cherish nature in her first concoction, and send their minds back to study in good tune and satisfaction. Where having followed it under vigilant eyes till about two hours before supper, they are, by a sudden alarum or watchword, to be called out to their military motions, under sky or covert, according to the season, as was the Roman wont; first on foot, then, as their age permits, on horseback, to all the art of cavalry; that having in sport, but with much exactness and daily muster, served out the rudiments of their soldiership in all the skill of embattling, marching, encamping, fortifying, besieging, and battering, with all the helps of ancient and modern stratagems, tactics, and warlike maxims, they may as it were out of a long war come forth renowned and perfect commanders in the service of their country. They would not then, if they were trusted with fair and hopeful armies, suffer them, for want of just and wise discipline, to shed away from about them like sick feathers, though they be never so oft supplied; they would not suffer their empty and unrecruitable colonels of twenty men in a company to quaff out or convey into secret hoards the wages of a delusive list and a miserable remnant; yet in the meanwhile to be overmastered with a score or two of drunkards, the only soldiery left about them, or else to comply with all rapines and violences. No, certainly, if they knew aught of that knowledge that belongs to good men or good governors they would not suffer these things.

But to return to our own institute: besides these constant exercises at home, there is another opportunity of gaining experience to be won from pleasure itself abroad; in those vernal seasons of the year when the air is calm and pleasant, it were an injury and sullenness against nature not to go out and see her riches, and partake in her rejoicing with heaven and earth. I should not, therefore, be a persuader to them of studying much then, after two or three years that they have well laid their grounds, but to ride out in companies, with prudent and staid guides, to all the quarters of the land; learning and observing all places of strength, all commodities of building and of soil, for towns and tillage, harbors and ports for trade. Sometimes taking sea as far as to our navy, to learn there also what they can in the practical knowledge of sailing and of sea-fight.

These ways would try all their peculiar gifts of nature; and if there were any secret excellence among them would fetch it out, and give it fair opportunities to advance itself by, which could not but mightily redound to the good of this nation, and bring into fashion again those old admired virtues and excellencies, with far more advantage now in this purity of Christian knowledge. Nor shall we then need the monsieurs of Paris to take our hopeful youth into their slight and prodigal custodies, and send them over back again transformed into mimics, apes, and kickshaws.[6] But if they desire to see other

[6]Superficial persons.

countries at three or four and twenty years of age, not to learn principles, but to enlarge experience and make wise observation, they will by that time be such as shall deserve the regard and honor of all men where they pass, and the society and friendship of those in all places who are best and most eminent. And perhaps then other nations will be glad to visit us for their breeding, or else to imitate us in their own country.

Now, lastly, for their diet there cannot be much to say, save only that it would be best in the same house; for much time else would be lost abroad, and many ill habits got; and that it should be plain, healthful, and moderate, I suppose is out of controversy.

Thus, Mr. Hartlib, you have a general view in writing, as your desire was, of that which at several times I had discoursed with you concerning the best and noblest way of education; not beginning, as some have done, from the cradle, which yet might be worth many considerations, if brevity had not been my scope. Many other circumstances also I could have mentioned, but this, to such as have the worth in them to make trial, for light and direction may be enough. Only I believe that this is not a bow for every man to shoot in[7] that counts himself a teacher, but will require sinews almost equal to those which Homer gave Ulysses; yet I am withal persuaded that it may prove much more easy in the assay than it now seems at distance, and much more illustrious; howbeit, not more difficult than I imagine, and that imagination presents me with nothing but very happy, and very possible according to best wishes, if God have so decreed, and this age have spirit and capacity enough to apprehend.

EDUCATION FOR LIVING[1]

Philip N. Youtz

THE function of American college and university education is to teach students how to live. Education is basically an anthropological problem. The purpose of the school is to develop the whole man and to prepare him to live efficiently and happily in the most intricate and rapidly changing culture this planet has produced.

Were we not primitive still, we should start long before school and college to breed students with the same care which we now devote to the breeding of plants and animals. The family institution, which we share with the higher animals, would be studied and either modified or supplanted to give our wellbred student the best possible environment during his early and most im-

[7]With.   [1]From *The Forum*, November, 1937.

pressionable years. Primary and secondary schools would be scrapped, and new and more refined educational instruments would be devised to serve the purpose of training the sensitive and growing student during the creative unfolding of his powers. The college and university would be discarded, and in their place we should provide a new instrumentality especially designed to teach the student all that is known about the art of living. In face of the ignorance, prejudice, and superstition which characterize our culture, such an intelligent approach to the educational problem is impossible. The best we can do is to focus attention on one step in the educational system and ask ourselves candidly whether it is not indeed the worst of possible instruments for the purpose intended and whether we are not justified in cautiously experimenting with a view to producing a new college and university capable of dealing with our present grade of students.

The most obvious difficulties with colleges today are easy to point out, though extremely hard to remedy.

First, the students are poorly bred, carelessly nurtured, and badly prepared. There seems very little that can be done about this situation as long as parenthood is the privilege of the unfit as well as the fit and as long as primary and secondary schools remain more political than educational institutions.

Second, the college today is a marriage of convenience between the medieval literary type of university and the modern scientific school. As might be expected from such an unnatural union there has arisen much dissent. The moderns have won to the extent of abandoning Greek and Latin, but the medieval partner has shown remarkable vitality, insisting that education remain largely an affair of words and books. Last, colleges and universities are generally run for faculties, not for students. They are designed to provide a pleasant academic retreat for professors who are deeply interested in their chosen subjects but who care very little about the job of education. The student is the forgotten man at most universities.

The graduate of twenty years' standing looks back at his futile struggles to apply a college education to the business of living with complete disillusionment. If he worked his way through school in part or in whole, he knows well that the four years of college and the four years of graduate work which followed were not worth the effort. He was the victim of America's best organized and most respected racket operating entirely within the law. His advice to the younger man who is just reaching the college age is (a) do not go to college at all or (b) accept the present college as a pleasant club where an intelligent man may enjoy four years of comparative leisure or (c) join with a group of other students and persuade some college president to try out the following curriculum.

The new curriculum will have the revolutionary aim of preparing students for twentieth-century living. Its most radical feature will be that it starts with the student.

What is a student? He is a physically mature and mentally adolescent animal who must compete in a civilization which moves a hundred times more rapidly than the one which his grandparents knew. As a healthy animal, he has sex as a dominant interest. Physiologically, he is ready for a mate. For social and economic reasons this mating must be postponed for a period of years. Muscularly, he is ready for the chase and for the warfare in which his not very remote ancestors delighted, though he lives in a culture which provides food without hunting and which regards warfare as a breakdown of civilization. He is very imaginative; he is subject to day-dreaming; he is emotionally unstable; intellectually, he is extremely naïve. Most of his attitudes are derived from his family and a narrow circle of friends. He is curious but not informed. He is personal in his judgments. He is earnest and trustful and eager to learn the mysteries of this modern world. Finally, he is away from home for the first time and knows nothing about taking care of himself or of planning his own life.

This young animal is an organism, and each part of his nature affects every other part. Ask him to write a paper on Shakespeare's use of the sonnet, and he is in such an emotional state over having succeeded or failed to make a fraternity that he writes gibberish. Demonstrate a mathematical solution to him, and he loses the thread of the reasoning because his fancy has wandered to the contemplation of some glamourous individual of the opposite sex. Lecture to him on Plato, and he falls asleep, in spite of having drunk three cups of strong coffee, because physically he is at the height of his powers and enjoys football so keenly that he plays until he is dead tired. You can't concentrate on training one part of him without having to reckon with the whole man. This fact is so fundamental that only college and university professors could have overlooked it.

Whether or not there is much organization or relation in the varied fields of human endeavor, each of us has to achieve a certain unity of experience in his own education. The mind is incessantly at work trying to integrate all the fragments of knowledge into one connected fabric. Subjects are separated, and courses of study are marked off chiefly for convenience. Because of the vast accumulation of knowledge, it is necessary to departmentalize to an ever increasing extent. But students, especially, in college, need less division and more unification of education. They need to have the vast panorama of human achievement with all its interrelation imprinted on their minds before they are bewildered by the job of exploring in detail minute parts of the wide terrain. Generations of college students have tried to assimilate five or six unrelated courses a semester without success. The task of organizing and unifying knowledge must be undertaken by the college, for it cannot successfully be achieved by an immature student.

Closely connected with this requirement is the need of bringing all teaching into relation with the student's own experience. Colleges are not offering subjects for their own sake but for the student's sake. It is just as simple to teach a course such as mathematics with dramatic examples from banking, insurance, and engineering as to teach it as an abstract and unrelated subject. Sound education should take the student's own limited experience as a base line and help him to triangulate from that to the most distant stars.

We may summarize by saying that the new curriculum must be developed as a unity for a young human animal who is himself an organic individual, not a collection of parts. To serve the whole man we must have a curriculum that is in itself well knit and well balanced—one which contains panoramic courses presenting the whole picture of culture. If we now discuss certain parts of this curriculum we must be on our guard to avoid thinking of these parts except as incomplete fragments of the whole structure.

Any sound education must begin by training the student physically. What kind of physical life is he going to live? One man in several thousand becomes a professional athlete or a director of physical training. A fair proportion becomes farmers or sportsmen, who need a well-developed physique. The great majority of college men and women, however, faces sedentary life in which large lung capacity and heavy muscles are a liability rather than an asset.

How can our youths be prepared to endure a sedentary life with its inevitable dangers of stooped shoulders and sagging abdomen? The answer is simple. They must be trained in habits of light exercise of a type which will tone up the entire body. If they are to persist in this exercise it must be enjoyable. If it is linked with games and sports it will have sufficient appeal to the individual to provide the motivation for lifelong practice.

Let us begin by requiring each student to learn to walk, run, dance, and swim correctly. Walking and running will teach proper carriage and breathing. Dancing is an acceptable form of physical exercise in college because it encourages natural attitudes toward the other sex and because it provides a wholesome outlet for the sex desires which are so imperious at college age. Socially, dancing is a great asset and gives the student poise and grace. More than any other training it teaches him to be at ease with his fellows. As for swimming, few of us will have the opportunity to make gallant rescues or save ourselves from a watery grave, but swimming is one of the most enjoyable and generally beneficial of exercises. These four physical arts can be appreciated keenly through life, and without them no life is complete.

Our next physical requirements are games of the type that can be enjoyed socially after college—golf, tennis, squash, handball, bowling, and badminton. Anyone who can play one or two of these games fairly well has taken out insurance for life against physical failure. He is sure of plenty of carefree recreation and wholesome exercise. No student should be allowed to graduate unless he is able to play some of these games well.

Students who reach college unable to ride a bicycle, drive a car, fly, ski, snowshoe, sail a boat, ride a horse, fish and shoot should be given individual instruction. These are physical skills which are in wide demand in the modern world and which have great recreational value.

In the new curriculum gymnasiums would be used only as places where games enjoyed in afterlife might be learned and where in individual cases certain corrective exercises might be taken under a doctor's orders. The whole tiresome rigmarole of calisthenics, weight pulling, and bending would be discarded as of doubtful benefit.

The sooner the public competitive sports are professionalized, the better it will be for American education. They have nothing to do with physical training, and are carried on simply for advertising and to satisfy the barbaric pleasure which college alumni find in gladiatorial combats. Football, soccer, baseball, hockey, basketball, and the rest are in the same class as bullfighting or prizefighting. They will always bring good gate receipts because people enjoy primitive competitive sports that require strength, skill, and courage. But they should be played by professionals, and colleges should devote themselves to educational pursuits. They are nearly valueless, educationally speaking, because they train only the few, they overtrain this minority, they do not carry over into afterlife, they consume a tremendous amount of time and energy, and they teach the nonparticipating majority the unwholesome habit of enjoying sports vicariously.

Along with the development of recreational skills there should be a brief course in applied physiology. The average man knows less about his bodily mechanism than he does about the design of his automobile or radio. Physiology, not the kind of thing that is usually taught in colleges under this name, is actually one of the most fascinating of all studies; and, because every human being possesses a body which he can come to know and control, it may become a major interest.

Each person has an individual physical problem, and it is keen sport to direct one's own physical mechanism in such a way as to obtain the highest possible performance. Yet most of us abuse ourselves physically during our youth and, as we get older, do little or nothing to cure our disabilities or to ward off impending ailments. One has only to recall the wild excesses of youth to realize that most students waste their physical resources futilely long before they appreciate their value.

Included in this section of our curriculum should be some sound dietetics calculated to train the student to regulate his eating for enjoyment and physical well-being. The promiscuous menu of the average student would destroy any other animal but man within a month. It leaves most students with a weakened digestion for the balance of their days.

In order to carry out this program, which will serve the purpose of developing physical resources and of establishing habits and skills that will keep a man fit throughout life, the college environment will have to be replanned. Much of the student's life which is now left to his own haphazard impulses must be controlled and directed. But the co-operation of the student himself will be an essential feature of any successful physical program, because the aim of the college must be students who are self-disciplined, not students who are faculty-disciplined.

A second division of our new college curriculum will be devoted to art in all its phases, both practical and theoretical. Traditionally the word *art*, at least in colleges, has stood for a somewhat rarefied and overaesthetic study of painting, sculpture, and architecture. In our curriculum art will include music, cinema, photography, dance, industrial design, costume design, interior design, landscape architecture, drama, poetry, the novel, and handcrafts, as well as painting, sculpture, and architecture. The art faculty will take pains to acquaint the student with all the current phases of art so that when he leaves college he will know every art tendency, whether it be a new technique in the cinema or the most recent trend in architecture. That is to say, he will not think of art as a term applied to one mode of expression but will be aware of the worth of all forms of creative activity and he will regard art not as something exhumed from the past but as a very vivid present enterprise.

Each student will be given the opportunity to participate in the practice of several of the arts and will be required to be proficient as an artist in one or more fields. He will be expected to live a creative life to the full extent of his abilities. For the majority of the students this participation will probably take the form of intelligent criticism and appreciation. For a few talented ones it will be a career.

As far as art is concerned, most of our college campuses are strongholds of barbarism. Student taste rarely rises above the lure of swing music, melodrama, and romantic movies. Most students are unaware that any other type of art exists. As to our college faculties—they are controlled by a profound intellectual snobbery toward any practical participation in the arts. They hide behind a long outmoded philosophical dualism which separates the things of the mind from the things of the body. They pursue the psychologically absurd theory that it is possible to educate the mind without considering the physical and emotional human being of which that mind is inseparably a part.

Far from being a rational creature, the student is actually controlled largely by his emotions. All his drives and most of his judgments are basically emotional. As he matures he gains some direction over these feelings, but to a great extent all human life is conditioned by emotion. The chief function of the arts is to afford pleasurable and creative outlets for this emotional nature with which we are endowed. Emotions, like any other human functions, may be trained and refined. Art supplies both the stimulus and the satisfaction for our emotional natures. Neglected, emotions may atrophy, thus robbing the individual of his sensitivity and imagination; or they may break out in animal-like behavior such as unrestrained anger and sexual indulgence; or they may, if repressed, produce some psychological abnormality.

Our Puritan tradition has conditioned us to shun emotional experiences as immoral. We have been taught to admire the Stoic and suspect the Epicurean. Emotions, however, are the source of most of our energy and ambition. It is through them that we experience our greatest satisfaction. They are the inspiration for all imaginative activity, for all creative thinking. Emotion is one of the greatest endowments of the human race.

Any education which neglects the training and satisfaction of the emotions is certain to produce intellectual sterility. For thinking depends on imagination, and imagination depends on emotional stimulus. Though we have built up the fiction that thinking is an abstract and cold process of reasoning, actually most of us do our best thinking when we are bodily and emotionally attuned to an intellectual problem.

The danger that our emotions will run away with our judgment is less hazardous than the danger that our judgments will lack imagination. Both dangers can be avoided by developing satisfying types of artistic experience in which we habitually participate. Emotionally it is quite as important for a man of affairs to play a piano or a violin after a day of activity as it is for a musician to enjoy his instrument. Though the man of affairs may not be sufficiently skilled to play in public, his playing may serve the useful purpose of restoring to him emotional equilibrium and poise.

In the usual type of college, emotional experience and training take place outside the curriculum. Whether the student chooses wine or women or prefers gambling or auto racing, the development of his emotions is sure to be controlled for the most part by fortuitous circumstances. On the other hand, if he plays in an orchestra, takes part in a drama, enjoys amateur photography, designs furniture, learns to sketch, paints during his vacation, or carves wood, he has already found a satisfying and wholesome outlet for his emotional life.

In the new curriculum each student will be required to play at least one musical instrument. He will be taught one of the graphic arts. He will be required to write poetry or stories. He will be given the opportunity of designing and making the furniture or other useful articles with which he is surrounded. Possibly he will never have a course in aesthetics. Certainly he will never be required to take history of art as a course distinct from other history but, on the other hand, he will never be offered any course in history which does not include the artistic development of man as well as his economic and social evolution.

Art education, like physical education, will be presented in such a way as to prepare the student for lifelong participation. The aim will be to make each man proficient in one or more of the arts, so that he will preserve an amateur or professional interest in it or them as long as he lives. Indeed, no instructor will really be able to certify that a student has passed this part of the curriculum until at the end of a lifetime it is discovered whether or not some form of art remained a hobby or a profession throughout the individual's career.

The purpose of the arts in the new curriculum will be to train the taste, to free the imagination, and to give the emotions pleasant and constructive expression. The emotional nature of the student will thus become an asset rather than a wasted resource or an impediment. Taste is the mark of an educated man, imagination the sign of a productive man, and emotional balance the token of a matured man.

In the third part of the new curriculum we approach for the first time the so-called intellectual phase of education. Our muscular and emotional human animal is also a thinking being. We may divide the field of knowledge into two parts; natural history and culture history, dealing respectively with man's physical surroundings and with his cultural environment.

Under the head of natural history we shall include all the natural sciences, together with mathematics. These will not be taught as a series of unrelated subjects, such as astronomy, geology, physics, chemistry, zoology, and mathematics, but as a well-rounded study of man's entire physical environment. They will culminate in a résumé of current problems in physical science. To teach such a course, a dozen or more instructors, each a specialist in a single science, will need to collaborate. Fortunately there will be no textbooks, and the student will be forced to rely on first-hand observation, laboratory experiments, source material, and classroom discussion and demonstration.

One of the major aims of such a course will be to acquaint the student with scientific method. He will be taught to make his own observations, to classify facts as he sees them, to make guarded inductions from these facts, to formulate tentative hypotheses to check his theories and determine whether they enable him to account for all the facts and to predict the future course of physical events. He will learn the difference between inductive, empirical thinking and deductive, rationalistic reasoning. He will discover the vagaries of his senses and the limitations of his mind. He will learn that mathematics is a way of thinking exactly about quantitative relations.

As the course develops it will unfold the entire cosmic system as we understand it. The student will learn of Lyell's great discovery of the geological forces at work in creating this earth and its familiar topography. He will be introduced to the microcosm within the chemical molecule. The evolution of plants and animals will be explained to him, and man's place indicated among the anthropoids. From such a course he will emerge not with a certain number of units of science but with a unified view of the whole cosmic panorama as far as it is understood today.

The values of such a course will be three-fold. First, it will give the student the discipline of laboratory observation and experiment; second, it will offer him practice in accurate, impersonal methods of thinking about physical problems; third, it will paint for him a unified picture of the physical world in which he lives. Such an introduction to physical science should endow the student with a sympathetic and an intelligent grasp of scientific procedure and research in the more important specialized fields. It should provide him with a pattern for meeting problems of his own and with confidence in developing an experimental answer.

In such a course both the content and the thinking are educationally significant, but the latter is the more vital for intelligent living. Ability to think scientifically should be the essence of the equipment which a student gains from college. The habit of using both the senses and the mind, of keen observation and accurate generalization, is one which must be practiced throughout life. Rigorous scientific thinking has advanced our culture further than have all the elaborate and pretentious philosophies ever propounded. It is safe to assert that the student will reap more benefit from a thorough study and practice of humble inductive logic than from all the dialectic brilliance of deductive logic. The modern world needs men with a grasp of facts, not facile, persuasive sophists.

The fourth and final division in our new curriculum will be culture history. Under this head will be included all the social sciences. Instead of being taught as separate subjects, they will be unified as far as possible. Unity will be achieved by a synthetic history of human development which will include anthropology, archaeology, ethnology, economics, sociology, politics, art, literature, and philosophy. This will begin with the dawn of culture, and during the first half of the course will come down to the present time. The latter half of the course will focus on current problems so that the student will have a complete picture of our contemporary culture.

The new all-inclusive history course will attempt to deal scientifically with culture, presenting not a eulogistic account of human achievement but the long hard struggle, with frequent defeats, through which modern civilization has been achieved. Contemporary culture will be analyzed with equal candor, so that the student will emerge from college not with a conception of an ideal republic such as Plato pictured but with a very intimate and realistic knowledge of the far from ideal republic in which we live.

The aim of the course will be to produce an intelligent citizen capable of living efficiently and co-operatively in a twentieth-century community. In our conventional college subjects there is very little carry-over into life after college. History somehow never reaches the present. At least half this fourth section of our curriculum will be devoted to a detailed analysis of our current social structure.

To teach such a course we shall again have to draw on the services of a corps of instructors from different departments. We shall have to find men who have not retreated into the security of the past but who are capable of analyzing and presenting the perplexing intricacies of the present. They must be men who believe that it is not beneath academic dignity to discuss political issues. They must have the background necessary to understand economic problems for which answers have not yet been found.

The source material for the latter half of this course must be life itself as we see it through our newspaper and periodical literature. Students must be given the opportunity of going to legislatures in session, of visiting industrial plants, of studying businesses at first hand, and of seeing public institutions from the inside, so that they can understand the working of our intricate social-economic machine. Here again the textbook must be discarded, and the student encouraged to go to source material. Not only that—but he must be taught to make impartial surveys and gather his own data.

The degradation of our democracy is due to pressure minorities which find that political plundering yields a far greater profit than the more primitive forms of plundering which marked earlier stages of human development. Our citizenry has been so engrossed in private interests and so apathetic and ignorant as regards public affairs that it has been easy for these groups to exploit the country. Our new education must aim at training a citizenry which is interested in government, which understands it and which participates effectively in it.

The latter part of our course in culture history might well be devoted to problems which democracy has hitherto found insoluble. Our cumbersome and often unjust judiciary system, our generally corrupt and inefficient city governments, our outmoded county governments, our State political machines, the spoils system as applied to the federal government—all represent problems which we devoutly hope the next generation will solve but to which our generation has made only modest contributions. Our great need is to orient the student so that he will be ready to assume his social obligations as a citizen and not devote his energies exclusively to his private affairs.

Culture history will introduce the student to a new pattern of purposeful thinking, the kind which men do when they attempt to create an orderly and pleasant society in which to live. This type of constructive thinking should be a lifelong practice. It must be as rigorous as scientific thinking yet serve social ends rather than purely impersonal goals of exact knowledge. It is the process by which literature, law, government, business, and industry are originated and are advanced. It actually is a kind of "poetic" thinking, for man is the "maker" of his culture rhythms.

The new curriculum contains but four courses; physical education, creative arts, natural history, and culture history. This curriculum is designed not around subject matter or educational theory but to meet the needs of a normal young human animal who must be prepared for the good life in the twentieth century. It begins with his physical training as a foundation, includes his emotional and imaginative life, considers his natural environment, and finally extends to the intricate structure of the cultural environment. Such a curriculum educates the whole man. It is strictly functional, aiming to shape habits, interests, and thinking in such a way as to serve the student equally well as a foundation for graduate school and as a basic pattern throughout life.

The new curriculum, while not despising content, is fundamentally concerned with teaching the student certain types of vital activity of body, imagination, senses, and mind. These trained modes of behavior all contribute to the full life. As a result of this curriculum the student should have learned to function effectively on each level of his being. He should be able to coordinate, to observe, to imagine, and to think easily and effectively. The new educational theory resembles the ancient Greek ideal of harmony between body and soul.

EDUCATION ON A MOUNTAIN[1]

Louis Adamic

EARLY last autumn—to get away for a while from the tempo and confusion of New York—I set out for the South. I had no definite plans. I thought of places to visit, but there was no "must" about any of them. One of these was Black Mountain College in North Carolina, of which I'd been hearing since it was started in 1933 by a group of teachers and students that, following a disagreement, had broken away from Rollins College, in Winter Park, Florida.

On my fifth day out, after a pleasant ramble through Virginia, I got to Black Mountain, a tiny town wedged between the Blue Ridge and Great Craggy ranges. Following a native's directions, I drove up a broad slope on the Blue Ridge side, freshly splashed with autumn reds and yellows, till I reached a great ramshackle of summer-hotel-like buildings which, I learned subsequently, the college leases from the Southern Y.M.C.A., which during July and August used it as a conference camp for its secretaries. Entering the vast barnlike lobby, I introduced myself to the first person I met, explaining I had heard of the place and wished to know more about it.

I had thought to stay an hour or so, then go on to inspect the TVA the next day; but the first thing I knew I was established in a guest-room. I laid it to Southern hospitality, though most of the people there seemed Northerners. I had a few talks with teachers and students, supper with the whole college, then more talks, lasting past midnight, and, to shorten a long tale, instead of staying overnight, I remained for two and a half months.

On the third day I found myself making notes about the place. And two weeks later I knew I had stumbled on what might eventually prove one of the most fascinating—and probably important—stories developing in America to-day.

The inception of BMC was incredibly fine. And I am not thinking particularly of Professor John Rice, who for years, while developing his philosophy of education, had openly criticized the American educational system and blasphemed the sacred cows grazing on the various campuses, and then become successively the leader of the rebels at Rollins College and the rector of the new college. Nor have I specially in mind the handful of professors and instructors who stood by Rice after his dismissal from Rollins College as troublemaker, thereby making the fracas national news and losing their own jobs. I admire the whole group that left Rollins and launched the new college in the turbulent wake of the Bank Holiday.

[1]From *My America* by Louis Adamic (1938). Harper & Brothers, publishers.

But I wish to commend particularly the fifteen boys and girls, average age twenty, including the president of the Rollins student body and the editor of the Rollins campus paper, who joined the rebel professors in the seemingly impossible enterprise of starting a new college when none of the professors had the least notion where they were to start it or what they were to use for money. Unlike the dismissed teachers, these fifteen students were not compelled to leave their comfortable dormitories in Winter Park and go looking for a spot on which to pitch their tents. Without them, Rice and his associates could not even have thought of starting a new school. And, after the new college was announced, these students helped the teachers to raise the minimum sum necessary to rent the hotel-like building they chanced to find at Black Mountain and buy the essential equipment for classes and food for the group for a few months, and to get four more students and three more instructors; so that when the college opened the teaching staff numbered nine and the student body nineteen.

Students and teachers pooled their personal book collections and called the result the college library, and agreed to contribute manual labor voluntarily. The teachers drew out of the treasury only what they needed for clothes and incidentals, which averaged $7.27 per month per person. But even so, the college nearly collapsed twice for lack of money, and was saved by the joint resourcefulness and self-denial of both the faculty and the students.

BMC is one of the smallest colleges in existence—at first inevitably, now deliberately so. It is not only a place where one can take most of the courses available in other colleges, but where one is obliged to live as an integral part of a close-knit social unit; so close-knit indeed that it has characteristics of a huge family—and this latter fact, as I shall show, is as important in the scheme as is class work.

Except for four faculty couples with small children occupying cottages near by, all members of the staff and all students live and do all their teaching and learning (save music, dramatics, and the dance), and all their studying, reading, and playing in the vast hotel-like structure I have mentioned. Everybody, including the families with little children, eats in a common mess-hall, connected with the main building by a passageway. Apart from a cook, his three assistants, a furnace-man in the winter, and two persons who clean the main hall, stairs, corridors, and lavatories, the college has no employees. All other chores are done by students and faculty without distinction, and altogether voluntarily. At meals students and teachers serve one another, though no one is detailed in advance to do anything specific. Food is brought to the tables, passed round, eaten; emptied dishes are taken to the kitchen and replenished, then the tables are cleared, someone brings the dessert, another tea and coffee; and all this takes place in perfect order. The students who pay less than the full fee, or nothing at all, are not expected to do extra service; the chief reason being that this is bad for those who are served—it gives them a feeling of unsound superiority.

The rebel students from Rollins were—naturally—the best sort of students. Some of those taken in during the first two years were perhaps not as good; for extreme poverty forced the college to accept nearly every applicant who could pay the fee or any part thereof. Last fall the number of applicants exceeded capacity; so in accepting students an effort was made to get a cross-section of American life by economic, cultural, and geographic distribution.

The students now in BMC, twenty-six boys and twenty-two girls, are between eighteen and twenty-five, but there is no set rule against older or younger people. Two requirements for admission are: ability to live in and profit from living in such a community as BMC (to be further discussed), and intelligence—not necessarily of a high order, but not too low. Among the desiderata are a capacity for deep dejection and a tendency to say every once in a while "I'm no good!"; a capacity for indignation and an inclination to get hot under the collar; a sense of order, a sense of form, and an inward love of truth. They take a few neurotics, partly because they feel they can help them become less neurotic and difficult, partly to give the "normal" people some training in living with difficult persons.

There are no required courses. Within his stay in the college, however, the student must, if he intends to graduate, submit to two tests of his knowledge: the first at the end of two years, the second about two years later, both depending upon his willingness and ability to work. How he is to obtain this knowledge is a matter for which he alone is responsible. He may work "on his own," under a tutor, or in classes. In general the work of the student is at first in classes; later on, almost entirely individual.

The BMC people hold that the range of knowledge at present is so nearly infinite that it is no longer possible to pick out a number of subjects and say of them "These a man must know." But before the student can make an intelligent choice of the subjects with which he is to deal, he must explore the fields of knowledge in the junior division, in order that he may not discover his real interests as late as his third or fourth year, as often happens in college.

The initiative in passing from the junior to the senior division, and from the latter to graduation, is always with the student, who must himself decide whether he is ready to make the move. Not that he is left, at this point or any throughout his stay, to flounder about alone; teachers are ready to give advice when requested. The first thing a student does during his first week, when he is not expected to register for any work but to spend the time planning what he is to do, is to choose some member of the faculty to be his adviser; a choice, however, that is not final.

The senior division is a period of specialization in a field or in cognate fields of knowledge. One of the requirements for entrance to this division is a carefully made plan of work to cover about two years. When the student thinks he has completed this work he petitions for the right to graduate, accompanying his request with a statement of what he professes to know in his chosen field. If this statement is satisfactory, the faculty invites some competent person not connected with the college to examine him in what he claims to know.

On the whole, the effort of BMC is to produce individuals rather than individualists, in the belief that the individualist is bound to be a misfit in modern life, while, at the other extreme, the subordination of men and women to a uniform and consistent pattern of action will inevitably prevent the creation of a better society than we now have. The first step in the process is to make the student aware of himself and his capacities, and a beginning is often best made by persuading him to submit himself to the discipline of one or more of the arts. For this reason, no classes are allowed to conflict in the schedule with elementary courses in music, dramatics, the fine arts. It is not expected that many students will become artists; in fact, the college regards it as a duty to discourage mere talent from thinking itself genius, but maintains there is something of the artist in everyone; and the development of this talent, however meager, carrying with it a severe discipline of its own, results in the student's becoming more sensitive to order than he can ever possibly become through intellectual effort alone.

But the individual must also be aware of his relation to others. In BMC, the whole community is his teacher. Wood-chopping, road-mending, working on the college farm, rolling the tennis courts, serving tea in the afternoon, getting the mail, policing the grounds, building a shed, driving the college truck, and other tasks done by individuals and groups of students and members of the faculty, help to rub off individualistic corners and give people training in assuming responsibility. The assistant treasurer is a student.

There is, naturally, an element of fun in all these tasks (which in a measure take the place of purely artificial sport activities in other schools), but in attending to them, the students gain a sense of participating in the vital day-to-day life of the place as a whole. They feel they belong, function. They have a sense of being important.

Though he is never told so, the student cannot help realizing that he is as important as the rector and the rest of the staff. He has all the freedom and privilege anyone else has. He is as free to criticize the teachers as they are to criticize him; free to open his mouth about anything, any time, anywhere, and take the consequences. Some teachers, including Rice, attend as students the classes which he is taking. He knows they are learning just as he is. He is an integral part of the community and, no matter what he does, he influences it. The place is so delicately organized (only "organized" is not the word) that he has it in his power to create a scandal and severely damage it. Conversely, he has the power to prevent—but only by persuasion—another student from creating such a scandal. Or he can do, or take part in doing, something which suddenly enhances the value of the place. Rice insists that the students have had as much to do with the making of the college as has the faculty.

Disagreeing with psychologists like Adler who say that everyone is trying to be superior, BMC holds that the average person is content when and where he "fits," where he functions in his unique way, when he feels he is in his job; and makes it not only possible but easy for a student to find out that he is not cut out to be a philosopher but a plumber; not a writer, but a scientist; not a chemist, but a grocery clerk. One of the efforts, in which the entire community continually participates, is to bring to each one's consciousness his uniqueness —and this not only as a potential scientist or plumber, but as a person who, being endowed with imagination, is an artist.

BMC realizes that in the past century America has undergone drastic changes and that education must begin to face the problems which have sprung out of those changes. To condense what several BMC people have said to me:

In the past the history of an individual has been that of reaching out gradually in acquaintance and understanding of people. First he became aware of his mother and began to understand humanity through her. Then came his adjustment to others in the family, all very gradual: for, fortunately, there were lots of them, and they represented, in little, what he would have to face later on. From some he could count on the necessary human emollient, unreasonable affection; from others, on guarded hostility. Old maid aunts and decrepit grandfathers were people he could begin cautiously to dislike, but with whom he had to get on. And he could count on the subtle thing, family feeling, to save him from disaster. He could escape no one; no one could escape him. He became adept in interpreting communication. The lifting of an eyebrow, the turn of a hand, every movement, every inflection of the voice had its meaning. He got ready for the village.

In the village he met open hostility, criticism unsugared by unreasonable affection or family decency, but, being not without experience, he could give as good as he got. And, as in the family, nobody could get away from anybody.

There they all were, in a Mountain, in a tight little world. Individualism had a hard time in the village, but the right to individuality was recognized per force. This explains why when you want to find characters you go to the village.

Now both the big family and the village have been largely wiped out of America, for even in villages that remain, those of Lewis's Main Street, the desire is to get to the city as quickly as possible, to escape—hence the old family and village lesson is not learned.

What we now have is the carefully restricted family, in which the child—often an only child—does not meet with open indifference, criticism, or hostility. The tendency is for him to be treated always as the center of his small world. He is intensely intimate with one or two persons who "share their every thought" with him.

Now, since the village is gone, the step he must take is from those he knows intimately to those he knows not at all. The immigrant into the world outside the home, in spite of his foretaste through schooling, finds himself among strangers; in the city, among potential enemies. He then carries on what he may have begun as a protective against too much affectionate prying in the home and against the intrusions of a schoolteacher; the building up of a superficial self to present to the world in lieu of reality. By the time he gets to college this superficial self is often a work of art. His best thoughts and ability have gone into its making.

The big family and the village are gone, but mankind needs them, especially the village. Only it must no longer be haphazard, a product of chance, but the best possible village that can be created, free of the old village narrowness, malice, cruelties, and obscurantism. . . . And we here in Black Mountain have stumbled on the idea that the college must be this new village. It must have also some of the characteristics of the big family.

A common saying in Black Mountain is that nearly everyone who comes here has to go through hell. The hell he goes through is the desperate attempt to preserve this superficial self, and the most awful moment in the process comes when he says to himself "Now they know me!" Imagine having scores of eyes focused on you, and you alone, and as many mouths saying, "Don't think you fool us! We see through you." These eyes and mouths turn the human spirit inside out.

This happens to nearly everyone who comes here. This college is the village with a touch of the old big family. It gets to work on the student a little late, at eighteen or later; so the experience is drastic, and he suffers and in his agony wants to hide or escape.

Gradually, however, the sufferer learns that others do for him something of what he has been doing for himself, appraising his virtues not so highly perhaps, as he has appraised them nor condemning his faults so relentlessly as he has condemned them. In other words, he at least discovers a measure of indifference, or charity, or humor, or even affection. This recalls him from his mad effort to hide or escape, or make a martyr of himself, or be a relentless judge of himself.

The BMC people have a name for this process—"group influence." It suggests psychoanalysis, but differs from it drastically. It implicitly disputes the modern psychologist's mechanistic concept of man, as a result of which people have come to regard themselves, not as entities, but as bundles of things that have been done to them and now cause them to do things they shouldn't do. BMC is less interested in the students' high school records and incidents in their past than in their potentialities as persons.

The new students come, then, unknown into an unknown world, which is also strangely and excitingly free. There are no rules in BMC. This is their chance. If they have been fools before, they are free to do something different now. If they have built up for themselves a reputation of angelic virtue which has grown uncomfortable, they are no longer obliged to be angels. Sometimes these noble people make asses of themselves within a short time after arrival, and within a short time, unless their asininity takes a form likely to make the place unlivable for others, they are allowed to go on making asses of themselves. Usually after a while they don't like it, and not because others don't like it (although, as already suggested, others have a share in bringing them to dislike it). The same procedure holds with those who have been fools before and elect to continue. It often takes a long time for them to realize that it is they who are the fools, nobody else.

In September the place is like a grand week-end party. Everybody is glad to be there. The place is beautiful; the view of the Craggies superb. Everybody is so free. And are they not of the elect? Have they not turned their backs on Harvard and Vassar? They feel superior. They form eternal friendships instantly, and implacable enmities: for, after all, a party is preliminary to vicious warfare—only formerly, back home, parties usually broke up before hostilities began.

Then they realize the first implication of freedom: that others also have taken the opportunity to be critical—and complaints are heard that there is too much talk about people; some go so far as to say that what they are and do is nobody's business. But no one goes so far as to say that he doesn't want his name mentioned except in his presence. This would be pressing logic too hard.

Consciousness of self begins. They don't think so much of BMC after all.

109

At moments they hate it. Gloom descends. This is what is desired; "without acute self-consciousness," one of the teachers said, "nothing can be accomplished."

"Group influence" works from elevation to depression and back again. When they achieve elevation from depression they think they have done it, and sit back and enjoy the peace of self-discovery. They swim in intelligence and desire to improve themselves. Then uncertainty steals upon them, and they sink again into depression. Not that the process ends here. There are continuous waves. Or, to change the figure, one's thoughts about oneself are abrasive. One rubs down and down till one touches the thing which is one's real self.

This is experience—education—of the most acute sort. Students are partly prepared for it intellectually by being told on their arrival that they must expect to change; that if they do not change then it is useless for them to have come; they can perfectly well remain what they are by returning home. Of course they don't realize then how they are to change.

Gradually, two things occur. One is that one's interest in others increases in both intensity and intelligence. The other is that one begins to like, almost enjoy, the process of being changed. BMC people explain this as follows:

Men suffer most from unacknowledged self-contempt. The characteristic of children, on the contrary, is self-respect. Somewhere between the kindergarten and college self-respect has been destroyed or so repressed and twisted that it is no longer evident to its possessor. But a man must have self-respect or a similitude of it to present to society. The movement is then from without. He tries to act in such a way that he will be respected by others, and he becomes confused into thinking finally that this assumed self-respect he has pawned off on others is a reality. But underneath he knows or feels that it is all a lie. Behind the front he offers to the world he is a disorderly person. He never knows when he walks into a room but that the enemy is waiting for him, ready to show him up for the liar he is. And yet, unconsciously, he longs for this very thing to happen to him. But at the first onslaught of the enemy he will fight as if he were a real enemy instead of a friend. He has constructed and elaborately decorated the superficial self that he is to present to society. It is as if he wore a carefully designed mask, to the making of which he has given his most tender care, and behind this lives the real man, growing increasingly chaotic, miserable, and unhappy, longing for his deliverer but ready to receive him as an enemy.

The task of the college is to be his enemy-friend: the bitter enemy of the superficial self, the friend of the real self. But the real one is starved, emaciated. It must be fed back to life, while the superficial one must be attacked without mercy.

110

BMC has a diet for the poor "real self." There is good will. Most of the talk about people is free of malice or pettiness. There is desire to help. Except when the issue is slight, no one ever goes completely without a champion. Also, as already said, one belongs, functions, is "important" in BMC. One, too, is constantly invited, verbally and by implication, to be intelligent, to be mature, which is slightly annoying but also rather pleasant. Older students try to find out what can be done to bring a newcomer to consciousness of his predicament. Candor, of which there is probably more at BMC than anywhere else in the United States, is discomfiting at times, yet it produces dramatic incidents which almost prove that truth is beauty. But the more important part of the diet for the "real self" is humor. Young students learn to laugh at themselves. And so, in one way or another, they discover that, their past experiences and a great mass of literature to the contrary notwithstanding, humanity is basically a rather decent breed.

The original BMC group began to develop this process back in 1933, mainly unconsciously and accidentally, when they abruptly found themselves in extremely tight quarters and had to get along on a basis of freedom, not only as students and teachers, but as persons endowed with various degrees of vitality. They had to rub the individualistic corners off one another's characters. Rice arrived at a faltering recognition of the virtues of the process and began cautiously to direct its development toward what it is now. He is of course not satisfied with it; nor is anyone else in BMC who understands it. It is still developing. Nearly every person who comes there adds something to it. This article, which brings it more or less into the open for the first time, is likely to affect it drastically. I write of it by permission of BMC, which was given me after considerable debate.

"Group influence," as I say, is one of the most important elements of BMC education. It already is stirring interest among psychologists, here and abroad, and among people studying human relations and kindred problems. What I tell of it here is a mere suggestion. To appreciate it fully one must experience it.

I might add that almost nothing can happen in that great hotel-like building which, though no one is spying, everyone cannot know in an hour; and that it is a rare person who comes there and stays two weeks and is not better known than where he lived before, no matter how long. The BMC community, so to speak, psychologically strips the individual, and there he stands revealed to everyone, including himself—and finally likes it.

One immediate aim of "group influence" is that no student should be able to make a mistake in his or her marriage. It should make one a connoisseur of people. I think it already has made connoisseurs of several students. Some of those who have been there longest can also exchange complicated communications without saying a word. The lift of an eyebrow to them is a sentence. They are most definitely being "resensitized."

Do BMC students marry BMC students? So far there has been one student marriage at the college. The couple are still there.

Sex morals? One is free to do anything, but the admonition always is "Be intelligent!" and on that basis nothing occurs that might create the possibility of a scandal to harm the college. The moral control pertaining to everything is within the group. It is not imposed on it. It comes partly from the fact that most people there, no matter how they may have resented certain phases of "group influence," develop a passionate devotion to the place.

Have people there no privacy? Students are two to a bedroom, but each person has a private study, on the door of which he can hang a "Don't disturb!" sign when alone in it.

Age, position, reputation are no basis for respect in BMC, and teachers are exposed to "group influence" no less than students. The result is a high proportion of effective and interesting teachers. Nowhere else do teachers work harder. In BMC they are geared to the whole purpose of the place, which is most insistent. Some students doubtless are not what they could be as students; many, however, want terribly to learn and know what they should be getting, and they must be satisfied. If they are not, they speak up; the unsatisfactory instructor is discussed—but, so far, never with the idea of getting rid of him; rather to see what can be done to help him develop his teaching technic and personality. Again, there is no malice and little pettiness. Usually the criticized teacher's ego is wounded. He resents being criticized by these chits and squirts in this so-called college; resents the fact that some of his colleagues agree with them. He discovers the place really is a new kind of college. Facts, results are unimportant; process, method, imagination are everything. Seeing how successful some of the others are in the classroom, he begins to suspect that their way may be right. He resents that he has not been told what was expected of him. He doesn't know he wasn't told anything because the idea is to let him develop, if possible uniquely. So he probably tries to imitate Rice and quickly discovers he cannot. More misery. He can develop only by unlearning much he had thought for a long time was all right.

He must revise his character and personality, become humble, a student more than a teacher. That he doesn't leave when this happens to him is due to the fact that, although his salary for the time is negligible, he is a free man. The most recent addition to the faculty said to me, "Here it's different. A man can stand up. He can find out why he is wrong or else go on being right. Walt Whitman might have felt at home here."

The weaknesses and difficulties of BMC as it stands to-day appear to one soon on arrival; if not, people there point them out.

Other colleges, with their buildings, equipment, and endowments, are concrete things. They are something everyone more or less understands. They get publicity, then more endowments, more buildings. BMC is built almost entirely of and on ideas and idealism, and as such is tenuous, imponderable. No quantitative evaluation of it is possible. There is no present in the life of BMC. Its moments have one foot in the past, the other in the future. The people there find it hard to tell what they are about. To most people they have nothing to say; they ask them to stay and find out. Two writers before me have vainly tried to put the place on paper; and I own that this article tells next to nothing about it. One can only experience it. And to give it any sort of support is an act of faith. Rice and his colleagues promise nothing. They dislike asking anyone for money. They can't tell what they want it for so that the potential philanthropist would know what they are talking about. Some are fearful of what money might do to the place, and are almost rabid about not wanting a dollar from anyone who may wish to dictate to them how to "run" the college, or make any demands upon them other than of politeness and of detailed accounts of expenditures. So BMC barely manages to exist from term to term. And they are in constant danger that the YMCA will sell the place to someone who will not want them to be there.

Some hope that before long an angel will fly over Black Mountain and drop a half-million dollars on them. They hope to buy the place they are renting; it is for sale. They have plans for "fixing it up," which would mean more opportunities for students to assume responsibility. They need an adequate library and equipment of all kinds. Now they blush with shame to admit they are forced to prefer the boy or girl whose parents can pay the full tuition fee to the boy or girl who can pay less or nothing at all. Some day they hope to have half the student body on full scholarships. Also, if they had a moderate sum of free money they could establish pensions, so that a permanent member of the staff could have the maximum security from financial worry now attainable. They could free students who are ready to leave but not sure of what they should do, from family pressure to "get a job" by allowing them to remain, or, if the thing they have chosen doesn't work out, to return and make another start. They would like to have as guests for long periods writers, artists, composers, dancers, scientists who would come there to work; for to see a person like that at work is to knock romance out of one's head.

But some of them know also that too much money might be even worse than their present poverty. Five million dollars, if it could not be laid aside for founding similar colleges in other localities, might ruin them. Greed might

113

enter it. Trips to Europe might become necessities. Fords mightn't be good enough. And, worse yet, they could not tell whether a new teacher had been attracted by the idea or the money.

Other dangers? Complacency and dilettantism. The BMC people feel pleased about themselves, especially those who have taught or studied elsewhere; and when visitors praise them, they cheerfully agree. "But," one of the teachers said to me, "the moment we think we have arrived, we shall be dead." Dilettantism, they realize, comes through a lack of seriousness; also, when there is too much teaching and not enough learning. There is no lack of seriousness now; but can they keep it up? I think they can and will; but who knows? Their future depends too on the developments in this country, in the world. War? Fascism? Communism? When asked about this, they raise their hands in a gesture of uncertainty.

I could give a list of lesser lacks and flaws, but by the time this reaches print they may no longer exist. Let me be as explicit as I can in saying that the place is a *process*, a way of education (which, in the BMC concept, is synonymous with life); that it is not only *a* process, but life's own process in miniature, with an intense reality of its own that is not unrelated to the world beneath the mountain: dynamic, creative, insistent not only on change, but improvement. It is self-corrective.

I have said that BMC is tenuous. But the idea is immense. It challenges the existing chaos and the methods of fascism and communism. It goes beyond all three and has the method to get there. It has the chance of becoming deeply attractive to millions of Americans who are sick of themselves, their own corruption, the corruption about them, and the stench of dissolution now filling the world; and who, weary of individualism, wish to lose themselves in, or identify themselves with, something bigger and better than themselves. The admonitions "Be intelligent!", "Be mature!" will have an increasingly great appeal to Americans. "Group influence" will draw also. People in BMC "die," burn up with self-contempt and despair; then, changed and "reborn," rise out of the ashes of their ex-selves. It is the old Phoenix myth, found in most religions: for there is something in nearly every human breast that craves death and rebirth. . . .[2]

[2]For a further discussion of Black Mountain College see "Another Consociate Family," by Bernard De Voto, *Harper's Magazine*, April, 1936.

SCHOOL FOR BARBARIANS[1]

Erika Mann

UNTIL recently, German schools had the world's respect: the relationship between teachers and pupils, especially just after the War, was human and dignified, and the teachers themselves were distinguished for thoroughness, discipline, and scientific exactness. The grammar schools and Gymnasien (high schools), colleges and universities, were open to all, and their moderate tuition fees were canceled for talented students of limited means. There were some, like the best American boarding schools, in beautiful, healthful places, whose modern methods allowed teacher and pupils to sit in the garden and have lessons that were remembered as stimulating conversation, or to make excursions over the hills and fields. There were performances in the school theaters, and films shown to supplement courses in natural science, history, and geography.

One subject, political propaganda, was missing from the curriculum. The German Republic refused to influence its citizens one way or the other, or to convince them of the advantages of democracy; it did not carry on any propaganda in its own favor. This proves to have been an error; and its atonement has been a terrible one. Whatever its cause, modesty or the waverings of a young and unconfident Republic, the error stands. What the Republic did toward education was done as a matter of course. Civic buildings, for peacetime use, were put up, and of these many were schools—airy, spacious, and happily adequate. They were set into service without propaganda or hullabaloo. The State was the people's servant; it served in quiet, believing that its master, the people, would be thankful. But the State was wrong.

Unused to self-rule, the German people submitted to a new State which made itself the master, and forced the people to be its servants. The State and its Führer entered their power in a frenzy of display. The Führer and his followers, shouting and raving, were the opposites of the old, submissive, quiet State. They praised their ideas as the only road to salvation; they commanded; they dictated.

What had been the field of politicians before, and known as "politics," was now a Weltanschauung (philosophy of life), no less, and there was no other than the National Socialist Weltanschauung. It soon forced itself into the schools, changing them, making rules, interdicting, innovating, and completely changing their character within a few months.

Had the "old-fashioned" educators tried to make civilized human beings of the children in their care? Had they encouraged them in their search for

[1]From *School For Barbarians* by Erika Mann (1938). Modern Age Books, Inc.

truth? Left youth as much personal freedom as they thought compatible with discipline? Taken them to theaters and movies to serve educational purposes? Had they done all of this? It must all go, according to the Nazis, immediately and radically. Morals, truth, freedom, humanitarianism, peace, education—they were errors that corrupted the young, stupidities with no value to the Führer. "The purpose of our education," he was crying, "is to create the political soldier. The only difference between him and the active soldier is that he is less specially trained."

The changes were extensive and thorough. Where good educational methods remained, they were not new ones, but those taken over from the Republican German Youth Movement, from the progressive schools, or from Russian or American experiments. The new methods were recognizable by their violence and brutality. There was only one entirely new and entirely different idea: the purpose to which the new education was dedicated. And that purpose was the aims and plans of the Führer.

In *Mein Kampf* there is a short chapter devoted to the problem of the education of children. It contains the proposals of the Führer in this field, and all German children grow up today in the materialism expressed in these twenty-five pages.

"Principles for scientific schools. . . . In the first place, the youthful brain must not be burdened with subjects, 90 per cent of which it does not need and therefore forgets again." And ". . . it is incomprehensible why, in the course of years, millions of men must learn two or three foreign languages which they can use for only a fraction of that time, and so, also in the majority, forget them completely; for of 100,000 pupils who learn French, for example, scarcely 2000 will have a serious use for this knowledge later, while 98,000 in the whole course of their lives will not be in a position to use practically what they have learned. . . . So, for the sake of the 2000 people to whom the knowledge of these languages is of use, 98,000 are deviled for nothing, and waste precious time. . . ."

His aversion for knowledge is strong and sincere. He has refused learning, and seems, even as a child, to have been "deviled for nothing." Also, it is necessary for the dictatorship to keep the people as ignorant as it can; only while the people remain unsuspecting, unaware of the truths of the past and present, can the dictatorship unleash its lies.

"Faith is harder to shake than knowledge," he continues. "Love succumbs less than respect to change, hate lasts longer than aversion, and the impetus toward the most powerful upheavals on this earth has rested at all times less in a scientific knowledge ruling the masses than in a fanaticism blessing them, and often in a hysteria that drove them forwards."

116

This is the positive force that is to take the place of the 90 per cent of school material which Hitler brands as superfluous. "Faith"—in the Führer, and the truth about him concealed; "Love"— for the Führer, with respect conceded as unworthy; "Hate"—of enemies whom mere "aversion" could not destroy; and, above all, the hysteria which is checked by scientific knowledge, the "fanaticism blessing" the masses.

The positive force is summed up: "The whole end of education in a people's State, and its crown, is found by burning into the heart and brain of the youth entrusted to it an instinctive and comprehended sense of race. . . . It is the duty of a national State to see to it that a history of the world is eventually written in which the question of race shall occupy a predominant position. . . . According to this plan, the curriculum must be built up with this point of view. According to this plan, education must so be arranged that the young person leaving school is not half pacifist, democrat or what have you, but a complete German. . . . Also, in this case (for girls), the greatest importance is to be given the development of the body, and only after that on the requirements of the mind, and finally of the soul. The aim of the education of women must be inflexibly that of the future mother."

The epilogue of *Mein Kampf* expresses in all clearness the whole purpose of education in Nazi Germany. "A state which, in the era of race-poisoning, devotes itself to the care of its best racial elements must one day become master of the world."

That is the aim: to make the Nazis the rulers of the world. It is towards this that Hitler stares, that Germany is equipping itself; this is fixed before the eyes of the children.

FRESHMAN ADVISER[1]

George Boas

WE ARE sitting pencil in hand, surrounded by college catalogues, rules and regulations, directories, handbooks, mimeographed slips with last-minute changes of courses on them, folders with big cards for the students' records, pads with two carbons on which to write out schedules. We are all washed and clean, fresh from a summer in which we were supposed to rest and which we spent making enough money to fill out the gap between our salaries and a living wage. We are all resigned to the winter that is before us, teaching, coal bills, committee meetings, those tonsils of Susie's, academic

[1]From *Harper's Magazine*, July, 1930.

freedom, subscription to the Symphony, student activities, what price a decent pair of shoes. . . . We smile at each other and sigh at the mass of paper. We have never learned all the rules. How can anyone learn them? Different ones for students in the college of arts and sciences, pre-meds, engineers. But what are rules anyway?

Here they come. . . .

His name is Rosburgh van Stiew. One can see he is one of the Van Stiews —and if one can't, he'll let one know soon enough. That suit of fuzzy tweed, that regimental cravat, that custom-made shirt. Right out of Vanity Fair. Already he has the Phi Pho Phum pledge button in his buttonhole.

He speaks with a drawl. It is the voice of his mother's face-à-main. He has slightly wavy blond hair—his mother still has a crinkly white pompadour, like Queen Mary's. He has weary eyes.

No use to smile.

"Very well, Mr. Van Stiew. Have you any idea of the courses you'd like to take?"

"No . . . aren't there some things you sort of have to take?"

"Freshman English and Gym."

"Well, I may as well take them."

"History?"

"Do you have to?"

"No. You can take Philosophy, Political Science, or Economics instead."

Mr. Van Stiew tightens his cravat.

"Guess I'll take History."

"Ancient or modern?"

"Well—when do they come?"

"Modern at 8:30, Wednesdays, Thursdays, and Saturdays; Ancient at 9:30, Mondays, Tuesdays, and Wednesdays."

"Oh, Ancient."

Mr. Van Stiew looks shocked that one should have asked.

One shouldn't have.

"Very well, Ancient History."

That leaves three more courses.

"One of the fellows said to take Art Appreciation."

"Yes, you could do that. But sooner or later you are required to take French and German and a laboratory science."

"Couldn't I put them off until next year?"

"You can until you're a senior."

"I think I'll put them off then. I don't want too heavy a schedule."

"Mathematics?"

"Do I have to?"

"It all depends. What are you going to major in?"

"Do I have to major?"

"More or less."

"When do I have to decide?"

"Next year."

So it goes with Mr. Van Stiew. He is using his right of election, his free will. His personality must not be crushed. He will have a Liberal Education, be a member of the Tennis Team, the Dramatic Club, and manager of the Glee Club. And as a prominent alumnus, he will see to it that the Football Team is never oppressed by a fastidious faculty.

Enter Mr. William Hogarth.

Hogarth is from the city Technical High School. Engineer. Red hair, freckles. Ready-made blue serge.

"Math, Physics, Philosophy, German—why can't I take Chemistry too? I'll make up my French this summer. . . . No, can't take any Saturday classes, working at the Universal Clothing Outlet Saturdays."

"English Literature?"

"Do I have to? . . . All right, Professor, put it down. Where do I get my textbooks? Don't they have any second-hand ones? . . . Classes begin to-morrow? All right. . . . Yes, I know about the Physical Exam. Had it already. . . . No, I guess I know everything now."

"If you need any information, Mr. Hogarth, I'm in my—"

"Thanks, don't believe I will."

He's gone.

Woof! One lights a cigarette.

A presence is before one, grinning. Lots of yellow hair parted in the middle, rising on each side of the part and falling like too ripe wheat. Head slightly to one side. Very red face.

Timidly shoves forward receipted bill from the Treasurer's Office.

Fred Wilkinson.

Mr. Wilkinson doesn't know what he's going to major in as yet—"you see, I may not stay here four years." A glance at his high-school record makes that more than probable.

"English and Physical Training, that is, Gym."

"Can't I be excused from that?"

"Have you a physical disability?"

"I'm not sure. . . ."

"Well, we'll put it down anyway and you can talk it over with the doctor."

"French? German?"

119

"I'm not very good on languages."

"Mathematics?"

"Heavens, no!"

"Philosophy?"

"What's that?"

"It's—it's part of the business of philosophy to find out, Mr. Wilkinson."

One stops in time.

"I don't believe you'd like Philosophy. Physics? You have to take one science."

"Isn't there one where you take a trip in the spring?"

"Geology?"

"Is that where you study rocks and things?"

"Yes." God forgive me.

"I guess I'll take that."

"History?"

Quick response. The eyes actually grow bright.

"Oh, yes, History. My brother said to take History."

"Good, that's that anyway. . . . Ancient or Modern?"

"A—what?"

"Ancient or Modern?"

Mr. Wilkinson looks as if he were going to cry. His lower lip seems to swell. His eyes blink. But he is only thinking.

"Which do you study Keats and Shelley in?"

"Which History course?"

"Yes. My brother studied Keats and Shelley. That's the course I want. Don't they come in History?"

"They are undoubtedly a part of history" (one grows pontifical) "but I don't believe they usually are discussed in the History courses."

"I'm sure my brother studied them here."

"Maybe it was the History of English Literature."

"Would that have Keats and Shelley?"

"I imagine so."

Mr. Wilkinson is dubious.

"Well, I tell you, Professor. Couldn't you put it down, and then if it isn't all right maybe I could change it afterwards. I could change it, couldn't I, you know, if I didn't like it, if they didn't teach Keats and Shelley in it, I could change it, couldn't I?"

Why not? Mr. Wilkinson will flunk out at mid-term anyway.

So we go.

The pad of the three carbons grows thinner and thinner. The atmosphere grows thicker and thicker. The advisers grow stupider and stupider. The day grows shorter and shorter. By night all schedules are made. To-morrow classes will begin. And after to-morrow Mr. Van Stiew, Mr. Hogarth, Mr. Wilkinson, and the rest will begin dropping courses, adding courses, shifting courses about until they have left of their original schedules only English Literature and Gym which are required in Freshman year.

FOOTBALL IS KING[1]

Frank Sullivan

John B. Smith takes the stand.

Q. Mr. Smith, are you familiar with the clichés used in football?

A. Naturally, as a football fan.

Q. What kind of football fan are you, may I ask?

A. I am a rabid football fan, sir.

Q. In that case, I suppose you attend a great many football games.

A. I go to a great many grid tilts, if that's what you mean.

Q. I see. Who attend these grid tilts?

A. Record crowds, or throngs.

Q. And what does a record crowd provide?

A. A colorful spectacle, particularly if it is the Army-Navy game.

Q. Mr. Smith, how do you know when the football season is about to start?

A. When there is a tang of autumn in the air I know that football will soon be king.

Q. Is there any other portent that helps you?

A. About September first, when the newsreels start showing pictures of coaches putting their charges through early practice, I know that football will soon hold sway—*undisputed* sway—over the hearts of sports lovers.

Q. Describe these pictures.

A. The candidates sit around on their haunches looking a little sheepish, while the coach stands in the middle holding a football—pardon *me*, a pigskin—and an announcer states that an atmosphere of optimism prevails in the Gopher camp despite a heavy schedule and the loss of several of their best men through graduation. Then the coach makes a short talk, the gist of which is that, while he will make no predictions, he *will* say that any team that comes up against the Gophers this fall will know they've been in a battle—how about it, men? Then the men line up and tackle a flying dummy.

[1]From *The Atlantic Monthly*, November, 1938.

Q. A shrewd summing up, Mr. Smith. Speaking of 'up,' what do football teams roll up?

A. A score.

Q. If they don't roll up a score what do they do?

A. They battle to a scoreless tie.

Q. What do they hang up?

A. A victory. Or, they pull down a victory.

Q. Which means that they do what to the opposing team?

A. They take the measure of the opposing team, or take it into camp.

Q. And the opposing team?

A. Drops a game, or bows in defeat.

Q. This dropping, or bowing, constitutes what kind of blow for the losing team?

A. It is a crushing blow to its hopes of annexing the Eastern championship. Visions of the Rose Bowl fade.

Q. So what follows as a result of the defeat?

A. A drastic shakeup follows as a result of the shellacking at the hands of Cornell last Saturday.

Q. And what is developed?

A. A new line of attack.

Q. Mr. Smith, how is the first quarter of a football game commonly referred to?

A. As the initial period.

Q. What kind of quarterbacks do you prefer?

A. Elusive quarterbacks.

Q. Who traditionally comprise the membership of Notre Dame's football team, the Fighting Irish?

A. Woszianko, Rumplemeyer, Kozlowski, Goldsmith, Ponzaneri, and so on.

Q. And who play on the Harvard team?

A. Mahoney, Grady, O'Halloran, Dolan, and Cabot.

Q. Very good. Now then, what does a young football player show?

A. An *embryo* football player? He shows great promise in high school.

Q. Why?

A. Because he is husky, powerful, sturdy, stout-hearted, fast on his feet, a tough man in a scrimmage, and tips the scales at two hundred pounds.

Q. Which makes him?

A. A magnificent physical specimen.

Q. What happens after the magnificent physical specimen shows great promise?

122

A. He goes to college.

Q. How?

A. On funds donated by wealthy alumni who are rabid football fans.

Q. And who are?

A. And who are dissatisfied with the coach, it is rumored.

Q. Once in college, what does the magnificent physical specimen become?

A. Promising football material.

Q. So he joins the candidates who are trying for positions on the football team, eh?

A. I wouldn't put it that way. I'd just say he goes out for football. By the way, Mr. Sullivan, now that I have amended your statement, how do you stand?

Q. I stand corrected.

A. Good. A bit of a cliché fancier yourself, eh?

Q. Oh, I dabble, I dabble. Now then, Mr. Smith, I suppose that in the course of time—the *due* course of time, to be exact—the magnificent physical specimen is appointed to a place on the regular team.

A. You waste so many words. He makes the varsity eleven.

Q. What kind of practice is he put through?

A. Hard, grueling practice.

Q. Where?

A. Under the eye of the coach.

Q. What kind of eye?

A. Watchful eye.

Q. So that he is?

A. In fine fettle, and a veritable human fighting machine.

Q. What does he shovel?

A. Passes.

Q. What kind of threats is he partial to?

A. Triple threats.

Q. What does he nurse?

A. Bruises.

Q. What does he break?

A. Training.

Q. What does he stave off?

A. Defeat.

Q. What kind of prowess does he boast?

A. Vaunted.

Q. What is a good football captain called?

A. An able field general.

123

Q. And the able field general leads his team through an unbroken series of victories, does he not?

A. He does unless he is declared ineligible.

Q. Where is he when he is declared ineligible?

A. He is behind in his studies.

Q. Now, Mr. Smith, what, according to tradition, does the coach call the players?

A. He calls them 'men.'

Q. And what does the captain call his teammates?

A. He calls them 'fellows.'

Q. What does the coach say in the locker room just before the game?

A. He says, 'Well, men, I guess that's about all. Now, get in there and fight!'

Q. What does the captain say?

A. He says, 'Come on, fellows, let's go!'

Q. So they go out there?

A. Determined to win.

Q. What for?

A. For the honor of the school; for dear old Alma Mater; for the glory of old Crimson; for God, for country, and for Yale; for dear old Rutgers, for good old coach; for Dad and Mother, and for A Certain Girl.

Q. For anything else?

A. For Delta Kappa Epsilon and good old Sigma Phi, for Scroll & Key and Skull & Bones, and Theta Delta Chi.

Q. Why, you're quite a poet, Mr. Smith!

A. Oh, I dabble, I dabble.

Q. Where is A Certain Girl during the game?

A. Up there in the stands, her heart glowing with pride.

Q. What is she wearing?

A. A chrysanthemum.

Q. Where are Mother and Dad?

A. Up there too, *their* hearts glowing with pride.

Q. When Son drops the punt do Dad's and Mother's hearts cease glowing with pride?

A. Dad's sinks, but not Mother's.

Q. Why not?

A. Because she thinks he has scored a point.

Q. Why else is Son determined to win?

A. Because he wants to emerge from that game as the greatest end since Larry Kelly.

124

Q. Why does he wish to be the greatest end?

A. So he can get his letter, and be a candidate for the All-American team.

Q. Why?

A. So that he can get a bid from a big pro team.

Q. Pro team?

A. Professional football.

Q. Why does he want to play pro football?

A. Because that may bring a bid from the movies to play magnificent physical specimen parts, such as Tarzan.

Q. Does he get his letter?

A. Yes.

Q. How?

A. By snatching victory from the jaws of defeat.

Q. How?

A. By carrying the ball seventy-five yards for a touchdown.

Q. When?

A. In the last minute of play.

Q. What was the crowd yelling?

A. 'Hold that line!'

Q. What else does the crowd yell?

A. 'Block that kick!'

Q. What does the rabid football fan sitting behind you do?

A. He jams my hat down over my head in his excitement.

Q. Why?

A. Because he is an old grad, and he is a little the worse for wear.

Q. You mean?

A. He is feeling good. He's in his cups.

Q. By the way, Mr. Smith, what would you call the annual game between Yale and Harvard?

A. It is a grid classic.

Q. And what is the Yale Bowl—or the Harvard Stadium—on the day of this grid classic?

A. A Mecca for football fans throughout the East.

Q. And the fans?

A. Jam the Bowl to its utmost capacity. Reporters estimate the crowd at 75,000.

Q. Just 75,000?

A. No. Pardon me. *Fully* 75,000.

Q. Do Yale or Harvard care whether they bow to any other eleven prior to their grid classic with each other?

A. Oh, no. They point to each other.

Q. Point?

A. Yes. Train for each other.

Q. Why?

A. Because of their age-old rivalry.

Q. Are they the only two colleges that have an age-old rivalry?

A. Good heavens, no! Every college worthy of the name has an age-old rivalry. Army and Navy. Cornell and Syracuse—you know.

Q. I see. What is it the rooters want Yale to hold?

A. ''Em.' You know—'Hold 'em, Yale!'

Q. If Harvard emerges triumphant over Yale, what does that constitute?

A. A moral victory for Yale.

Q. And the game itself?

A. It was a good game from the spectators' point of view.

Q. Why?

A. Because there were plenty of thrills.

Q. What happens after a football game?

A. The undergraduates tear down the goal posts.

Q. What reigns on the campus of the winning team that night?

A. Joy, or pandemonium.

Q. And the cops?

A. The cops wink.

Q. Mr. Smith, as an expert, what lesson do you draw from the game of football?

A. Life is a game of football, Mr. Sullivan, and we the players. Some of us are elusive quarterbacks, some of us are coaches and some of us are old grads, slightly the worse for wear, up in the stands. Some of us thump the people in front of us on the head in our excitement, some of us are the people who always get thumped. But the important thing to remember is—Play the Game!

Q. How true!

Vocations and Professions

THE WAY TO WEALTH[1]

Benjamin Franklin

It would be thought a hard Government that should tax
its People one tenth Part of their *Time*, to be employed in its Service. But
Idleness taxes many of us much more, if we reckon all that is spent in absolute
Sloth, or doing of nothing, with that which is spent in idle Employments or
Amusements, that amount to nothing. *Sloth,* by bringing on Diseases, absolutely shortens Life. *Sloth, like Rust, consumes faster than Labour wears,
while the used Key is always bright,* as *Poor Richard* says. But *dost thou love
Life, then do not squander Time, for that's the Stuff Life is made of,* as *Poor
Richard* says.—How much more than is necessary do we spend in Sleep! forgetting that *The Sleeping Fox catches no Poultry,* and that *there will be
sleeping enough in the Grave,* as *Poor Richard* says. If Time be of all Things
the most precious, *wasting of Time* must be, as *Poor Richard* says, *the greatest
Prodigality,* since, as he elsewhere tells us, *Lost Time is never* found again;
and what we call *Time-enough, always proves little enough.* Let us then be
up and doing, and doing to the Purpose; so by Diligence shall we do more
with less Perplexity. *Sloth makes all things difficult, but Industry all Things
easy,* as *Poor Richard* says; and *He that riseth late, must trot all Day, and shall
scarce overtake his Business at night.* While *Laziness travels so slowly, that
Poverty soon overtakes him,* as we read in *Poor Richard,* who adds, *Drive thy
Business, let not that drive thee; and, Early to Bed, and early to rise, makes a
Man healthy, wealthy, and wise.*

So what signifies *wishing* and *hoping* for better times. We may make
these Times better if we bestir ourselves. *Industry need not wish* as *Poor
Richard* says, and *He that lives upon Hope will die fasting. There are no
Gains, without Pains;* then *Help Hands, for I have no Lands,* or if I have,
they are smartly taxed. And as *Poor Richard* likewise observes, *He that hath
a Trade hath an Estate,* and *He that hath a Calling hath an Office of Profit
and Honour*; but then the *Trade* must be worked at, and the *Calling* well
followed, or neither the *Estate,* nor the *Office,* will enable us to pay our Taxes.
—If we are industrious we shall never starve; for as *Poor Richard* says, *At the
working Man's House Hunger looks in, but dares not enter.* Nor will the
Bailiff or the Constable enter, for *Industry pays Debts while Despair en-
creaseth them,* says *Poor Richard.*—What though you have found no Treasure,
nor has any rich Relation left you a Legacy; *Diligence is the Mother of Good-
luck,* as *Poor Richard* says, *and God gives all things to Industry.* Then *plough*

[1]From "Father Abraham's Speech," forming the preface to *Poor Richard's Almanac*
for 1758.

deep, while Sluggards sleep, and you shall have Corn to sell and to keep, says *Poor Dick*. Work while it is called To-day, for you know not how much you may be hindered To-morrow, which makes *Poor Richard* say, *One To-day is worth two To-morrows*; and farther, *Have you somewhat to do To-morrow, do it To-day*. If you were a Servant, would you not be ashamed that a good Master should catch you idle? Are you then your own Master, *be ashamed to catch yourself idle*, as *Poor Dick* says. When there is so much to be done for yourself, your Family, your Country, and your gracious King, be up by Peep of Day; *Let not the Sun look down and say, Inglorious here he lies*. Handle your Tools without Mittens; remember that *the Cat in Gloves catches no Mice*, as *Poor Richard* says. 'Tis true there is much to be done, and perhaps you are weak-handed, but stick to it steadily, and you will see great Effects, for *constant Dropping wears away Stones*, and by *Diligence and Patience, the Mouse ate in two the Cable*; and *little Strokes fell great Oaks*, as *Poor Richard* says in his Almanack, the Year I cannot just now remember.

Methinks I hear some of you say, *Must a Man afford himself no Leisure?* —I will tell thee My Friend, what *Poor Richard* says, *Employ thy Time well if thou meanest to gain Leisure*; and, *since thou art not sure of a Minute, throw not away an Hour*. Leisure is Time for doing something useful; this Leisure the diligent man will obtain, but the lazy man never; so that, as *Poor Richard* says, *a Life of leisure and a Life of Laziness are two Things*. Do you imagine that Sloth will afford you more comfort than Labour? No, for as *Poor Richard* says, *Trouble springs from Idleness, and grievous Toil from needless Ease. Many without Labour, would live by their WITS only, but they break for want of stock.* Whereas Industry gives Comfort, and Plenty and Respect: *Fly Pleasures and they'll follow you. The diligent Spinner has a large Shift; and now I have a Sheep and a Cow every Body bids me Good morrow*, all which is well said by *Poor Richard*.

But with our Industry, we must likewise be *steady, settled*, and *careful*, and oversee our own Affairs *with our own Eyes*, and not trust too much to others; for, as *Poor Richard* says,

> *I never saw an oft removed Tree,*
> *Nor yet an oft removed Family,*
> *That throve so well as those that settled be.*

And again, *Three Removes is as bad as a Fire*; and again, *Keep thy Shop, and thy Shop will keep thee*; and again, *If you would have your Business done, go; if not, send*. And again,

> *He that by the Plough would thrive,*
> *Himself must either hold or drive.*

130

And again, *The Eye of a Master will do more Work than both his Hands*; and again, *Want of Care does us more Damage than Want of Knowledge*; and again, *Not to oversee Workmen, is to leave them your Purse open.* Trusting too much to others' Care is the Ruin of many; for, as the *Almanack* says, *In the Affairs of this World, Men are saved, not by Faith, but by the Want of it*; but a Man's own Care is profitable; for, saith *Poor Dick, Learning is to the Studious*, and *Riches to the Careful*, as well as *Power to the Bold*, and *Heaven to the Virtuous.* And, farther, *If you would have a faithful Servant, and one that you like, serve yourself.* And again, he adviseth to Circumspection and Care, even in the smallest Matters, because sometimes, *a little Neglect may breed great Mischief*, adding *for want of a Nail, the Shoe was lost; for want of a Shoe the Horse was lost; and for want of a Horse the Rider was lost*, being overtaken and slain by the Enemy; all for want of Care about a Horse-shoe Nail.

So much for Industry, my Friends, and Attention to one's own Business; but to these we must add *Frugality*, if we would make our *Industry* more certainly successful. A man may, if he knows not how to save as he gets, *Keep his Nose all his Life to the Grindstone*, and die not worth *a Groat* at last. *A fat Kitchen makes a lean Will*, as Poor Richard says; and

> *Many Estates are spent in the Getting,*
> *Since Women for Tea forsook Spinning and Knitting,*
> *And Men for Punch forsook Hewing and Splitting.*

If you would be wealthy, says he, in another Almanack, *think of Saving as well as of Getting: The* Indies *have not made Spain rich, because her* Outgoes *are greater than her* Incomes. Away then with your expensive Follies, you will not have so much cause to complain of hard Times, heavy Taxes, and chargeable Families; for, as *Poor Dick* says,

> *Women and Wine, Game and Deceit,*
> *Make the Wealth small, and the Wants great.*

And farther, *What maintains one Vice would bring up two Children.* You may think, perhaps, that a *little* Tea or a *little* Punch now and then, Diet a *little* more costly, Clothes a *little* finer, and a *little* Entertainment now and then, can be no *great* Matter: but remember what *Poor Richard* says, *Many a* Little *makes a Mickle*; and farther, *Beware of little Expenses; a small Leak will sink a great Ship*; and again, *Who Dainties love shall Beggars prove*; and moreover, *Fools make Feasts and wise Men eat them.*

Here you are all got together at this Vendue of *fineries* and *Knicknacks*. You call them *Goods*, but if you do not take Care, they will prove *Evils* to some of you. You expect they will be sold *cheap,* and perhaps they may for less than they cost; but if you have no Occasion for them, they must be *dear* to you. Remember what *Poor Richard* says, *Buy what thou hast no Need of, and ere long thou shalt sell thy Necessaries.* And again, *At a great Penny-worth pause a while*: He means, that perhaps the Cheapness is *apparent* only, and not *real*; or the Bargain, by straitning thee in thy Business, may do thee more Harm than Good. For in another Place he says, *Many have been ruined by buying good Pennyworths.* Again *Poor Richard* says, *'Tis foolish to lay out Money in a Purchase of Repentance*; and yet this Folly is practised every Day at Vendues, for want of minding the Almanack. *Wise Men,* as *Poor Dick* says, *learn by others' Harms, Fools scarcely by their own*; but *Felix quem faciunt aliena Pericula cautum.* Many a one, for the Sake of Finery on the Back, have gone with a hungry Belly, and half starved their Families; *Silks and Satins, Scarlet and Velvets,* as *Poor Richard* says, *put out the Kitchen Fire.* These are not the *Necessaries* of Life; they can scarcely be called the *Conveniences,* and yet only because they look pretty, how many *want* to *have* them. The *artificial* Wants of Mankind thus become more numerous than the *natural*; and as *Poor Dick* says, *For one* poor *Person there are an hundred* indigent. By these, and other Extravagancies the Genteel are reduced to Poverty, and forced to borrow of those whom they formerly despised, but who through *Industry* and *Frugality,* have maintained their Standing; in which case it appears plainly that a Ploughman on his Legs is higher than a Gentleman on his Knees, as *Poor Richard* says. Perhaps they have had a small Estate left them, which they knew not the Getting of,—they think *'tis Day and will never be Night*; that a little to be spent out of *so much,* is not worth minding; (*a Child and a Fool,* as *Poor Richard* says, *imagine Twenty Shillings and Twenty Years can never be spent*) but, *always taking out of the meat-tub and never putting in, soon comes to the Bottom*; then, as *Poor Dick* says, *When the Well's dry, they know the Worth of Water.* But this they might have known before, if they had taken his Advice; *If you would know the Value of Money, go and try to borrow some; for he that goes a borrowing goes a sorrowing*; and, indeed, so does he that lends to such People, when he goes *to get it in again.*—*Poor Dick* farther advises, and says,

> *Fond* Pride of Dress *is sure a very Curse*;
> *Ere* Fancy *you consult, consult your Purse.*

And again, *Pride is as loud a Beggar as Want, and a great deal more saucy.* When you have bought one fine Thing you must buy ten more, that your appearance may be all of a Piece; but *Poor Dick* says, *'Tis easier to* suppress *the first Desire, than to* satisfy *all that follow it.* And 'tis as truly Folly for the Poor to ape the Rich, as for the Frog to swell, in order to equal the Ox.

> *Great Estates may venture more,*
> *But little Boats should keep near Shore.*

'Tis, however, a Folly soon punished; for, *Pride that dines on Vanity sups on Contempt,* as *Poor Richard* says. And in another Place, *Pride breakfasted with Plenty, dined with Poverty, and supped with Infamy.* And after all, of what Use is this *Pride of Appearance,* for which so much is risked, so much is suffered! It cannot promote Health, or ease Pain; it makes no Increase of Merit in the Person, creates Envy, it hastens Misfortune.

> *What is a Butterfly? At best*
> *He's but a Caterpillar drest.*
> *The gaudy Fop's his Picture just.*

as *Poor Richard* says.

But what Madness must it be to *run in Debt* for these Superfluities! We are offered by the Terms of this Vendue Six Months' Credit; and that perhaps has induced some of us to attend it, because we cannot spare the ready Money, and hope now to be fine without it. But, ah, think what you do when you run in Debt; *You give to another Power over your Liberty.* If you cannot pay at the Time, you will be ashamed to see your Creditor; you will be in Fear when you speak to him; you will make poor, pitiful, sneaking Excuses, and by Degrees come to lose your Veracity, and sink into base, downright lying; for as *Poor Richard* says, *The second Vice is Lying, the first is running in Debt.* And again, to the same Purpose, *Lying rides upon Debt's Back;* whereas a freeborn *Englishman* ought not to be ashamed or afraid to see or speak to any Man living. But Poverty often deprives a man of all Spirit and Virtue; *'Tis hard for an empty Bag to stand upright,* as *Poor Richard* truly says. What would you think of that Prince, or that Government, who should issue an Edict forbidding you to dress like a Gentleman or a Gentlewoman, on Pain of Imprisonment or Servitude! Would you not say, that you are free, have a Right to dress as you please, and that such an Edict would be a Breach of your Privileges, and such a Government tyrannical! And yet you are about to put yourself under that Tyranny when you run in Debt for such Dress! Your Creditor has Authority at his Pleasure to deprive you of your Liberty by confining you in Gaol for Life, or to sell you for a Servant, if you should not be able to pay him! When you have got your Bargain, you may, perhaps, think little of Payment! But, *Creditors, Poor Richard* tells us, *have better*

Memories than Debtors; and in another Place says, *Creditors are a super-stitious Sect, great Observers of set Days and Times.* The Day comes round before you are aware, and the Demand is made before you are prepared to satisfy it, Or if you bear your Debt in Mind, the Term, which at first seemed so long, will, as it lessens, appear extremely short. Time will seem to have added Wings to his Heels as well as Shoulders. *Those have a short Lent,* saith *Poor Richard, who owe Money to be paid at Easter.* Then, since as he says, *The Borrower is a Slave to the Lender, and the Debtor to the Creditor,* disdain the Chain, preserve your Freedom; and maintain your Independency; Be *industrious* and *free*; be *frugal* and *free*. At present, perhaps, you may think yourself in thriving Circumstances, and that you can bear a little Extravagance without Injury; but

> *For Age and Want save while you may;*
> *No Morning Sun lasts a whole Day,*

as *Poor Richard* says.—Gain may be temporary and uncertain, but ever while you live Expense is constant and certain; and *'tis easier to build two Chimnies than to keep one in Fuel,* as *Poor Richard* says. *So rather go to Bed supperless than rise in Debt.*

> *Get what you can, and what you get hold.*
> *'Tis the stone that will turn all your Lead into Gold,*

as *Poor Richard* says. And when you have got the Philosopher's Stone, sure you will no longer complain of the bad Times or the Difficulty of paying Taxes.

This Doctrine, my Friends, is *Reason* and *Wisdom*; but after all, do not depend too much on your own *Industry* and *Frugality,* and *Prudence,* though excellent Things; for they may all be blasted without the Blessing of Heaven; and therefore ask that Blessing humbly, and be not uncharitable to those that at present seem to want it, but comfort and help them, Remember *Job* suffered, and was afterwards prosperous.

And now, to conclude, *Experience keeps a dear School,* but *Fools will learn in no other, and scarce in that*; for it is true, *we may give Advice, but we cannot give Conduct,* as *Poor Richard* says: However, remember this, *They that won't be counselled, can't be helped,* as *Poor Richard* says: and farther, That *if you will not hear Reason, she'll surely wrap your Knuckles.*

HAPPY[1]

Thomas Carlyle

ALL WORK, even cotton-spinning, is noble; work is alone noble: be that here said and asserted once more. And in like manner too, all dignity is painful; a life of ease is not for any man, nor for any god. The life of all gods figures itself to us as a Sublime Sadness,—earnestness of Infinite Battle against Infinite Labour. Our highest religion is named the 'Worship of Sorrow.' For the son of man there is no noble crown, well worn or even ill worn, but is a crown of thorns!—These things, in spoken words, or still better, in felt instincts alive in every heart, were once well known.

Does not the whole wretchedness, the whole *Atheism* as I call it, of man's ways, in these generations, shadow itself for us in that unspeakable Life-philosophy of his: The pretension to be what he calls 'happy'? Every pitifulest whipster that walks within a skin has his head filled with the notion that he is, shall be, or by all human and divine laws ought to be 'happy.' His wishes, the pitifulest whipster's, are to be fulfilled for him; his days, the pitifulest whipster's, are to flow on in ever-gentle current of enjoyment, impossible even for the gods. The prophets preach to us, Thou shalt be happy; thou shalt love pleasant things, and find them. The people clamour, Why have we not found pleasant things?

We construct our theory of Human Duties, not on any Greatest-Nobleness Principle, never so mistaken; no, but on a Greatest-Happiness Principle. 'The word *Soul* with us, as in some Slavonic dialects, seems to be synonymous with *Stomach*.' We plead and speak, in our Parliaments and elsewhere, not as from the Soul, but from the Stomach;—wherefore indeed our pleadings are so slow to profit. We plead not for God's Justice; we are not ashamed to stand clamouring and pleading for our own 'interests,' our own rents and trade-profits; we say, They are the 'interests' of so many; there is such an intense desire in us for them! We demand Free-trade, with much just vocifera-tion and benevolence, That the poorer classes, who are terribly ill-off at present, may have cheaper New-Orleans bacon. Men ask on Free-trade platforms, How can the indomitable spirit of Englishmen be kept up without plenty of bacon? We shall become a ruined Nation!—Surely, my friends, plenty of bacon is good and indispensable: but, I doubt, you will never get even bacon by aiming only at that. You are men, not animals of prey, well-used or ill-used! Your Greatest-Happiness Principle seems to me fast becoming a rather unhappy one.—What if we should cease babbling about 'happiness,' and leave *it* resting on its own basis, as it used to do!

[1]This selection and "Labour," which follows, are from Carlyle's *Past and Present*, 1843.

A gifted Byron rises in his wrath; and feeling too surely that he for his part is not 'happy,' declares the same in very violent language, as a piece of news that may be interesting. It evidently has surprised him much. One dislikes to see a man and poet reduced to proclaim on the streets such tidings: but on the whole, as matters go, that is not the most dislikable. Byron speaks the *truth* in this matter. Byron's large audience indicates how true it is felt to be.

'Happy,' my brother? First of all, what difference is it whether thou art happy or not! Today becomes Yesterday so fast, all Tomorrows become Yesterdays; and then there is no question whatever of the 'happiness,' but quite another question. Nay, thou hast such a sacred pity left at least for thyself, thy very pains once gone over into Yesterday become joys to thee. Besides, thou knowest not what heavenly blessedness and indispensable sanative virtue was in them; thou shalt only know it after many days, when thou art wiser!

LABOUR

For there is a perennial nobleness, and even sacredness, in Work. Were he never so benighted, forgetful of his high calling, there is always hope in a man that actually and earnestly works: in Idleness alone is there perpetual despair. Work, never so Mammonish, mean, *is* in communication with Nature; the real desire to get Work done will itself lead one more and more to truth, to Nature's appointments and regulations, which are truth.

The latest Gospel in this world is, Know thy work and do it. 'Know thyself': long enough has that poor 'self' of thine tormented thee; thou wilt never get to 'know' it, I believe! Think it not thy business, this of knowing thyself; thou art an unknowable individual: know what thou canst work at; and work at it, like a Hercules! That will be thy better plan.

It has been written, 'an endless significance lies in Work'; a man perfects himself by working. Foul jungles are cleared away, fair seed-fields rise instead, and stately cities; and withal the man himself first ceases to be a jungle and foul unwholesome desert thereby. Consider how, even in the meanest sorts of Labour, the whole soul of a man is composed into a kind of real harmony, the instant he sets himself to work! Doubt, Desire, Sorrow, Remorse, Indignation, Despair itself, all these like helldogs lie beleaguering the soul of the poor dayworker, as of every man: but he bends himself with free valour against his task, and all these are stilled, all these shrink murmuring far off into their caves. The man is now a man. The blessed glow of Labour in him, is it not as purifying fire, wherein all poison is burnt up, and of sour smoke itself there is made bright blessed flame!

Destiny, on the whole, has no other way of cultivating us. A formless Chaos, once set it *revolving*, grows round and ever rounder; ranges itself, by mere force of gravity, into strata, spherical courses; is no longer a Chaos, but a round compacted World. What would become of the Earth, did she cease to revolve? In the poor old Earth, so long as she revolves, all inequalities, irregularities disperse themselves; all irregularities are incessantly becoming regular. Hast thou looked on the Potter's wheel,—one of the venerablest objects; old as the Prophet Ezechiel and far older? Rude lumps of clay, how they spin themselves up, by mere quick whirling, into beautiful circular dishes. And fancy the most assiduous Potter, but without his wheel; reduced to make dishes, or rather amorphous botches, by mere kneading and baking! Even such a Potter were Destiny, with a human soul that would rest and lie at ease, that would not work and spin! Of an idle unrevolving man the kindest Destiny, like the most assiduous Potter without wheel, can bake and knead nothing other than a botch; let her spend on him what expensive colouring, what gilding and enamelling she will, he is but a botch. Not a dish; no, a bulging, kneaded, crooked, shambling, squint-cornered, amorphous botch,— a mere enamelled vessel of dishonour! Let the idle think of this.

Blessed is he who has found his work; let him ask no other blessedness. He has a work, a life-purpose; he has found it, and will follow it! How, as a free-flowing channel, dug and torn by noble force through the sour mud-swamp of one's existence, like an ever-deepening river there, it runs and flows; —draining-off the sour festering water, gradually from the root of the remotest grass-blade; making, instead of pestilential swamp, a green fruitful meadow with its clear-flowing stream. How blessed for the meadow itself, let the stream and *its* value be great or small! Labour is Life: from the inmost heart of the Worker rises his god-given Force, the sacred celestial Life-essence breathed into him by Almighty God; from his inmost heart awakens him to all nobleness,—to all knowledge, 'self-knowledge' and much else, so soon as Work fitly begins. Knowledge? The knowledge that will hold good in working, cleave thou to that; for Nature herself accredits that, says Yea to that. Properly thou hast no other knowledge but what thou hast got by working: the rest is yet all a hypothesis of knowledge; a thing to be argued of in schools, a thing floating in the clouds, in endless logic-vortices, till we try it and fix it. 'Doubt, of whatever kind, can be ended by Action alone.'

WHAT ARE YOU FIT FOR?[1]

William Seabrook

Fifteen years ago a now famous young Harvard psychologist named Johnson O'Connor began to test aptitudes and potential abilities in employees and applicants at General Electric. His work widened and has evolved into the Human Engineering Laboratory now located at Stevens Institute of Technology, Hoboken, New Jersey, with branches in Boston, Chicago, and Washington and field activities covering most of the United States.

The aim of the Laboratory is not vocational guidance but rather to give to a person, through a series of ingenious tests, a *conscious inventory of his natural aptitudes and potential capabilities.*

Dr. O'Connor likes to say, "We have only a little lantern in the dark," and, "Goodness, man, we don't pretend to predict an individual's future or settle his life for ten dollars in two hours!" He does feel, however, that the tests can always shed *some* definite light on inherent aptitude and that, by choosing work in accord with his natural aptitudes, the individual is more likely to be successful and happy.

These limited pretensions seemed so at variance with reports of astounding "successes" and "adjustments" engineered by O'Connor and his crew that I went to Hoboken to report on just what they have accomplished there.

Headquarters of Human Engineering Laboratory are located on the campus of Stevens Institute (one of the four ranking technological schools in America), which sprawls on heights overlooking the Hoboken waterfront, in an old converted brownstone mansion which hums all day long. Director O'Connor, still around forty, is smallish, dark, wiry, kinetic, pleasant, with a thick, black beard of the sort occasionally worn in the French Academy but seldom seen in America or on anybody named O'Connor anywhere. He is surrounded by a staff of sixteen men and women, mostly specialists from Yale, Columbia, Cornell, Wellesley, Smith, etc.

LEARNING ABOUT YOURSELF

No matter who you are, male or female, so long as you are nine years of age or older, you can go and take the tests, regardless of whether you are in a job, out of a job, bright or dumb. A fee ranging from $10 to $20 is charged but doesn't cover the actual cost of the testing.

Of the 20,000 persons they've tested here and in field work (about 70 per cent of whom they have definitely helped toward better adjustment), the first 13,000 were employees in industry, tested at the request of their employers; the

[1]From *The Forum*, August, 1938.

subsequent 12,000 were about half adults and about half college students and school children.

The tests should work at all ages, because inherent aptitudes, if they exist at all, are basic and cannot be acquired. Whether these things are immutably fixed in the womb or on the nursery floor is outside their pragmatic province. What difference does it make, if there's nothing you can do about it afterward? They have succeeded up to now in isolating only ten testable inherent aptitudes, yet suspect there are probably 90 to 100 which may some day be discovered.

"We have paralleled thus far very closely the history of chemistry," O'Connor said. "Originally, fire, air, earth, and water were thought to be the chemical elements. It was not until chemists stumbled upon and isolated hydrogen, chlorine, oxygen, and carbon that it began to lead into a new science. I think we are just beginning to isolate some real mental elements. When we began trying to sift out the bright, mediocre, and the dull applicants for jobs, we presently found that there didn't seem to be any such thing as general intelligence or general aptitude. We began to discover a few basic, highly *specific* elements which some individuals had and some did not or had in different combinations—and that was the real beginning, just as the real beginning of chemistry began with the isolation of hydrogen, chlorine, etc. It required, I believe, nearly a hundred and fifty years to isolate the other chemical elements. It may require a hundred and fifty years to isolate all the mental elements.

"Despite scientific evidence to the contrary, most of us still think of men in terms of general intelligence. Even parents do not always recognize ability in their own children.

"Some time ago a white-haired grandmother brought her nineteen-year-old grandson to the Laboratory. He had failed and had been asked to leave a well-known preparatory school. His parents, both brilliantly successful, had given him up as hopeless. Only the grandmother hoped that some hidden ability might be discovered. When measured, the boy excelled in every measurable characteristic—except one. He was poor in clerical aptitude and consequently did poorly not merely in arithmetic but in other written examinations where attention to detail counted. He had become discouraged and finally accepted the teachers' estimate that he was dull. Assured now that he had real brains, he plugged cheerfully at the detail work and came through with honors."

"Do you ever get miracles like that with grownups?"

"I wish you wouldn't call them miracles," O'Connor said, "but we often get surprises."

"Such as what?" I asked, and he told me the queer case of an accountant in a big manufacturing firm who was going to be let out. His associates and superiors didn't like him.

The head of his department had said to O'Connor, "You might as well test him. We're going to fire him anyway. He's able, but his heart's not in the work, and we don't like that kind of employee."

When the Laboratory began the tests, his aptitude for accounting proved extremely high—and he became immediately an interesting problem: but he scored equally high in engineering aptitude (recently renamed structural visualization). He had been doing auditing, which consisted simply of juggling groups or columns of figures. Dr. O'Connor persuaded the company, instead of firing him, to shift him to cost accounting, which required blueprints, graphs, etc., almost like those in an engineer's office. Here he not only *could* use but would be *forced* to use his second high aptitude, i.e., structural visualization, along with the other ability he thought he hated.

O'Connor urged me to beware of emphasizing miracles, but what happened was that at the end of four years the man was head of the cost-accounting department, and at the end of five years, which is today, he is head of the whole organization and boss of the executives who were going to fire him!

DISCOVERING THE REAL YOU

My curiosity had now been violently aroused about the tests themselves. I wanted now to see the wheels go round.

You begin by sitting opposite an amiable man at an ordinary flat-top desk. If they decide to give you the works, as it were, you will be tested on the following ten counts:

1. Observation.
2. Type of personality, whether subjective or objective.
3. Engineering ability (or structural visualization).
4. Accounting or clerical ability.
5. Tweezer dexterity.
6. Finger dexterity.
7. Creative imagination.
8. Inductive reasoning.
9. Visual memory.
10. Tonal memory.

They may also test you for "interest," but about the first thing I learned is that interest is no guide to aptitude. One of the strange discoveries at the

Laboratory has been that interest tests are not only frequently inconclusive, but sometimes actually misleading. Aptitudes remain constant through life, while interests change frequently with chameleonic rapidity. Every kid, at some adolescent point, wants passionately to be a cop or fireman. And the grownup, too, will unconsciously give misleading answers in all sincerity, in order to "make a better impression" or to seem to have more ambition or simply as a lollypop to his deluded ego. Generally speaking, *real* interests run parallel with aptitudes, but O'Connor prefers to deduce interests generally from aptitudes—rather than the other way round. They almost say, "*You can't trust your interests*," and do say you can't trust your seeming interests at any given period in your age or career.

When the aptitude battery gets going, you are first asked a series of quite ordinary questions and wonder why the set is called a battery. Soon, however, varied artillery is introduced, including fantastic photographs which would delight surrealists; innocent-looking wooden blocks that frustrated gentlemen have been known to hurl through the plate-glass window; phonograph records which you might guess had been made in China during the first Ming dynasty; metal blocks with holes to stick pegs in, if you can. When you have finished, which is generally at the end of about two and a half hours, you understand full well why they chose the word *battery*.

Personality is not an aptitude in the true sense of the word. It is a distinction in temperament and, as such, governs the contentment of a person in group contact or in individual work. Objective personality correlates with salesmanship, high-school teaching, social group activities, and social-service work. Subjective personality is found among writers, doctors, engineers, and scientists.

To decide whether you have a subjective or an objective personality, they read a rapid list of words to you, with a slight pause after each word, during which you answer automatically, instantly and without reflection, with the first word which pops into your head. The words in the key list have no sequence or connection. For example, they may run *cat, girl, umbrella*.

If your automatic responses are something like *cat-Alcibiades, girl-Nellie, umbrella-aunt*, you have a subjective personality. In other words, if you tend automatically to make highly personalized responses, naming your own tom-cat and some girl in particular and recalling that your sainted aunt from Haw-kinsville, Georgia, never goes without her umbrella, this is being "subjective," and you probably work best when withdrawn into yourself and alone. If you answer in terms of impersonal, world-embracing generality, being objective, you enjoy human contacts, work better with other people.

For engineering aptitude, which they now prefer to call structural visualization, the tester trots out and places tenderly on the desk in front of you a block of wood about the shape and size of a thick dictionary. It has been trisected by a wave line cut into nine parts. It is a sort of three-dimensional jigsaw puzzle, looks simple and innocent. He lets you stare at it and study the lines as it stands there assembled. Then he takes it apart slowly, giving you time to note how it is put together. Then he shuffles the parts, and you try to put them together again.

If you have an inherent aptitude for structural visualization, you may put them together in a couple of minutes. If you are mediocre and do it by the trial-and-error method, it may take you from six to ten minutes. If you are deficient in this inherent aptitude, even though you be a doctor of philosophy or executive head of vast industries, you may hurl them through the window as that one irate gentleman did a couple of years ago. Surgeons, dentists, die-makers, and architects, as well as engineers, score high in structural visualization.

THE CASE COMPLETED

For accounting or clerical aptitude, you'll be surprised they don't ask you to do any adding or subtracting or lightning calculating. They hand you a sheet on which are printed columns of figures in groups of two each. They begin with sets composed of three numerals each, like this:

| 326 | 236 | Same | Different |

All you do is to glance quickly at them and indicate at the right whether the figures are identical or different. Subsequent lines have increasingly more numerals in each group, until you get to the bottom of the sheet, when you have lines like:

| 412573386 | 412753386 | Same | Different |

Speed is the essence of this test. The test administrator is working now with a couple of stop watches, and your aptitude or deficiency is judged solely by the time it takes you in split seconds to recognize whether the figures are the same or different. They are certain this digs down to *inherent* aptitude. Any tests involving the actual working of problems in arithmetic would be useless because they would drag in the extraneous elements of study, schooling, and practice. Accounting aptitude enters into typing, bookkeeping, arithmetical operations in statistics, banking, copy-desk work in newspaper offices, proofreading, and printing.

For tweezer dexterity they give you a flat metal block in which are 100 holes ranged symmetrically in rows of 10; also 100 blunt, headless brass pins, about the size of ordinary pins but a little thicker, which you pick up, one by one, with a pair of ordinary tweezers and insert in the holes. There are no tricks or problems. The tester has the stop watch, and aptitude is decided solely by the time you take. This test shows aptitude or lack of aptitude for working with any small tool or instrument. The tool might be a surgeon's scalpel, a scientist's microscope slide, a sewing woman's needle, a carpenter's punch, or a garage mechanic's screw driver.

Next comes the test for finger dexterity, with a similar metal block, in which you use the fingers of one hand only and insert similar pins in larger holes, in groups of three pins to each hole.

An unexpected result from these tests has been the discovery that tweezer dexterity and finger dexterity have no necessary correlation whatever. You may be good at one and clumsy as an ape at the other. Finger dexterity is used in basket weaving and in manual factory assembly jobs, whereas tweezer dexterity is used by surgeons, dentists, nurses, bacteriologists, and most laboratory workers in the physical sciences and by those doing miniature instrument assembly work in factories.

There are other tests less graphic in the telling but not less important in sizing up your powers.

The visual-memory test, for example, is an unmitigated horror to persons not gifted with that aptitude. (O'Connor himself takes it every once in a while and generally makes a score somewhere between D and zero). A motion-picture machine projects a series of scrambled numbers like those on a freight car, motor license, or bill of lading. Each is shown you only for a second. Then the machine squawks and dies, and you are merely supposed to remember all the numbers if you can! The horror lies in the fact that people who possess this fantastic aptitude often easily remember all of them! It gives them a terrific advantage in expediting shipments, production following, handling order numbers. Dealers in the stock market generally possess it to a high degree.

For aptitude in tonal memory, you listen to a set of phonograph records, consisting of grouped musical notes—but not from any symphony or song. The record repeats a phrase in a group of three notes—*do, re, fa,* for instance. Then it's followed by groups in which one (and one only) of the three notes changes. You're given a pad and asked to indicate, as you listen, whether note 1, 2, or 3 has changed. The change may be a full tone or a half-tone, or the tone may be merely off key.

O'Connor does not believe vocabulary is an inherent aptitude, but he tests for it because it seems to have a greater correlation with success in all fields than any other one quality. High-up executives seem generally to have the largest vocabulary of anybody—larger (and this was a surprise) than uni-

143

versity professors, journalists, and authors. The test goes far beyond mere parrot definitions, into the realm of shaded meanings, synonyms and antonyms.

In two or three weeks you receive by mail a report on your scores, an analysis of what they seem to imply, and a statement of what would seem to be, from that analysis, the general sort of endeavor in which you are most likely to be successful and happy.

The Laboratory workers keep insisting that vocational guidance is not their function and will refrain from advising too specifically what precise career would be best for you. This does not evade the basic purpose, however, for they tell you clearly the *kind* or *kinds* of work in which they are sure you will do best.

If contradictory evidence has been disclosed, you may be invited back for a conference and discussion, based on their scientific knowledge and your mutual common sense, as to what you should do about it.

PROOF OF THE PUDDING

I got a clearer idea of how these tests work and what they accomplish from studying completed cases than from watching the Laboratory operate. I was helped by its director, David Mack, the smooth-faced young giant who plays a sort of Plato to O'Connor's bearded Socrates. He kept worrying about my wanting to pick "miracle" cases, and said, "Putting all of our work into a nutshell, I think that what we want to do more than anything else is simply to point out to a person certain things that he can do well and certain things that he can do poorly and to help him as nearly as possible locate some field, *rather than any one kind of job in particular*, in which he will be called upon to do the things which he can do well and where he will not be called upon to do the things which he does poorly."

A now celebrated individual went several years ago to take the tests. He had specialized in radio engineering but didn't seem to be getting anywhere. He had a lot of technical knowledge, but the tests proved him poor in natural engineering aptitude. It was a blow to him—and a puzzle. Tests in other aptitudes were merely so-so—until they reached tonal memory, when his score jumped sky-high! This shed light on something he'd been hiding from himself. With the help of O'Connor's psychologists, he was presently realizing and confessing that his passionate emotional interest had always been in music, about which he knew very little. His real reason for wanting to break into radio was love of music, and he had taken up engineering as a means because he had no musical training and didn't dream he had any natural musical ability. He had been a rotten engineer but soon became an expert in the fields

144

his latent musical potentialities opened up—and now he's a big shot on a nationwide network.

A shift in one's field of activity is not always indicated. Adjustment will do the needed trick.

Recently a successful writer went to take the tests because he hated writing. His books are occasional best sellers, and he writes regularly for big magazines. Yet he loathed writing. He said he had secretly hoped O'Connor would advise him to give it up and become a carpenter. They disclosed a deplorable mediocrity at everything—almost. The only ones he rated high in were precisely those required for writing—creative imagination, inductive reasoning, observation. He rated high also in vocabulary. But he turned out to be an "objective" type —liked meeting and talking and playing with people and loathed applying the seat of the pants to the seat of a chair in solitude. That was why he hated writing. O'Connor advised him to recognize the facts, go on suffering and writing, since it was the only craft for which he had natural aptitude, but to take up lecturing, too, and to write about things which involved contact with others. He told him that he'd go bankrupt if he ever went into business and that he'd make a lousy carpenter.

A young woman doing a finger job in a factory was going to be fired, not so much because her ability was mediocre as because she was sullen and quarrelsome. The tests showed that, while she had learned to do the job with her fingers not too badly, her inherent finger dexterity was very poor. On the contrary, though she had never been employed at any job requiring tweezer dexterity, she made a high score in that. Purely as an experiment, O'Connor persuaded her foreman to shift her to a job in which she used small tools instead of her fingers. She still holds the job and is one of the most popular workers in the factory. Her ill nature came from a sense of frustration in work for which she had no natural aptitude.

EDUCATIONAL GUIDANCE

Despite these marvelous adult adjustments, it still seemed to me that the testing of pupils and students might be the Laboratory's most important contribution to the future welfare of humanity.

"Many youngsters never really get interested in education," says O'Connor. "They worry about where they are going. They are not going to college because they have no idea what they are going to do afterwards. A youngster is bound to be more interested if he has some notion of where he is going. Our purpose, therefore, is to help him direct his education toward some aim.

"Another reason for aptitude testing among younger children is to help them avoid difficulties. A boy who is low in clerical aptitude is almost certain to be bored by the routine, clerical schoolwork. He is very apt to have so much trouble with arithmetic that he never goes on into higher mathematics, which he can very often do and do well. He is very apt to make so many foolish mistakes that teachers do not realize that he is thinking correctly and that his mistakes are not errors of thinking but merely errors of bookkeeping."

The tests for young people are identical with those given adults, and here are some proof-of-the-pudding cases.

A boy who had failed repeatedly in Latin, French, and English scored well only in the tests indicating aptitude for scientific and engineering work. This was explained not only to him but to his prep-school headmaster. The boy had previously been told that because of his failure to pass the language requirements he should abandon all thought of college. The headmaster planned the boy's next year with care: senior physics and advanced laboratory work; chemistry, perhaps somewhat less structural than physics but a science; and geometry—three subjects in which he could make practical use of high structural-visualization aptitude. As a fourth course the boy took English, but he was told that he would be judged only by his sciences. At the end of the year he took college-board examinations in his three scientific subjects and averaged high. The result was most satisfactory. The boy acquired a confidence in himself which he had never had before, and the faculty of the school had confidence in him. No teacher is ordinarily interested in struggling with a boy who fails repeatedly in language examinations, but a boy who does well in science is a challenge to the masters who teach language.

A father who teaches in a large metropolitan high school was worried because his boy was introspective, shrinking from contacts, apathetic toward school and social activities. To everybody's surprise, the boy scored extremely objective in personality and high in a wide range of inherent aptitudes. Somewhere in life he had had some experience which had caused him to acquire on the surface the mannerisms of a subjective person but down deep he was objective—enjoyed people and contacts. He was prevailed on, in the light of the tests, to admit it. Six months later his father came in to tell Mack that the boy was a totally different person, that he was getting A's instead of C's in his schoolwork, that he had been elected president of one of the school social organizations and vice president of another.

On the other hand, a truly subjective young man who had taken the tests was accepted, after having failed in two colleges, by a third college, which studied the adjustments of the individual. The shrinking youth was told that he would not be called on to recite in class; and this was impressed on every member of the faculty. A senior scholarship man was assigned to work in the same room with the boy evenings, not to tutor him but to be on hand if some question arose—for an extremely subjective person often wastes hours on a problem rather than make a simple query which might instantly clear up the difficulty. This student attended all his classes but for eight weeks sat without a word. Not until he discovered, at mid-term, that he had passed everything did he begin at rare intervals to take part in class discussion. He remained subjective and aloof but graduated in the top ten of his class.

A young girl had flunked out of one of the best Eastern colleges for women in the middle of her freshman year. She came in to take the tests and proved high in structural visualization. She enrolled the next year for a course in architecture. The last heard of her was that she had won two prizes and that one of her architectural layouts was on display in the lobby of the college architectural building.

The importance of early testing is shown by the sad case of the son of an engineer. He came to the Laboratory at eighteen, after barely managing to scrape through high school. This boy had inherited his father's talent without knowing it. His brilliant scores in structural-visualization tests made it seem desirable that he enter engineering, architecture, surgery, or some profession which offers similar opportunity to capitalize the gift for visualizing solid forms. Each of these fields, however, demands highly specialized college training; and four years of high-school floundering, without scientific guidance, had given this young man nothing which the college he needed could accept for entrance.

In addition to the many students who are sent by parents or come voluntarily to Hoboken, Boston, and Chicago, the Laboratory is continually doing field work, by request, in public and private schools. It also tests for various industries, including chain stores, two New York banks, one of the national radio organizations, an aeronautical concern, as well as for individual adults who apply voluntarily.

The Laboratory makes no claim to have discovered a panacea, but if a person is fundamentally sound timber, whether rare mahogany or common pine, whether he is a square or round peg, O'Connor and his associates have definitely discovered a way to help him find the right sort of hole.

THE DECLINE OF THE PROFESSIONS[1]

Harold J. Laski

THE lawyer and the doctor have been the professional men *par excellence* since the Industrial Revolution. With the clergy, they have almost by common consent been accorded a special social pre-eminence in our civilization. Few of them may have won great pecuniary rewards; but they have had in compensation a status which only statesmen, a few outstanding business men, and the survivors of an aristocracy could hope to rival. Even in the English cathedral town—the rampart of the feudal spirit in Western Europe—the lawyer and the doctor have dined with the bishop and the dean these sixty or seventy years. The law has been one of the acknowledged highroads to the peerage, and the successful physician has enjoyed distinguished social patronage at least since the reign of George II. In America, as Tocqueville noted, the lawyer has always had a place apart; and the American physician has outdistanced all other types as the embodiment of public virtues.

Inherent in this recognition has been the sense that they exist to perform a public service in a way not open to business men. They enter their professions upon the basis of approved standards of competence. They have a special code of ethical conduct. They have the obligation freely to make research regarding their problems to the common advantage. They are debarred from habits which the world accepts from business men because it assumes that personal gain is their primary objective. Tradition tells us that the law and medicine are vocations in which public service is more vital than private profit. Behind the status they have acquired is the belief that there is an essential idealism in these professions more honorable than the business world can evoke from its members.

It is impossible to draw up an indictment against a profession; and there is no doubt a subtle alchemy in historic tradition which communicates at least to some of those who inherit it a special sense of public obligation. Everyone can think of doctors, from the humblest rural practitioner to men like Osler and Koch, whose devoted service to mankind is part of the glory of our time. Everyone also can think, if more rarely, of great lawyers whose attitude to, and achievement in, their vocation has added to the stature of the human race. But we must not judge a profession by the achievement of its men of genius. Rather we must inquire into the predominant characteristic of the contribution it writes into our daily life. And we must seek to relate that characteristic to the end which a profession is supposed to serve. Our business is to assess in a given social environment the way in which it is organized for the purposes it

[1]From *Harper's Magazine*, November, 1935.

needs to fulfill. It is only when this has been examined that we are really in a position to pronounce our verdict.

The thesis I desire to maintain in this paper has at least the merit of simplicity. It is that the individualistic organization of these professions is now fatal to the fulfilment of their function. They cannot, I shall argue, give of their best to the civilization in which they play so large a part so long as their members offer their services for private hire and sale. In a world organized as our world is organized the result is that only the exceptional man can give his best to a community which needs his best. A world in which the lawyer's skill is bought in the market like any other commodity is one in which the lawyer becomes concerned not with justice but with the satisfaction of his client. A world in which, at least predominantly, the medical man competes with his fellows in the market for patients is one in which neither his skill nor his knowledge is the primary basis of success. Each of these professions, I shall urge, can serve the public in a full degree only as it is organized as a public profession. So long, that is, as the motive of personal gain is the primary basis of their activities the true end of a profession becomes subordinate to it. And in addition, in the present state of civilization the prospect of their fulfilling their end as a profession declines rather than grows. It has become an urgent matter, therefore, to consider the foundations of professionalism if we are to realize what it could contribute to the public good.

The most influential type of American lawyer to-day is the corporation lawyer. He may fairly be called the legal strategist of high finance, the annex of the millionaire class. His business is corporate reorganization, the legal handling of the issues of taxation, the manipulation of receiverships, the penetration, on behalf of his clients, of those bulwarks erected by legislatures to safeguard the public from the depredations of high finance. His firms become household names. They are an organized regiment of officers and soldiers protecting the wealthy from the graver consequences of social legislation. All their interests are affiliated to those of the class they serve. In that service the good of the public largely shrinks from their horizon. They too become rich. Their habits of life become dependent upon their ability to preserve their clients. They play precisely the same part in the modern business world that the mercenary soldier plying his sword for hire played before the advent of national armies. Their reward is wholly a function of their success; and their success is incompatible with the public good.

The evidence to support this somber view has reached immense proportions in recent years. Some of it has been revealed in the legal habits displayed in histories like that in which Mr. Lowenthal has shown how the investor was robbed in the bankruptcy of a Western railroad. Other parts are recorded in the record of attempts to violate the Sherman Act. The public utility, the investment banks, the oil industry, all contribute their grim quota. Behind the Securities Act is nothing so much as an effort to protect the public from the labyrinthine ingenuities of the Wall Street lawyer; and the Federal Trade Commission is largely concerned with the same objective. It was this type of lawyer who invented for Mr. Mellon, and a thousand lesser men, ways and means of avoiding the income tax. He is not, of course, the crude type who breaks the law. He is the more elegant type of hireling who devotes all his skill and learning to finding ways round the law of which, to the public detriment, his clients can take advantage. He sees to it that the law is bent to the service of those who control the financial power of society.

But the evil he can do does not end with the advice he gives as consultant. Not seldom he is promoted to the Bench; for the rich lawyer likes at the close of long years of work like this the independence and dignity which high judicial rank confers. Then, only too often, as we have learned from the private papers of Mr. Justice Miller, he merely acts for his clients on the Bench instead of advising them in chambers. It is not, of course, that he is avowedly dishonest. It is simply that his experience at the Bar has implanted in him what Mr. Justice Holmes has called "inarticulate major premises" in favor of property from which he cannot shake himself free simply because he does not know he is moved by them. Even the New York *Sun* could say of Mr. Justice Matthews that his appointment was equivalent to placing Jay Gould upon the Supreme Court of the United States. Blachford, Field, and Lamar were all the type of judge who, whatever his ability, reads into his decisions the habits of an advocacy limited by service to the interests of rich men. It is not without significance that in the early eighties of last century there were only two judges of the Supreme Court whose distinction had not been won by their devotion to railroad interests.

The judge, in fact, is rare whose outlook as a judge is not an expression of his habits as counsel and the prejudices which these shape. But the influence of high finance over the lawyer is more subtle than this. The lawyer must if he is to win clients of this caliber get the reputation of a thoroughly "sound" man. Radical beliefs, a constant service to some radical cause, are fatal in the majority of instances to a successful career at the Bar. The eminent lawyer who became Attorney-General to the Labor Government of 1924 almost ruined his practice by so doing; it was notable that shortly after its close he announced his withdrawal from active politics. Everyone who knows the inner history of the Roosevelt Administration knows of the pressure brought to bear upon those of its members who previously were engaged in legal practice; and, even when they have been professors of law, influence has been brought to play by rich alumni on the presidents of their universities to prevent their services from being available to the President. The corporation lawyer is the head of his profession and he sets the tone and habits of his lesser brethren. But below him is a horde almost infinite in number, of the semi-successful in whom also the standards of public service are largely devoid of meaning. The ambulance-chaser; the lawyer who specializes in protecting the professional criminal from the results of his crime; the lawyer who lives by professional lobbying in a State legislature, who may even get elected to its membership and live by a retainer from some powerful corporation; the type who preserves himself by service to the owner of small properties whom he saves, by what artifices he can, from full observance of the building and health laws; the type, again, who takes the kind of speculative case which arises out of motor accidents, workmen's compensation, or the patent laws—these are all instances of the prostitution of a profession. Partly no doubt, their existence is due to an overcrowded market which almost places a premium on undesirable practice; the average earnings of a lawyer may not be much over a thousand dollars a year. Partly also, the standards of the profession necessarily reflect the general social environment to which it belongs; in a society in which money is the unequivocal test of success most things will be pardoned to those who are successful.

But a profession in which these habits are widely prevalent cannot hope to give the public the service it requires. An inadequate Bar does not mean only an inadequate Bench; it means also inattention to overdue legal reform and to the research which is the essential basis of the reform. It is striking that the impulse to the first, both in Great Britain and in America, comes from outside the practitioners of the profession; and it is significant that legal research in both countries also is mainly sponsored either by law teachers or by social workers whose experience gives them insight into the clinical difficulties of the law. Taken as a whole, neither Bench nor Bar has shown any zeal in the past sixty or seventy years for equating law with justice. In Great Britain it is notable that the Bar Council has not throughout its history proposed a single law reform of public importance; while the council of the judges has been either hostile or indifferent to any major proposals that have been made.

The reason, I suggest, lies in the commercialization of the legal profession. Having been made a dependency of the business empire, it has had to adapt its habits to the standards of its protector. Its independence has gone; and, with its independence, there has gone also any profound social consciousness it may once have professed. It is, I think, significant that the great names in modern law are either those of judges like Holmes who came to the Bench via scholarship, or Brandeis, whose radical opinions earned him the hostility of the profession; while among those who remained at the Bar, the creative impulse has been almost wholly confined to the great names in the law schools. The fact seems to be that the requirements of modern practice largely stifle those qualities which go to earn for the lawyer recognition that the service of the public is an integral part of his vocation. He still insists no doubt that this is an essential part of his professional obligation. But the intensity of competition, on the one hand, and the requirements of big business, on the other, make this insistence no more than a formal piece of rhetoric in which no one takes any particular credence.

The problems of the medical profession are of a different kind. For the most part, from the angle of public interest, they are threefold in their nature. There is the intense fight of the average medical man to win, and to hold, a practice, especially when he lacks private means; there are the issues connected with the etiquette of the profession; and there are the related matters of the adjustment between medicine and disciplines like that of osteopathy which are still struggling for professional recognition.

Each of these as a problem is mostly a matter in which the public interest is seriously jeopardized by the competitive nature of the profession. The average doctor who becomes a general practitioner is largely a prisoner serving a life-sentence. His success depends only partially on his scientific skill. His bedside manner, his political outlook, his religious creed, the social graces of his wife, his ability to play golf or bridge, any one or all of these may be terms in the equation he has to solve. He may fail to make headway because he is inadequately attentive to some rich neurasthenic. He may suffer because he takes part in a campaign against the slums or in favor of birth control. He may find himself made because a rich and influential patient calls him in suddenly when his ordinary doctor is away. He may fail because his visits are too businesslike and brief. He lacks the one thing in his ordinary work which is fundamental to the preservation of the scientific temper—security. Until that comes, if it comes, the things to which he has to pay attention are all of them extraneous to the technic he possesses and the service he has been trained to perform.

And that is not all. Unless he is well-established, he has little hope of keeping up with the development of medicine in any continuously profound way. He dare not take a long holiday for fear that his practice disappear to rivals. He cannot afford, for the same reason, the luxury of a period at some graduate school of medicine to refresh his knowledge. An occasional conference apart, he has little chance of rubbing shoulders with the heads of his profession. The chance of serious research hardly comes his way. Unless a tired man at the end of a long day's work can find inspiration in the medical journals he reads, the chances, especially for a rural practitioner, are strongly in favor of his technic remaining all through life much what it was when he began to practice. Experience, no doubt, will mature his judgment; but it will not give him a really profound awareness of progress in medicine unless he is an exceptional man.

Nor does the etiquette of the profession help the public. The relation of the general practitioner to the specialist is a labyrinth of complicated punctilio. The problem of access to the hospitals, the costs of a major operation, the connection, or the lack of it, with dental work in ophthalmology, are distressing. Some of this, no doubt, we have sought to meet in recent years by the development of the medical "firm"; but this as yet only touches the fringe of the population. And we have no medical attitude of any coherent and effective kind to some of the vital medical problems of our time—abortion, for instance, and birth control. In relation to neither of these issues is the preparation provided by medical training even approximately adequate, even though knowledge of, and decision upon, the issues they raise are vital to the happiness and well-being of the public. Anyone who analyzes the profession from this angle will find it difficult not to conclude that its rules are significant less as a protection for the patient than as a safeguard for the economic interests of doctors. As a profession, medicine has not even begun to consider the social implications of its organization.

Nor is the profession enlightened about its relation to peripheral disciplines. That it has a case against the osteopath may well be true; that it has, especially in England, fought him less from the angle of the public than to safeguard its own monopoly of the right to practice will be obvious to anyone who seeks to scrutinize the evidence. There is nothing whatever to be said for the General Medical Council's savage persecution in England of Dr. Axham for his association with the famous bonesetter, Sir Herbert Barker. Hardly more satisfactory is the absence of any coherent relations with the dentist and the psychologist. The relation of the profession to proprietary products in drugs, especially of the patent medicine variety, is a curious example of a deficient public sense; in the recent fight in Congress for pure drugs there should have been an organized and irresistible medical opinion. Progress in this realm is hampered at every turn by the fact that the economic insecurity of the profession prevents it from offering that definite guidance to the public of which it stands in so great a need.

Nor must one forget the different treatment of rich and poor in medicine. With noble and notable exceptions, it is largely true in Great Britain that a successful panel-doctor under the insurance system cannot hope to grapple adequately with his patients. In the hospitals as compared with the private nursing-homes the long hours of waiting, the early hours of waking, the frequent impossibility of effective convalescence, all point to an absence of a socially adequate attitude in the medical profession. It is notable that a rich man who fights a charge of being drunk when driving a car is almost invariably able to bring a private physician to counter police evidence brought against him; it is also notable that a poor man under a similar charge rarely appears able to secure such evidence on his behalf. Defective standards of housing, of wages, of hours of labor, with the toll they take of the health of the general population far too infrequently invoke any organized expression of medical protest. The doctor's social opinions indeed tend to be less an inference from the plain lessons of his medical experience than the expression of the middle- or upper-class environment to which he belongs. Either he regards these matters as outside his purview or he is afraid to jeopardize his standing by embracing unpopular opinions. In the field of public health the pressure for great social reforms has too often come from without the profession, even when the facts leading to that pressure have been gathered by doctors who, because they were in the service of State or city, could afford to make the revelations urgent to an advance of public well-being.

One does not read of fashionable physicians in Harley Street or Park Avenue leading an attack upon the slums. The medical man who fights for the right of the poor to that birth-control information he sells daily to the middle class is rare; in England the author of the most popular handbook on this theme published it under a pseudonym lest he injure his standing in the profession by association with it. Our inability to make a serious impression upon the long unchanging statistics of maternal morbidity is in large part the outcome of the profession's silence upon their meaning. The diet of poor children in relation to the quality of their school-work, the absence of adequate recreational facilities in the great cities, the vast problem of sex-hygiene in schools, the standards of relief in relation to nutrition for the unemployed—upon all these things, to take only some of the outstanding issues of the time, what is notable about the medical profession as a whole is its absence of any coherent civic sense. The occasional doctor may care profoundly about these things. The profession as a profession lacks that sense of urgent obligation to the public which alone could effect the radical reforms that are essential.

Broadly speaking, the indictment brought against the medical profession by Graham Wallas half a generation ago remains as true as when he wrote it. It shrinks from the effort to think out afresh its foundations, and this, "combined with a narrow calculation of individual advantage, prevents the community from receiving the full benefit of that transformation." His economic uncertainties compel the average doctor to seek, so far as he can obtain it, a local monopoly enforced by as effective a boycott as he can impose upon the intruder. Within his area he can give any treatment he thinks fit with little need to keep up to date and little fear of expert criticism or legal action. When he retires he can sell his practice to the highest bidder as though he deals in soap or wine instead of human life. He needs at every point the help of the specialist, the skill of the nurse, the microscope of the bacteriologist. But he knows also that, save in dramatic cases, he can recommend the use of these only to his richer patients. All his emphasis is on curative medicine; with the major aspect of prevention he has hardly any concern. In a fundamental way he is fighting a battle he cannot win because he is not organized to combat the forces against which he is fighting.

A sane world surely would approach these issues from a different angle. These professions are integrally related to public well-being. Their purposes cannot be fulfilled so long as their members are dependent upon the hazards of a commercial market. It is notable that in each of them the best work is done, the highest public spirit displayed by those of their members from whom the virus of insecurity has been removed. The professor in the law school like Harvard or Yale, the medical man in the public health service, whether Gorgas in America or Sir David Bruce in England, the servant of a great medical institution, like Hughlings Jackson or Carrel or Alfred Cohn, represents an achievement of the kind which gives to the profession its essential meaning. They represent a continuous attention to standards, an independence of pressure from privilege, a power to contemplate only the highest ends, which are attainable only because their services are not bought and sold under competitive pressure. Until we can make their spirit permeate the professions as a whole, we cannot prevent them from declining in the way that they have done in recent times.

The way out, therefore, is to organize them as public services. The legal profession should be a great corporation under government control, the members of which should work for the public on a fixed salary at fixed charges. Instead of plying for hire, they should act as public servants who undertake cases in terms of the public import they reveal. In this fashion we could end the corporation lawyer, the ambulance chaser, the defaulting attorney, the lawyer who devotes his energies to helping rich men to evade the income tax. Each area could have its contingent of lawyers, largely self-governing, disinterested, eager, because they were disinterested, to secure the continuous improvement of the law. We should not, as we do now, have, as so largely we have, one law for the rich and another for the poor. We should escape the danger of judges biased by their existence to one side of the social equation. We could make the standards of legal education adequate. We could properly relate the academic to the practical side of the profession. We should not meet at every turn of the road to reform the vested interests of lawyers themselves hostile to change which might jeopardize their financial position. We could assure the poor client, not less than the rich, of an adequate attention to his problems.

It is of course an immense reform; but the experience of Soviet Russia shows that it is a practicable one. There the private lawyer has gone. He has been replaced by a body of public servants organized not to benefit themselves, but to serve the public merely. Under a control partly of themselves, partly of the Bench and the Ministry of Justice, they give the ordinary citizen a quality of service far more profound than anything he could even hope for in the days of the Tzar. They have no financial interest in either the content or the number of their cases. Their advancement in the profession is dependent solely upon the profession's own judgment of the quality of the work they perform. They can freely devote themselves to research if they feel the call to do so. They can change from teaching to practice or practice to teaching whenever, under reasonable circumstances, they wish for the change. The result of the system in Russia is quite unquestionably one of the triumphs of the regime. It has shown that the legal profession, once it is freed from dependence on property, can become one of the most powerful instruments of social well-being which a community possesses; for it is notable that, whereas with ourselves, the lawyer is regarded, not unjustly, as the enemy of social progress, in Russia Bench and Bar alike are looked upon as among the most essential of its guardians.

It is of course true that in a society like ours the attainment of such an ideal would, for the law, be a long and arduous adventure; perhaps it is possible of achievement only in a socialist state. But of the medical profession this is emphatically not the case. Already its public side is a vast organization; already also the preventive and research sides of medicine are predominantly in public, or quasi-public hands. The change required to give a full public context to the whole is much smaller than in the case of the law. To make the whole profession a public one, even in a capitalist society, we require only to extend the idea of insurance for medical care to all members of the population. Upon that basis the cost of an adequate service for each section of the population could be assured without difficulty. The doctor would then be a public servant assigned, according to his preference and qualities, to the appropriate branch and area of the service. He could be promoted, as he is now promoted in the public health departments of English county and city, in terms of proven achievement. He would work as a member of a team constantly in touch with the latest developments of research. He could from time to time be given leave for postgraduate training or research. He would be free from the need to win the support of his patients upon considerations independent of his professional skill. He would not need to vary the treatment he recommended in terms of his patients' means. He could develop a proper relation not only to other members of his profession, but also to the peripheral disciplines, without the fear that he was jeopardizing his practice. He would be free from that haunting fear of insecurity which today poisons the wellsprings of his effort.

To the layman a development such as this surely presents immense advantages. His insurance would afford him, as of right, access to adequate medical care. He need not fear, as he now has to fear, the cost of an operation, the possible expense of a specialist, the hazard of a diagnosis made by a man whose last serious contact with scientific medicine may be as much as a generation old. He could have the assurance that the profession was not, at every point, defending, at his cost, vested interests from invasion. He could feel confident that the public attitude in medicine was determined by the only consideration which should govern it—the standard of health in the community. For in matters like housing or birth control a great public profession organized in this way need not fear the economic pressure of privilege. It would have the power to make its objective findings upon them, and the disinterestedness to fight for their acceptance. The average doctor, on such a scheme, could become in the full sense a citizen; for the simple reason that his science could then become conscious of its social obligations in a way that is not now open to him. That a profession will, given the opportunity, act in this way has been proved to demonstration by British experience of its public health services. For it is notable that when, after the crisis of 1931, the government sought to economize upon the health services of the nation, it was the pressure of medical officers of health and school doctors, and the objective testimony of their impartial reports which awakened public opinion to the significance of governmental opinion. The doctor who is free from the pressure of competition can combine the functions of scientist and citizen so that the lessons of the one permeate and control the obligations of the other. Our present system is a standing and organized denial of that opportunity.

What has here been said of lawyer and doctor is not confined to their professions. The sickness of an acquisitive society, above all in its present phase of contraction, poisons every vocation in which the principle of disinterestedness should be paramount. The indictment I have made of them could be brought, not less urgently, against the teacher and the journalist, the engineer and the architect. There are thousands of teachers in every society driven by the pressure of privilege to subordinate the truth that is in them to economic necessity. There are few journalists, not working for an endowed journal which does not need to consider profit, who have not at some time been compelled to sacrifice the truth in the news to a point of view demanded either because it paid or because it was exacted by the proprietor of the journal he served. It is well known that the mine-managers of Great Britain in 1919 were in favor of the socialization of the mines in the national interest; but they did not dare to say so for fear that they might be adversely affected if the Royal Commission of that year did not result in the nationalization of the mines. There are architects and to spare—as our slums bear witness—who have lent themselves to building schemes which outrage every canon of decency their profession claims to uphold.

What, in fact, I have said of lawyers and doctors represents a general truth about our society from the consequences of which there is no escape within the confines of the present social system. So long as its predominant motive is the making of profit for private persons, the demand which will shape all its habits will be that which ministers to the successful operation of that motive. Its operation will create vested interests of privilege; and these will fight with all their resources against a communal well-being which seeks either to modify or to extinguish them.

From the operation of this rule there is no reason, on the evidence, to suppose that the professions can escape. And when, as now, a society based on the motive of private profit runs into heavy weather, its privileged class will fight more ardently than ever to preserve its privileges; and professions like the law and journalism, which have a special service to render to privilege, will find themselves more particularly degraded by reason of the demands made upon them. Nothing perhaps illustrates this better than the degradation of German scholarship under the Hitler regime. A body of learned professors, whose vocation was the disinterested service of truth, were there willing to prostitute their scholarship to ends which hundreds of them knew to be mean and false. They were willing to do so, with hardly an exception; and thereby they showed that when privilege in a decaying social system arms itself for battle it demands from its dependents the sacrifice even of their last shred of self-respect.

A society accordingly which aims at the utilization of scientific learning has two principles upon which it must build its life. It must, in the first place, expunge from its habits the privilege that is built upon economic power; for this in the end shapes the use of science to its own preservation and, therefore, frustrates its objective. It must also, in the second place, so organize all professions which are important for the daily life of the society as to render them independent of the profit-making motive. To fail in either of these is to leave the well-being of the community at the mercy of men who make learning the hired lackey of their zest for power. A society so founded has inherent in it the roots of inescapable conflict. It has placed its organized authority at the service of men whose interests are antithetic to its own. The conflict may be concealed when the society is in process of expansion. When, as with crisis, its presence is revealed, the result is to jeopardize that social heritage which gives life all its grace and dignity.

VOCABULARY AND SUCCESS[1]

Johnson O'Connor

WHAT is success? And how is it gained? Whether one thinks of success as financial reward, or as assured social position, or as satisfaction in able work accomplished and recognized, or as a combination of the three and something more, many factors contribute. Most of them elude our understanding and remain intangibly beyond definition. A vital force drives some individuals over every obstacle. With others that great generalization, character, adds strength of a different sort. Neither may ever be restricted to a hard and fast formula; certainly, at the moment, neither can be measured. But other more concrete constituents of success have been isolated and studied in the laboratory. One of these is a large English vocabulary.

An extensive knowledge of the exact meanings of English words accompanies outstanding success in this country more often than any other single characteristic which the Human Engineering Laboratories have been able to isolate and measure.

What is meant by vocabulary? Just what the word signifies. Does the word *enervating* mean *soothing, exciting, distressing, invigorating*, or *weakening*? For most well-educated persons the choice is between *invigorating* and *weakening*. Fifty-two per cent of the college graduates whom we have measured choose *invigorating* as the synonym; only sixteen per cent choose *weakening*, the dictionary definition. Does *stilted* in the phrase 'his stilted manner' mean *irresolute, improper, cordial, stiffly formal*, or *vicious*? A majority of

---

[1]From *The Atlantic Monthly*, February, 1934. Introduction to *English Vocabulary Builder* by Johnson O'Connor, Human Engineering Laboratory.

educated persons mark *stiffly formal*, but more than a third mark *irresolute*. Answers to the meaning of *scurrilous*, in the phrase 'scurrilous rogue,' divide themselves more or less evenly between *hurrying, desperate, abusive, frantic,* and *diseased*, with *desperate* the most popular. For *peremptory*, a majority mark *decisive*, but many choose *persuasive, uncertain,* and *angry*. *Pleasant,* the fifth choice, is not as popular. *Linguist* and *glutton* are equally enticing as synonyms for *polyglot*. For *refulgent*, in 'a refulgent smile,' *repellent* is most intriguing and *very bright* next, with *mischievous, flattering,* and *sour* all following closely in popularity. For *monograph* forty per cent choose *soliloquy* and less than twenty per cent *treatise* and *epitaph* each.

The word *vocabulary*, as used in this article, signifies a knowledge of the dictionary meaning of just such words as *enervating, stilted, scurrilous, peremptory, polyglot, refulgent,* and *monograph*. Not until one attempts to pick an exact synonym does one realize the difficulty. One may like the sound of a word and use it in a picturesque way without being accurate in its meaning.

To measure the vocabulary of an individual, the Laboratory uses a list of one hundred and fifty test words. Each is printed in italics in a short phrase and is followed by five choices, all of which fit the phrase but only one of which is a synonym of the test word. The instructions are: 'Underline that one of the five choices which is nearest in meaning to the word in italics.' The words to be defined were selected by Alexander Inglis of the Graduate School of Education, Harvard University. His intention was to include words which appear once or twice in 100,000 words of printed matter. It is a general reader's vocabulary from which technical terms have been excluded. The test words vary from some that are quite easy, such as

Thrilling experiences: dangerous, exciting, unusual, digusting, profitable,

to others that are more difficult, such as

Glabrous heads: bald, over-sized, hairy, square, round,

which only twenty-one per cent of college graduates mark correctly. Since one fifth, or twenty per cent, should guess the correct answer, the meaning of *glabrous* is practically unknown. The test measures knowledge of words one recognizes, not necessarily of those one uses. The words one uses accurately are, no doubt, fewer than those one recognizes, but there is probably a relation between the two.

Three hundred high-school freshmen average 76 errors in the list of 150 words. Seven hundred college freshmen average 42 errors. One thousand college graduates from a wide variety of colleges—most of them, however, in the eastern part of the United States—average 27 errors, and vary from the one person in a thousand who achieves a perfect score to the one who knows less than 50 of the 150 items. The college professors whom we have measured average 8 errors; major executives average 7 errors. Major executives score higher in this English vocabulary test than any other selected group with which we have experimented.

By the term 'major executives' is meant all individuals who, for five years or longer, have held the position of president or vice president in a business organization. Such a definition includes both successful and unsuccessful executives, provided only that they have survived five years; it includes alike forceful personalities and figureheads; but it has the great advantage of excluding our personal judgment from the process of selection. Major executives as thus defined average in the top ten per cent of college graduates as a whole.

Although it is impossible to define success rigidly or scientifically, it seems to be true, nevertheless, that a large vocabulary is typical, not exclusively of executives, but of successful individuals. It happens that in the business world successful men and women are designated by this special appellation, 'executive.' The successful lawyer or doctor is marked by no such name. But if, to the best of one's ability, one selects successful persons in the professions, they also score high in vocabulary.

For one meaning of success the Century dictionary gives 'a high degree of worldly prosperity.' The measured English vocabulary of an executive correlates with his salary. This does not mean that every high-vocabulary person receives a large salary, but the relation between the two is close enough to show that a large vocabulary is one element, and seemingly an important one.

Furthermore, the executive level which a man or woman reaches is determined to some extent by vocabulary. In many manufacturing organizations the first step in the executive ladder is the leading hand, called sometimes the working foreman. This man is in charge of half a dozen or a dozen others. He works at the bench or at a machine as they do, but is the executive of the group. The next step is the foreman, who may be in charge of as many as a hundred or more individuals. He does no bench work, he is not a producer, but devotes full time to his executive duties, to the keeping of records and to the handling of the personnel. The next step in many large organizations is the department head or superintendent or manager, who ordinarily does not come in direct contact with the workers, but handles them through his foremen. The final step is the major executive or official, the vice president or president of the organization.

These four executive ranks represent four degrees of success, in one sense in which that word is used. One is *advanced* from leading hand to foreman, from foreman to manager, from manager to president. As far as we can determine by measurements, the leading hand and the official have much the same inherent aptitudes. They differ primarily in vocabulary. Typical non-college-graduate shop foremen average, as a group, about as high as college graduates. Department heads score higher, roughly fifteen errors, and major executives the highest of all, averaging only seven errors. Whether the word 'executive' refers only to the major group or is used in the broader sense to mean anyone in charge of other workers, it is still true that the executive scores higher than those under him and higher than other persons of similar age and education.

An interesting sidelight on the high vocabulary scores of executives is that they were unforeseen. When a scientist expects a result and finally achieves it there is always the feeling that, regardless of the care he has taken, personal bias may have entered. Six or eight years ago the Human Engineering Laboratories tested forty major executives of the Telephone Company who had offered themselves as victims to be experimented upon in a search for executive characteristics. At the same time the Laboratory was also revising the vocabulary test, not with the notion of using it with executives, but with the hope that it might prove of value in education. One day, with no thought of the consequences, I gave it to an executive, and from then on was asked for it regularly because of the interest it aroused. I paid little heed to the results until one day an executive refused to take the test. He had been obliged by lack of money to leave school at fourteen, and had earned his own living since. With no further formal education, he had worked his way to a major position. He had taken the aptitude tests without hesitation, but vocabulary seemed to him so directly the result of schooling that he knew in advance he would fail. His own words were that he had made his way without being found out and he was not willing to give himself away. But in scientific work one cannot test only those who think they will do well, and we finally persuaded him to try the vocabulary test. He made two errors where the average college graduate makes twenty-seven.

Was it luck? Or was it significant of something which we had not recognized? The Laboratory listed the vocabulary scores of one hundred executives and, parallel with them, the scores of one hundred miscellaneous college graduates. The difference between the two arrays was striking. Only nine per cent of the college graduates scored as high as the average major executive.

Why do large vocabularies characterize executives and possibly outstanding men and women in other fields? The final answer seems to be that words are the instruments by means of which men and women grasp the thoughts of others and with which they do much of their own thinking. They are the tools of thought.

Before accepting so far-reaching a conclusion several more obvious explanations must be examined and excluded. The first and most natural supposition is that successful persons acquire words with age and with the experiences of life. Success does not usually occur early. The successful group were necessarily older in both years and experience than the general run of college graduates with whom they were compared; and their large vocabularies might be the inevitable result of age.

To probe this point a study of the growth of vocabulary with age was undertaken. From twelve, the earliest age for which we have a large number of measurements, to twenty-two or twenty-three vocabulary expands steadily and at a uniform rate. Through this school period the score on the vocabulary test of one hundred and fifty items improves five words a year. From twenty-three to fifty vocabulary continues to increase, but changes no more in these twenty-five years than in two school years—not enough to explain the high scores of executives. Normally, vocabulary is acquired early in life, before most men have made appreciable progress toward a responsible position. The large vocabularies of successful individuals come before success rather than after. Age and the experiences of life may contribute new words, but certainly do not explain in full the high vocabulary scores of business executives.

The next thought is that effective schooling may be the source both of a wide vocabulary and of executive success. It is known, from the work which the American Telephone and Telegraph Company has undertaken, that there is a relationship between school success and business success later in life. Although not everyone who leads his class becomes a brilliant executive, and although not everyone who fails in school fails in life, in general school success preludes executive success. Schooling may be the vital factor of which the large vocabularies which we are measuring are but by-products.

To obtain evidence bearing on this point, we measured the vocabularies of twenty men who had left school at the age of fifteen and who had worked their way into major positions. They also averaged only seven errors. Their scores equaled those of the college-graduate executives. In the case of these twenty men it is their vocabularies which are important rather than their formal school education. Their large vocabularies are not the result of schooling and must, we therefore conclude, be significant for some other reason than as a by-product of an educational background.

Is, then, a college background of no importance? Has the non-college man the same chance of becoming an executive as has the college graduate? This fact seemed worth determining. Of the major executives in a large industrial organization, sixty per cent are college graduates, forty per cent non-college.

At first glance, college would seem to have done little, for almost half are not college men. But, to be fair to education, there is another angle from which to view this result. Of the college graduates with this same company, more than three quarters are in executive positions, whereas, of the non-college men, well under a tenth are in similar positions. College graduates, in general, average measurably higher in vocabulary than do non-college persons. Furthermore, of the college group a significantly larger percentage are executives.

One would like to conclude without further preamble that the vocabularies of the college group are large because of directed effort and that these purposefully gained vocabularies have contributed to executive success. Non-college executives, then, are those rare individuals who pick up words so easily that their vocabularies are large without effort. But there is one further possibility which must be investigated.

Although the vocabulary test was designed to measure knowledge which must have come through books or by word of mouth, a high score may reveal an underlying aptitude for language. It may be this flair which is the contributing factor in both vocabulary and success later in life.

It should be possible to isolate and measure diathesis apart from knowledge. We have worked on this approach for a number of years, thus far unproductively. For the time being we must leave the conclusion of this part of the research in abeyance and admit that the vocabularies of successful executives may reveal an aptitude.

Vocabularies may always be consciously increased regardless of the presence or absence of any gift. A knowledge of the meaning of each word at one's command must have been obtained by word of mouth or through reading, by some educational process.

Furthermore, with groups of individuals of apparently similar aptitudes, the amount of vocabulary added in a given period varies with different educational techniques. At Stevens Institute of Technology the freshman class is divided alphabetically into four sections. Each of these studies freshman English under a different member of the faculty. Four years ago the entire class took the vocabulary test the first week of freshman year. The four sections averaged about the same in vocabulary, and there was no reason to suppose that, selected as they were, one would score higher than another or have more ability. Yet, when remeasured nine months later, two of the sections had improved more than average academic freshmen, one section had improved only half this amount, and the fourth had retrogressed slightly.

The improvement of one section may have been due to the fact that the instructor was interested in the vocabulary test and its implications. The important fact is that differences in vocabulary improvement were caused by differences in teaching techniques—in other words, that an improvement in vocabulary score can be produced by education.

Those boys and girls whom the Laboratory has measured and urged to better their vocabularies, and then remeasured at the end of two or three years, have shown more than average improvement. Here again vocabulary is induced independent of aptitude. It is for this reason that the Human Engineering Laboratories, in helping a youngster to find himself and start in the right direction, use a vocabulary test in lieu of a general intelligence test.

We come now to the question of whether or not that increment of vocabulary directly due to educational stimulation contributes to success. The four sections of the freshman class at Stevens Institute of Technology to which reference has been made, which took freshman English with different members of the faculty and improved different amounts in vocabulary, were followed to see the effect of these new vocabularies on school work the next year. The four sections averaged nearly the same in school marks freshman year. Sophomore year the two sections which had enlarged their vocabularies the previous year showed general gain in all school subjects—not strikingly, not enough to prove the point once and for all time, but enough to suggest that a vocabulary acquired consciously reflects in general school improvement the next year.

It is always possible that the improvement in school work was due to inspired teaching, to added incentive, but if this were true it would seem as if the improvement in school work should appear immediately freshman year, whereas it did not appear until sophomore year after the vocabulary had been acquired. This seems to indicate that it is the additional words themselves which are the tools used the next year, that words are important in and for themselves.

Granted that diction is important, and many would agree without elaborate proof of the point, how, from the standpoint of the school, can it best be given; and, from that of the individual, how best achieved? Is it a knowledge of Latin and Greek which lays a sound foundation for a real understanding of words? Or is it constant reading? Or the assiduous perusal of the dictionary? Probably all contribute; as yet we have found no straight and easy road.

In the search for a road to vocabulary we have unearthed several facts which throw light on the learning process. One of these, which, if rightly interpreted, may prove to be of far-reaching importance to education, is that vocabulary advances with an almost unbroken front. The words at the command of an individual are not a miscellany gathered from hither and yon. With a very few exceptions they are all of the words in the dictionary up to those of an order of difficulty at which his vocabulary stops abruptly, and almost no words beyond. In the revised form of the test which is now available for school use, the items are arranged in order of difficulty as determined by actual test results. The first fifteen or twenty words of the test are known to the average high-school freshman or sophomore. The next thirty to forty are on the border line of his knowledge. Some he recognizes, others are vaguely familiar, and others he has not yet encountered. The balance are so far beyond him that he marks correctly no more than the one in five which he guesses by pure chance.

For convenience of scoring, the words are divided into ten groups of constantly increasing difficulty. One who knows the words of Group II, second in difficulty, almost invariably marks correctly every word of Group I. Another youngster who may know the words of, let us say, Group VI rarely fails on a single word in any of the first five easier groups. Similarly, one who fails on twelve of the fifteen words in any one group—that is, marks correctly only the one word in five which he guesses—almost never knows a word in any more difficult group. There are not, as we had expected, stray words in the difficult part which one who fails earlier in the test has stumbled upon and remembered. These unusual words, if previously encountered as they must have been in reading and conversation, are too far beyond the point he has reached to make any lasting impression.

The one exception to this rule is the foreign student who may know difficult words because of their similarity to his own language, but miss much easier ones. Thus the Southern European often marks correctly such difficult words as *cephalic*, *garrulity*, and *piscatorial*, because of knowledge of Italian and French, but fails to know much easier words of Old English origin, such as, for instance, *knack*, *blotch*, and *cope*.

In the region where learning is taking place, the commonest error is the confusion of a word with its exact opposite. Among seventh- and eighth-grade and first-year high-school pupils, nearly a third mark *found guilty* as the correct meaning of *acquitted*. *Upright* is the most popular misconception for the meaning of *reclining*; and, strange as it may seem, *neat* is the commonest misconception of *untidy*. The seventh-grade youngster berated for keeping an untidy room quite often evidently receives the impression that he is too orderly. The failing is not limited to the high-school group. For *incontrovertible* the correct answer *indisputable* is usually marked by college men, but of the remaining four choices *unsound* is by far most popular. In the phrase 'You *allay* my fears,'—where the five choices are *justify*, *calm*, *arouse*, *increase*, and *confirm*,—*calm* is usually answered by the educated group, but *arouse* is next most popular. In the phrase 'He *retracts* his criticism,' *withdraws* is the correct answer and *repeats* is the most common delusion. In 'He

166

vented his wrath,' *poured forth* is correct and *restrained* is the commonest misapprehension.

One need but turn to words of which one is not quite certain to see how difficult it is to distinguish opposites. One evening at dinner with a delightful Dean of education, we fell to discussing this question. He recognized *cathode* and *anode* instantly as electrical terms designating the two poles, but hesitated a moment before saying which was which. *Port* and *starboard* he admitted he had never straightened out and resorted to some such phrase as 'Jack left port.' *Gee* and *haw* were beyond him. He surmised that they meant *up* and *down*, but said frankly he did not know the words. When told that they were used in ploughing, he was instantly interested, but did not care at all which was which. He was taking the first step in the learning process, placing them in their correct environment. The fifty-two per cent of college graduates who choose *invigorating* as the meaning of *enervating* are on the verge of knowing the word. The dictum of modern education, never to teach what a thing is not, has perhaps come from a realization of this confusion of opposites. The confusion seems, however, to be a natural step in the learning process.

In the study of human beings the factors involved are so numerous and so intertwined with one another that the experimenter, in unraveling the strands, must pause periodically to make certain that he is progressing. What then has been discovered? An exact and extensive vocabulary is an important concomitant of success. So much is known. Furthermore, such a vocabulary can be acquired. It increases as long as an individual remains in school or college, but without conscious effort does not change materially thereafter.

There may be some subtle distinction between a natural vocabulary picked up at home, at meals, and in reading, and one gained by a study of the dictionary. The latter may not be as valuable as the former. But there is nothing to show that it is harmful and the balance of evidence at the moment suggests that such a consciously, even laboriously, achieved vocabulary is an active asset.

Government

LIFE IN UTOPIA[1]

Thomas More

HUSBANDRY is a science common to them all in general, both men and women, wherein they be all expert and cunning. In this they be all instructed even from their youth; partly in schools with traditions and precepts, and partly in the country nigh the city, brought up as it were in playing, not only beholding the use of it, but by occasion of exercising their bodies practising it also.

Besides husbandry, which (as I said) is common to them all, every one of them learneth one or other several and particular science, as his own proper craft. That is most commonly either clothworking in wool or flax, or masonry, or the smith's craft, or the carpenter's science. For there is none other occupation that any number to speak of doth use there. For their garments, which throughout all the island be of one fashion (saving that there is a difference between the man's garment and the woman's, between the married and the unmarried), and this one continueth for evermore unchanged, seemly and comely to the eye, no let to the moving and wielding of the body, also fit both for winter and summer: as for these garments (I say), every family maketh their own. But of the other foresaid crafts every man learneth one; and not only the men, but also the women. But the women, as a weaker sort, be put to the easier crafts. They work wool and flax. The other more laboursome sciences be committed to the men. For the most part every man is brought up in his father's craft, for most commonly they be naturally thereto bent and inclined. But if a man's mind stand to any other, he is by adoption put into a family of that occupation which he doth most fancy, whom not only his father, but also the magistrates do diligently look to, that he be put to a discreet and honest householder. Yea, and if any person, when he hath learned one craft, be desirous to learn also another, he is likewise suffered and permitted. When he hath learned both, he occupieth whether he will, unless the city hath more need of the one than of the other.

The chief and almost the only office of the syphogrants[2] is to see and take heed that no man sit idle, but that every one apply his own craft with earnest diligence; and yet for all that not to be wearied from early in the morning to late in the evening with continual work, like labouring and toiling beasts. For this is worse than the miserable and wretched condition of bondmen; which nevertheless is almost everywhere the life of workmen and artificers,

[1]From the *Utopia* by Sir Thomas More (1515).
[2]Every thirty families or farms chose annually an officer whom they called in their language "syphogrant," meaning "The Elders of the Sty."

saving in Utopia. For they, dividing the day and the night into twenty-four just hours, appoint and assign only six of those hours to work, three before noon, upon which they go straight to dinner: and after dinner, when they have rested two hours, then they work three: and upon that they go to supper. About eight of the clock in the evening (counting one of the clock at the first hour after noon) they go to bed; eight hours they give to sleep. All the void time, that is between the hours of work, sleep, and meat, that they be suffered to bestow, every man as he liketh best himself: not to the intent they should misspend this time in riot, or slothfulness, but, being then licensed from the labour of their own occupations to bestow the time well and thriftily upon some other good science, as shall please them. For it is a solemn custom there, to have lectures daily early in the morning, where to be present they only be constrained that be namely chosen and appointed to learning. Howbeit a great multitude of every sort of people, both men and women, go to hear lectures: some one and some another, as every man's nature is inclined. Yet, this notwithstanding, if any man had rather bestow this time upon his own occupation (as it chanceth in many, whose minds rise not in the contemplation of any science liberal) he is not letted or prohibited, but is also praised and commended as profitable to the commonwealth.

After supper they bestow one hour in play: in summer in their gardens, in winter in their common halls, where they dine and sup. There they exercise themselves in music, or else in honest and wholesome communication. Dice-play, and such other foolish and pernicious games, they know not, but they use two games not much unlike the chess. The one is the battle of numbers, wherein one number stealeth away another. The other is wherein vices fight with virtues, as it were in battle array, or a set field. In the which game is very properly shewed both the strife and discord that vices have among themselves, and again their unity and concord against virtues: and also what vices be repugnant to what virtues; with what power and strength they assail them openly; by what wiles and subtlety they assault them secretly, with what help and aid the virtues resist and overcome the puissance of the vices; by what craft they frustrate their purposes; and finally by what sleight or means the one getteth the victory.

But here, lest you be deceived, one thing you must look more narrowly upon. For seeing they bestow but six hours in work, perchance you may think that the lack of some necessary things hereof may ensue. But this is nothing so. For that small time is not only enough, but also too much, for the store and abundance of all things that be requisite, either for the necessity or commodity of life. The which thing you also shall perceive, if you weigh and consider with yourselves how great a part of the people in other countries liveth idle. First, almost all women, which be the half of the whole number, or else if the women be anywhere occupied, there must commonly in their stead the men be idle. Besides this, how great, and how idle a company is there of priests and religious men, as they call them? Put thereto all rich men, specially all landed men, and noblemen. Take into this number also their servants: I mean all that flock of stout, bragging rushbucklers. Join to them also sturdy and valiant beggars, cloaking their idle life under the colour of some disease or sickness. And truly you shall find them much fewer than you thought, by whose labour all these things be gotten that men use and live by. Now consider with yourself, of these few that do work, how few be occupied in necessary works. For where money beareth all the swing, there many vain and superfluous occupations must needs be used, to serve only for riotous superfluity and unhonest pleasure. For the same multitude that now is occupied in work, if they were divided into so few occupations as the necessary use of nature requireth, in so great plenty of things, as then of necessity would ensue, doubtless the prices would be too little for the artificers to maintain their livings. But if all these, that be now busied about unprofitable occupations, with all the whole flock of them that live idly and slothfully, which consume and waste every one of them more of these things that come by other men's labour than two of the workmen themselves do; if all these (I say) were set to profitable occupations, you easily perceive how little time would be enough, yea, and too much, to store us with all things that may be requisite either for necessity, or for commodity; yea, or for pleasure, so that the same pleasure be true and natural.

And this in Utopia the thing itself maketh manifest and plain. For there in all the city, with the whole country or shire adjoining to it, scarcely five hundred persons of all the whole number of men and women, that be neither too old nor too weak to work, be licensed from labour. Among them be the syphogrants (which though they be by the laws exempt and privileged from labour), yet they exempt not themselves; to the intent they may the rather by their example provoke other to work. The same vacation from labour do they also enjoy, to whom the people, persuaded by the commendation of the priests and secret election of the syphogrants, have given a perpetual licence from labour to learning. But if any one of them prove not according to the expectation and hope of him conceived, he is forthwith plucked back to the company of artificers. And contrariwise, often it chanceth that a handicraftsman doth so earnestly bestow his vacant and spare hours in learning, and through diligence so profit therein, that he is taken from his handy occupation and promoted to the company of the learned.

Out of this order of the learned be chosen ambassadors, priests, tranibores,[3] and finally the prince himself; whom they in their old tongue call Barzanes, and by a newer name, Adamus.[4] The residue of the people being neither idle, neither occupied about unprofitable exercises, it may be easily judged in how few hours how much good work by them may be done towards those things that I have spoken of. This commodity they have also above other, that in the most part of necessary occupations they need not so much work as other nations do. For first of all, the building or repairing of houses asketh everywhere so many men's continual labour, because that the unthrifty heir suffereth the houses that his father builded in continuance of time to fall and decay. So that which he might have upholden with little cost, his successor is constrained to build it again anew, to his great charge. Yea, many times also the house that stood one man in much money, another is of so nice and so delicate a mind that he setteth nothing by it. And it being neglected, and therefore falling shortly into ruin, he buildeth up another in another place with no less cost and charge. But among the Utopians, where all things be set in good order and the commonwealth in a good stay, it very seldom chanceth that they choose a new plot to build an house upon. And they do not only find speedy and quick remedies for present faults, but also prevent them that be like to fall. And by this means their houses continue and last very long with little labour and small reparations, insomuch that that kind of workmen sometimes have almost nothing to do; but that they be commanded to hew timber at home, and to square and trim up stones, to the intent that if any work chance, it may the more speedily rise.

Now, Sir, in their apparel, mark, I pray you, how few workmen they need. First of all, whiles they be at work, they be covered homely with leather or skins that will last seven years. When they go forth abroad, they cast upon them a cloak which hideth the other homely apparel. These cloaks throughout the whole island be all of one colour, and that is the natural colour of the wool. They therefore do not only spend much less woollen cloth than is spent in other countries, but also the same standeth them in much less cost. But linen cloth is made with less labour, and is therefore had more in use. But in linen cloth only whiteness, in woollen only cleanliness, is regarded. As for the smallness or fineness of the thread, that is no thing passed for. And this is the cause wherefore in other places four or five cloth gowns of divers colours, and as many silk coats, be not enough for one man. Yea, and if he be of the delicate and nice sort, ten be too few, whereas their one

---

[3]Every ten syphogrants with their thirty families were under an officer called in their language "tranibore."

[4]Latin, *Ademus*, without a people.

174

garment will serve a man most commonly two years. For why should he desire more? seeing if he had them, he should not be the better hapt or covered from cold, neither in his apparel any whit the comelier.

Wherefore, seeing they be all exercised in profitable occupations, and that few artificers in the same crafts be sufficient, this is the cause that, plenty of all things being among them, they do sometimes bring forth an innumerable company of people to amend the highways, if any be broken. Many times also, when they have no such work to be occupied about, an open proclamation is made that they shall bestow fewer hours in work. For the magistrates do not exercise their citizens against their wills in unneedful labours. For why? in the institution of that weal publique this end is only and chiefly pretended and minded, that what time may possibly be spared from the necessary occupations and affairs of the commonwealth, all that the citizens should withdraw from the bodily service to the free liberty of the mind and garnishing of the same. For herein they suppose the felicity of this life to consist.

IN BROBDINGNAG[1]

Jonathan Swift

THE King, who, as I before observed, was a prince of excellent understanding, would frequently order that I should be brought in my box, and set upon the table in his closet. He would then command me to bring one of my chairs out of the box, and sit down within three yards distance upon the top of the cabinet, which brought me almost to a level with his face. In this manner I had several conversations with him. I one day took the freedom to tell his Majesty, that the contempt he discovered towards Europe, and the rest of the world, did not seem answerable to those excellent qualities of the mind he was master of. That reason did not extend itself with the bulk of the body: on the contrary, we observed in our country that the tallest persons were usually least provided with it. That among other animals, bees and ants had the reputation of more industry, art and sagacity, than many of the larger kinds. And that, as inconsiderable as he took me to be, I hoped I might live to do his Majesty some signal service. The King heard me with attention, and began to conceive a much better opinion of me than he had ever before. He desired I would give him as exact an account of the government of England as I possibly could; because, as fond as princes

[1]From "A Voyage to Brobdingnag," in *Gulliver's Travels* by Jonathan Swift (1726).

commonly are of their own customs (for so he conjectured of other monarchs, by my former discourses), he should be glad to hear of anything that might deserve imitation.

Imagine with thyself, courteous reader, how often I then wished for the tongue of Demosthenes or Cicero, that might have enabled me to celebrate the praise of my own dear native country in a style equal to its merits and felicity.

I began my discourse by informing his Majesty that our dominions consisted of two islands, which composed three mighty kingdoms under one sovereign, beside our plantations in America. I dwelt long upon the fertility of our soil, and the temperature of our climate. I then spoke at large upon the constitution of an English Parliament, partly made up of an illustrious body called the House of Peers, persons of the noblest blood, and of the most ancient and ample patrimonies. I described that extraordinary care always taken of their education in arts and arms, to qualify them for being counsellors born to the king and kingdom, to have a share in the legislature, to be members of the highest Court of Judicature, from whence there could be no appeal, and to be champions always ready for the defence of their prince and country, by their valour, conduct, and fidelity. That these were the ornament and bulwark of the kingdom, worthy followers of their most renowned ancestors, whose honour had been the reward of their virtue, from which their posterity were never once known to degenerate. To these were joined several holy persons, as part of that assembly, under the title of Bishops, whose peculiar business it is to take care of religion, and of those who instruct the people therein. These were searched and sought out through the whole nation, by the prince and his wisest counsellors, among such of the priesthood as were most deservedly distinguished by the sanctity of their lives, and the depth of their erudition; who were indeed the spiritual fathers of the clergy and the people.

That the other part of the Parliament consisted of an assembly called the House of Commons, who were all principal gentlemen, freely picked and culled out by the people themselves, for their great abilities and love of their country, to represent the wisdom of the whole nation. And these two bodies make up the most august assembly in Europe, to whom, in conjunction with the prince, the whole legislature is committed.

I then descended to the Courts of Justice, over which the Judges, those venerable sages and interpreters of the law, presided, for determining the disputed rights and properties of men, as well as for the punishment of vice, and protection of innocence. I mentioned the prudent management of our treasury; the valour and achievements of our forces by sea and land. I com-

176

puted the number of our people, by reckoning how many millions there might be of each religious sect, or political party among us. I did not omit even our sports and pastimes, or any other particular which I thought might redound to the honour of my country. And I finished all with a brief historical account of affairs and events in England for about an hundred years past.

This conversation was not ended under five audiences, each of several hours, and the King heard the whole with great attention, frequently taking notes of what I spoke, as well as memorandums of several questions he intended to ask me.

When I had put an end to these long discourses, his Majesty in a sixth audience, consulting his notes, proposed many doubts, queries, and objections, upon every article. He asked what methods were used to cultivate the minds and bodies of our young nobility, and in what kind of business they commonly spent the first and teachable part of their lives. What course was taken to supply that assembly when any noble family became extinct. What qualifications were necessary in those who were to be created new lords. Whether the humour of the prince, a sum of money to a court lady, or a prime minister, or a design of strengthening a party opposite to the public interest, ever happened to be motives in those advancements. What share of knowledge these lords had in the laws of their country, and how they came by it, so as to enable them to decide the properties of their fellow-subjects in the last resort. Whether they were always so free from avarice, partialities, or want, that a bribe, or some other sinister view, could have no place among them. Whether those holy lords I spoke of were always promoted to that rank upon account of their knowledge in religious matters, and the sanctity of their lives, had never been compliers with the times while they were common priests, or slavish prostitute chaplains to some nobleman, whose opinions they continued servilely to follow after they were admitted into that assembly.

He then desired to know what arts were practised in electing those whom I called commoners: whether a stranger with a strong purse might not influence the vulgar voters to choose him before their own landlord, or the most considerable gentleman in the neighbourhood. How it came to pass, that people were so violently bent upon getting into this assembly, which I allowed to be a great trouble and expense, often to the ruin of their families, without any salary or pension: because this appeared such an exalted strain of virtue and public spirit, that his Majesty seemed to doubt it might possibly not be always sincere: and he desired to know whether such zealous gentlemen could have any views of refunding themselves for the charges and trouble they were at, by sacrificing the public good to the designs of a weak and vicious prince in conjunction with a corrupted ministry. He multiplied his questions, and sifted me thoroughly upon every part of this head, proposing numberless enquiries and objections, which I think it not prudent or convenient to repeat.

Upon what I said in relation to our Courts of Justice, his Majesty desired to be satisfied in several points: and this I was the better able to do, having been formerly almost ruined by a long suit in chancery, which was decreed for me with costs. He asked, what time was usually spent in determining between right and wrong, and what degree of expense. Whether advocates and orators had liberty to plead in causes manifestly known to be unjust, vexatious, or oppressive. Whether party in religion or politics were observed to be of any weight in the scale of justice. Whether those pleading orators were persons educated in the general knowledge of equity, or only in provincial, national, and other local customs. Whether they or their judges had any part in penning those laws which they assumed the liberty of interpreting and glossing upon at their pleasure. Whether they had ever at different times pleaded for and against the same cause, and cited precedents to prove contrary opinions. Whether they were a rich or a poor corporation. Whether they received any pecuniary reward for pleading or delivering their opinions. And particularly whether they were ever admitted as members in the lower senate.

He fell next upon the management of our treasury; and said he thought my memory had failed me, because I computed our taxes at about five or six millions a year, and when I came to mention the issues, he found they sometimes amounted to more than double; for the notes he had taken were very particular in this point, because he hoped, as he told me, that the knowledge of our conduct might be useful to him, and he could not be deceived in his calculations. But, if what I told him were true, he was still at a loss how a kingdom could run out of its estate like a private person. He asked me, who were our creditors; and where we should find money to pay them. He wondered to hear me talk of such chargeable and expensive wars; that certainly we must be a quarrelsome people, or live among very bad neighbours, and that our generals must needs be richer than our kings. He asked what business we had out of our own islands, unless upon the score of trade or treaty, or to defend the coasts with our fleet. Above all, he was amazed to hear me talk of a mercenary standing army in the midst of peace, and among a free people. He said, if we were governed by our own consent in the persons of our representatives, he could not imagine of whom we were afraid, or against whom we were to fight; and would hear my opinion, whether a private man's house might not better be defended by himself, his children, and family, than by half a dozen rascals picked up at a venture in the streets, for small wages, who might get an hundred times more by cutting their throats.

He laughed at my odd kind of arithmetic (as he was pleased to call it) in reckoning the numbers of our people by a computation drawn from the several sects among us in religion and politics. He said he knew no reason why those who entertain opinions prejudicial to the public should be obliged to change, or should not be obliged to conceal them. And as it was tyranny in any government to require the first, so it was weakness not to enforce the second: for a man may be allowed to keep poisons in his closet, but not to vend them about for cordials.

He observed that among the diversions of our nobility and gentry I had mentioned gaming. He desired to know at what age this entertainment was usually taken up, and when it was laid down; how much of their time it employed; whether it ever went so high as to affect their fortunes; whether mean, vicious people, by their dexterity in that art, might not arrive at great riches, and sometimes keep our very nobles in dependence, as well as habituate them to vile companions, wholly take them from the improvement of their minds, and force them, by the losses they have received, to learn and practise that infamous dexterity upon others.

He was perfectly astonished with the historical account I gave him of our affairs during the last century, protesting it was only an heap of conspiracies, rebellions, murders, massacres, revolutions, banishments, the very worst effects that avarice, faction, hypocrisy, perfidiousness, cruelty, rage, madness, hatred, envy, lust, malice, or ambition could produce.

His Majesty in another audience was at the pains to recapitulate the sum of all I had spoken, compared the questions he made with the answers I had given, then taking me into his hands, and stroking me gently, delivered himself in these words, which I shall never forget nor the manner he spoke them in: My little friend Grildrig,[2] you have made a most admirable panegyric upon your country; you have clearly proved that ignorance, idleness, and vice, may be sometimes the only ingredients for qualifying a legislator; that laws are best explained, interpreted, and applied by those whose interest and abilities lie in perverting, confounding, and eluding them. I observe among you some lines of an institution, which in its original might have been tolerable, but these half erased, and the rest wholly blurred and blotted by corruptions. It doth not appear from all you have said, how any one virtue is required towards the procurement of any one station among you; much less that men are ennobled on account of their virtue, that priests are advanced for their piety or learning, soldiers for their conduct or valour, judges for their in-

[2]The name given to Gulliver by the child who cared for him in Brobdingnag. According to Swift, "The word imports what the Latins call *manunculus*, the Italians *homunceletina*, and the English *mannikin*."

tegrity, senators for the love of their country, or counsellors for their wisdom. As for yourself (continued the King) who have spent the greatest part of your life in travelling, I am well disposed to hope you may hitherto have escaped many vices of your country. But by what I have gathered from your own relation, and the answers I have with much pains wringed and extorted from you, I cannot but conclude the bulk of your natives to be the most pernicious race of little odious vermin that nature ever suffered to crawl upon the surface of the earth.

ON DEMOCRACY[1]

Thomas Carlyle

. . . W HAT *is* Democracy; this huge inevitable Product of the Destinies, which is everywhere the portion of our Europe in these latter days? There lies the question for us. Whence comes it, this universal big black Democracy; whither tends it; what is the meaning of it? A meaning it must have, or it would not be here. If we can find the right meaning of it, we may, wisely resisting and controlling, still hope to live in the midst of it; if we cannot find the right meaning, if we find only the wrong or no meaning in it, to live will not be possible! The whole social wisdom of the Present Time is summoned, in the name of the Giver of Wisdom, to make clear to itself, and lay deeply to heart with an eye to strenuous valiant practice and effort, what the meaning of this universal revolt of the European populations, which calls itself Democracy, and decides to continue permanent, may be.

Certainly it is a drama full of action, event fast following event; in which curiosity finds endless scope, and there are interests at stake, enough to rivet the attention of all men, simple and wise. Whereat the idle multitude lift up their voices, gratulating, celebrating sky-high; in rhyme and prose announcement, more than plentiful, that *now* the New Era, and long-expected Year One of Perfect Human Felicity has come. Glorious and immortal people, sublime French citizens, heroic barricades; triumph of civil and religious liberty—O Heaven! one of the inevitablest private miseries, to an earnest man in such circumstances, is this multitudinous efflux of oratory and psalmody, from the universal foolish human throat; drowning for the moment all reflection whatsoever, except the sorrowful one that you are fallen in an evil, heavy-laden, long-eared age, and must resignedly bear your part in the same. The front wall of your wretched old crazy dwelling, long de-

[1]From the first of the *Latter-Day Pamphlets* by Thomas Carlyle (1850).

nounced by you to no purpose, having at last fairly folded itself over, and fallen prostrate into the street, the floors, as may happen, will still hang on by the mere beam-ends, and coherency of old carpentry, though in a sloping direction, and depend there till certain poor rusty nails and worm-eaten dovetailings give way:—but is it cheering, in such circumstances, that the whole household burst forth into celebrating the new joys of light and ventilation, liberty and picturesqueness of position, and thank God that now they have got a house to their mind? My dear household, cease singing and psalmodying; lay aside your fiddles, take out your work-implements, if you have any; for I can say with confidence the laws of gravitation are still active, and rusty nails, worm-eaten dovetailings, and secret coherency of old carpentry, are not the best basis for a household! In the lanes of Irish cities, I have heard say, the wretched people are sometimes found living, and perilously boiling their potatoes, on such swing-floors and inclined planes hanging on by the joist-ends; but I did not hear that they sang very much in celebration of such lodging. No, they slid gently about, sat near the back wall, and perilously boiled their potatoes, in silence for most part!

High shouts of exultation, in every dialect, by every vehicle of speech and writing, rise from far and near over this last avatar[2] of Democracy in 1848: and yet, to wise minds, the first aspect it presents seems rather to be one of boundless misery and sorrow. What can be more miserable than this universal hunting out of the high dignitaries, solemn functionaries, and potent, grave, and reverend signiors of the world; this stormful rising up of the inarticulate dumb masses everywhere, against those who pretended to be speaking for them and guiding them? These guides, then, were mere blind men only pretending to see? These rulers were not ruling at all; they had merely got on the attributes and clothes of rulers, and were surreptitiously drawing the wages, while the work remained undone? The Kings were Sham-Kings, play-acting as at Drury Lane;—and what were the people withal that took them for real? . . .

Democracy, once modelled into suffrages, furnished with ballot-boxes and such-like, will itself accomplish the salutary universal change from Delusive to Real, and make a new blessed world of us by and by? To the great mass of men, I am aware, the matter presents itself quite on this hopeful side. Democracy they consider to be a kind of "Government." The old model, formed long since, and brought to perfection in England now two hundred years ago, has proclaimed itself to all Nations as the new healing for every woe: "Set up a Parliament," the Nations everywhere say, when the old King is detected to be a Sham-King, and hunted out or not; "set up a Parliament;

[2]Extraordinary appearance.

let us have suffrages, universal suffrages; and all either at once or by due degrees will be right, and a real Millennium come." Such is their way of construing the matter.

Such, alas, is by no means my way of construing the matter; if it were, I should have had the happiness of remaining silent, and been without call to speak here. It is because the contrary of all this is deeply manifest to me, and appears to be forgotten by multitudes of my contemporaries, that I have had to undertake addressing a word to them. The contrary of all this;—and the farther I look into the roots of all this, the more hateful, ruinous, and dismal does the state of mind all this could have originated in appear to me. To examine this recipe of a Parliament, how fit it is for governing Nations, nay how fit it may now be, in these new times, for governing England itself where we are used to it so long: this, too, is an alarming inquiry, to which all thinking men, and good citizens of their country, who have an ear for the small still voices and eternal intimations, across the temporary clamours and loud blaring proclamations, are now solemnly invited. Invited by the rigorous fact itself; which will one day, and that perhaps soon, demand practical decision or redecision of it from us,—with enormous penalty if we decide it wrong! I think we shall all have to consider this question, one day; better perhaps now, than later, when the leisure may be less. If a Parliament, with suffrages and universal or any conceivable kind of suffrages, *is* the method, then certainly let us set about discovering the kind of suffrages, and rest no moment till we have got them. But it is possible a Parliament may not be the method! Possible the inveterate notions of the English People may have settled it as the method, and the Everlasting Laws of Nature may have settled it as not the method! Not the whole method; not the method at all, if taken as the whole? If a Parliament with never such suffrages is *not* the method settled by this latter authority, then it will urgently behove us to become aware of the fact, and to quit such methods;—we may depend upon it, however unanimous *we* be, every step taken in that direction will, by the Eternal Law of things, be a step *from* improvement, not towards it.

Not towards it, I say, if so! Unanimity of voting,—that will do nothing for us if *so*. Your ship cannot double Cape Horn by its excellent plans of voting. The ship may vote this and that, above decks and below, in the most harmonious exquisitely constitutional manner: the ship, to get round Cape Horn, will find a set of conditions already voted for, and fixed with adamantine rigour by the ancient Elemental Powers, who are entirely careless how you vote. If you can, by voting or without voting, ascertain these conditions, and valiantly conform to them, you will get round the Cape: if you cannot,— the ruffian Winds will blow you ever back again; the inexorable Icebergs, dumb privy-counselors from Chaos, will nudge you with most chaotic "admonition"; you will be flung half-frozen on the Patagonian cliffs, or admonished into shivers by your iceberg councilors, and sent sheer down to Davy Jones, and will never get round Cape Horn at all! Unanimity on board ship;—yes indeed, the ship's crew may be very unanimous, which doubtless, for the time being, will be very comfortable to the ship's crew, and to their Phantasm Captain if they have one: but if the tack they unanimously steer upon is guiding them into the belly of the Abyss, it will not profit them much! Ships accordingly, do not use the ballot-box at all; and they reject the Phantasm species of Captains: one wishes much some other Entities,—since all entities lie under the same rigorous set of laws,—could be brought to show as much wisdom, and sense at least of self-preservation, the *first* command of Nature. Phantasm Captains with unanimous votings: this is considered to be all the law and all the prophets at present.

A divine message, or eternal regulation of the Universe, there verily is, in regard to every conceivable procedure and affair of man: faithfully following this, said procedure or affair will prosper, and have the whole Universe to second it, and carry it, across the fluctuating contradictions, towards a victorious goal; not following this, mistaking this, disregarding this, destruction and wreck are certain for every affair. How find it? All the world answers me, "Count heads; ask Universal Suffrage, by the ballot-boxes, and that will tell." Universal Suffrage, ballot-boxes, count of heads? Well,—I perceive we have got into strange spiritual latitudes indeed. Within the last half century or so, either the Universe or else the heads of men must have altered very much. Half a century ago, and down from Father Adam's time till then, the Universe, wherever I could hear tell of it, was wont to be of somewhat abstruse nature: by no means carrying its secret written on its face, legible to every passer-by; on the contrary, obstinately hiding its secret from all foolish, slavish, wicked, insincere persons, and partially disclosing it to the wise and noble-minded alone, whose number was not the majority in my time! . . .

Historically speaking, I believe there was no Nation that could subsist upon Democracy. Of ancient Republics, and *Demoi* and *Populi*, we have heard much; but it is now pretty well admitted to be nothing to our purpose;—a universal-suffrage republic, or a general-suffrage one, or any but a most-limited-suffrage one, never came to light, or dreamed of doing so in ancient times. When the mass of the population were slaves, and the voters intrinsically a kind of *kings*, or men born to rule others; when the voters were *real* "aristocrats" and manageable dependents of such,—then doubtless voting, and confused jumbling of talk and intrigue, might, without immediate destruction, or the need of a Cavaignac to intervene with cannon and sweep the streets clear of it, go on; and beautiful developments of manhood might be possible beside it, for a season. Beside it; or even, if you will, by means of it, and in virtue of it, though that is by no means so certain as is often supposed. Alas, no: the reflective constitutional mind has misgivings as to the origin of old Greek and Roman nobleness; and indeed knows not how this or any other human nobleness could well be "originated," or brought to pass, by voting or without voting, in this world, except by the grace of God very mainly;—and remembers, with a sigh, that of the Seven Sages themselves no fewer than three were bits of Despotic Kings, Τύραννοι, "Tyrants" so-called (such being greatly wanted there); and that the other four were very far from Red Republicans, if of any political faith whatever! We may quit the Ancient Classical concern, and leave it to College clubs and speculative debating societies, in these late days.

Of the various French Republics that have been tried, or that are still on trial,—of these also it is not needful to say any word. But there is one modern instance of Democracy nearly perfect, the Republic of the United States, which has actually subsisted for threescore years or more, with immense success as is affirmed; to which many still appeal, as to a sign of hope for all nations, and a "Model Republic." Is not America an instance in point? Why should not all Nations subsist and flourish on Democracy, as America does?

Of America it would ill beseem any Englishman, and me perhaps as little as another, to speak unkindly, to speak *unpatriotically*, if any of us even felt so. Sure enough, America is a great, and in many respects a blessed and hopeful phenomenon. Sure enough, these hardy millions of Anglo-Saxon men prove themselves worthy of their genealogy; and, with the axe and plough and hammer, if not yet with any much finer kind of implements, are triumphantly clearing out wide spaces, seedfields for the sustenance and refuge of mankind, arenas for the future history of the world; doing, in their day and generation, a creditable and cheering feat under the sun. But as to a Model Republic, or a model anything, the wise among themselves know too well that there is nothing to be said. Nay the title hitherto to be a Commonwealth or Nation at all, among the ἔθνη [3] of the world, is, strictly considered, still a thing they are but striving for, and indeed have not yet done much towards attaining. Their Constitution, such as it may be, was made here, not there; went over with them from the Old Puritan English workshop ready-made. Deduct what they carried with them from England ready-made,—their common English Language, and that same Constitution, or rather elixir of constitutions, their inveterate and now, as it were, inborn reverence for the Constable's Staff; two quite immense attainments, which England had to spend much blood, and valiant sweat of blood and brain, for centuries long, in achieving;—and what new elements

[3] Races.

of polity or nationhood, what noble new phasis of human arrangement, or social device worthy of Prometheus or of Epimetheus,[4] yet comes to light in America? Cotton-crops and Indian corn and dollars come to light; and half a world of untilled land, where populations that respect the constable can live, for the present *without* Government: this comes to light; and the profound sorrow of all nobler hearts, here uttering itself as silent patient unspeakable ennui, there coming out as vague elegiac wailings, that there is still next to nothing more. "Anarchy *plus* a street-constable": that also is anarchic to me, and other than quite lovely!

I foresee, too, that, long before the waste lands are full, the very street-constable, on these poor terms, will have become impossible: without the waste lands, as here in our Europe, I do not see how he could continue possible many weeks. Cease to brag to me of America, and its model institutions and constitutions. To men in their sleep there is nothing granted in this world: nothing, or as good as nothing, to men that sit idly *caucusing* and ballot-boxing on the graves of their heroic ancestors, saying, "It is well, it is well!" Corn and bacon are granted: not a very sublime boon, on such conditions; a boon moreover which, on such conditions, cannot last! No: America too will have to strain its energies, in quite other fashion than this; to crack its sinews, and all but break its heart, as the rest of us have had to do, in thousandfold wrestle with the Pythons and mud-demons, before it can become a habitation for the gods. America's battle is yet to fight; and we, sorrowful though nothing doubting, will wish her strength for it. New Spiritual Pythons, plenty of them; enormous Megatherions, as ugly as were ever born of mud, loom huge and hideous out of the twilight Future on America; and she will have her own agony, and her own victory, but on other terms than she is yet quite aware of. Hitherto she but ploughs and hammers, in a very successful manner; hitherto, in spite of her "roast-goose with apple-sauce," she is not much. "Roast-goose with apple-sauce for the poorest working-man": well, surely that is something,—thanks to your respect for the street-constable, and to your continents of fertile waste land;—but that, even if it could continue, is by no means enough; that is not even an instalment towards what will be required of you. My friend, brag not yet of our American cousins! Their quantity of cotton, dollars, industry and resources, I believe to be almost unspeakable; but I can by no means worship the like of these. What great human soul, what great thought, what great noble thing that one could worship, or loyally admire, has yet been produced there? None: the American cousins have yet done none of these things. "What have they done?" growls Smelfungus,[5] tired of the subject:

[4]Brother of Prometheus.

[5]A nickname for a pessimistic grumbler. Used originally by Sterne in *Tobias Smollett.*

"They have doubled their population every twenty years. They have begotten, with a rapidity beyond recorded example, Eighteen Millions of the greatest *bores* ever seen in this world before,—that hitherto is their feat in History!"— And so we leave them, for the present; and cannot predict the success of Democracy, on this side of the Atlantic, from their example.

Alas, on this side of the Atlantic and on that, Democracy, we apprehend, is forever impossible! So much, with certainty of loud astonished contradiction from all manner of men at present, but with sure appeal to the Law of Nature and the ever-abiding Fact, may be suggested and asserted once more. The Universe itself is a Monarchy and Hierarchy; large liberty of "voting" there, all manner of choice, utmost free-will, but with conditions inexorable and immeasurable annexed to every exercise of the same. A most free common-wealth of "voters"; but with Eternal Justice to preside over it, Eternal Justice enforced by Almighty Power! This is the model of "constitutions"; this: nor in any Nation where there has not yet (in some supportable and withal some constantly increasing degree) been confided to the *Noblest*, with his select series of *Nobler*, the divine everlasting duty of directing and controlling the Ignoble, has the "Kingdom of God," which we all pray for, "come," nor can "His will" even *tend* to be "done on Earth as it is in Heaven" till then. My Christian friends, and indeed my Sham-Christian and Anti-Christian, and all manner of men, are invited to reflect on this. They will find it to be the truth of the case. The Noble in the high place, the Ignoble in the low; that is, in all times and in all countries, the Almighty Maker's Law.

To raise the Sham-Noblest, and solemnly consecrate *him* by whatever method, new-devised, or slavishly adhered to from old wont, this, little as we may regard it, is in all times and countries, a practical blasphemy, and Nature will in no wise forget it. Alas, there lies the origin, the fatal necessity, of modern Democracy everywhere. It is the Noblest, not the Sham-Noblest; it is God-Almighty's Noble, not the Court-Tailor's Noble, nor the Able-Editor's Noble, that must in some approximate degree be raised to the supreme place; he and not a counterfeit,—under penalties! Penalties deep as death, and at length terrible as hell-on-earth, my constitutional friend! Will the ballot-box raise the Noblest to the chief place; does any sane man deliberately believe such a thing? That nevertheless is the indispensable result, attain it how we may: if this is attained, all is attained; if not that, nothing. He that cannot believe the ballot-box to be attaining it, will be comparatively indifferent to the ballot-box. Excellent for keeping the ship's crew at peace under their Phantasm Captain; but unserviceable, under such, for getting round Cape Horn. Alas, that there should be human beings requiring to have these things argued of, at this late time of day!

186

I say, it is the everlasting privilege of the foolish to be governed by the wise; to be guided in the right path by those who know it better than they. This is the first "right of man"; compared with which all other rights are as nothing,—mere superfluities, corollaries which will follow of their own accord out of this; if they be not contradictions to this, and less than nothing! . . .

One thing I do know, and can again assert with great confidence, supported by the whole Universe, and by some two hundred generations of men, who have left us some record of themselves there, That the few Wise will have, by one method or another, to take command of the innumerable Foolish; that they must be got to take it;—and that, in fact, since Wisdom, which means also Valour and heroic Nobleness, is alone strong in this world, and one wise man is stronger than all men unwise, they can be got. That they must take it; and having taken, must keep it, and do their God's-Message in it, and defend the same, at their life's peril, against all men and devils. This I do clearly believe to be the backbone of all Future Society, as it has been of all Past; and that without it, there is no Society possible in the world. And what a business *this* will be, before it end in some degree of victory again, and whether the time for shouts of triumph and tremendous cheers upon it is yet come, or not yet by a great way, I perceive too well! A business to make us all very serious indeed. A business not to be accomplished but by noble manhood, and devout all-daring, all-enduring loyalty to Heaven, such as fatally *sleeps* at present,—such as is not *dead* at present either, unless the gods have doomed this world of theirs to die! . . .

THE UTOPIANS[1]

H. G. Wells

THE earlier curiosities of the Earthlings turned upon methods of government. This was perhaps natural in the presence of two such statesmen as Mr. Burleigh and Mr. Catskill.

"What form of government do you have?" asked Mr. Burleigh. "Is it a

[1]From *Men Like Gods* by H. G. Wells, 1922, The Macmillan Company. In this novel a group of Englishmen called Earthlings, including Mr. Barnstaple an editor, Rupert Catskill, Secretary of State for War, Mr. Burleigh a conservative leader, and a clergyman. Father Amerton, suddenly find themselves transported to Utopia. This is a land which has passed through the Age of Confusion (which still reigns on earth) into a period of scientific enlightenment. In this selection the Utopians, among them Lychnis, a woman, and two men, Urthred and Lion, attempt to explain to the Earthlings the new order of society which exists in Utopia.

monarchy or an autocracy or a pure democracy? Do you separate the executive and the legislative? And is there one central government for all your planet, or are there several governing centres?"

It was conveyed to Mr. Burleigh and his companions with some difficulty that there was no central government in Utopia at all.

"But surely," said Mr. Burleigh, "there is someone or something, some council or bureau or what not, somewhere, with which the final decision rests in cases of collective action for the common welfare. Some ultimate seat and organ of sovereignty, it seems to me, there *must* be." . . .

No, the Utopians declared, there was no such concentration of authority in their world. In the past there had been, but it had long since diffused back into the general body of the community. Decisions in regard to any particular matter were made by the people who knew most about that matter.

"But suppose it is a decision that has to be generally observed? A rule affecting the public health, for example? Who would enforce it?"

"It would not need to be enforced. Why should it?"

"But suppose someone refused to obey your regulation?"

"We should inquire why he or she did not conform. There might be some exceptional reason."

"But failing that?"

"We should make an inquiry into his mental and moral health."

"The mind doctor takes the place of the policeman," said Mr. Burleigh.

"I should prefer the policeman," said Mr. Rupert Catskill.

"You *would*, Rupert," said Mr. Burleigh as who should say: "*Got* you that time."

"Then do you mean to say," he continued, addressing the Utopians with an expression of great intelligence, "that your affairs are all managed by special bodies or organizations—one scarcely knows what to call them—without any co-ordination of their activities?"

"The activities of our world," said Urthred, "are all co-ordinated to secure the general freedom. We have a number of intelligences directed to the general psychology of the race and to the interaction of one collective function upon another."

"Well, isn't that group of intelligences a governing class?" said Mr. Burleigh.

"Not in the sense that they exercise any arbitrary will," said Urthred. "They deal with general relations, that is all. But they rank no higher, they have no more precedence on that account than a philosopher has over a scientific specialist."

"This is a republic indeed!" said Mr. Burleigh. "But how it works and

188

how it came about I cannot imagine. Your state is probably a highly socialistic one?"

"You still live in a world in which nearly everything except the air, the high roads, the high seas and the wilderness is privately owned?"

"We do," said Mr. Catskill. "Owned—and competed for."

"We have been through that stage. We found at last that private property in all but very personal things was an intolerable nuisance to mankind. We got rid of it. An artist or a scientific man has complete control of all the material he needs, we all own our tools and appliances and have rooms and places of our own, but there is no property for trade or speculation. All this militant property, this property of manoeuvre, has been quite got rid of. But how we got rid of it is a long story. It was not done in a few years. The exaggeration of private property was an entirely natural and necessary stage in the development of human nature. It led at last to monstrous results, but it was only through these monstrous and catastrophic results that men learnt the need and nature of the limitations of private property."

Mr. Burleigh had assumed an attitude which was obviously habitual to him. He sat very low in his chair with his long legs crossed in front of him and the thumb and fingers of one hand placed with meticulous exactness against those of the other.

"I must confess," he said, "that I am most interested in the peculiar form of Anarchism which seems to prevail here. Unless I misunderstand you completely every man attends to his own business as the servant of the state. I take it you have—you must correct me if I am wrong—a great number of people concerned in the production and distribution and preparation of food; they inquire, I assume, into the needs of the world, they satisfy them and they are a law unto themselves in their way of doing it. They conduct researches, they make experiments. Nobody compels, obliges, restrains or prevents them. ("People talk to them about it," said Urthred with a faint smile.) And again others produce and manufacture and study metals for all mankind and are also a law unto themselves. Others again see to the habitability of your world, plan and arrange these delightful habitations, say who shall use them and how they shall be used. Others pursue pure science. Others experiment with sensory and imaginative possibilities and are artists. Others again teach."

"They are very important," said Lychnis.

"And they all do it in harmony—and due proportion. Without either a central legislature or executive. I will admit that all this seems admirable—but impossible. Nothing of the sort has ever been even suggested yet in the world from which we come."

"Something of the sort was suggested long ago by the Guild Socialists," said Mr. Barnstaple.

"Dear me!" said Mr. Burleigh. "I know very little about the Guild Socialists. Who were they? Tell me."

Mr. Barnstaple tacitly declined that task. "The idea is quite familiar to our younger people," he said. "Laski calls it the pluralistic state, as distinguished from the monistic state in which sovereignty is concentrated. Even the Chinese have it. A Pekin professor, Mr. S. C. Chang, has written a pamphlet on what he calls 'Professionalism.' I read it only a few weeks ago. He sent it to the office of the *Liberal*. He points out how undesirable it is and how unnecessary for China to pass through a phase of democratic politics on the Western model. He wants China to go right straight on to a collateral independence of functional classes, mandarins, industrials, agricultural workers and so forth, much as we seem to find it here. Though that of course involves an educational revolution. Decidedly the germ of what you call Anarchism here is also in the air we come from."

"Dear me!" said Mr. Burleigh, looking more intelligent and appreciative than ever. "And is that so? I had *no* idea—!"

The conversation continued desultory in form and yet the exchange of ideas was rapid and effective. Quite soon, as it seemed to Mr. Barnstaple, an outline of the history of Utopia from the Last Age of Confusion onward shaped itself in his mind.

The more he learnt of the Last Age of Confusion the more it seemed to resemble the present time on earth. In those days the Utopians had worn abundant clothing and lived in towns quite after the earthly fashion. A fortunate conspiracy of accidents rather than any set design had opened for them some centuries of opportunity and expansion. Climatic phases and political chances had smiled upon the race after a long period of recurrent shortage, pestilence and destructive warfare. For the first time the Utopians had been able to explore the whole planet on which they lived, and these explorations had brought great virgin areas under the axe, the spade and the plough. There had been an enormous increase in real wealth and in leisure and liberty. Many thousands of people were lifted out of the normal squalor of human life to positions in which they could, if they chose, think and act with unprecedented freedom. A few, a sufficient few, did. A vigorous development of scientific inquiry began and, trailing after it a multitude of ingenious inventions, produced a great enlargement of practical human power.

There had been previous outbreaks of the scientific intelligence in Utopia, but none before had ever occurred in such favourable circumstances or lasted

long enough to come to abundant practical fruition. Now in a couple of
brief centuries the Utopians, who had hitherto crawled about their planet like
sluggish ants or travelled parasitically on larger and swifter animals, found
themselves able to fly rapidly or speak instantaneously to any other point on
the planet. They found themselves, too, in possession of mechanical power
on a scale beyond all previous experience, and not simply of mechanical
power; physiological and then psychological science followed in the wake of
physics and chemistry, and extraordinary possibilities of control over his own
body and over his social life dawned upon the Utopian. But these things
came, when at last they did come, so rapidly and confusingly that it was only
a small minority of people who realized the possibilities, as distinguished from
the concrete achievements, of this tremendous expansion of knowledge. The
rest took the novel inventions as they came, haphazard, with as little adjustment as possible of their thoughts and ways of living to the new necessities
these novelties implied.

The first response of the general population of Utopia to the prospect of
power, leisure and freedom thus opened out to it was proliferation. It behaved
just as senselessly and mechanically as any other animal or vegetable species
would have done. It bred until it had completely swamped the ampler opportunity that had opened before it. It spent the great gifts of science as rapidly
as it got them in a mere insensate multiplication of the common life. At one
time in the Last Age of Confusion the population of Utopia had mounted to
over two thousand million. . . .

"But what is it now?" asked Mr. Burleigh.

About two hundred and fifty million, the Utopians told him. That had
been the maximum population that could live a fully developed life upon the
surface of Utopia. But now with increasing resources the population was
being increased.

A gasp of horror came from Father Amerton. He had been dreading this
realization for some time. It struck at his moral foundations. "And you dare
to *regulate* increase! You control it! Your women consent to bear children
as they are needed—or refrain!"

"Of course," said Urthred. "Why not?"

"I feared as much," said Father Amerton, and leaning forward he covered
his face with his hands murmuring, "I felt this in the atmosphere! The
human stud farm! Refusing to create souls! The *wickedness* of it! Oh,
my God!"

Mr. Burleigh regarded the emotion of the reverend gentleman through
his glasses with a slightly shocked expression. He detested catchwords. But
Father Amerton stood for very valuable conservative elements in the com-

munity. Mr. Burleigh turned to the Utopian again. "That is extremely interesting," he said. "Even at present our earth contrives to carry a population
of at least five times that amount."

"But twenty millions or so will starve this winter, you told us a little while
ago—in a place called Russia. And only a very small proportion of the rest
are leading what even you would call full and spacious lives?"

"Nevertheless the contrast is very striking," said Mr. Burleigh.

"It is terrible!" said Father Amerton.

The overcrowding of the planet in the Last Age of Confusion was, these
Utopians insisted, the fundamental evil out of which all the others that
afflicted the race arose. An overwhelming flood of newcomers poured into
the world and swamped every effort the intelligent minority could make to
educate a sufficient proportion of them to meet the demands of the new and
still rapidly changing conditions of life. And the intelligent minority was
not itself in any position to control the racial destiny. These great masses of
population that had been blundered into existence, swayed by damaged and
decaying traditions and amenable to the crudest suggestions, were the natural
prey and support of every adventurer with a mind blatant enough and a
conception of success coarse enough to appeal to them. The economic system,
clumsily and convulsively reconstructed to meet the new conditions of mechanical production and distribution, became more and more a cruel and
impudent exploitation of the multitudinous congestion of the common man
by the predatory and acquisitive few. That all too common common man was
hustled through misery and subjection from his cradle to his grave; he was
cajoled and lied to, he was bought, sold and dominated by an impudent
minority, bolder and no doubt more energetic, but in all other respects no
more intelligent than himself. It was difficult, Urthred said, for a Utopian
nowadays to convey the monstrous stupidity, wastefulness and vulgarity to
which these rich and powerful men of the Last Age of Confusion attained.

("We will not trouble you," said Mr. Burleigh. "Unhappily—we know.
. . . We know. Only too well do we know.")

Upon this festering, excessive mass of population disasters descended at
last like wasps upon a heap of rotting fruit. It was its natural, inevitable
destiny. A war that affected nearly the whole planet dislocated its flimsy
financial system and most of its economic machinery beyond any possibility
of repair. Civil wars and clumsily conceived attempts at social revolution
continued the disorganization. A series of years of bad weather accentuated
the general shortage. The exploiting adventurers, too stupid to realize what
had happened, continued to cheat and hoodwink the commonalty and burke
any rally of honest men, as wasps will continue to eat even after their bodies

have been cut away. The effort to make passed out of Utopian life, triumphantly superseded by the effort to get. Production dwindled down towards the vanishing point. Accumulated wealth vanished. An overwhelming system of debt, a swarm of creditors, morally incapable of helpful renunciation, crushed out all fresh initiative.

The long diastole in Utopian affairs that had begun with the great discoveries, passed into a phase of rapid systole. What plenty and pleasure was still possible in the world was filched all the more greedily by the adventurers of finance and speculative business. Organized science had long since been commercialized, and was "applied" now chiefly to a hunt for profitable patents and the forestalling of necessary supplies. The neglected lamp of pure science waned, flickered and seemed likely to go out again altogether, leaving Utopia in the beginning of a new series of Dark Ages like those before the age of discovery began.

"It is really *very* like a gloomy diagnosis of our own outlook," said Mr. Burleigh. "Extraordinarily like. How Dean Inge would have enjoyed all this!"

"To an infidel of his stamp, no doubt, it would seem most enjoyable," said Father Amerton a little incoherently.

These comments annoyed Mr. Barnstaple, who was urgent to hear more. "And then," he said to Urthred, "what happened?"

What happened, Mr. Barnstable gathered, was a deliberate change in Utopian thought. A growing number of people were coming to understand that amidst the powerful and easily released forces that science and organization had brought within reach of man, the old conception of social life in the state, as a limited and legalized struggle of men and women to get the better of one another, was becoming too dangerous to endure. There had to be new ideas and new conventions of human association if history was not to end in disaster and collapse.

All societies were based on the limitation by laws and taboos and treaties of the primordial fierce combativeness of the ancestral man-ape; that ancient spirit of self-assertion had now to undergo new restrictions commensurate with the new powers and dangers of the race. The idea of competition to possess, as the ruling idea of intercourse, was, like some ill-controlled furnace, threatening to consume the machine it had formerly driven. The idea of creative service had to replace it. To that idea the human mind and will had to be turned if social life was to be saved. Propositions that had seemed, in former ages, to be inspired and exalted idealism began now to be recognized not simply as sober psychological truth but as practical and urgently necessary

193

truth. In explaining this Urthred expressed himself in a manner that recalled to Mr. Barnstaple's mind certain very familiar phrases; he seemed to be saying that whosoever would save his life should lose it, and that whosoever would give his life should thereby gain the whole world.

Father Amerton's thoughts, it seemed, were also responding in the same manner. For he suddenly interrupted with: "But what you are saying is a quotation!"

Urthred admitted that he had a quotation in mind, a passage from the teachings of a man of great poetic power who had lived long ago in the days of spoken words.

He would have proceeded, but Father Amerton was too excited to let him do so. "But who was this teacher?" he asked. "Where did he live? How was he born? How did he die?"

A picture was flashed upon Mr. Barnstaple's consciousness of a solitary-looking, pale-faced figure, beaten and bleeding, surrounded by armoured guards, in the midst of a thrusting, jostling, sun-bit crowd which filled a narrow, high-walled street. Behind, some huge, ugly implement was borne along, dipping and swaying with the swaying of the multitude. . . .

"Did he die upon the Cross in *this* world also?" cried Father Amerton. "Did he die upon the Cross?"

This prophet in Utopia they learnt had died very painfully, but not upon the Cross. He had been tortured in some way, but neither the Utopians nor these particular Earthlings had sufficient knowledge of the technicalities of torture to get any idea over about that, and then apparently he had been fastened upon a slowly turning wheel and exposed until he died. It was the abominable punishment of a cruel and conquering race, and it had been inflicted upon him because his doctrine of universal service had alarmed the rich and dominant who did not serve. Mr. Barnstaple had a momentary vision of a twisted figure upon that wheel of torture in the blazing sun. And, marvellous triumph over death! out of a world that could do such a deed had come this great peace and universal beauty about him!

But Father Amerton was pressing his questions. "But did you not realize who he was? Did not this world suspect?"

A great many people thought that this man was a God. But he had been accustomed to call himself merely a son of God or a son of Man.

Father Amerton stuck to his point. "But you worship him now?"

"We follow his teaching because it was wonderful and true," said Urthred.

"But worship?"

"No."

"But does nobody worship? There *were* those who worshipped him?"

194

There were those who worshipped him. There were those who quailed before the stern magnificence of his teaching and yet who had a tormenting sense that he was right in some profound way. So they played a trick upon their own uneasy consciences by treating him as a magical god instead of as a light to their souls. They interwove with his execution ancient traditions of sacrificial kings. Instead of receiving him frankly and clearly and making him a part of their understandings and wills they pretended to eat him mystically and make him a part of their bodies. They turned his wheel into a miraculous symbol, and they confused it with the equator and the sun and the ecliptic and indeed with anything else that was round. In cases of ill-luck, ill-health or bad weather it was believed to be very helpful for the believer to describe a circle in the air with the forefinger.

And since this teacher's memory was very dear to the ignorant multitude because of his gentleness and charity, it was seized upon by cunning and aggressive types who constituted themselves champions and exponents of the wheel, who grew rich and powerful in its name, led people into great wars for its sake and used it as a cover and justification for envy, hatred, tyranny and dark desires. Until at last men said that had that ancient prophet come again to Utopia, his own triumphant wheel would have crushed and destroyed him afresh. . . .

Father Amerton seemed inattentive to this communication. He was seeing it from another angle. "But surely," he said, "there is a remnant of believers still! Despised perhaps—but a remnant?"

There was no remnant. The whole world followed that Teacher of Teachers, but no one worshipped. On some old treasured buildings the wheel was still to be seen carved, often with the most fantastic decorative elaborations. And in museums and collections there were multitudes of pictures, images, charms and the like.

"I don't understand this," said Father Amerton. "It is too terrible. I am at a loss. I do not understand."

A fair and rather slender man with a delicately beautiful face whose name, Mr. Barnstaple was to learn later, was Lion, presently took over from Urthred the burthen of explaining and answering the questions of the Earthlings.

He was one of the educational co-ordinators in Utopia. He made it clear that the change over in Utopian affairs had been no sudden revolution. No new system of laws and customs, no new methods of economic co-operation based on the idea of universal service to the common good, had sprung abruptly into being complete and finished. Throughout a long period, before and during the Last Age of Confusion, the foundations of the new state were laid by a growing multitude of inquirers and workers, having no set plan or preconceived method, but brought into unconscious co-operation by a common impulse to service and a common lucidity and veracity of mind. It was only towards the climax of the Last Age of Confusion in Utopia that psychological science began to develop with any vigour, comparable to the vigour of the development of geographical and physical science during the preceding centuries. And the social and economic disorder which was checking experimental science and crippling the organized work of the universities was stimulating inquiry into the processes of human association and making it fearless and desperate.

The impression given Mr. Barnstaple was not of one of those violent changes which our world has learnt to call revolutions, but of an increase of light, a dawn of new ideas, in which the things of the old order went on for a time with diminishing vigour until people began as a matter of common sense to do the new things in the place of the old.

The beginnings of the new order were in discussions, books, and psychological laboratories; the soil in which it grew was found in schools and colleges. The old order gave small rewards to the school-master, but its dominant types were too busy with the struggle for wealth and power to take much heed of teaching: it was left to any man or woman who would give thought and labour without much hope of tangible rewards, to shape the world anew in the minds of the young. And they did so shape it. In a world ruled ostensibly by adventurer politicians, in a world where men came to power through floundering business enterprises and financial cunning, it was presently being taught and understood that extensive private property was socially a nuisance, and that the state could not do its work properly nor education produce its proper results, side by side with a class of irresponsible rich people. For, by their very nature, they assailed, they corrupted, they undermined every state undertaking; their flaunting existences distorted and disguised all the values of life. They had to go, for the good of the race.

"Didn't they fight?" asked Mr. Catskill pugnaciously.

They had fought irregularly but fiercely. The fight to delay or arrest the coming of the universal scientific state, the educational state, in Utopia, had gone on as a conscious struggle for nearly five centuries. The fight against it was the fight of greedy, passionate, prejudiced and self-seeking men against the crystallization into concrete realities of this new idea of association for service. It was fought wherever ideas were spread; it was fought with dismissals and threats and boycotts and storms of violence, with lies and false accusations, with prosecutions and imprisonments, with lynching-rope, tar and feathers, paraffin, bludgeon and rifle, bomb and gun.

But the service of the new idea that had been launched into the world never failed; it seized upon the men and women it needed with compelling power. Before the scientific state was established in Utopia more than a million martyrs had been killed for it, and those who had suffered lesser wrongs were beyond all reckoning. Point after point was won in education, in social laws, in economic method. No date could be fixed for the change. A time came when Utopia perceived that it was day and that a new order of things had replaced the old. . . .

"So it must be," said Mr. Barnstaple, as though Utopia were not already present about him. "So it must be."

A question was being answered. Every Utopian child is taught to the full measure of its possibilities and directed to the work that is indicated by its desires and capacity. It is born well. It is born of perfectly healthy parents; its mother has chosen to bear it after due thought and preparation. It grows up under perfectly healthy conditions; its natural impulses to play and learn are gratified by the subtlest educational methods; hands, eyes and limbs are given every opportunity of training and growth; it learns to draw, write, express itself, use a great variety of symbols to assist and extend its thought. Kindness and civility become ingrained habits, for all about it are kind and civil. And in particular the growth of its imagination is watched and encouraged. It learns the wonderful story of its world and its race, how man has struggled and still struggles out of his earlier animal narrowness and egotism towards an empire over being that is still but faintly apprehended through dense veils of ignorance. All its desires are made fine; it learns from poetry, from example and the love of those about it to lose its solicitude for itself in love; its sexual passions are turned against its selfishness, its curiosity flowers into scientific passion, its combativeness is set to fight disorder, its inherent pride and ambition are directed towards an honourable share in the common achievement. It goes to the work that attracts it and chooses what it will do.

If the individual is indolent there is no great loss, there is plenty for all in Utopia, but then it will find no lovers, nor will it ever bear children, because no one in Utopia loves those who have neither energy nor distinction. There is much pride of the mate in Utopian love. And there is no idle rich "society" in Utopia, nor games and shows for the mere looker-on. There is nothing for the mere looker-on. It is a pleasant world indeed for holidays, but not for those who would continuously do nothing.

For centuries now Utopian science has been able to discriminate among births, and nearly every Utopian alive would have ranked as an energetic creative spirit in former days. There are few dull and no really defective

197

people in Utopia; the idle strains, the people of lethargic dispositions or weak imaginations, have mostly died out; the melancholic type has taken its dismissal and gone; spiteful and malignant characters are disappearing. The vast majority of Utopians are active, sanguine, inventive, receptive, and good tempered.

"And you have not even a parliament?" asked Mr. Burleigh, still incredulous.

Utopia has no parliament, no politics, no private wealth, no business competition, no police nor prisons, no lunatics, no defectives nor cripples, and it has none of these things because it has schools and teachers who are all that schools and teachers can be. Politics, trade and competition are the methods of adjustment of a crude society. Such methods of adjustment have been laid aside in Utopia for more than a thousand years. There is no rule nor government needed by adult Utopians because all the rule and government they need they have had in childhood and youth.

Said Lion: *"Our education is our government."*

THE COMING VICTORY
OF DEMOCRACY[1]

Thomas Mann

For the moment, I am concerned with a definition of democracy, and every definition of democracy is insufficient—insufficient for belief in it—if it is confined to the technical-political aspects. It is insufficient to define the democratic principle as the principle of majority rule and to translate democracy literally, all too literally, as government by the people, an expression of double meaning which could also signify mob rule, for that is more nearly the definition of fascism. It is even inadequate—correct as it may be—to reduce the democratic idea to the idea of peace, and to assert that the right of a free people to determine its own destiny includes respect for the rights of foreign people and thus constitutes the best guarantee for the creation of a community of nations and for peace. We must reach higher and envisage the whole. We must define democracy as that form of government and of society which is inspired above every other with the feeling and consciousness of the dignity of man.

[1]Reprinted from *The Coming Victory of Democracy* by Thomas Mann (1938), by permission of and special arrangement with Alfred A. Knopf, Inc., authorized publishers.

The dignity of man—do we not feel alarmed and somewhat ridiculous at the mention of these words? Do they not savour of optimism grown feeble and stuffy—of after-dinner oratory, which scarcely harmonizes with the bitter, harsh, everyday truth about human beings? We know it—this truth. We are well aware of the nature of man, or, to be more accurate, the nature of men— and we are far from entertaining any illusions on the subject. The nature of man is transfixed in the sacred words: "The imagination of man's heart is evil from his youth." It has been described with philosophical cynicism in the phrase of Frederick II: "the accursed race—*cette race maudite*." Yes, yes, humanity—its injustice, malice, cruelty, its average stupidity and blindness are amply demonstrated, its egoism is crass, its deceitfulness, cowardice, its anti-social instincts, constitute our everyday experience; the iron pressure of disciplinary constraint is necessary to keep it under any reasonable control. Who cannot embroider upon the depravity of this strange creature called man, who does not often despair over his future or sympathize with the contempt felt by the angels of heaven from the day of creation for the incomprehensible interest which the heavenly Father takes in this problematical creature? And yet it is a fact—more true today than ever—that we cannot allow ourselves, because of so much all too well-founded scepticism, to despise humanity. Despite so much ridiculous depravity, we cannot forget the great and the honourable in man, which manifest themselves as art and science, as passion for truth, creation of beauty and the idea of justice; and it is also true that insensitiveness to the great mystery which we touch upon when we say "man" or "humanity" signifies spiritual death. That is not a truth of yesterday or the day before yesterday, antiquated, unattractive, and feeble. It is the new and necessary truth of today and tomorrow, the truth which has life and youth on its side in opposition to the false and withering youthfulness of certain theories and truths of the moment.

Did I say too much when I spoke of man as a great mystery? Whence does he come? From nature, animal nature, and thereby his conduct is unmistakably conditioned. But in him nature becomes conscious, it seems to have produced him not only to make him master over himself—that is merely the expression of something more profound; for in him nature opens a door to the spiritual, questions, admires, and judges itself in a being which belongs at the same time to itself and to a higher order of things. To become conscious means to acquire conscience, means the knowledge of what is good and what is evil. Nature that is infra-human does not know this difference. It is without guilt. In humanity nature becomes responsible. Man is nature's fall from grace, only it is not a fall, but just as positively an elevation as conscience is higher than innocence. What Christianity calls "original sin" is more than priestly trickery designed to suppress and control humanity—it is the deep feeling of man as a spiritual being for his natural infirmities and limitations, above which he raises himself through spirit. Is that infidelity to nature? By no means. It is according to nature's deepest intent. Because it is for its own spiritualization that nature produced mankind.

This dignity which the mysterious confers upon man, democracy recognizes and honours; democracy's understanding and respect for this quality, it calls "humanity." The anti-human, dictatorial mentality of our day ignores "original sin," or what may be called spiritual conscience. It considers the consciousness of sin, or spirituality, as injurious to military prowess. It teaches optimistic heroics—in direct and stupid contradiction of the extreme contempt for humanity, which it exalts in the same breath. For all men of violence, tyrants, those who seek to stupefy and stultify the masses, and all those who are intent upon turning a nation into an unthinking war-machine in order to control free and thinking citizens—these necessarily despise humanity. They give the pretext, to be sure, that they wish to restore to mankind the honour which Christianity has sullied, by freeing him from original sin and forcing Germanic heroics down his throat. Under all circumstances they set themselves up as the leaders who have restored their country's honour. Even to Germany they have "restored its honour," if we are to believe their radio broadcasts. But in reality they practise a truly grotesque contempt of humanity—grotesque if we think of the victims, grotesque if we consider those who exercise the contempt, since they are themselves the most contemptible creatures.

I am willing to accept contempt which comes from on high, the contempt of the great personality that has outgrown ordinary human limitations. But it is impossible to understand how completely despicable creatures, lacking every moral and spiritual attribute, could undertake to be contemptuous. It is, to be sure, the kind of contempt which strives with all its might to degrade and corrupt humanity in order to force the people to do its will. Terror destroys people, that is clear. It corrupts character, releases every evil impulse, turns them into cowardly hypocrites and shameless informers. It makes them contemptible—that is the reason why these contemners of humanity love terrorism. Their delight in the abuse of people is dirty and pathological. The treatment of the Jews in Germany, the concentration camps and the things which took place and are still taking place in them, are the illustration and proof of this. Every kind of dishonour, disgrace, ignominious distinctions such as the cutting of the hair and the yellow spot, the compulsion to moral suicide, the destruction of mind and soul through bodily torture, and the corruption of justice through force until men, overcome by extreme horror, despair of justice and abjure it for the worship of force—these are all expedients of this lust for human degradation which it would be too much honour to call devilish, for it is simply diseased. Can the flagrant actions which dictatorship permits itself be considered anything but diseased—the lies, the annihilation of truth, the deception—a deception so crass that it, too, amounts to violence? And is there not something diseased in the boundless confidence which the dictators place in a population that has been stultified and intellectually enfeebled to meet their desires and needs? There is but one public voice—theirs. Every other voice has been silenced. There is no contradiction, not even the slightest memory of opposition; they can say what they like. Undisturbed and to their heart's content they can crack the whip of lies over the heads of the populace—the whip of lies called propaganda.

Democracy, whatever may be its conception of humanity, has only the best of intentions toward it. Democracy wishes to elevate mankind, to teach it to think, to set it free. It seeks to remove from culture the stamp of privilege and disseminate it among the people—in a word, it aims at education. Education is an optimistic and humane concept; and respect for humanity is inseparable from it. Hostile to mankind and contemptuous of it is the opposing concept called propaganda, which tries to stultify, stupefy, level, or regiment men for the purpose of military efficiency and, above all, to keep the dictatorial system in power. I do not wish to imply that propaganda could not be used in the sense of education—that is, in the democratic sense. It may be that all over the world and even in this country democracy has heretofore made too little use of it in its own educational sense. But certainly in the hands of the dictators propaganda is an instrument of cynical contempt for humanity.

Thus we see contradiction on both sides—apparently there is no escaping it in life. Democracy being a fertile ground for intellect and literature, for the perception of psychological truth and the search for it, contradicts itself inasmuch as it has an acute appreciation and makes a critical analysis of the comical wickedness of man, but nevertheless insists resolutely upon the dignity of man and the possibility of educating him. Dictatorship contradicts itself inasmuch as it declares the Christian idea of original sin abolished, frees man of conscience, and teaches him noble heroics (in order to make him a better fighter in its defence), but at the same time degrades and enslaves him without the slightest feeling for his dignity, convinced that he deserves no better fate and that every other attitude is antiquated, sentimental talk. Both are illogical. But which form of illogical thinking is the more decent?

I spoke of the characteristic friendliness of democracy to intellect and also to the arts, to literature; and it is scarcely necessary to add that this, in itself, distinguishes it very definitely from dictatorship, which because of its belief in force is thereby obligated to be remote, foreign, and hostile to intellectual pursuits. But this assertion only acquires real value as a definition of democracy if the concept of intellectual life is not understood as one-sided, isolated, abstract, superior to life and remote from it, but is characterized as closely related to life, as directed toward life and action—for only that and specifically that is the democratic spirit. That is the spirit of democracy. Democracy is not intellectualistic in an old and outworn sense. Democracy is thought; but it is thought related to life and action. Otherwise it would not be democratic, and herewith I give a definition which contributes to the modernity and the originality of democracy. The French philosopher Bergson sent to a philosophical congress which recently met in Paris a message in which he set up this imperative; "Act as men of thought, think as men of action." That is a thoroughly democratic slogan. No intellectual of the pre-democratic era ever thought of action, nor of what kind of action would result if his thinking were put into practice. It is characteristic of undemocratic or of democratically uneducated nations that their thinking goes on without reference to reality, in pure abstraction, in complete isolation of the mind from life itself, and without the slightest consideration for the realistic consequences of thought. That indicates a lack of pragmatism which is reprehensible. As a result thought meets with a horrible defeat through reality, and thinking, in general, is compromised. Goethe said: "The man of action is always conscienceless; conscience belongs only to the observer." That is true, but because it is true, the observer must also be conscientious on behalf of the man of action—a requirement which is of course most happily fulfilled when both thought and action reside in one and the same person.

We call the recently deceased founder and first President of the Czechoslovak Republic a great democrat. Why? Because he embodied a new and modern relationship between mind and life, because he represented the organic association of the philosopher and the statesman—a philosopher as statesman, and as a statesman a philosopher. Plato's insistence that philosophers should rule the state would create a dangerous Utopia if it merely implied that the ruler should be a philosopher. The philosopher must also be a ruler—for that, primarily, creates the relationship of mind and life which we call democratic. What we admire today in Descartes, the philosopher who stands at the beginning of modern thought, is specifically the proximity to life and action of his mode of thinking; and the longer European philosophy pursued this democratic trend of thought since that Cartesian era, the more decisive it became. Even so extremely individualistic and aristocratic a thinker as Nietzsche is a democrat in this specifically modern sense; his battle against the theorist, his almost excessive and dangerous glorification of life at the expense of thought and abstract truth, is of a philosophic-democratic character, and of a very artistic one, at that. For the artist is not a theorist, or, at least, only in immediate reference to the kind of action, the creative activity, that arises out of the mind. In more than one way Nietzsche brought art and scientific thinking close together, allowed them to fuse one into the other; through him the borderline between them faded away. But to come close to art means to come close to life, and if an appreciation of the dignity of man is the moral definition of democracy, then its psychological definition arises out of its determination to reconcile and combine knowledge and art, mind and life, thought and deed.

To be sure, misunderstanding and misuse of this concept lie close at hand. There exists a caricature of this modern anti-intellectualism which has nothing whatever to do with democracy, but which lands us in the middle of the base demagogic world of fascism. This is the contempt of pure reason, the denial and violation of truth in favour of power and the interests of the state, the appeal to the lower instincts, to so-called "feeling," the release of stupidity and evil from the discipline of reason and intelligence, the emancipation of black-guardism—in short, a barbaric mob-movement, beside which what we call democracy certainly stands out as aristocratic to the highest degree. In fact, the contrast between democracy and aristocracy is only inadequately justified by life itself; the one is not always the real antithesis of the other. If aristoc-racy really and always meant "the rule of the good, of the best," then it would be the most desirable of all things because it would be exactly what we under-stand by democracy. Masaryk the democrat, Roosevelt the democrat, Léon Blum the democrat, are certainly more aristocratic as individual types of men and of statesmen than such types as Hitler or Mussolini, who are both out-right plebeians. But it is logical that people of an aristocratic bent should represent the principle of democracy politically, because intellect confers dis-tinction and is in itself an expression of refinement and of a higher category. Moreover, because of its association and solidarity with knowledge, truth, justice, and as the opposite of violence and vulgarity, intellect becomes the ad-vocate and representative of democracy on earth.

Real democracy, as we understand it, can never dispense with aristocratic attributes—if the word "aristocratic" is used, not in the sense of birth or any sort of privilege, but in a spiritual sense. In a democracy which does not respect the intellectual life and is not guided by it, demagogy has free play, and the level of national life is depressed to that of the ignorant and uncultivated. But this cannot happen if the principle of education is allowed to dominate and the tendencies prevail to raise the lower classes to an appreciation of cul-ture and to accept the leadership of the better elements. If the conception of culture and its level are determined from below, according to the ideas and understanding of the mob—this, precisely, is nothing but demagogy; and we have its perfect exemplification in the so-called "*Kultur*" speeches of the above-mentioned Hitler. One of these speeches had the practical result that contemporary German painters of world renown such as Corinth, Kokoschka, Pechstein, Klee, Hofer, Marck, and Nolde were figuratively and, one might say, personally pilloried. Their works were exposed in an exhibition of "degenerate art," to the ridicule of those whose greatest exponent is the same "*Kultur*" orator. The nonsense which this new kind of ruler talks in an authoritative manner upon art and intellect, upon sculpture, painting, literature, will make clear to future generations what could happen in the war-damaged Germany of our day, a country which once enjoyed a great intellectual position; it will show them what "degenerate democracy" is like. I know nothing about the art of government—it is possible that this zealot is leading Germany toward a glorious future, although William II also promised that. But on the subject of culture I am somewhat at home. That I can legitimately discuss. And since Germany is wrapped in the funereal silence of dictatorship, since there all opposition is choked, human dignity demands that, at least, here in freedom it should be asserted that these "*Kultur*" orations are nothing but low and vulgar babble and that their only value is to prove how democracy degenerates when it loses the necessary influences of intellectual leadership. . . .

I am aware, ladies and gentlemen, that today's lecture had to be a trifle theoretical, in its attempt to define the exalted and comprehensive concept of democracy. And so I feel certain that you will forgive me if in conclusion I say a few words of a personal nature. I do not know how many of you are familiar with my written works. I am no sans-culotte, no Jacobin, no revolutionary—my whole being is that of a conservative; that is to say that I stand by tradition. I am a man who regards it as his task in life to advance the German heritage, though with modern means and in the modern spirit; who, if his friends are to be believed, may hope one day to assume a place in the history of German culture. No one, I am sure, will interpret anything I have said as a desire to destroy cultural values. I left Germany because in the Germany of today the traditional values underlying Western culture have been rejected and trodden under foot. I have made many sacrifices in order to save one thing which was denied me in Germany: freedom of thought and expression. What better use could I make of this freedom than to tell of my experience during my last years in Germany and what it taught me.

To me the chief lesson of those years is that we must not be afraid to attempt a reform of freedom—in the conservative sense. I believe it to be the duty of every thinking man to take an active part in this task—which is tantamount to the preservation of culture—and to give freely of himself. I must regretfully own that in my younger years I shared that dangerous German habit of thought which regards life and intellect, art and politics as totally separate worlds. In those days we were all of us inclined to view political and social matters as nonessentials that might as well be entrusted to politicians. And we were foolish enough to rely on the ability of these specialists to protect our highest interests. Not long after the war, however, I recognized the threat to liberty which was beginning to take form in Germany, and almost alone among writers I warned the public to the best of my powers. When subsequently the spectre became reality and National-Socialism achieved absolute power, I realized at once that I should not be able to breathe in this air, that I should have to leave my home. In Switzerland, one of Europe's oldest democracies, I found an honourable haven, for which I am duly grateful. Even more do I owe thanks to the Republic of Czechoslovakia, which most generously made a gift of its citizenship to me who was robbed of my German nationality. Especially at this moment, when the heavens of central Europe are darkening so threateningly, it is a heartfelt necessity to give expression to my faithful loyalty to this courageous and lovable democratic republic.

Four years ago I visited America for the first time, and since then I have come here each year. I was delighted with the atmosphere that I found here, because it was almost free of the poisons that fill the air of Europe—because here, in contrast to the cultural fatigue and inclination to barbarism prevalent in the Old World, there exists a joyful respect for culture, a youthful sensitivity to its values and its products. I feel that the hopes of all those who cherish democratic sentiments in the sense in which I have defined them, must be concentrated on this country. Here it will be possible—here it *must* be possible—to carry out those reforms of which I have spoken; to carry them out by peaceful labour, without crime and bloodshed. It is my own intention to make my home in your country, and I am convinced that if Europe continues for a while to pursue the same course as in the last two decades, many good Europeans will meet again on American soil. I believe, in fact, that for the duration of the present European dark age, the centre of Western culture will shift to America. America has received much from Europe, and that debt will be amply repaid if, by saving our traditional values from the present gloom, she can preserve them for a brighter future that will once again find Europe and America united in the great tasks of humanity.

THE TAMING OF POWER[1]

Bertrand Russell

'IN PASSING by the side of a Mount Thai, Confucius came on a woman who was weeping bitterly by a grave. The Master pressed forward and drove quickly to her; then he sent Tze-lu to question her. "Your wailing," said he, "is that of one who has suffered sorrow on sorrow." She replied, "That is so. Once my husband's father was killed here by a tiger. My husband was also killed, and now my son has died in the same way." The Master said, "Why do you not leave the place?" The answer was, "There is no oppressive government here." The Master then said, "Remember this, my children: oppressive government is more terrible than tigers." '

The subject of this paper is the problem of ensuring that government shall be *less* terrible than tigers.

The problem of the taming of power is, as the above quotation shows, a very ancient one. The Taoists thought it insoluble, and advocated anarchism; the Confucians trusted to a certain ethical and governmental training which should turn the holders of power into sages endowed with moderation and benevolence. At the same period, in Greece, democracy, oligarchy, and tyranny were contending for mastery; democracy was intended to check abuses of power, but was perpetually defeating itself by falling a victim to the temporary popularity of some demagogue. Plato, like Confucius, sought the solution in a government of men trained to wisdom. This view has been revived by Mr. and Mrs. Sidney Webb, who admire an oligarchy in which power is confined to those who have the 'vocation of leadership.' In the interval between Plato and the Webbs, the world has tried military autocracy, theocracy, hereditary monarchy, oligarchy, democracy, and the Rule of the Saints—the last of these, after the failure of Cromwell's experiment, having been revived in our day by Lenin, Mussolini, and Hitler. All this suggests that our problem has not yet been solved.

To anyone who studies either history or human nature, it must be evident that democracy, while not a complete solution, is an essential part of the solution. The complete solution is not to be found by confining ourselves to political conditions; we must take account also of economics, of propaganda, and of psychology as affected by circumstances and education. Our subject thus divides itself into four parts: (1) political conditions, (2) economic conditions, (3) propaganda conditions, and (4) psychological and educational conditions. Let us take these in succession.

The merits of democracy are negative: it does not ensure good government,

[1]From *Power* by Bertrand Russell (1938), published by W. W. Norton & Company, Inc.

but it prevents certain evils. Until women began to take part in political affairs, married women had no control over their own property, or even over their own earnings; a charwoman with a drunken husband had no redress if he prevented her from using her wages for the support of her children. The oligarchical Parliament of the eighteenth and early nineteenth centuries used its legislative power to increase the wealth of the rich by depressing the condition of both rural and urban labor. Only democracy has prevented the law from making trade-unionism impossible. But for democracy, Western America, Australia, and New Zealand would be inhabited by a semi-servile yellow population governed by a small white aristocracy. The evils of slavery and serfdom are familiar, and wherever a minority has a secure monopoly of political power the majority is likely to sink, sooner or later, into either slavery or serfdom. All history shows that, as might be expected, minorities cannot be trusted to care for the interests of majorities.

There is a tendency, as strong now as at any former time, to suppose that an oligarchy is admirable if it consists of 'good' men. The government of the Roman Empire was 'bad' until Constantine, and then it became 'good.' In the Book of Kings, there were those who did right in the sight of the Lord, and those who did evil. In English history as taught to children, there are 'good' kings and 'bad' kings. An oligarchy of Jews is 'bad,' but one of Nazis is 'good.' The oligarchy of Tsarist aristocrats was 'bad,' but that of the Communist Party is 'good.'

This attitude is unworthy of grown-up people. A child is 'good' when it obeys orders, and 'naughty' when it does not. When it grows up and becomes a political leader, it retains the ideas of the nursery, and defines the 'good' as those who obey its orders and the 'bad' as those who defy it.

Such a point of view, if taken seriously, makes social life impossible. Only force can decide which group is 'good' and which 'bad,' and the decision, when made, may at any moment be upset by an insurrection. Neither group, if it attains power, will care for the interests of the other, except in so far as it is controlled by the fear of rousing rebellion. Social life, if it is to be anything better than tyranny, demands a certain impartiality. But since, in many matters, collective action is necessary, the only practicable form of impartiality, in such matters, is the rule of the majority.

Democracy, however, though necessary, is by no means the only political condition required for the taming of power. It is possible, in a democracy, for the majority to exercise a brutal and wholly unnecessary tyranny over a minority. In the period from 1885 to 1922, the government of the United Kingdom was (except for the exclusion of women) democratic, but that did not prevent the oppression of Ireland. Not only a national, but a religious or political minority may be persecuted. The safeguarding of minorities, so far as is compatible with orderly government is an essential part of the taming of power.

This requires a consideration of the matters regarding which the community must act as a whole, and those regarding which uniformity is unnecessary. The most obvious questions concerning which a collective decision is imperative are those that are essentially geographical. Roads, railways, sewers, gas mains, and so on, must take one course and not another. Sanitary precautions, say against plague or rabies, are geographical: it would not do for Christian Scientists to announce that they will take no precautions against infection, because they might infect others.

Where there is a geographically concentrated minority, such as the Irish before 1922, it is possible to solve a great many problems by devolution. But when the minority is distributed throughout the area concerned, this method is largely inapplicable. Where Christian and Mohammedan populations live side by side, they have, it is true, different marriage laws, but except where religion is concerned they all have to submit to one government. It has been gradually discovered that theological uniformity is not necessary to a State, and that Protestants and Catholics can live peaceably together under one government. But this was not the case during the first one hundred and thirty years after the Reformation.

The question of the degree of liberty that is compatible with order is one that cannot be settled in the abstract. The only thing that can be said in the abstract is that, where there is no technical reason for a collective decision, there should be some strong reason connected with public order if freedom is to be interfered with. In the reign of Elizabeth, when Roman Catholics wished to deprive her of the throne, it is not surprising that the government viewed them with disfavor. Similarly in the Low Countries, where Protestants were in revolt against Spain, it was to be expected that the Spaniards would persecute them. Nowadays theological questions have not the same political importance. Even political differences, if they do not go too deep, are no reason for persecution. Conservatives, Liberals, and Labor people can all live peaceably side by side, because they do not wish to alter the Constitution by force; but Fascists and Communists are more difficult to assimilate. Where there is democracy, attempts of a minority to seize power by force, and incitements to such attempts, may reasonably be forbidden, on the ground that a law-abiding majority has a right to a quiet life if it can secure it.

I come now to the economic conditions required in order to minimize arbitrary power. This subject is of great importance, both on its own account and because there has been a very great deal of confusion of thought in relation to it.

Political democracy, while it solves a part of our problem, does not by any means solve the whole. Marx pointed out that there could be no real equalization of power through politics alone, while economic power remained monarchical or oligarchic. It followed that economic power must be in the hands of the State, and that the State must be democratic. Those who profess, at the present day, to be Marx's followers have kept only the half of his doctrine, and have thrown over the demand that the State should be democratic. They have thus concentrated both economic and political power in the hands of an oligarchy, which has become, in consequence, more powerful and more able to exercise tyranny than any oligarchy of former times.

Both old-fashioned democracy and new-fashioned Marxism have aimed at the taming of power. The former failed because it was only political, the latter because it was only economic. Without a combination of both, nothing approaching to a solution of the problem is possible.

The arguments in favor of state ownership of land and the large economic organizations are partly technical, partly political. The technical arguments have not been much stressed except by the Fabian Society, and to some extent in America in connection with such matters as the Tennessee Valley Authority. Nevertheless they are very strong, especially in connection with electricity and water power, and cause even Conservative governments to introduce measures which, from a technical point of view, are socialistic. We have seen how, as a result of modern technique, organizations tend to grow and to coalesce and to increase their scope; the inevitable consequence is that the political State must either increasingly take over economic functions or partially abdicate in favor of vast private enterprises which are sufficiently powerful to defy or control it. If the State does not acquire supremacy over such enterprises, it becomes their puppet, and they become the real State. In one way or another, wherever modern technique exists, economic and political power must become unified. This movement towards unification has the irresistible impersonal character which Marx attributed to the development that he prophesied. But it has nothing to do with the class war or the wrongs of the proletariat.

Socialism as a political movement has aimed at furthering the interests of industrial wage earners; its technical advantages have been kept comparatively in the background. The belief is that the economic power of the private capitalist enables him to oppress the wage earner, and that since the wage earner cannot, like the handicraftsman of former times, individually own his means of production, the only way of emancipating him is collective ownership by the whole body of workers. It is argued that if the private capitalist were expropriated the whole body of the workers would constitute the State; and that consequently the problem of economic power can be solved completely by state ownership of land and capital, and in no other way.

Before examining the argument, I wish to say unequivocally that I consider it valid, provided it is adequately safeguarded and amplified. *Per contra*, in the absence of such safeguarding and amplifying I consider it very dangerous, and likely to mislead those who seek liberation from economic tyranny so completely that they will find they have inadvertently established a new tyranny at once economic and political, more drastic and more terrible than any previously known.

In the first place, 'ownership' is not the same thing as 'control.' If, say, a railway is owned by the State, and the State is considered to be the whole body of the citizens, that does not ensure, of itself, that the average citizen will have any power over the railway. Let us revert, for a moment, to what Messrs. Berle and Means say in *The Modern Corporation and Private Property* about ownership and control in large American corporations. They point out that in the majority of such corporations all the directors together usually own only about one or two per cent of the stock, and yet, in effect, have complete control:—

In the election of the board the stockholder ordinarily has three alternatives. He can refrain from voting, he can attend the annual meeting and personally vote his stock, or he can sign a proxy transferring his voting power to certain individuals selected by the management of the corporation, the proxy committee. As his personal vote will count for little or nothing at the meeting unless he has a very large block of stock, the stockholder is practically reduced to the alternative of not voting at all or else of *handing over his vote to individuals over whom he has no control and in whose selection he did not participate.* In neither case will he be able to exercise any measure of control. Rather, control will tend to be in the hands of those who select the proxy committee. . . . Since the proxy committee is appointed by the existing management, the latter can virtually dictate their own successors.

The helpless individuals described in the above passage are, it should be noted, not proletarians, but capitalists. They are part owners of the corporation concerned, in the sense that they have legal rights which may, with luck, bring them in a certain income; but, owing to their lack of control, the income is very precarious. When I first visited the United States in 1896, I was struck by the enormous number of railways that were bankrupt; on inquiry, I found that this was not due to incompetence on the part of directors, but to skill: the investments of ordinary shareholders had been transferred, by one device or another, to other companies in which the directors had a large interest. This was a crude method, and nowadays matters are usually managed in a more decorous fashion, but the principle remains the same. In any large corporation, power is necessarily less diffused than ownership, and carries with it advantages which, though at first political, can be made sources of wealth to an indefinite extent. The humble investor can be politely and legally robbed; the only limit is that he must not have such bitter experiences as to lead him to keep his future savings in a stocking.

The situation is in no way essentially different when the State takes the place of a corporation; indeed, since it is the size of the corporation that causes the helplessness of the average stockholder, the average citizen is likely to be still more helpless as against the State. A battleship is public property, but if, on this ground, you try to exercise rights of ownership, you will be soon put in your place. You have a remedy, it is true: at the next General Election you can vote for a candidate who favors a reduction in the Navy Estimates, if you can find one; or you can write to the papers to urge that sailors should be more polite to sight-seers. But more than this you cannot do.

But, it is said, the battleship belongs to a capitalist State, and when it belongs to a workers' State everything will be different. This view seems to me to show a failure to grasp the fact that economic power is now a matter of government rather than ownership. If the United States Steel Corporation, say, were taken over by the United States Government, it would still need men to manage it; they would be either the same men who now manage it or men with similar abilities and a similar outlook. The attitude which they now have towards the shareholders they would then have towards the citizens. True, they would be subject to the government, but, unless it was democratic and responsive to public opinion, it would have a point of view closely similar to that of the officials.

Marxists, having retained, as a result of the authority of Marx and Engels, many ways of thinking that belong to the forties of last century, still conceive of businesses as if they belonged to individual capitalists, and have not learned the lessons to be derived from the separation of ownership and control. The important person is the man who has control of economic power, not the man who has a fraction of the nominal ownership. The Prime Minister does not own No. 10 Downing Street, and Bishops do not own their palaces; but it would be absurd to pretend, on this account, that they are no better off than the average wage earner. Under any form of socialism which is not democratic, those who control economic power can, without 'owning' anything, have palatial official residences, the use of the best cars, a princely entertainment allowance, holidays at the public expense in official holiday resorts, and so on and so on. And why should they have any more concern for the ordinary worker than those in control have now? There can be no reason why they should have, unless the ordinary worker has power to deprive them of their positions. Moreover the subordination of the small investor in existing large corporations shows how easy it is for the official to overpower the democracy, even when the 'democracy' consists of capitalists.

Not only, therefore, is democracy essential if state ownership and control of economic enterprises are to be in any degree advantageous to the average citizen, but it will have to be an effective democracy and this will be more difficult to secure than it is at present, since the official class will, unless very carefully supervised, combine the powers at present possessed by the government and the men in control of industry and finance, and since the means of agitating against the government will have to be supplied by the government itself, as the sole owner of halls, paper, and all the other essentials of propaganda.

While, therefore, public ownership and control of all large-scale industry and finance is a necessary condition for the taming of power, it is far from being a sufficient condition. It needs to be supplemented by a democracy more thoroughgoing, more carefully safeguarded against official tyranny, and with more careful provision for freedom of propaganda, than any purely political democracy that has ever existed.

I come now to the propaganda conditions for the taming of power. It is obvious that publicity for grievances must be possible; agitation must be free provided it does not incite to breaches of the law; there must be ways of impeaching officials who exceed or abuse their powers. The government of the day must not be in a position to secure its own permanence by intimidation, falsification of the register of electors, or any similar method. There must be no penalty, official or unofficial, for any well-grounded criticism of prominent men. Much of this, at present, is secured by party government in democratic countries, which causes the politicians in power to be objects of hostile criticism by nearly half the nation. This makes it impossible for them to commit many crimes to which they might otherwise be prone.

All this is more important when the State has a monopoly of economic power than it is under capitalism, since the power of the State will be vastly augmented. Take a concrete case: that of women employed in the public service. At present they have a grievance, because their rates of pay are lower than those of men; they have legitimate ways of making their grievance known, and it would not be safe to penalize them for making use of these ways. There is no reason whatever for supposing that the present inequality would necessarily cease with the adoption of socialism, but the means of agitating about it would cease, unless express provision were made for just such cases. Newspapers and printing presses would all belong to the government, and would print only what the government ordered.

Can it be assumed as certain that the government would print attacks on its own policy? If not, there would be no means of political agitation by way of print. Public meetings would be just as difficult, since the halls would all belong to the government. Consequently, unless careful provision were made for the express purpose of safeguarding political liberty, no method would exist of making grievances known, and the government, when once elected, would be as omnipotent as Hitler, and could easily arrange for its own re-election to the end of time. Democracy might survive as a form, but would have no more reality than the forms of popular government that lingered on under the Roman Empire.

To suppose that irresponsible power, just because it is called Socialist or Communist, will be freed miraculously from the bad qualities of all arbitrary power in the past is mere childish nursery psychology; the wicked prince is ousted by the good prince, and all is well. If a prince is to be trusted, it must be not because he is 'good,' but because it is against his interest to be 'bad.' To ensure that this shall be the case is to make power innocuous; but it cannot be rendered innocuous by transforming men whom we believe to be 'good' into irresponsible despots.

The British Broadcasting Corporation is a state institution which shows what is possible in the way of combining freedom of propaganda with government monopoly. At such a time as that of the General Strike, it must be admitted, it ceases to be impartial; but at ordinary times it represents different points of view, as nearly as may be, in proportion to their numerical strength. In a Socialist State, similar arrangements for impartiality would have to be made in regard to the hiring of halls for meetings and the printing of controversial literature. It might be found desirable, instead of having different newspapers representing different points of view, to have only one, with different pages allocated to different parties. This would have the advantage that readers would see all opinions, and would tend to be less one-sided than those who, at present, never see in a newspaper anything with which they disagree.

There are certain regions, such as art and science, and (so far as public order allows) party politics, where uniformity is not necessary or even desirable. These are the legitimate sphere of competition, and it is important that public feeling should be such as to bear differences on such matters without exasperation. Democracy, if it is to succeed and endure, demands a tolerant spirit, not too much hate, and not too much love of violence. But this brings us to the psychological conditions for the taming of power.

213

The psychological conditions for the taming of power are in some ways the most difficult. Fear, rage, and all kinds of violent collective excitement tend to make men blindly follow a leader, who in most cases takes advantage of their trust to establish himself as a tyrant. It is therefore important, if democracy is to be preserved, both to avoid the circumstances that produce general excitement and to educate in such a way that the population shall be little prone to moods of this sort. When a spirit of ferocious dogmatism prevails, any opinion with which men disagree is liable to provoke a breach of the peace. Schoolboys are apt to illtreat a boy whose opinions are in any way odd, and many grown men have not got beyond the mental age of schoolboys. A diffused liberal sentiment, tinged with skepticism, makes social cooperation much less difficult, and liberty correspondingly more possible.

Revivalist enthusiasm, such as that of the Nazis, rouses admiration in many through the energy and apparent self-abnegation that it generates. Collective excitement, involving indifference to pain and even to death, is historically not uncommon. Where it exists, liberty is impossible. The enthusiasts can only be restrained by force, and if they are not restrained they will use force against others. I remember a Bolshevik whom I met in Peking in 1920, who marched up and down the room exclaiming with complete truth, 'If vee do not keel zem, zey vill keel us!' The existence of this mood on one side of course generates the same mood on the other side; the consequence is a fight to a finish, in which everything is subordinated to victory. During the fight, the government acquires despotic power for military reasons; at the end, if victorious, it uses its power first to crush what remains of the enemy, and then to secure the continuance of its dictatorship over its own supporters. The result is something quite different from what was fought for by the enthusiasts. Enthusiasm, while it can achieve certain results, can hardly ever achieve those that it desires. To admire collective enthusiasm is reckless and irresponsible, for its fruits are fierceness, war, death, and slavery.

War is the chief promoter of despotism, and the greatest obstacle to the establishment of a system in which irresponsible power is avoided as far as possible. The prevention of war is therefore an essential part of our problem— I should say, the most essential. I believe that if once the world were free from the fear of war, under no matter what form of government or what economic system, it would in time find ways of curbing the ferocity of its rulers. On the other hand all war, but especially modern war, promotes dictatorship by causing the timid to seek a leader and by converting the bolder spirits from a society into a pack.

The risk of war causes a certain kind of mass psychology, and reciprocally this kind, where it exists, increases the risk of war, as well as the likelihood of despotism. We have therefore to consider the kind of education which will make societies least prone to collective hysteria, and most capable of successfully practising democracy.

Democracy, if it is to succeed, needs a wide diffusion of two qualities which seem, at first sight, to tend in opposite directions. On the one hand men must have a certain degree of self-reliance and a certain willingness to back their own judgment; there must be political propaganda in opposite directions, in which many people take part. But on the other hand men must be willing to submit to the decision of the majority when it goes against them. Either of these conditions may fail; the population may be too submissive, and may follow a vigorous leader into dictatorship; or each party may be too self-assertive, with the result that the nation falls into anarchy.

If democracy is to be workable, the population must be as far as possible free from hatred and destructiveness, and also from fear and subservience. These feelings may be caused by political or economic circumstances, but what I want to consider is the part that education plays in making men more or less prone to them.

Some parents and some schools begin with the attempt which is almost bound to produce either a slave or a rebel, neither of which is what is wanted in a democracy. As to the effects of a severely disciplinary education, the view that I hold is held by all the dictators of Europe. After the war, almost all the countries of Europe had a number of free schools, without too much discipline or too much show of respect for the teachers; but one by one the military autocracies, including the Soviet Republic, have suppressed all freedom in schools and have gone back to the old drill, and to the practice of treating the teacher as a miniature Führer or Duce. The dictators, we may infer, all regard a certain degree of freedom in school as the proper training for democracy, and autocracy in school as the natural prelude to autocracy in the State.

Every man and woman in a democracy should be neither a slave nor a rebel, but a citizen—that is, a person who has, and allows to others, a due proportion, but no more, of the governmental mentality. Where democracy does not exist, the governmental mentality is that of masters towards dependents; but where there is democracy it is that of equal cooperation, which involves the assertion of one's own opinion up to a certain point, but no further.

This brings us to a source of trouble to many democrats—namely, what is called 'principle.' Most talk about principle, self-sacrifice, heroic devotion to a cause, and so on, should be scanned somewhat skeptically. A little psychoanalysis will often show that what goes by these fine names is really something quite different, such as pride, or hatred, or desire for revenge, that has become idealized and collectivized and personified as a noble form of idealism. The warlike patriot, who is willing and even anxious to fight for his country, may reasonably be suspected of a certain pleasure in killing. A kindly population, a population who in their childhood had received kindness and been made happy, and who in youth had found the world a friendly place, would not develop that particular sort of idealism called patriotism, or class war, or what not, which consists in joining together to kill people in large numbers. I think the tendency to cruel forms of idealism is increased by unhappiness in childhood, and would be lessened if early education were emotionally what it ought to be. Fanaticism is a defect which is partly emotional, partly intellectual; it needs to be combated by the kind of happiness that makes men kindly, and the kind of intelligence that produces a scientific habit of mind.

The temper required to make a success of democracy is, in the practical life, exactly what the scientific temper is in the intellectual life; it is a halfway house between skepticism and dogmatism. Truth, it holds, is neither completely attainable nor completely unattainable; it is attainable, to a certain degree, and that only with difficulty.

Autocracy, in its modern forms, is always combined with a creed; that of Hitler, that of Mussolini, or that of Stalin. Wherever there is autocracy, a set of beliefs is instilled into the minds of the young before they are capable of thinking, and these beliefs are taught so constantly and so persistently that it is hoped the pupils will never afterwards be able to escape from the hypnotic effect of their early lessons. The beliefs are instilled, not by giving any reason for supposing them true, but by parrotlike repetition, by mass hysteria and mass suggestion. When two opposite creeds have been taught in this fashion, they produce two armies which clash, not two parties that can discuss. Each hypnotized automaton feels that everything most sacred is bound up with the victory of his side, everything most horrible exemplified by the other side. Such fanatical factions cannot meet in Parliament and say, 'Let us see which side has the majority'; that would be altogether too pedestrian, since each side stands for a sacred cause. This sort of dogmatism must be prevented if dictatorships are to be avoided, and measures for preventing it ought to form an essential part of education.

If I had control of education, I should expose children to the most vehement and eloquent advocates on all sides of every topical question, who should speak to the schools from the B.B.C. The teacher should afterwards invite the children to summarize the arguments used, and should gently insinuate the view that eloquence is inversely proportional to solid reason. To acquire immunity to eloquence is of the utmost importance to the citizens of a democracy.

Modern propagandists have learned from advertisers, who led the way in the technique of producing irrational belief. Education should be designed

to counteract the natural credulity and the natural incredulity of the uneducated; the habit of believing an emphatic statement without reasons, and of
disbelieving an unemphatic statement even when accompanied by the best of
reasons. I should begin in the infant school, with two classes of sweets between
which the children should choose; one very nice, recommended by a coldly
accurate statement as to its ingredients; the other very nasty, recommended by
the utmost skill of the best advertisers. A little later I should give them a
choice of two places for a country holiday; a nice place recommended by a
contour map, and an ugly place recommended by magnificent posters.

The teaching of history ought to be conducted in a similar spirit. There
have been in the past eminent orators and writers who defended, with an
appearance of great wisdom, positions which no one now holds: the reality of
witchcraft, the beneficence of slavery, and so on. I should cause the young to
know such masters of eloquence, and to appreciate at once their rhetoric and
their wrong-headedness. Gradually I should pass on to current questions. As
a sort of *bonne bouche* to their history, I should read to them what is said about
Spain (or whatever at the moment is most controversial), first by the *Daily
Mail*, then by the *Daily Worker*; and I should then ask them to infer what
really happened. For undoubtedly few things are more useful to a citizen of a
democracy than skill in detecting, by reading newspapers, what it was that
took place. For this purpose it would be instructive to compare the newspapers
at crucial moments during the Great War with what subsequently appeared
in the official history. And when the madness of war hysteria, as shown in the
newspapers of the time, strikes your pupils as incredible, you should warn
them that all of them, unless they are very careful to cultivate a balanced and
cautious judgment, may fall overnight into a similar madness at the first
touch of government incitement to terror and blood lust.

I do not wish, however, to preach a purely negative emotional attitude.
I am not suggesting that all strong feelings should be subjected to destructive
analysis. I am advocating this attitude only in relation to those emotions which
are the basis of collective hysteria, for it is collective hysteria that facilitates
wars and dictatorships. But wisdom is not *merely* intellectual: Intellect may
guide and direct, but does not generate the force that leads to action. The
force must be derived from the emotions. Emotions that have desirable social
consequences are not so easily generated as hate and rage and fear. In their
creation, much depends upon early childhood; much, also, upon economic circumstances. Something, however, can be done, in the course of ordinary education, to provide the nourishment upon which the better emotions can grow,
and to bring about the realization of what may give value to human life.

This has been, in the past, one of the purposes of religion. The churches, however, have also had other purposes, and their dogmatic basis causes difficulties. For those to whom traditional religion is no longer possible, there are other ways. Some find what they need in music, some in poetry. For some others, astronomy serves the same purpose. When we reflect upon the size and antiquity of the stellar universe, the controversies on this rather insignificant planet lose some of their importance, and the acerbity of our disputes seems a trifle ridiculous. And when we are liberated by this negative emotion we are able to realize more fully, through music or poetry, through history or science, through beauty or pain, that the really valuable things in human life are individual, not such things as happen on a battlefield or in the clash of politics or in the regimented march of masses of men towards an externally imposed goal. The organized life of the community is necessary, but it is necessary as mechanism, not something to be valued on its own account. What is of most value in human life is more analogous to what all the great religious teachers have spoken of. Those who believe in the Corporate State maintain that our highest activities are collective, whereas I should maintain that we all reach our best in different ways, and that the emotional unity of a crowd can only be achieved on a lower level.

The essential difference between the liberal outlook and that of the totalitarian State is that the former regards the welfare of the State as residing ultimately in the welfare of the individual, while the latter regards the State as the end and individuals merely as indispensable ingredients, whose welfare must be subordinated to a mystical totality which is a cloak for the interest of the rulers. Ancient Rome had something of the doctrine of State-worship, but Christianity fought the Emperors and ultimately won. Liberalism, in valuing the individual, is carrying on the Christian tradition; its opponents are reviving certain pre-Christian doctrines. From the first, the idolaters of the State have regarded education as the key to success. This appears, for example, in Fichte's *Addresses to the German Nation*, which deal at length with education. What Fichte desires is set forth in the following passage:—

If anyone were to say: 'How could anyone demand more of an education than that it should show the pupil the right and strongly recommend it to him; whether he follows these recommendations is his own affair, and if he does not do it, his own fault; he has free will, which no education can take from him': I should answer, in order to characterize more sharply the education I contemplate, that just in this recognition of and counting on the free will of the pupil lies the first error of education hitherto, and the distinct acknowledgment of its impotence and emptiness. For inasmuch as it admits that, after all its strongest operation, the will remains free,— that is, oscillating undecidedly between good and bad,—it admits that it neither can nor wishes to mould the will, or, since will is the essential root of man, man himself;

and that it holds this to be altogether impossible. The new education, on the contrary, would have to consist in a complete annihilation of the freedom of the will in the territory that it undertook to deal with.

His reason for desiring to create 'good' men is not that they are in themselves better than 'bad' men; his reason is that 'only in such [good men] can the German nation persist, but through bad men it will necessarily coalesce with foreign countries.'

All this may be taken as expressing the exact antithesis of what the liberal educator will wish to achieve. So far from 'annihilating the freedom of the will,' he will aim at strengthening individual judgment; he will instill what he can of the scientific attitude towards the pursuit of knowledge; he will try to make beliefs tentative and responsive to evidence; he will not pose before his pupils as omniscient, nor will he yield to the love of power on the pretense that he is pursuing some absolute good. Love of power is the chief danger of the educator, as of the politician; the man who can be trusted in education must care for his pupils on their own account, not merely as potential soldiers in an army or propagandists for a cause.

Fichte and the powerful men who have inherited his ideals, when they see children, think: 'Here is material that I can manipulate, that I can teach to behave like a machine in furtherance of my purposes; for the moment I may be impeded by joy of life, spontaneity, the impulse to play, the desire to live for purposes springing from within, not imposed from without; but all this, after the years of schooling that I shall impose, will be dead; fancy, imagination, art, and the power of thought will have been destroyed by obedience; the death of joy will have bred receptiveness to fanaticism; and in the end I shall find my human material as passive as stone from a quarry or coal from a mine. In the battles to which I shall lead them, some will die, some will live; those who die will die exultantly, as heroes, those who live will live on as my slaves, with that deep mental slavery to which my schools will have accustomed them.'

All this, to any person with natural affection for the young, is horrible; just as we teach children to avoid being destroyed by motorcars if they can, so we should teach them to avoid being destroyed by cruel fanatics, and to this end we should seek to produce independence of mind, somewhat skeptical and wholly scientific, and to preserve, as far as possible, the instinctive joy of life that is natural to healthy children. This is the task of a liberal education; to give a sense of the value of things other than domination, to help to create wise citizens of a free community, and, through the combination of citizenship with liberty in individual creativeness, to enable man to give to human life that splendor which some few have shown that it can achieve.

RUSSIA AND THE SOCIALIST IDEAL[1]

Max Eastman

THE Russian revolution has failed of its essential objectives. The "dictatorship of the proletariat," instead of providing a transition toward the "society of the free and equal," has led to a crude and bloody personal despotism resting on a privileged bureaucracy which exploits the wage worker much as he is exploited elsewhere. This is perhaps the greatest tragedy in human history, terrible in the breadth of its impact, terrible in the depth of its significance, terrible in its personal details. Other revolutionary martyrs have been permitted a heroic death. The heroes of the Russian revolution have been shot like dogs in the cellar and swept out with the refuse.

If this tragedy, when at last it is faced by loyal and thoughtful men, is not to throw them back into cynicism or despair it must be faced as the unhappy result of a legitimate experiment. To cry "Socialism is dead! Long live socialism!" may satisfy a momentary impulse but will not long sustain a thinking will. When an experiment fails, intelligence demands that we re-examine the theory upon which it was constructed and rectify this in the light of the result. The whole result of the Russian development is of course not yet in sight, but plenty is in sight to show that it will have little in common with the aims of socialists, whether utopian or scientific. Plenty is in sight to warrant a re-examination of the principles from which it set out.

Trotsky, the ablest exponent of the theory and natural critic of the experiment, declines to take this step. In *The Revolution Betrayed* he raises the question of "radically revising our traditional views of the socialist society," but only to decide against it. Asserting that the prodigious success of the Soviet Union in increasing production has demonstrated the "practicability of socialist methods," he blames its equally prodigious failure to show the beginnings of freedom and equality upon "lack of the means of subsistence resulting from the low productivity of labor" in a backward country. That and the "tardiness" of the revolution in more advanced countries are for him adequate explanations of the whole disaster. And he has drawn the vigorous moral: "All those for whom the word 'socialism' is not a hollow sound but the content of their moral life—forward!"

Socialism is not the content of my moral life. I have always regarded socialism as an effort to solve a specific problem, and one only of the engrossing problems that confront our human nature. And this perhaps emboldens me to perceive a little more adequately than Trotsky does the scope and significance of the Russian failure. I do not believe either in the Marxian legend of

[1]From *Harper's Magazine*, March, 1938.

universal "upward" evolution which supports him in his somewhat cursory reaction to this collapse of our hopes. Moreover, I am completely detached from party struggle and not vitally concerned about revolutionary prestige. I am in a position to regard Stalin and his dictatorship not as an enemy, but as a result. For these reasons, although not in some ways equipped as Trotsky is for the task, I am going to suggest what seem to me the main points in that "revision of our traditional views" which he declines to make.

I have spoken of the Russian revolution as an experiment. But it was not an experiment to those believers in the Marxian philosophy who stood at the head of it. To them it was a step in a general process of whose "historic necessity" they were convinced in advance. Only its details were experimental. A great many of their miscalculations were due to this fact, so many that we must begin our revision of the socialist theory by removing from it this element of philosophical belief. We must restate the theory in the form of hypothesis before we can revise it with a free mind in the light of experiment.

Marx inherited his philosophical belief from Hegel. It is a belief that the world is evolving of its own necessary motion, and by a "dialectic" procedure, "from the lower to the higher." He attributed this kind of evolution to a world which he called, in opposition to Hegel, material. But he did not, and could not, define the word "higher" merely in a material sense. He meant by "higher" more ideal.[2] And the ideal he had in mind, so far as concerns human society, was that of the utopian socialists. It is the simple conception of men living together reasonably, generously, and justly, without class exploitation, without war, and with freedom for everybody and a fair chance to grow. Such a state of affairs is approximated in any good-natured and happily situated family, and that is why it seems so natural a hope for humanity at large. The Christian evangel and the doctrine of "natural rights" have made it seem still more axiomatic to many minds.

Marx assumed, on no other basis but a turning other side up of Hegel's philosophy, that the world about him was in process of realizing this ideal. He was studious both of books and events; he was rich in ideas; he made many contributions to knowledge; but he never questioned that assumption. He never, therefore, really tried to prove it. The essential labor of his mind was to discover how a material and yet dialectic world would evolve from capitalism toward a "society of the free and equal," and to find his place and that of all

[2]Engels, in an exposition of their common philosophy read and endorsed by Marx, replaced the word "higher" in eulogizing the dialectic universe by "more magnificent." "The celestial bodies, like the formations of the organisms . . . arise and perish and the courses that they run . . . take on eternally more magnificent dimensions."

serious-minded socialists in the process. And the result of his labor, to summarize it briefly and therefore inadequately, was this:

A dialectic process, according to Hegel, is a process of advance by inner conflict or self-contradiction, and the resolution of this conflict in a "higher unity." In human society this inner conflict is to be found in the economic phenomenon of class struggle. And in modern society it is to be found in the struggle, not so well known in Marx's time, of the proletariat against the capitalists. It is this new struggle which is destined to resolve itself in the higher unity foreseen and advocated in so detached and impractical a manner by the utopian socialists. The ideas of the utopians are, indeed, only a "symptom" in the mental world of this approaching material change. The mere development of the technic of production will bring it about "with iron necessity" that the workers will seize the power, expropriate the capitalists, and "socialize" the means of production. A period of proletarian dictatorship must intervene, but this dictatorship will inevitably die away as the new and higher form of social life emerges. Nobody can describe this "higher social form" in detail, but obviously it will be that "society of the free and equal" which is striven after in so soft and foolishly impractical a way by the utopian socialists.

The way to strive after it is to join the harsh struggle of the workers against the capitalists, make the struggle revolutionary, make it "conscious of its destiny," make it lead as rapidly as possible to the seizure of power, the inauguration of class dictatorship, and the beginning of the process of socialization.

That is the Marxian theory stripped of the prodigious wealth of factual and ideational material which Marx and his followers have brought under it, or built into it, or remarkably illumined by means of it. It enables the Marxians, notwithstanding the extreme humaneness of their idea, to be hardheaded, realistic, ruthless, and even to a degree cynical, in their pursuit of the ideal. It is through clash and bloody conflict that society advances; good and evil are merely names for the two forces through whose contradiction "higher forms" are born. The only ultimate good in a world thus inevitably going upward through struggle is to be on the right side of the struggle. And the only valid knowledge is hostile criticism from the point of view of the class destined to conquer.

Marx believed that this ingenious philosophy, besides reconciling toughminded realism with tender-minded aspirations, removed the mystical or utopian element from such aspirations. He thought that, since he had attributed his ideals as end-terms to the natural evolution of a "material" world, it became perfectly sensible and scientific, and indeed a kind of super-science, to believe in them. But it is not sensible to take utopian aspirations out of your own head and attribute them to the external world. And no matter how much you disguise the process by calling the world "material," and by in-

222

voking the word *scientific*, it is not science to do this. It is just the opposite—religion. It is primitive, unverified, and unverifiable belief in what you want to have come true.

There exists no proof that the world is traveling of necessity and by its own motion toward something "higher" in the human sense—much less in the sense of the utopian socialists. To minds trained in experimental science the very pretense to know the "historically necessary" result of capitalist evolution, even did it not fall in so pat with the author's wishes, would have, if proposed today, the aspect of a grandiose delusion. The apparent success of the Russian revolution has given an adventitious prestige even among scientific minds to this austere pretense at knowledge. But the failure of the revolution will rapidly destroy it. Notwithstanding his notable contributions to science, Marx's system as a whole will be set down as wish-fulfillment thinking in a form as crude and antiquated as it is ingenious. Marx will take a place in history not unlike that of Rousseau—a man behind the highest scientific attitudes of his time but borne to great heights because he created a new *Weltanschauung*, and one which fell in with the passions, aims, and tactics of a great social movement.

The *Weltanschauung* will live forever, a priceless treasure, comparable to those of Sophocles, of Dante, of Aquinas, of Spinoza. The incidental contributions to verified knowledge will also live and be acknowledged. But as a system pretending to be scientific, and indeed to be a kind of super-science, Marxism will be laid away with Thomism, Calvinism, and the rest. The sole use science has for *isms* made out of a man's name is to ridicule subjective and unverified emotional beliefs. Only in a general return to medieval darkness could this romantic metaphysics, "saturated" as Trotsky truly says "with the optimism of progress," really conquer modern minds.

We have no certain knowledge where the world is going, whether "higher" or "lower." We have no knowledge how much we, any one or all of us, by taking thought can swerve it. But we care where it is going. And it does not seem impossible that by a process of experimentation, if we hold ourselves free to learn all we can from each experiment, we may succeed in drawing up some plan for arriving at a more reasonable and decent general form of social life.

What made the Marxian metaphysics so acceptable of course was that the *action* proposed by it seemed reasonable. Restated in the form of a working hypothesis, a plan to be tried out, Marxian socialism was as good as anything anybody in its epoch had to propose. So restated, it would read somewhat as follows:

223

The opinion of the utopian socialists, that men might live together in society much as they do in happy families, if land and the instruments of production were owned in common, and wealth justly distributed, is perfectly reasonable; the aim may be attained. It cannot be attained, however, by regarding present-day society as a unit and preaching to everybody the reasonableness of the idea. Society is too sharply divided into classes for that, and people in general react to ideas too much on a basis of class interest. That very fact, however, can be turned to account by those who believe in the socialist idea.

Let them enter into the present-day class struggle on the side of the exploited classes. The difficulties of capitalist production are such that crises are bound to occur. As foreign markets are used up these crises will become more and more severe and far-reaching. In some nation-wide and perhaps world-wide crisis if a political party having socialist aims and resting essentially on the workers has made adequate preparations, it will be possible to seize the political power by main force, expropriate the capitalists, and declare the land and instruments of production the common property of all.

After that, the processes of education and evangelism, so futile under the present class system, will become effective. Men are reasonable and malleable enough, and life will be enough happier in such a society, so that after a brief period of dictatorship by the new ruling class, co-operative relations will become established in custom and habit. No dictatorship, and in fact no public power whatever, will long be necessary. The state will quite naturally die away, and men will find themselves living together in large societies, and indeed ultimately all over the planet, in a state of equality and freedom, tolerance and mutual helpfulness.

This is the revolutionary socialist hypothesis, abridged and stripped of detail just as we stripped the Marxian dialectic theory. To persons buffaloed by intellectuality as such, it will sound more naive, but to those who know what thinking is, it is obviously more mature. And it indicates, of course, the same general line of action:

Join the harsh struggle of the workers against the capitalists, make it revolutionary, make it conscious of its possibilities, make it lead as rapidly as possible to the seizure of power, the inauguration of class dictatorship, and the beginning of the process of socialization.

Only the substitution of *possibilities* for *destiny* differentiates the two programs. And yet in the long run the difference is deep between those who are consciously trying out an hypothesis based upon quantitative judgments and probability and those who conceive themselves as co-operating with a process expressing the ultimate nature of the universe, and who assume that their destined goal is knowable on other grounds than the experiment itself. It is as deep a difference as can separate two minds interested in the same project.

Some people think that only the religiously believing minds will be resolute enough to wage a serious struggle. But the evidence of history is against them. Struggles of this kind have been waged, and waged with great violence— notably the American Revolution—with a clear sense of the hazards involved and no philosophy but naked resolution. Indeed, the characteristic function of optimistic systems of belief is not to sustain action, but to offer consolation when it is abandoned. The Mensheviks, in trying to postpone the proletarian revolution of 1917, were as much supported emotionally by their certainty of its ultimate triumph as the Bolsheviks were in speeding it on. Lenin himself, in all particular crises of action, explicitly rejected that sense of sure victory which in a more general way his philosophy gave him. "There is no situation," he asserted, "of which only one outcome is possible." And in the critical days before October he repeated in a thousand different variants the thought: "We must take the hazard of action now!"

Those who persuade themselves that in order to win a social struggle we must bandage our eyes and go in like blind bulls are worse than historical reactionaries. They are biological defeatists. Man has no superiority over the powers of nature but his intelligence, and any proposal to set a limit to the free growth and movement of that is an attack against man, no matter how accompanied with trumpets and triumphal banners. What has to be done with blinders on had better not be done.

Once the Marxian theory is restated as a working hypothesis, or in other words a simple plan of action, its chief defect becomes quite obvious. In any well-deliberated plan of action three elements can be distinguished: definition of the end to be attained, examination of the conditioning facts, and mode of procedure by which it is proposed to pass from the facts to the end. It is in the definition of the end that Marxism falls most obviously short of the standards of science, and it is of this only that the present article will treat.[3]

The fact is that Marx, owing to his belief that Reality-as-Such is a dialectic procedure toward something "higher," did not bother to define his end at all. He left that task to Reality-as-Such.

It is not a question [he said in early life] of putting through some utopian system, but of taking a conscious part in the process of social transformation which is going on before our very eyes.

To those able to identify science with an optimistic philosophy such a cavalier attitude to the crux of the practical problem seemed worthy to be

[3]Marxians will understand that I am reserving for future discussion the theory of history and the analysis of capitalism, as well as the class and party struggle toward proletarian dictatorship.

called scientific. And the whole mid-nineteenth century was so "saturated" with optimism that this was actually put across as scientific socialism. I have been bitterly criticized for calling Marxism a religion, and yet what is Marx actually saying in that famous sentence but this:

The way to avoid utopian schemes is to have no schemes at all—put forth your efforts in the right direction and leave the rest to God.

And he said the same thing a quarter of a century later when commenting on the Paris Commune:

The workers well know that in order to realize their own emancipation, and at the same time the higher form toward which the present society tends *by its own economic forces*, they will have to pass through long periods of struggle which will transform both circumstances and men. *They have no ideal to realize, they have only to set free the elements of the new society which the old bourgeois society carries in its womb.*[4] Italics mine.

Any engineer can tell you that the first thing to do if you want to build something is to make a blueprint. Specify what you are going to build. And be guided, moreover, from the first strokes of the pencil, by a consideration of the materials at your disposal. This does not mean of course that a scientific socialist should ignore the creativeness of future evolution or go foolishly into the details of an earthly paradise. He should, indeed, know that there will be no earthly paradise. Nor does it mean that science in general, when concerned with human society, can have the exactitude of physics or astronomy—or even of agronomics or expert stock-breeding. It does mean that when proposing to "build a new society" a scientific mind would raise the question what qualities in the material, human nature, can be relied upon to make it function successfully and hold together. Even the "utopian" socialists, Marx's predecessors in the early nineteenth century, had raised this question and attempted to answer it. Robert Owen began his career with a series of essays designed to prove that man's moral character is wholly due to external circumstances, and that given the proper environment, especially in early life, he will be as just, reasonable, and intelligent as a co-operative commonwealth demands. St. Simon relied upon a new and more brotherly-intelligent kind of religious feeling to accomplish the required change. Fourier wrote a whole psychology to establish that a passion of social attraction, which he called *Unitéisme*, would harmonize all

[4]This sentence provides perhaps the best refutation of those who, in the effort to hold up Marx's philosophy in the environment of modern science, have contrived to identify it with John Dewey's instrumental theory of ideas. No one who believed in that theory could conceivably write such a sentence.

226

other passions once conditions were established enabling us to function as our Maker had intended.

Marx never criticized these amateurish but obviously essential inquiries. He never said: "Well, let us look into this! What *is* there in human nature to give assurance that a society can really operate on the principle, 'From each according to his abilities, to each according to his needs'?"

To answer this question would have involved independent biological and psychological investigations. And Marx's system of philosophy made such investigations not only unnecessary, but, if you can believe it, impossible. Marx knew primarily on philosophic grounds—which is to say, on faith—that the present society "tends by its own economic forces" toward a "higher form," and he knew that this higher form was indicated in a rough way by the utopian socialists. In order to "know" that he had to make human nature a function of those economic forces. He had to "integrate" man, as he put it, in the economically evolving society.

The individual . . . has no real existence outside the milieu in which he lives, and in order to understand the true nature of man it is necessary to integrate him in society, in social life. . . .
All history is nothing but a continual transformation of human nature.

That is the whole of Marx's contribution to this primary problem. And it is of course no contribution at all. These statements are advertised by his disciples as a wondrous prevision of modern psychology with its emphasis upon the social nature of the brain and nervous system. And they are that, incidentally; Marx was full of wondrous previsions. But their essential function in his system was to make unnecessary, and impossible, *any* independent science of psychology. Marx was on this head less scientific, not more so, than his predecessors. And there is consequently just as much utopianism in his idea of the future society as in theirs. He merely discusses it less often and more sketchily.

"The workers have no ideal to realize, they have only to set free the elements of the new society . . ." and yet we may remark in passing that "in the higher phase of the Communist society . . . the limited horizon of capitalist right will be left behind entirely and society will inscribe upon its banners: *From each according to his abilities, to each according to his needs!*"

That in brief—and substantially in the words of Marx—is the Marxist's attitude toward his goal.

It must be remembered of course that this scheme of revolutionary metaphysics was devised before the birthday of modern psychology, and while biology was still speculative and sociology hardly imagined. It antedates Fechner and Herbert Spencer, Darwin and Huxley, and all the hardheaded fact-finders in these organic sciences. Marxism was in its own time and place a noble, as well as a fertile, intellectual construction. It does seem astonishing, however, that throughout these ninety years filled stupendously with advancing knowledge of life, and particularly of man's life and mind, not one Marxian has ever raised the simple question: Is human nature, as it has developed in the struggle for survival, sufficiently self-dependent and sufficiently co-operative, or sufficiently capable of self-dependence and malleable in a co-operative direction, so that a collectivization of property would actually lead to the society of the free and equal, the dying away of state power, the condition of felicity described in the formula: "From each according to his abilities, to each according to his needs"? Even Darwin's theory of species and of how their characters are determined did not provoke an inquiry on this head. It was only grabbed in as another evidence of the generality of upward evolution, a further proof that because of the nature of the universe —and never mind about man's nature!—we are bound to arrive at an earthly paradise.

Since the scientific socialists were never scientific enough to ask that simple preliminary question, it is natural that their first experiment should surprise them with a most conclusive, bloody, and implacable answer: No!

It is hardly necessary to go into the details of Stalin's murderous and hypocritical regime. It has been described as it looks to those who believed in the socialist ideal, and yet believe also in telling the bitter truth, by Andrew Smith in *I Was a Soviet Worker*; by Fred E. Beal, the Gastonia strike leader, in *Proletarian Journey*; by Boris Souvarine, first secretary of the French Communist Party, in his monumental book, *Staline, Aperçu Historique de Bolshevisme*; by Victor Serge in *Russia Twenty Years After*; by Trotsky in *The Revolution Betrayed*; and above all, for Americans, by Eugene Lyons in his candid and absorbing personal history, *Assignment in Utopia*.

That these truth-telling books by initiated minds are few, and are not always welcomed by publishers, need not cause any doubts of their reliability. After "socialization" was accomplished in Russia on paper, and after the revolution as a dynamic reality, a seizure of power by workers and peasants, was checkmated and its threat on the international field expressly withdrawn, the Western intelligentsia "went over" to Bolshevism almost in a body and with a very natural alacrity. For it is, alas, natural to an intelligentsia to want to believe with its mind in an extreme program and yet be assured in its heart that the program holds no serious threat to present adjustments. This wholesale conversion, just because safely belated, was impetuous and intense, and it involved an immense investment both of emotion and of intellectual prestige. Its momentum, therefore, is great, and one finds it almost as hard now to get liberals to confront the cruel facts about Stalin's regime as it was once to make the reactionary press print the glowing truth about Lenin and Trotsky and the Workers' State. Facts, as Lenin said, are stubborn things; the only things equally stubborn are those who will not see them.

Suffice it to say then, for those who hold their eyes open, that together with that collectivization or nationalization of the means of production which was supposed to emancipate the working class, and therewith make "all society" free, and permit the state to "die away," there has grown up as the substance of the state a caste or class of bureaucrats who have enslaved the proletariat more effectively than before, appropriating all that can well be taken of the increasing product of their labor, and depriving them of every means of protest, and that besides enslaving the proletariat, these bureaucrats have perfected the enslavement of "all society." Trotsky says boldly and truly, after describing socialism as "a classless society based upon solidarity and the harmonious satisfaction of all needs," that "in this fundamental sense there is not a hint of socialism in Russia." We might further say that there is not a hint of many of the liberties and equalities, to say nothing of the fraternities, which normally prevail under competitive capitalism. Indeed, although there is in some respects a greater equality, there is far less liberty in Russia than there was under the semi-feudal regime of the tzars. As to fraternity—or, in Marx's phrase, the rendering of "all the everyday relations of man to man perfectly intelligible and reasonable"—it is difficult to speak temperately. Bureaucratic usurpation and concealed class-rule have made Russia, so far as she is public and articulate politically, a nation of informers, spies, hypocrites, lickspittles, and mass-murderers. Her men and women of most noble and humane feeling are in jail or in exile or in concentration camps or in hiding or in traitors' graves or cowed into absolute silence. Human relations have, I dare say, never on a large scale sunk so low. The deliberate murder by starvation of four to six million peasants in the name of a "workers' and peasants' republic," and the wholesale execution in the name of the "complete triumph of socialism" of the sincerest and most clear-sighted leaders of the movement toward socialism, are but high points in a total system based on lies and held erect by cruelty and terror.

Any mind realistically devoted to the aims of socialism emerges from the library after reading the journals out of Stalin's Russia with the very feeling recorded by the socialist mechanic, Andrew Smith, on leaving the country itself after his years of service there:

As soon as we crossed the border it was as if we had suddenly been released from some dark, terrifying jail into the bright golden sunlight. The passengers broke out into lively conversation and ecstatic cries of joy, of freedom. They laughed, they cried, they sang.

It is impossible, after reading those journals, filled now these many months ago with shrieking rituals of obscene toadyism and insanely raging hate, to deny the extreme statement of Boris Souvarine in a recent article in *La Revue de Paris*:

All respect for man having disappeared, life and human dignity having lost their value, nothing moderates the bestiality of the strong and abasement of the weak. One sees no longer any limit to the savagery that has been unchained.

After such statements from others who made sacrifices to the cause of communism in Russia, Fred Beal seems cool and moderate when he says:

The more I saw of Russia, the more convinced I became that not only the homeless children but all the common people of the country were a nuisance to the Soviet Government.

Fred Beal declined a frank invitation to a career of luxury and self-deception as a Soviet bureaucrat, in order to come home to the United States and, with a twenty-year prison sentence standing against him, told the American workers the truth of what he saw. Although he can be criticized for publishing chapters of his book in the reactionary press, the book is honest and will bring no ultimate reward to him but self-respect.

I found [he says] that the Stalinist road leads to calamity and darkness. But I am as convinced as ever that there is another road to a free and classless humanity, a road which is worth the quest, and which can be found only by minds liberated from the worship of false gods and by spirits strong enough to face the truth.

Beal says significantly, speaking of the radical books he read in youth: "I could not understand Karl Marx." This inability of clear-headed Americans to understand Karl Marx is wholly due to the fact that Marx was constrained by his German philosophical training to keep up a perpetual pretense that his simple practical plan for changing the world was an abstruse, theoretical understanding of how the world is changing itself. Beal's innocence of this metaphysical hokum was an essential part of his preparation for the task of telling American workers the truth about Soviet Russia. He is far more reliable because of his naïve freedom to see a few unintellectualized vital facts than Trotsky is, with his colossal power to marshal all the facts, from the price of pig-iron to the forms of lyric poetry, within the framework of a romantic German philosophy.

In *The Revolution Betrayed*, Trotsky answers all the horrors to which the insurrection organized by him has led, with the assertion that socialism according to the Marxian theory was never supposed to be achieved in a single country, especially a backward one, and that the leaders of the Russian revolution thought of it only as a fuse to revolution in more advanced countries. He explains the absence of even a "hint of socialism" in Russia as due to her backward economy, low industrialization, low productivity of labor, lack of enough goods to go round, survival of "petty bourgeois psychology," etc., together with the pressure of world imperialism. He has very solemnly assured us (in an article in *Liberty*) that in America, because of her high industrial developments, "communism, far from being an intolerable bureaucratic tyranny and individual regimentation, will be the means of greater individual liberty and shared abundance. . . . Control over individual consumption—whether by money or administration—will no longer be necessary when there is more than enough of everything for everybody." Coming from a leader of the revolution, these statements are impressive, and I think Trotsky's Marxian analysis of the Soviet society in *The Revolution Betrayed* is a prodigious feat of intellect. The amount of free and fluid judgment he achieves within the framework of a rationalistic metaphysics is amazing—a tribute to his dexterity and the ingenuity of old Hegel. His sustained sense of human society as a process rather than a thing—the real wisdom concealed under the cant about "dialectic"—is also admirable. I find much truth too in his concrete demonstrations of the results of Russia's backwardness, and much empirical good sense in his insistence upon the interdependence of the nations in any basic economic change they make. The idea of capitalistic encirclement and the war danger—used by Stalinists to "blackmail the intellectuals and keep down the workers," as James T. Farrell truly says—is used by Trotsky with honesty and a just sense of its significance.

As to his essential thesis about Russia, however, I remain unconvinced. It is an exaggeration, in the first place, to say that the Russian revolution was always thought of by its leaders as an initiator of world revolution. In his most vigorous polemic against those who maintained that proletarian action should have been postponed in October because Russia was not yet "ripe" for socialism, Lenin never mentions the world revolution or the idea that socialism in Russia had to wait upon it. He says:

How utterly mechanical is that idea which they learned by heart during the development of western European social democracy, that we in Russia have not yet grown up to socialism, that we lack—as various learned gentlemen among them express it—the objective economic premises for socialism. . . .

If the creation of socialism demands a definite level of culture (although nobody can say just exactly what that definite level is) then why can we not begin by winning with a revolution the premises for that definite level of culture, and then afterward on the basis of the workers' and peasants' power and the soviet structure, set out to catch up to the other peoples? . . .

Trotsky is of course wholly right in insisting that Lenin's Marxian policies demand the continued support of world revolution. He is wrong, however, in my opinion, when he implies that Lenin's hopes would not have been tragically disappointed by the developments in Russia even as an isolated proletarian state.

In the second place, Trotsky offers no real proof, except the tenets of the dialectic philosophy, that the sole decisive cause within Russia of the failure of socialist hopes is her backward technic of production. Like all true Marxians, he builds that fact into, or up under, all the failures in every phase of the national life. And like all true Marxians, he ignores in doing this the very existence of the hereditary nature of man. No independent psychological or biological problems exist for him. Developments that to the most ordinary shrewd good sense reveal a conflict between Marxian theory and the universal attributes of human nature are attributed by him to survivals in a backward country of a "petty bourgeois psychology." The Marxian romantic idealization of the proletariat—based on no study of its character, based solely on its metaphysical position in the dialectic schema as the progressive factor in an upward-going contradiction—becomes almost a wilful blindness in this book. The book is indeed "saturated" with optimism.

To my more skeptical and yet far from pessimistic mind, it seems obvious that if the socialist idea of a free and equal co-operative commonwealth emerging from the dictatorship of the proletariat were practical under an economy of abundance, we should find under an economy of scarcity some lame approximation to it. Instead of the germ of the Society of the Free and Equal, we find in Russia the perfected fruit of the Totalitarian State. We find that collective ownership of all wealth-producing capital makes it possible for a shrewd politician who gets hold of the state power to exercise a more absolute tyranny over the lives and minds of men than has been seen before. To the powers of an old-line political despot, he adds those of an apotheosized factory boss, and those of an armed Pope, an absolute censor of all printed or audibly spoken wish or opinion. And we find that this concentrated power is used—as indeed in the long run such power must be used—to restore in disguised forms the old system of class exploitation. That, it seems to me, is an already obvious lesson of the Russian revolution.

You can of course reply that the new bureaucracy and their privileges developed as rapidly as the process of collectivization, so that in reality "Socialism was never tried in Russia." The same thing is often said about Christianity, and I suppose always will be. There are people whose greatest need in life is a lost cause to believe in. And a lost cause surrounded by an edifice of scientifically plausible wish-fulfillment metaphysics, a kind of socio-economic Talmud in which to enjoy the delights of intellectual superiority and endless disputation, will unquestionably live forever. To a practical mind, however, the fact that after a completely successful revolution led by extreme and audacious Marxists, it proved impossible to show a "hint" of the authentic goal of Marxism can only suggest a drastic reconsideration—or rather, since that is the lamentable fact about it, a belated preliminary consideration—of the goal.

I said that there is just as much utopianism in Marx's ideal as in that of his predecessors. I will illustrate it with the following casual remark:

Socialism will abolish both architecture and barrow-pushing as professions, and the man who has given half an hour to architecture will also push the cart a little until his work as an architect is again in demand. It would be a pretty sort of socialism which perpetuated the business of barrow-pushing.

Other phrases which reveal the goal Marx had in mind, are these: "Society of the free and equal"; "leap from the Kingdom of Necessity to the Kingdom of Freedom"; disappearance of "the enslaving subordination of the individual under the division of labor"; "society by regulating the common production will make it possible for me to do this to-day and that to-morrow, to hunt in the morning, fish in the afternoon, carry on cattle-breeding in the evening . . . without becoming hunter, fisherman, or cattle-breeder"; disappearance of "the opposition between manual and intellectual labor"; "labor becomes not only a means of life, but the highest desire of life"; "from each according to his abilities, to each according to his needs"; "an association which will exclude classes and their antagonisms"; "the practical relations of everyday life [will] offer to man none but perfectly intelligible and reasonable relations to his fellow men and to nature."

All these aspirations, natural to anyone in a mood of wholesale revolt against the irrationality and meanness of human civilization, were lumped together by the Marxists, and for no other reason but that they are obviously unattainable under present conditions, asserted to be the necessary end-products of an evolving technic of production. And for good measure Marx

233

added in the early Christian, or anarchist, idea of getting along without any government. It was first said, I believe, by the Anabaptists and Diggers in the seventeenth century that if property were held in common no government would be necessary. And Marx, while telling us what a universe rising eternally of its own motion "from the lower to the higher" must ultimately arrive at, quite properly threw in this happy prospect too:

> There will no longer be political power, properly speaking, since political power is simply the official form of the antagonism in civil society.

Most of these formulae, if seriously considered in the light of present-day knowledge about human nature, can be thrown out offhand as fantastic. It hardly required the failure of the Russian revolution to inform modern minds that "labor" will never become, in the majority of mankind, the "highest desire of life"; that the opposition between manual and intellectual labor will never disappear; that no amount of collectivization can remove the division of labor or the subordination of the individual entailed by it; that the slogan "from each according to his abilities, to each according to his needs" is the very definition of utopia; that the conception of a "leap from the Kingdom of Necessity to the Kingdom of Freedom" is but a translation into this-worldly terms of the Christian myth of the resurrection; that the dream of man's having none but "perfectly intelligible and reasonable relations to his fellow-men and to nature" is also not of this world. And if there is a more preposterous notion in the history of religion than that of the "scientific socialists" that when the gigantic mechanism of a concentrated capitalist industry is taken over by a proletarian state, and the attempt made to operate it on a basis of revolutionary justice, the state will immediately begin to "die away," I do not know where it is to be found. It was only by not thinking about these things, that shrewd and hardheaded realists like Marx and Lenin managed to believe that they believed in them.

Our first step, then, must be to eliminate from our conception of the future society all those elements which require a belief in miracles, whether at the hands of the Divine Spirit or the Technic of Production. After that is done we shall still find that we have in hand a perfectly thoughtless combination of two opposing political principles which, if pushed to an extreme, are incompatible. And we shall find that they are not only pushed to an extreme by Marxists, but pushed to the absolute. The Jeffersonian ideal of freedom and rank individualism and as little government as possible arose in and—according to Marx's own ways of thinking—might seem properly to belong to an agrarian society without highly developed industries or big cities. The devel-

234

opment of these cities and industries has at any rate steadily forced this system into the background, and advanced into its place a system which stresses instead equality, co-operativeness, and governmental regulation for the good of all. Marxism ignores this vital contrast and this momentous change, one of the most momentous in the history of political thought.

Marxism simply tosses into its pot at the end of the rainbow of future history all the ideals in both systems, and as though that were not utopian enough, decrees that each and all are destined to be realized in as extreme a form as they can be conceived. Jefferson's shrewd and skeptical idea of very little government becomes in Marx's believing mind the total disappearance of the state. The healthy notion supported by Lincoln that a man is entitled to the product of his labor is dismissed by Marx as "bourgeois." In the society to which the dictatorship of the proletariat inevitably conducts, his dialectic faith assures us, men will not receive according to their labor but according to their needs. In my opinion anyone who, contemplating the results of the Russian revolution, can still dwell believingly in these myths of the absolute ideal is unwilling to learn and unfit to teach. It is not a matter for emotions, whether of loyalty or despair. It is not a question, as Trotsky thinks, of being "frightened by defeat" or "holding one's positions." It is a question of moving forward or being stuck in the mud. No mind not bold enough to reconsider the socialist hypothesis in the light of the Russian experiment can be called intelligent.

Russia's political ideals during her ten years of violent industrialization have passed through in fevered form the very development upon which ours spent a century. The freedom-individuality-and-less-government element has been forgotten, or deliberately withdrawn from circulation, and the equality-co-operation-and-state-regulation element tends to be presented as though it were the single aim for which the revolution had been fought. Lenin's writings in the months preceding the October revolution were filled with such expressions as these:

One must *build* democracy directly, from the bottom, on the initiative of the masses themselves, and with their active participation in the entire life of the state, without "supervision" from above, without officialdom. . . . Abolish the police, the bureaucracy and the standing army. Create a *militia* consisting of the whole people, women included, generally and universally armed. This is the practical business which should be launched without delay. The more initiative, variety, daring creativeness are brought into play by the masses, the better.

And in his little book on *Problems of Culture*, the first word on these problems after the revolution, Trotsky expressed the same view: "The revolution is above all an awakening of personality in those masses who have been heretofore condemned to be impersonal."

Only a few years after those lines were written, Mr. René Fülöp-Miller was able, with but his usual exaggeration, to attribute to Bolsheviks as such a belief that "the collective-impersonal is alone real and the separate existence of the single individual is an illusion." The ideals of initiative, variety, daring creativeness, awakened personality have now so far dropped from view that even a transplanted American like Anna Louise Strong can solemnly reproach me that I fail to understand what is going on in Russia because I have not learned the millennial art of "collective thinking."

One of the first problems, then, for a new and more scientific social movement is to effect an adjustment between the two conflicting halves of the socialist ideal. It might have been deduced by a process of meditation, if anybody had done any meditating on these subjects, that the concept of extreme individualism is in conflict with that of extreme co-operativeness. The Russian experiment provokes the further query: To what extent is the principle of equality, vigorously applied, incompatible with a vigorous assertion of personal freedom? The resurrection of the death-penalty for theft after all wealth-producing property had-been "socialized," must induce some reflection, it seems to me, beyond the remark that Russia's wealth-production is not high. It might well serve as a symbol of the thinking that we socialists have still to do.

If life is to have dignity and richness the principles of freedom and individualism must be sacredly preserved. That they arose in a pre-industrial era, and will be difficult to cherish in an industrial one, only makes this issue the more pressing. But if life is to flourish in an age of machinery and mass production, there must also be a new co-operativeness, one involving a new degree of discipline and subordination to the collective purpose, and to that end more state control than would have been good sense in the time of Jefferson.

One cannot of course revise his aim completely in independence of his definition of the conditioning facts, or his program of action. Tentatively, however, and in a too negative manner, we might sum up our revision of the socialist ideal in the light of science and the Russian experiment as follows:

1. Instead of being attributed as an end term to an omnipotent process of historic evolution, the ideal should be regarded as a purpose in the minds of those who strive to reach it.

2. Problems of being and of universal history arising from this situation should be acknowledged to exist, but not solved by the device of pretending to know what is not known.

3. The various components of the ideal should be analyzed and considered separately.

4. Those obviously fantastic in the light of modern biological and psychological knowledge, to say nothing of modern common sense, should be thrown out.

5. None of those remaining should be conceived as absolute.

6. The incompatibility between the liberty-and-individuality principles and the equality-and-co-operation principles should be adjusted, where necessary, by mutual concessions.

7. We must surrender to co-operation and the attending state control as much of our individual freedom as is indispensably necessary to the operation of a complicated wealth-producing machinery.

8. We must guard with eternal vigilance the rest.

THIRD INAUGURAL ADDRESS
JANUARY 20, 1941

Franklin Delano Roosevelt

On each national day of Inauguration since 1789, the people have renewed their sense of dedication to the United States.

In Washington's day the task of the people was to create and weld together a nation.

In Lincoln's day the task of the people was to preserve that nation from disruption from within.

In this day the task of the people is to save that nation and its institutions from disruption from without.

To us there has come a time, in the midst of swift happenings, to pause for a moment and take stock—to recall what our place in history has been, and to rediscover what we are and what we may be. If we do not, we risk the real peril of inaction.

Lives of nations are determined not by the count of years, but by the lifetime of the human spirit. The life of a man is three-score years and ten: a little more, a little less. The life of a nation is the fullness of the measure of its will to live.

There are men who doubt this. There are men who believe that democracy, as a form of government and a frame of life, is limited or measured by a kind of mystical and artificial fate—that, for some unexplained reason, tyranny and slavery have become the surging wave of the future—and that freedom is an ebbing tide.

But we Americans know that this is not true.

Eight years ago, when the life of this Republic seemed frozen by a fatalistic terror, we proved that this is not true. We were in the midst of shock—but we acted. We acted quickly, boldly, decisively.

These later years have been living years—fruitful years for the people of this democracy. For they have brought to us greater security and, I hope, a better understanding that life's ideals are to be measured in other than material things.

Most vital to our present and our future is this experience of a democracy which successfully survived crisis at home; put away many evil things; built new structures on enduring lines; and, through it all, maintained the fact of its democracy.

For action has been taken within the three-way framework of the Constitution of the United States. The co-ordinate branches of the government continue freely to function. The Bill of Rights remains inviolate. The freedom of elections is wholly maintained. Prophets of the downfall of American democracy have seen their dire predictions come to naught.

Democracy is not dying.

We know it because we have seen it revive—and grow.

We know it cannot die—because it is built on the unhampered initiative of individual men and women joined together in a common enterprise—an enterprise undertaken and carried through by the free expression of a free majority.

We know it because democracy alone, of all forms of government, enlists the full force of men's enlightened will.

We know it because democracy alone has constructed an unlimited civilization capable of infinite progress in the improvement of human life.

We know it because, if we look below the surface, we sense it still spreading on every continent—for it is the most humane, the most advanced, and in the end the most unconquerable of all forms of human society.

A nation, like a person, has a body—a body that must be fed and clothed and housed, invigorated and rested, in a manner that measures up to the objectives of our time.

A nation, like a person, has a mind—a mind that must be kept informed and alert, that must know itself, that understands the hopes and the needs of its neighbors—all the other nations that live within the narrowing circle of the world.

And a nation, like a person, has something deeper, something more permanent, something larger than the sum of all its parts. It is that something which matters most to its future—which calls forth the most sacred guarding of its present.

It is a thing for which we find it difficult—even impossible—to hit upon a single, simple word.

And yet we all understand what it is—the spirit—the faith of America. It is the product of centuries. It was born in the multitudes of those who came from many lands—some of high degree, but mostly plain people—who sought here, early and late, to find freedom more freely.

The democratic aspiration is no mere recent phase in human history. It *is* human history. It permeated the ancient life of early peoples. It blazed anew in the Middle Ages. It was written in Magna Carta.

In the Americas its impact has been irresistible. America has been the New World in all tongues, to all peoples, not because this continent was a new-found land, but because all those who came here believed they could create upon this continent a new life—a life that should be new in freedom.

Its vitality was written into our own Mayflower Compact, into the Declaration of Independence, into the Constitution of the United States, into the Gettysburg Address.

Those who first came here to carry out the longings of their spirit, and the millions who followed, and the stock that sprang from them—all have moved forward constantly and consistently toward an ideal which in itself has gained stature and clarity with each generation.

The hopes of the Republic cannot forever tolerate either undeserved poverty or self-serving wealth.

We know that we still have far to go; that we must more greatly build the security and the opportunity and the knowledge of every citizen, in the measure justified by the resources and the capacity of the land.

But it is not enough to achieve these purposes alone. It is not enough to clothe and feed the body of this nation, and instruct and inform its mind. For there is also the spirit. And of the three, the greatest is the spirit.

Without the body and the mind, as all men know, the nation could not live.

But if the spirit of America were killed, even though the nation's body and mind, constricted in an alien world, lived on, the America we know would have perished.

That spirit—that faith—speaks to us in our daily lives in ways often unnoticed, because they seem so obvious. It speaks to us here in the Capital of the nation. It speaks to us through the processes of governing in the sovereignties of forty-eight States. It speaks to us in our counties, in our cities, in our towns, and in our villages. It speaks to us from the other nations of the

Hemisphere, and from those across the seas—the enslaved, as well as the free. Sometimes we fail to hear or heed these voices of freedom because to us the privilege of our freedom is such an old, old story.

The destiny of America was proclaimed in words of prophecy spoken by our first President in his first Inaugural in 1789—words almost directed, it would seem, to this year of 1941: "The preservation of the sacred fire of liberty and the destiny of the republican model of government are justly considered . . . deeply, . . . finally, staked on the experiment intrusted to the hands of the American people."

If we lose that sacred fire—if we let it be smothered with doubt and fear—then we shall reject the destiny which Washington strove so valiantly and so triumphantly to establish. The preservation of the spirit and faith of the nation does, and will, furnish the highest justification for every sacrifice that we may make in the cause of national defense.

In the face of great perils never before encountered, our strong purpose is to protect and to perpetuate the integrity of democracy.

For this we muster the spirit of America, and the faith of America.

We do not retreat. We are not content to stand still. As Americans, we go forward, in the service of our country, by the will of God.

Propaganda

THE CRISIS[1]

Thomas Paine

THESE are the times that try men's souls. The summer soldier and the sunshine patriot will, in this crisis, shrink from the service of their country; but he that stands it *now*, deserves the love and thanks of man and woman. Tyranny, like hell, is not easily conquered; yet we have this consolation with us, that the harder the conflict, the more glorious the triumph. What we obtain too cheap, we esteem too lightly: it is dearness only that gives everything its value. Heaven knows how to put a proper price upon its goods; and it would be strange indeed, if so celestial an article as *Freedom* should not be highly rated. Britain, with an army to enforce her tyranny, has declared that she has a right (*not only to* TAX) but "*to* BIND *us in* ALL CASES WHATSOEVER," and if being *bound in that manner*, is not slavery, then is there not such a thing as slavery upon earth. Even the expression is impious; for so unlimited a power can belong only to God.

Whether the independence of the continent was declared too soon, or delayed too long, I will not now enter into as an argument; my own simple opinion is, that had it been eight months earlier, it would have been much better. We did not make a proper use of last winter, neither could we, while we were in a dependent state. However, the fault, if it were one, was all our own; we have none to blame but ourselves. But no great deal is lost yet. All that Howe has been doing for this month past, is rather a ravage than a conquest, which the spirit of the Jerseys, a year ago, would have quickly repulsed, and which time and a little resolution will soon recover.

I have as little superstition in me as any man living, but my secret opinion has ever been, and still is, that God Almighty will not give up a people to military destruction, or leave them unsupportedly to perish, who have so earnestly and so repeatedly sought to avoid the calamities of war, by every decent method which wisdom could invent. Neither have I so much of the infidel in me, as to suppose that He has relinquished the government of the world, and given us up to the care of devils; and as I do not, I cannot see on what grounds the king of Britain can look up to heaven for help against us: a common murderer, a highwayman, or a house-breaker, has as good a pretence as he.

'Tis surprising to see how rapidly a panic will sometimes run through a country. All nations and ages have been subject to them: Britain has trembled like an ague at the report of a French fleet of flat-bottomed boats; and in the

---

[1]Paper Number 1 from *The Crisis Papers* by Thomas Paine. Published December 23, 1776.

fourteenth century the whole English army, after ravaging the kingdom of France, was driven back like men petrified with fear; and this brave exploit was performed by a few broken forces collected and headed by a woman, Joan of Arc. Would that heaven might inspire some Jersey maid to spirit up her countrymen, and save her fair fellow sufferers from ravage and ravishment! Yet panics, in some cases, have their uses; they produce as much good as hurt. Their duration is always short; the mind soon grows through them, and acquires a firmer habit than before. But their peculiar advantage is, that they are the touchstones of sincerity and hypocrisy, and bring things and men to light, which might otherwise have lain forever undiscovered. In fact, they have the same effect on secret traitors, which an imaginary apparition would have upon a private murderer. They sift out the hidden thoughts of man, and hold them up in public to the world. Many a disguised tory has lately shown his head, that shall penitentially solemnize with curses the day on which Howe arrived upon the Delaware.

As I was with the troops at Fort Lee, and marched with them to the edge of Pennsylvania, I am well acquainted with many circumstances, which those who live at a distance know but little or nothing of. Our situation there was exceedingly cramped, the place being a narrow neck of land between the North River and the Hackensack. Our force was inconsiderable, being not one fourth so great as Howe could bring against us. We had no army at hand to have relieved the garrison, had we shut ourselves up and stood on our defence. Our ammunition, light artillery, and the best part of our stores, had been removed, on the apprehension that Howe would endeavour to penetrate the Jerseys, in which case fort Lee could be of no use to us; for it must occur to every thinking man, whether in the army or not, that these kind of field forts are only for temporary purposes, and last in use no longer than the enemy directs his force against the particular object, which such forts are raised to defend. Such was our situation and condition at fort Lee on the morning of the 20th of November, when an officer arrived with information that the enemy with 200 boats had landed about seven miles above: Major General Green, who commanded the garrison, immediately ordered them under arms, and sent express to General Washington at the town of Hackensack, distant by the way of the ferry, six miles. Our first object was to secure the bridge over the Hackensack, which laid up the river between the enemy and us, about six miles from us, and three from them. General Washington arrived in about three quarters of an hour, and marched at the head of the troops towards the bridge, which place I expected we should have a brush for; however, they did not choose to dispute it with us, and the greatest part of our troops went over the bridge, the rest over the ferry, except some which passed at a mill on a small creek, between the bridge and the ferry, and made their way through some marshy grounds up to the town of Hackensack, and there passed the river. We brought off as much baggage as the wagons could contain, the rest was lost. The simple object was to bring off the garrison, and march them on till they could be strengthened by the Jersey or Pennsylvania militia, so as to be enabled to make a stand. We staid four days at Newark, collected our out-posts with some of the Jersey militia, and marched out twice to meet the enemy, on being informed that they were advancing, though our numbers were greatly inferior to theirs. Howe, in my little opinion, committed a great error in generalship in not throwing a body of forces off from Staten Island through Amboy, by which means he might have seized all our stores at Brunswick, and intercepted our march into Pennsylvania; but if we believe the power of hell to be limited, we must likewise believe that their agents are under some providential controul.

I shall not now attempt to give all the particulars of our retreat to the Delaware; suffice it for the present to say, that both officers and men, though greatly harassed and fatigued, frequently without rest, covering or provision, the inevitable consequences of a long retreat, bore it with a manly and martial spirit. All their wishes centered in one, which was, that the country would turn out and help them to drive the enemy back. Voltaire has remarked that King William never appeared to full advantage but in difficulties and in action; the same remark may be made on General Washington, for the character fits him. There is a natural firmness in some minds which cannot be unlocked by trifles, but which, when unlocked, discovers a cabinet of fortitude; and I reckon it among those kind of public blessings, which we do not immediately see, that God hath blessed him with uninterrupted health, and given him a mind that can even flourish upon care.

I shall conclude this paper with some miscellaneous remarks on the state of our affairs; and shall begin with asking the following question, Why is it that the enemy have left the New-England provinces, and made these middle ones the seat of war? The answer is easy: New-England is not infested with tories, and we are. I have been tender in raising the cry against these men, and used numberless arguments to show them their danger, but it will not do to sacrifice a world either to their folly or their baseness. The period is now arrived, in which either they or we must change our sentiments, or one or both must fall. And what is a tory? Good God! what is he? I should not be afraid to go with a hundred whigs against a thousand tories, were they to attempt to get into arms. Every tory is a coward; for servile, slavish, self-interested fear is the foundation of toryism; and a man under such influence, though he may be cruel, never can be brave.

But, before the line of irrecoverable separation be drawn between us, let us reason the matter together: Your conduct is an invitation to the enemy, yet not one in a thousand of you has heart enough to join him. Howe is as much deceived by you as the American cause is injured by you. He expects you will all take up arms, and flock to his standard, with muskets on your shoulders. Your opinions are of no use to him, unless you support him personally, for 'tis soldiers, and not tories, that he wants.

I once felt all that kind of anger, which a man ought to feel, against the mean principles that are held by the tories: a noted one, who kept a tavern at Amboy, was standing at his door, with as pretty a child in his hand, about eight or nine years old, as I ever saw, and after speaking his mind as freely as he thought was prudent, finished with this unfatherly expression, "*Well! give me peace in my day.*" Not a man lives on the continent but fully believes that a separation must some time or other finally take place, and a generous parent should have said, "*If there must be trouble, let it be in my day, that my child may have peace*"; and this single reflection, well applied, is sufficient to awaken every man to duty. Not a place upon earth might be so happy as America. Her situation is remote from all the wrangling world, and she has nothing to do but to trade with them. A man can distinguish himself between temper and principle, and I am as confident, as I am that God governs the world, that America will never be happy till she gets clear of foreign dominion. Wars, without ceasing, will break out till that period arrives, and the continent must in the end be conqueror; for though the flame of liberty may sometimes cease to shine, the coal can never expire.

America did not, nor does not want force; but she wanted a proper application of that force. Wisdom is not the purchase of a day, and it is no wonder that we should err at the first setting off. From an excess of tenderness, we are unwilling to raise an army, and trusted our cause to the temporary defence of a well-meaning militia. A summer's experience has now taught us better; yet with those troops, while they were collected, we were able to set bounds to the progress of the enemy, and, thank God! they are again assembling. I always considered militia as the best troops in the world for a sudden exertion, but they will not do for a long campaign. Howe, it is probable, will make an attempt on this city[2]; should he fail on this side the Delaware, he is ruined: if he succeeds, our cause is not ruined. He stakes all on his side against a part on ours; admitting he succeeds, the consequence will be, that armies from both ends of the continent will march to assist their suffering friends in the middle states; for he cannot go everywhere, it is impossible. I consider Howe as the greatest enemy the tories have; he is bringing a war

[2]Philadelphia.

into their country, which, had it not been for him and partly for themselves, they had been clear of. Should he now be expelled, I wish with all the devotion of a Christian, that the names of whig and tory may never more be mentioned; but should the tories give him encouragement to come, or assistance if he come, I as sincerely wish that our next year's arms may expel them from the continent, and the congress appropriate their possessions to the relief of those who have suffered in well-doing. A single successful battle next year will settle the whole. America could carry on a two years war by the confiscation of the property of disaffected persons, and be made happy by their expulsion. Say not that this is revenge, call it rather the soft resentment of a suffering people, who, having no object in view but the *good* of *all*, have staked their *own all* upon a seemingly doubtful event. Yet it is folly to argue against determined hardness; eloquence may strike the ear, and the language of sorrow draw forth the tear of compassion, but nothing can reach the heart that is steeled with prejudice.

Quitting this class of men, I turn with the warm ardour of a friend to those who have nobly stood, and are yet determined to stand the matter out: I call not upon a few, but upon all: not on *this* state or *that* state, but on *every* state; up and help us; lay your shoulders to the wheel; better have too much force than too little, when so great an object is at stake. Let it be told to the future world, that in the depth of winter, when nothing but hope and virtue could survive, that the city and the country, alarmed at one common danger, came forth to meet and to repulse it. Say not that thousands are gone, turn out your tens of thousands; throw not the burden of the day upon Providence, but *"show your faith by your works,"* that God may bless you. It matters not where you live, or what rank of life you hold, the evil or the blessing will reach you all. The far and the near, the home counties and the back, the rich and the poor, will suffer or rejoice alike. The heart that feels not now, is dead: the blood of his children will curse his cowardice, who shrinks back at a time when a little might have saved the whole, and made *them* happy. I love the man that can smile in trouble, that can gather strength from distress, and grow brave by reflection. 'Tis the business of little minds to shrink; but he whose heart is firm, and whose conscience approves his conduct, will pursue his principles unto death. My own line of reasoning is to myself as straight and clear as a ray of light. Not all the treasures of the world, so far as I believe, could have induced me to support an offensive war, for I think it murder; but if a thief breaks into my house, burns and destroys my property, and kills me or threatens to kill me, or those that are in it, and, to *"bind me in all cases whatsoever,"* to his absolute will, am I to suffer it? What signifies it to me, whether he who does it is a king or a common man; my countryman

247

or not my countryman; whether it be done by an individual villain, or an army of them? If we reason to the root of things we shall find no difference; neither can any just cause be assigned why we should punish in the one case and pardon in the other. Let them call me a rebel, and welcome, I feel no concern from it; but I should suffer the misery of devils, were I to make a whore of my soul by swearing allegiance to one whose character is that of a sottish, stupid, stubborn, worthless, brutish man. I conceive likewise a horrid idea in receiving mercy from a being, who at the last day shall be shrieking to the rocks and mountains to cover him, and fleeing with terror from the orphan, the widow, and the slain of America.

There are cases which cannot be overdone by language, and this is one. There are persons, too, who see not the full extent of the evil which threatens them; they solace themselves with hopes that the enemy, if he succeed, will be merciful. It is the madness of folly, to expect mercy from those who have refused to do justice; and even mercy, where conquest is the object, is only a trick of war; the cunning of the fox is as murderous as the violence of the wolf, and we ought to guard equally against both. Howe's first object is, partly by threats and partly by promises, to terrify or seduce the people to deliver up their arms and receive mercy. The ministry recommended the same plan to Gage, and this is what the tories call making their peace, "*a peace which passeth all understanding*" indeed! A peace which would be the immediate forerunner of a worse ruin than any we have yet thought of. Ye men of Pennsylvania, do reason upon these things! Were the back counties to give up their arms, they would fall an easy prey to the Indians, who are all armed: this perhaps is what some tories would not be sorry for. Were the home counties to deliver up their arms, they would be exposed to the resentment of the back counties, who would then have it in their power to chastise their defection at pleasure. And were any one state to give up its arms, *that* state must be garrisoned by all Howe's army of Britons and Hessians to preserve it from the anger of the rest. Mutual fear is the principal link in the chain of mutual love, and woe be to that state that breaks the compact. Howe is mercifully inviting you to barbarous destruction, and men must be either rogues or fools that will not see it. I dwell not upon the powers of imagination; I bring reason to your ears; and, in language as plain as *A, B, C*, hold up truth to your eyes.

I thank God, that I fear not. I see no real cause for fear. I know our situation well, and can see the way out of it. While our army was collected, Howe dared not risk a battle; and it is no credit to him that he decamped from the White Plains, and waited a mean opportunity to ravage the defenceless Jerseys; but it is great credit to us, that, with a handful of men, we sustained an orderly retreat for near an hundred miles, brought off our ammunition, all our field pieces, the greatest part of our stores, and had four rivers to pass. None can say that our retreat was precipitate, for we were near three weeks in performing it, that the country might have time to come in. Twice we marched back to meet the enemy, and remained out till dark. The sign of fear was not seen in our camp, and had not some of the cowardly and disaffected inhabitants spread false alarms through the country, the Jerseys had never been ravaged. Once more we are again collected and collecting; our new army at both ends of the continent is recruiting fast, and we shall be able to open the next campaign with sixty thousand men, well armed and clothed. This is our situation, and who will may know it. By perseverance and fortitude we have the prospect of a glorious issue; by cowardice and submission, the sad choice of a variety of evils—a ravaged country—a depopulated city—habitations without safety, and slavery without hope—our homes turned into barracks and bawdy-houses for Hessians, and a future race to provide for, whose fathers we shall doubt of. Look on this picture and weep over it! and if there yet remains one thoughtless wretch who believes it not, let him suffer it unlamented.

THE AMERICAN MIND IN WARTIME[1]

James R. Mock and Cedric Larson

WE HAD gone to war. We had decided to send our boys over to France to save democracy. But even as indignation against Germany had surged higher and higher in those last tense days before 3:12 A.M., April 6, 1917, no one could say just what the American people would do after their eloquent leader had urged them into war.

The great majority of Americans, it seemed, wanted to fight, but people wondered anxiously how large and how determined the minority might be. Minorities are dangerous when the fate of civilization is hanging in the balance. Who felt quite easy with Senator LaFollette and his "little group of wilful men" still in Congress? How could we count on the millions of Germans, Austrians, Hungarians, Poles, Russians and other "aliens in our midst"? Wasn't there something very disquieting in the widely quoted opinion of Dr. Aleš Hrdlicka that the Melting Pot had failed to melt? How many people still believed there was such a thing as being too proud to fight? How many remembered the President's statement that there was no essential

[1]From *Words That Won The War*. Princeton University Press, 1939.

difference in the expressed war aims of the belligerents? What of enemy spies, of whom there were said to be 100,000 or more at large, and their allies, the pacifists, Socialists, and labor agitators? What about the success of Wilson's campaign slogan, "He kept us out of war"? What about warnings against entanglement in Europe's quarrels which still echoed in countless homes?

And what, above all, about the unknown thousands of Americans who might not feel very strongly one way or the other but thought Europe was a long way off and might find it too much bother to make the sacrifices which a modern war demands of the entire population?

We had pledged "our lives, our fortunes, and our sacred honor," but could we fulfill that pledge? When a peaceful nation, jealous of individual liberty and proud of its freedom from militarism, attempted to mobilize its men, money, resources, and emotions for one mighty effort, even a rather small minority could bring disaster. "Widespread cooperation" was not good enough when the nation's life was at stake. Nothing less than complete solidarity would do.

America was not unified when war was declared. The necessary reversal of opinion was too great to be achieved overnight. The agonizing question in official Washington, the question on which hung the fate of the country's entire wartime effort, was whether the inner lines at home would hold as effectively as the lines in France.

The Committee on Public Information was assigned the staggering task of "holding fast the inner lines." The story of how it fulfilled that mission is a dramatic record of vigor, effectiveness, and creative imagination. The Committee was America's "propaganda ministry" during the World War, charged with encouraging and then consolidating the revolution of opinion which changed the United States from anti-militaristic democracy to an organized war machine. This work touched the private life of virtually every man, woman, and child; it reflected the thoughts of the American people under the leadership of Woodrow Wilson; and it popularized what was for us a new idea of the individual's relation to the state.

President Wilson created the Committee on Public Information by executive order dated April 13, 1917, and appointed George Creel as civilian chairman, with the Secretaries of State, War, and Navy as the other members. Mr. Creel assembled as brilliant and talented a group of journalists, scholars, press agents, editors, artists, and other manipulators of the symbols of public opinion as America had ever seen united for a single purpose. It was a gargantuan advertising agency the like of which the country had never known, and the breathtaking scope of its activities was not to be equalled until the rise of totalitarian dictatorships after the war. George Creel, Carl Byoir, Edgar

Sisson, Harvey O'Higgins, Guy Stanton Ford, and their famous associates were literally public relations counsellors to the United States government, carrying first to the citizens of this country and then to those in distant lands the ideas which gave motive power to the stupendous undertaking of 1917–1918.

Whether or not one accepts the interpretation of Charles Beard, the Nye Committee, Walter Millis, or someone else, it is clear that *ideas*, for whatever reason they were held, took us into the war and kept alive the fiercely burning fires of industrial and military and naval activity. Without the driving force of those ideas there would have been no A.E.F. in France, no destroyer squadron at Queenstown, no sub-chasers in the Mediterranean, no "Bridge of Ships" spanning the Atlantic, no Liberty Bonds, no Draft Law, no food rationing, no coal shortage, no seizure of railroads and ammunition plants, no abridgment of free speech and free press.

And it was the Committee on Public Information that both mobilized and expressed the thoughts and emotions supporting these extraordinary dislocations of peaceful life. The story of its career holds a strategic place in the history of the war, and it presses for current attention as America anxiously considers what it will do in the current European War.

Through every known channel of communication the Committee carried straight to the people its message of Wilson's idealism, a war to end war, and America to the rescue of civilization. "Fireside chats" via radio did not in that day give national leaders the present easy avenue of approach to the family circle, but the Committee was nevertheless able to address itself directly to the minds and hearts of Americans, however isolated they might appear to be from the main stream of martial activity.

If they included misinformation in their complex of ideas about the war, at least it was misinformation shared with them by editors and college professors, the country's greatest intellectual and spiritual leaders, and by public figures in the shadow of the White House. History had not yet separated true and false, and many things were believed in 1918 that scholars would deny today. But there was little expressed difference of opinion. It was illegal to express dissent of certain kinds, but for most people no law was necessary. The Committee on Public Information had done its work so well that there was a burning eagerness to believe, to conform, to feel the exaltation of joining in a great and selfless enterprise.

When facts were known or convictions held by any considerable number of the people they were common to all—to simple folk on the edge of the prairie, to department store clerks and subway guards in the metropolis, to lumbermen deep in the forest of the Northwest, and to maintenance men set down in squalid huts along a desert right-of-way. Americans stood close together in the comradeship of battle in 1917 and 1918, and it was largely the doing of the Committee on Public Information.

Consider the case of one mid-western family. They lived on a quarter-section of farmland a dozen miles from the railroad, telegraph, and postoffice. The nearest daily newspaper was published at the far end of the next county, seventy-five miles away. No through road passed near their farm, they had seen pavement only a few times in their lives, and they had no phone. Normally they paid scant attention to public affairs. Their only aim in life, so it seemed, was to bring in the golden harvest.

Yet when this simple, uneducated family, far from urban centers of information and five thousand miles across sea and land from the battlefields of France, sat down to a threshers' supper in the summer of 1918 they were more conscious of the World War than many more literate people had been of any war since fighting began.

And every item of war news they saw—in the county weekly, in magazines, or in the city daily picked up occasionally in the general store—was not merely officially approved information but precisely the same kind that millions of their fellow citizens were getting at the same moment. Every war story had been censored somewhere along the line—at the source, in transit, or in the newspaper office in accordance with "voluntary" rules issued by the CPI. The same mimeograph machines furnished most of the Washington news, and the same cable censorship had passed all items from abroad.

Patriotic advertising in all of these papers had been prepared by the CPI, and even commercial announcements had a patriotic twist which had been suggested by someone in the Committee office. Cartoons were those inspired by the Committee staff. At the state fair the family viewed war exhibits under Committee sponsorship, and the movies at the county seat began with one of the Committee's patriotic films and paused briefly for oratory by one of the Committee's Four-Minute Men, who had gained his ideas for the talk from the Committee's "suggestions."

At the township school the children saw war photographs issued by the Committee, recited war verse from a Committee brochure, learned current events from a Committee newspaper, studied war maps with a teacher who had acquired her knowledge of international politics through the Committee's pamphlets, and when they came home at night bore more literature for their parents.

The postoffice bulletin board was adorned with copies of the Committee's *Official Bulletin*, and posters in the general store and on telephone poles up and down the countryside were those designed by the Committee's artists, the same pictures appearing again and again with the persuasive insistence of modern cigarette advertising. Both the children and their mother read war stories suggested or actually briefed by the Committee. On Sunday the pastor thanked Providence for blessings that had been listed by one of the Committee's copywriters, and prayed for achievement of an objective glowingly described by another. When the Ladies' Aid held its monthly meeting, the program was that suggested by the Committee's division of women's war work, and the speaker came bearing credentials from the Committee's speakers' bureau. He delivered an address which he thought was his own but which actually paraphrased one of the Committee pamphlets, and his talk was illustrated with lantern slides which the Committee had prepared.

Some people in the community were of foreign extraction, some unable to read English, but that did not make them ineligible to join the crusade against despotism, in fact it seemed to single them out for special attention. Their foreign-language newspapers carried translations of the same news the rest of the community was reading in English, and many of the pamphlets were also given in a number of tongues. Some of these people belonged to the Friends of German Democracy, others to the John Ericsson League of Patriotic Service, the American-Hungarian Loyalty League, and so on, according to their several countries of origin—and almost all of these groups were either openly or secretly supported by the CPI.

Everyone wore the same patriotic buttons, put up the same window stickers, passed the same clichés, knew the same rumors. The wool buyer who visited the various farms in the spring had carried a little pamphlet, which the Committee had designed especially for travelling men, enabling him to speak with the exciting authority of inside information, and everyone assumed that the stories must be true because salesmen who stopped at the general store brought with them the same thrilling narrative.

Uniformity of testimony is convincing.

And testimony seemed nearly uniform not only in the heart of the Great Plains country but throughout the nation. Dissenters merely intensified the vigor with which their fellow citizens presented the prevailing view of the war, of international morality, and of world politics. Scholars will long discuss the precise division of "real opinion" in America when war was declared, but there can be no uncertainty regarding articulate opinion as it was expressed in newspapers, books, pamphlets, cartoons, and public addresses—it was overwhelmingly and wholeheartedly on the side of the Allies and in favor of our belligerence.

Search for the reasons behind this has engaged the energy of many brilliant investigators, and they offer varying interpretations. But all seem agreed that in the years of our neutrality, as the calendar turned through 1915, 1916, and the first fatal months of 1917, there was a steady and progressively rapid solidifying of opinion around the concepts which President Wilson was to present in their familiar aspect only as the country stood at the very brink of the abyss. These concepts of a "War to End War" and "Make the World Safe for Democracy" had taken form slowly at first, but as our actual entry neared there was a coagulation of opinion, and this process was hastened by many forces, such as economic interest, Anglo-American friendship, British propaganda, exposure of German plots in America, the uplifting sweep of President Wilson's eloquence, America's Big Brother complex, the hope of making a better world, and so on.

Many agencies were at work to bring more and ever more American citizens within the magnetic field of the war spirit. The National Security League, the American Defense Society, the Navy League, General Leonard Wood, many of the leaders of the League to Enforce Peace—all these and many more undertook deliberate campaigns for military preparedness. Most of them also favored war at least a year before our entry.

Almost from the invasion of Belgium in 1914, a growing number of Americans believed that France and England were fighting our battle. These people set about converting their fellow citizens. Friends of Germany, anglophobes, pacifists, and isolationists attempted to check this movement, but they lost ground steadily. More and more Americans came to believe that defeat of the Allies would mean eventual doom for democracy everywhere; many feared actual and immediate armed invasion or at least bombardment of North America. Special economic interests both nurtured and exploited these fears, and every sensational development in Germany's submarine warfare, in the occupation of Belgium, or in the inept German plotting in this country was used by all of the war groups—the idealists as well as the special interests —to gain new supporters for their contention that German military might must be struck to earth.

Through it all rang the voice of Woodrow Wilson, a clear call to the American people, lifting them to heights of spiritual excitement from which they were not to descend until the back-to-normalcy days of President Harding.

When war was declared there was a sharp intensification of feeling, a speeding up in the process of unifying opinion, but there was not the sharp break with the past that we sometimes think of. From August 1914 to April 1917 a host of disparate groups had carried the burden of propaganda and education which the Committee on Public Information assumed under George Creel when war actually came.

The Committee performed an almost incredible task in the marshalling of opinion, in building strong walls of national solidarity. But it is important to realize that the Committee was no inner clique imposing unwanted views on the general public. Scarcely an idea may be found in all the work of the CPI that was not held by many Americans before war was declared. The Committee was representative of the articulate majority in American opinion.

What the Committee did do was to codify and standardize ideas already widely current, and to bring the powerful force of the emotions behind them. It is true that the whipping-in of stragglers through application of social pressure held a vitally important place in the work, but the greatest effort was directed toward vitalizing convictions already held and toward developing the will to fight for ideas already familiar.

The job was to keep the Wilson program before the people and to make it seem like something worth dying for.

With the CPI viewed in this light, George Creel's selection for the post of chairman was natural. He had been a Wilson man "before 1912"; for years he had expressed in the language of front-page journalism very much the same sort of thing that President Wilson expressed in the language of the library and the pulpit. Mr. Creel has given the authors his own report on the reasons for his selection:

"As editor of the *Rocky Mountain News* in Denver, I advocated Woodrow Wilson's nomination as early as 1911, and had correspondence with him throughout his first administration. Going to New York in 1913, I played a rather important part in the 1916 campaign, contributing syndicated articles to the press and also publishing *Wilson and the Issues*. After the election he asked me to come to Washington as a member of his official family, but my finances would not permit acceptance of the offer. When we entered the war on April 6, 1917, and the papers carried the news that some rigid form of censorship would be adopted, I wrote a letter of protest to the President in which I explained to him that the need was for expression not repression, and urged a campaign that would carry our war aims and peace terms not only to the United States, but to every neutral country, and also in England, France, and Italy. As for censorship, I insisted that all proper needs could be met by some voluntary methods. He sent for me and after approving my proposal, drafted me to act as active chairman. No other person was considered for the place."

Mr. Creel suggests here not only his political kinship with Wilson but also his determination to carry out the work of the CPI along Wilsonian lines— by bold appeal to the people.

Two methods of handling public opinion were available to the United

States. An ironclad censorship could be established, with a great bureaucracy attempting to judge the "loyalty" of every item in every newspaper, every word in every conversation—to probe, in fact, into the innermost thoughts of every citizen. On the other hand, a policy could be adopted whereby the hand of censorship was held back but the channels of communication were literally choked with official, approved news and opinion, leaving little freeway for rumor or disloyal news.

George Creel took the affirmative line.

Consistently to the end of the war, he placed his faith in a censorship which was at least technically voluntary. The newspapers accepted this censorship, though they also contributed in full measure the expected criticism of Mr. Creel himself. He was one of the most disliked and traduced members of the national government while the war was in progress, and the 1918 caricature of him carries over to the present day.

This picture is unfair, as the reader will discover, but Mr. Creel was in a sense hoist with his own petard. For he, more than any other one man aside from the President, helped to produce the 1917 temper in which the tossing about of symbols became a substitute for an intellectual transaction, and in which people thought together and thought in stereotypes.

Truth, George Creel knew, is the first casualty in war, but he shared with his chief and with millions of their fellow citizens the hope that "this war will be different." As the story of the CPI unfolds it will be clear in how many ways George Creel attempted to protect truth. But the emotional climate in which Ora Buffington, a Pennsylvania attorney, urged the CPI to import for public exhibition some of the Belgian children whose hands had been cut off was the very climate that Mr. Creel had to maintain for the support of President Wilson's most ennobling political ideals.

The CPI hoped that it could direct the nation's emotional energy into channels of constructive patriotism, not hysteria, but it was not always successful. Though only too well aware of how hysteria begins and grows, the Committee was forced to deal constantly with the material of panic, fear, and intolerance.

Preposterous or frightening evidences of "national jitters" were continually received.

Joseph P. Tumulty, the President's secretary, had been imprisoned as a German spy . . . he had been shot. . . .

Five Americans, former prisoners of war with their tongues cut out, were in a hospital ship lying in the Potomac. . . .

The assistant to the chairman of the U. S. Shipping Board protested against the cover of the *Hog Island News*, a shipbuilder's house organ, which showed a huge porker carrying an American flag—he thought it might be used for German propaganda. . . .

Newspapers reported a TEUTON PLAN TO TORTURE CAPTURED SAMMIES. . . .

U-boat captains were believed to have landed on the Atlantic Coast and then to have made their way inland, poisoning wells en route. . . .

Suspected pro-Germans were lynched. . . .

A report was syndicated that a man in a training camp near Chillicothe, Ohio, had never received any mail. Shortly after this publication, he received 1200 letters, nineteen special-delivery messages, and fifty-four packages . . . "As it happens," the tired postmaster reported to Washington, "—— can neither read or write. He is not just right and was not accepted by the army but refuses to leave. . . ."

All of this was socially unwholesome. It was also dangerous. During the Spanish-American War, as at other times, civilian hysteria had forced the United States to change its disposition of forces and threatened strategical plans. But the CPI was caught in a dilemma. It was forced to return again and again to the methods of arousing opinion which brought the very atmosphere of hate and fear which might endanger national safety and was surely incompatible with the consecrated mission on which President Wilson was leading the country.

George Creel has been charged with being too eager, too impetuous and flamboyant. Each of these adjectives is properly applied to him. Evidence is abundant, however, that countless citizens wished public opinion to be whipped to higher and higher fury. The independent patriotic groups such as the National Security League, perhaps jealous of government interference with private enterprise, frequently charged the CPI with malingering. Even more sober observers feared public apathy and called ever and again for more dramatic action.

In August 1917, for instance, Grosvenor Clarkson, secretary (later director) of the Council of National Defense, wrote to a number of prominent men, calling attention to lack of war enthusiasm and asking their opinions. Clarkson sent copies of the replies to Creel.

Roy W. Howard of the Scripps papers and United Press, who had just returned from the Pacific Coast, concurred in Clarkson's judgment and said: "This weakness must be remedied before the nation will go to war with its heart as well as its hands and feet." Frederick Dixon, editor of the *Christian Science Monitor*: "The country is not awake . . . invaluable time is being wasted." Frank Cobb, editor of the *New York World*: "There are plenty of soap-boxes and some of them might well be occupied by men who believe in the United States and in the justice of its cause." R. J. Cuddihy, treasurer of

Funk and Wagnalls: "The churches of the country should be counted on to reach the spiritual and emotional side of our people, and . . . this is the side that must be fully awakened."

Typical of many letters that came to Creel through all the months of the war was one from S. H. Church, president of Carnegie Institute of Technology. In January 1918 he wrote that the CPI must emphasize "in season and out of season, the fact that we are engaged in a bloody and remorseless war with the most pitiless and despicable nation that has ever attacked the peace and dignity of civilization, and that this high note of raging battle ought to be sounded throughout the world until we shall receive a definite assurance that peace is within our grasp and upon our own terms."

The "high note of raging battle," however, produced not only the will to fight Germany but also the mood for spy hunts. Spies there undoubtedly were, but their number was infinitesimal compared with the excitement they caused. After the war John Lord O'Brian, head of the War-Emergency Division of the Department of Justice, said that "No other one cause contributed so much to the oppression of innocent men as the systematic and indiscriminate agitation against what was claimed to be an all-pervasive system of German espionage." Captain Henry T. Hunt, head of the Military Intelligence counter-espionage section during the war, has told the authors that in addition to unfounded spy stories innocently launched there were many started with the apparent object of removing or inconveniencing political, business, or social rivals. As an illustration of the complexity of charges and counter-charges, he reports that on one occasion two of his own men were taken into custody by the Department of Justice, while seeking to determine the loyalty of the headwaiter in a Washington hotel.

The nervousness illustrated by this incident was exploited and turned to devious uses. Professor S. H. Clark of the Department of Public Speaking at the University of Chicago, for instance, wrote to Creel: "Many public men and many of our prominent newspapers who have always bitterly fought socialism, the I.W.W.'s, and even labor unions, are taking advantage of the present crisis in an effort not purely patriotic to squelch all of these more or less radical organizations without regard to the effect upon the future of our country, to say nothing of the effect in the present war."

One man who emphatically agreed with this was the famous I.W.W. agitator, Big Bill Haywood, who wrote to Creel from Cook County Jail: "Perhaps some day when the pendulum swings back, when a war-mad world can assume something of a normal attitude of thought, when the ideas and ideals of a New Freedom will not be misinterpreted, I may ask you to do something for *us*. I still hate autocracy and Russian Oligarchy from the bottom of my

258

heart, but even more the Industrial Oligarchy so rapidly developing in this country—which must be fought after the World War if democracy is to endure."

From the very opposite end of the social and economic scale—from Thomas W. Lamont, the Morgan partner who had just purchased the *New York Evening Post*—Creel received yet another letter showing appreciation of what happens in wartime: "There is altogether too great a tendency to call people names just because they happen to talk intelligently on certain topics. I have heard people dubbed Socialists just because they happened to be students of sociology and, looking forward, were convinced that in the future labor would have to have an even squarer deal than it has had in the past. I have heard other people called pro-Germans just because they expressed the hope that war would not last forever. . . . I think we are apt, in time of war, to fall into a mood of more or less intolerance, if the other fellow doesn't agree with us."

But perhaps the most interesting of all the letters which came to George Creel on this subject was that from the wealthy but radical lawyer and publicist, Amos Pinchot, whose political position lay somewhere between Big Bill Haywood and Thomas Lamont. He wrote:

"Has Wilson changed? Is he going back on himself and on us? Has he seen a new vision of world peace, founded on things un-American, based on old-world imperialist aggression, which he so lately condemned? Have we got to die tomorrow for principles that yesterday the President told us were wrong?

"What has changed Wilson? Who has put it over on him?

"We have got to remember that before we went into the war, the Administration, and the liberal press, the Scripps papers, the Cloverleaf syndicate, the N.E.A., and even much of the reactionary press, for two solid years carried on anti-war propaganda. They were pro-Ally, but they said that we had no business in it. At the end of this period the President went to the country on the issue that he kept us out of war—and won. . . .

"Considering our approaches to the war, the President's own attitude, his distinct downright repudiation of the Allies' annexation policies, the anti-imperialist feeling in America, it seems fairly evident that even for Wilson the task of swinging the public into line for the present war aims of the Allies would be too big a task, even if it were a right and necessary course.

"If the President attempts it he will fail. He will fall as an American leader, and fall farther and harder than any modern liberal statesman."

There is no evidence of a reply from Creel, but from many other records we know what he would have said. He would have granted the change in the President's attitude toward the war, granted the perils of entanglement in European politics, granted the dangers to democracy which militarism had brought to this country. But he would have said that we were fighting not for Europe's war aims but for Wilson's, and that the hope of a new world, of universal democracy, and of permanent peace made any temporary concessions richly justified.

Creel did not, however, push from his mind the knowledge of how "patriotism" was being turned to selfish uses, and how much work remained to be done for democracy at home. In March 1918 he wrote to Joseph E. Davies: "I shall support every necessary measure directed to the supreme end of defeating . . . the unholy combination of autocracy, militarism, and predatory capitalism which rules Germany and threatens liberty and self-government everywhere. . . . [But] I ask and expect only support of those who believe that for the sake of political liberty and social progress, America must win this war while it consolidates at home every position won from the forces of reaction and political bigotry."

George Creel, as Woodrow Wilson, faced the tragic dilemma of a war on behalf of democracy. In the record of the Committee on Public Information one may find evidence of their success or lack of success in meeting it. This book can present only part of the evidence, but the files of the CPI contain some of the most important material of American history. For it is not only George Creel that is to be judged but the entire national policy of a democracy at war. The problem boils down to this: Can any wartime compromise be "temporary"? Can modern war, a war of populations, be waged without permanent loss of some of the things for which America entered the World War in 1917?

Every observer will have his own answer to these questions, but no one can afford to evade them.

HOW TO DETECT
AND ANALYZE PROPAGANDA[1]

Clyde R. Miller

IN EXAMINATION of propaganda the first logical thing to do is to define the term. A little over a year ago a group of scholars organizing the Institute for Propaganda Analysis, after a good many hours of argument, arrived at this definition: "As generally understood, propaganda is an expression of opinion or action by individuals or groups, deliberately designed to influence opinions or actions of other individuals or groups with reference to pre-determined ends."

That means if you and I have an opinion and express it with intent to influence some individual or group, we are, to that extent, propagandists. And are acts propaganda too? Yes. The Boston Tea Party was a propaganda act plotted and planned and beautifully timed by that master propagandist of the American Revolution, Samuel Adams, to crystallize the feeling of hatred of the Colonists against the British Tories. The burning of the Reichstag when Hitler came to power may have been a propaganda act. Certainly Hitler took advantage of it by placing blame for it on "Jews" and "Communists," labeling those whom he did not like "Jews" and "Communists" whether they were or not, blaming them for the fire and putting them in prison. By such propaganda acts Hitler was able to dispose of many of his enemies at the very outset of his dictatorship. Everybody engages in propaganda acts. For example, if you refuse to buy silk because you don't want to give the Japanese money to buy bombs to kill the Chinese that very act of refusal is a propaganda act. So, too, is the deliberate purchase of goods to help the Japanese or Chinese.

Observe that we don't have opinions in vacuum. We have opinions about issues on which we feel strongly, on which we take sides for or against.

Was Franco right or wrong in trying to bring a fascist regime into Spain?

Were Hitler and Mussolini and Chamberlain and the Catholic Church right or wrong in supporting Franco?

Was Roosevelt right or wrong in keeping up the embargo and thus permitting Franco to win?

Do we approve or disapprove Hitler's policy of expansion in Austria, in Czecho-Slovakia, in Southeastern Europe, in Western Europe?

Do we approve or disapprove Mussolini's demand for French territory?

[1] A lecture delivered at New York Town Hall, February 20, 1939. Reprinted by permission of Town Hall, Inc., and of the author, Clyde R. Miller, Secretary of the Institute for Propaganda Analysis.

Did we approve or disapprove Chamberlain's policy of appeasing Hitler and Mussolini with respect to Austria, Czecho-Slovakia, and Spain?

Were we for or against the help which Mr. Roosevelt gave to Mr. Chamberlain in his policy of appeasement?

If we stand on either one side or the other and express our opinions or commit acts intended to influence the acts and opinions of others, we are propagandists.

Now there are three things to observe about propaganda. If we see these clearly we have a key to enable us to recognize it, understand it, and help us to analyze it. First, observe that propaganda is associated with conflict, either as cause or as result or as cause and result. The Czecho-Slovakian crisis was a synthetic conflict created by Hitler's sending propagandists into the Sudeten area of Czecho-Slovakia to agitate for a partitioning.

Let's imagine a blackboard here. Let's imagine that we make a big **X** and call that **X** *conflict*—call it the number one element in propaganda. Now we don't see many of these conflicts directly, face to face. We see the pictures of them and we meet the propagandas associated with them through various channels of communication, various avenues or lenses. So let's draw a line straight out from that **X** and let it represent channels of communication, the number two aspect of propaganda. Channels of communication include press, radio, newsreel, cinema, school, church, labor union, business organization, women's club, patriotic group, civic organization, as well as individuals who spread propaganda by word of mouth. We see our pictures of reality through these channels. I have used the word lens. A newspaper is like a lens. We are not in China today seeing Japanese planes bombing the Chinese nor are we in Spain to see the last stand or collapse of the Loyalists. We are not in Italy or Berlin or London or Washington. We are here. The pictures of realities, the conflicts and propagandas which come from these places come to us through these channels, these lenses. Maybe the lenses distort the pictures. As we look at the world of reality through the Communist *Daily Worker* we see a world entirely different from that we view through the lens which is the *New York Times*. And if we look at the world through the *Herald Tribune* we see a world yet different, and still different worlds through the *World Telegram* or the *Nation* or the *New Republic* or the Catholic magazine *Commonweal*, or the Catholic magazine *America*; we see still different worlds through Protestant publications like the *Christian Century* and the bulletin of the Methodist Federation for Social Service.

Lenses have factors of distortion as those of us who wear spectacles know. We have had the experience of sitting in the optician's chair, trying to read

262

the letters on the chart, having our eyes tested one at a time. The optician puts a lens in the slot and says: "What do you see there now?"

"Well," you say, "I see the first letter all right, that big letter at the top."

"What's on the second line?"

"Well, that first letter is an *E* or an *F* and the second is a *D* or an *O*."

He drops another lens in the slot.

"How is it now?"

"That's better. That first letter really is an *F* and the second isn't either a *D* or an *O*; it's a *Q*."

And so he puts in one lens after another until finally you see nearly all the letters on the chart, sharp and clear. What has the optician done? He has cancelled out factors of distortion. That, of course, is what we must do in our newspaper reading, our radio listening, in listening to individuals express opinions, in appraising propaganda acts.

But suppose we do have all the factors cancelled out. Let's take the chalk again and draw a perpendicular line at the end of the horizontal line. Let's call this the camera film—the human mind—the number three element in propaganda. Upon this camera film are focussed the pictures which travel through the channels of communication—press, newsreel, radio, etc., the lenses of which I have spoken. But do we get true pictures on this camera film? Let's use an analogy. Suppose I happen to be a guest at some country place on Long Island or up in Westchester; suppose it's a hot day next summer. I am seated on the porch looking upon a beautiful yard. Over at my right are great clumps of yellow roses. Then there is the greenest lawn imaginable. To the left, beds of red and yellow tulips. I say to myself, "My, isn't this lovely." I say, "Wouldn't Aunt Sadie enjoy this?"

Aunt Sadie, say, is an aunt who lives out in Davenport, Iowa. I think of her because she has made a hobby of yellow roses and I know she would love these. So I say I must send her a picture of this. But I am lazy and do not disturb myself to do it until a black and white cat walks slowly out upon the lawn, blinks his eyes, and lies down to sleep. That moves me. Aunt Sadie has a black and white cat, too. So I step into the house and bring out a camera which has a lens from which every factor of distortion has been cancelled out. I point the camera right, I give it the right exposure, the right timing. I press the shutter. It ought to be a perfect picture, but is it? Do I get the yellow of the roses, the green of the grass, the red and yellow of the tulips? The answer is—I do not. But I get a perfect picture of the black and white cat. Why? Because the camera film is conditioned to take pictures only in black and white. If I want the yellow of the roses and the red and yellow of the tulips and the green of the grass I'll have to get one of those new color films. The camera film is like our mind. We can have a mind conditioned to hate Catholics or Jews or Protestants or foreigners. We can have minds conditioned to put a Gene Debs in jail, and then we can have them reconditioned to have respect for Jews and Catholics and Protestants and foreigners and Gene Debs.

This number three element, the camera film of the mind, is important to all of us who would analyze propaganda, because we must begin the analysis with understanding how our own minds have been conditioned and how because of that conditioning they might refuse to receive pictures of reality.

One further point while we have the blackboard in mind. Draw upon it two triangles; label one "A" and the other one "D."

These triangles represent two distinct types of human organization. That labeled "A" represents the authoritarian type; that marked "D," the democratic type. We see both types in families, schools, churches, labor unions, business organizations, and governments. In the authoritarian type of human organization in government, we have an excellent example, marked by high efficiency, in Nazi Germany. A good example of the democratic type is seen in our own government.

In the authoritarian organization, such as we observe in the dictator state, authority flows from the top down; and from the bottom up comes obedience, blind, instant, and unquestioning. Here there is just one will, that of the dictator or dictator-group at the top of the triangle. Because there is just one will, there is just one opinion. That means, according to our definition, just one propaganda. In short, we find in the authoritarian organization a *monopoly* of propaganda. We see the dictator controlling all opinion, using concentration camp and terrorism for that purpose, if need be. His most important means of control, however, lies in his ability to control the number three element in our diagram—that camera film, the human mind. School, youth organizations, adult groups, labor and business organizations, even the home and church must have their activities carefully prescribed in order that the minds of the people will be made receptive to just one propaganda, that of the dictator, and in order that their minds will reject any other propaganda which might chance to reach them. All the channels of communication carry precisely the distortion which the dictator wants them to carry. Even the conflicts with which propaganda is associated are made to order by the dictator. Thus, Hitler created the Sudeten issue, which led to the war crisis in September, 1938. Before last spring few had heard of any Sudeten discontent; but after Hitler's propagandists got to work on the issue, the whole world knew about it. Similarly, the Spanish issue seems to have been planned and plotted by Hitler and Mussolini with the approval later of Baldwin and Chamberlain in England and Daladier in France.

In Germany, the persecution of minority groups of Jews, Catholics, Protestants, Masons, and Communists represents the creation of conflicts which serve as the springboard for vast volumes of propaganda inciting the people to fear and hatred of these groups. Nobody can oppose the dictator unless he is prepared to go to a concentration camp or kneel at the headsman's block. Hence, there is no counter-propaganda to be heard or read save that which may be surreptitiously circulated.

Contrast with this the democratic type of human organization. Here, too, authority flows from the top down and obedience from the bottom up; but there are important differences. The obedience is not necessarily instant, blind, or unquestioning. Further, authority flows from the bottom up and obedience from the top down.

What does this mean in terms of propaganda? In a nation of democratic organization, such as the United States, we see not one will, but many wills. Hence we find many opinions, many propagandas. In short, in a democracy there is a *competition* of propagandas, as contrasted with a *monopoly* of propagandas in the dictatorship.

Superficially, the dictatorship seems more efficient. Everything seems to run like clockwork. Everybody has a job to do and does it. Everybody seems to like what is going on and to voice approval of it. It is quite natural that travellers returning from Germany tell how happy everybody is. They must say they're happy, for to express disapproval or discontent is a crime, punishable in extreme cases by death and in trivial cases by imprisonment. And always there is fear of expressing adverse opinion. Young people, especially, are conditioned not to have opinions other than those the dictator wishes them to have; they are trained not to think for themselves but to accept as their own thought those thoughts which the Führer wishes them to have. How long a human organization can exist when its members are not encouraged to think critically is a question. If such an organization has sufficient material power, it may exist indefinitely as a new kind of feudal society, with thought static, with individual personalities suppressed.

The democratic type of organization, with its many conflicting propagandas, seems inefficient. Here we have a confusion of tongues, a Babel of voices, warnings, charges, counter-charges, assertions, and contradictions continually assailing us through press, radio, newsreel. These propagandas are disseminated by political parties, labor unions, chambers of commerce, patriotic societies, churches, schools, and also by word of mouth of millions of individuals. It is all very confusing; but there is hope in this confusion. It is an evidence that people—at least, some people—are thinking critically and creatively. True, most of the propagandas may be parrot-repetitions of opinions by persons who do not think critically or creatively themselves; but some of the opinions or propagandas represent new thought. Out of new thought come better ways of living and working together.

In October, 1937, the Institute for Propaganda Analysis was organized by a group of scholars to help the intelligent citizen detect and analyze propaganda. The Institute is a non-profit, educational organization. It issues a monthly bulletin and occasional special bulletins dealing with today's propagandas, for these are the propagandas which concern us most. Cooperating with the Institute in devising more effective methods of recognizing and analyzing propaganda are approximately 500 high schools and colleges and adult groups in churches, forums, and various civic associations.

The Institute holds that propaganda differs from scientific analysis. The propagandist is trying to "put something across," good or bad, whereas the scientist is trying to discover truth and fact. Often the propagandist does not want careful scrutiny and criticism; he wants to bring about a specific action. Because the action may be socially beneficial or socially harmful to millions of people, it is necessary to focus upon the propagandist and his activities the searchlight of scientific scrutiny. Socially desirable propaganda will not suffer from such examination, but the opposite type will be detected and revealed for what it is.

Propaganda which concerns us most is that which alters public opinion on matters of large social consequence, often to the detriment of the majority of the people. Such propaganda, for example, is involved in issues such as these: Henry Ford should or should not recognize the C.I.O.; Hitler and Mussolini and many dignitaries of the Catholic Church are right or wrong in siding against the Spanish Loyalists; Japan is right or wrong in attacking China; anti-New Deal senators and representatives are right or wrong in approving or opposing a program of social legislation; Chamberlain did or did not betray the democratic peoples by his policy of appeasing Hitler, Mussolini, and Franco.

Opinions or propagandas associated with issues like these are highly charged with emotion, prejudice, bitterness. People make a virtue of defending their own opinions or propagandas. Many would deal with opinions or propagandas they don't like by suppressing them, by violence if need be. But suppression of unpopular opinions or propagandas is contrary to democratic conceptions of government. A "heresy" or an unpopular propaganda or opinion may be "bad" or "good." One way to find out is by analysis and

266

classification according to types and interests. This way the Institute for Propaganda Analysis follows.

To deal with propaganda by suppression through federal legislation would violate the Constitution of the United States. "Congress shall make no law respecting an establishment of religion, or prohibiting the free exercise thereof; or abridging the freedom of speech, or of the press; or the right of the people peaceably to assemble, and to petition the government for a redress of grievances."

These freedoms are the essence of democracy. In terms of them, the Institute subjects propagandas to scientific analysis, seeks to indicate whether they conform or not to the American principles of democracy.

When does a propaganda conform to democratic principles? It conforms when it tends to preserve and extend democracy; it is antagonistic when it undermines or destroys democracy.

Democracy has four parts, set forth or implied in the Constitution and federal statutes:

1. *Political.* Freedom to vote on public issues; freedom of press and speech to discuss those issues in public gatherings, in press, radio, motion pictures, etc.

2. *Economic.* Freedom to work and to participate in organizations and discussions to promote better working standards and higher living conditions for the people.

3. *Social.* Freedom from oppression based on theories of superiority or inferiority.

4. *Religious.* Freedom of worship, with separation of church and state.

With all of these freedoms are associated responsibilities. Thus, with freedom of the press goes the responsibility for accuracy in news and honesty in editorials.

Propagandas of those who pay only lip service to the Constitution, if crystallized in action or law, would destroy one or more of these freedoms. Propagandas of others could preserve and extend these freedoms.

Inseparable from propaganda analysis are periodic appraisals of controls over the channels through which opinions and propagandas flow: press, radio, motion pictures, labor unions, business and farm organizations, patriotic societies, churches, schools, and political parties.

What convictions, biases, and interests do these channels represent or express? Do these channels, by reason of bias, support and disseminate certain opinions or propagandas, and facts and alleged facts relating to them? Are other opinions or propagandas opposed by means of distortion, false emphasis, or censorship? The Institute of Propaganda Analysis is attempting to set up standards for appraising channels of propaganda as well as analyzing propaganda itself. It is today's propagandas flowing from today's conflicts which interest and concern us most. For example, analysis of World War propagandas of 1914–1918 is significant today primarily in terms of analysis of propagandas preparing perhaps for the next World War. The emphasis which high schools and colleges have given to dead issues of yesterday to the neglect of the living issues of today accounts for the fact that many high school and college graduates can be easily misled by anti-democratic propaganda.

What is the chief danger of propaganda? It appeals to emotion, and decisions made under stress of emotion often lead to disaster when the emotion crowds out cool, dispassionate thought.

Students and teachers especially should know how to deal with propaganda unemotionally.

Approximately sixteen million young people between the ages of fourteen and twenty in the next seven years will become voters. As such they will decide issues affecting every aspect of democratic freedom—political, economic, social, and religious. They cannot wait until they are twenty-one to learn how to decide issues unemotionally, critically, thoughtfully. They must be learning now how to avoid decisions antagonistic to democracy.

"Free propaganda," wrote the *Springfield Republican*, Sept. 3, 1937, "is nothing but free publicity for the views, interpretations, arguments, pleadings, truths and untruths, half-lies and lies of all creation. Propaganda is good as well as bad. 'We are surrounded by clouds of propaganda. . . .' It is up to each of us to precipitate from those clouds the true and false, the near-true and the near-false, identifying and giving to each classification its correct label."

We are fooled by propaganda chiefly because we don't recognize it when we see it. It may be fun to be fooled, but, as the cigarette ads used to say, it is more fun to know. We can more easily recognize propaganda when we see it if we are familiar with the seven common propaganda devices. These are:

1. The Name Calling Device
2. The Glittering Generalities Device
3. The Transfer Device
4. The Testimonial Device
5. The Plain Folks Device
6. The Card Stacking Device
7. The Band Wagon Device

Why are we fooled by these devices? Because they appeal to our emotions rather than to our reason. They make us believe and do something we might not believe or do if we thought about it calmly, dispassionately. In examining

268

these devices, note that they work most effectively at those times when we are too lazy to think for ourselves; also, they tie into emotions which sway us to be "for" or "against" nations, races, religions, ideals, economic and political policies and practices, and so on through automobiles, cigarettes, radios, toothpastes, presidents, and wars. With our emotions stirred, it may be fun to be fooled by these propaganda devices, but it is more fun and infinitely more to our own interests to know how they work.

Lincoln must have had in mind citizens who could balance their emotions with intelligence when he made his remark: ". . . but you can't fool all of the people all of the time."

Let's talk of three of these devices.

Name Calling is a device to make us form a judgment without examining the evidence on which it should be based. Here the propagandist appeals to our hate and fear. He does this by giving "bad names" to those individuals, groups, nations, races, policies, practices, beliefs, and ideals which he would have us condemn and reject. For centuries the name "heretic" was bad. Thousands were oppressed, tortured, or put to death as heretics. Anybody who dissented from popular or group belief or practice was in danger of being called a heretic. In the light of today's knowledge, some heresies were bad and some were good. Many of the pioneers of modern science were called heretics; witness the cases of Copernicus, Galileo, Bruno. Today's bad names include: Fascist, demagogue, dictator, Red, financial oligarchy, Communist, alien, outside agitator, economic royalist, Utopian, rabble-rouser, troublemaker, Tory.

Al Smith called Roosevelt a Communist by implication when he said, "There can be only one capital, Washington or Moscow." When Al Smith was running for the presidency many called him a tool of the Pope, saying in effect, "We must choose between Washington and Rome." That implied that Mr. Smith, if elected President, would take his orders from the Pope. Recently Secretary Ickes has called Congressman Dies a "zany"; and Congressman Dies has called those who oppose the Dies Committee "intellectual tomtits."

Use of "bad names" without presentation of their essential meaning, without all their pertinent implications, comprises perhaps the most common of all propaganda devices. Those who want to maintain the status quo apply bad names to those who would change it. For example, the Hearst press applies bad names to Communists and Socialists. Those who want to change the status quo apply bad names to those who would maintain it. For example, the *Daily Worker* and the *American Guardian* apply bad names to conservative Republicans and Democrats.

269

Glittering Generalities is a device by which the propagandist identifies his program with virtue by use of "virtue words." Here he appeals to our emotions of love, generosity, and brotherhood. He uses words like truth, freedom, honor, liberty, social justice, public service, the right to work, loyalty, progress, democracy, the American way. These words suggest shining ideals. All persons of good will believe in these ideals. Hence the propagandist, by identifying his individual group, nation, race, policy, practice, or belief with such ideals, seeks to win us to his cause. As Name Calling is a device to make us form a judgment to reject and condemn, without examining the evidence, Glittering Generalities is a device to make us accept and approve, without examining the evidence.

See the Communist *Daily Worker* for a good example of glittering generalities. On page one it always refers to itself as "People's Champion of Liberty, Progress, Peace, and Prosperity." Another example, equally good, is to be found daily in the words printed at the top of William Randolph Hearst's *Journal-American*: "Truth, Justice, Public Service."

In the Name Calling and Glittering Generalities devices, words are used to stir up our emotions and to befog our thinking. In one device "bad words" are used to make us mad; in the other "good words" are used to make us glad.

The propagandist is most effective in use of these devices when his words make us create devils to fight or gods to adore. By use of the "bad words" we personify as a "devil" some nation, race, group, individual, policy, practice, or ideal; we are made fighting mad to destroy it. By use of "good words" we personify as a god-like idol some nation, race, group, etc. Words which are "bad" to some are "good" to others, or may be made so. Thus, to some the New Deal is a "prophecy of social salvation" while to others it is an "omen of social disaster."

Transfer is a device by which the propagandist carries over the authority, sanction, and prestige of something we respect and revere to something he would have us accept. For example, most of us respect and revere our church and our nation. If the propagandist succeeds in getting church or nation to approve a campaign in behalf of some program, he thereby transfers its authority, sanction, and prestige to that program. Thus we may accept something which otherwise we might reject.

In the Transfer device symbols are constantly used. The cross represents the Christian Church. The flag represents the nation. Cartoons like Uncle Sam represent a consensus of public opinion. Those symbols stir emotions. At their very sight, with the speed of light, is aroused the whole complex of feelings we have with respect to church or nation. A cartoonist by having Uncle Sam disapprove a budget for unemployment relief would have us feel

270

that the whole United States disapproves relief costs. By drawing an Uncle Sam who approves the same budget, the cartoonist would have us feel that American people approve it. Thus, the Transfer device is used both for and against causes and ideas.

In war time propagandists of all countries use the cross, the symbol of the Church, either to approve or condemn the war. Note England's wartime slogan: "For God, for King and country"; and Germany's "Gott mit uns."

Observe that in all these devices our emotion is the stuff with which propagandists work. Without it they are helpless; with it, harnessing it to their purposes, they can make us glow with pride or burn with hatred, they can make us zealots in behalf of the program they espouse.

To say this is not to condemn emotion, an essential part of life, or to assert that all predetermined ends of propagandists are "bad." It is simply to say that the intelligent citizen does not want propagandists to utilize his emotions, even to the attainment of "good" ends, without knowing what is going on. He does not want to be "used" in the attainment of ends he may later consider "bad." He does not want to be gullible. He does not want to be fooled. He does not want to be duped, even in a "good" cause. He wants to know the facts and among these is included the fact of the utilization of his emotions.

To sum up, note these points:

First. All propaganda is associated with conflict in some form—either as a cause, or as effect, or as both cause and effect.

Second. If we check our own opinions with respect to conflicts about which we feel strongly—on which we take sides—we see the direction of our own propagandas or opinions.

Third. Propaganda which concerns us most is *today's* propaganda associated with today's conflicts. It affects our incomes, our businesses, our working conditions, our health, our education, our rights and responsibilities in fields political, economic, social, and religious.

Fourth. Our own opinions, even with respect to today's propagandas, have been largely determined for us by mental conditioning, environment. We are born white or black, Jew or Gentile, Catholic or Protestant, rich or poor. We have been reared in urban or rural communities, North or South, East or West. Our parents have been devout believers, ardent free-thinkers, or indifferent to religious doctrine. Our beliefs and actions mirror the conditioning influences of home and neighborhood, church and school, vocation and political party. We resemble those whose inheritance and environment are similar to ours; we are bound to them by ties of common experience. We tend

271

to respond favorably to their opinions and propagandas because they are "our kind of people." We tend to distrust the opinions of those who differ from us in inheritance and environment. Only drastic changes in our life conditions, with new and different experiences, associations, and influences can offset or cancel out the effect of inheritance and long years of environment.

Fifth. A fundamental step in propaganda analysis, therefore, is to analyze ourselves, to make clear *why* we act and believe as we do with respect to various conflicts and issues—political, economic, social and religious. Do we believe and act as we do because we are Jews, Protestants, Catholics; because our fathers were strong Republicans or lifelong Democrats; because our parents were Methodists or Seventh Day Adventists; because our fathers belonged to labor unions; because our fathers were employers who fought labor unions?

Sixth. The most effective way to deal with propaganda, once we recognize it, is to suspend our judgment until we obtain essential facts and implications involved in the propaganda. We must ask: Who is the propagandist? Is he consciously and intentionally trying to influence our thoughts and actions? For what purpose does he use words and symbols? What are their exact meanings? What do they mean to the propagandist? What do they mean to us? What are the propagandist's interests? Do his interests coincide with the interests of most citizens?

Seventh. The fact that some words are omnibus words makes many the easy dupes of propagandists. Omnibus words are words extraordinarily difficult to define. They carry all meanings to all men. Therefore, the best test for the factual content of propaganda lies in specific, concrete definition of the words and symbols used by the propagandist.

The best test for *purpose* of propaganda is, if possible, to know the purpose of the propagandist. Who is he? Whom does he represent? Does he represent some group or person, consciously or unconsciously? Does this group or individual have an axe to grind? If we did what the propagandist wants us to do, would we be serving our own interests or the selfish interests of the group or individual?

Eighth. Remember that there are three ways to deal with propaganda—first, to suppress it; second, to answer it by counter-propaganda; third, to analyze it.

Suppression of propaganda is contrary to democratic principles, specifically contrary to the provisions of the United States Constitution.

Counter-propaganda is legitimate but often intensifies cleavages.

Analysis of propaganda, on the other hand, cannot hurt propaganda for a cause that we consider "good." Of course, "good" and "bad" are relevant.

Most persons everywhere would consider propaganda to eliminate tuberculosis, infantile paralysis, and other diseases "good." The dictator-propagandist would consider "bad" much that believers in democracy would consider "good." For example, he would consider a propaganda campaign for education to encourage critical thought on social issues as "bad," whereas in a democracy believers in democracy would consider such propaganda "good."

A final word about two current propaganda issues before the American people. Many would suppress the propaganda of Father Coughlin. It seems to me this would be a foolish thing to do. *Father Coughlin ought to have radio time, and he ought to have it free of charge, but with the stipulation that when he speaks others have an opportunity to speak on the same program to express different points of view.* All listeners might well be invited to analyze all points of view on such a program.

The same holds for Congressman Dies. Despite sharp opinion or propaganda to the contrary, I express the opinion or propaganda that the idea of a Congressional Committee to investigate propaganda is altogether admirable. It is a good thing to have this committee continued. Perusal of the published volumes of the committee indicates that it has revealed in its investigation a great many propagandas. It is true also that some members of the committee, including Mr. Dies himself, and particularly in public speeches, have themselves disseminated propaganda which could be called un-American. When Mr. Dies speaks as a propagandist, I think the conditions ought to be exactly the same as those suggested for Father Coughlin. Indeed, those ought to be the conditions for anyone who expresses opinions or views on controversial issues. Good examples of this method are found in such radio programs as the Town Meeting of the Air, the University of Chicago Round Table, and the People's Platform.

Direct, penetrating thought, examination of sources, and the constant recollection of our own conditioning—these are the things which are needed in propaganda analysis. These are the things needed to make democracy function more effectively in all its aspects—political, economic, social, and religious.

THE FIFTH COLUMN[1]

THE other day, in Baltimore, a man parked his car across the street from a German restaurant. Its name is best left unmentioned. A passerby threw a lighted cigarette butt into the car. The butt set fire to the cushions. Somebody saw the smoke and called for help. The restaurant owner ran over with a fire extinguisher and put out the blaze. Police radio cars arrived. The restaurant owner chatted for a few minutes with some of the policemen. They left and he went back into his restaurant. Normally that would have been the end of the incident.

But the temperature of public opinion is now far from normal. Within forty-eight hours rumors had spread about the city that the restaurant had been raided as a center of Fifth Column activities. It was said that a police patrol backed up to the place and officers brought out no less than twenty-four big, square boxes, each of them containing a huge bomb. It was whispered that the restaurant owner had been subjected to a severe cross-examination in the local F.B.I. offices. People claimed to have heard these stories from eye-witnesses or from people who had talked with eye-witnesses. One woman phoned a columnist on a Baltimore daily[2] and asked in a great fury: "Why do the Baltimore newspapers conceal the fact that the F.B.I. discovered a Fifth Column nest? Are they sympathetic to the Fifth Columnists?" A cigarette butt, as Louis Azrael, Baltimore *News-Post* columnist said, had ignited Baltimore.

Fifth Column hysteria is not limited to Baltimore. One can pick up few newspapers without reading that somebody has called somebody else a Fifth Columnist. The President and his associates have been termed Fifth Columnists. New Dealers have called Lindbergh Fifth Columnist for advocating isolation. Congress has begun to pass legislation against Communists and Bundists as Fifth Columnists. From the far Right has come the cry that all liberals are Fifth Columnists. On the far Left Communists have applied the term to big business and their own heretic sectlets. Fascists have applied the term to interventionists. Above all the feeling has grown that to be opposed to American aid to the Allies or to a more active "non-belligerency" in the present war is to lay oneself open to the suspicion of being a Fifth Columnist.

Propaganda's chief weapon in whipping up fear and hatred before America's entrance into the last war was the atrocity story. This time the same purposes seem to be served by stories of the Fifth Column. The atrocity story— the raped nuns and the Belgian babies with their hands cut off—were too

[1] A Bulletin of the Institute for Propaganda Analysis.

[2] This account is taken from Louis Azrael's column in the Baltimore *News-Post* of June 10, 1940.

274

thoroughly discredited after the last war to be effective in this one. This time the Fifth Column, sinister symbol of treachery and lurking danger, has seized on the popular imagination. It is effective as war propaganda because it creates fear, and fear stirs hostility far better than does sympathy with victims of the German blitzkrieg or animosity toward Nazi-Fascist principles. Pity is a luxury and ideology is subject for debate, but the shadow of the Fifth Column is a direct and immediate menace to ourselves. We read little in the press about atrocities, much about the Fifth Column. "In the prosecution of this war," the Sons of the American Revolution declared at their 51st annual Congress in Washington, "military success is sought . . . by flouting international law, disregarding all neutral rights and inviting treason and by planting Fifth Columns within the confines of the countries attacked."[3]

THE GREEKS HAD A WORD . . .

The tactic represented by the Fifth Column is far older than the name itself. It is used interchangeably with the term Trojan Horse, and that goes back, of course, to Homer's story of how the Greeks effected an entry into Troy by smuggling their men into the city in a hollow horse, presented to Troy as a gift. Fifth Columns operated in the Peloponnesian War, 500 years before Christ. The great Greek historian, Thucydides, tells us that the democratic Athenians depended on democratic sympathizers within the cities they attacked, while their chief enemies, the Spartans, relied on sympathizers with their own oligarchic and "National Socialist" form of government. The same tactic played its part in the World War. The Germans permitted Lenin to pass from Switzerland into Russia in the famous "sealed train" in the hope that he would act as a revolutionary Fifth Column to overthrow the Russian government and take Russia out of the war. The Wilson Administration established secret contacts with German democrats during the World War and sent the Hungarian pacifist Rozika Schwimmer (later refused American citizenship because she wouldn't bear arms) on a Fifth Column mission into Austro-Hungary to contact democratic elements and give them copies of Wilson's messages.[4] At home during America's participation in the war travelling salesmen were warned, "throughout the land the Kaiser's paid agents and sympathizers are spreading by word of mouth rumors, criticisms and lies that aim to disrupt our national unity . . ."[5]

The term Fifth Column originated when a Franco general before Madrid

[3]Washington *Post*, May 22, 1940.

[4]James R. Mock and Cedric Larson, *Words That Won the War*, pp. 276–278. Princeton University Press, 1939.

[5]*Ibid.*, p. 176, "The Kaiserite in America."

boasted in 1936, "We have four columns of soldiers and the 'fifth column' will rise up from within Madrid to help us."[6] But the phrase was given new prominence and the hysteria associated with it touched off by Leland Stowe's famous Fifth Column cable from Stockholm to the Chicago *Daily News* syndicate, April 15. "For the first time," Stowe cabled, "the story behind Germany's paralyzing twelve-hour conquest of Norway last Tuesday can be told. . . . Norway's capital and great seaports were not captured by armed force. They were seized with unparalleled speed by means of a gigantic conspiracy which must undoubtedly rank among the most audacious, most perfectly oiled, political plots of the last century." Stowe said, "By bribery and extraordinary infiltration on the part of Nazi agents, and by treason on the part of a few highly placed Norwegian civilian and defense officials, the German dictatorship built a Trojan Horse inside of Norway. Then, when the hour struck, the German plotters spiked the guns of the Norwegian navy and reduced its formidable fortresses to impotence."[7]

WHAT HAPPENED IN NORWAY

The full story of the German blitzkrieg against Norway will not be known until after this war is over. Whether Norway was the victim of a Fifth Column or of a surprise attack launched by a military machine that has proved too powerful for bigger countries remains to be determined. But there is evidence that the Stowe Fifth Column report was exaggerated. Before the guns of the Norwegian navy were "spiked" they took a heavy toll of the German navy. The Norwegian minelayer Olaf Tryggvason sank three Nazi cruisers, the Emden, the Karlsruhe and a third cruiser said to be the Blucher as the German flotilla came into Oslo Fjord. The forts of Oskarsburg and Seierstein were reported to have sunk a battleship further up the Fjord before mysterious capitulation orders stopped firing.[8]

Were these capitulation orders the work of Norwegian treachery—of a Fifth Column—or of Nazi duplicity? On April 18 the Norwegian legation at Washington issued a statement saying that fake orders and not treason or sabotage were responsible for the confusion in the defense of Norway during the first impact of the Nazi attack.[9] The Norwegian legation in Stockholm cabled, "Sensational rumors of treason and sabotage must be received with the greatest reservation."[10] General Carl Johan Erichsen, commander of the first

[6]N. Y. *World Telegram*, June 4, 1940. See also Ernest Hemingway's play *The Fifth Column*.
[7]Chicago *Daily News*, New York *Post* and other papers, April 15, 1940.
[8]New York *Times*, April 16, 1940.
[9]New York *Times*, April 19, 1940.   [10]*Ibid.*

division in southeastern Norway, denied stories of Fifth Column treason. "In these days when we Norwegians are living through such terrible happenings," he said, "it is to be deeply regretted that our burden should be increased by rumors which are entirely without foundation in fact. These rumors must be regarded as a part of a strong propaganda which is being conducted by the enemy in order to destroy us by such means as well."[11] Pulitzer Prize winner Otto D. Tolischus cabled the New York *Times* on April 27 that unpreparedness rather than a Fifth Column was the cause of the Norwegian defeat. Tolischus reported that the German element in Norway was smaller than in almost any other country, with only about 500 German citizens, most of them Jewish refugees, in the country at the time.[12]

Much was made at first of the role played by Major Vikdun Quisling, head of the Norwegian Nazi party, in the conquest of the country. In a communique of April 15, the Norwegian government declared that on the first contact between itself and the invaders it was informed that Hitler's personal wish was that Quisling should head the government.[13] But two days after the attack on Norway Berlin had recognized that the Norwegian Nazis were "a hopelessly small minority" and was holding aloof from Major Vikdun Quisling's "opportunist cabinet" in Oslo.[14] The last heard of Quisling was when the British Under Secretary of Foreign Affairs Butler announced in the Commons on June 12 that the Norwegian Nazi's name had been stricken from the Order of the British Empire. Butler said Quisling was made an honorary commander of the order on November 22, 1939, in recognition of services rendered to the British government in Russia while serving in Moscow on the Norwegian legation staff.[15] The nature of the services was not explained.

NAZI TROJAN HORSES

Whatever the true causes of the Norwegian disaster, pro-Nazi elements had aided in the seizure of Austria, the disruption of Czechoslovakia, and the annexation of Memel and Danzig. Fear of the Nazi Fifth Column became world wide. In Yugoslavia German homes were raided. "We want no Quislings, no Henleins, no Hachas, no Seyss-Inquarts in Yugoslavia," one official said, calling the roll of the Nazi Fifth Columnists who figured in Norway, the Sudetenland, Bohemia-Moravia and Austria.[16] On May 4 prominent Nazis and Nazi sympathizers were arrested in Holland and Belgium. On May 18 Hungary arrested 200 Communists as Fifth Columnists. On May 23 there

---

[11]*Ibid.*
[12]New York *Times*, April 28, 1940.
[13]New York *Times*, April 16, 1940.
[14]New York *Times*, April 12, 1940.
[15]New York *Herald Tribune*, June 13, 1940.
[16]New York *Times*, April 19, 1940.

was a roundup of Fascists and alleged Fascist sympathizers in England, Sir Oswald Mosley, British Fascist leader, and Captain Archibald H. M. Ramsay, Conservative M.P., being among those arrested.[17] In South Africa and the Philippines, in Egypt and in Latin America there was talk of Fifth Columnists. "America's defenders," the Associated Press reported from Washington on June 8, "are watching warily the foreign agents operating in the lands below the Rio Grande. In national capitals from Mexico City down to Santiago and Buenos Aires, the governments are alert to the danger from within. They call it *quinta columna*—the same old Fifth Column that be-devils the neutrals of Europe." Danger was seen "lurking in close-knit German settlements of the São Paulo coffee district; in the German pilots who, even when their country is at war, guide commercial planes over the South American mountains; in settlements of Japanese farmers and fishing folk on land well-suited to air base uses—and close to the Panama Canal." In Canada, Adrien Arcand, Fascist leader, and many of his aides were seized by the authorities on May 30.

A flood of Fifth Column stories came from Mexico, to the annoyance of the Cardenas government. Dies proposed that the Monroe Doctrine be extended to cover Fifth Column activities in Latin America.[18] An unofficial spokesman for the Cardenas regime called these charges ridiculous. "The fantastic charges of Mr. Dies—who is from Texas, an oil state—are seconded by political groups and Mexican newspapers whose connections with the oil companies are well known, for which reason it is believed that the American Congressman is simply doing his part to increase the tension of the situation, in order to bring pressure on the Mexican government and to prepare the way for serious future events."[19] What these serious future events are is not explained but Paul Mallon, Hearst Washington columnist, reported recently that Mr. Roosevelt wanted authority to call out the National Guard in order "to cope with possible local disturbances" in Latin American countries.[20]

FIFTH COLUMN CLASSIC

Wildest of the Fifth Column stories was that reported in Ludwig Lore's column in the New York *Post* on May 18. Lore attributed it to the Jewish Telegraphic Agency and said he would not have reprinted it "if it were not given on the authority of the Dutch government." According to this story Nazi spies entered the Netherlands last February 16 in the guise of Jewish

[17]New York *Times*, May 23, 1940.

[18]New York *Journal American*, June 6, 1940.

[19]"The Crisis in Mexico" by Alejandro Carrillo. *Virginia Quarterly Review*, Summer, 1940.

[20]New York *Journal American*, June 7, 1940.

refugees "even taking the precaution of being circumcized." They were un-masked—so the report has it—when a rabbi determined that they had not been circumcized according to the Jewish ritual. The story appeared originally in the French newspaper *L'Œuvre*: "The Gestapo had selected sixteen men who looked Jewish, had them attend synagogue services for several weeks, furnished them with passports stamped with 'J' (Jew) and sent them to Holland. The Netherlands anti-espionage service, suspecting that they were spies, had them arrested." This may become a classic of Fifth Column propaganda.

NAME CALLING

From the point of view of propaganda analysis the most important aspect of the Fifth Column is its use as the newest and most effective form of Name Calling. The extent and variety of those who have been called Fifth Colum-nists in the few weeks since the Norwegian conquest brought the phrase into prominence is amazing. It is noteworthy that although the Fifth Column originally denoted Nazi sympathizers and has been extended to Communists because of the Nazi-Soviet Non-Aggression Pact, it is being used with ever greater frequency against the New Deal and its liberal supporters. This was first called sharply to public attention on May 15 when Hendrik Willem Van Loon announced his resignation from the Dutch Treat Club because its president, Clarence Budington Kelland, said, "The Fifth Column in this country is headed by that fellow in the White House."[21] Similarly on May 20 Bainbridge Colby, Secretary of State under Woodrow Wilson and a frequent contributor to the Hearst press, told the General Society of Colonial Wars in New York City, "In Europe the Fifth Column is in disguise. With us, the Fifth Column is in office."[22] Congressman J. Parnell Thomas of New Jersey said over a nation-wide radio hookup, "The Fifth Column in the United States has flourished under New Deal rule. In some respects it is synonymous to the New Deal, so the surest way of removing the Fifth Column from our shores is to remove the New Deal from the seat of the government." Borough President Harvey of Queens, in an address warning the New York Kiwanis Club against subversive elements in the city's educational and police depart-ments, said "Fifth Column parachute troops" had been landing in the United States for two decades. "Our advance guards," Harvey explained, "don't wear uniforms or bristle with guns. They are disguised as so-called 'liberals' . . ."[23]

[21] New York *World Telegram*, May 15, 1940.
[22] New York *Journal American*, May 21, 1940.
[23] New York *Sun*, May 22, 1940.

Fifth Column Name Calling has not been limited to the New Deal or even to politics. Thomas F. Woodlock, Wall Street *Journal* columnist, attacked John Dewey's educational theories as "a dangerous 'Fifth Column' in the nation's life." Senator Norris made a four hour speech in the Senate denouncing J. Edgar Hoover as a peril to civil liberties and "the greatest publicity hound on the American continent,"[24] but the F.B.I. director told the New York City Federation of Women's Clubs that recent attacks upon him were a cover up for Fifth Column activities.[25] Wendell Willkie at Kansas City on May 24 declared that if the Republican party gave up its opposition to a third term it would become a Fifth Column.[26]

COMMUNISTS ACCUSE MR. MORGAN

The *Daily Worker* pinned the label on its old friend, J. P. Morgan: "There is a real Fifth Column in our country.... Their chief is J. P. Morgan, fattening like a vampire off the blood of young men."[27] William Z. Foster spoke of the wiping out of a "Trotskyite-Zinovievite-Bukharinite Fifth Column"[28] in the Soviet Union. Dorothy Thompson saw a Fifth Column "in our great industries ... the line taken with them is that Nazism represents the logical quintessence of industrial—as opposed to financial—capitalism. . . ."[29] Senator Barbour of New Jersey hinted that his Democratic opponent, James H. R. Cromwell, was a Fifth Columnist. He called Cromwell "an admitted seditionist" for making what Barbour interpreted as slurring references to the Constitution in a book called *The Voice of Young America*.[30] A speaker before the New York State Association of Young Republican Clubs, referring to the anti-Dewey bloc, said, "In this time of crisis it is our duty to see that no Fifth Column operates in the Republican party."[31] A Fifth Columnist, it soon began to seem, was anybody who disagreed with you.

More particularly, a Fifth Columnist was someone who did not wish to help the Allies or to enter the war. This, though rarely given open statement, was the implication of a growing volume of pro-Ally propaganda. "Fifth Columnists are already active in America," said Senator Byrnes in his reply to Lindbergh, "and those who consciously or unconsciously retard the efforts of this government to provide for the defense of the American people are the Fifth Columnists' most effective fellow travellers."[32] Colonel Frank Knox in a Chicago *Daily News* editorial called anti-New Deal die-hards among busi-

[24]*Congressional Record*, May 7, 1940. [29]New York *Herald Tribune*, May 27, 1940.
[25]New York *Times*, May 5, 1940. [30]New York *Times*, June 3, 1940.
[26]New York *Herald Tribune*, May 25, 1940. [31]New York *Times*, May 18, 1940.
[27]*Daily Worker*, May 22, 1940. [32]New York *Times*, May 23, 1940.
[28]*Ibid.*, June 12, 1940.

ness men Fifth Columnists. "It is easy to spot these elements of the Fifth Column," he said. "Today they are unusually conspicuous because of attitudes and utterances that seem to show they would prefer to leave this country wide open to invasion rather than to support a national administration they do not like. . . ."[33] The Committee to Defend America by Aiding the Allies, in the full page advertisements it placed in the nation's press June 10, said, "The Fifth Column is led in this as in other countries by Nazis and Communists and their fellow travellers. . . . Their object is to destroy national unity . . . sabotaging all aid to the Allies."[34]

AMERICA'S "PEACE FRONT"

"Italian Pro-Fascists," said a New York *Post* headline after Italy joined the war, "In U. S. Join Peace Front. Two Newspapers Here Take Communist-Nazi Isolationist Line."[35] "Peace Front Here," the New York *World Telegram* discovered, "Linked to Communists."[36] War feeling, Senator Nye protested to the Sales Executive Club in New York, is at a stage where "if you are not ready to go the whole way you must be pro-Nazi, pro-Italian, pro-Communist, or anything except pro-American. . . ."[37]

The Administration has warned against hysteria but has also warned against the Fifth Column. "We have seen the treacherous use of the Fifth Column," the President told Congress on May 16 in his famous 50,000-planes message, "by which persons supposed to be peaceful visitors were actually part of an enemy occupation."[38] On May 24 he told a press conference that he considered the Dies committee records a good source of information on Fifth Column activities.[39] Two days earlier he asked Congress to transfer the Bureau of Immigration and Naturalization from the Labor Department to the Department of Justice in order to permit a closer check on Fifth Columnists. Mr. Roosevelt said that this reflected no intention to deprive aliens of "their civil liberties" but that it would enable the government "to deal quickly with those aliens who conduct themselves in a manner that conflicts with the public interest."[40] And in his defense message of May 26 the President warned again against "The Fifth Column that betrays a nation unprepared for treachery."[41]

[33]Reprinted in *The Progressive*, June 1, 1940.   [38]New York *Times*, May 17, 1940.
[34]New York *Times*, June 10, 1940.   [39]New York *Journal American*, May 24, 1940.
[35]New York *Post*, June 11, 1940.   [40]New York *Times*, May 23, 1940.
[36]New York *World Telegram*, June 4, 1940.   [41]New York *Times*, May 27, 1940.
[37]New York *Times*, June 12, 1940.

THE SUPREME COURT ACTS

The demand for national unity made itself felt even on the Supreme Court where Justice Frankfurter for the majority, with only Justice Stone dissenting, upheld the expulsion from school of members of the Jehovah's Witnesses sect for refusing to salute the flag. When members of this sect were attacked in Maine a few days later the New York *Herald Tribune* protested, "We have the 'liberal' members of the Supreme Court to thank ... the Supreme Court's recent decision that the Jehovah's Witnesses must salute the flag seems to have convinced several hundred Maine rustics that it is their personal responsibility to see this decree carried out. The national 'Fifth Column' hysteria had added fuel to the flames. ..."[42]

In Texas and in Maine members of the Jehovah's Witnesses, anti-Nazi but also anti-war, were attacked by mobs. Legion posts organized to "fight the Fifth Column." The New York National Guard revived its Intelligence Unit, which ordinarily operates only in war-time, to watch for Fifth Columnists.[43] In Sparta, Michigan, a foundry worker confessed that he shot and killed his neighbor because he suspected that the neighbor was a Fifth Columnist.[44] A Technocrat was jailed in Sapulpa, Oklahoma, as a Fifth Columnist.[45] A professional parachutist sent a letter to an Omaha, Nebraska, newspaper begging people not to shoot anyone seen descending in a parachute during the county fair season.[46] A group of fifty women organized an anti-parachutist rifle club in New York City with the acting regional director of the National Legion of Mothers of America as their head. A naval reserve lieutenant presented the women with two rifles to start practicing.[47] An Erase-The-Fifth-Column, Inc., was formed in Los Angeles. Jeff Davis, King of the Hoboes, announced formation of a group to be known as the Jungle Bulls headed by One-Eye Connolly to watch for the Fifth Column. "People don't realize it," Davis said, "but the hoboes are the best friends this country has. They're loyal."[48]

JANITORS HELP TOO

Janitors were organized in New York City to spy on late parties[49] and the noted Italian anti-Fascist writer, G. A. Borgese, deplored the abuse of free speech by Fifth Columnists.[50] Volunteer firemen, in national convention at

[42]New York *Herald Tribune* editorial, June 13, 1940.
[43]New York *Times*, May 23, 1940.
[44]Milwaukee *Evening Post*, May 28, 1940.
[45]*American Guardian*, May 31, 1940.
[46]United Press dispatch from Omaha in Milwaukee *Evening Post*, May 31, 1940.
[47]New York *Times*, May 23, 1940. [49]New York *Sun*, May 25, 1940.
[48]New York *Times*, May 29, 1940. [50]New York *Times*, May 22, 1940.

Philadelphia, pledged themselves to fight the Fifth Column.[51] Aliens were ordered registered in Georgia and New Jersey and deputy sheriffs were posted at the polls in Andover Township, New Jersey, to bar Bund members from the polls.[52]

A bill was introduced in the New York City Council to guard against the Fifth Column by forcing all aliens to register.[53] Harold G. Campbell, superintendent of New York City schools, told Kindergarten-6B teachers they must help fight the Fifth Column.[54] The Erie County, New York, American Legion mobilized to keep Fifth Columnists from crossing the border at Niagara Falls.[55] The 300,000 members of the National Rifle Association were warned to keep a watch for Fifth Columnists along our borders.[56] On Long Island, Nassau County officials set up a clearing house for news of subversive activities because residents expressed concern over the county's proximity to New York City.[57] The Longshoremen's Union refused to permit the discharge of Italian members[58] and the House by a vote of 330–42 passed a bill ordering the deportation of Harry Bridges, West Coast longshoremen's leader, as a "symbol of the fifth column."[59] "Deluge of Tips On 'Fifth Column' Swamps the F.B.I.," said a headline in the New York *Herald Tribune*, May 30.

THE ASSOCIATED FARMERS

Leading the hue and cry against the Fifth Column were some odd organizations and characters, not always associated in the public mind with devotion to American principles. The Associated Farmers of California[60] issued a press release in June declaring that they were "throwing every resource at their command into a fight against the Fifth Column in this State...." This was too much for the New York *Times* which warned in an editorial on the Fifth Column on June 13: "It is highly important that no group should be permitted to act on the assumption that persons who disagree with it or stand in its way economically should therefore be treated as 'Fifth Columns.'..." The *Times* mentioned the Associated Farmers and said: "This country is likely to become a madhouse if anyone with an interest or grievance may use the country's danger to promote the interest or satisfy the grievance."

[51]New York *Times*, May 27, 1940.   [56]New York *Journal American*, June 7, 1940.

[52]New York *Journal American*, May 22, 1940.   [57]New York *Times*, May 26, 1940.

[53]New York *Herald Tribune*, May 25, 1940.   [58]New York *Sun*, June 13, 1940.

[54]New York *Times*, May 25, 1940.   [59]New York *Times*, June 14, 1940.

[55]New York *Times*, June 5, 1940.

[60]See Institute for Propaganda Analysis Bulletin, Volume II, No. 12, "The Associated Farmers."

Of the four "top men" who met to organize the Associated Farmers for action against the "Fifth Column" one, Colonel Walter E. Garrison of Lodi, has led attacks on strikers and another, Philip Bancroft, had many kind things to say of the Hitler regime after a visit to Germany a few years ago.

Foremost in the ranks of those attacking the Fifth Column was William Randolph Hearst and on May 30 the New York *Journal American* took credit for pioneering in the battle. "The Hearst papers have for years warned the country against all forms of subversion, no matter under what mask it parades." The final reference was not explained, but readers may have recalled Hearst's frequent attacks on the New Deal as "Communistic." Another strange bedfellow in the fight against the Fifth Column was Senator Robert R. Reynolds of North Carolina. The April 14 issue of William Dudley Pelley's anti-Semitic and pro-Nazi *Liberation* devoted two full columns to praise of "the good work" being done by Reynolds. Reynolds' own native Fascist paper, *The American Vindicator*, is often sold at Silvershirt meetings. "There are many herds of Trojan horses grazing in the fertile fields of America," Reynolds said in asking for a broad Congressional investigation of Fifth Column activities on May 22. His words were echoed in the Stop Hitler Now advertisement run by the Committee to Help the Allies on June 10. "We cannot ignore the fact," the ad said, "that Trojan horses are grazing in all the fertile fields of North and South America."

MAYOR HAGUE ENLISTS

Mayor Hague of Jersey City has also enlisted in the fight against the Fifth Column. The New York *Daily Mirror* on June 4 reported that Hague, recently rebuked by the Supreme Court for violation of the Constitution in Jersey City, was working with war veterans to "clamp down" on the Fifth Column there. Borough President Harvey of Queens, as we have seen, is also taking credit for having long ago warned against "liberal" Fifth Columnists, and Martin Dies left Washington on May 26 for Buffalo to begin an investigation of Fifth Column elements in New York State.[61] Ex-Congressman John J. O'Connor, who has attacked the New Deal as "Communistic" in the past, announced organization of a First Column to fight the Fifth Column.[62]

PROTESTS ARE FEW

Protests were made against the hysteria but they were few. "Before long," Raymond Clapper said in his column in the New York *World Telegram* of May 28, "any little pants presser will be able to put a competitor out of the

[61]New York *Herald Tribune*, May 27, 1940.   [62]New York *Times*, June 10, 1940.

way by turning him in as a Fifth Columnist. Any fellow who wants 30 cents an hour when the boss is paying 25 cents will be suspected as a Fifth Columnist. If this business goes on what will be the difference between a Communist criticizing President Roosevelt or a Republican criticizing him? They will both be stirring up dissension." Samuel Grafton in the New York *Post* of June 1 said, "There is a $4\frac{1}{2}$ column in this country. The $4\frac{1}{2}$ column consists of men who are trying to make political capital for themselves by exploiting the public's proper fear of the Fifth Column." And in characteristic vein H. L. Mencken in the Baltimore *Sun* on June 9 said of the Fifth Column hysteria, "Nothing could be better adapted to the uses of demagogy. It gives every boob a chance to harry and defame his neighbors in the name of Service, and it secures him against any hazard of reprisal for most of his operations may be carried out in whispers, and whenever he is dragged into the open he will have a gang behind him and not only a gang, but the full force of the state." "My own fear," Jonathan Daniels, editor of the Raleigh *News and Observer*, said on June 9 in declining to sign a statement calling for an American declaration of war against Germany, "is that we may embrace fascism at home in the guise of defense against fascism abroad." America needs to be on guard against a Fifth Column. It also needs to be on guard against Fifth Column hysteria.

War

THE ARMY IN BROBDINGNAG[1]

Jonathan Swift

IN HOPES to ingratiate myself farther into his Majesty's favour, I told him of an invention discovered between three and four hundred years ago, to make a certain powder, into an heap of which the smallest spark of fire falling, would kindle the whole in a moment, although it were as big as a mountain, and make it all fly up in the air together, with a noise and agitation greater than thunder. That a proper quantity of this powder rammed into an hollow tube of brass or iron, according to its bigness, would drive a ball of iron or lead with such violence and speed, as nothing was able to sustain its force. That the largest balls thus discharged, would not only destroy whole ranks of an army at once, but batter the strongest walls to the ground, sink down ships, with a thousand men in each, to the bottom of the sea; and, when linked together by a chain, would cut through masts and rigging, divide hundreds of bodies in the middle, and lay all waste before them. That we often put this powder into large hollow balls of iron, and discharged them by an engine into some city we were besieging, which would rip up the pavements, tear the houses to pieces, burst and throw splinters on every side, dashing out the brains of all who came near. That I knew the ingredients very well, which were cheap, and common; I understood the manner of compounding them, and could direct his workmen how to make those tubes of a size proportionable to all other things in his Majesty's kingdom, and the largest need not be above an hundred foot long; twenty or thirty of which tubes, charged with the proper quantity of powder and balls, would batter down the walls of the strongest town in his dominions in a few hours, or destroy the whole metropolis, if ever it should pretend to dispute his absolute commands. This I humbly offered to his Majesty, as a small tribute of acknowledgment in return of so many marks that I had received of his royal favour and protection.

The King was struck with horror at the description I had given of those terrible engines, and the proposal I had made. He was amazed how so impotent and grovelling an insect as I (these were his expressions) could entertain such inhuman ideas, and in so familiar a manner as to appear wholly unmoved at all by the scenes of blood and desolation, which I had painted as the common effects of those destructive machines, whereof he said some evil genius, enemy to mankind, must have been the first contriver. As for himself, he protested that although few things delighted him so much as new discoveries in art or in nature, yet he would rather lose half his kingdom than be

[1]From "A Voyage to Brobdingnag" in *Gulliver's Travels* by Jonathan Swift (1726).

privy to such a secret, which he commanded me, as I valued my life, never to mention any more.

A strange effect of narrow principles and short views! that a prince possessed of every quality which procures veneration, love, and esteem; of strong parts, great wisdom, and profound learning, endued with admirable talents for government, and almost adored by his subjects, should from a nice unnecessary scruple, whereof in Europe we can have no conception, let slip an opportunity put into his hands, that would have made him absolute master of the lives, the liberties, and the fortunes of his people. Neither do I say this with the least intention to detract from the many virtues of that excellent King, whose character I am sensible will on this account be very much lessened in the opinion of an English reader: but I take this defect among them to have risen from their ignorance, they not having hitherto reduced politics into a science, as the more acute wits of Europe have done. For I remember very well, in a discourse one day with the King, when I happened to say there were several thousand books among us written upon the art of government, it gave him (directly contrary to my intention) a very mean opinion of our understandings. He professed both to abominate and despise all mystery, refinement, and intrigue, either in a prince or a minister. He could not tell what I meant by secrets of state, where an enemy or some rival nation were not in the case. He confined the knowledge of governing within very narrow bounds; to common sense and reason, to justice and lenity, to the speedy determination of civil and criminal causes; with some other obvious topics, which are not worth considering. And he gave it for his opinion, that whoever could make two ears of corn or two blades of grass grow upon a spot of ground where only one grew before, would deserve better of mankind, and do more essential service to his country than the whole race of politicians put together.

As to their military affairs, they boast that the King's army consists of an hundred and seventy-six thousand foot and thirty-two thousand horse: if that may be called an army which is made up of tradesmen in the several cities, and farmers in the country, whose commanders are only the nobility and gentry, without pay or reward. They are indeed perfect enough in their exercises, and under very good discipline, wherein I saw no great merit; for how should it be otherwise, where every farmer is under the command of his own landlord, and every citizen under that of the principal men in his own city, chosen after the manner of Venice by ballot?

I have often seen the militia of Lorbrulgrud[2] drawn out to exercise in a great field near the city of twenty miles square. They were in all not above

[2]Name of the metropolis in Brobdingnag, meaning Pride of the Universe.

twenty-five thousand foot, and six thousand horse; but it was impossible for me to compute their number, considering the space of ground they took up. A cavalier mounted on a large steed, might be about an hundred foot high. I have seen this whole body of horse, upon a word of command, draw their swords at once, and brandish them in the air. Imagination can figure nothing so grand, so surprising, and so astonishing. It looked as if ten thousand flashes of lightning were darting at the same time from every quarter of the sky.

I was curious to know how this prince, to whose dominions there is no access from any other country, came to think of armies, or to teach his people the practice of military discipline. But I was soon informed, both by conversation and reading their histories. For in the course of many ages they have been troubled with the same disease to which the whole race of mankind is subject; the nobility often contending for power, the people for liberty, and the King for absolute dominion. All which, however happily tempered by the laws of the kingdom, have been sometimes violated by each of the three parties, and have once or more occasioned civil wars, the last whereof was happily put an end to by this prince's grandfather by a general composition;[3] and the militia, then settled with common consent, hath been ever since kept in the strictest duty.

IN THE LAND OF THE HOUYHNHNMS[1]

Jonathan Swift

THE reader may please to observe, that the following extract of many conversations I had with my master, contains a summary of the most material points which were discoursed at several times for above two years; his Honour often desiring fuller satisfaction as I farther improved in the Houyhnhnm tongue. I laid before him, as well as I could, the whole state of Europe; I discoursed of trade and manufactures, of arts and sciences; and the answers I gave to all the questions he made, as they arose upon several subjects, were a fund of conversation not to be exhausted. But I shall here only set down the substance of what passed between us concerning my own country, reducing it into order as well as I can, without any regard to time or other circumstances, while I strictly adhere to truth. My only concern is that I shall hardly be able to do justice to my master's arguments and expressions, which must

[3]General agreement.
[1]From "A Voyage to the Houyhnhnms" in *Gulliver's Travels* by Jonathan Swift (1726).

needs suffer by my want of capacity, as well as by a translation into our barbarous English.

In obedience therefore to his Honour's commands, I related to him the Revolution under the Prince of Orange; the long war with France entered into by the said prince, and renewed by his successor the present Queen, wherein the greatest powers of Christendom were engaged, and which still continued: I computed at his request that about a million of Yahoos[2] might have been killed in the whole progress of it, and perhaps a hundred or more cities taken, and thrice as many ships burnt or sunk.

He asked me what were the usual causes or motives that made one country go to war with another. I answered they were innumerable, but I should only mention a few of the chief. Sometimes the ambition of princes, who never think they have land or people enough to govern; sometimes the corruption of ministers, who engage their master in a war in order to stifle or divert the clamour of the subjects against their evil administration. Difference in opinions hath cost many millions of lives: for instance, whether flesh be bread, or bread be flesh; whether the juice of a certain berry be blood or wine; whether whistling be a vice or a virtue; whether it be better to kiss a post, or throw it into the fire; what is the best colour for a coat, whether black, white, red, or gray; and whether it should be long or short, narrow or wide, dirty or clean; with many more. Neither are any wars so furious and bloody, or of so long continuance, as those occasioned by difference in opinion, especially if it be in things indifferent.

Sometimes the quarrel between two princes is to decide which of them shall dispossess a third of his dominions, where neither of them pretend to any right. Sometimes one prince quarrelleth with another, for fear the other should quarrel with him. Sometimes a war is entered upon, because the enemy is too strong, and sometimes because he is too weak. Sometimes our neighbours want the things which we have, or have the things which we want; and we both fight, till they take ours or give us theirs. It is a very justifiable cause of a war to invade a country after the people have been wasted by famine, destroyed by pestilence, or embroiled by factions among themselves. It is justifiable to enter into war against our nearest ally, when one of his towns lies convenient for us, or a territory of land, that would render our dominions round and complete. If a prince sends forces into a nation where the people are poor and ignorant, he may lawfully put half of them to death, and make slaves of the rest, in order to civilize and reduce them from their barbarous way of living. It is a very kingly, honourable, and frequent prac-

[2]Term used by Swift for the human brutes who were subject to the horses in the land of the Houyhnhnms.

tice, when one prince desires the assistance of another to secure him against an invasion, that the assistant, when he hath driven out the invader, should seize on the dominions himself, and kill, imprison or banish the prince he came to relieve. Alliance by blood or marriage is a frequent cause of war between princes; and the nearer the kindred is, the greater is their disposition to quarrel: poor nations are hungry, and rich nations are proud; and pride and hunger will ever be at variance. For these reasons, the trade of a soldier is held the most honourable of all others; because a soldier is a Yahoo hired to kill in cold blood as many of his own species, who have never offended him, as possibly he can.

There is likewise a kind of beggarly princes in Europe, not able to make war by themselves, who hire out their troops to richer nations, for so much a day to each man; of which they keep three fourths to themselves, and it is the best part of their maintenance; such are those in Germany and other northern parts of Europe.

What you have told me, (said my master) upon the subject of war, does indeed discover most admirably the effects of that reason you pretend to; however, it is happy that the shame is greater than the danger; and that nature hath left you utterly uncapable of doing much mischief.

For your mouths lying flat with your faces, you can hardly bite each other to any purpose, unless by consent. Then as to the claws upon your feet before and behind, they are so short and tender, that one of our Yahoos would drive a dozen of yours before him. And therefore in recounting the numbers of those who have been killed in battle, I cannot but think that you have *said the thing which is not*.

I could not forbear shaking my head and smiling a little at his ignorance. And being no stranger to the art of war, I gave him a description of cannons, culverins, muskets, carabines, pistols, bullets, powder, swords, bayonets, battles, sieges, retreats, attacks, undermines, countermines, bombardments, sea fights; ships sunk with a thousand men, twenty thousand killed on each side; dying groans, limbs flying in the air, smoke, noise, confusion, trampling to death under horses' feet; flight, pursuit, victory; fields strewed with carcasses left for food to dogs, and wolves, and birds of prey; plundering, stripping, ravishing, burning, and destroying. And to set forth the valour of my own dear countrymen, I assured him that I had seen them blow up a hundred enemies at once in a siege, and as many in a ship, and beheld the dead bodies come down in pieces from the clouds, to the great diversion of the spectators.

I was going on to more particulars, when my master commanded me silence. He said whoever understood the nature of Yahoos might easily believe it possible for so vile an animal to be capable of every action I had named, if their strength and cunning equalled their malice. But as my discourse had increased his abhorrence of the whole species, so he found it gave him a disturbance in his mind, to which he was wholly a stranger before. He thought his ears being used to such abominable words, might by degrees admit them with less detestation. That although he hated the Yahoos of this country, yet he no more blamed them for their odious qualities, than he did a *gnnayh* (a bird of prey) for its cruelty, or a sharp stone for cutting his hoof. But when a creature pretending to reason could be capable of such enormities, he dreaded lest the corruption of that faculty might be worse than brutality itself. He seemed therefore confident, that instead of reason, we were only possessed of some quality fitted to increase our natural vices; as the reflection from a troubled stream returns the image of an ill-shapen body, not only larger, but more distorted.

He added, that he had heard too much upon the subject of war, both in this and some former discourses. . . .

WAR AND FOOTBALL[1]

Donald Moffat

ON THE way out to Soldiers Field Mr. Pennyfeather annoyed me by giving an imitation of an Old Grad. He groused, morosely. He complained that we shouldn't find parking space in the same county, that he'd have a drunk in his lap at the game, that football was a fool pastime anyway,—they'd complicated the rules so it took a lawyer to understand them,—and that we were a couple of idiots to come out in a cold, gray drizzle to watch a lot of boys slither round in the mud. He predicted that Harvard would fumble whenever they got inside the Yale fifteen-yard line. They always did, he said: they were taught to, just as the backs were taught to run very, very slowly into the middle of the line three times and then punt. I patiently reminded him that he hadn't been out to the Stadium lately. 'They've given up all that sort of thing for good,' I said bravely. Anything to shut him up.

'Conant told 'em not to, I suppose?' he jeered.

'Harlow. You'll see.'

Pennyfeather laughed harshly. 'Conant ought to lend 'em a couple of his roving professors for the backfield. I wonder which job the public really thinks more important: the President's or the Head Coach's?'

[1]From *The Atlantic Monthly*, January, 1938.

A more loyal 'Harvard man' than Pennyfeather doesn't exist. I suspect that he, like many another old grad, takes Harvard's superiority so for granted that he can't bear to see her in second place even in the relatively unimportant field of athletics, and so covers up his genuine chagrin by a show of pessimism. When Harvard wins he finds it only reasonable and natural; when Harvard loses he's sore. I'd had a hard time persuading him to come out to the game at all; and now I was beginning to wish I hadn't, and told him so. But he cheered up when he found that our seats were on the thirty-five-yard line, and that beside him sat, instead of the predicted drunk, a young lady who, he whispered, might take his mind off the game if he didn't watch out.

'The gals look pretty good at football games, don't they?' I whispered back.

'Yes,' he admitted grudgingly, 'even damp ones. Till they begin to yell. Of course, they only come here to see men hurt.'

I usually grunt—and did so now—whenever he makes an unnecessarily outrageous generality. Nevertheless, he seemed to be sniffing the old familiar attar of Stadium with some relish. It's an air I like to breathe, whatever the circumstances,—even when its consistency is that of thin, cold soup; even when the sky is the color of threatening steel instead of blue and hazy gold,— and I suspected that Pennyfeather too was beginning to enjoy the smell of it more than he was ready to admit.

He sat quietly through the first half. When Harvard scored the first touchdown he called it a fluke—'Anybody's likely to catch a pass,' he said. And when Daughters presently dropped another pass on the Yale goal line he looked almost pleased at the vindication of his own pessimism. 'Watch those damned Elis when they come back for the second half,' he muttered darkly.

But he did have the decency to look glum when the Elis promptly made his prediction come true ('That Hessburg!' he muttered. 'Slippery!') and his relief when the try for goal was blocked seemed as wholehearted as my own. I, as an old, addicted fan, continued to feel my customary prayerful, tense hysteria; uttered shrill spontaneous yelps and oaths, sprinkled with groans torn from the heart and sharp breath-hissings. Pennyfeather sat with his collar turned up and his hands in his pockets, gazing stolidly through the murky curtain of wet snow. What was my surprise then, when Foley trickled round right end in the last quarter for the winning touchdown, to find Pennyfeather on his feet beside me, roaring, one fist high above his head, the other pounding my dripping hat to a pulp. I laughed at him, the girl on the other side smiled, and he took it.

'Brrrr—those last three minutes! They ought to be ruled out,' I heard him say, relief in his voice, as we shuffled towards the exit. 'The boys seem to have something at last. Good coaching, I expect.' Then he was humming to

himself, to the air of the old hymn, 'Foley, Foley, Foley, Lord God Almighty
. . .' I smiled, and said nothing.

'Doesn't it tire you, though, watching a game?' he continued in a drowsy
voice when we'd found the car and begun the battle of fenders in the parking
space. 'I'm absolutely exhausted. Too bad prohibition's over—I could use a
flask.' He yawned, and set me yawning, enormously. 'Oh, but it's an irritating
game—a fool game when you stop to think of it. Whistles! Penalties! Rules!
Referees! I suppose it satisfies some instinct in us. Force, speed, smartness,
deception—perfect expression of the national spirit. Oh, I know, it's supposed
to be a jolly, character-building sport, teaching fair play and teamwork. My
eye! It's a game of trickery.'

'Of course it is,' I interrupted in surprise.

'I don't mean secret signals and hidden ball plays; I mean beating the
law. How the devil can a game teach fair play when winning depends
on superior cleverness in taking advantage of the rules? Like faking an
injury to get an illegal breathing spell. None of that to-day, I know. Nevertheless—! Of course the decent coaches and players don't like it, but they
do it just the same. It's part of the game. And putting in subs to stop the
clock and gain more time; and stalling when you're ahead—deliberately
going off side, for instance, to delay the game, and suchlike trickeries. Stalling has become such a matter of technique that it has a technical name:
freezing, they call it—did you hear that man behind us explaining it to his
son? Then next morning you read in the paper, "Head Coach Brown has
made great progress in teaching his boys how to move fast and think fast.
Smith's ability to fake an injury in the fourth period was one bit of quick
thinking which marks him as a youngster who plays with his head as well
as his feet."

'You remember the famous accident last year when Kelley kicked the
loose ball and won the Navy game for Yale? Against the rules to do it on
purpose. No doubt it was an accident; but did the papers admit it? Not they!
They said Kelley had always shown himself to be a smart player, and that
if it was an accident it was the first he'd ever been mixed up in. They assumed
he'd taken deliberate advantage of the rules, and gave him full credit. If that's
the sign of a character-building sport, I'm Mussolini. Don't blame the reporters. They simply reflect the spirit of the game as they find it.'

'Come off it,' I said. 'Why not take things as they are?'

'Never!' retorted Pennyfeather with passion. 'Look out for this sportsman
in the yellow job here—he's got a nasty face.'

I was easing ahead on my clutch towards the narrow exit, my bumper
inches behind the car in front. I slowed up to let the yellow job cut in ahead,

and the sportsman driving it, instead of giving me a nod of thanks, sneered at me in a superior way as if he'd successfully bluffed me. I got mad.

'Son of a ——!' I mutter conventionally. 'He'd cut out of line at his own grandmother's funeral.'

'There, there,' Pennyfeather soothed me. 'What's the hurry? Pretend they're subhuman. You wouldn't be far wrong, either.'

I relaxed and drove in silence, the parking space behind us, thinking of what he'd said. 'All the same,' I observed finally, 'it's the best game in the world, with all its faults, and you know it.'

'Why?'

'Because it's the most exciting, the most dramatic, to play or to watch. You just like to grouse.'

He grinned. 'Have it your own way: best game in the world. It must have something, to pack 'em in the way it does. It can't go on forever, though, the way it's heading. Too much like war. The only things it lacks right now are poison gas and machine guns. And I expect they're on the way. Soldiers Field is well named.'

I drove on homeward. 'There's an idea in that,' he went on presently. 'War and football: why not substitute one for the other—let the nations fight it out on the gridiron? Like the Davis Cup. Why not?'

'Fine,' I agreed. 'Except for the little matter of getting rid of war first. How are you going to do that?'

'Bottle up the Hotspurs,' he answered promptly, as we drew up in front of my house. 'Hotspur, the typical halfback. And the professional patriots. Muzzle 'em! Chain 'em!'

My daughter Mary came in with a tall young man, at cocktail time, and after dinner I took him into the library for coffee with Pennyfeather and me. His name was Prentiss, a Junior at Harvard. He stood very straight and had very blue eyes and serious manners, in which he differed agreeably from Mary's last, who had been short and dark, and with no manners to speak of. He listened politely to Pennyfeather's account of the game, and was properly amused by his idea for replacing war by football. During the course of the ensuing conversation about the various states of peace now raging in the world, Prentiss admitted, a little hesitantly, that as for war, he was against it.

Pennyfeather pricked up his ears. 'Good for you, Prentiss,' he said. 'Why? Are you sure? Thought about it a lot? Not just one of these undergraduate Peace Day faddists, I hope?'

'I helped organize the Peace Day—yes, sir. But I'm no faddist. It simply seems to me that war is the last and stupidest error, and since governments aren't capable of preventing it, it's up to the individual. If enough private citizens refuse to go, there can't very well be any war. At least that's the way I look at it.'

'Conscientious objector?' Pennyfeather asked him. 'Pacifist?'

I thought Prentiss looked a little uncomfortable, so I played host. 'Those are just words, you know—don't be afraid of them.' I switched the current to Pennyfeather. 'How about yourself?' I asked him. 'Would you go again?'

'Me?' He looked startled. 'Good God, no!'

'How the devil can you be so sure?' I persisted. 'You don't even know whom we'll be fighting, or how the angle of hate will be drawn for us by the powers that be.' Having suffered all my life from double vision, the kind that makes me see both sides of a question, I am ever freshly appalled—and amused—and made a little envious, to tell the truth—by Pennyfeather's magnificent single-mindedness.

'Because I've been to war,' he answered promptly. 'I know about war. One part excitement, nine parts boredom, childishness, and futility. Going to war twice would be like going up twice in an airplane: you've had the thrill—nothing left but the noise and monotony. I'm a conscientious objector, too,' he smiled at Prentiss. 'I conscientiously object to discomfort, for one thing, especially when I know that it won't do anyone any good. But then, I've been through it once. Are you sure of yourself?' he demanded of Prentiss. 'Do you understand the consequences?'

'Yes. It's really a question of principle.' Prentiss spoke with the appealing arrogance of youth, which knows best. (And does know best, and swears never to make the mistakes the old men made, and doesn't; but makes a new set of its own, just as fatal to its dreams.)

'All right,' said Pennyfeather, 'and I'm all for you—as long as you keep from feeling like a martyr about it,' he added, shaking a finger. 'A pleasant sensation, but bad for the morals.' He drew a deep breath, and let it out slowly. 'There's so much bunk written about war—God knows it's bad enough without that. If I had a son your age,' he went on, looking suddenly serious, 'and he should ask my advice,—which you haven't done; this is purely gratuitous,'—he smiled apologetically,—'I'd tell him to go ahead, in spite of my own belief in war's futility. To keep him safe would be to cheat him of something precious: the chance of proving himself in adventure, of knowing one of life's fundamental experiences, of sharing the spiritual release of self-forgetfulness in a common effort.

'But I would urge him to go with his eyes open, keeping his loyalties free. I'd say to him, Don't believe anything they tell you, either that you're engaged in a holy crusade, or that there is anything to be won for your country or humanity. Don't go in the name of democracy, I'd say, or patriotism, or for revenge, or principle, or even for glory. "He who did well in war just earns the right to begin doing well in peace." Browning said that, of all people, in *Luria*. It ought to be carved over every war office in the world.

'In the last war I believed every blasted thing I was told. My God, but I was young! I loyally hated the Kaiser, believed every word of Allied propaganda, detested slackers, loved the generals, literally believed that in going to France I was defending my country against ultimate invasion and helping make the world safe for democracy. Yes, sir, I was the original push-over. I was not only ready to die for the cause—and I thought of it as a Cause!— I felt vaguely cheated when the war ended and I found myself still alive. The reaction was bad. It wasn't shell shock: it was war shock. For years nothing mattered, nothing seemed worth doing. Disillusion! The stale taste! Death would have been trivial in comparison. Well, I'd still rather see a man die young in battle than watch him slowly decay, grow soft, covetous, timid, mean, afraid of life and its insecurity. Peace is hard on some people—especially hard, I think, on those who are temperamentally unable to see it for what it is: the chance to live quietly from day to day, without hope of fame or expectation of heaven, but simply for the sake of ordinary decency and self-respect.'

'Come, come, Pennyfeather,' I interrupted. 'Be careful: that's almost Christianity!'

He didn't even hear me. 'I'd tell him, this son, not to fool himself about war the way my generation did. I'd paint it black because black is its color: pain, sickness, dirt, fear, boredom, humiliation. *But,* I'd go on, he couldn't afford to miss it, even so. For war means battle, and battle has its great moments of disciplined fury when men's souls rise and mingle in a divine comradeship. The exaltation of battle is one of humanity's deepest experiences. It's like the exaltation of love, or of creation, but more easily attainable. Not every man is spiritually capable of exaltation in love; those who have the gift, the genius, to lose themselves in the creation of a sonnet, or a symphony, or a painting, are even rarer. But almost anyone can swing a right hook, and most of us do, at times, and the emotion at the moment of impact is good. That's why men play football, and love it. So I'd say: Go to war, go ahead! But go with your eyes open. For your own sake you can't afford to miss it. Over your tomb, instead of "Died Gloriously for His Country," I'd carve, "Died Gloriously in Search of His Soul."'

Pennyfeather broke off, looking a little embarrassed. 'But then,' he smiled, 'I haven't got a son. Pardon the oration. Any more coffee? Thanks.'

I said, 'Very interesting, Oscar. But I don't believe you'll find many people going to war on those grounds. You always sound so sure of yourself.'

'Sure of myself?' he retorted indignantly. 'I'm sure of nothing—nothing on earth. Just ideas. I like fooling with them. Have you read the war books?' he asked Prentiss.

'Some of them. It all sounds pretty unreal to read about, though. I was only five when the war ended.'

'No, you can't learn anything from reading about it. I've read them all, and I'd say not one gives a true objective picture of war as it is—not even the best of them, *War and Peace*. They're not content to show us war; they all try to sell an idea, in terms of propaganda. The current fashion is to emphasize the horrors, and so frighten humanity away from it. And a worthy impulse too, except that man has never shown himself capable of being frightened by anything for long. The war books don't tell the truth. War isn't divisible. The truth must show all sides. The books that make war seem a fairly agreeable kind of romantic picnic—like *The First Hundred Thousand*, for instance—are just as true in their way as the books of disillusionment and despair, such as *All Quiet*, *Three Soldiers*, *Captain Conan*, *Paths of Glory*, *Journey's End*, *The General*, to name the first that occur to me. Bairnsfather's cartoons, and Poulbot's, are just as true as Raemaekers's. War is not divisible.'

'How about *Seven Pillars*?' I asked.

'Yes, that one tells the truth—all of it; especially about the insane confusion of war. But it's really more a portrait of a man's soul than of a campaign. Still, it ranks well up with Tolstoy. The history books are the worst—at least the ones I read when I was young. Sheer patriotic propaganda. Look at the Civil War histories. Plenty about the Boys in Blue springing to arms, very little about the scandal and corruption that saturated the Northern effort. I've been reading Professor Shannon's *Organization and Administration of the Union Army*, a grownup history that gives the facts, and the facts aren't pretty. It's a picture of supply scandals, desertions, an army organized and officered, during the early years, by the politicians for the politicians, in the holy light of the spoils system. Northern workmen didn't want the slaves freed to compete with them—they rioted at the first suggestion. Neither did their employers, especially in the industrial Northeast, see anything in the war but a glorious chance to profit. The Northern creed was a simple Business First. Here's a passage I copied down from Shannon, a quotation from the *New York Tribune* of August 8, 1863. It seems to be the *Tribune*'s best advice on the popular topic of avoiding the draft.' Pennyfeather took a slip of paper from his wallet and read aloud:—

300

'If you are drafted, and can possibly leave your business, go; if you cannot go, send your substitute, the best whom money will obtain; if you cannot possibly get one, pay the commutation; but pay $500 for a substitute rather than $300 as commutation, if for no other reason than that, if you send a substitute, you cannot be drafted again while he continues to serve in your stead; whereas, if you commute, that suffices only for this draft, and leaves you clearly liable to the next, if next there shall be.

'People weren't slow to take such advice. Business first. In the draft of July 1863, if I remember the figures, of 292,000 men enrolled 26,000 furnished substitutes and about twice that number paid commutation. Incidentally, only about 10,000 of the whole enrollment actually served. The rest either enlisted as volunteers or were exempted for physical disability or business and political reasons, or simply never showed up at all. There were great waves of emigration to Canada and the Far West coinciding with the four drafts. Shannon quotes a contemporary cartoon in *Harper's Weekly* on the subject of draft avoidance—a picture of a husky citizen pleading before the draft board, "I'm over age, a negro, a minister, a Cripple, a British subject, and an habitual Drunkard."

'There were 268,000 desertions from the Union armies during the Civil War—did you ever read that in a history book? It's fair to add that many of the deserters were bounty jumpers—mercenary gents who enlisted for the state bounty paid to volunteers, then deserted and reenlisted for a different state bounty under an assumed name. Then there was—'

'Out for all they could get, eh?' I broke in. 'Just like the American Legion and the bonus.'

'Yes—except that the Legionnaires didn't have to do any deserting. Just like all men everywhere after every war, as a matter of fact. And during wars, too. It's a rare man who doesn't holler for a bonus for merely doing his duty, in war or peace.'

Pennyfeather paused to light his pipe. Prentiss cleared his throat and leaned forward earnestly. 'I think perhaps the conception of patriotic duty is changing,' he said.

'I'm sure it's changing,' Pennyfeather answered eagerly. 'There are plenty of signs—like the Veterans of Future Wars with their poppy seeds: that's my favorite. But is it changing fast enough? Some day, of course, we'll look back on patriotism as a sort of primitive tribal creed, but it hasn't run its course yet. Some day we'll have its equivalent in world-wide form, real international solidarity. I suppose nothing would hurry it along so fast as an attack by a League of Planets; but we can hardly count on that. Some people think Trotsky has a strangle hold on the one idea that might save us. I don't happen to, myself, but—well, prophets are seldom prophets to their own generation.'

'In the meantime,' said Prentiss, returning to his original declaration, 'it may not be so long before there are enough people who oppose war on principle—enough of us who see it as a patriotic duty to oppose war—to swing the balance. I may be wrong, but I mean to give it a try, anyhow.'

'I'm sure you think you can swing the balance,' Pennyfeather agreed pleasantly, 'and I respect you for it. But what you can't conceive, before you're in it, is the wartime atmosphere, the hysteria, the rule of mob opinion. Will you be able to stick to your principles when the drums and bugles and flags go by? And the women start yelling—they're the noisiest of all. For a while, yes, you probably will. But remember this: never before in the world's history has government had at its disposal such powerful agencies for spreading propaganda; never before has the great public ear been so trained to listen, or so fixed in the habit of believing what it is told.

'You'll start with high principles and heroic determination, and some of you will stick. But most of you won't be strong enough. You'll drift off, one by one, all armed with the best excuses: "This war is different," you'll say. "It's a defensive war; I won't attack, but I've got to defend my home." "My sister was killed by a bomb—let me at 'em!" "If we don't lick 'em over there, we'll have to do it later on over here." Oh, there'll be plenty of good reasons, all old as time itself—not to mention the other strings tugging at you: the relief of joining the mob, the surrender of responsibility, the secret hope of glory; and the question that sensitive men—all conscientious objectors are sensitive men—are eternally asking, "Am I being honest with myself? Or am I really just afraid? Of course I know I'm not afraid, but will other people?" And then the conviction that every man clings to—if he didn't there wouldn't be any war, ever—that *he'll* get through alive anyway. Oh, it's a mess, a tangle of emotions, all pulling every which way. Don't fool yourself: pacifism isn't enough. Not yet. The world isn't ready for it.'

'Then what's the answer?' Prentiss asked a little sadly.

'I don't think there is any clear-cut answer. None that will serve present generations. Future hope, I think, lies in a league of the nations; not this league, necessarily, but the one that will grow out of the seed of this one—maybe not till another general war has made all the nations understand that they *must* unite or perish.'

'And in the meantime?'

'There are signs. I think the Mediterranean anti-submarine patrol is a hopeful one. It's just such a form of cooperative international police as Malinowski, for one, predicts, or hopes for. The only possible agency for maintaining peace until such time as the will to war has disappeared from the face of the earth. He's a pretty wise man. Yet he places no reliance on human goodwill. He thinks the world needs an international superstate to ride herd on the gangster nations.'

'Do you really believe the human instinct for war will ever die?' I asked.

'Sure. Some day.'

'It's been with us a long time now.'

'Oh, but that's a stale argument,' Pennyfeather said disgustedly. 'As Malinowski points out, theologians used to maintain that human slavery was ordained by God—until it stopped paying. Then they discovered that it was immoral. Well, everyone knows to-day that war doesn't pay—even the field marshals know it; but nobody dares act on that knowledge, yet. Give 'em time. In the meantime, an international army. Would you enlist in that, Prentiss?'

Prentiss didn't answer at once. Presently he looked up, grinning, and said, 'I think your idea of replacing war with football is a better bet, on the whole.'

'Maybe you're right at that,' said Pennyfeather. 'Think how easy the shift would be. Practically all you'd have to do would be to change the name of the Secretary of War to Secretary of Football. Otherwise they're about the same. Sure, I mean it: spirit, background, organization, everything. Most men play football for the same reason they enter aviation in wartime—for glory. To-day's ace flier will be to-morrow's star halfback. Look at the way intercollegiate football is organized: each college has its general staff of coaches; its secret service—scouts to-day, but out-and-out spies not so long ago; its recruiting branch, made up of old grads; its QM corps; its press department for propaganda; its treasury, selling tickets instead of Liberty Bonds, and for the same purpose; its diplomatic branch, for writing notes and breaking off relations—everything, even intercollegiate leagues and conferences to keep the game clean, just like the League of Nations.'

'How would you recruit the squad?' I queried.

'Oh, conscription, of course. Bred from infancy to die for dear old Latvia. Federal training camps for candidates, and none of this nonsense about getting an education. That's what ruins so many college teams to-day.'

'I should think the politicians might give trouble, though,' I suggested.

'Politicians always give trouble,' he replied, 'but I don't see how they could give any worse trouble than they ordinarily do. They'd go on swapping votes. A senatorial tackle appointment, say, for a vote on a favorite constitutional amendment. I can't see a flaw in the scheme. And think how pleased the colleges will be. No more hiring of mercenaries under athletic scholarships, hence nothing but intercollegiate love, peace, fraternity. Would you enlist if your country should declare football on England, Prentiss?'

'You bet,' said Prentiss. 'I like to play football.'

'I didn't know you did play,' Pennyfeather said in surprise, as I got up, suggesting a move into the other room.

Prentiss seemed embarrassed, as if he'd been found out. 'Yes, sir,' he said hesitantly. 'I was out there this afternoon, as a matter of fact. I went in at right end.'

'I'll be damned,' Pennyfeather laughed. 'And you like to smack 'em down?'

'Well—yes, sir; to tell the truth, I do.'

'And you a pacifist!' said Pennyfeather.

BACKGROUND FOR WAR[1]

1063 WEEKS

For nine years the whole world (pop. 2,134,000,000), with brief exceptions here and there, has been in a Great Depression. At some point in these bitter years, the post-War world became a pre-War world— that is, a world anticipating World War. Millions and millions of young men, in the U. S. as elsewhere, had War marked fatalistically on their private calendars.

Since the big guns began to go off or to be wheeled into place, most U. S. readers have followed current European history closely and anxiously. Not so familiar to them is the history of the period immediately before it—the sequence of post-War settlements, conferences, treaties that began when the Armistice was signed. Briand with his drooping lips and shaggy head, Strese- mann with his dueling scars, Sir Austen Chamberlain with his monocle, his glassy stare and elegance of dress, are names in history books for high-school students, dim recollections for those students' parents.

Only voluminous histories can retrace the steps of post-War diplomacy, unravel post-War complexities. But refreshing memories of events since the Armistice makes last week's war news seem less abrupt, the transition from post-War to pre-War less startling. Against the broad sweep of history, that period is brief—246 months, 1063 weeks, 7453 days, time for 20 wheat crops, for 20 classes to graduate.

[1]From *Time, The Weekly Newsmagazine*, May 1, 1939.

WAR'S END

In periods of sweeping change history is measured by days and hours, not by years. In the last weeks of the War events followed each other so rapidly that General Foch himself could not believe that the end was in sight. Only one month before the end, when he was launching what he called "the greatest of all battles," Foch was making plans for campaigns the next year. Then, in 300 hours:

Turkey appealed for an armistice; Belgrade, Trieste, fell to the Allies; Austria-Hungary signed an armistice; sailors of the German Grand Fleet, ordered to sea in a move of desperation, mutinied; Socialist Kurt Eisner led a monster demonstration in Munich which culminated in the proclaiming, November 8, of the Bavarian Socialist Republic; the German Majority Socialists served the Kaiser with an ultimatum to abdicate; revolution spread to Frankfort, Cologne, Düsseldorf, Leipzig, Stuttgart, Madgeburg, Brunswick; the rulers of Brunswick, Bavaria, Mecklenburg-Schwerin, abdicated; the Kaiser fled; the German Republic was proclaimed; Croatian independence was proclaimed in Zagreb; a revolt in Budapest put liberal Count Karolyi in power.

The German Army, which had already retreated 100 miles, with a loss by capture of 390,000 men and 6600 guns—the largest in the history of military operations—fled through Belgium, Holland, over the Rhine, swiftly and efficiently, in a manner that Liddell Hart viewed not as a rout but as a skilful military movement.

The Allied pursuit through Belgium, Luxemburg, Alsace-Lorraine penetrated Germany to the left bank of the Rhine and 30 kilometers beyond the bridgeheads at Mainz, Coblentz, Cologne. By the terms of the Armistice, Germany delivered 5000 locomotives, 150,000 railroad cars, 5000 trucks to the Allies, and U. S. General Tasker Bliss, astute observer, anti-militarist general, feared the sort of peace that generals and politicians would dictate.

The War was over. It ended in bewildering darkness, and, said General Bliss, happiness at its ending was subdued. The old States, the old ways of life, the old political and social organizations of Europe were shattered; 9,000,000 men had been killed in battle or had died of their wounds; 22,000,000 had been wounded; an unknown number of civilians died as a result of the War. "Not until our children's time can the former joy of life come into the world," Bliss remarked. "And it can come then only if our culminating work makes it impossible for them ever to see another such war."

The War was over. Except:

In Russia, the Bolsheviks fought the Whites and the Allies on a great wavering battle line that reached from Archangel to Vladivostok.

In the Balkans, Greece invaded Turkey, occupied Anatolia, was driven back after more than a year of fighting. Rumanian, Czech and Yugoslavian armies overran Hungary, seized livestock, locomotives, battled the Communist Government of Bela Kun.

Poland seized Vilna; Lithuania seized Memel; Yugoslavia seized Montenegro.

In Dublin, a Sinn Fein Government was established within two months of the establishment of a republic in Vienna. For three years the Irish fought the English. At the same time, in Morocco, Riffs fought Spaniards.

Savage and costly though they were, these clashes were minor compared with the titanic conflict that had ended; they were the death struggles of the World War, rather than the War itself. And they were dwarfed by political developments that moved as swiftly, as bewilderingly. In the first 500 days of peace:

Thirty-five new Governments came into existence in Europe, struggled to establish themselves.

The Treaty of Versailles set up Poland, Czecho-Slovakia, Lithuania, Latvia, Estonia, Finland; wiped off the map Montenegro, Croatia, Bohemia, Transylvania, Galicia, Livonia, Courland, Schleswig; established a League of Nations, which 42 nations soon joined.

The German, Russian, Austro-Hungarian Empires, under whose political organizations most Europeans lived, were swallowed up in the cataclysm—the Austrian ministry appointed for liquidation found the Empire had disappeared before it could map its program. With them went bureaucrats, ruling cliques, political leaders, military castes, police functionaries, armies of officeholders, diplomats, the props and supports of the ruling dynasties. Replacing them came, along with the States, new political organizations employing new methods to realize new social theories. In Russia a brilliant group of social theorists under Lenin struggled with rival theoricians, Tsarist generals, Allied intervention, for control of the former Russian Empire, but everywhere social experimentation—good or bad, radical or reactionary—was in the air. It was administered by politicians of a new type—professors like Masaryk, artists like Paderewski, literary figures like Kurt Eisner or D'Annunzio, trade unionists like Ebert, visionaries like Karolyi, soldiers like Pilsudski—and as they consolidated their power or went under, they fitted into a Europe in which the demand for peace dominated everything else.

GERMANY

Defeated, exhausted, blockaded, Germany passed through a staggering cycle of panics, revolutionary and counter-revolutionary outbreaks, financial debacles, governmental upheavals. Her Army was disarmed, her fleet scuttled, her merchant marine forfeited, but 62,000,000 Germans nevertheless remained to be fed, clothed, housed, organized in some political community. Europe's new States outside Germany emerged slowly, bumped shoulders, clashed over boundaries, made alliances. But Germany remained Europe's central problem, while Russia was still split with civil war. For the first five years of peace, from the Armistice to the Ruhr, the biggest development in Europe, outside of Russia, was France's policy of keeping Germany weak.

Weak Germany certainly was. At the War's end, after the Versailles Treaty, she had lost:

1,700,000 killed in battle, 4,200,000 wounded, 1,150,000 missing.

Alsace-Lorraine, most of Posen and West Prussia, all her colonies, other territorial concessions.

18,000,000 of her population, over 1,000,000 square miles of her territory, 45% of her coal, 65% of her iron ore, 15% of her arable lands, 10% of her factories, 5,100,000 tons of her merchant fleet.

To France she agreed to deliver 105,000 tons of benzol, 105,000 tons of coal tar, 90,000 tons of sulfate of ammonia, 500 stallions, 30,000 mares, 2000 bulls, 90,000 cows, 1000 rams, 100,000 sheep, 10,000 goats, and she agreed to pay (but paid only in part) $5,000,000,000 reparations before May 1921.

But 62,000,000 Germans weakened to desperation seemed as menacing to the rest of the world as, to France in her post-War mood, they seemed reassuring. Inside Germany political chaos became almost normal, marked by Communist and reactionary uprisings, the brief soviet of Bavaria, by *Putsche* like those of Kapp, Hitler, and Ludendorff. Walther Rathenau, brilliant economist, industrialist, Foreign Minister, was assassinated by two young nationalists who sped past his automobile on the way to the Foreign Office, tossed hand grenades into it, riddled his mangled body with shots from a Lewis gun, then committed suicide in a castle hideout in Thuringia. But Rathenau's murder was not the only one: Liberal Matthias Erzberger and Socialist Kurt Eisner were killed; Revolutionists Rosa Luxemburg and Karl Leibknecht were kidnapped and murdered.

Outside Germany the States created by the Treaty of Versailles and the treaties which followed it were linked to France in a chain of alliances. Poland and France in the treaty of February 19, 1921 pledged themselves to mutual assistance in the event of German aggression. When Belgium and Czecho-

Slovakia also signed with France, the ring around Germany was closed. When Czecho-Slovakia, Yugoslavia, Rumania, formed another such ring around Hungary—and this ring was coordinated with the other by the Franco-Czecho-Slovakian alliance—French security against possible German ambitions seemed as solid as diplomatic measures, military might, economic dominance, could make it.

Out-worn in the post-War world were measures of national revenge backed by military strength. Revulsion at the Treaty of Versailles was revulsion at its territorial and reparations clauses, not only at its idealistic plans for war's prevention, which these contradicted. By 1921, despite U. S. rejection of the League of Nations, the U. S. had taken the lead in proposing naval limitation, and at the Washington Conference, when Charles Evans Hughes proposed that the U. S., Great Britain, and Japan scrap 1,876,000 tons of their battleships, Balfour with poker-faced aplomb called it: ". . . the basis of the greatest reform in the matter of armament and preparation for war that has ever been conceived or carried out by the courage and patriotism of statesmen," and the work of scaling down war vessels began. In 1922, when Germany requested a three-year moratorium on reparations, Great Britain was favorable to the idea, Poincaré refused. Outside the ring that France had built around Germany, hostility to the defeated ebbed fast. It ebbed faster when, in 1922, German recognition of the Soviet Union brought fears of a Russian-German alliance. And when Poincaré, on January 11, 1923, sent French troops to seize 80% of Germany's coal, iron and steel sources, in "the mad and ruinous Ruhr episode," Great Britain's criticism swelled, Great Britain's sympathies shifted. Lloyd George, who four years before had been re-elected on a platform of punishment for Germany, later called it ". . . the dismal and tragic episode of the Ruhr occupation," and said that it caused "untold misery to many millions of Central Europe, had put back the clock of post-War reconstruction throughout the world, intensified unemployment problems and industrial depression, and had signally failed in its main object of extracting reparations from Germany."

For 600 of the maddest days in history French troops patrolled the Ruhr: 147,000 German citizens were driven from the district in eleven months.

Burgomasters of every major city in the land of 4,000,000 people were expelled or imprisoned.

Funds and records of manufacturing companies were seized and their offices taken over; at least 100 people lost their lives; newspapers were suppressed; 19,000 officials in the area of the French-sponsored "Autonomous Government of the Palatinate" were deported.

In Munich, Ludendorff and Hitler attempted to set up a dictatorship.

German workers in the Ruhr downed their tools, supported by the German Government, which printed more paper currency to pay them.

Germany's economy was swept away in an avalanche which threatened to break the ring around her, sweep over Europe. In December, shortly before the French occupied the Ruhr, a U. S. dollar would buy 7000 marks. In a month it would buy 50,000. By June it would buy 100,000. Prices were quoted by the hour; workmen paid by the day; savings wiped out; housewives rushed to spend money before nightfall, knowing morning would make it worth less. In August one U. S. dollar would buy 5,000,000 marks. By the middle of November the U. S. dollar was quoted at 2,500,000,000,000 in Berlin, and 4,000,000,000,000 at Cologne 300 miles away.

Occupation cost France more proportionately than she got out of it. It brought Germany to the edge of revolution. It unleashed a whirlwind—big guns could not bombard a falling mark, diplomats could not make treaties around it. By the beginning of 1924, powerful France jittered defiantly as she prepared to back down—her own currency was skidding fast. First stage of post-war policy had ended.

Inside her ring of States, Germany spun like the whirling dervish, tossing off bits of old treaties, remnants of old economies, fragments of old customs, large chunks of old moralities, and threatening at any moment to fly apart. State power, in Charles Beard's phrase, lay in the streets. And it threshed around like a live wire, destroying whoever seized it. Awed and appalled, the new States of Europe looked on; if that was post-War democracy, most of them wanted dictatorship.

Outside Germany stabilization came fast: Czecho-Slovakia prospered; Poland and the Soviet Union made peace; Mussolini, still working with regularly elected deputies, was known primarily as a theatrical figure who, by some process that involved castor-oil applied to his opponents and the suppression of free speech, had made the trains of Italy run on time. But inside Germany the great problem remained: 62,000,000 Germans had to be fed, clothed, housed, organized in some political system and, as the Ruhr occupation had demonstrated, organized economically as well.

LOCARNO

Grapes were ripe on the white dusty hills around Locarno, the blue water. of Lake Maggiore were warm, when Briand, Stresemann, Sir Austen Chamberlain and representatives from four other countries assembled to make the Locarno Treaties. Those treaties are dead letters now. But the Locarno spirit in 1925 was Europe's biggest hope. And as it radiated out, promising an easement of armaments, a solution of war debts, new dreams of a warless Europe and even of a European Federation of States, it coincided with the world-wide prosperity of 1925–29.

As treaties, the Locarno pacts were not so much. Stresemann, Foreign Minister through ten German ministries, met Aristide Briand, unpunctual, disorderly French Foreign Minister who held portfolios in 26 French Governments. Stresemann drank beer with German journalists, Chamberlain rode around in a glittering red-cushioned Rolls-Royce that had been built for an Indian Maharaja, Briand took the delegates sailing in a small lake steamer, as for eleven days they consulted. They worked out five important agreements. In four of these the clumsy, nervous Stresemann pledged Germany to settle by arbitration disputes with France, Belgium, Czecho-Slovakia, Poland. These were the States allied in the ring around Germany. In a Treaty of Mutual Guarantee, however, Germany, France, Belgium, Italy, Great Britain, guaranteed the inviolability of the Franco-German and Franco-Belgian frontiers. France's fear of Germany, source of her post-War policy, seemed over.

In the evening of October 16, the treaty was signed while church bells rang and a crowd clamored outside the town hall. It was brought to the window, lighted like an ikon. Mussolini took a special train from Rome to Milan, drove a racing car from Milan to Stresa, a speedboat from Stresa to Locarno. Briand, always in bed by nine if possible, was asleep two hours after the signing. But he was stirred: "It is ended," he said later, "that long war between us. Ended those long veils of mourning for the pains that will never be assuaged. Away with the rifles, the machine guns and the cannon! Here come conciliation, arbitration and peace!"

The post-War world now began to seem not only warless, but prospering. The years of German loans, of the building of the *Bremen*, the *Graf Zeppelin*, of reconstruction, of speculation, of U. S. financial dominance unaccompanied by an increase of U. S. political responsibility, were also years that saw the production of the world's goods reach new heights. They were the years when Coolidge said of war debts, "They hired the money," when Charles Dawes was Coolidge's vicegerent in Europe, wearing laurels won with the Dawes plan.

They were the years in which the German steel production approached its pre-War level; Germany's merchant marine climbed from 400,000 to 3,700,000 tons. They were the years in which France stabilized her currency, recovering from the post-Ruhr crisis that swept six ministries out of office in 15 months. They were the years when Edward, Prince of Wales, was known as the Empire's greatest salesman. And though England was laboring with an unemployment problem and China was torn by internal revolt, advocates of international cooperation flourished in the capitals of Europe as trade grew, production increased.

On New Year's Day, 1929, a spectator from any place but Mars might have seen, beneath the hysteria and hangover of the boom years, a perspective of peace ahead. The ribbons of trenches that crisscrossed Europe had been filled in, the post-War statesmen of revenge were out of office, the Soviet Union had turned from its program of international revolution to its program of international development under the Five-Year Plan. U. S. tourist spending in Europe jumped over 350% between 1920 and 1928, building went on as rapidly as in any period of history, and if for a moment a steadily rising standard of living seemed an approachable goal for mankind, it was a measure of what continued peace meant, of what might happen in a community of nations that was not haunted by dreams of the last War, or by premonitions of the next.

COLLAPSE

On October 24, 1929, the market crashed in New York, and in that year world unemployment swelled to 30,000,000. By 1931:

The price of copper slumped from 18¢ to 8¢ a pound; U. S. wheat fell from $1.30 to 53¢ a bushel; cotton from 16¢ to 6¢ per pound; beef from $9 to $5 per 100 pounds.

In the summer of 1929 in Germany there were 720,000 unemployed. That winter there were 2,000,000. Looming bigger in a new crisis was a 40-year-old World War corporal named Adolf Hitler. If he looked back on his last nine years, on the growth of his National Socialist Party, he could see gains more impressive to him than to Germany's rulers. Nine years before he had joined seven men in one of the innumerable visionary parties of desperation that post-War Germany produced. There were then seven and one-half marks in the party treasury. With his colleagues he had worked out a 25-point program, designed a flag and uniform, floated a newspaper, taken the party itself from its founders. Now it had 108,000 dues-paying members. Now it had twelve members in the Reichstag (out of a total of 490). It had 13 deputies in the Berlin City Council. It won more than eleven percent of the total vote in an election in Thuringia. It had become important enough to be courted by Hugenberg, leader of the powerful Nationalists.

For the first time since the War, history began to be measured in days. The Müller Government, socialist and conciliatory, gave way to the Brüning Government. In the Reichstag election the Nazis gained 107 seats, 6,401,200 votes (out of a total of 35,000,000). Hitler was no longer a rival of von Papen, von

Schleicher, Brüning, but of Hindenburg himself. The Brüning Government ruled by decree, the von Papen ministry lasted 170 days, was followed by the von Schleicher ministry that lasted 56. On January 30, 1933, Hitler became Chancellor of Germany.

PRE-WAR

Simultaneously U. S. citizens, previously preoccupied by three long years of Depression, were compelled to take a new interest in foreign news. Strange news it was at first, confused, murky, seething, a sequence of brutal events, of medieval vengeance wreaked with modern weapons, news of German book-burnings, of anti-Semitic outbreaks, of a bloody purge, news of statesmen who seemed only masters of vituperation and violence. What could be expected from a country whose leaders believed, in Propaganda Minister Goebbels' words, that their mission was "to unchain volcanic passions, to cause outbreaks of fury, to set the masses of men on the march, to organize hate and suspicion with ice-cold calculation"?

Beneath the surface of the news, bigger forces were in motion. Hitler's Germany warned that the post-War world had ended. Its end was soon thundered by the renewed sound of big guns pounding in Japan's 1932 attack on Shanghai. Crises began to come so fast, were reported so fully, speculated about so constantly, that they became horrifyingly familiar: a crisis over the League censure of Japan for seizing Manchukuo, followed by crises over the brief civil war in Austria, the assassinations of Dollfuss and of King Alexander of Yugoslavia, over the invasion of Ethiopia, the remilitarization of the Rhineland, the civil war in Spain, the German seizure of Austria, the Russian-Japanese clash in the Far East, the menacing gestures of Hitler against Czecho-Slovakia—until at Munich the sequence of bluffs, threats, swift moves, force and the threat of force culminated in the panicky weeks of Europe's worst war scare in 20 years.

History is at best violent, doubly so in such periods. Bombers over Shanghai and Guernica, refugees from Barcelona and Prague, tell stories whose raw horror blurs the minds of those who try to understand the causes of war. When philosophers, economists, historians try to penetrate the wild surface of events, to see the forces that have created them, their dry generalizations and statistics seem cold beside the living reality of the headlines. In different terms they state the causes of international conflict—as rivalry between the Haves and the Have-nots, between the countries struggling to keep what they have and the countries struggling to expand. Or they see it as the clash of rival ideologies or of rival imperialists, with a vast segment of the world looking to Great Britain to maintain order while protecting her remote dominions,

312

and another segment threatening to block her channels of communication with them. Or they see it as a problem of overpopulation in the crowded centres of the world, the masses of Europe and Japan swelling and pressing against the barriers that block them from the sparsely inhabited areas of the globe. Or they see it as a problem of armaments, the countries jockeying desperately for first place in a race whose only end is death. But however they state it, their theories, analyses, guesses and figures come out the same and say, as do events, that war is inevitable.

But one great difference separates the new period from the one before the World War. Citizens of that pre-War world had no knowledge of what lay ahead of them, had no historical precedent for the tragedy toward which they were moving, and even the statesmen who tried to avert it had no conception of its terrible scope. On the evening of Aug. 3, 1914, when Great Britain pondered war, Sir Edward Grey stood at the window of the Foreign Office, watching the lamps being lit in the summer dusk, and said: "The lamps are going out all over Europe; we shall not see them lit again in our lifetime." To those who expect another war, his phrase seems optimistic; many are in a mood to say: "They will never be lit again."

WHY MEN FIGHT[1]

Will Durant

PERSPECTIVE

In the year 1830 a French customs official unearthed, in the valley of the Somme, strange implements of flint now recognized by the learned as the weapons with which the men of the Old Stone Age made war. These stones are called *coups de poing*, or "blows of the fist," for one end was rounded to be grasped in the hand, while the other end was pointed for persuasion. With these modest tools of death, it seems, Neanderthal men from what is now Germany, and Cro-Magnon men from what is now France, fought fifty thousand years ago for the mastery of the continent, and, after a day of lusty battle, left perhaps a score of dead on the field. Twenty years ago, modern Germans and modern Frenchmen fought again, in that same valley, for that same prize, with magnificent tools of death that killed ten thousand

[1]From *The Saturday Evening Post*, July 10, 1937.

313

men in a day. One art alone has made indisputable progress in history, and that is the art of war.

For five hundred centuries, two thousand generations have struggled for that terrain in a calendar of wars whose beginning is as distant as its end. Our own children rest there, some of them, lured by fear or nobility into that ancient strife. Even the sophisticated mind, accustomed to magnitude and marvels, is appalled by the panorama of historic war, from the occasional brawls and raids of normally peaceful "savages," through the sanguinary annals of Sumer, Babylonia and Assyria, the endless fratricide of the Greek city states, the merciful conquests of Alexander and Caesar, the brutal triumphs of Imperial Rome, the holy carnage of expanding Islam, the glorious slaughters of Genghiz Khan, Tamerlane's pyramid of skulls, the destruction of Vijayanagar, the Hundred Years' War, the War of the Spanish Succession, the Seven Years' War, the English, American, French, and Russian Revolutions, the Civil Wars of England and America, the Napoleonic Wars, the War of 1812, the Crimean War, the Franco-Prussian War, the Spanish-American War, the Boer War, the Russo-Japanese War, the First World War, the suicide of Spain, the Sino-Japanese War, the Second World War. . . . This, in our pessimistic moments, seems to be the main and bloody current of history, beside which all the achievements of civilization, all the illumination of letters and the arts, all the tendernesses of women and the courtesies of men, are but graceful incidents on the bank, helpless to change the course or character of the stream.

Such a chronicle of conflict exaggerates, without doubt, the rôle of war in the records of our race. Strife is dramatic, and, to most of our historians, peaceful generations appear to have no history. So our chroniclers leap from battle to battle, and unwittingly deform the past into a shambles. In our saner moments we know that it is not so; that lucid intervals of peace far outweigh, in any nation's story, the mad seizures of war and revolution; that the history of civilization—of science and invention, law and morals, religion and philosophy, literature and art—runs like hidden gold in the river bed of time. Even war cannot quite blacken the picture of man's development.

Nevertheless, war has always been. Will it always be? What are its causes in the nature of men and in the structure of societies? What are its effects, for good or evil, upon the soul, the species, and the state? Can it be prevented, or diminished in frequency, or in any measure controlled? Let us consider these questions as objectively as may be permitted to men and women standing on the brink of what may be the most brutal war that history has ever known.

CAUSES

The causes of war are psychological, biological, economic, and political—that is, they lie in the impulses of men, the competition of groups, the material needs of societies, and fluctuations of national power.

The basic causes are in ourselves, for the state is an enlarged picture of the soul. The five major instincts of mankind—food-getting, mating, parental love, fighting, and association—are the ultimate sources of war. Our inveterate habit of eating is the oldest and deepest cause of war. For thousands, perhaps millions, of years, men were uncertain of their food supply. Not knowing yet the bounty of the soil, they trusted to the fortunes of the hunt. Having captured prey, they tore or cut it to pieces, often on the spot, and gorged themselves to their cubic capacity with the raw flesh and the hot gore; how could they tell when they might eat again? Greed is eating, or hoarding, for the future; wealth is originally a hedge against starvation; war is at first a raid for food. All vices were once virtues, indispensable in the struggle for existence; they became vices only in the degree to which social order and increasing security rendered them unnecessary for survival. Once men had to chase, to kill, to grasp, to overeat, to hoard; a hundred millenniums of insecurity bred into the race those acquisitive and possessive impulses which no laws or ideals, but only centuries of security, can mitigate or destroy.

The desire for mates and the love of children write half of the private history of mankind, but they have only rarely been the direct causes of war. The fighting instinct enters more obviously into the analysis, even if it operates most freely in persons above military age. Nature develops it vigorously as an aid in getting or keeping food or mates; it arms every animal with organs of offense and defense, and lends to the physically weaker species the advantages of cunning and association. Since, by and large, those individuals and groups survived that excelled in food-getting, mate-getting, caring for children, and fighting, these instincts have been selected and intensified with every generation, and have budded into a hundred secondary forms of acquisition, venery, kindliness, and contention.

As the quest for food has grown into the amassing of great fortunes, so the fighting instinct has swelled into the lust for power and the waging of war. The lust for power is in most men a wholesome stimulus to ambition and creation, but in exceptional men, dressed in great and lasting authority, it becomes a dangerous disease, an elephantiasis of the soul, which goads them on to fight a thousand battles by proxy. Nietzsche, nervous and sickly and disqualified for military service, thrilled at the sight and sound of cavalry galloping along a Frankfort street, and at once composed a paean in honor

315

of war and the "will to power." Mussolini and Hitler have read Nietzsche, and may, by replacing parliaments with supermen, and the religion of peace with the religion of war, justify the gentle maniac's prediction that the future would divide history into B. N. and A. N.—Before Nietzsche and After Nietzsche. Nothing is so improbable as the future.

The instinct of flight is hardly a source of war, though war gives it an extensive field of operations. The instinct of action enters into the picture as a love of adventure, an escape from relative and routine. A richer source is the instinct of association. Men fear solitude, and naturally seek the protection of numbers. Slowly a society develops within whose guarded frontiers men are free to live peaceably, to accumulate knowledge and goods, and to worship their gods. Since our self-love overflows into love of our parents and children, our homes and possessions, our habits and institutions, our wonted environment and transmitted faith, we form in time an emotional attachment for the nation and the civilization of which these are constituent parts; and when any of them is threatened, our instinct of pugnacity is aroused to the limit determined by the natural cowardice of mankind. Such patriotism is reasonable and necessary, for without it the group could not survive, and the individual could not survive without the group. Prejudice is fatal to philosophy, but indispensable to a people.

Put all these passions together, gather into one force the acquisitiveness, pugnacity, egoism, egotism, affection, and lust for power of a hundred million souls, and you have the psychological sources of war. It may be that these sources are not completely instinctive, not inevitably rooted in the blood; contemporary psychology is chary of instincts, and suspects that many of them are but habits formed in early years through the imitation of corrupt adults. We need not spend ourselves on the dispute, for in any case the practical problem would remain—we should still have to change the parents before we could change the children.

The experience of Russia indicates that the business of pursuing food and mates, of fighting and gathering together, of loving children and money and power, is more deeply ingrained in human character than fashionable theory believes. Or was it that the lenience of the Ogpu allowed too many adults to survive? It is hard to build tomorrow's society with the day-after-tomorrow's men. *Historia non facit saltum*: History, like nature, makes no leaps.

These psychological impulses, taken in their social mass, become the biological sources of war. The group, too, as well as the individual, can be hungry or angry, ambitious or proud; the group, too, must struggle for existence, and be eliminated or survive. The protective fertility of organisms soon multiplies mouths beyond the local food supply; the hunger of the parts, as in the body, becomes the hunger of the whole, and species wars against species, group against group, for lands or waters that may give more support to abounding life. Euripides, twenty-three hundred years ago, attributed the Trojan War to the rapid multiplication of the Greeks. "States that have a surplus population," said the ancient Stoic philosopher Chrysippus, "send great numbers out to colonies, and stir up wars against their neighbors." If that was the case when infanticide and Greek friendship were tolerated as means of controlling population, consider the results where statesmen encourage fertility. For then the birth rate must be raised to provide soldiers for war; war must be waged to conquer land for an expanding population; and population expands because the birth rate is so high. It is a very pinwheel of logic, bright and frail, a form of reasoning puzzlingly whimsical until we add its concealed premise—the will to power.

Group hunger begets group pugnacity, and pugnacity develops in the group, as in the individual, organs of protection and attack. In the group these are called armament; and when they are powerful, they may themselves, like the boy's biceptual consciousness, become a secondary source of war. On either scale some armament is necessary, for struggle is inevitable, and competition is the trade of life. The tragedy of our ideals is that we hitch them to the falling stars of equality and peace, while nature blithely bases her inescapable machinery of development upon difference and inequality of endowment and ability, upon competition and war; what chance have our ideals, nurtured in the mutual aid of the family, against that supremest court of all? Even mutual aid becomes an organ of struggle: We cooperate as individuals that we may the better compete as groups; morality and order have been developed because they strengthened the group in the inexorable competition of the world. Only when another star attacks us will the earth know internal peace; only a war of the planets can produce, for a moment, the brotherhood of man.

These psychological and biological forces are the ultimate origins of human conflict. From them flow the national rivalries that generate the proximate causes of war—those economic and political causes with which superficial analysis so readily contents itself.

The basic economic cause is rivalry for land: Land to receive a designedly expanding population, land to provide material resources, land to open up new subjects to conscription and taxation. So the ancient Greeks fought their way through the Aegean isles to the coasts of Asia Minor and the Black Sea, and through the Mediterranean to Africa, Sicily, Italy, France, and Spain; so the English spread through the world in the last two centuries; so the Italians begin to spread today. There is, in history, a law of colonial expansion almost as explosive as any law of expansion in physics: Whenever a population fails to exploit the resources of its soil, it will sooner or later be conquered by a people able to exploit those resources, and to pour them into the commerce and uses of mankind.

These ancient provocations to conquest have been sharpened and magnified by the Industrial Revolution. To make war successfully a modern nation must be wealthy; to be wealthy it must develop industry; to maintain industry it must, in most cases, import food, fuel, and raw materials; to pay for these it must export manufactured goods; to sell these it must find foreign markets; to win these it must undersell its competitors or wage successful war. As likely as not, it will make war for any of the goods it must import, or for control of the routes by which it imports them.

Even in antiquity semi-industrial Athens waged war for the control of the Aegean, the Hellespont, and the Black Sea, because it was dependent upon Russian grain; Rome had to conquer Egypt because it needed markets for its handicrafts and fortunes for its politicians. Egyptian wheat, Near Eastern oil, and Indian cotton explain many a battle in British history; Spanish silver explains the wars of Rome with Carthage; Spanish copper, not Fascist theory, explains in our time the German help to the insurgent forces in Spain. Our sinless selves had a taste for sugar in 1898; and far back in 1853 we pointed our presents and cannon at a frightened shogun and persuaded him to allow a peaceful, agricultural, self-contained nation to transform itself into industrial, imperial, militaristic Japan. Those chickens have come home to roost.

The business cycle adds its own contribution to the causes of modern war. Since men are by nature unequal—some strong and some weak, some able and some (as they tell us) virtuous—it follows that in any society a majority of abilities will be possessed by a minority of men; from which it follows that sooner or later, in any society, a majority of goods will be possessed by a minority of men. But this natural concentration of wealth impedes the wide spread of purchasing power among the people; production, perpetually accelerated by invention, leaps ahead of consumption; surpluses rise and generate either depression or war. For either production must stop to let consumption catch up, or foreign markets must be found to take the surplus unbought at home. Foreign markets can be secured by underselling competitors or defeating them in war. To undersell our competitors is impracticable; our standard of living is too high for that; to lower it to the level of Japan's would bring revolution; apparently the choice is between depression and war. But another major depression, possibly made worse through the increased displacement of costly labor by economical machines, might also

318

bring revolution. What is left but war—or an unprecedented change in the behavior of men?

Add a few political causes, and our recipe for war will be complete. The first law of governments is self-preservation; their appetite grows by what they feed on, and they are seldom content. But further, the distribution of power among nations is always changing—through the discovery or development of new natural resources, through the rise or decline of population, through the weakening of religion, morals, and character, or through some other material, or biological or psychological circumstance; and the nation that has become strong soon asserts itself over the nation that has become weak. Hence the impossibility of writing a peace pact that will perpetuate a *status quo*; hence the absurdity of Article X of the League of Nations Covenant; hence the failure of sanctions and the breakdown of the Treaty of Versailles. Excellent indeed is the peace treaty that does not generate a war.

These, then, are the causes of war. How natural it seems now, in the perspective of science and history; how ancient its sources and how inscrutable its destiny!

Is it any wonder that peace is so often but invisible war, in which the nations rest only to fight again?

EFFECTS

Consider briefly the effects of war. We think of these too often, too seldom of the causes. A reminding summary will suffice.

There are psychological effects. A certain exaltation of spirit may come to a country embarked upon what it believes to be a just war; the mind and heart of the people are unified, hyphens drop out, and the diverse elements of the population are more closely fused into a homogeneous nation. The citizens acquire habits of order and discipline, of courage and tenacity; if they are not destroyed, they are made stronger. Against these gains there is the silent gloom of parents and children bereaved, the disorders of demobilization, the demoralization of men new-trained to habits of violence, promiscuity, and deceit.

For a time there is a revulsion against war: pacifism flourishes so long as the evils of war are fresh in the memory; generous men like the Abbé of St. Pierre and Immanuel Kant and Woodrow Wilson offer plans for perpetual peace, and many humane resolutions are made. But as a fresh generation grows up, pacifism subsides; aged reminiscence idealizes the past, and the young are ready to believe that war is 99 per cent glory, and only 1 per cent diarrhea. War loses some of its terrors; to give one's life for one's country is again sweet and beautiful; and to die in bed becomes a shameful fate reserved for noncombatants and generals.

Biologically, war reduces the pressure of population upon the means of subsistence—which is an academic way of saying that some millions of people have been killed. Probably as a result of this, the birth rate has, before our Malthusian days, risen after war; and for some unknown reason, the ratio of male to female births has increased. Dysgenic and eugenic processes go on side by side. The strong and brave go to meet their deaths; the weak remain, and the timid return, to multiply their kind. Pugnacity and brutality are diminished by the superior death rate of the pugnacious and the brutal, both in war and in peace. But usually the finer, more cultured and artistic societies are crushed out, or dominated, by the cruder and more warlike groups: Athens by Sparta, Greece by Macedonia and Rome, T'ang China by the Tatars, Sung China by the Mongols, Gupta India by the Huns, Rome by the barbarians, Renaissance Italy by France, France by Germany, Samurai Japan by the United States. History is a war between war and art, as life is a war between life and death; life and art are always defeated, and always reborn.

To most participating nations, a modern war brings complex economic results. Science and industry are occasionally advanced by researches derived from the stimulus and energy of war. Life and property are destroyed; vast sums are consumed in armament; impossible debts accumulate. Repudiation in some form becomes inevitable; currencies are depreciated or annulled, inflation relieves debtor governments and individuals, savings and investments are wiped out, and men patiently begin to save and lend again. Overexpansion in war is followed by a major depression in peace. International trade is disrupted by intensified nationalism, exalted tariffs, and the desire to develop at home all industries requisite in war. The vanquished are enslaved —physically, as in antiquity, financially and by due process of law today. The victorious masses gain little except in self-conceit; the ruling minority among the victors may gain much in conquered lands, markets, spheres of influence, supplies, and taxable population. This is the little point that Sir Norman Angell forgot.

Politically, war may bring, to the conquered, revolution; to the victors, a strengthened government, the domination of the exchequer by returning soldiers, and the transformation of good generals into bad statesmen.

The methods and institutions that won the war tend to spread abroad and to replace the methods and institutions that lost. The pride of triumph and the appetite for spoils encourage further war, until men and materials are thrown recklessly into the lap of Mars, and the victor, like Assyria and Rome, destroys itself with its victories.

NOSTRUMS

If the foregoing analysis is substantially correct, we shall be spared from any detailed examination of the usual plans for ending war; it is clear that most of these plans have ignored the multiple and tenacious roots of war in the nature of man.

William James, in his kindly way, hoped that the enrollment of the nation's youth, for a year or two, in a wideflung "war against Nature" would give creative expression to the impulses of action, adventure, and association, and so provide a "moral equivalent for war." It is evident that such a procedure would not offer an outlet for the other and major causes of international strife.

The League of Nations, except under Briand and Stresemann, was a conspiracy of the victors to preserve the gains they had made; it had to fail as soon as the fertility and industry of the defeated had altered the balance of national power left by the Treaty of Versailles. An organization of peace designed to perpetuate the spoils of war defeats itself by definition. The life of nations cannot be strait-jacketed into immutability.

Pacifism would be a cure for war, and doubtless for sovereignty, if it could survive the call to arms or the visible peril of attack. Pacifism in England, in our time, was strong enough to endanger the British Empire through unpreparedness and timidity; but a few Fascist twists of the Lion's tail restored the latent vigor of the beast, and pacifists voted great sums for rearmament. A wise people will love peace and keep its powder dry.

Vague appeals to the conscience of mankind to put an end to war have had little effect in history, for there is no conscience of mankind. Morality is a habit of order generated by centuries of compulsion; international morality awaits international order; international order awaits international force. Conscience follows the policeman.

An effective approach to the problem of war will proceed, not by large and generous emotions but by the specific study and patient adjustment of specific causes and disputes. Peace must be planned and organized as realistically as war—with provision for every factor, and prevision for every detail. This cannot be done in an occasional moment stolen by statesmen from internal affairs; it requires the full-time attention of able minds. It should be a major function of the Department of State to wage peace vigorously and continuously on every front; to isolate the germs of war at their source and to sterilize them with understanding and negotiation. It is our good fortune that our Department of State is headed by Cordell Hull, a man who has a will, rather than merely a wish, for peace.

If now we look again at the causes of war, we shall recognize at once that, even with the best will and intelligence available, these causes can be at best mitigated, but not soon removed. We may slowly lessen the greed that breeds war, by reducing the economic insecurity of individuals and states. As the food supply becomes more secure, fear and pugnacity will decrease. As painful taxes melt back into the public mint the great fortunes generated by the contact of free ability with great natural resources, the stimulus to excessive acquisition will be reduced. Perhaps in time we shall distribute among a cabinet of first-class men appointed by and responsible to Congress, many of the burdens and powers now unbearably concentrated in the presidency; then the temptations and opportunities of the will to power will be diminished, though doubtless superior ability will still polarize power to its purposes. Possibly, the Civilian Conservation Corps can be developed as a "moral equivalent" for the impulses to action, wanderlust, adventure, and association. Conceivably, religion may achieve again the international unity and influence by which it reduced, in the Middle Ages, the frequency, extent, and barbarity of war. The slow internationalization of culture through greater ease of communication and travel, and the restoration of trade in ideas as well as goods, may diminish the egotism in patriotism, as happened in the Hellenistic world, and may win more adherents to the International of the Mind. How could a people trained to love art and music go to war with Italy or Germany, or a people matured to relish great literature make war upon England, Russia, or France?

Since the chief biological source of war is the pressure of population upon the means of life, the falling birth rate in the democratic countries is a subtle stimulus to peace. The rise of the birth rate in Germany and Russia is probably temporary; even dictators are helpless before the great tides of imitation that change the mores, or customs, of mankind. It may be possible—after the next holocaust—to organize international agreements pledging governments to refrain from artificial provocations to fertility. Such a move, however, would demand as a prerequisite the reduction of the economic incentives to war.

Those incentives are so numerous and powerful that each of them should be the major concern of an international commission specifically appointed for its consideration and adjustment. There are so many specialists, economists, and diplomats lying about—to use this verb in a purely geographical sense—that we might well distribute them into commissions severally assigned to examine the economic causes of war, to hear the disputing groups patiently, to investigate possibilities of conciliation, to do their work without the explosive excitement of publicity, and to make specific and practicable recommendations to their governments.

322

One such commission would study the problem of fertility, and seek territorial outlets for congested populations; another would consider the access of agriculturally limited peoples to foreign food supplies; another, the access of industrial nations to foreign or colonial raw materials and fuels; another, the breaking down of barriers to world trade; another, the opening of opportunities to investment and enterprise. It might be economical to offer to Germany and Italy access to coal and iron, copper and cotton and wheat, in return for cooperation in the reduction of armaments, imperialistic sorties, birth bonuses, and warlike orations. If the democratic nations prefer the arbitrament of battle to such tentatives of peace, it will be hard to absolve them from partial responsibility for the next world war. It is true that nations so aided would be strengthened, but they would be less dangerous in their prosperity than in their need.

Meanwhile, it is good to organize peace throughout the Western Hemisphere, and to give an example of pacific policy at home. It is good to support democracy wherever we can do it without war; for democracies are less likely to make war than nations whose powers are concentrated in a small number of irresponsible men. It may be that the growing weight and terror of rival armaments will generate, before this year passes, such secret willingness to peace as may make another world conference a practicable and hopeful thing, instead of a windy and mischievous futility. A gathering of this kind might seek, not solutions but a year's truce in arming and talking, while commissions examine the causes of conflict, explore avenues of adjustment, and prepare their reports for a reconvened conference. The more briefly such commissions sit, and the more continuously such commissions labor, the better it will be for the peace of mankind. Perhaps oratory should be added to the major causes of war.

Other proposals swarm into the imagination, but we may be sure that they involve more difficulties than are dreamt of by amiable philosophers. Many are tempted toward the idea of a federation of the English-speaking peoples of the world; here, perhaps, would be a force able to forge an international order, conscience, and peace. But, presumably, such a federation would evoke an equal and opposite federation; it would make government too powerful for the good of our public liberties; and, even if secure from without, it would not end strife within—war would merely become "civil." We do not want a crushing conformity of minds and wills to however admirable a Titan of American virtue and British order; variety and freedom are worth the price we pay for them, even the price of war.

In the end we must steel our hearts against utopias and be content, like Aristotle, with a slightly better state. We must not expect the world to improve much faster than ourselves. Perhaps, if we can broaden our borders with intelligent study, modest travel, and honest thought, if we can become conscious of the natural hunger and needs of other peoples, and sensitive to the varied beauties of many cultures and diverse lands, we shall not so readily plunge into a competitive homicide, but shall find room in our hearts for a wider understanding and an almost universal sympathy. We, above all, who enjoy beyond our merits the grace of peace and unity conferred upon us by our encompassing seas, owe it as a debt of honor to see more generously the problems of nations divided by hostile frontiers, conflicting necessities, dissimilar languages, and unfamiliar ways. We shall find in all these people qualities and accomplishments from which we may learn and refresh ourselves, and by which we may enrich our inheritance and our posterity. Someday, let us hope, it will be permitted us to love our country without betraying mankind.

Art of Living

OF LOVE[1]

Francis Bacon

THE stage is more beholding to Love, than the life of man.
For as to the stage, love is ever matter of comedies, and now and then of
tragedies; but in life it doth much mischief, sometimes like a syren, sometimes
like a fury. You may observe, that amongst all the great and worthy persons
(whereof the memory remaineth, either ancient or recent), there is not one
that hath been transported to the mad degree of love: which shews that great
spirits and great business do keep out this weak passion. You must except
nevertheless Marcus Antonius, the half partner of the empire of Rome, and
Appius Claudius, the decemvir and lawgiver; whereof the former was indeed
a voluptuous man, and inordinate; but the latter was an austere and wise
man: and therefore it seems (though rarely) that love can find entrance not
only into an open heart, but also into a heart well fortified, if watch be not
well kept. It is a poor saying of Epicurus, *Satis magnum alter alteri theatrum
sumus*[2]; as if man, made for the contemplation of heaven and all noble objects,
should do nothing but kneel before a little idol, and make himself a subject,
though not of the mouth (as beasts are), yet of the eye; which was given him
for higher purposes. It is a strange thing to note the excess of this passion,
and how it braves[3] the nature and value of things, by this; that the speaking
in a perpetual hyperbole is comely in nothing but in love. Neither is it merely
in the phrase; for whereas it hath been well said that the arch-flatterer, with
whom all the petty flatterers have intelligence, is a man's self; certainly the
lover is more. For there was never proud man thought so absurdly well of
himself as the lover doth of the person loved; and therefore it was well said,
That it is impossible to love and to be wise. Neither doth this weakness appear
to others only, and not to the party loved; but to the loved most of all, except
the love be reciproque. For it is a true rule, that love is ever rewarded either
with the reciproque or with an inward and secret contempt. By how much
the more men ought to beware of this passion, which loseth not only other
things, but itself. As for the other losses, the poet's relation doth well figure
them; That he that preferred Helena, quitted the gifts of Juno and Pallas.
For whosoever esteemeth too much of amorous affection quitteth both riches
and wisdom. This passion hath his floods in the very times of weakness;
which are great prosperity and great adversity; though this latter hath been
less observed; both which times kindle love, and make it more fervent, and

---

[1]This essay and the two following are from Francis Bacon's *Essays* (1612).
[2]To one another we are a spectacle great enough.
[3]Exaggerates.

therefore shew it to be the child of folly. They do best, who if they cannot but admit love, yet make it keep quarter; and sever it wholly from their serious affairs and actions of life; for if it check[4] once with business, it troubleth men's fortunes, and maketh men that they can no ways be true to their own ends. I know not how, but martial men are given to love: I think it is but as they are given to wine; for perils commonly ask to be paid in pleasures. There is in man's nature a secret inclination and motion towards love of others, which if it be not spent upon some one or a few, doth naturally spread itself towards many, and maketh men become humane and charitable; as it is seen sometime in friars. Nuptial love maketh mankind; friendly love perfecteth it; but wanton love corrupteth and embaseth it.

OF FRIENDSHIP

Francis Bacon

It had been hard for him that spake it to have put more truth and untruth together in few words, than in that speech, *Whosoever is delighted in solitude is either a wild beast or a god*. For it is most true that a natural and secret hatred and aversation[1] towards society in any man, hath somewhat of the savage beast; but it is most untrue that it should have any character at all of the divine nature; except it proceed, not out of a pleasure in solitude, but out of a love and desire to sequester a man's self for a higher conversation[2]: such as is found to have been falsely and feignedly in some of the heathen; as Epimenides the Candian, Numa the Roman, Empedocles the Sicilian, and Apollonius of Tyana; and truly and really in divers of the ancient hermits and holy fathers of the church. But little do men perceive what solitude is, and how far it extendeth. For a crowd is not company; and faces are but a gallery of pictures; and talk but a tinkling cymbal, where there is no love. The Latin adage meeteth with it a little: *Magna civitas, magna solitudo*[3]; because in a great town friends are scattered; so that there is not that fellowship, for the most part, which is in less neighbourhoods. But we may go further, and affirm most truly that it is a mere and miserable solitude to want true friends; without which the world is but a wilderness; and even in this sense also of solitude, whosoever in the frame of his nature and affections is unfit for friendship, he taketh it of the beast, and not from humanity.

---

[4]Interfere.   [1]Aversion.   [2]Way of living.   [3]A great city is a great solitude.

A principal fruit of friendship is the ease and discharge of the fulness and swellings of the heart, which passions of all kinds do cause and induce. We know diseases of stoppings and suffocations are the most dangerous in the body; and it is not much otherwise in the mind; you may take sarza[4] to open the liver, steel to open the spleen, flower of sulphur for the lungs, castoreum[5] for the brain; but no receipt openeth the heart, but a true friend; to whom you may impart griefs, joys, fears, hopes, suspicions, counsels, and whatsoever lieth upon the heart to oppress it, in a kind of civil shrift or confession.

It is a strange thing to observe how high a rate great kings and monarchs do set upon this fruit of friendship whereof we speak: so great, as they purchase it many times at the hazard of their own safety and greatness. For princes, in regard of the distance of their fortune from that of their subjects and servants, cannot gather this fruit, except (to make themselves capable thereof) they raise some persons to be as it were companions and almost equals to themselves, which many times sorteth to inconvenience. The modern languages give unto such persons the name of favourites, or privadoes; as if it were matter of grace, or conversation. But the Roman name attaineth the true use and cause thereof, naming them *participes curarum*[6]; for it is that which tieth the knot. And we see plainly that this hath been done, not by weak and passionate princes only, but by the wisest and most politic that ever reigned; who have oftentimes joined to themselves some of their servants; whom both themselves have called friends, and allowed others likewise to call them in the same manner; using the word which is received between private men.

L. Sylla, when he commanded Rome, raised Pompey (after surnamed the Great) to that height, that Pompey vaunted himself for Sylla's over-match. For when he had carried the consulship for a friend of his, against the pursuit of Sylla, and that Sylla did a little resent thereat, and began to speak great, Pompey turned upon him again, and in effect bade him be quiet; *for that more men adored the sun rising than the sun setting*. With Julius Caesar, Decimus Brutus had obtained that interest, as he set him down in his testament for heir in remainder after his nephew. And this was the man that had power with him to draw him forth to his death. For when Caesar would have discharged the senate, in regard of some ill presages, and specially a dream of Calpurnia; this man lifted him gently by the arm out of his chair, telling him he hoped he would not dismiss the senate till his wife had dreamt a better dream. And it seemeth his favour was so great, as Antonius, in a letter which is recited *verbatim* in one of Cicero's Philippics, calleth him *venefica*, *witch*; as if he had enchanted Caesar. Augustus raised Agrippa (though of

[4]Sarsaparilla.   [5]Secretion of the beaver.   [6]Sharers of cares.

mean birth) to that height, as when he consulted with Maecenas about the marriage of his daughter Julia, Maecenas took the liberty to tell him, *that he must either marry his daughter to Agrippa, or take away his life: there was no third way, he had made him so great*. With Tiberius Caesar, Sejanus had ascended to that height, as they two were termed and reckoned as a pair of friends. Tiberius in a letter to him saith, *haec pro amicitiâ nostrâ non occultavi*[7]; and the whole senate dedicated an altar to Friendship, as to a goddess, in respect of the great dearness of friendship between them two. The like or more was between Septimius Severus and Plautianus. For he forced his eldest son to marry the daughter of Plautianus; and would often maintain Plautianus in doing affronts to his son; and did write also in a letter to the senate, by these words: *I love the man so well, as I wish he may over-live me*. Now if these princes had been as a Trajan or a Marcus Aurelius, a man might have thought that this had proceeded of an abundant goodness of nature; but being men so wise, of such strength and severity of mind, and so extreme lovers of themselves, as all these were, it proveth most plainly that they found their own felicity (though as great as ever happened to mortal men) but as an half piece, except they mought have a friend to make it entire; and yet, which is more, they were princes that had wives, sons, nephews; and yet all these could not supply the comfort of friendship.

It is not to be forgotten what Comineus observeth of his first master, Duke Charles the Hardy; namely, that he would communicate his secrets with none; and least of all, those secrets which troubled him most. Whereupon he goeth on and saith that towards his latter time *that closeness did impair and a little perish his understanding*. Surely Comineus mought have made the same judgment also, if it had pleased him of his second master Lewis the Eleventh, whose closeness was indeed his tormentor. The parable of Pythagoras is dark, but true; *Cor ne edito: Eat not the heart*. Certainly, if a man would give it a hard phrase, those that want friends to open themselves unto are cannibals of their own hearts. But one thing is most admirable (wherewith I will conclude this first fruit of friendship), which is, that this communicating of a man's self to his friend works two contrary effects; for it redoubleth joys, and cutteth griefs in halfs. For there is no man that imparteth his joys to his friend, but he joyeth the more: and no man that imparteth his griefs to his friend, but he grieveth the less. So that it is in truth of operation upon a man's mind, of like virtue as the alchymists use to attribute to their stone for man's body; that it worketh all contrary effects, but still to the good and benefit of nature. But yet without praying in aid of alchymists, there is a manifest image of this in the ordinary course of nature. For in bodies, union strengtheneth

[7]Because of our friendship, I have not hidden these things.

and cherisheth any natural action; and on the other side weakeneth and dulleth any violent impression: and even so it is of minds.

The second fruit of friendship is healthful and sovereign for the understanding, as the first is for the affections. For friendship maketh indeed a fair day in the affections, from storm and tempest; but it maketh daylight in the understanding, out of darkness and confusion of thoughts. Neither is this to be understood only of faithful counsel, which a man receiveth from his friend; but before you come to that, certain it is that whosoever hath his mind fraught with many thoughts, his wits and understanding do clarify and break up, in the communicating and discoursing with another; he tosseth his thoughts more easily; he marshalleth them more orderly; he seeth how they look when they are turned into words: finally, he waxeth wiser than himself; and that more by an hour's discourse than by a day's meditation. It was well said by Themistocles to the king of Persia, *That speech was like cloth of Arras, opened and put abroad; whereby the imagery doth appear in figure; whereas in thoughts they lie but as in packs.* Neither is the second fruit of friendship, in opening the understanding, restrained only to such friends as are able to give a man counsel; (they indeed are best;) but even without that, a man learneth of himself, and bringeth his own thoughts to light, and whetteth his wits as against a stone, which itself cuts not. In a word, a man were better relate himself to a statua or picture, than to suffer his thoughts to pass in smother.

Add now, to make this second fruit of friendship complete, that other point which lieth more open and falleth within vulgar observation; which is faithful counsel from a friend. Heraclitus saith well in one of his enigmas, *Dry light is ever the best.* And certain it is, that the light that a man receiveth by counsel from another, is drier and purer than that which cometh from his own understanding and judgment; which is ever infused and drenched in his affections and customs. So as there is as much difference between the counsel that a friend giveth, and that a man giveth himself, as there is between the counsel of a friend and of a flatterer. For there is no such flatterer as is a man's self; and there is no such remedy against flattery of a man's self, as the liberty of a friend. Counsel is of two sorts: the one concerning manners, the other concerning business. For the first, the best preservative to keep the mind in health is the faithful admonition of a friend. The calling of a man's self to a strict account is a medicine, sometime, too piercing and corrosive. Reading good books of morality is a little flat and dead. Observing our faults in others is sometimes improper for our case. But the best receipt (best, I say, to work, and best to take) is the admonition of a friend. It is a strange thing to behold what gross errors and extreme absurdities many (especially of the greater sort) do commit, for want of a friend to tell them of them; to the great damage both of their fame and fortune: for, as St. James saith, they are as men *that look sometimes into a glass, and presently forget their own shape and favour.* As for business, a man may think, if he will, that two eyes see no more than one; or that a gamester seeth always more than a looker-on; or that a man in anger is as wise as he that hath said over the four and twenty letters[8]; or that a musket may be shot off as well upon the arm as upon a rest; and such other fond[9] and high imaginations, to think himself all in all. But when all is done, the help of good counsel is that which setteth business straight. And if any man think that he will take counsel, but it shall be by pieces; asking counsel in one business of one man, and in another business of another man; it is well, (that is to say, better perhaps than if he asked none at all;) but he runneth two dangers: one, that he shall not be faithfully counselled; for it is a rare thing, except it be from a perfect and entire friend, to have counsel given, but such as shall be bowed and crooked to some ends which he hath that giveth it. The other, that he shall have counsel given, hurtful and unsafe, (though with good meaning,) and mixed partly of mischief and partly of remedy; even as if you would call a physician that is thought good for the cure of the disease you complain of, but is unacquainted with your body, and therefore may put you in way for a present cure, but overthroweth your health in some other kind; and so cure the disease and kill the patient. But a friend that is wholly acquainted with a man's estate will beware, by furthering any present business, how he dasheth upon other inconvenience. And therefore rest not upon scattered counsels; they will rather distract and mislead, than settle and direct.

After these two noble fruits of friendship, (peace in the affections, and support of the judgment,) followeth the last fruit; which is like the pomegranate, full of many kernels; I mean aid and bearing a part in all actions and occasions. Here the best way to represent to life the manifold use of friendship, is to cast and see how many things there are which a man cannot do himself; and then it will appear that it was a sparing speech of the ancients, to say, *that a friend is another himself*; for that a friend is far more than himself. Men have their time, and die many times in desire of some things which they principally take to heart; the bestowing of a child, the finishing of a work, or the like. If a man have a true friend, he may rest almost secure that the care of those things will continue after him. So that a man hath, as it were, two lives in his desires. A man hath a body, and that body is confined to a

---

[8] According to Ben Jonson in his *English Grammar*, the English alphabet was limited to twenty-four letters.
[9] Foolish.

place; but where friendship is, all offices of life are as it were granted to him and his deputy. For he may exercise them by his friend. How many things are there which a man cannot, with any face or comeliness, say or do himself? A man can scarce allege his own merits with modesty, much less extol them; a man cannot sometimes brook to supplicate or beg; and a number of the like. But all these things are graceful in a friend's mouth, which are blushing in a man's own. So again, a man's person hath many proper relations which he cannot put off. A man cannot speak to his son but as a father; to his wife but as a husband; to his enemy but upon terms: whereas a friend may speak as the case requires, and not as it sorteth with the person. But to enumerate these things were endless; I have given the rule, where a man cannot fitly play his own part: if he have not a friend, he may quit the stage.

OF MARRIAGE AND SINGLE LIFE

Francis Bacon

HE THAT hath wife and children hath given hostages to fortune; for they are impediments to great enterprises, either of virtue or mischief. Certainly the best works, and of greatest merit for the public, have proceeded from the unmarried or childless men; which both in affection and means have married and endowed the public. Yet it were great reason that those that have children should have greatest care of future times; unto which they know they must transmit their dearest pledges. Some there are, who though they lead a single life, yet their thoughts do end with themselves, and account future times impertinences. Nay, there are some other that account wife and children but as bills of charges. Nay more, there are some foolish rich covetous men, that take a pride in having no children, because they may be thought so much the richer. For perhaps they have heard some talk, *Such an one is a great rich man*, and another except to it, *Yea, but he hath a great charge of children*; as if it were an abatement to his riches. But the most ordinary cause of a single life is liberty, especially in certain self-pleasing and humorous[1] minds, which are so sensible of every restraint, as they will go near to think their girdles and garters to be bonds and shackles. Unmarried men are best friends, best masters, best servants; but not always best subjects; for they are like to run away; and almost all fugitives are of that condition. A single life doth well with churchmen; for charity will hardly water the ground where

[1]Whimsical.

it must first fill a pool. It is indifferent for judges and magistrates; for if they be facile and corrupt, you shall have a servant five times worse than a wife. For soldiers, I find the generals commonly in their hortatives[2] put men in mind of their wives and children; and I think the despising of marriage amongst the Turks maketh the vulgar soldier more base. Certainly wife and children are a kind of discipline of humanity; and single men, though they may be many times more charitable, because their means are less exhaust, yet, on the other side, they are more cruel and hardhearted, (good to make severe inquisitors,) because their tenderness is not so oft called upon. Grave natures, led by custom, and therefore constant, are commonly loving husbands; as was said of Ulysses, *vetulam suam proetulit immortalitati.*[3] Chaste women are often proud and froward, as presuming upon the merit of their chastity. It is one of the best bonds both of chastity and obedience in the wife, if she think her husband wise; which she will never do if she find him jealous. Wives are young men's mistresses; companions for middle age; and old men's nurses. So as a man may have a quarrel,[4] to marry when he will. But yet he was reputed one of the wise men, that made answer to the question when a man should marry?—*A young man not yet, an elder man not at all.* It is often seen that bad husbands have very good wives; whether it be that it raiseth the price of their husband's kindness when it comes; or that the wives take a pride in their patience. But this never fails, if the bad husbands were of their own choosing, against their friends' consent; for then they will be sure to make good their own folly.

A BUSY LIFE[1]

Joseph Addison

—Fruges consumere nati.[2]

HORACE

Augustus, a few moments before his death, asked his friends who stood about him if they thought he had acted his part well; and upon receiving such an answer as was due to his extraordinary merit, Let me then, says he, go off the stage with your applause, using the expression with which the Roman actors made their exit at the conclusion of a dramatic

[2]Exhortations.   [3]He preferred his aged wife to immortality.   [4]Excuse.
[1]This essay and the two following by Addison are from *The Spectator* (1711–12).
[2]"Born but to feed."—Sir Theodore Martin.

piece. I could wish that men, while they are in health, would consider well the nature of the part they are engaged in, and what figure it will make in the minds of those they leave behind them: whether it was worth coming into the world for, whether it be suitable to a reasonable being; in short, whether it appears graceful in this life, or will turn to an advantage in the next. Let the sycophant, or buffoon, the satirist, or the good companion, consider with himself, when his body shall be laid in the grave, and his soul pass into another state of existence, how much it will redound to his praise to have it said of him that no man in England eat better, that he had an admirable talent at turning his friends into ridicule, that nobody outdid him at an ill-natured jest, or that he never went to bed before he had dispatched his third bottle. These are, however, very common funeral orations, and eulogiums on deceased persons who have acted among mankind with some figure and reputation.

But if we look into the bulk of our species, they are such as are not likely to be remembered a moment after their disappearance. They leave behind them no traces of their existence, but are forgotten as though they had never been. They are neither wanted by the poor, regretted by the rich, nor celebrated by the learned. They are neither missed in the common-wealth, nor lamented by private persons. Their actions are of no significancy to mankind, and might have been performed by creatures of much less dignity than those who are distinguished by the faculty of reason. An eminent French author speaks somewhere to the following purpose: I have often seen from my chamber window two noble creatures, both of them of an erect countenance, and endowed with reason. These two intellectual beings are employed, from morning to night, in rubbing two smooth stones one upon another; that is, as the vulgar phrase it, in polishing marble.

My friend, Sir Andrew Freeport, as we were sitting in the Club last night, gave us an account of a sober citizen who died a few days since. This honest man, being of greater consequence in his own thoughts than in the eye of the world, had for some years past kept a journal of his life. Sir Andrew showed us one week of it. Since the occurrences set down in it mark out such a road of action as that I have been speaking of, I shall present my reader with a faithful copy of it; after having first informed him that the deceased person had in his youth been bred to trade, but finding himself not so well turned for business, he had for several years last past lived altogether upon a moderate annuity.

Monday, Eight o'clock. I put on my clothes and walked into the parlor. Nine o'clock, ditto. Tied my knee-strings, and washed my hands.

Hours ten, eleven, and twelve. Smoked three pipes of Virginia. Read the *Supplement* and *Daily Courant*. Things go ill in the north. Mr. Nisby's opinion thereupon.

One o'clock in the afternoon. Chid Ralph for mislaying my tobacco-box.

Two o'clock. Sat down to dinner. Mem. Too many plums, and no suet.

From three to four. Took my afternoon's nap.

From four to six. Walked into the fields. Wind, S.S.E.

From six to ten. At the Club. Mr. Nisby's opinion about the peace.

Ten o'clock. Went to bed, slept sound.

Tuesday, being holiday, Eight o'clock. Rose as usual.

Nine o'clock. Washed hands and face, shaved, put on my double soled shoes.

Ten, eleven, twelve. Took a walk to Islington.

One. Took a pot of Mother Cob's Mild.

Between two and three. Returned, dined on a knuckle of veal and bacon. Mem. Sprouts wanting.

Three. Nap as usual.

From four to six. Coffee house. Read the news. A dish of twist. Grand Vizier strangled.

From six to ten. At the Club. Mr. Nisby's account of the Great Turk.

Ten. Dream of the Grand Vizier. Broken sleep.

Wednesday, Eight o'clock. Tongue of my shoe-buckle broke. Hands, but not face.

Nine. Paid off the butcher's bill. Mem. To be allowed for the last leg of mutton.

Ten, eleven. At the coffee house. More work in the north. Stranger in ,. black wig asked me how stocks went.

From twelve to one. Walked in the fields. Wind to the south.

From one to two. Smoked a pipe and a half.

Two. Dined as usual. Stomach good.

Three. Nap broke by the falling of a pewter-dish. Mem. Cook-maid in love, and grown careless.

From four to six. At the coffee house. Advice from Smyrna, that the Grand Vizier was first of all strangled, and afterwards beheaded.

Six o'clock in the evening. Was half an hour in the Club before anybody else came. Mr. Nisby of opinion that the Grand Vizier was not strangled the sixth instant.

Ten at night. Went to bed. Slept without waking till nine next morning.

Thursday, Nine o'clock. Stayed within till two o'clock for Sir Timothy, who did not bring me my annuity according to his promise.

Two in the afternoon. Sat down to dinner. Loss of appetite. Small beer sour. Beef overcorned.

Three. Could not take my nap.

Four and five. Gave Ralph a box on the ear. Turned off my cookmaid. Sent a message to Sir Timothy. Mem. I did not go to the Club tonight. Went to bed at nine o'clock.

Friday. Passed the morning in meditation upon Sir Timothy, who was with me a quarter before twelve.

Twelve o'clock. Bought a new head to my cane, and a tongue to my buckle. Drank a glass of purl to recover appetite.

Two and three. Dined, and slept well.

From four to six. Went to the coffee house. Met Mr. Nisby there. Smoked several pipes. Mr. Nisby of opinion that laced coffee is bad for the head.

Six o'clock. At the Club as steward. Sat late.

Twelve o'clock. Went to bed, dreamt that I drank small beer with the Grand Vizier.

Saturday. Waked at eleven, walked in the fields. Wind N.E.

Twelve. Caught in a shower.

One in the afternoon. Returned home, and dried myself.

Two. Mr. Nisby dined with me. First course marrow-bones. Second ox-cheek, with a bottle of Brook's and Hellier.

Three o'clock. Overslept myself.

Six. Went to the Club. Like to have fallen into a gutter. Grand Vizier certainly dead, etc.

I question not but the reader will be surprised to find the above-mentioned journalist taking so much care of a life that was filled with such inconsiderable actions and received so very small improvements; and yet, if we look into the behavior of many whom we daily converse with, we shall find that most of their hours are taken up in those three important articles of eating, drinking, and sleeping. I do not suppose that a man loses his time, who is not engaged in public affairs, or in an illustrious course of action. On the contrary, I believe our hours may very often be more profitably laid out in such trans-actions as make no figure in the world than in such as are apt to draw upon them the attention of mankind. One may become wiser and better by several methods of employing one's self in secrecy and silence, and do what is laudable without noise or ostentation. I would, however, recommend to every one of my readers the keeping a journal of their lives for one week, and setting down punctually their whole series of employments during that space of time. This kind of self-examination would give them a true state of themselves, and incline them to consider seriously what they are about. One day would rectify the omissions of another, and make a man weigh all those indifferent actions, which, though they are easily forgotten, must certainly be accounted for.

THE BEAU'S HEAD

Joseph Addison

—tribus Anticyris caput insanabile.[1]
JUVENAL

I WAS yesterday engaged in an assembly of virtuosos, where one of them produced many curious observations, which he had lately made in the anatomy of an human body. Another of the company communicated to us several wonderful discoveries, which he had also made on the same subject, by the help of very fine glasses. This gave birth to a great variety of uncommon remarks, and furnished discourse for the remaining part of the day.

The different opinions which were started on this occasion presented to my imagination so many new ideas that, by mixing with those which were already there, they employed my fancy all the last night, and composed a very wild extravagant dream.

I was invited, methought, to the dissection of a beau's head, and of a coquette's heart, which were both of them laid on a table before us. An imaginary operator opened the first with a great deal of nicety, which upon a cursory and superficial view, appeared like the head of another man; but, upon applying our glasses to it, we made a very odd discovery, namely, that what we looked upon as brains, were not such in reality, but an heap of strange materials wound up in the shape and texture, and packed together with wonderful art in the several cavities of the skull. For, as Homer tells us that the blood of the gods is not real blood, but only something like it; so we found that the brain of a beau is not real brain but only something like it.

[1]"Their heads, which three Anticyras cannot heal."—Translated by Ben Jonson.

338

The pineal gland, which many of our modern philosophers suppose to be the seat of the soul, smelt very strong of essence and orange-flower water, and was encompassed with a kind of horny substance, cut into a thousand little faces or mirrors, which were imperceptible to the naked eye; insomuch that the soul, if there had been any here, must have been always taken up in contemplating her own beauties.

We observed a large antrum or cavity in the sinciput, that was filled with ribbons, lace, and embroidery, wrought together in a most curious piece of network, the parts of which were likewise imperceptible to the naked eye. Another of these antrums or cavities was stuffed with invisible billets-doux, love-letters, pricked dances, and other trumpery of the same nature. In another we found a kind of powder, which set the whole company a sneezing, and by the scent discovered itself to be right Spanish. The several other cells were stored with commodities of the same kind, of which it would be tedious to give the reader an exact inventory.

There was a large cavity on each side of the head, which I must not omit. That on the right side was filled with fictions, flatteries, and falsehoods, vows, promises, and protestations; that on the left with oaths and imprecations. There issued out a duct from each of these cells, which ran into the root of the tongue, where both joined together, and passed forward in one common duct to the tip of it. We discovered several little roads or canals running from the ear into the brain, and took particular care to trace them out through their several passages. One of them extended itself to a bundle of sonnets and little musical instruments. Others ended in several bladders which were filled either with wind or froth. But the large canal entered into a great cavity of the skull, from whence there went another canal into the tongue. This great cavity was filled with a kind of spongy substance, which the French anatomists call *galimatias*,[2] and the English nonsense.

The skins of the forehead were extremely tough and thick, and, what very much surprised us, had not in them any single blood-vessel that we were able to discover, either with or without our glasses; from whence we concluded that the party when alive must have been entirely deprived of the faculty of blushing.

The os cribriforme[3] was exceedingly stuffed, and in some places damaged with snuff. We could not but take notice in particular of that small muscle which is not often discovered in dissections, and draws the nose upwards, when it expresses the contempt which the owner of it has, upon seeing anything he does not like, or hearing anything he does not understand. I need not tell my learned reader, this is that muscle which performs the motion so

[2]Gibberish.   [3]Driveling mouth.

often mentioned by the Latin poets, when they talk of a man's cocking his nose, or playing the rhinoceros.

We did not find anything very remarkable in the eye, saving only that the *musculi amatorii*, or as we may translate it into English, the ogling muscles, were very much worn and decayed with use; whereas on the contrary, the elevator or the muscle which turns the eye toward heaven did not appear to have been used at all.

I have only mentioned in this dissection such new discoveries as we were able to make, and have not taken any notice of those parts which are to be met with in common heads. As for the skull, the face, and indeed the whole outward shape and figure of the head, we could not discover any difference from what we observe in the heads of other men. We were informed that the person to whom this head belonged, had passed for a man above five and thirty years: during which time he eat and drank like other people, dressed well, talked loud, laughed frequently, and on particular occasions had acquitted himself tolerably at a ball or an assembly, to which one of the company added that a certain knot of ladies took him for a wit. He was cut off in the flower of his age, by the blow of a paving shovel, having been surprised by an eminent citizen, as he was tendering some civilities to his wife.

When we had thoroughly examined this head with all its apartments, and its several kinds of furniture, we put up the brain, such as it was, into its proper place, and laid it aside under a broad piece of scarlet cloth, in order to be prepared, and kept in a great repository of dissections, our operator telling us that the preparation would not be so difficult as that of another brain, for that he had observed several of the little pipes and tubes which ran through the brain were already filled with a kind of mercurial substance, which he looked upon to be true quicksilver.

He applied himself in the next place to the coquette's heart, which he likewise laid open with great dexterity. There occurred to us many particularities in this dissection; but, being unwilling to burden my reader's memory too much, I shall reserve this subject for the speculation of another day.

THE COQUETTE'S HEART

Joseph Addison

Pectoribus inhians spirantia consulit exta.[1]

VIRGIL

HAVING already given an account of the dissection of a beau's head, with the several discoveries made on that occasion, I shall here, according to my promise, enter upon the dissection of a coquette's heart, and communicate to the public such particularities as we observed in that curious piece of anatomy.

I should perhaps have waived this undertaking, had not I been put in mind of my promise by several of my unknown correspondents, who are very importunate with me to make an example of the coquette, as I have already done of the beau. It is, therefore, in compliance with the request of friends that I have looked over the minutes of my former dream, in order to give the public an exact relation of it, which I shall enter upon without further preface. . . .

Our operator, before he engaged in this visionary dissection, told us that there was nothing in his art more difficult than to lay open the heart of a coquette, by reason of the many labyrinths and recesses which are to be found in it, and which do not appear in the heart of any other animal.

He desired us first of all to observe the pericardium, or outward case of the heart, which we did very attentively; and by the help of our glasses discerned in it millions of little scars, which seemed to have been occasioned by the points of innumerable darts and arrows, that from time to time had glanced upon the outward coat; though we could not discover the smallest orifice by which any of them had entered and pierced the inward substance.

Every smatterer in anatomy knows that this pericardium, or case of the heart, contains in it a thin reddish liquor, supposed to be bred from the vapors which exhale out of the heart, and being stopped here, are condensed into this watery substance. Upon examining this liquor, we found that it had in it all the qualities of that spirit which is made use of in the thermometer to show the change of weather.

Nor must I here omit an experiment one of the company assured us he himself had made with this liquor, which he found in great quantity about the heart of a coquette whom he had formerly dissected. He affirmed to us that he had actually enclosed it in a small tube made after the manner of a

---

[1]"And gazing greedily on the . . . breasts, consults the entrails, yet quivering with life."—John Conington.

weatherglass; but that, instead of acquainting him with the variations of the atmosphere, it showed him the qualities of those persons who entered the room where it stood. He affirmed also that it rose at the approach of a plume of feathers, an embroidered coat, or a pair of fringed gloves; and that it fell as soon as an illshaped periwig, a clumsy pair of shoes, or an unfashionable coat came into his house: Nay, he proceeded so far as to assure us that upon his laughing aloud, when he stood by it, the liquor mounted very sensibly, and immediately sunk again upon his looking serious. In short, he told us that he knew very well by this invention whenever he had a man of sense or a coxcomb in his room.

Having cleared away the pericardium, or the case and liquor above mentioned, we came to the heart itself. The outward surface of it was extremely slippery, and the mucro, or point, so very cold withal that, upon endeavoring to take hold of it, it glided through the fingers like a smooth piece of ice.

The fibers were turned and twisted in a more intricate and perplexed manner than they are usually found in other hearts; insomuch, that the whole heart was wound up together like a Gordian knot, and must have had very irregular and unequal motions, whilst it was employed in its vital function.

One thing we thought very observable, namely, that upon examining all the vessels which came into it or issued out of it, we could not discover any communication that it had with the tongue.

We could not but take notice, likewise, that several of those little nerves in the heart which are affected by the sentiments of love, hatred, and other passions, did not descend to this before us from the brain, but from the muscles which lie about the eye.

Upon weighing the heart in my hand, I found it to be extremely light, and consequently very hollow; which I did not wonder at when, upon looking into the inside of it, I saw multitudes of cells and cavities running one within another, as our historians describe the apartments of Rosamond's Bower.[2] Several of these little hollows were stuffed with innumerable sorts of trifles, which I shall forbear giving any particular account of, and shall therefore only take notice of what lay first and uppermost, which upon our unfolding it and applying our microscope to it appeared to be a flame-colored hood.

We were informed that the lady of this heart, when living, received the addresses of several who made love to her, and did not only give each of them encouragement, but made everyone she conversed with believe that she regarded him with an eye of kindness; for which reason we expected to have seen the impression of multitudes of faces among the several plates and foldings of the heart, but to our great surprise not a single print of this nature

[2]Bower where Henry II is supposed to have sheltered Rosamond Clifford.

discovered itself till we came into the very core and center of it. We there observed a little figure, which, upon applying our glasses to it, appeared dressed in a very fantastic manner. The more I looked upon it, the more I thought I had seen the face before, but could not possibly recollect either the place or time; when at length one of the company, who had examined this figure more nicely than the rest, showed us plainly by the make of its face, and the several turns of its features, that the little idol that was thus lodged in the middle of the heart was the deceased beau, whose head I gave some account of in my last Tuesday's paper.

As soon as we had finished our dissection, we resolved to make an experiment of the heart, not being able to determine among ourselves the nature of its substance, which differed in so many particulars from that of the heart in other females. Accordingly we laid it into a pan of burning coals, when we observed in it a certain salamandrine quality, that made it capable of living in the midst of fire and flame, without being consumed, or so much as singed.

As we were admiring this strange phenomenon, and standing round the heart in a circle, it gave a most prodigious sigh, or rather crack, and dispersed all at once in smoke and vapor. This imaginary noise, which methought was louder than the burst of a cannon, produced such a violent shake in my brain, that it dissipated the fumes of sleep, and left me in an instant broad awake.

PORTRAIT OF A GENTLEMAN[1]

John Henry Newman

HENCE it is that it is almost a definition of a gentleman to say he is one who never inflicts pain. This description is both refined and, as far as it goes, accurate. He is mainly occupied in merely removing the obstacles which hinder the free and unembarrassed action of those about him; and he concurs with their movements rather than takes the initiative himself. His benefits may be considered as parallel to what are called comforts or conveniences in arrangements of a personal nature; like an easy chair or a good fire, which do their part in dispelling cold and fatigue, though nature provides both means of rest and animal heat without them. The true gentleman in like manner carefully avoids whatever may cause a jar or a jolt in the minds of those with whom he is cast;—all clashing of opinion, or collision of feeling, all restraint, or suspicion, or gloom, or resentment; his great concern being to

[1]From *Idea of a University* by John Henry Newman (1852).

343

make every one at their ease and at home. He has his eyes on all his company; he is tender towards the bashful, gentle towards the distant, and merciful towards the absurd; he can recollect to whom he is speaking; he guards against unseasonable allusions, or topics which may irritate; he is seldom prominent in conversation, and never wearisome. He makes light of favours while he does them, and seems to be receiving when he is conferring. He never speaks of himself except when compelled, never defends himself by a mere retort, he has no ears for slander or gossip, is scrupulous in imputing motives to those who interfere with him, and interprets everything for the best. He is never mean or little in his disputes, never takes unfair advantage, never mistakes personalities or sharp sayings for arguments, or insinuates evil which he dare not say out. From a long-sighted prudence, he observes the maxim of the ancient sage, that we should ever conduct ourselves towards our enemy as if he were one day to be our friend. He has too much good sense to be affronted at insults, he is too well employed to remember injuries, and too indolent to bear malice. He is patient, forbearing, and resigned, on philosophical principles; he submits to pain, because it is inevitable, to bereavement, because it is irreparable, and to death, because it is his destiny. If he engages in controversy of any kind, his disciplined intellect preserves him from the blundering discourtesy of better, perhaps, but less educated minds; who like blunt weapons, tear and hack instead of cutting clean, who mistake the point in argument, waste their strength on trifles, misconceive their adversary, and leave the question more involved than they find it. He may be right or wrong in his opinion, but he is too clear-headed to be unjust; he is as simple as he is forcible, and as brief as he is decisive. Nowhere shall we find greater candour, consideration, indulgence; he throws himself into the minds of his opponents, he accounts for their mistakes. He knows the weakness of human reason as well as its strength, its province and its limits. If he be an unbeliever, he will be too profound and large-minded to ridicule religon or to act against it; he is too wise to be a dogmatist or fanatic in his infidelity. He respects piety and devotion; he even supports institutions as venerable, beautiful, or useful, to which he does not assent; he honours the ministers of religion, and it contents him to decline its mysteries without assailing or denouncing them. He is a friend of religious toleration, and that, not only because his philosophy has taught him to look on all forms of faith with an impartial eye, but also from the gentleness and effeminacy of feeling, which is the attendant on civilization.

Not that he may not hold a religion too, in his own way, even when he is not a Christian. In that case his religion is one of imagination and sentiment; it is the embodiment of those ideas of the sublime, majestic, and beautiful, without which there can be no large philosophy. Sometimes he acknowledges the being of God, sometimes he invests an unknown principle or quality with the attributes of perfection. And this deduction of his reason, or creation of his fancy, he makes the occasion of such excellent thoughts, and the starting-point of so varied and systematic a teaching, that he even seems like a disciple of Christianity itself. From the very accuracy and steadiness of his logical powers, he is able to see what sentiments are consistent in those who hold any religious doctrine at all, and he appears to others to feel and to hold a whole circle of theological truths, which exist in his mind no otherwise than as a number of deductions.

Such are some of the lineaments of the ethical character, which the cultivated intellect will form, apart from religious principle. They are seen within the pale of the Church and without it, in holy men, and in profligate; they form the *beau-ideal* of the world; they partly assist and partly distort the development of the Catholic. They may subserve the education of a St. Francis de Sales or a Cardinal Pole; they may be the limits of the contemplation of a Shaftesbury or a Gibbon. Basil and Julian were fellow-students at the schools of Athens; and one became the Saint and Doctor of the Church, the other her scoffing and relentless foe.

ON TALK [1]

Oliver Wendell Holmes

Don't flatter yourselves that friendship authorizes you to say disagreeable things to your intimates. On the contrary, the nearer you come into relation with a person, the more necessary do tact and courtesy become. Except in cases of necessity, which are rare, leave your friend to learn unpleasant truths from his enemies; they are ready enough to tell them. Good-breeding *never* forgets that *amour-propre* is universal. When you read the story of the Archbishop and Gil Blas,[2] you may laugh, if you will, at the poor old man's delusion; but don't forget that the youth was the greater fool of the two, and that his master served such a booby rightly in turning him out of doors.

[1] From *The Autocrat of the Breakfast Table* by Oliver Wendell Holmes (1858). Houghton Mifflin Company, publishers.

[2] See *Gil Blas* by Lesage. Gil Blas, a poor orphan, by turns enters the service of a physician, a lady of fashion, an archbishop, a prime minister, all with equal confidence, accepting luxury or destitution, palace or prison, with equal philosophy. While in service with the Archbishop of Granada, the archbishop invites Gil Blas to criticize his sermons and deeply resents the criticism when given.

You need not get up a rebellion against what I say, if you find everything in my sayings is not exactly new. You can't possibly mistake a man who means to be honest for a literary pickpocket. I once read an introductory lecture that looked to me too learned for its latitude. On examination, I found all its erudition was taken ready-made from Disraeli. If I had been ill-natured, I should have shown up the little great man, who had once belabored me in his feeble way. But one can generally tell these wholesale thieves easily enough, and they are not worth the trouble of putting them in the pillory. I doubt the entire novelty of my remarks just made on telling unpleasant truths, yet I am not conscious of any larceny.

Neither make too much of flaws and occasional overstatements. Some persons seem to think that absolute truth, in the form of rigidly stated propositions, is all that conversation admits. This is precisely as if a musician should insist on having nothing but perfect chords and simple melodies,—no diminished fifths, no flat sevenths, no flourishes, on any account. Now it is fair to say, that, just as music must have all these, so conversation must have its partial truths, its embellished truths, its exaggerated truths. It is in its higher forms an artistic product, and admits the ideal element as much as pictures or statues. One man who is a little too literal can spoil the talk of a whole tableful of men of *esprit*.—"Yes," you say, "but who wants to hear fanciful people's nonsense? Put the facts to it, and then see where it is!"—Certainly, if a man is too fond of paradox,—if he is flighty and empty,—if, instead of striking those fifths and sevenths, those harmonious discords, often so much better than the twinned octaves, in the music of thought,—if, instead of striking these, he jangles the chords, stick a fact into him like a stiletto. But remember that talking is one of the fine arts,—the noblest, the most important, and the most difficult,—and that its fluent harmonies may be spoiled by the intrusion of a single harsh note. Therefore conversation which is suggestive rather than argumentative, which lets out the most of each talker's results of thought, is commonly the pleasantest and the most profitable. It is not easy, at the best, for two persons talking together to make the most of each other's thoughts, there are so many of them.

[The company looked as if they wanted an explanation.]

When John and Thomas, for instance, are talking together, it is natural enough that among the six there should be more or less confusion and misapprehension.

[Our landlady turned pale;—no doubt she thought there was a screw loose in my intellects,—and that involved the probable loss of a boarder. A severe-looking person, who wears a Spanish cloak and a sad cheek, fluted by the passions of the melodrama, whom I understand to be the professional ruffian of the neighboring theatre, alluded, with a certain lifting of the brow, drawing down of the corners of the mouth, and somewhat rasping *voce di petto*, to Falstaff's nine men in buckram. Everybody looked up; I believe the old gentleman opposite was afraid I should seize the carving-knife; at any rate, he slid it to one side, as it were carelessly.]

I think, I said, I can make it plain to Benjamin Franklin here, that there are at least six personalities distinctly to be recognized as taking part in that dialogue between John and Thomas.

Three Johns

> 1. The real John; known only to his Maker.
> 2. John's ideal John; never the real one, and often very unlike him.
> 3. Thomas's ideal John; never the real John, nor John's John, but often very unlike either.

Three Thomases

> 1. The real Thomas.
> 2. Thomas's ideal Thomas.
> 3. John's ideal Thomas.

Only one of the three Johns is taxed; only one can be weighed on a platform-balance; but the other two are just as important in the conversation. Let us suppose the real John to be old, dull, and ill-looking. But as the Higher Powers have not conferred on men the gift of seeing themselves in the true light, John very possibly conceives himself to be youthful, witty, and fascinating, and talks from the point of view of this ideal. Thomas, again, believes him to be an artful rogue, we will say; therefore he *is*, so far as Thomas's attitude in the conversation is concerned, an artful rogue though really simple and stupid. The same conditions apply to the three Thomases. It follows, that, until a man can be found who knows himself as his Maker knows him, or who sees himself as others see him, there must be at least six persons engaged in every dialogue between two. Of these, the least important, philosophically speaking, is the one that we have called the real person. No wonder two disputants often get angry, when there are six of them talking and listening all at the same time.

[A very unphilosophical application of the above remarks was made by a young fellow answering to the name of John, who sits near me at table. A certain basket of peaches, a rare vegetable, little known to boarding-houses, was on its way to me *via* this unlettered Johannes. He appropriated the three that remained in the basket, remarking that there was just one apiece for him. I convinced him that his practical inference was hasty and illogical, but in the mean time he had eaten the peaches.]

347

ON MARRIAGE[1]

Robert Louis Stevenson

WITH the single exception of Falstaff, all Shakespeare's characters are what we call marrying men. Mercutio, as he was own cousin to Benedick and Biron, would have come to the same end in the long run. Even Iago had a wife, and, what is far stranger, he was jealous. People like Jaques and the Fool in *Lear*, although we can hardly imagine they would ever marry, kept single out of a cynical humor or for a broken heart, and not, as we do nowadays, from a spirit of incredulity and preference for the single state. For that matter, if you turn to George Sand's French version of *As You Like It* (and I think I can promise you will like it but little), you will find Jaques marries Celia just as Orlando marries Rosalind.

At least there seems to have been much less hesitation over marriage in Shakespeare's days; and what hesitation there was was of a laughing sort, and not much more serious, one way or the other, than that of Panurge. In modern comedies the heroes are mostly of Benedick's way of thinking, but twice as much in earnest, and not one-quarter so confident. And I take this diffidence as a proof of how sincere their terror is. They know they are only human after all; they know what gins and pitfalls lie about their feet; and how the shadow of matrimony waits, resolute and awful, at the cross-roads. They would wish to keep their liberty; but if that may not be, why, God's will be done! "What, are you afraid of marriage?" asks Cécile, in *Maître Guerin*. "Oh, mon Dieu, non!" replies Arthur; "I should take chloroform." They look forward to marriage much in the same way as they prepare themselves for death: each seems inevitable; each is a great Perhaps, and a leap into the dark, for which, when a man is in the blue devils, he has specially to harden his heart. That splendid scoundrel, Maxime de Trailles, took the news of marriages much as an old man hears the deaths of his contemporaries. "C'est désespérant," he cried, throwing himself down in the arm-chair at Madame Schontz's; "c'est désespérant, nous nous marions tous!" Every marriage was like another gray hair on his head; and the jolly church bells seemed to taunt him with his fifty years and fair round belly.

The fact is, we are much more afraid of life than our ancestors, and cannot find it in our hearts either to marry or not to marry. Marriage is terrifying, but so is a cold and forlorn old age. The friendships of men are vastly agreeable, but they are insecure. You know all the time that one friend will marry and put you to the door; a second accept a situation in China, and become

[1]From *Virginibus Puerisque*, by Robert Louis Stevenson (1881). Charles Scribner's Sons.

no more to you than a name, a reminiscence, and an occasional crossed letter, very laborious to read; a third will take up with some religious crotchet and treat you to sour looks thenceforward. So, in one way or another, life forces men apart and breaks up the goodly fellowships forever. The very flexibility and ease which make men's friendships so agreeable while they endure, make them the easier to destroy and forget. And a man who has a few friends, or one who has a dozen (if there be any one so wealthy on this earth), cannot forget on how precarious a base his happiness reposes; and how by a stroke or two of fate—a death, a few light words, a piece of stamped paper, a woman's bright eyes—he may be left, in a month, destitute of all. Marriage is certainly a perilous remedy. Instead of on two or three, you stake your happiness on one life only. But still, as the bargain is more explicit and complete on your part, it is more so on the other; and you have not to fear so many contingencies; it is not every wind that can blow you from your anchorage; and so long as Death withholds his sickle, you will always have a friend at home. People who share a cell in the Bastille, or are thrown together on an uninhabited island, if they do not immediately fall to fisticuffs, will find some possible ground of compromise. They will learn each other's ways and humors, so as to know where they must go warily, and where they may lean their whole weight. The discretion of the first years becomes the settled habit of the last; and so, with wisdom and patience, two lives may grow indissolubly into one.

But marriage, if comfortable, is not at all heroic. It certainly narrows and damps the spirits of generous men. In marriage, a man becomes slack and selfish, and undergoes a fatty degeneration of his moral being. It is not only when Lydgate misallies himself with Rosamond Vincy, but when Ladislaw marries above him with Dorothea, that this may be exemplified. The air of the fireside withers out all the fine wildings of the husband's heart. He is so comfortable and happy that he begins to prefer comfort and happiness to everything else on earth, his wife included. Yesterday he would have shared his last shilling; to-day "his first duty is to his family," and is fulfilled in large measure by laying down vintages and husbanding the health of an invaluable parent. Twenty years ago this man was equally capable of crime or heroism; now he is fit for neither. His soul is asleep, and you may speak without constraint; you will not wake him. It is not for nothing that Don Quixote was a bachelor and Marcus Aurelius married ill. For women, there is less of this danger. Marriage is of so much use to a woman, opens out to her so much more of life, and puts her in the way of so much more freedom and usefulness, that, whether she marry ill or well, she can hardly miss some benefit. It is true, however, that some of the merriest and most genuine of women are old maids; and that those old maids, and wives who are unhappily married, have often most of the true motherly touch. And this would seem to show, even for women, some narrowing influence in comfortable married life. But the rule is none the less certain: if you wish the pick of men and women, take a good bachelor and a good wife.

I am often filled with wonder that so many marriages are passably successful, and so few come to open failure, the more so as I fail to understand the principle on which people regulate their choice. I see women marrying indiscriminately with staring burgesses and ferret-faced, white-eyed boys, and men dwelling in contentment with noisy scullions, or taking into their lives acidulous vestals. It is a common answer to say the good people marry because they fall in love; and of course you may use and misuse a word as much as you please, if you have the world along with you. But love is at least a somewhat hyperbolical expression for such lukewarm preference. It is not here, anyway, that Love employs his golden shafts; he cannot be said, with any fitness of language, to reign here and revel. Indeed, if this be love at all, it is plain the poets have been fooling with mankind since the foundation of the world. And you have only to look these happy couples in the face, to see they have never been in love, or in hate, or in any other high passion, all their days. When you see a dish of fruit at dessert, you sometimes set your affections upon one particular peach or nectarine, watch it with some anxiety as it comes round the table, and feel quite a sensible disappointment when it is taken by some one else. I have used the phrase "high passion." Well, I should say this was about as high a passion as generally leads to marriage. One husband hears after marriage that some poor fellow is dying of his wife's love. "What a pity!" he exclaims; "you know I could so easily have got another!" And yet that is a very happy union. Or again: A young man was telling me the sweet story of his loves. "I like it well enough as long as her sisters are there," said this amorous swain; "but I don't know what to do when we're alone." Once more: A married lady was debating the subject with another lady. "You know, dear," said the first, "after ten years of marriage, if he is nothing else, your husband is always an old friend." "I have many old friends," returned the other, "but I prefer them to be nothing more." "Oh, perhaps I might *prefer* that also!" There is a common note in these three illustrations of the modern idyll; and it must be owned the god goes among us with a limping gait and blear eyes. You wonder whether it was so always; whether desire was always equally dull and spiritless, and possession equally cold. I cannot help fancying most people make, ere they marry, some such table of recommendations as Hannah Godwin wrote to her brother William anent her friend, Miss Gay. It is so charmingly comical, and so pat to the occasion, that I must quote a few phrases. "The young lady is in every sense formed to make one of your disposition really happy. She has a pleasing voice, with which she accompanies her musical instrument with judgment. She has an easy politeness in her manners, neither free nor reserved. She is a good house-keeper and a good economist, and yet of a generous disposition. As to her internal accomplishments, I have reason to speak still more highly of them: good sense without vanity, a penetrating judgment without a disposition to satire, with about as much religion as my William likes, struck me with a wish that she was my William's wife." That is about the tune: pleasing voice, moderate good looks, unimpeachable internal accomplishments after the style of the copy-book, with about as much religion as my William likes; and then, with all speed, to church.

To deal plainly, if they only married when they fell in love, most people would die unwed; and among the others, there would be not a few tumultuous households. The Lion is the King of Beasts, but he is scarcely suitable for a domestic pet. In the same way, I suspect love is rather too violent a passion to make, in all cases, a good domestic sentiment. Like other violent excitements, it throws up not only what is best, but what is worst and smallest, in men's characters. Just as some people are malicious in drink, or brawling and viru-lent under the influence of religious feeling, some are moody, jealous, and exacting when they are in love, who are honest, downright, good-hearted fellows enough in the everyday affairs and humors of the world.

How then, seeing we are driven to the hypothesis that people choose in comparatively cold blood, how is it they choose so well? One is almost tempted to hint that it does not much matter whom you marry; that, in fact, marriage is a subjective affection, and if you have made up your mind to it, and once talked yourself fairly over, you could "pull it through" with anybody. But even if we take matrimony at its lowest, even if we regard it as no more than a sort of friendship recognized by the police, there must be degrees in the freedom and sympathy realized, and some principle to guide simple folk in their selection. Now what should this principle be? Are there no more definite rules than are to be found in the Prayer-book? Law and religion forbid the bans on the grounds of propinquity or consanguinity; society steps in to separate classes; and in all this most critical matter, has common-sense, has wisdom, never a word to say? In the absence of more magisterial teaching, let us talk it over between friends: even a few guesses may be of interest to youths and maidens.

In all that concerns eating and drinking, company, climate, and ways of life, community of taste is to be sought for. It would be trying, for instance, to keep bed and board with an early riser or a vegetarian. In matters of art and intellect, I believe it is of no consequence. Certainly it is of none in the companionships of men, who will dine more readily with one who has a good heart, a good cellar, and a humorous tongue, than with another who shares all their favorite hobbies and is melancholy withal. If your wife likes Tupper, that is no reason why you should hang your head. She thinks with the majority, and has the courage of her opinions. I have always suspected public taste to be a mongrel product out of affectation by dogmatism; and felt sure, if you could only find an honest man of no special literary bent, he would tell you he thought much of Shakespeare bombastic and most absurd, and all of him written in very obscure English and wearisome to read. And not long ago I was able to lay by my lantern in content, for I found the honest man. He was a fellow of parts, quick, humorous, a clever painter, and with an eye for certain poetical effects of sea and ships. I am not much of a judge of that kind of thing, but a sketch of his comes before me sometimes at night. How strong, supple, and living the ship seems upon the billows! With what a dip and rake she shears the flying sea! I cannot fancy the man who saw this effect, and took it on the wing with so much force and spirit, was what you call commonplace in the last recesses of the heart. And yet he thought, and was not ashamed to have it known of him, that Ouida was better in every way than William Shakespeare. If there were more people of his honesty, this would be about the staple of lay criticism. It is not taste that is plentiful, but courage that is rare. And what have we in place? How many, who think no otherwise than the young painter, have we not heard disbursing second-hand hyperboles? Have you never turned sick at heart, O best of critics! when some of your own sweet adjectives were returned on you before a gaping audience? Enthusiasm about art is become a function of the average female being, which she performs with precision and a sort of haunting sprightliness, like an ingenious and well-regulated machine. Sometimes, alas! the calmest man is carried away in the torrent, bandies adjectives with the best, and out-Herods Herod for some shameful moments. When you remember that, you will be tempted to put things strongly, and say you will marry no one who is not like George the Second, and cannot state openly a distaste for poetry and painting.

The word "facts" is, in some ways, crucial. I have spoken with Jesuits and Plymouth Brethren, mathematicians and poets, dogmatic republicans and dear old gentlemen in bird's-eye neckcloths; and each understood the word "facts" in an occult sense of his own. Try as I might, I could get no nearer the principle of their division. What was essential to them, seemed to me trivial or untrue. We could come to no compromise as to what was, or what was not, important in the life of man. Turn as we pleased, we all stood back to back in a big ring, and saw another quarter of the heavens, with different mountain-tops along the sky-line and different constellations overhead. We had each of us some whimsy in the brain, which we believed more than anything else, and which discolored all experience to its own shade. How would you have people agree, when one is deaf and the other blind? Now this is where there should be community between man and wife. They should be agreed on their catchword in *"facts of religion,"* or *"facts of science,"* or *"society, my dear"*; for without such an agreement all intercourse is a painful strain upon the mind. "About as much religion as my William likes," in short, that is what is necessary to make a happy couple of any William and his spouse. For there are differences which no habit nor affection can reconcile, and the Bohemian must not intermarry with the Pharisee. Imagine Consuelo as Mrs. Samuel Budgett, the wife of the successful merchant! The best of men and the best of women may sometimes live together all their lives, and, for want of some consent on fundamental questions, hold each other lost spirits to the end.

A certain sort of talent is almost indispensable for people who would spend years together and not bore themselves to death. But the talent, like the agreement, must be for and about life. To dwell happily together, they should be versed in the niceties of the heart, and born with a faculty for willing compromise. The woman must be talented as a woman, and it will not much matter although she is talented in nothing else. She must know her *métier de femme*, and have a fine touch for the affections. And it is more important that a person should be a good gossip, and talk pleasantly and smartly of common friends and the thousand and one nothings of the day and hour, than that she should speak with the tongues of men and angels; for awhile together by the fire, happens more frequently in marriage than the presence of a distinguished foreigner to dinner. That people should laugh over the same sort of jests, and have many a story of "grouse in the gun-room," many an old joke between them which time cannot wither nor custom stale, is a better preparation for life, by your leave, than many other things higher and better sounding in the world's ears. You could read Kant by yourself, if you wanted; but you must share a joke with some one else. You can forgive people who do not follow you through a philosophical disquisition; but to find your wife laughing when you had tears in your eyes, or staring when you were in a fit of laughter, would go some way toward a dissolution of the marriage.

I know a woman who, from some distaste or disability, could never so much as understand the meaning of the word *politics*, and has given up trying to distinguish Whigs from Tories; but take her on her own politics, ask her about other men or women and the chicanery of everyday existence—the rubs, the tricks, the vanities on which life turns—and you will not find many more shrewd, trenchant, and humorous. Nay, to make plainer what I have in mind, this same woman has a share of the higher and more poetical understanding, frank interest in things for their own sake, and enduring astonishment at the most common. She is not to be deceived by custom, or made to think a mystery solved when it is repeated. I have heard her say she could wonder herself crazy over the human eyebrow. Now in a world where most of us walk very contentedly in the little lit circle of their own reason, and have to be reminded of what lies without by specious and clamant exceptions—earthquakes, eruptions of Vesuvius, banjos floating in mid-air at a *séance*, and the like—a mind so fresh and unsophisticated is no despicable gift. I will own I think it a better sort of mind than goes necessarily with the clearest views on public business. It will wash. It will find something to say at an odd moment. It has in it the spring of pleasant and quaint fancies. Whereas I can imagine myself yawning all night long until my jaws ached and the tears came into my eyes, although my companion on the other side of the hearth held the most enlightened opinions on the franchise or the ballot.

The question of professions, in as far as they regard marriage, was only interesting to women until of late days, but it touches all of us now. Certainly, if I could help it, I would never marry a wife who wrote. The practice of letters is miserably harassing to the mind; and after an hour or two's work, all the more human portion of the author is extinct; he will bully, backbite, and speak daggers. Music, I hear, is not much better. But painting, on the contrary, is often highly sedative; because so much of the labor, after your picture is once begun, is almost entirely manual, and of that skilled sort of manual labor which offers a continual series of successes, and so tickles a man, through his vanity, into good-humor. Alas! in letters there is nothing of this sort. You may write as beautiful a hand as you will, you have always something else to think of, and cannot pause to notice your loops and flourishes; they are beside the mark, and the first law stationer could put you to the blush. Rousseau, indeed, made some account of penmanship, even made it a source of livelihood, when he copied out the *Héloïse* for *dilettante* ladies; and therein showed that strange eccentric prudence which guided him among so many thousand follies and insanities. It would be well for all of the *genus irritabile* thus to add something of skilled labor to intangible brain-work. To find the right word is so doubtful a success and lies so near to failure, that there is no satisfaction in a year of it; but we all know when we have formed a letter perfectly; and a stupid artist, right or wrong, is almost equally certain he has found a right tone or a right color, or made a dexterous stroke with his brush. And, again, painters may work out of doors; and the fresh air, the deliberate seasons, and the "tranquillizing influence" of the green earth, counterbalance the fever of thought, and keep them cool, placable, and prosaic.

354

ON MARRIAGE · ROBERT LOUIS STEVENSON

A ship captain is a good man to marry if it is a marriage of love, for absences are a good influence in love and keep it bright and delicate; but he is just the worst man if the feeling is more pedestrian, as habit is too frequently torn open and the solder has never time to set. Men who fish, botanize, work with the turning-lathe, or gather sea-weeds, will make admirable husbands; and a little amateur painting in water-color shows the innocent and quiet mind. Those who have a few intimates are to be avoided; while those who swim loose, who have their hat in their hand all along the street, who can number an infinity of acquaintances and are not chargeable with any one friend, promise an easy disposition and no rival to the wife's influence. I will not say they are the best of men, but they are the stuff out of which adroit and capable women manufacture the best of husbands. It is to be noticed that those who have loved once or twice already are so much the better educated to a woman's hand; the bright boy of fiction is an odd and most uncomfortable mixture of shyness and coarseness, and needs a deal of civilizing. Lastly (and this is, perhaps, the golden rule), no woman should marry a teetotaller, or a man who does not smoke. It is not for nothing that this "ignoble tabagie," as Michelet calls it, spreads over all the world. Michelet rails against it because it renders you happy apart from thought or work; to provident women this will seem no evil influence in married life. Whatever keeps a man in the front garden, whatever checks wandering fancy and all inordinate ambition, whatever makes for lounging and contentment, makes just so surely for domestic happiness.

These notes, if they amuse the reader at all, will probably amuse him more when he differs than when he agrees with them; at least they will do no harm, for nobody will follow my advice. But the last word is of more concern. Marriage is a step so grave and decisive that it attracts light-headed, variable men by its very awfulness. They have been so tried among the inconstant squalls and currents, so often sailed for islands in the air or lain becalmed with burning heart, that they will risk all for solid ground below their feet. Desperate pilots, they run their sea-sick, weary bark upon the dashing rocks. It seems as if marriage were the royal road through life, and realized, on the instant, what we have all dreamed on summer Sundays when the bells ring, or at night when we cannot sleep for the desire of living. They think it will sober and change them. Like those who join a brotherhood, they fancy it needs but an act to be out of the coil and clamor forever. But this is a wile of the devil's. To the end, spring winds will sow disquietude, passing faces leave a regret behind them, and the whole world keep calling and calling in their ears. For marriage is like life in this—that it is a field of battle, and not a bed of roses.

THE DAILY MIRACLE[1]

Arnold Bennett

"Yes, he's one of those men that don't know how to manage. Good situation. Regular income. Quite enough for luxuries as well as needs. Not really extravagant. And yet the fellow's always in difficulties. Somehow he gets nothing out of his money. Excellent flat—half empty! Always looks as if he'd had the brokers in. New suit—old hat! Magnificent necktie—baggy trousers! Asks you to dinner: cut glass—bad mutton, or Turkish coffee—cracked cup! He can't understand it. Explanation simply is that he fritters his income away. Wish I had the half of it! I'd show him—"

So we have most of us criticised, at one time or another, in our superior way.

We are nearly all chancellors of the exchequer: it is the pride of the moment. Newspapers are full of articles explaining how to live on such and such a sum, and these articles provoke a correspondence whose violence proves the interest they excite. Recently, in a daily organ, a battle raged round the question whether a woman can exist nicely in the country on £85 a year. I have seen an essay, "How to live on eight shillings a week." But I have never seen an essay, "How to live on twenty-four hours a day." Yet it has been said that time is money. That proverb understates the case. Time is a great deal more than money. If you have time you can obtain money—usually. But though you have the wealth of a cloak-room attendant at the Carlton Hotel, you cannot buy yourself a minute more time than I have, or the cat by the fire has.

Philosophers have explained space. They have not explained time. It is the inexplicable raw material of everything. With it, all is possible; without it, nothing. The supply of time is truly a daily miracle, an affair genuinely astonishing when one examines it. You wake up in the morning, and lo! your purse is magically filled with twenty-four hours of the unmanufactured tissue of the universe of your life! It is yours. It is the most precious of possessions. A highly singular commodity, showered upon you in a manner as singular as the commodity itself!

For remark! No one can take it from you. It is unstealable. And no one receives either more or less than you receive.

Talk about an ideal democracy! In the realm of time there is no aristocracy of wealth, and no aristocracy of intellect. Genius is never rewarded by even an extra hour a day. And there is no punishment. Waste your infinitely

[1]From *How to Live on Twenty-Four Hours a Day*, by Arnold Bennett. Copyright 1910 by Doubleday, Doran & Company, Inc.

precious commodity as much as you will, and the supply will never be withheld from you. No mysterious power will say:—"This man is a fool, if not a knave. He does not deserve time; he shall be cut off at the meter." It is more certain than consols, and payment of income is not affected by Sundays. Moreover, you cannot draw on the future. Impossible to get into debt! You can only waste the passing moment. You cannot waste tomorrow; it is kept for you. You cannot waste the next hour; it is kept for you.

I said the affair was a miracle. Is it not?

You have to live on this twenty-four hours of daily time. Out of it you have to spin health, pleasure, money, content, respect, and the evolution of your immortal soul. Its right use, its most effective use, is a matter of the highest urgency and of the most thrilling actuality. All depends on that. Your happiness—the elusive prize that you are all clutching for, my friends!— depends on that. Strange that the newspapers, so enterprising and up-to-date as they are, are not full of "How to live on a given income of time," instead of "How to live on a given income of money"! Money is far commoner than time. When one reflects, one perceives that money is just about the commonest thing there is. It encumbers the earth in gross heaps.

If one can't contrive to live on a certain income of money, one earns a little more—or steals it, or advertises for it. One doesn't necessarily muddle one's life because one can't quite manage on a thousand pounds a year; one braces the muscles and makes it guineas, and balances the budget. But if one cannot arrange that an income of twenty-four hours a day shall exactly cover all proper items of expenditure, one does muddle one's life definitely. The supply of time, though gloriously regular, is cruelly restricted.

Which of us lives on twenty-four hours a day? And when I say "lives," I do not mean exists, nor "muddles through." Which of us is free from that uneasy feeling that the "great spending departments" of his daily life are not managed as they ought to be? Which of us is quite sure that his fine suit is not surmounted by a shameful hat, or that in attending to the crockery he has forgotten the quality of the food? Which of us is not saying to himself— which of us has not been saying to himself all his life: "I shall alter that when I have a little more time"?

We never shall have any more time. We have, and we have always had, all the time there is. It is the realisation of this profound and neglected truth (which, by the way, I have not discovered) that has led me to the minute practical examination of daily time-expenditure.

FRIENDSHIPS[1]

George Santayana

FRIENDSHIP is almost always the union of a part of one mind
with a part of another; people are friends in spots. Friendship sometimes rests
on sharing early memories as do brothers and schoolfellows, who often, but
for that now affectionate familiarity with the same old days, would dislike and
irritate one another extremely. Sometimes it hangs on passing pleasures and
amusements, or on special pursuits; sometimes on mere convenience and
comparative lack of friction in living together. One's friends are that part of
the human race with which one can be human. But there are youthful friendships of quite another quality, which I seem to have discovered flourishing
more often and more frankly in England than in other countries; brief echoes,
as it were, of that love of comrades so much celebrated in antiquity. I do not
refer to the "friendship of virtue" mentioned by Aristotle, which means, I
suppose, community in allegiance or in ideals. It may come to that in the end,
considered externally; but community in allegiance or in ideals, if genuine,
expresses a common disposition, and its roots are deeper and more physical
than itself. The friendship I have in mind is a sense of this initial harmony
between two natures, a union of one whole man with another whole man, a
sympathy between the centres of their being radiating from those centres on
occasion in unanimous thoughts, but not essentially needing to radiate. Trust
here is inwardly grounded; likes and dislikes run together without harness,
like the steeds of Aurora; you may take agreement for granted without words;
affection is generously independent of all tests or external bonds; it can even
bear not to be mutual, not to be recognized; and in any case it shrinks from
the blatancy of open vows. In such friendships there is a touch of passion
and of shyness; an understanding which does not need to become explicit or
complete. There is wine in the cup; it is not to be spilled nor gulped down
unrelished, but to be sipped slowly, soberly, in the long summer evening, with
the window open to the college garden, and the mind full of all that is
sweetest to the mind.

Now there is a mystery here—though it need be no mystery—which some
people find strange and distressing and would like to hush up. This profound
physical sympathy may sometimes, for a moment, spread to the senses; that is
one of its possible radiations, though fugitive; and there is a fashionable
psychology at hand to explain all friendship, for that reason, as an aberration
of sex. Of course it is such in some people, and in many people it may seem
to be such at rare moments; but it would be a plain abuse of language to

'From *Soliloquies in England and Later Soliloquies* (1923), Charles Scribner's Sons.

call a mother's love for her children sexual, even when they are boys, although certainly she could not have that love, nor those children, if she had no sex. Perhaps if we had no sex, we should be incapable of tenderness of any sort; but this fact does not make all forms of affection similar in quality nor in tendency. The love of friends is not, like the love of woman, a lyrical prologue to nest-building. Engaging, no doubt, the same radical instincts, in a different environment and at another phase of their development, it turns them whilst still plastic, in other directions. Human nature is still plastic, especially in the region of emotion, as is proved by the ever-changing forms of religion and art; and it is not a question of right and wrong, nor even, except in extreme cases, of health and disease, but only a question of alternative development, whether the human capacity to love is absorbed in the family cycle, or extends to individual friendships, or to communion with nature or with God. The love of friends in youth, in the cases where it is love rather than friendship, has a mystical tendency. In character, though seldom in intensity, it resembles the dart which, in ecstatic vision, pierced the heart of Saint Theresa, bursting the normal integument by which the blood is kept coursing through generation after generation, in the closed channel of human existence and human slavery. Love then escapes from that round; it is, in one sense, wasted and sterilized; but in being diverted from its earthly labors it suffuses the whole universe with light; it casts its glowing colors on the sunset, upon the altar, upon the past, upon the truth. The anguished futility of love corrects its own selfishness, its own illusion; gradually the whole world becomes beautiful in its inhuman immensity; our very defeats are transfigured, and we see that it was good for us to have gone up into that mountain.

That such mystic emotions, whether in religion or in friendship, are erotic was well known before the days of Freud. They have always expressed themselves in erotic language. And why should they not be erotic? Sexual passion is itself an incident in the life of the Psyche, a transitive phase in the great cycle by which life on earth is kept going. It grows insensibly out of bodily self-love, childish play, and love of sensation; it merges in the end, after its midsummer night's dream, into parental and kingly purposes. How casual, how comic, the purely erotic impulse is, and how lightly nature plays with it, may be seen in the passion of jealousy. Jealousy is inseparable from sexual love, and yet jealousy is not itself erotic either in quality or in effect, since it poisons pleasure, turns sympathy into suspicion, love into hate, all in the interests of proprietorship. Why should we be jealous, if we were simply merry? Nature weaves with a wide loom, and crosses the threads; and erotic passion may be as easily provoked peripherally by deeper impulses as be itself the root of other propensities. Lovers sometimes pretend at first to be only friends, and friends have sometimes fancied, at first blush, that they were lovers; it is as easy for one habit or sentiment as for the other to prove the radical one, and to prevail in the end. As for Englishmen, the last thing they would do would be to disguise some base prompting in high-flown language; they would call a spade a spade, if there were occasion. They are shy of words, as of all manifestations; and this very shyness, if it proves that there is at bottom a vital instinct concerned, also proves that it is not intrinsically more erotic than social, nor more social than intellectual. It is each of these things potentially, for such faculties are not divided in nature as they are in language; it may turn into any one of them if accident leads it that way; but it reverts from every casual expression to its central seat, which is the felt harmony of life with life, and of life with nature, with everything that in the pulses of this world beats our own measure, and swells the music of our thoughts.

LIVING PHILOSOPHY[1]

Albert Einstein

STRANGE is our situation here upon earth. Each of us comes for a short visit, not knowing why, yet sometimes seeming to divine a purpose.

From the standpoint of daily life, however, there is one thing we do know: that man is here for the sake of other men—above all for those upon whose smile and well-being our own happiness depends, and also for the countless unknown souls with whose fate we are connected by a bond of sympathy. Many times a day I realize how much my own outer and inner life is built upon the labors of my fellow-men, both living and dead, and how earnestly I must exert myself in order to give in return as much as I have received. My peace of mind is often troubled by the depressing sense that I have borrowed too heavily from the work of other men.

I do not believe we can have any freedom at all in the philosophical sense, for we act not only under external compulsion but also by inner necessity. Schopenhauer's saying—"A man can surely do what he wills to do, but he cannot determine what he wills"—impressed itself upon me in youth and has always consoled me when I have witnessed or suffered life's hardships. This conviction is a perpetual breeder of tolerance, for it does not allow us to take ourselves or others too seriously; it makes rather for a sense of humor.

To ponder interminably over the reason for one's own existence or the meaning of life in general seems to me, from an objective point of view, to be

[1]From *Living Philosophies* (1931), Simon and Shuster.

sheer folly. And yet everyone holds certain ideals by which he guides his aspiration and his judgment. The ideals which have always shone before me and filled me with the joy of living are goodness, beauty and truth. To make a goal of comfort or happiness has never appealed to me; a system of ethics built on this basis would be sufficient only for a herd of cattle.

Without the sense of collaborating with like-minded beings in the pursuit of the ever unattainable in art and scientific research, my life would have been empty. Ever since childhood I have scorned the commonplace limits so often set upon human ambition. Possessions, outward success, publicity, luxury— to me these have always been contemptible. I believe that a simple and un-assuming manner of life is best for everyone, best both for the body and the mind.

My passionate interest in social justice and social responsibility has always stood in curious contrast to a marked lack of desire for direct association with men and women. I am a horse of single harness, not cut for tandem or team work. I have never belonged wholeheartedly to country or state, to my circle of friends, or even to my own family. These ties have always been accom-panied by a vague aloofness, and the wish to withdraw into myself increases with the years.

Such isolation is sometimes bitter, but I do not regret being cut off from the understanding and sympathy of other men. I lose something by it, to be sure, but I am compensated for it in being rendered independent of the cus-toms, opinions, and prejudices of others, and am not tempted to rest my peace of mind upon such shifting foundations.

My political ideal is democracy. Everyone should be respected as an in-dividual, but no one idolized. It is an irony of fate that I should have been showered with so much uncalled-for and unmerited admiration and esteem. Perhaps this adulation springs from the unfulfilled wish of the multitude to comprehend the few ideas which I, with my weak powers, have advanced.

Full well do I know that in order to attain any definite goal it is impera-tive that *one* person should do the thinking and commanding and carry most of the responsibility. But those who are led should not be driven, and they should be allowed to choose their leader. It seems to me that the distinctions separating the social classes are false; in the last analysis they rest on force. I am convinced that degeneracy follows every autocratic system of violence, for violence inevitably attracts moral inferiors. Time has proved that illus-trious tyrants are succeeded by scoundrels.

For this reason I have always been passionately opposed to such régimes as exist in Russia and Italy today. The thing which has discredited the Eu-ropean forms of democracy is not the basic theory of democracy itself, which some say is at fault, but the instability of our political leadership, as well as the impersonal character of party alignments.

I believe that those in the United States have hit upon the right idea. A President is chosen for a reasonable length of time and enough power is given him to acquit himself properly of his responsibilities. In the German Government on the other hand, I like the state's more extensive care of the individual when he is ill or unemployed. What is truly valuable in our bustle of life is not the nation, I should say, but the creative and impressionable individuality, the personality—he who produces the noble and sublime while the common herd remains dull in thought and insensible in feeling.

This subject brings me to that vilest offspring of the herd mind—the odious militia. The man who enjoys marching in line and file to the strains of music falls below my contempt; he received his great brain by mistake—the spinal cord would have been amply sufficient. This heroism at command, this senseless violence, this accursed bombast of patriotism—how intensely I despise them! War is low and despicable, and I had rather be smitten to shreds than participate in such doings.

Such a stain on humanity should be erased without delay. I think well enough of human nature to believe that it would have been wiped out long ago had not the common sense of nations been systematically corrupted through school and press for business and political reasons.

The most beautiful thing we can experience is the mysterious. It is the source of all true art and science. He to whom this emotion is a stranger, who can no longer pause to wonder and stand rapt in awe, is as good as dead; his eyes are closed. This insight into the mystery of life, coupled though it be with fear, has also given rise to religion. To know that what is impenetrable to us really exists, manifesting itself as the highest wisdom and the most radiant beauty which our dull faculties can comprehend only in their most primitive forms—this knowledge, this feeling, is at the center of true religiousness. In this sense, and in this sense only, I belong in the ranks of devoutly religious men.

I cannot imagine a God who rewards and punishes the objects of his creation, whose purposes are modeled after our own—a God, in short, who is but a reflection of human frailty. Neither can I believe that the individual survives the death of his body, although feeble souls harbor such thoughts through fear or ridiculous egotism. It is enough for me to contemplate the mystery of conscious life perpetuating itself through all eternity, to reflect upon the marvelous structure of the universe which we can dimly perceive, and to try humbly to comprehend even an infinitesimal part of the intelligence manifested in nature.

362

THREE BLIND MICE[1]

George Boas

A MAN would be a fool to attempt a complete list of the sick souls who inhabit this globe, but after one has reached middle age certain ailments begin to stand out and lead one to think that if they could be cured the most important of our troubles would be over. There are three of these maladies which I have been observing for the last twenty-five years, and I should hazard the guess that they are among our most pernicious. They are three forms of blindness.

The first is that of the people who hate to be moral. I should be the last to admit that one could tell whether a bouillabaisse is good or not by applying the standards of ethics. There is nothing right or wrong ethically about a flavor. There are obviously scores of things which we have the right to praise or blame without reference to morality. But there are other things which it is insane to judge aesthetically or logically or whatever the other alternatives are, and a person who doesn't see that simply doesn't know how to think.

But when an occasion arises on which moral standards ought to be applied the first of our Three Blind Mice begins to squirm. He will object strongly to the behavior he is judging, but will immediately add, 'Not that I have any *moral* objections,' when moral objections are precisely the kind most in order. I heard a young graduate of a women's college recently condemning a friend for her disloyalty. 'I don't care what she does or doesn't do. Her life is her own. But to act like that is so *ugly*.'

'Why don't you call it wrong?' I asked from the heights of senility.

'Oh, I don't say it was *wrong*. I shouldn't *dream* of calling it wrong. Moral standards are changing and we must be *tolerant*. But it's so *ugly*.'

It is, of course, true that moral standards are changing; so are metric standards. And a change in standards is always bewildering. But because one is bewildered doesn't prove that there is nothing to be bewildered about. The point is not that moral standards are changing, but that they are bad form. It is considered more sophisticated to call a thing 'ugly' than to call it 'wrong.' But even if one uses an adjective from the field of aesthetics, one has simply added to its already large burden of ambiguity—unless one has robbed it of all meaning.

So radical is this blindness to moral values that some people have been known to take on a disguise of immorality though living almost puritanical lives. I know of one couple in New York who, though legally married, insist on preserving all the outward signs of living in sin, thus making life at least

[1]From *The Contributors' Club* in *The Atlantic Monthly*, December, 1935.

twice as inconvenient as it normally is. The wife wears no wedding ring, keeps her maiden name, refuses to accept mail and telephone calls addressed to Mrs. Unetelle, has her own name as well as her husband's over the mailbox, and has a wonderful time raising Ned with what she calls 'conventions.' She forgets that her own little convention is as narrow as those of society at large and much more annoying.

The second Blind Mouse hates to be intelligent, having been blinded by truth, I suppose. He has a deadly fear of seeming highbrow. This afflicts men more than women in this country, where the kingdom of the mind is largely in the hands of the Amazons. 'We are each of,' says Plotinus, 'an intelligible world,' but it is considered very ill-bred to admit it. Thus, if someone is discussing a play or a picture or a book, he will avoid fine discriminations and feel it enough to distinguish between the 'swell' and the 'lousy.' There must be some things in the world which are neither swell nor lousy: for instance, the novels of Jane Austen, the pictures of Hubert Robert, the music of Gluck, the Institut de France. But the second Blind Mouse does not find them. Or, if he does, he is ashamed to say so. For the discovery of even one of the grosser nuances might be a mark of intelligence; and that would degrade him in the eyes not only of his fellows but of himself.

College professors find this individual one of their greatest problems. For to teach him is to combat the resistance not so much of an individual as of a social class. It is as if one should try to induce the football squad to take up embroidery. Just how one can mould taste on a social scale is not very well understood and is probably impossible for one who stands without the group.

Why the fear of intelligence should be so strong is difficult to understand. Intelligence, it is true, is often critical, analytical, and destructive of custom. But at the same time, it is creative, solves problems, and is utilized by the very people who fear it most. Americans are very proud of their inventions, and yet inventions cannot be made without deeply novel ways of thinking. One would imagine that here of all countries intelligence would be honored. But I think it was Edith Wharton who once said that no language other than our own has a term of reproach the equivalent of our 'highbrow.'

The third Blind Mouse is more pathetic than the others. He is the person who is afraid to be himself. By the time a person has reached maturity his character is pretty well determined and most people by then have access to their inner natures. Yet, instead of taking stock and being faithful to their real desires and abilities, most of them try to be anything other than what they are. Here again social pressure has its influence; there are certain approved occupations in every group and it is next to impossible to persuade anyone to engage in any other. Mothers, fathers, rich relatives, teachers, clergymen, friends, professional writers—everyone is ready and eager to advise the young on what they should be. But they already are. And all the advice in the world won't turn a girl who really wants to be a woman into a happy archaeologist or a highly paid secretary or a musician. In the case of girls, womanhood is definitely looked down upon; a woman who is in love with her husband and happy in educating her children feels disgraced. How often one hears remarks like these: 'What a pity Clara has done nothing with her music!' 'Poor Helen hasn't written a line since her marriage!' 'Mary used to be the life of the Current Events Club, but now it's nothing but John and the children.' No one stops to think that Clara and Helen and Mary are much better off—and society is too—than would be the case were they playing Liszt in a concert hall or banging out short stories on a typewriter or delivering 'reports' on the Future of Democracy.

But women are not the only victims. Every year I have five or ten students who go into law or business or medicine because Dad would be sore if they didn't. Good mechanics, farmers, haberdashers, are lost every year because boys are afraid to be what they are. Like Peter Bell's primrose, they must be everything but a primrose.

Started off with so devious a push, it is no wonder that they land in strange places. I have done my share of lecturing about the country, God forgive me, and am constantly saying to myself, as my deep-bosomed hostess tells me how much they all adored the lecture she thinks I gave, 'You, dear Madame, were you true to yourself, would be in the Maison Tellier,' or, 'What took you out of the kitchen?' or, 'If you only knew how ashamed I am to be telling *you* such stuff.'

When the Three Blind Mice ran after the Farmer's Wife, she cut off their tails with a carving knife. How effective such therapy was the song does not tell. But it must have relieved the poor woman's feelings. I have no carving knife; I have only a mirror. But, alas, these mice are blind.

Fine Arts

A CHAPTER ON EARS[1]

Charles Lamb

I HAVE no ear.—

Mistake me not, reader,—nor imagine that I am by nature destitute of those exterior twin appendages, hanging ornaments, and (architecturally speaking) handsome volutes to the human capital. Better my mother had never borne me.— I am, I think, rather delicately than copiously provided with those conduits; and I feel no disposition to envy the mule for his plenty, or the mole for her exactness, in those ingenious labyrinthine inlets—those indispensable side-intelligencers.

Neither have I incurred, nor done anything to incur, with Defoe, that hideous disfigurement, which constrained him to draw upon assurance—to feel "quite unabashed,"[2] and at ease upon that article. I was never, I thank my stars, in the pillory; nor, if I read them aright, is it within the compass of my destiny, that I ever should be.

When therefore I say that I have no ear, you will understand me to mean—*for music*.— To say that this heart never melted at the concourse of sweet sounds, would be a foul self-libel.— "*Water parted from the sea*" never fails to move it strangely. So does "*In infancy*." But they were used to be sung at her harpsichord (the old-fashioned instrument in vogue in those days) by a gentlewoman—the gentlest, sure, that ever merited the appellation—the sweetest—why should I hesitate to name Mrs. S——, once the blooming Fanny Weatheral of the Temple—who had power to thrill the soul of Elia, small imp as he was, even in his long coats; and to make him glow, tremble, and blush with a passion that not faintly indicated the day-spring of that absorbing sentiment, which was afterwards destined to overwhelm and subdue his nature quite, for Alice W——n.

I even think that *sentimentally* I am disposed to harmony. But *organically* I am incapable of a tune. I have been practising "*God save the King*" all my life; whistling and humming of it over to myself in solitary corners; and am not yet arrived, they tell me, within many quavers of it. Yet hath the loyalty of Elia never been impeached.

I am not without suspicion that I have an undeveloped faculty of music within me. For, thrumming, in my wild way, on my friend A.'s piano, the other morning, while he was engaged in an adjoining parlour,—on his return he was pleased to say, "*he thought it could not be the maid!*" On his first

---

[1]From *London Magazine*, March, 1821.

[2]"Earless on high stood, unabashed, Defoe." [Lamb's note] *Dunciad*. Defoe had his ears cropped and was placed in the pillory.

surprise at hearing the keys touched in somewhat an airy and masterful way, not dreaming of me, his suspicions had lighted on *Jenny*. But a grace, snatched from a superior refinement, soon convinced him that some being,—technically perhaps deficient, but higher informed from a principle common to all the fine arts,—had swayed the keys to a mood which Jenny, with all her (less cultivated) enthusiasm, could never have elicited from them. I mention this as proof of my friend's penetration and not with any view of disparaging Jenny.

Scientifically I could never be made to understand (yet have I taken some pains) what a note in music is; or how one note should differ from another. Much less in voices can I distinguish a soprano from a tenor. Only sometimes the thorough bass I contrive to guess at, from its being supereminently harsh and disagreeable. I tremble, however, for my misapplication of the simplest terms of *that* which I disclaim. While I profess my ignorance, I scarce know what to *say* I am ignorant of. I hate, perhaps, by misnomers. *Sostenuto* and *adagio* stand in the like relation of obscurity to me; and *Sol, Fa, Mi, Re,* is as conjuring as *Baralipton.*

It is hard to stand alone—in an age like this,—(constituted to the quick and critical perception of all harmonious combinations, I verily believe, beyond all preceding ages, since Jubal stumbled upon the gamut) to remain, as it were, singly unimpressible to the magic influences of an art, which is said to have such an especial stroke at soothing, elevating and refining the passions.— Yet rather than break the candid current of my confessions, I must avow to you, that I have received a great deal more pain than pleasure from this so cried-up faculty.

I am constitutionally susceptible to noises. A carpenter's hammer, in a warm summer noon, will fret me into more than mid-summer madness. But those unconnected, unset sounds are nothing to the measured malice of music. The ear is passive to those single strokes; willingly enduring stripes, while it hath no task to con. To music it cannot be passive. It will strive—mine at least will—'spite of its inaptitude to thrid the maze; like an unskilled eye painfully poring upon hieroglyphics. I have sat through an Italian Opera, till, for sheer pain, and inexplicable anguish, I have rushed out into the noisiest places of the crowded streets, to solace myself with sounds which I was not obliged to follow, and get rid of the distracting torment of endless, fruitless, barren attention! I take refuge in the unpretending assemblage of honest, common-life sounds;—and the purgatory of the Enraged Musician becomes my paradise.

I have sat at an Oratorio (that profanation of the purposes of the cheerful playhouse) watching the faces of the auditory in the pit (what a contrast to Hogarth's Laughing Audience!) immovable, or affecting some faint emotion,

—till (as some have said, that our occupations in the next world will be but a shadow of what delighted us in this) I have imagined myself in some cold Theatre in Hades, where some of the *forms* of the earthly one should be kept up, with none of the *enjoyment*; or like that—

> —Party in a parlour,
> All silent, and all Damned.

Above all, those insufferable concertos, and pieces of music, as they are called, do plague and embitter my apprehension.— Words are something; but to be exposed to an endless battery of mere sounds; to be long a dying, to lie stretched upon a rack of roses; to keep up languor by unintermitted effort; to pile honey upon sugar, and sugar upon honey, to an interminable tedious sweetness; to fill up sound with feeling, and strain ideas to keep pace with it; to gaze on empty frames, and be forced to make the pictures for yourself; to read a book, *all stops*, and be obliged to supply the verbal matter; to invent extempore tragedies to answer to the vague gestures of an unexplicable rambling mime—these are faint shadows of what I have undergone from a series of the ablest-executed pieces of this empty *instrumental music*.

I deny not, that in the opening of a concert, I have experienced something vastly lulling and agreeable:—afterwards followeth the languor, and the oppression. Like that disappointing book in Patmos; or, like the comings on of melancholy, described by Burton, doth music make her first insinuating approaches;—"Most pleasant it is to such as are melancholy given, to walk alone in some solitary grove, betwixt wood and water, by some brook side, and to meditate upon some delightsome and pleasant subject, which shall affect him most, *amabilis insania*,[3] and *mentis gratissimus error*.[4] A most incomparable delight to build castles in the air, to go smiling to themselves, acting an infinite variety of parts, which they suppose, and strongly imagine, they act, or that they see done.— So delightsome these toys at first, they could spend whole days and nights without sleep, even whole years in such contemplations, and fantastical meditations, which are like so many dreams, and will hardly be drawn from them—winding and unwinding themselves as so many clocks, and still pleasing their humours, until at last the scene turns upon a sudden, and they being now habitated to such meditations, and solitary places, can endure no company, can think of nothing but harsh and distasteful subjects. Fear, sorrow, suspicion, *subrusticus pudor*,[5] discontent, cares, and weariness of life, surprise them on a sudden, and they can think of nothing else: continually suspecting, no sooner are their eyes open, but this infernal plague of melancholy seizeth on them, and terrifies their souls, representing

[3]Pleasing madness.   [4]Most delightful delusion.   [5]Rustic shyness.

some dismal object to their minds; which now, by no means, no labour, no persuasions they can avoid, they cannot be rid of it, they cannot resist."

Something like this "SCENE-TURNING" I have experienced at the evening parties, at the house of my good Catholic friend *Nov*—; who, by the aid of a capital organ, himself the most finished of players, converts his drawing-room into a chapel, his week days into Sundays, and these latter into minor heavens.[6]

When my friend commences upon one of those solemn anthems which peradventure struck upon my heedless ear, rambling in the side aisles of the dim abbey, some five and thirty years since, waking a new sense and putting a soul of old religion into my young apprehension—whether it be *that*, in which the psalmist, weary of the persecutions of bad men, wisheth to himself dove's wings—or *that other*, which, with a like measure of sobriety and pathos, inquireth by what means the young man shall best cleanse his mind—a holy calm pervadeth me,—I am for the time

—rapt above earth,
And possess joys not promised at my birth.

But when this master of the spell, not content to have laid a soul prostrate, goes on, in his power, to inflict more bliss than lies in her capacity to receive,—impatient to overcome her "earthly" with his "heavenly,"—still pouring in, for protracted hours, fresh waves and fresh from the sea of sound, or from that inexhausted *German* ocean, above which, in triumphant progress, dolphin-seated, ride those Arions *Haydn* and *Mozart*, with their attendant tritons, *Bach, Beethoven*, and a countless tribe, whom to attempt to reckon up would but plunge me again in the deeps,—I stagger under the weight of harmony, reeling to and fro at my wit's end;—clouds, as of frankincense, oppress me—priests, altars, censers, dazzle before me—the genius of *his* religion hath me in her toils—a shadowy triple tiara invests the brow of my friend, fate so naked, so ingenious—he is Pope,—and by him sits, like as in the anomaly of dreams, a she-Pope too,—tri-coroneted like himself! I am converted, and yet a Protestant;—at once *malleus hereticorum*,[7] and myself grand heresiarch: or three heresies centre in my person:—I am Marcion, Ebion, and Cerinthus—Gog and Magog—what not?—till the coming in of the friendly suppertray dissipates the figment, and a draught of true Lutheran beer (in which chiefly my friend shows himself no bigot) at once reconciles me to the rationalities of a purer faith; and restores to me the genuine unterrifying aspects of my pleasant-countenanced host and hostess.

[6]I have been there, and still would go;   [7]**Hammer of the heretics.**
'Tis like a little heaven below.—Dr. Watts
[Lamb's note]

GREATNESS IN ART[1]

John Ruskin

In the 15th Lecture of Sir Joshua Reynolds, incidental notice is taken of the distinction between those excellences in the painter which belong to him as such, and those which belong to him in common with all men of intellect, the general and exalted powers of which art is the evidence and expression, not the subject. But the distinction is not there dwelt upon as it should be, for it is owing to the slight attention ordinarily paid to it, that criticism is open to every form of coxcombry, and liable to every phase of error. It is a distinction on which depend all sound judgment of the rank of the artist, and all just appreciation of the dignity of art.

Painting, or art generally, as such, with all its technicalities, difficulties, and particular ends, is nothing but a noble and expressive language, invaluable as the vehicle of thought, but by itself nothing. He who has learned what is commonly considered the whole art of painting, that is, the art of representing any natural object faithfully, has as yet only learned the language by which his thoughts are to be expressed. He has done just as much toward being that which we ought to respect as a great painter, as a man who has learned how to express himself grammatically and melodiously has toward being a great poet. The language is, indeed, more difficult of acquirement in the one case than in the other, and possesses more power of delighting the sense, while it speaks to the intellect; but it is, nevertheless, nothing more than language, and all those excellences which are peculiar to the painter as such, are merely what rhythm, melody, precision, and force are in the words of the orator and the poet, necessary to their greatness, but not the test of their greatness. It is not by the mode of representing and saying, but by what is represented and said, that the respective greatness either of the painter or the writer is to be finally determined.

Speaking with strict propriety, therefore, we should call a man a great painter only as he excelled in precision and force in the language of lines, and a great versifier, as he excelled in precision and force in the language of words. A great poet would then be a term strictly, and in precisely the same sense, applicable to both, if warranted by the character of the images or thoughts which each in their respective languages conveyed.

Take, for instance, one of the most perfect poems or pictures (I used the words as synonymous) which modern times have seen:—the "Old Shepherd's Chief-mourner." Here the exquisite execution of the glossy and crisp hair of the dog, the bright sharp touching of the green bough beside it, the clear

[1]From *Modern Painters*, Vol. I, Pt. 1, §1, Ch. 2 (1843).

painting of the wood of the coffin and the folds of the blanket, are language—language clear and expressive in the highest degree. But the close pressure of the dog's breast against the wood, the convulsive clinging of the paws, which has dragged the blanket off the trestle, the total powerlessness of the head laid, close and motionless, upon its folds, the fixed and tearful fall of the eye in its utter hopelessness, the rigidity of repose which marks that there has been no motion nor change in the trance of agony since the last blow was struck on the coffin-lid, the quietness and gloom of the chamber, the spectacles marking the place where the Bible was last closed, indicating how lonely has been the life, how unwatched the departure of him who is now laid solitary in his sleep;—these are all thoughts—thoughts by which the picture is separated at once from hundreds of equal merit, as far as mere painting goes, by which it ranks as a work of high art, and stamps its author, not as the neat imitator of the texture of a skin, or the fold of a drapery, but as the Man of Mind.

It is not, however, always easy, either in painting or literature, to determine where the influence of language stops, and where that of thought begins. Many thoughts are so dependent upon the language in which they are clothed, that they would lose half their beauty if otherwise expressed. But the highest thoughts are those which are least dependent on language, and the dignity of any composition, and praise to which it is entitled, are in exact proportion to its independency of language or expression. A composition is indeed usually most perfect, when to such intrinsic dignity is added all that expression can do to attract and adorn; but in every case of supreme excellence this all becomes as nothing. We are more gratified by the simplest lines or words which can suggest the idea in its own naked beauty, than by the robe and the gem which conceal while they decorate; we are better pleased to feel by their absence how little they could bestow, than by their presence how much they can destroy.

There is therefore a distinction to be made between what is ornamental in language and what is expressive. That part of it which is necessary to the embodying and conveying of the thought is worthy of respect and attention as necessary to excellence, though not the test of it. But that part of it which is decorative has little more to do with the intrinsic excellence of the picture than the frame or the varnishing of it. And this caution in distinguishing between the ornamental and the expressive is peculiarly necessary in painting; for in the language of words it is nearly impossible for that which is not expressive to be beautiful, except by mere rhythm or melody, any sacrifice to which is immediately stigmatized as error. But the beauty of mere language in painting is not only very attractive and entertaining to the spectator, but requires for its attainment no small exertion of mind and devotion of time by the artist.

Hence, in art, men have frequently fancied that they were becoming rhetoricians and poets when they were only learning to speak melodiously, and the judge has over and over again advanced to the honor of authors those who were never more than ornamental writing-masters.

Most pictures of the Dutch school, for instance, excepting always those of Rubens, Vandyke, and Rembrandt, are ostentatious exhibitions of the artist's power of speech, the clear and vigorous elocution of useless and senseless words; while the early efforts of Cimabue and Giotto are the burning messages of prophecy, delivered by the stammering lips of infants. It is not by ranking the former as more than mechanics, or the latter as less than artists, that the taste of the multitude, always awake to the lowest pleasures which art can bestow, and blunt to the highest, is to be formed or elevated. It must be the part of the judicious critic carefully to distinguish what is language, and what is thought, and to rank and praise pictures chiefly for the latter, considering the former as a totally inferior excellence, and one which cannot be compared with nor weighed against thought in any way nor in any degree whatsoever. The picture which has the nobler and more numerous ideas, however awkwardly expressed, is a greater and a better picture than that which has the less noble and less numerous ideas, however beautifully expressed. No weight, nor mass, nor beauty of execution, can outweigh one grain or fragment of thought. Three penstrokes of Raffaelle are a greater and a better picture than the most finished work that ever Carlo Dolci polished into inanity. A finished work of a great artist is only better than its sketch, if the sources of pleasure belonging to color and realization—valuable in themselves—are so employed as to increase the impressiveness of the thought. But if one atom of thought has vanished, all color, all finish, all execution, all ornament, are too dearly bought. Nothing but thought can pay for thought, and the instant that the increasing refinement or finish of the picture begins to be paid for by the loss of the faintest shadow of an idea, that instant all refinement or finish is an excrescence and a deformity.

Yet although in all our speculations on art, language is thus to be distinguished from, and held subordinate to, that which it conveys, we must still remember that there are certain ideas inherent in language itself, and that, strictly speaking, every pleasure connected with art has in it some reference to the intellect. The mere sensual pleasure of the eye, received from the most brilliant piece of coloring, is as nothing to that which it receives from a crystal prism, except as it depends on our perception of a certain meaning and intended arrangement of color, which has been the subject of intellect. Nay, the term idea, according to Locke's definition of it, will extend even to the sensual impressions themselves as far as they are "things which the mind occupies itself about in thinking"; that is, not as they are felt by the eye only, but as they are received by the mind through the eye. So that, if I say that the greatest picture is that which conveys to the mind of the spectator the greatest number of the greatest ideas, I have a definition which will include as subjects of comparison every pleasure which art is capable of conveying. If I were to say, on the contrary, that the best picture was that which most closely imitated nature, I should assume that art could only please by imitating nature; and I should cast out of the pale of criticism those parts of works of art which are not imitative, that is to say, intrinsic beauties of color and form, and those works of art wholly, which, like the Arabesques of Raffaelle in the Loggias, are not imitative at all. Now I want a definition of art wide enough to include all its varieties of aim. I do not say, therefore, that the art is greatest which gives most pleasure, because perhaps there is some art whose end is to teach, and not to please. I do not say that the art is greatest which teaches us most, because perhaps there is some art whose end is to please, and not to teach. I do not say that the art is greatest which imitates best, because perhaps there is some art whose end is to create and not to imitate. But I say that the art is greatest which conveys to the mind of the spectator, by any means whatsoever, the greatest number of the greatest ideas; and I call an idea great in proportion as it is received by a higher faculty of the mind, and as it more fully occupies, and in occupying, exercises and exalts, the faculty by which it is received.

If this, then, be the definition of great art, that of a great artist naturally follows. He is the greatest artist who has embodied, in the sum of his works, the greatest number of the greatest ideas.

PREFACE[1]

Joseph Conrad

A work that aspires, however humbly, to the condition of art should carry its justification in every line. And art itself may be defined as a single-minded attempt to render the highest kind of justice to the visible universe, by bringing to light the truth, manifold and one, underlying its every aspect. It is an attempt to find in its forms, in its colors, in its light, in its shadows, in the aspects of matter and in the facts of life, what of each is fundamental, what is enduring and essential—their one illuminating and convincing quality—the very truth of their existence. The artist, then, like

---

[1]From *The Nigger of the Narcissus*, by Joseph Conrad. Copyright 1897, 1914 by Doubleday, Doran & Company, Inc.

the thinker or the scientist, seeks the truth and makes his appeal. Impressed by the aspect of the world the thinker plunges into ideas, the scientist into facts—whence, presently, emerging they make their appeal to those qualities of our being that fit us best for the hazardous enterprise of living. They speak authoritatively to our common-sense, to our intelligence, to our desire of peace or to our desire of unrest; not seldom to our prejudices, sometimes to our fears, often to our egoism—but always to our credulity. And their words are heard with reverence, for their concern is with weighty matters; with the cultivation of our minds and the proper care of our bodies: with the attainment of our ambitions: with the perfection of the means and the glorification of our precious aims.

It is otherwise with the artist.

Confronted by the same enigmatical spectacle the artist descends within himself, and in that lonely region of stress and strife, if he be deserving and fortunate, he finds the terms of his appeal. His appeal is made to our less obvious capacities; to that part of our nature which, because of the warlike conditions of existence, is necessarily kept out of sight within the more resisting and hard qualities—like the vulnerable body within a steel armor. His appeal is less loud, more profound, less distinct, more stirring—and sooner forgotten. Yet its effect endures forever. The changing wisdom of successive generations discards ideas, questions facts, demolishes theories. But the artist appeals to that part of our being which is not dependent on wisdom; to that in us which is a gift and not an acquisition—and, therefore, more permanently enduring. He speaks to our capacity for delight and wonder, to the sense of mystery surrounding our lives: to our sense of pity, and beauty, and pain: to the latent feeling of fellowship with all creation—and to the subtle but invincible conviction of solidarity in dreams, in joy, in sorrow, in aspirations, in illusions, in hope, in fear, which binds men to each other, which binds together all humanity—the dead to the living and the living to the unborn.

It is only some such train of thought, or rather of feeling, that can in a measure explain the aim of the attempt, made in the tale which follows, to present an unrestful episode in the obscure lives of a few individuals out of all the disregarded multitude of the bewildered, the simple and the voiceless. For, if there is any part of truth in the belief confessed above, it becomes evident that there is not a place of splendor or a dark corner of the earth that does not deserve, if only a passing glance of wonder and pity. The motive, then, may be held to justify the matter of the work: but this preface, which is simply an avowal of endeavor, cannot end here—for the avowal is not yet complete.

Fiction—if it at all aspires to be art—appeals to temperament. And in truth it must be, like painting, like music, like all art, the appeal of one temperament to all the other innumerable temperaments whose subtle and resistless power endows passing events with their true meaning, and creates the moral, the emotional atmosphere of the place and time. Such an appeal to be effective must be an impression conveyed through the senses; and, in fact, it cannot be made in any other way, because temperament, whether individual or collective, is not amenable to persuasion. All art, therefore, appeals primarily to the senses, and the artistic aim when expressing itself in written words must also make its appeal through the senses, if its high desire is to reach the secret spring of responsive emotions. It must strenuously aspire to the plasticity of sculpture, to the color of painting, and to the magic suggestiveness of music—which is the art of arts. And it is only through complete, unswerving devotion to the perfect blending of form and substance; it is only through an unremitting never-discouraged care for the shape and ring of sentences that an approach can be made to plasticity, to color; and the light of magic suggestiveness may be brought to play for an evanescent instant over the commonplace surface of words: of the old, old words, worn thin, defaced by ages of careless usage.

The sincere endeavor to accomplish that creative task, to go as far on that road as his strength will carry him, to go undeterred by faltering, weariness or reproach, is the only valid justification for the worker in prose. And if his conscience is clear, his answer to those who, in the fullness of a wisdom which looks for an immediate profit, demand specifically to be edified, consoled, amused; who demand to be promptly improved, or encouraged, or frightened, or shocked, or charmed, must run thus:—My task which I am trying to achieve is, by the power of the written word, to make you hear, to make you feel—it is, before all, to make you see. That—and no more, and it is everything. If I succeed, you shall find there according to your deserts: encouragement, consolation, fear, charm—all you demand and, perhaps, also that glimpse of truth for which you have forgotten to ask.

To snatch in a moment of courage, from the remorseless rush of time, a passing phase of life, is only the beginning of the task. The task approached in tenderness and faith is to hold up unquestioningly, without choice and without fear, the rescued fragment before all eyes and in the light of a sincere mood. It is to show its vibration, its color, its form; and through its movement, its form, and its color, reveal the substance of its truth—disclose its inspiring secret: the stress and passion within the core of each convincing moment. In a single-minded attempt of that kind, if one be deserving and fortunate, one may perchance attain to such clearness of sincerity that at last the presented vision of regret or pity, of terror or mirth, shall awaken in the hearts of the beholders that feeling of unavoidable solidarity; of the solidarity in mysterious origin, in toil, in joy, in hope, in uncertain fate, which binds men to each other and all mankind to the visible world.

It is evident that he who, rightly or wrongly, holds by the convictions expressed above cannot be faithful to any one of the temporary formulas of his craft. The enduring part of them—the truth which each only imperfectly veils—should abide with him as the most precious of his possessions, but they all: Realism, Romanticism, Naturalism, even the unofficial sentimentalism (which like the poor, is exceedingly difficult to get rid of) all these gods must, after a short period of fellowship, abandon him—even on the very threshold of the temple—to the stammerings of his conscience and to the outspoken consciousness of the difficulties of his work. In that uneasy solitude the supreme cry of Art for Art, itself, loses the exciting ring of its apparent immorality. It sounds far off. It has ceased to be a cry, and is heard only as a whisper, often incomprehensible, but at times and faintly encouraging.

Sometimes, stretched at ease in the shade of a roadside tree, we watch the motions of a laborer in a distant field, and after a time, begin to wonder languidly as to what the fellow may be at. We watch the movements of his body, the waving of his arms, we see him bend down, stand up, hesitate, begin again. It may add to the charm of an idle hour to be told the purpose of his exertions. If we know he is trying to lift a stone, to dig a ditch, to uproot a stump, we look with a more real interest at his efforts; we are disposed to condone the jar of his agitation upon the restfulness of the landscape; and even, if in a brotherly frame of mind, we may bring ourselves to forgive his failure. We understood his object, and, after all, the fellow has tried, and perhaps he had not the strength—and perhaps he had not the knowledge. We forgive, go on our way—and forget.

And so it is with the workman of art. Art is long and life is short, and success is very far off. And, thus, doubtful of strength to travel so far, we talk a little about the aim—the aim of art, which, like life itself, is inspiring, difficult—obscured by mists. It is not in the clear logic of a triumphant conclusion; it is not in the unveiling of one of those heartless secrets which are called the Laws of Nature. It is not less great, but only more difficult.

To arrest, for the space of a breath, the hands busy about the work of the earth, and compel men entranced by the sight of distant goals to glance for a moment at the surrounding vision of form and color, of sunshine and shadows; to make them pause for a look, for a sigh, or a smile—such is the aim, difficult and evanescent, and reserved only for a very few to achieve. But sometimes, by the deserving and the fortunate, even that task is accomplished. And when it is accomplished—behold!—all the truth of life is there: a moment of vision, a sigh, a smile—and then return to an eternal rest.

THE GREAT RICH VINE[1]

John Holmes

THE poet is an accident combining a boundless variety of sympathies, quick physical responses, a tough saneness of resistance, an incredible conviction that he stands under the middle of the arch of the world, and a hard necessity to share, to teach, to tell—all these in one body owning a set of five sharp senses, a heart always a little too full, an eagerly curious mind, and a greed for every possible experience.

It is no easier for him to cultivate his inward estate to something like orderly productivity and endurable habitation than it is for someone else to bound that area and enclose it with a sturdy definition. His borders are forever shifting. He hopes they are enlarging, and his peculiar acquisitiveness for lively memories from the country of the mind makes it rather certain that they are. Sometimes his estate seems to shape itself with a wide emphasis south southeast, while his customary latitudes are abandoned. Sometimes his residence and activities are at the opposite direction of the compass. But in the course of time he pushes his borders farther and farther out from the centre, and makes them symmetrical; within he seeds here and harvests there, repairs highroads and tramps out fresh bypaths, inspects old ideas and fences in new ones. Some fields he passes by and looks the other way. He is as patient as nature with others, and eager as the wind with still others. And somewhere in this soil the deep-thrust roots of the tree of life draw nourishment, and find it rich.

Having language, the poet is able to tell what it is he feels about his world, both the inner and the outer. Before he had language, we do not know what he did; he may have run up a hill and looked abroad, like stout Balboa on a peak in Darien, and shouted loudly. But a shout cannot be written down for second performance. He may have found satisfaction in pounding the trunk of a tree with a good thick club; but that, too, would be a little difficult to record. He may have danced his delight, or his terror, or hatred, or reverence, and probably did; the dance could be remembered and repeated.

But when there was a language, and therefore determined meanings for certain sounds, it was his great pleasure to make words dance with the exact posture, the same swiftness, the same satisfaction of rhythm that patterned his dance. There is even a mode of taste that returns through the nameless centuries to catch again that shout, that hearty tree-drubbing, in what is also called poetry. However, in imitation by words lies the art of poetry; and at last, when the words themselves have come to have such rolling reverberations

[1]From *The Poet's Work* by John Holmes. Oxford University Press, 1939.

of meaning, such ghostly genealogies of memory, such Saturn rings of light around them, all the dance is in the words: poetry is words. The poet finds himself under a compulsion to arrange words in patterns, the most tangible parts of which seem to be printer's ink on a white page. Actually what drives him is a necessity for summoning these ancestries of meaning into significant order; for arranging these overtones into a symphony; for translating the subtly outgoing signals into a newer message. These intangibilities rise from the black letters into the astonished and illumined brain of the reader, and that is poetry.

It is when words have been put together, and words so plain in themselves joined to make phrases like 'this goodly frame, the earth . . . this majestic roof fretted with golden fire,' or 'the bright boroughs, the quivering citadels there,' or 'how sweet the moonlight sleepes upon this banke,' that there falls that inexplicable radiance upon the page, and round the very room where the page is read. It has taken more than words to do this; there was an urgency in the poet that brimmed and he could not help it; it overflowed and he was glad. Unless that surge of wonder, that intolerable beating of wings in the poet's mind, had found the right words, we never should have cared. There is poetry in words, much blood in words, but there is a thing that moves behind them, a spirit that puts them on like a garment and wears them, filling the infinite possibilities of their drapery with a body that lives and moves, and goes up and down to delight us with its grace and stir us with its vigor.

It is the sum of what the poet teaches himself that determines his quality. In the midst of external activity, he may, like Yeats rehearsing a play, suddenly perceive that 'tragedy must always be a drowning and breaking of the dykes that separate man from man'; or gradually come to place, like George Moore, the capacity for revision of the written page above all the virtues. All this and much more is hidden behind the greatness of the poetry we read, and has added its beam to the light. The poet may have learned Mozart's lesson, that 'when I am feeling well and in good humor, thoughts come in swarms and with marvelous ease,' or it may be that, as an artist, those are not at all the conditions for getting things done. Analogies may teach him, if he has the eyes for them, like the one Hazlitt drew between the writer and the Indian jugglers of knives. Or he may discover, because of his knowledge of the poetry of the past, that one of his contemporaries, by adapting, accepting, exaggerating old methods, has fashioned and used a new one.

Failure teaches him that all failure in the arts may possibly be mended in the next attempt. Praise teaches him, perhaps, how imperfectly he has transmitted himself, so unpredictable and often so absurd praise is. All pronounce-

ments on style, by poets of his own generation or those of years ago, help him
to shape the idea of his own, for he knows that his style must be his own or
nothing. He learns, by experiences he would hardly care to tell about, what
medicine cures or eases an unwillingness to make an imaginative effort. The
weather of his mind is an affair of low pressure areas and sudden storms that
he must learn to predict with unfailing accuracy. He watches the least stirring
of leaves that indicates a rising wind, and he knows what planets draw his
tides. He supports the findings of an almost instrumental skill in self-
knowledge of this kind with an old native wisdom of intuition and shrewd
speculation. Time concerns him, that he may not waste it; no waking day is
ever quite long enough for creation. And at last he learns what all great artists
know, each in their kind: to hold to a single ruthlessness of purpose, and that
purpose poetry.

Any description of the poet as human being must underline his inclusive-
ness and his intensity; and it is easy to translate that truth into the part truth
that this means an abundance of all that is good and happy and affirmative.
But when Walt Whitman said that he, too, 'knitted the old knot of contrariety,
had guile, lust, hot wishes I dared not speak, was wayward, vain, greedy,
shallow,' he gave evidence of one extreme. But there was also Keats, 'happy
as a man may be . . . with the yearning passion I have for the beautiful, connected and made one with the ambition of my intellect'; and there is William
Butler Yeats, in one mood 'blest by everything, everything I look upon is
blest,' and in another, 'timid, entangled, empty, and abashed.'

T. W. H. Crosland helps the variety with the 'furious wise will and heart
of stone,' and D. H. Lawrence with his cry of 'My great religion is a belief in
the blood!' Sir Thomas Browne had 'all Africa and her prodigies' in him.
Conrad Aiken bids us 'laugh with fool's delight that heavenly folly made the
world so bright'; Bliss Perry reminds us that the poet has always been *genus
irritabile*—the irritable kind; John Donne must have the soul descend to affections and to faculties, 'else a great Prince in prison lies'; and Shakespeare
marks bitterly 'the expense of spirit in a waste of shame.' John Masefield
remembers, as most poets do, that 'man with his burning soul has but an hour
of breath'; Emerson walks across Cambridge Common, 'glad almost to the
brink of fear'; Katherine Mansfield in the grimness of grief writes in her
journal, 'To-day I am hardening my heart. I am walking all around my heart
and building up the defenses'; and Keats feels 'an awful warmth about my
heart like a load of immortality.'

And yet all these are not a fraction of the poet's capacity for life. There
was Milton, who knew the courts of heaven, and Villon, who knew the alleys
of Paris. Chaucer rode down to Canterbury with priests, shipmen, millers,

knights, and nuns; George Herbert lived in the retirement of a country parish and his mother's house. Blake was mad (or was he sane?) and Alexander Pope was very sane.

'Not only poems, but songs, snatches and raptures of a flaming spirit,' said a seventeenth-century writer, of the psalms of David. It is the heat of the blood that differentiates the poet. It was clever of Oscar Wilde to say that several drinks of whiskey can induce an effect very similar to intoxication. But in one of the mightiest of short English poems James Thomson says, 'he reeleth with his own heart, that great rich vine.'

It is not an accident that the poet is articulate; for sometimes one feels that writers of all kinds have an unearned advantage over the rest of the world because they can get a hearing for their pains and joys, as if no one else felt at all. But the special quality of the poet includes the involuntary voice. With such a necessity laid upon him, seeing as he does the golden outline that defines people standing between one's self and the low sun, he may not silence the vivid sense of life in him. It beats and surges into words. The sum and total of the words may be only a declaration of being, an emphatic I AM: the world was thus when I was in it—active, growing, decaying, complex, passionate, pitiful, miraculous. It is simply that a current passes through his body; sometimes it convulses him with its enormous voltage, but more often he is a good conductor, pure metal, and passes on the flow of life to later times and other men.

For people who are afraid of the life in the wires, poetry is dangerous to read. Because the drift of days seldom makes the average man shiver and glow with a sudden shock of life, he feels in the unusual behavior of the poet something deplorable and not quite brave, because it is unusual. The average man has also had unpleasant experience of the poet of mixed and baser metal, the imperfect conductor of the current. But the real poet is the norm for mankind; in his quality of living, the man all would wish to be. It is T. W. H. Crosland who reminds us of the old falsehood to the effect that a writer of poems, especially of sonnets, is a person in precarious health, or of abnormal behavior. But, he says, as a matter of fact, the great poets 'are not only the sanest people in the world, but physically and temperamentally the toughest.' How could this not be so? Men and women weak in body and nerves burn out after a little of the current. But in the great spirits, Shakespeare, Goethe, Whitman, Yeats, there is a calmness, and a confident strength. They are in accord with the force flowing through them; there is room enough in them, and no obstructions.

But all metaphors are a view from one side. To speak of poets as good conductors is to imply passive reception and release; the figure is not the whole truth. This is because the poet also imparts a special quality to the life flowing through him, so that it is changed by the passage. One element of this change is the new rhythm he gives to the stream of life. Each poet is tuned to a different pitch, not necessarily higher or lower, but more intense than another, or less so in a special way. It has been his study to discover his inner rhythm, and to make himself a resonant instrument for its music. All life that enters his perception beats thereafter to that unmistakable vibration.

Another and essential element of the change in the life the poet feels is his powerful affection for it. Proust, though not a versifier, transmitted his sense of life colored by love that dwells in every scene, on every hour, reluctant to be called away even to the next hour and the following episode. The poet knows that loving particularity. James Stephens says the poet makes grief beautiful—'caring for grief he cares his grief away.' It may be, too, that sharp sense of the appalling limits of time is what makes the poet wish to linger— 'the lyf so short,' as Chaucer knew. But after all, the poet is one who, because he feels in the air time rushing by, knows more than most men about it, and has power over it. He can stop time. By his passionately scrupulous examination of one moment, he can re-create it as it is and let it go. Nothing is ever lost, no experience is ever in vain.

And the poet, who can free all men as well as himself from time, loves what he writes of, and writes of what he loves. If he protests, if he mourns, if he hates, and writes about that, love is not far; it is that powerful affection thwarted of which he speaks. And to a certain extent he loves the hateful thing, if only it has life in it. 'As to the poetic character itself,' wrote Keats in a letter, 'it lives in gusto, be it foul or fair, high or low, rich or poor, mean or elevated—it has as much delight in conceiving an Iago as an Imogen.'

In containing and changing the flow of life, the artist who is a poet has enemies and allies, some within himself, and some, the least important, outside himself. The indifferent, the stubborn, the willfully blind, never cease to reproduce themselves in the world, and they are the enemies of art. But the temptation to publish what will satisfy nearly everyone, and not, in his own heart, himself, is the poet's more immediate adversary. Time is always a potential enemy. In merciless and unforeseen ways Time destroys all but the most honest poetry. Yet victory over the temptation to haste can conquer both indifference and Time.

Sudden inspiration, bringing completion of the poem, is a treacherous friend, for it glosses the surface with what seems to be the light of poetry. But the light fades, and the workmanship loosens in its joints, and the poem that creation without toil had fashioned falls apart. Or the waste of emptiness may threaten; but here, as Ben Jonson says, 'the mind is like a bow, the stronger by being unbent.' Infertile hours are not failure or defeat, but a part of the process of writing, a process that has, like green things growing, spaces of rest. Danger may come in an excess of loyalty to some one method, or poet, or audience, till proportion is destroyed. The complex pull of affections, habits, duties, or pleasures in one's life as a private citizen may also distort artistry; since these things go very deep into existence, one or another is sometimes the most corruptive enemy of all, having place and power within and without. It is an expensive but important chapter in the poet's history that tells how he learned to adjust his poetic to his private life, and both to his life in public. It is a story of the unfailing renewal of an exact balance between the three.

His allies in self-preservation are his self-respect as an artist, the attraction of the goal still before him, and the height of his old vows. Knowledge of life and of all poetry is obviously a loyal part of his forces. Mastery of his creative power is something he has learned slowly and thoroughly, and can usually summon to the endeavor, and control. In composition his allies serve with a vital allegiance, but not always with their presence when it is most fervently asked. Health and peace of mind are his allies, or lacking them, the drive of such a necessity from within that the writing gets done, but this is costly. The support of the subconscious mind, while powerful, is unpredictable. In the crisis a memory of things he had forgotten may rush in, and a knowledge of things he had never learned. But the subconscious mind may not add its final impetus at all, and it may desert at the time when it is most needed and used.

The object of all this complex and endless study, all this tireless application to the acquisition of knowledge of himself, of life, of the genius of language, is to write poetry. The poet wants that poetry to be an exact representation of his own peculiar inner rhythm, and that rhythm so confirmed and set free that it will sound its own note, original and significant, in the poetry of his age. And who will know whether or not he has succeeded? He will know. That is his greatest satisfaction, even though he may have found readers who have been pleased and moved by poetry he has written ever since before he knew what poetry really was. He knows, too, that other poets will know. He has learned to value most the praise of equals, and next the confidence of living men. To those of his contemporaries whose sense of life he has enriched he is grateful for their attendance on his work, and he is fulfilled by it. As an artist he wants approval by his kind. 'The oration is to the orator,' said Whitman, 'the acting is to the actor and actress, not to the audience.' The poet values their response because they understand as artists, not only the finished thing, but the rigors of devotion to the art.

Wherever the poet stands, the hills and houses and the thinking of mankind centre on him like the spokes of a wheel or the threads of a spider's web. He looks out in every direction with as fresh an excitement as if the world had never been thrust upon the eyes of man till then. This is a mad conviction, but it is the key to the mystery of the universe, what Goethe calls the 'open secret,' open to all, seen by almost none. It never occurs to him not to dare to say what he sees and feels; to him it is an overwhelming wonder that he is there at all, and it seems only natural that, so placed, he should communicate his astonishment and delight. This confidence is an element of genius, but every poet shares it. He feels a kind of godhead; not egotistic assumption, but the fullness of life and his nearness to the source. In vision he has time and space for latitude, as well as such intense apprehension that the commonplace is miraculous and the near-at-hand a wonder fetched home for his pleasure. Whenever the scale of things seems meagre to him, because the gods were tired, or daylight not illumination enough, he heightens through his own creativeness the proportions, and he focuses a single beam of light which the sun will not dim by its going down. When natural music is faint to the ears of mankind, the poet magnifies it. Gaps in the created order are his to fill, and the future, however impenetrable a curtain it seems to drop between it and ourselves, is his to prophesy. To do these things, to sharpen, to reënforce, to heighten, to prophesy, is to exercise his highest power, that of creator.

THE ROAD TO MUSIC[1]

Catherine Drinker Bowen

It has become an irresistible temptation, with me, to ask musicians by what road they came home. Some, like Henry, achieve music by rebellion; their innate musicality flourishes upon negation; a wall to kick against, far from breaking their shins, only fattens their artistic marrow, strengthens their artistic muscle. Patience, my little Quaker pupil, is like that. Once I abandoned her altogether. 'I cannot teach you, Patience,' I told her, 'because you do not learn anything.' After some months she called me on the telephone to ask if I would object to her playing for assembly, at school? She

---

[1]From *Friends and Fiddlers* (1934), by Catherine Drinker Bowen. Reprinted by permission of Little, Brown & Company.

had, she assured me, been practising; the violin did not sound badly at all, and would I like to hear her play 'Cinquantaine' some day? Tuesday, perhaps, at her old lesson hour?

'Cinquantaine' emerged from under her bow with an actual lilt—the first lilt ever achieved by Patience. She must, in her vacation, have practised her fingers callous; I sat down and pondered, but I knew I should never dare this method with a soul less hardy than Patience. Not every fiddler has a Quaker genius for stubbornness.

Every year, on Cynthia's birthday, Anton Horner comes to play the Brahms Horn Trio with Cynthia and her father. For twenty years Horner played first horn in the Philadelphia Orchestra; it was Cynthia who asked him how he happened to choose his instrument. 'Oh,' he said, 'for the same reason every German boy in my day wanted to learn the horn. We all had to be soldiers, sometime, and the army brass has a good place in the rear.' But Horner's name tells his true story; his father and his grandfather and his great-grandfather were master horners. It is miraculous what Tony can do with a horn; he can sing you to sleep or he can march you to battle, but he says it was not always so. His father had to beat him to make him practise; he used to be locked in his room, first with a violin, then with a horn. 'That's the way to do it,' Tony said, looking benevolently round at our family assortment of young fiddlers. 'Keep 'em at it, whether they like it or no!'

We used to be afraid to 'keep 'em at it,' afraid of our own parental enthusiasm and the possible mistake of overemphasis. How much music could be pushed down a child's throat without fatal indigestion? But we fear this no longer; we have seen our young revolt; around the piano of an evening we have mourned the loss of one child and another from the fiddler's ranks— and then, eventually, they have come back. All but one, and him we await with confidence.

Even Cynthia tried to desert us—tried passionately, when she was fourteen. She practised with a scowl upon her face. 'What good does music do me?' she asked me one day in fury, holding her violin at arm's length as if it were a serpent and would bite her. 'Playing the fiddle won't get me into Omega Tau. It won't get me partners at dances. It just interferes with all those things. I *hate* music. What good can music do me?'

Nobody in her senses would try to put off a young and healthy Cynthia with middle-aged comfort, with 'You wait. When you're older, you'll know.' I hesitated and Cynthia looked full at me.

'You!' she said belligerently, 'Aunt Kay, you play more music than anyone I know, except Father. I suppose you've always been like that? I suppose *you* never wanted to throw your fiddle in the sink?'

I never did, and no possible expediency of auntly compromise could make me say so. I felt suddenly, ridiculously, as passionate as Cynthia. 'You're spoiled,' I said. 'Put your fiddle in the sink and go sing Omega Tau. You're not worthy of a violin.'

And then I went home and tried to remember what it was like to be fourteen. . . .

At fourteen, three brothers flooded our house with members of the team (John had by then passed beyond teams). Large, muscular youths eyed my violin with curiosity, requested me to play upon it, and, as I played, lay dreamily upon their stomachs before the fire, smoking their cigarettes. Thus far, good. Song, melody, they could understand—but if I attempted to talk about music they fidgeted. They looked embarrassed and slunk away in search of easier game, of companions less intense, more comfortable. I saw this,—what girl could help seeing it—and I learned to keep silence when silence was in order. That I hated this restriction and rebelled against it in my heart made me no less the traitor. This was a decade before the word 'highbrow' had been coined to crown the confusion of those whose blood leads them—flings them, willy-nilly—into embarrassing and lonely passions for Bach fugues. By the time that dread word was born, I was safe in music school.

Many a man who has known himself at ten forgets himself utterly between ten and thirty; I was fortunate in that my years of self-deception were short, my disloyalties brief. The largest of these took place, I remember, at Cynthia's exact age of rebellion—fourteen. There was a choice between playing in a recital at the Acorn Club, in Philadelphia, and going to a hometown affair called the 'Prep Dance.' After weeks of musical preparation I told my mother I could not play well enough for the recital, I told my music teacher I could not endure the Wieniawski Minuet, and I went to the dance. My teacher, who had come up from Philadelphia every Saturday for five years to give me a lesson, shook me from his list, spurned me eloquently in a letter to my parents, and I never saw him again.

Recalling these things, I wondered if all adolescents rebel against art, as they rebel against everything of parental instigation. If there were some way they could discover music for themselves, and not be pulled to it, sulking under the harness! Never to mention music, never to urge one's son to the piano—and then to have him come, suddenly and alone, upon beauty! Impossible; by the time his emotional apparatus was ready for music, his muscles would have grown too old to train.

Horner was right; we have to keep them at it. I have seen children pass through months of violent rebellion against music and months of warm devotion to it; the bridging periods of lukewarm tolerance are due, I think, to habit. Once in a while fortune aids the despairing parent by presenting the child with a new deskmate or roommate who can or cannot play, but who loves music. In the very nick, the very crack and needlepoint of time, Cynthia acquired a beau—transient as summer, but as welcome—who thought a violin more engaging even than curls, and said so.

I know not how it may be with genius; I have had no traffic with genius or even with superior talent; my children and my nieces and nephews are intelligent and ambitious, but without musical gift. No perfect pitch, no golden voice, no limber wrist of magic is ours for the showing; we exist merely as examples of how far the normal person may come into possession of music. Perhaps 'average' is a word less offensive to the gods—do they, having created us in their image, look upon perfect pitch as the norm? However that may be, here upon earth I have found but one key to a child's heart, musically speaking, but one bait to which he will rise eagerly, repeatedly: active participation in ensemble performance.

How many mothers have said to me, 'My little Freddy is only two years old,'—or five or six,—'but I am sure he is going to be very musical because he will sit for *hours* listening to really *good* music on the radio'—or the victrola or whatever. With difficulty I suppress the reply, 'Yes, my dear madam, and I have seen cretins in the asylum do the same for even longer hours, with the identical expression of sleepy wonderment displayed upon the face of your Freddy. And cretin and Freddy would enjoy the same sensation if stroked gently on either side of the backbone.'

And this raises the question of cheap music, jazz, the radio, and all the competitions and comparisons that good music meets to-day. It is of no use to outlaw cheap mechanical music from the home; it is, indeed, dangerous. If the age decree jazz, let our defense lie not in prohibition but in education; let us teach the young to differentiate, to know that 'Hello, Beautiful,' however tickling to the palate, bears no more relationship to music than does soda pop to vintage wine. Verbal persuasion is unwise; exposure, repetitive exposure, to good music is what turns the trick; but the exposure must include more than listening. Children—I cannot say it too often—cannot prove things in the abstract; they think with their bodies. Do not ask them, therefore, to listen to Haydn; ask them to play Haydn, no matter how unskillfully. Children are savages—more difficult still, they are savages thrust by us into a sophisticated society, and they have prepared for themselves defenses against this society. Tell a modern child that Beethoven is beautiful and he will not believe you—until he has proved it by the repeated testimony of his own finger tips.

Cynthia has a victrola in her room; often, passing her door, I have heard her caroling to the tune of 'A Dream Walking,' or the most recent and appealing torch song. She invites me to listen. 'Isn't that tune,' she will demand, 'simply divine?' But invite her to play the divine tune on her fiddle and she will turn up her nose. 'Too thin,' she told me once. 'Those tunes, they're boring to play.' Cynthia still thinks Handel is boring to play, too. 'It's too *smooth*. Father, let's do the Horn Trio. There's some *excitement* to Brahms.'

I never saw a child that was not bored by soloism—his own performance as well as somebody else's. What boy wants to sit on a piano stool and play pieces for mother's visitors? He is shy and uncomfortable, and his resentment has a solid psychological foundation. A child detects instantly a false situation; in the name of music or culture or the acquisition of poise, he is being sacrificed to his mother's vanity; is it any wonder he only bides his time before flinging off music forever?

Once I had a violin pupil, a little girl of eleven whose talent was equaled only by her powers of resistance to pedagogy. A fond mother had set up a flourishing case of musical hatred ('Mother says music is beautiful as prayer, but I only practise because I get a dollar an hour for it'). One day I asked Mary if she would care to come to our house next Sunday evening. She eyed me suspiciously and asked if there would be music. I said that there would be some children her age and we might sing a little. 'There will be,' I said, 'a string quartet and you can double with Cynthia on second fiddle if you think you can keep the place. But nobody has to play. We just do it for fun.'

At home the bets were five to one against Mary's arrival, but on Sunday the stroke of six announced her—silent, very much on the defensive. She refused to take a part in the singing and wandered about the room with a fine show of indifference, but from the corner of my eye I saw her pause by the fire and reach up a furtive hand to touch the old French horn on the mantel, saw her pause again to pluck a string on the cello in the corner. When we stopped singing she had come to anchor by the cupboard which holds the fiddles. 'Is this the Maggini violin?' she asked. 'That boy,' nodding coldly toward John Junior, 'sang off key.'

Quickly, before John Junior could pick up this gauntlet, I replied that yes, it was the Maggini and we were going to play a Haydn quartet. I told her I was sure she would be wanting to go home before we began. Avoiding that sharp childish eye, 'Will you please,' I said rapidly, 'get the Maggini ready for me while I answer the telephone?'

I left the room. The telephone had not rung and my lie had emerged from the larynx in a silly falsetto; did Mary know I was playing my last card? When I came back she was sitting comfortably before one of the quartet stands, John's Maggini on her knee. 'I tuned it,' she said, 'and I dusted off the rosin. It sounds fine on the G string. I'll stay if you'll let me play it.'

Even very small children love to handle a violin; its glossy smooth surface, the vibration of its plucked strings, exercise the fascination—but in superlative degree—of a perfect conch shell found upon the seashore. I honestly believe the privilege of dusting the Maggini has won more childish converts to music than many an endured symphony concert. All the radios in the world playing 'Cock-a-Doodle-Doo,' all the tickets for all the Youth Symphonies, would not have availed against Mary's rebellion. . . . Perhaps it is not so complicated as this. Perhaps any two-legged, deep-hearted creature fashioned by the Lord, if he held a fiddle in his hands, would know beneath his chin a cold emptiness, would itch to unfurl his right elbow in the balance of a long, strong bow.

This exercise of musical participation cannot begin too early. Let the child sing nursery rhymes with his mother, turn pages for the pianist as soon as he can read music, or sound A for the visiting fiddler to tune. Also, it can do no harm to leave the nursery door open when there is music. Music that drifts upstairs to a child's dark bedroom possesses a peculiar potency. Going to sleep to music at night, waking to music in the morning—absurdly enough, these experiences are, in some unaccountable way, musical participation; they define music, for the child, as a thing natural and homely, as much a part of a day as breakfast, dinner, and supper.

There are people who hate radios, and people—I say it with regret—who hate pianos and violins. Most families possess a well-rounded example of each species, and this is something we melomaniacs must acknowledge or see our family music crash dissonantly into family dispute. We who practise upon the flute are so taken up with making a wrong noise into a right one that we forget the persons to whom even a right noise upon the flute is maddeningly wrong. But there is a way to solve this problem.

When my brother John built his new house the architect said, 'I understand the main feature of this residence is to be the music room? That is why you are building the house?'

John shook his head. 'I want a room big enough for two pianos and at least a hundred people in comfortable chairs singing Bach. That will be the music room. But that is not at all what you call the main feature of the residence, and it is not at all the reason'—he turned to me and grinned—'why we are building the house.'

Over his blueprints the architect raised the patient inevitable eyebrows of architects in conference with clients. 'We had a music room in the other house,' I explained, 'and in the house before that, too.'

Impossible for me to speak of John's houses in any but the possessive case, although I have never actually lived in any of them. A house in which one's fiddle and one's children's fiddles repose under the piano can be spoken of in no other case than the possessive.

'In all of the houses,' John was saying with a large gesture of impatience, 'in all the houses we had music rooms. Pianos, fiddles, flutes—Lord, yes. But what good did it do us?' He turned to me again. 'There was no place to sit downstairs except the music room and a library that opened off it with double doors. Every time we wanted to play, the family had to stop talking or roll those sticky doors shut or go somewhere else. When we had people for dinner we couldn't play or sing because the Browns didn't like music. Wasted evenings,'—his voice grew indignant,—'wasted Saturday afternoons. And as likely as not a batch of newly published trios just arrived from Breitkopf and Hartel's.'

John's eye was gloomy with remembered wrongs.

'So what we want,' I began helpfully . . .

'Is a retreat,' finished the architect, 'for musicians.'

'Nothing of the kind!' John shouted. '*We* aren't going to retreat. We're going to play music. It's the audience that's going to retreat. The people that don't play . . . Look here!' John's finger was on the blueprint. 'You see those steps? Well, they lead up from the music room to the hall. I want that hall a mile long. I don't care how it looks. It can look like a public school or a hospital or a lunatic asylum—I don't care. Then away down here at the end of the hall I want a room, nice and cheerful, with books in it, and a fireplace. Card tables, easy-chairs—*anything* in it,' said John, 'as long as it has a door that will stay shut.'

'With a keyhole,' interrupted the architect, suddenly inspired, 'on the outside?'

'That's it,' John said, in his voice a rich and eager satisfaction. 'That's why we are building this house.'

Speaking practically, I know of nothing more fatal to the musical progress of a growing family than a piano in a common sitting room. Particularly if grandparents live in the house, or a husband who, however sweet-tempered, is not sufficiently interested in music to endure those loud bleating sounds produced by a piano under striving small fingers. Sounds even more excruciating can be achieved by beginning violinists. I myself battled with such a situation until so lately as a year ago, when, against vigorous protest, I had the piano moved upstairs. I put it—hideous but well-used upright—into one of those rooms possessed by every sizable family and known by such titles as the sewing room, Aunt Eliza's (deceased) room, or Uncle Jim's (deceased) study. I did this in secret, when the children were at school and their grand-parents taking their afternoon siesta. Three large, grimy, pleasant men appeared at my door and with astonishing rapidity took the piano apart and flourished it up the stairs. In husky Irish whispers they requested a duster and delicately dusted its insides until the sewing room was dim with dust, after which they put the instrument together again and, with no more disturbance than three sneezes, took their pay, grinned, and disappeared.

I may call this one of the two major strategic musical victories of my life. The other was achieved when I moved the radio into the kitchen. Radios in the right place are as welcome as pianos in the right place, but in the wrong place, radios are . . . Let me tell a story.

On a boat going from Philadelphia to Boston I met a large genial man of middle age. He was the kind of man who carries a heavy elaborate camera and takes pictures of everyone on the boat—the very person I should have thought would love a radio. Upon the second evening of our voyage, a warm, soft summer night, I put my children to bed and went forward to enjoy the stars. As I hurried along the lighted deck a spirited raffle was taking place in the main saloon, with three radios as prizes. No one was on the bow deck; I stood alone by the rail thinking with satisfaction of my children tucked into starboard bunks and my automobile tucked into cavernous places below deck. Broken water slipped gently, monotonously past our bows; a mild contented revery possessed me, and I wondered why all the people who must go from Philadelphia to Boston in summer, instead of screaming through the night on heated wheels, do not tread thus softly upon the starlit wave.

A voice at my side said, 'What more could anybody want?'—and I recognized the camera man. 'Why,' he continued, 'don't people who have to go places remember about boats—and why aren't you down there buying chances on radios?'

I inquired if the gentleman so much wanted to win a radio, and he replied with gusto that he certainly did. To which I asked a little wearily *why* he wanted to win a radio.

He turned to me quite ferociously and said with a bitter, startling distinctness, 'So I can carry it up here and drop it over the bow.' His voice was exultant. 'So I can watch myself drop a radio, brand-new and shiny, over this rail—splash!—into that black, irrecoverable grave. Into that bourn,' he continued with a large gesture, and with magnificent disregard for the triteness of the quotation, 'from which no traveler . . .'

'Returns,' I finished, and extended my hand. He shook it gravely, and we resumed our starry watch.

It was that moment which told me Music in the right place is what domestic America needs—and it was that moment which, cherished all summer, inspired me to move our radio from living room to kitchen. The kitchen— is it not the hearth, the altar, the very sanctum of domestic life? Does it not deserve, therefore, as ornament, the very cream of modern invention? Also, is it not the room farthest from fiddledom and the piano bench? Since that night, peace has graced our home.

To revert to the fascinating query, 'By what road do men come to music?' I advise against asking this question of a singer. The answer lies too wide of the mark. Fate, or God, or the circumstances of heredity shaped Fiorella's vocal cords with a beautiful physiological exactitude of proportion: Fiorella opens her mouth and a lark flies forth. But, we may ask, what has this to do with music? Seven toes on each foot would lead home as surely. Many a Fiorella have I met with a throat of bird, brain of wax, and heart of putty.

On the other hand, I have seen converts made, more unbelievers brought to Jordan, by singing than by any other blandishment of the muse. I have watched Sarah lead in the baptized by the dozens, and I have admired her technique, which is compounded less of enthusiasm than of an unshakable conviction that anybody in the world, if he will open his mouth wide enough, can sing—more important still, that he will like it. Sarah herself learned singing long ago—wise Sarah, who would have been drowned, deafened, lost completely in the vociferation of husbandly *arpeggios*, the urgent fiddle strings of her progeny. She had no voice; she could not, indeed, stay on the tune; but ten years ago an idea seized her, and with Sarah an idea is *fait accompli* no matter how long the way. At that time, no one in the family sang; John went about in trains and buses with Magnificats and B Minor Masses under his arm, but he never sang. It had not occurred to him.

Sarah sat down and trained—not her voice, but her ear. She began with 'Three Blind Mice.' Eventually she induced seven other women to sing with her once a week, on Wednesday morning. After a decent interval they procured a professional leader; the chorus now numbers ninety members, few of whom ever miss a Wednesday. The chorus does not sing in public; its aim is to read the literature of choral music. Sarah is herself astonished at the direction in which the wind of music has blown her straws; John, whom one would surely never think of as a straw, has become as enthusiastic a singer as his wife. Sarah and he hold Sunday-night singing parties; sometimes twenty people come, sometimes a hundred and twenty. John takes off his coat and leads the chorus; Sarah sits in the front row, singing, and somehow her very presence seems to balance the affair.

John has a very useful loud voice; while he conducts, he sings bass or tenor, whichever seems to need support at the moment. He does not know if the room is hot or cold; half of us could faint from exhaustion and John would notice nothing save an annoyingly reduced volume of sound. It is Sarah to whom we turn in extremity. 'We have sung enough,' she tells John. 'We must rest awhile. It is time for supper.'

Sarah and John are themselves surprised at the choice of persons who elect to sing with them. Professional instrumentalists of the first water, not to speak of singers. Magic flautists from the Philadelphia Orchestra, harp pluckers, fiddlers, and pianists of glittering fame sit modestly sharing a Brahms Gypsy Song, a Palestrina Mass, with a red-cheeked, golf-playing importer of sisal hemp, a singing grandmother, or somebody's nephew who happens to be home from school for the holidays. . . .

We sing from six to seven-thirty; then, conversing in whispers,—only the professional singers seem to know how to use a voice without losing it,—we have supper. After supper some hardy soloist entertains us until we are recovered sufficiently to sing again. Names of these soloists—no matter how renowned—never appear on the invitations, but only the music to be sung and the names of the composers. This leads to occasional misunderstanding. One day Sarah, hurriedly preparing invitations, instead of writing out Beethoven, Opus 132, wrote at the end of the programme, 'An early and a late Beethoven quartet'—phrases as familiar to musicians as 'three-minute egg' to a cook. A group of people, arriving at nine, said they had come late because they were especially fond of Beethoven and understood it was to be played *later*.

To us it is a matter of enormous pleasure that our one persistent rebel-to-music, my nephew David, the real musical talent in the family, who in his teens did fling his cello, so to speak, down the sink—David sometimes sings with us at these parties. He never talks about music; like my brother's friends when I was young, he would strangle rather than admit he likes it, but, an infallibly correct sight reader, he sits with the basses and breathes deep, and we pretend not to know he is there.

Sarah's peculiar method of learning to sing is, I think, what fascinates everybody; perhaps I had rather say, her very individual outlook upon the arts. Sarah was not reared, as were the rest of us, in a school which lets go, which roars its enthusiasm, turns red in the face, and pounds its feet when pleased. Sarah takes art for granted in the same calm, extremely practical way that she takes life and dinner time.

One Sunday we were singing a Handel duet with the children, and Sarah read the alto part at sight. John was playing our accompaniment; he turned and stared at his wife. 'Got that D natural, by heaven, didn't you? Where did you learn to sing fourths? I never heard you practise them.'

Sarah replied easily that she had learned them driving the automobile. 'Every time I turn a right-hand corner I sing a fourth, and every time I turn a left-hand corner I sing a fifth. I've been doing it for months.'

Not a child in the room, upon hearing this, but wanted to try the vocal leap of one-to-four, with all its variations. Perhaps it is not art, that kind of effort, perhaps it is not even music. But it is a game, and a good game.

One winter afternoon another fiddler and I were playing sonatas with Pamela at her house in Bryn Mawr—old sonatas for two violins and piano. Tea was laid before the fire; between movements we snatched at buttered toast and conversation. Pamela was at that time a candidate for the state senate; present was an enthusiastic young man who had called to discuss political matters with her. His enthusiasm concerned not music, but the autumn elections, and what he wanted was *talk*; it was obvious he neither knew music nor cared to know it. As I played I could see him where he crouched by the fire, a look upon his face half exasperation, half puzzlement. What, he was wondering, is Pamela up to now? Why do these people fling themselves so violently from the attainable concrete to the unattainable abstract?

After an hour he got up and, walking over to us, stood watching closely until we played the last chord. We played it—bang!—with a ring and a smash, and all three rose laughing—I do not know exactly why—from our seats. The young man laughed too. 'Well, I'm damned!' he said. 'It's *fun*, doing that, isn't it?'

Fun! I remember one child who played second violin with us at home for years. 'It's fun,' she would say, as she put up her instrument when we were done. 'Mozart is fun to play. I had to count sixteen measures rest, and I got back exactly on time. And I'll bet nobody saw my feet move, either.' (Like the indignant Briton, this child—who was not Cynthia—belongs to the school which thinks rhythm should be felt, not tapped with the foot. Cynthia herself counts, she says, all *andantes* with her stomach.) 'Let's try a new Mozart, next Sunday,' the child would say—and then one night when she was sixteen she laid her fiddle on her knee and looked at me wide-eyed across the stands. A long adagio cadence trembled on the air; the child's eyes were bright, bewildered. 'It's beautiful,' she said softly. 'That Mozart—why, it's beautiful.'

The long road or the short, the straight or the crooked,—as aesthete, poacher, or as sportsman,—I care not how nor by what road men come home to music. I care only that they come.

SOCIAL SIGNIFICANCE
OF CONTEMPORARY ART[1]

Lewis Mumford

On the surface, there seems to be a great stir in the graphic and plastic arts today. The artist is no longer skulking behind the lines: his work is one of the first things either to be attacked, or to lead the attack. When the Nazis got into power in Germany they assaulted the artist in the same breath that they struck at the communists and the Jews; they threatened George Grosz, the savage satirist of decadent post-war Germany, with death, and even expressed disapproval of a dyed-in-the-wool German of the purest Nordic lineage, Barlach, whose war memorial in Hamburg, one of the few restrained and poetic monuments of modern times, they probably hated for its very tenderness.

When Plato banished the artist from his Republic as an enemy, he merely set the fashion for the present-day totalitarians. For art is not innocuous: images have power to stir men, and beliefs and attitudes may be expressed in painting and sculpture that would be easily recognized and suppressed if they were stated in so many words. So the artist has been alternately reproached by the reactionaries for being out of touch with the people, and banned because of his dangerous political potentialities. In short, the arts today occupy a position that is full of ambiguities, paradoxes, and contradictions. And even those who espouse the social role of the artist or who seek to use art as a means of social propaganda do not, perhaps, fully realize the implications of their position.

The first contradiction that confronts us is that there is still a gap between the artist and the body of people who should normally share his interests and enjoy his creations. During the last centuries, the arts came more and more to be regarded as a badge of caste. Popular taste was vulgarized and debased, while an isolated connoisseurship took over the appreciation and patronage of the arts. By habit and temperament the artist often belonged to the working classes; even when Cézanne inherited a fortune from his father he lived on a modest scale. Indeed, the Bohemianism of the artist has often been misunderstood and undervalued. His defiance of bourgeois standards of reputability, his general contempt for money and the things money will buy, were very sturdy social virtues; and the painter may be looked upon as one of the few surviving handicraftsmen who escaped complete debasement by commercial competition. But the industrial workers lacked the means and

[1]From *The Social Frontier*, December, 1935.

the leisure, and, therefore, the sensibility and education, to respond to the art of the painters. After days and weeks and years of coarse brutalizing toil or dull routine, they needed equally coarse stimulants to stir their esthetic senses.

The contemporary artist has sought to lessen this breach in a number of different ways. He has demanded public walls and sought release from the individual patronage of the bourgeoisie by proclaiming his interest in mural painting. By turning to public art he has sought direct popular stimulus and appreciation. He has accepted work at day wages, like the painters of the Middle Ages and the Renascence, instead of proving his worth by bourgeois standards—that is, by setting a fabulously high price upon it. All these methods of bridging the gap between the artist and the public have been pragmatically useful; they have been valuable even when—as in the renewal of fresco painting in a fixed, undetachable, wall space—they are in opposition to the canons and interests of modern architecture. As a result of the painter's earnest desire to be treated as a fellow worker and a responsible member of society, the importance of painting and sculpture as social activities is almost reëstablished. In this sense, the position of the artist is, perhaps, better than it has been for over a hundred years; all the more because these practical steps have been accompanied by a broader educational recognition of the place of the arts in a living culture. Gradgrind, and Gradgrind's conception that art is mere idleness and sentimentality, a distraction from the important work of the world, are no longer fashionable.

But while these preparatory steps are important, they still leave a number of questions unanswered. How, apart from his current employment in schools, and workers' centers and union headquarters and post-offices, shall the painter or the sculptor express his social interest? How does this interest alter the contents and significance of his art? To what extent is art propaganda, and to what extent can propaganda be art? Are social content and conscious political purpose or indoctrination the same things? All these questions require clarification.

At present, the painters who have attempted to use themes that shall be intelligible to everyone and that escape the vices of bourgeois refinement are divided into two camps: the "proletarians" and the "patriots." In interest, the first group follows the tradition of William Morris; they recognize the need for a social revolution which will establish a basis of justice and equality between men and will make it possible for everyone to work heartily in the service of the community as a whole. To express their identification with the working classes, they deal with workers and with the commonplace or dramatic scenes of their daily life—with scenes of starvation, terrorism, or struggle. This is not altogether a new note: it was expressed in Rembrandt's tender pictures of the poor and the outcast and in Pieter Breughel the Elder's marvelous interpretations of work and play in the Netherlands; the chord sounded more sonorously and directly in the paintings of Daumier and Van Gogh, which had all the stir of the French revolutions of '89 and '48 behind them, and, in a lesser degree, in those of Millet and in our day it came forth again, strong and resonant, in the paintings of the Mexicans, Rivera, Orozco, Siquieros, and their followers.

Today, artists like Lurçat, who had played with the distorted dream-image of surréalisme, now feel that they must face sharper realities and more serious duties. Work and the struggles of the worker; the drama of labor, men working in the foundry and the blast furnace and the cotton and wheat fields, as in the paintings of Thomas Benton or Joe Jones, men toiling on the farm or in the mine, as in the paintings of Eugene Higgins, participating in strikes and mass-movements, as in Rivera and William Gropper, arising in blind protest and sober strength, as in the great Orozco murals at Dartmouth—the common occupations and interests of men, part of the new ideology of our day, begin to occupy a place once occupied in the Middle Ages by the Holy Family and the saints, and in the Renascence by the images of gods and princes.

But doctrine and esthetic achievement do not necessarily go hand in hand: the face of Lenin or Marx, so often used by the proletarian artist, does not spell the *promise* of revolution unless the spectator is already a Leninist or a Marxist. Clarity of political program and conscious revolutionary energy do not necessarily make effective propaganda art; and the mere use of proletarian material does not necessarily prove that the artist has solved the crucial problems that concern his relation with his spectators. I shall revert to this presently.

The other social movement in painting parallels that of the "proletarian" artists as fascism parallels communism: it exhibits some of the same energies and some of the same defects.

The men who belong to the more "patriotic" school are not necessarily conscious nationalists or fascists, although the justification of their mode of painting by a reactionary critic like Thomas Craven is usually tunnelled with fascist prejudices and raw nationalistic attitudes. Underlying this nationalist art is the notion that nationalism is an absolute and unconditioned fact; that membership in this or that national group is the highest human good; specifically, the belief that by selecting certain images and looking at certain moments of life one can and should identify oneself as American. Not merely this: the American artist has a duty to use only certain pat symbols that refer to exclusively American experience; and to perform this duty he must exclude from eye and mind and practice any influence drawn from outside his own country. Carried out rigorously in every department of life, this doctrine would denude our country of most of its institutions, its inventions, and its physical and cultural wealth; and it is just as violent a piece of folly in art as it would be in life. The fact is that it is only second rate painters who want to exclude foreign competitors by edict, who do not wish to face comparison with the artists of other countries, and who seek to raise the fact of nationality into the crazy political doctrine of nationalism.

Truly national painters, like Eakins or Ryder, do not need the props of political nationalism. And Ryder is as much the interpreter of American life when he paints a scene from Wagner as when he paints an obscure fishing boat on a cold moonlit sea. Nor is realism a necessary mark of American art: perhaps the very finest products we have produced in art, outside a handful of paintings, are the best of the patchwork quilts done in the 'forties and 'fifties: pure abstract design. Moreover, as painters of America, the patriotic school is singularly limited; their images of America overstress the humdrum, the tumble-down, the dull, the pathetic, and the defeated, or—as in the paintings of Grant Wood—the prim and the sweet. And with all the great fuss and bother about achieving a purely American art, free from foreign taint or influence, most of the painters of contemporary Americana—I would perhaps except Hopper and Benton—are only stale replicas of the inferior European genre painters. Indeed Grant Wood, who has become the chief political symbol for the patriots, is technically without any sources except European ones, not having come for an instant, apparently, under the sway of Ryder, or Eakins, or Homer, as so many of the better painters in America have done. For a fuller interpretation of the American scene, with something of its confidence, its energy, and its originality, as well as its limitations, one must turn to such non-political painters as O'Keeffe, Marin, Sheeler, Kantor, Brook, Karfiol, Gropper, or Peggy Bacon, Adolf Dehn, and Howard Cook, among the printmakers.

Perhaps the only points upon which the painters of Americana have been effective is their intelligibility: people look at their pictures and see at once what they mean. But immediate intelligibility and a large audience is not a test of esthetic achievement; if that were so, Edgar Guest would be a greater poet than Shakespeare, and Landseer a more important painter than Turner. For immediate and widespread intelligibility must be based upon fixed signs and accepted attitudes; whereas art of the highest quality transforms the fixed sign and alters attitudes. Let me sum up this situation in two statements that only on their surface present a contradiction. First: art is by its very nature propaganda, that is, it seeks to share and widen a particular kind of experience; and it succeeds in this to the extent that it alters the feelings, the emotions, and the attitudes of the participant. Propagandist art, on the other hand, is limited because it is tempted to utilize an emblem instead of creating a symbol. That emblem, which is a rallying point for the believer by its very character, warns off the non-believer or puts him in an attitude of aggressive defense, insulating him against the possibility of a fresh experience. Whether propagandist or non-propagandist, art is social *in intention*: an abstraction of three cylinders is just as social by nature as a painting of a subway rush at Times Square; and it is social even in this respect, that it may tell as much about the nature of the society from which it emanates as the most photographic realist could.

At the bottom of this paradox lies the essential difference between a sign, a symbol, and an emblem. Once this is cleared up, the political and social mission of the artist should be plainer.

Signs, symbols, and emblems are means of social intercourse and co-operation. The first is an instrument of communication, the second an instrument of communion, and the third is an instrument of cohesion. Each of these means has its place in society; but the graphic and plastic arts serve mainly for communion, and unless this purpose dominates the expression even the accessory functions of communication or cohesion cannot be served. Communion attempts not to convey a meaning but to establish an attitude and rouse, by sympathy and empathy, an appropriate response. The complex symbols of painting represent clusters of perceptions, feelings, sentiments. They are the condensation of an experience even more complex. These symbols cannot be translated into signs, or reduced to emblems, without great loss of content and effect. Even when communion is forced to make use of signs (as in poetry) it contrives to give such signs a different value from what they have in logical communication. The aim of communication is complete intelligibility, and signs tend to perfection as they approach the accuracy and economy and objectivity of mathematical expressions. Communion, on the other hand, attempts to give to the varied members of a community the same concrete experience in all its thickness and richness: it aims, not so much at rational acceptance, as at providing a common background in emotions and feelings: color and form, like pure music, have deep physiological effects, which are beyond arguments. The arts may indeed echo Whitman: "I and mine do not convince by arguments, we convince by our presence." As for the emblem, it is for the most part antagonistic to symbolic expression since it is purely an instrument of action, and its main business is by repetition to produce certain automatic effects of obedience and common discipline. Emblems and badges are useful; all groups and societies resort to them for purposes of prompt cohesion; but the artist must not confuse the acceptance of an emblem with his true social task: that is the creation of new symbols, leading to new attitudes and new expressions of life. The social problem of the artist, in fact, is how to get beyond the emblem: which means, how to break through the order whose cohesion the emblem seeks to promote.

The rationalist would like to limit social expression to communication. Carried out thoroughly this would practically wipe out the painter and the sculptor; for in this line, he can do nothing that the scholar or the scientist cannot do much better. The drill-sergeant and the bureaucrat and the dictator would like to limit art to the emblem: from the standpoint of totalitarian politics, this is the only kind of art that can be effectually controlled.

But the more ready the artist is to espouse social attitudes, to throw his own lot in with that of the community, to make his appeal to his fellow workers as a worker and a citizen, the more careful must he be to avoid these two pitfalls and the more zealously must he concentrate upon his special function. For by altering the feelings and attitudes of men, projecting in paint or marble or wood all those forces and interests that remain tangled and obscure, or dumb and sterile, until they are translated into an objective medium, he is performing his peculiar social function. When the artist of the Renascence organized his pictures by means of linear perspective, established through a network of Cartesian co-ordinates, he was making men ready for the new conquest of mathematics, for the new physical science and technology: his symbols foretold the world of Descartes and Newton and Watt by almost two centuries. It is in that fashion that the best artists today are making ready for profound social transformations: not merely by showing the strife and torment of the present conflict between classes, but by relating man and nature and the machine within a new framework which will express, and thereby help make possible, a new social order.

ART FOR OUR SAKE[1]

Charles W. Ferguson

Now that the surrealist and dada exhibit has made the rounds, it is time to speak plainly of the sad estate to which the national mind seems in imminent danger of falling. For the fact which bludgeons one who confronts surrealism and allied whimsies is not that men will paint such pictures and fashion such objects, but that the common fellow of our time, holding no passion for art and less for the abstract, should patronize the transcontinental jaunt of the exhibit and, if not exactly genuflect, at least confess upon emerging from the menage of phantasmagoric objects that he has been touched.

I went, somewhat painfully, to the show in Manhattan. There I beheld four floors overflowing with disembodied ash cans and populated with an assortment of impressed beholders who had come to scoff and remained sheepishly to grin. Eavesdropping, I caught gasps as well as snickers and I discovered that objects which seemed hardly more than giant typographical errors had hooked the fancy of not a few from all walks of life. One young woman told me that, whereas she could not admire the collection, she did feel a certain exhilaration.

In talking later with others who had attended the show, I got a hint of bated breath—a humility which does not seem to embarrass us on other topics. I heard capable artists admit, not waggishly, but in sober earnest, that some of the stuff on exhibit was beyond their depth.

Thus the incomprehensible has acquired followers and the revolt against meaning is in full cry. While this fact is essentially funny, it is likewise important. No matter how much one smiles at the spectacle of men enthralled by ten-cent mysteries, one must not miss the point: The confusion, mental and emotional, of the average person has become so pronounced and terrifying that he seeks outside support and validation of it. Confronting an unassimilable body of facts, the modern mind retreats comfortably into gibberish, substitutes an entertaining brand of madness for effort, and is delighted to find that its mistakes can be dignified by the term art.

If this interpretation seems far-fetched, one need only have his memory refreshed on the salient gewgaws exhibited. Or, for that matter, he may dip again into the blotto works of those who started it all. One of Gertrude Stein's poems begins:

> Sweet sweet sweet sweet sweet tea.
> Susie Asado.

[1]From *Harper's Magazine*, July, 1937.

The young Roumanian Jew who was the founder of dadaism issued the following manifesto: "We want works straightforward, strong, accurate, and forever not understood. Logic is a complication." Started in France, dada societies sprang up in Germany and elsewhere. There were public meetings, spectacular and rousing speeches. A young artist spilled an irregular blot of ink on a sheet of white paper and called it The Virgin Mary. Here is one of the founder's poems:

> A e ou o youyouyou i e ou o
> youyouyou
> drrrr drrr drrr grrr grrr grrrrrrr
> bit of green duration flutter
> in my room
> a e x o i ii i e a ou ii ii belly
> shows the center I want to take it
> ambran bran bran and restore
> center of the four
> beng bong beng bang

Now come with me to the most recent display of the extremists. Here is a small birdcage filled with block sugar somewhat the worse for wear. And what is this object? The caption, if that will help you any, is "Why Not Sneeze?" Turn from this to an overpowering piece of wood some six feet high and three feet across, carved roughly in the manner of a hallowe'en prank. Upon the surface of the wood you find, if you take the pains and stand before it long enough, the following objects, among others: a black bow tie, two baby shoes, an old discarded umbrella, a toothbrush, a bustle, a bottle top, a typewriter ribbon, the lid of a garbage pail, a pencil, cigar butts, and all the other ill-assorted items one might uncover if one cleaned the garage, his desk, and the attic on the same day. The objects are not arranged with any view to symmetry but are fastened in such places as might appear to be handy.

These works are not singular oddities in a chamber of horrors but tolerably representative of the whole eerie collection. To be sure, there are others which range closer to the norm, if any conception of the norm remains after a glance round the walls. There is a felicitous picture of a piece of cold ham on a cold plate flanked by a bottle of wine, and the ham has a glassy eye in the center of it. There is a picture of a buxom and obtuse woman seated stolidly on a horsehair sofa in the middle of a luxuriant jungle, the foliage of which barely conceals the smug and uninterested countenances of two toothless and amiable lions. There is a fur-bearing cup and saucer. And on another floor there are the almost conventional paintings of Dali, one of which shows a woman of lovely shape filled with drawers, some half-empty and all carrying the assorted objects of the boudoir.

The same kind of performance goes on apace to-day in the realm of dissonant music, unpunctuated and occult verse, stream-of-unconsciousness novels. A not inconsiderable crowd of those whose high business it is to interpret the impulses and emotions of our times have seen fit to do so in terms of studied nonsense. Indeed, deference for the meaningless has even found its way into modern education, so that when a child draws a picture of a frog and it resembles a tumor, it is not good form to chide the child. It's a frog to him and it behooves you to see it as he does. There is no longer any simple conviction that a frog is a frog.

Can it be said that there is something too deep to plumb in all this? Not at all. Paul Jordan Smith, the critic, gave the lie to such a notion when, largely to deride the neo-artists, he executed several years ago a magnificent series of hoaxes under a gaga pseudonym. These he caused to be shown and lauded throughout the civilized world as authentic pictures in the modernist manner. Moguls and public fell as heartily for his dazzling travesties as they have since for the more genuine but not less outrageous works of the new masters. A fake is as good as the true in the latterday art with its hallmark of incoherence. The whole array of modern objets d'art have meaning chiefly because they are meaningless.

Not long ago I found myself going down a village street with two things in mind. One was a Mickey-Mouse-Merry-Go-Round and the other was hepicoleum compound. When the average mind comes to entertain in a single instant two such extraneous concepts it is not remarkable that it should find some meaning in a picture which showed a stovepipe playing the piano and brushing its teeth with a Christmas tree. If you dare, you can freeze your thoughts at any one instant during the day and find a menagerie of ideas and objects not a whit less preposterous than you will see at a prize-winning dada show.

This is true in part because of the increasing multitude of objects which in this day and time assail our conscious mind and—to a regrettable degree— enter it. Added to this are such bewildering items as trade indices, extraterritoriality, nationalism, reprisals, sanctions, balance of trade, bonded indebtedness, international law, and other properties of the modern setting that at best make only a slight sense to the average person.

We come to live more and more by symbols and to deal with objects that are several paces removed from our understanding. Faced with a jungle of things, haunted by peering eyes of uncertainty, we assume that all these objects and symbols, in their disheveled state, have significance to us. But when we try to assert their significance we talk foolishness, and this is precisely what the new art and the newer literature tend to do.

The artist of course ought to occupy a singular position—one not far removed from the priest. It is his function, though he seldom admits it, to reveal what is significant and to play into obscurity what is not. That is why it seems to me that the more cockeyed forms of modern art do us common people such a profound disservice. We know well enough that the life we lead every day tends to become distracted. We have reason to expect from the artist some god-like resolution of order out of chaos. We may at moments be grateful if he reveals mercilessly the contents of our minds. He may even do good deeds with this method, giving body to the abstract. In the main though the artist needs—as we need—to select, not to choose willy-nilly from the garbled contents of our daily ash heap. These dadaists and the frightful imps who slavishly follow their lack of pattern teach us indiscriminateness, a feeling that one thing is as good as another and that the aggregate is appalling.

In a world less distraught there would be less cause to regret that the artist is inclined to forsake his last. The modern vogue of the monstrous though is more than a pastime. It has the intent and thrust of drama. Nay, more, it has the shadowy compulsion of a religion. It is a kind of worship in a creepy cathedral peopled by the authoritatively insane. The droning chant of half-formed, jumbled words breaking now and then into the cry of a distant loon; the sight of unsightly objects where the statues of saints ought to be; the explosive, industrial cacophony of music without melody; the audience, spectral and agape, yapping its approval: these are not the pyrotechnics of exhibitionism but the dreadful Te Deum of men beset by furies.

If you can imagine coming out of the night for solace into such a service, you can understand what the common run of us experience when we confront this sort of modern art. We find no relief save the momentary one of knowing that others are muddled too. We get none of the transfiguration which ideas should bring.

And the great pity of this is that now more than ever the arts are the property of us all. For the first time they are in a position to serve as evangels of perfection, touching millions that they have not touched before. Hence the high importance and obligation of those who give art expression.

To blame the artist solely of course is only to evade the issue for ourselves. The schizophrenic craftsman is no more responsible for imbalance than a riveter is for noise. The new art merely echoes the jangle of our age. It is but a sign of the centrifugal forces at work. The aberrant artists have not created a promiscuity of values. Their fault is only that they do nothing to clear up our ghastly bewilderment but rather, if taken seriously and accorded continued obeisance, tend to make it intolerable.

What we, the people, ask of the artist is no more than we must do ourselves. The world is so full of a number of things that we need now to be saved, or to save ourselves, from multiplicity. Schiller said you could tell an artist by what he leaves out. Let art forsake its function of selectiveness, and the task is thrown squarely back on us. We must have some toughness of mind if we are to avoid losing all semblance of character and stamina in an age of con-fusion. We must select and concentrate on that which is significant. This is the high command which art could give to us. Even if it does not supply this we can at least ask it not to attach pseudo-meaning through artistry and cunning to that which we know is grotesque.

Science

SALOMON'S HOUSE[1]

Francis Bacon

"God bless thee, my son; I will give thee the greatest jewel I have. For I will impart unto thee, for the love of God and men, a relation of the true state of Salomon's House.[2] Son, to make you know the true state of Salomon's House, I will keep this order. First, I will set forth unto you the end of our foundation. Secondly, the preparations and instruments we have for our works. Thirdly, the several employments and functions whereto our fellows are assigned. And fourthly, the ordinances and rites which we observe.

"This end of our foundation is the knowledge of causes and secret motions of things; and the enlarging of the bounds of human empire, to the effecting of all things possible.

"The preparations and instruments are these. We have large and deep caves of several depths; the deepest are sunk 600 fathoms; and some of them are digged and made under great hills and mountains; so that if you reckon together the depth of the hill and the depth of the cave, they are, some of them, above three miles deep. For we find that the depth of an hill, and the depth of a cave from the flat, is the same thing; both remote alike from the sun and heaven's beams, and from the open air. These caves we call the lower region. And we use them for all coagulations, indurations, refrigerations, and conservations of bodies. We use them likewise for the imitation of natural mines and the producing also of new artificial metals, by compositions and materials which we use and lay there for many years. We use them also sometimes (which may seem strange) for curing of some diseases, and for prolongation of life, in some hermits that choose to live there, well accommodated of all things necessary, and indeed live very long; by whom also we learn many things.

"We have burials in several earths, where we put divers cements, as the Chinese do their porcelain. But we have them in greater variety of composts and soils, for the making of the earth fruitful.

"We have high towers, the highest about half a mile in height, and some of them likewise set upon high mountains, so that the vantage of the hill with the tower is in the highest of them three miles at least. And these places we call the upper region, accounting the air between the high places and the low as a middle region. We use these towers, according to their several heights and situations, for insolation, refrigeration, conservation, and for the view

[1]From *The New Atlantis* by Francis Bacon (1626).
[2]This was the name given to the ideal order of society in Bacon's *The New Atlantis*.

of divers meteors—as winds, rain, snow, hail; and some of the fiery meteors also. And upon them, in some places, are dwellings of hermits, whom we visit sometimes, and instruct what to observe.

"We have great lakes, both salt and fresh, whereof we have use for the fish and fowl. We use them also for burials of some natural bodies, for we find a difference in things buried on earth or in the air below the earth, and things buried in water. We have also pools, of which some do strain fresh water out of salt, and others by art do turn fresh water into salt. We have also some rocks in the midst of the sea, and some bays upon the shore for some works, wherein is required the air and vapour of the sea. We have likewise violent streams and cataracts, which serve us for many motions; and likewise engines for multiplying and enforcing of winds to set also on going divers motions.

"We have also a number of artificial wells and fountains, made in imitation of the natural sources and baths, as tincted upon vitriol, sulphur, steel, brass, lead, nitre, and other minerals; and again, we have little wells for infusions of many things, where the waters take the virtue quicker and better than in vessels or basins. And amongst them we have a water, which we call water of Paradise, being by that we do to it made very sovereign for health and prolongation of life.

"We have also great and spacious houses, where we imitate and demonstrate meteors—as snow, hail, rain, some artificial rains of bodies and not of water, thunders, lightnings; also generations of bodies in air—as frogs, flies, and divers others.

"We have also certain chambers, which we call chambers of health, where we qualify the air as we think good and proper for the cure of divers diseases and preservation of health.

"We have also fair and large baths, of several mixtures, for the cure of diseases and the restoring of man's body from arefaction; and others for the confirming of it in strength of sinews, vital parts, and the very juice and substance of the body.

"We have also large and various orchards and gardens, wherein we do not so much respect beauty as variety of ground and soil, proper for divers trees and herbs, and some very spacious, where trees and berries are set, whereof we made divers kinds of drinks, besides the vineyards. In these we practise likewise all conclusions of grafting and inoculating, as well of wild trees as fruit-trees, which produceth many effects. And we make by art, in the same orchards and gardens, trees and flowers, to come earlier or later than their seasons, and to come up and bear more speedily than by their natural course they do. We make them also by art greater much than their nature;

412

and their fruit greater and sweeter, and of differing taste, smell, colour, and figure, from their nature. And many of them we so order, as that they become of medicinal use.

"We have also means to make divers plants rise by mixtures of earths without seeds, and likewise to make divers new plants, differing from the vulgar, and to make one tree or plant turn into another.

"We have also parks, and enclosures of all sorts, of beasts and birds; which we use not only for view or rareness, but likewise for dissections and trials, that thereby we may take light what may be wrought upon the body of man. Wherein we find many strange effects: as continuing life in them, though divers parts, which you account vital, be perished and taken forth; resuscitating of some that seem dead in appearance, and the like. We try also all poisons and other medicines upon them, as well of chirurgery as physic. By art likewise we make them greater or smaller than their kind is, and contrariwise dwarf them and stay their growth; we make them more fruitful and bearing than their kind is, and contrariwise barren and not generative. Also we make them differ in colour, shape, activity, many ways. We find means to make commixtures and copulations of divers kinds, which have produced many new kinds, and them not barren, as the general opinion is. We make a number of kinds of serpents, worms, flies, fishes, of putrefaction, whereof some are advanced (in effect) to be perfect creatures, like beasts or birds, and have sexes, and do propagate. Neither do we this by chance, but we know beforehand of what matter and commixture what kind of those creatures will arise.

"We have also particular pools where we make trials upon fishes, as we have said before of beasts and birds.

"We have also places for breed and generation of those kinds of worms and flies which are of special use; such as are with you your silkworms and bees.

"I will not hold you long with recounting of our brewhouses, bakehouses, and kitchens, where are made divers drinks, breads, and meats, rare and of special effects. Wines we have of grapes, and drinks of other juice, of fruits, of grains, and of roots, and of mixtures with honey, sugar, manna, and fruits dried and decocted; also of the tears or woundings of trees, and of the pulp of canes. And these drinks are of several ages, some to the age or last of forty years. We have drinks also brewed with several herbs, and roots, and spices; yea, with several fleshes, and white meats; whereof some of the drinks are such as they are in effect meat and drink both, so that divers, especially in age, do desire to live with them with little or no meat or bread. And above all we strive to have drinks of extreme thin parts, to insinuate into the body,

413

and yet without all biting, sharpness, or fretting; insomuch as some of them, put upon the back of your hand, will with a little stay pass through to the palm, and yet taste mild to the mouth. We have also waters, which we ripen in that fashion, as they become nourishing, so that they are indeed excellent drink, and many will use no other. Breads we have of several grains, roots, and kernels; yea, and some of flesh and fish dried; with divers kinds of leavenings and seasonings; so that some do extremely move appetites, some do nourish so as divers do live of them, without any other meat, who live very long. So for meats, we have some of them so beaten, and made tender, and mortified, yet without all corrupting, as a weak heat of the stomach will turn them into good chylus, as well as a strong heat would meat otherwise prepared. We have some meats also and bread and drinks, which taken by men, enable them to fast long after; and some other, that, used, make the very flesh of men's bodies sensibly more hard and tough, and their strength far greater than otherwise it would be.

"We have dispensatories or shops of medicines; wherein you may easily think, if we have such variety of plants and living creatures more than you have in Europe (for we know what you have), the simples, drugs, and ingredients of medicines must likewise be in so much the greater variety. We have them likewise of divers ages and long fermentations. And for their preparations, we have not only all manner of exquisite distillations, and separations, and especially by gentle heats and percolations through divers strainers, yea, and substances; but also exact forms of composition, whereby they incorporate almost as they were natural simples.

"We have also divers mechanical arts, which you have not; and stuffs made by them, as papers, linen, silks, tissues, dainty works of feathers of wonderful lustre, excellent dyes, and many others, and shops likewise as well for such as are not brought into vulgar use amongst us, as for those that are. For you must know that, of the things before recited, many of them are grown into use throughout the kingdom; but yet, if they did flow from our invention, we have of them also for patterns and principals.

"We have also furnaces of great diversities, and that keep great diversity of heats; fierce and quick, strong and constant, soft and mild, blown, quiet, dry, moist, and the like. But above all we have heats in imitation of the sun's and heavenly bodies' heats, that pass divers inequalities and as it were orbs, progresses, and returns, whereby we produce admirable effects. Besides, we have heats of dungs, and of bellies and maws of living creatures and of their bloods and bodies, and of hays and herbs laid up moist, of lime unquenched, and such like. Instruments also which generate heat only by motion. And further, places for strong insolations; and again, places under the earth, which by nature or art yield heat. These divers heats we use as the nature of the operation which we intend requireth.

"We have also perspective houses, where we make demonstrations of all lights and radiations, and of all colours; and out of things uncoloured and transparent we can represent unto you all several colours, not in rainbows, as it is in gems and prisms, but of themselves single. We represent also all multiplications of light, which we carry to great distance, and make so sharp as to discern small points and lines. Also all colorations of light: all delusions and deceits of the sight, in figures, magnitudes, motions, colours; all demonstrations of shadows. We find also divers means, yet unknown to you, of producing of light, originally from divers bodies. We procure means of seeing objects afar off, as in the heaven and remote places; and represent things near as afar off, and things afar off as near; making feigned distances. We have also helps for the sight, far above spectacles and glasses in use; we have also glasses and means to see small and minute bodies perfectly and distinctly; as the shapes and colours of small flies and worms, grains, and flaws in gems which cannot otherwise be seen, observations in urine and blood not otherwise to be seen. We make artificial rainbows, halos, and circles about light. We represent also all manner of reflections, refractions, and multiplications of visual beams of objects.

"We have also precious stones of all kinds, many of them of great beauty and to you unknown; crystals likewise, and glasses of divers kinds; and amongst them some of metals vitrificated, and other materials, besides those of which you make glass. Also a number of fossils and imperfect minerals, which you have not. Likewise loadstones of prodigious virtue: and other rare stones, both natural and artificial.

"We have also sound-houses, where we practise and demonstrate all sounds and their generation. We have harmony which you have not, of quarter-sounds and lesser slides of sounds. Divers instruments of music likewise to you unknown, some sweeter than any you have; with bells and rings that are dainty and sweet. We represent small sounds as great and deep, likewise great sounds extenuate and sharp; we make divers tremblings and warblings of sounds, which in their original are entire. We represent and imitate all articulate sounds and letters, and the voices and notes of beasts and birds. We have certain helps which, set to the ear, do further the hearing greatly; we have also divers strange and artificial echoes, reflecting the voice many times, and as it were tossing it; and some that give back the voice louder than it came, some shriller and some deeper; yea, some rendering the voice differing in the letters of articulate sound from that they receive. We have all means to convey sounds in trunks and pipes, in strange lines and distances.

415

"We have also perfume-houses, wherewith we join also practices of taste. We multiply smells, which may seem strange: we imitate smells, making all smells to breathe out of other mixtures than those that give them. We make divers imitations of taste likewise, so that they will deceive any man's taste. And in this house we contain also a confiture-house, where we make all sweetmeats, dry and moist, and divers pleasant wines, milks, broths, and salads, far in greater variety than you have.

"We have also engine-houses, where are prepared engines and instruments for all sorts of motions. There we imitate and practise to make swifter motions than any you have, either out of your muskets or any engine that you have; and to make them and multiply them more easily and with small force, by wheels and other means, and to make them stronger and more violent than yours are, exceeding your greatest cannons and basilisks. We represent also ordnance and instruments of war and engines of all kinds; and likewise new mixtures and compositions of gunpowder, wildfires burning in water and unquenchable; also fireworks of all variety, both for pleasure and use. We imitate also flights of birds; we have some degrees of flying in the air. We have ships and boats for going under water and brooking of seas, also swimming-girdles and supporters. We have divers curious clocks, and other like motions of return, and some perpetual motions. We imitate also motions of living creatures by images of men, beasts, birds, fishes, and serpents; we have also a great number of other various motions, strange for equality, fineness and subtilty.

"We have also a mathematical-house, where are represented all instruments, as well of geometry as astronomy, exquisitely made.

"We have also houses of deceits of the senses, where we represent all manner of feats of juggling, false apparitions, impostures and illusions, and their fallacies. And surely you will easily believe that we, that have so many things truly natural which induce admiration, could in a world of particulars deceive the senses, if we would disguise those things and labour to make them more miraculous. But we do hate all impostures and lies, insomuch as we have severely forbidden it to all our fellows, under pain of ignominy and fines, that they do not show any natural work or thing adorned or swelling, but only pure as it is, and without all affectation of strangeness.

"These are, my son, the riches of Salomon's House.

"For the several employments and offices of our fellows, we have twelve that sail into foreign countries under the names of other nations (for our own we conceal), who bring us the books and abstracts, and patterns of experiments of all other parts. These we call merchants of light.

"We have three that collect the experiments which are in all books. These we call depredators.

"We have three that collect the experiments of all mechanical arts, and also of liberal sciences, and also of practices which are not brought into arts. These we call mystery-men.

"We have three that try new experiments, such as themselves think good. These we call pioneers or miners.

"We have three that draw the experiments of the former four into titles and tables, to give the better light for the drawing of observations and axioms out of them. These we call compilers. We have three that bend themselves, looking into the experiments of their fellows, and cast about how to draw out of them things of use and practice for men's life and knowledge, as well for works as for plain demonstration of causes, means of natural divinations, and the easy and clear discovery of the virtue and parts of bodies. These we call dowrymen or benefactors.

"Then, after divers meetings and consults of our whole number, to consider of the former labours and collections, we have three that take care out of them to direct new experiments, of a higher light, more penetrating into Nature than the former. These we call lamps.

"We have three others that do execute the experiments so directed, and report them. These we call inoculators.

"Lastly, we have three that raise the former discoveries by experiments into greater observations, axioms, and aphorisms. These we call interpreters of Nature.

"We have also, as you must think, novices and apprentices, that the succession of the former employed men do not fail; besides a great number of servants and attendants, men and women. And this we do also: we have consultations, which of the inventions and experiences which we have discovered shall be published, and which not: and take all an oath of secrecy for the concealing of those which we think fit to keep secret: though some of those we do reveal sometimes to the State, and some not.

"For our ordinances and rites we have two very long and fair galleries: in one of these we place patterns and samples of all manner of the more rare and excellent inventions; in the other we place the statues of all principal inventors. There we have the statue of your Columbus, that discovered the West Indies: also the inventor of ships: your monk that was the inventor of ordnance and of gunpowder: the inventor of music: the inventor of letters: the inventor of printing: the inventor of observations of astronomy: the inventor of works in metal: the inventor of glass: the inventor of silk of the worm: the inventor of wine: the inventor of corn and bread: the inventor of sugars; and all these by more certain tradition than you have. Then we have divers inventors of our own of excellent works; which since you have not seen, it were too long to make descriptions of them; and besides, in the right understanding of those descriptions you might easily err. For upon every invention of value we erect a statue to the inventor, and give him a liberal and honourable reward. These statues are some of brass, some of marble and touchstone, some of cedar and other special woods gilt and adorned; some of iron, some of silver, some of gold.

"We have certain hymns and services, which we say daily, of laud and thanks to God for His marvellous works. And forms of prayers, imploring His aid and blessing for the illumination of our labours; and turning them into good and holy uses.

"Lastly, we have circuits or visits of divers principal cities of the kingdom; where, as it cometh to pass, we do publish such new profitable inventions as we think good. And we do also declare natural divinations of diseases, plagues, swarms of hurtful creatures, scarcity, tempest, earthquakes, great inundations, comets, temperature of the year, and divers other things; and we give counsel thereupon, what the people shall do for the prevention and remedy of them."

And when he[3] had said this, he stood up; and I, as I had been taught, knelt down; and he laid his right hand upon my head, and said, "God bless thee, my son, and God bless this relation which I have made. I give thee leave to publish it for the good of other nations; for we here are in God's bosom, a land unknown." And so he left me, having assigned a value of about two thousand ducats for a bounty to me and my fellows. For they give great largesses, where they come, upon all occasions.

[3]The account was given by one of the fathers of Salomon's House.

THE METHOD OF SCIENTIFIC
INVESTIGATION[1]

Thomas Henry Huxley

THE method of scientific investigation is nothing but the expression of the necessary mode of working of the human mind. It is simply the mode at which all phenomena are reasoned about, rendered precise and exact. There is no more difference, but there is just the same kind of difference, between the mental operations of a man of science and those of an ordinary person, as there is between the operations and methods of a baker or of a butcher weighing out his goods in common scales, and the operations of a chemist in performing a difficult and complex analysis by means of his balance and finely graduated weights. It is not that the action of the scales in the one case, and the balance in the other, differ in the principles of their construction or manner of working; but the beam of one is set on an infinitely finer axis than the other, and of course turns by the addition of a much smaller weight.

You will understand this better, perhaps, if I give you some familiar example. You have all heard it repeated, I dare say, that men of science work by means of induction and deduction, and that by the help of these operations, they, in a sort of sense, wring from Nature certain other things, which are called natural laws, and causes, and that out of these, by some cunning skill of their own, they build up hypotheses and theories. And it is imagined by many, that the operations of the common mind can be by no means compared with these processes, and that they have to be acquired by a sort of special apprenticeship to the craft. To hear all these large words, you would think that the mind of a man of science must be constituted differently from that of his fellow men; but if you will not be frightened by terms, you will discover that you are quite wrong, and that all these terrible apparatus are being used by yourselves every day and every hour of your lives.

There is a well-known incident in one of Molière's plays, where the author makes the hero express unbounded delight on being told that he had been talking prose during the whole of his life. In the same way, I trust, that you will take comfort, and be delighted with yourselves, on the discovery that you have been acting on the principles of inductive and deductive philosophy during the same period. Probably there is not one here who has not in the course of the day had occasion to set in motion a complex train of reasoning,

---

[1]From the third of six lectures given to workingmen by **Huxley** on *The Causes of the Phenomena of Organic Nature* (1863).

of the very same kind, though differing of course in degree, as that which a scientific man goes through in tracing the causes of natural phenomena.

A very trivial circumstance will serve to exemplify this. Suppose you go into a fruiterer's shop, wanting an apple,—you take up one, and, on biting it, you find it is sour; you look at it, and see that it is hard and green. You take up another one, and that too is hard, green, and sour. The shopman offers you a third; but, before biting it, you examine it, and find that it is hard and green, and you immediately say that you will not have it, as it must be sour, like those that you have already tried.

Nothing can be more simple than that, you think; but if you will take the trouble to analyse and trace out into its logical elements what has been done by the mind, you will be greatly surprised. In the first place, you have performed the operation of induction. You found that, in two experiences, hardness and greenness in apples went together with sourness. It was so in the first case, and it was confirmed by the second. True, it is a very small basis, but still it is enough to make an induction from; you generalise the facts, and you expect to find sourness in apples where you get hardness and greenness. You found upon that a general law, that all hard and green apples are sour; and that, so far as it goes, is a perfect induction. Well, having got your natural law in this way, when you are offered another apple which you find is hard and green, you say, "All hard and green apples are sour; this apple is hard and green, therefore this apple is sour." That train of reasoning is what logicians call a syllogism, and has all its various parts and terms,—its major premiss, its minor premiss, and its conclusion. And, by the help of further reasoning, which, if drawn out, would have to be exhibited in two or three other syllogisms, you arrive at your final determination, "I will not have that apple." So that, you see, you have, in the first place, established a law by induction, and upon that you have founded a deduction, and reasoned out the special conclusion of the particular case. Well now, suppose, having got your law, that at some time afterwards, you are discussing the qualities of apples with a friend: you will say to him, "It is a very curious thing,—but I find that all hard and green apples are sour!" Your friend says to you, "But how do you know that?" You at once reply, "Oh, because I have tried them over and over again, and have always found them to be so." Well, if we were talking science instead of common sense, we should call that an experimental verification. And, if still opposed, you go further, and say, "I have heard from the people in Somersetshire and Devonshire, where a large number of apples are grown, that they have observed the same thing. It is also found to be the case in Normandy, and in North America. In short, I find it to be the universal experience of mankind wherever attention has been directed to the subject."

Whereupon, your friend, unless he is a very unreasonable man, agrees with you, and is convinced that you are quite right in the conclusion you have drawn. He believes, although perhaps he does not know he believes it, that the more extensive verifications are,—that the more frequently experiments have been made, and results of the same kind arrived at,—that the more varied the conditions under which the same results are attained, the more certain is the ultimate conclusion, and he disputes the question no further. He sees that the experiment has been tried under all sorts of conditions, as to time, place, and people, with the same result; and he says with you, therefore, that the law you have laid down must be a good one, and he must believe it.

In science we do the same thing;—the philosopher exercises precisely the same faculties, though in a much more delicate manner. In scientific inquiry it becomes a matter of duty to expose a supposed law to every possible kind of verification, and to take care, moreover, that this is done intentionally, and not left to a mere accident, as in the case of the apples. And in science, as in common life, our confidence in a law is in exact proportion to the absence of variation in the result of our experimental verifications. For instance, if you let go your grasp of an article you may have in your hand, it will immediately fall to the ground. That is a very common verification of one of the best established laws of nature—that of gravitation. The method by which men of science establish the existence of that law is exactly the same as that by which we have established the trivial proposition about the sourness of hard and green apples. But we believe it in such an extensive, thorough, and unhesitating manner because the universal experience of mankind verifies it, and we can verify it ourselves at any time; and that is the strongest possible foundation on which any natural law can rest.

So much, then, by way of proof that the method of establishing laws in science is exactly the same as that pursued in common life. Let us now turn to another matter (though really it is but another phase of the same question), and that is, the method by which, from the relations of certain phenomena, we prove that some stand in the position of causes towards the others.

I want to put the case clearly before you, and I will therefore show you what I mean by another familiar example. I will suppose that one of you, on coming down in the morning to the parlour of your house, finds that a tea-pot and some spoons which had been left in the room on the previous evening are gone,—the window is open, and you observe the mark of a dirty hand on the window-frame, and perhaps, in addition to that, you notice the impress of a hob-nailed shoe on the gravel outside. All these phenomena have struck your attention instantly, and before two seconds have passed you say, "Oh, somebody has broken open the window, entered the room, and run off with the spoons and the tea-pot!" That speech is out of your mouth in a moment. And you will probably add, "I know there has; I am quite sure of it." You mean to say exactly what you know; but in reality you are giving expression to what is, in all essential particulars, an hypothesis. You do not know it at all; it is nothing but an hypothesis rapidly framed in your own mind. And it is an hypothesis founded on a long train of inductions and deductions.

What are those inductions and deductions, and how have you got at this hypothesis? You have observed in the first place, that the window is open; but by a train of reasoning involving many inductions and deductions, you have probably arrived long before at the general law—and a very good one it is—that windows do not open of themselves; and you therefore conclude that something has opened the window. A second general law that you have arrived at in the same way is, that tea-pots and spoons do not go out of a window spontaneously, and you are satisfied that, as they are not now where you left them, they have been removed. In the third place, you look at the marks on the window-sill, and the shoe-marks outside, and you say that in all previous experience the former kind of mark has never been produced by anything else but the hand of a human being; and the same experience shows that no other animal but man at present wears shoes with hob-nails in them such as would produce the marks in the gravel. I do not know, even if we could discover any of those "missing links" that are talked about, that they would help us to any other conclusion! At any rate the law which states our present experience is strong enough for my present purpose. You next reach the conclusion that, as these kinds of marks have not been left by any other animals than men, or are liable to be formed in any other way than by a man's hand and shoe, the marks in question have been formed by a man in that way. You have, further, a general law, founded on observation and experience, and that, too, is, I am sorry to say, a very universal and unimpeachable one,—that some men are thieves; and you assume at once from all these premises—and that is what constitutes your hypothesis—that the man who made the marks outside and on the window-sill, opened the window, got into the room, and stole your tea-pot and spoons. You have now arrived at a *vera causa*;—you have assumed a cause which, it is plain, is competent to produce all the phenomena you have observed. You can explain all these phenomena only by the hypothesis of a thief. But that is a hypothetical conclusion, of the justice of which you have no absolute proof at all; it is only rendered highly probable by a series of inductive and deductive reasonings.

I suppose your first action, assuming that you are a man of ordinary common sense, and that you have established this hypothesis to your own satisfaction, will very likely be to go off for the police, and set them on the track of the burglar, with the view to the recovery of your property. But just as you are starting with this object, some person comes in, and on learning what you are about, says, "My good friend, you are going on a great deal too fast. How do you know that the man who really made the marks took the spoons? It might have been a monkey that took them, and the man may have merely looked in afterwards." You would probably reply, "Well, that is all very well, but you see it is contrary to all experience of the way tea-pots and spoons are abstracted; so that, at any rate, your hypothesis is less probable than mine." While you are talking the thing over in this way, another friend arrives, one of that good kind of people that I was talking of a little while ago. And he might say, "Oh, my dear sir, you are certainly going on a great deal too fast. You are most presumptuous. You admit that all these occurrences took place when you were fast asleep, at a time when you could not possibly have known anything about what was taking place. How do you know that the laws of Nature are not suspended during the night? It may be that there has been some kind of supernatural interference in this case." In point of fact, he declares that your hypothesis is one of which you cannot at all demonstrate the truth, and that you are by no means sure that the laws of Nature are the same when you are asleep as when you are awake.

Well, now, you cannot at the moment answer that kind of reasoning. You feel that your worthy friend has you somewhat at a disadvantage. You will feel perfectly convinced in your own mind, however, that you are quite right, and you say to him, "My good friend, I can only be guided by the natural probabilities of the case, and if you will be kind enough to stand aside and permit me to pass, I will go and fetch the police." Well, we will suppose that your journey is successful, and that by good luck you meet with a policeman; that eventually the burglar is found with your property on his person, and the marks correspond to his hand and to his boots. Probably any jury would consider those facts a very good experimental verification of your hypothesis, touching the cause of the abnormal phenomena observed in your parlour, and would act accordingly.

Now, in this supposititious case, I have taken phenomena of a very common kind, in order that you might see what are the different steps in an ordinary process of reasoning, if you will only take the trouble to analyse it carefully. All the operations I have described, you will see, are involved in the mind of any man of sense in leading him to a conclusion as to the course he should take in order to make good a robbery and punish the offender. I say that you are led, in that case, to your conclusion by exactly the same train of reasoning as that which a man of science pursues when he is endeavouring to discover the origin and laws of the most occult phenomena. The process is, and always must be, the same; and precisely the same mode of reasoning was employed by Newton and Laplace in their endeavours to discover and define the causes of the movements of the heavenly bodies, as you, with your own common sense, would employ to detect a burglar. The only difference is, that the nature of the inquiry being more abstruse, every step has to be most carefully watched, so that there may not be a single crack or flaw in your hypothesis. A flaw or crack in many of the hypotheses of daily life may be of little or no moment as affecting the general correctness of the conclusions at which we may arrive; but, in a scientific inquiry, a fallacy, great or small, is always of importance, and is sure to be in the long run constantly productive of mischievous, if not fatal results.

Do not allow yourselves to be misled by the common notion that an hypothesis is untrustworthy simply because it is an hypothesis. It is often urged, in respect to some scientific conclusion, that, after all, it is only an hypothesis. But what more have we to guide us in nine-tenths of the most important affairs of daily life than hypotheses, and often very ill-based ones? So that in science, where the evidence of an hypothesis is subjected to the most rigid examination, we may rightly pursue the same course. You may have hypotheses, and hypotheses. A man may say, if he likes, that the moon is made of green cheese: that is an hypothesis. But another man, who has devoted a great deal of time and attention to the subject, and availed himself of the most powerful telescopes and the results of the observations of others, declares that in his opinion it is probably composed of materials very similar to those of which our own earth is made up: and that is also only an hypothesis. But I need not tell you that there is an enormous difference in the value of the two hypotheses. That one which is based on sound scientific knowledge is sure to have a corresponding value; and that which is a mere hasty random guess is likely to have but little value. Every great step in our progress in discovering causes has been made in exactly the same way as that which I have detailed to you. A person observing the occurrence of certain facts and phenomena asks, naturally enough, what process, what kind of operation known to occur in Nature applied to the particular case, will unravel and explain the mystery? Hence you have the scientific hypothesis; and its value will be proportionate to the care and completeness with which its basis had been tested and verified. It is in these matters as in the commonest affairs of practical life: the guess of the fool will be folly, while the guess of the wise man will contain wisdom. In all cases, you see that the value of the result depends on the patience and faithfulness with which the investigator applies to his hypothesis every possible kind of verification.

CAN SCIENCE POINT THE WAY?[1]

Arthur H. Compton

THE LABORATORY APPROACH TO LIFE

Around the white-haired wizard of Menlo Park were gathered hundreds of the leading citizens of his country, assembled to do him honor. Ether waves had brought messages from England and Germany. The President of the United States was speaking. Great as had been the influence of Thomas Edison's inventions in improving the lot of mankind, yet more significant was his introduction of the industrial research laboratory as an effective means of applying the powerful methods of science to man's immediate needs. Said President Hoover:

Scientific research means more than its practical results in living comfort. The future of the nation is not merely a question of the development of our industries and of reducing the cost of living or multiplying our harvests or even of larger leisure. We must constantly strengthen the fiber of national life by the inculcation of that veracity of thought which springs alone from the search for truth. From its pursuit we shall discover the unfolding of beauty, we shall stimulate the aspiration for knowledge, we shall ever widen human undertaking.

In considering the human value of science, we are accustomed to think of the great changes in man's attitude toward life. Increased knowledge has ushered man into a new world, with a challenge for him to shape his destiny on a more heroic scale. Can science go further and point the way man's greater life should follow?

It was in the effort to find man's place in nature and to lay a reliable basis for life that the first studies of science were undertaken. *Of what and how is the world made?* was the problem set by Thales. To him and his successors science was of value if it would enable men to find a more satisfactory way of life. Likewise Pythagoras, on the basis of his broad knowledge of the physical world, established a semireligious order whose aim it was to bring about the rule of reason and morality. This ambitious objective is as yet far from achievement. Nevertheless, the many benefits that have come through learning the laws of nature have had their effect in influencing men to organize their lives on the basis of tested truth.

It is frequently overlooked that the scientific approach to life has not always been acceptable to thinking men. There was the historic protest of Socrates against the science of the Atomists, which he felt destroyed the basis

[1]From *The Forum*, May, 1937.

of morality. In the hands of the Neo-Platonists this protest led to an anti-scientific philosophy which overwhelmed struggling Greek science and opened the way for the flood of oriental magic and mysticism which followed upon Alexander's conquests. Then came a thousand dark years during which credulity in all forms of magic and witchcraft prevailed. Man thought himself in a world governed by the whims of demons and angels.

Even more than to the Aristotelian philosophy of Thomas Aquinas we owe to physics and astronomy the rescue of Western civilization from these depths of superstition. Galileo's studies of dynamics as well as his telescope showed that facts were to be found by observing nature rather than by searching ancient writings. Newton's success in solving the riddle of the motion of planets established in men's minds the fact that we live in a world of law. Great improvements in our welfare have come through applications of the principles of science. It has thus become evident to all that if we wish to make the best of life we must learn nature's laws and use them as our guides.

Auguste Comte once remarked that there are three approaches to truth—the religious, the philosophical, and the scientific. Let us follow his suggestion and compare the expressions of initiators of thought in these three fields as they consider the principles on which men should organize their lives. For the religious approach we may consider some of Jesus' statements, as given in Goodspeed's translation of the Gospels of Luke and John:

See how the lilies grow. They do not toil or spin, but, I tell you, even Solomon in all his splendour was never dressed like one of them. But if God so dresses the wild grass, which is alive today and is thrown into the furnace tomorrow, how much more surely will he clothe you, who have so little faith? So you must not ask what you are to have to eat or drink, and you must not be anxious about it. . . . But you must strive to find his kingdom, and you will have these other things besides.

. . . .

I am the Way and Truth and Life. No one can come to the Father except through me. . . . It is he who has my commands and observes them that really loves me, and whoever loves me will be loved by my Father, and I will love him and show myself to him. . . . What I command you to do is to love one another.

Here we find the broadest of principles, the love of God and of one's fellowman, given to guide our way. There is little suggestion as to how this principle is to be applied, though Jesus indicates that it is sufficient, if faithfully followed, to gain the desired end of God's love.

Perhaps the best early discussion by a philosopher of the organization of society is that supplied in Plato's *Republic*. Let us follow Shorey's translation.

"Wise in very deed I think the city that we have described is, for it is well counselled, is it not?" "Yes." "And surely this very thing, good counsel, is a form of wisdom. For it is not by ignorance but by knowledge that men counsel well." "Obviously." "But there are many and manifold knowledges or sciences in the city." "Of course." "Is it then owing to the science of her carpenters that a city is to be called wise and well advised?" "By no means for that, but rather mistress of the arts of building." "Then a city is not to be styled wise because of the deliberations of the science of wooden utensils for their best production?" "No, I grant you." "Is it then because of the brass implements or any other of that kind?" "None whatsoever," he said. . . . "Then," said I, "is there any science in the city just founded by us residing in any of its citizens which does not take counsel about some particular thing in the city but about the city as a whole and the betterment of its relations with itself and other states?" "Why yes, there is." "What is it," I said, "and in whom is it found?" "It is the science of guardianship or government and it is to be found in those rulers to whom we just now gave the name of guardians in the full sense of the word."

There follows a discussion of the place of the brave soldiers and the sober artisans in the justly adjusted society. In Plato's mind it is, however, clear that the primary requirement of the ideal society is that its policies shall be determined by the wise ruler-philosophers.

A different emphasis is given by that practical statesman-philosopher, Francis Bacon, sometimes mistakenly called the father of modern science, as he describes the organization of the New Atlantis. The Good Jew is speaking:

Ye shall understand that amongst the excellent acts of that king, one above all hath the pre-eminence. It was the erection and institution of an Order or Society, which we call *Salomon's House*: the noblest foundation (as we think) that ever was on the earth; and the lanthorn of this kingdom. It is dedicated to the study of the works and creatures of God.

Second only to the king is the president of their university, known as the Father of Salomon's House, who continues the account:

The end of our foundation is the knowledge of causes, and secret motions of things; and the enlarging of the bounds of human empire, to the effecting of all things possible. . . .

We have large and various orchards and gardens, wherein we do not so much respect beauty, as variety of ground and soil, proper for divers trees and herbs. . . .

We have also glasses and means to see small and minute bodies perfectly and distinctly; as in the shapes and colours of small flies and worms, grains, observations in urine and blood not otherwise to be seen. . . . [Such as] these are . . . the riches of Salomon's House. . . .

427

We have consultations, which of the inventions and experiences which we have discovered shall be published and which not: and take all an oath of secrecy for the concealing of those which we see fit to keep secret; though some of those we do reveal to the state and some not.

If we view these three statements with the eye of a biologist, we see in each an effort of man to adjust himself more satisfactorily to his surroundings. The scientist sees the possibility through increased knowledge of the laws of nature to increase man's powers, "enlarging the bounds of human empire," thus giving to man a fuller life. The philosopher would find Utopia in a world whose civic life is suitably organized. The religionist sees in the social attitude of each individual toward his neighbor the fundamental problem of human ecology. The question of the means of living is to religion of negligible importance, to philosophy of secondary interest, and to practical science occupies the center of the stage. As we view the social changes that have resulted from the technical application of science, we see that these are more profound and probably more permanent than those which have resulted from changes in our method of government. Yet, as the circle of our neighbors has extended from the house next door to the far corners of the earth, the need for adequate social attitudes if the human species is to thrive has become even more evident.

A common feature of these approaches to the human problem is their agreement as to the fundamental objective of life. The satisfaction of appetite and desire, the strife for preferment and fame are to religion of only temporary and illusory value. To the philosopher these goods are balanced by the equivalent pains of disappointment at failure to obtain one's objective and of disillusionment if one dwells on his successes. To the biologist these appetites and ambitions are of value if they lead the individual to act for the welfare of the human species but, if followed to its detriment, are unmitigated evils.

All are agreed, however, that life has an adequate and satisfying objective: the welfare of mankind. To religion this appears as the love of one's fellows. To the philosopher human values are the only true ones, from which humanism is the necessary deduction. The scientist sees that nature is not concerned with the individual but with the species. From the standpoint of evolution, all our effort to learn the laws of nature and use them to our advantage is an aspect of an organism's adapting itself to its environment. A species can thrive only in so far as it is successful in making this adaptation. Biologically speaking, the good man is thus he who does his part in enabling his group to live successfully. Mankind the world over now forms, however, a biological unit. Thus science, with all the weight of its body of tested truth, re-emphasizes the conclusion of religion and philosophy: *The only adequate objective of man's life is the welfare of man.*

If the objective of life is thus agreed on, the study of the best procedure for approaching that objective is the peculiar field of applied science. Its noteworthy successes in meeting the practical needs of man in supplying the means of livelihood and living comfort and of improved health have given general confidence in the scientific method. Gradually its use is being extended into other fields.

In view of the unusual breadth of the problem now before us it will be well to consider what we mean by the scientific method. Francis Bacon, in his suggestion of "inductive" logic, outlines a procedure which, though it has been extensively used, is nevertheless of interest by way of contrast with that generally employed. Bacon proposed the accumulation of all the facts available, with the hope that from them it might be found possible to draw some generalization. The method almost universally used is to draw some carefully considered hypothesis on the basis of the known facts and seek for observations which will test the hypothesis. If no such test is possible, the hypothesis is scientifically useless. If the test is made, the hypothesis will be rejected, confirmed, or modified according as the results demand. The confirmed or modified hypothesis will then be subjected to further tests, until it is so well established that we can include it as a part of the organized body of tested truth which constitutes scientific knowledge.

The distinction between the scientific and the philosophical approach is illuminating. It is clear that philosophy, which concerns itself with all knowledge, must include science as one aspect. The distinctive feature of science is that it deals with aspects of knowledge which depend for their reliability on the test of experience, which in the natural sciences is usually an experiment devised for the purpose. Science differs in this way from logic, such as mathematics, whose validity is independent of such tests. Thus the formation of anatomic theory as compared with a continuum theory of matter is philosophical but is not scientific until the deductions from the alternative hypotheses can be tested. Similarly, Plato's philosophy of the organization of the state, according to which monarchy is preferable to a democracy, would become scientific if it were possible to set up two such states under controlled conditions and find which worked out more satisfactorily. The obvious difficulties of performing such an experiment show how the scientific method must be modified when applied to social problems.

In general it may be said that, if it makes any difference whether a statement is true or false, the statement is subject to test and may thus be approached, at least ideally, by the scientific method. The characteristic feature of science is thus that it approaches understanding by the cautious method of testing each step as it goes. It is for making such tests that exact, particular facts are needed. Occasionally these tests are inadequate, and mistakes are made. But it is evident that the procedure is much more reliable than if the tests were omitted.

In common with other types of philosophical thought, the very essence of science is the ideas which it embodies. At the early stage when a science is chiefly concerned with classification, these ideas may appear heterogeneous. When, however, the science becomes concerned with explanations and interpretations, the ideas become a closely knit and unified structure. Thus the sciences of heat and sound are incorporated within mechanics, and mechanics itself, as well as optics, have become aspects of electrodynamics. The dividing lines between physics, astronomy, and chemistry have completely disappeared, except for administrative purposes. Psychology calls on physiology and chemistry and itself becomes fundamental to sociology. Within its own domain of truth that can be tested it is thus as much the function of science as of philosophy to organize and to unify its knowledge. In fact, such unification is an important trend of present-day science.

When it comes to solving life's practical problems, science has its technique well developed. The general problem is split into specific problems, each of which is approached in the appropriate way. In the present case this means, first, finding the conditions on which man's welfare depends and, second, determining the most suitable methods for realizing those conditions.

Such questions as the provision of adequate food and shelter and of maintenance of health are demonstrably subject to effective scientific approach. The more human problem of enabling the individuals of a society to reach the best development of their various possibilities is an aspect of education, which involves aesthetic as well as quantitative factors and is an art as well as a science. Final solutions to such problems are never obtainable, because of the continually changing social conditions. Similarly the principles of a stable form of government best suited to man's welfare will always be difficult to establish on a scientific basis, because of the obvious difficulties of making adequate tests of proposed schemes. It is clear, however, that the continuous, active study of these problems by a group of unprejudiced and highly qualified investigators would supply a body of knowledge which would serve as an invaluable guide for the administrators who must determine the form of our society.

I have had a small share in the deliberations of a group of some hundreds of research men who are concerned with supplying this country with better light for less money. It is a profitable enterprise for the electrical industry. Near the campus of our university the meat packers' institute is helping to solve a specific aspect of our food problem. A recent census showed some 1,400 similar industrial research organizations actively at work in this country. Research centers, great and small, for finding methods for fighting disease are to be found.

But, as Plato asks, "Is it owing to the science of her carpenters that a city is to be called wise and well advised?" Would not the well-demonstrated effectiveness of these research institutes indicate the importance of a greater emphasis of the same method in connection with the more general aspects of the organization of our society? A few of our universities have research departments of education. There is a Brookings Institution for the study of economic and political problems. But the need is great.

In a recently published article I called attention to the fact that the United States occupies a central position regarding scientific development. In India it remains possible for a Gandhi to persuade his followers that the works of technology are harmful and should be kept out of their lives. The Oxford don may decry the dehumanizing influence of science, prefer a pen (though a fountain pen) to the typewriter, and walk rather than ride in a motorcar. The American, however, cannot question the value of science and technology. They are his very life. Railroads, automobiles, airplanes; agricultural machinery, mechanized meat packing, pasteurized milk; telephones, radios, movies; electric power—if these were gone he could not live. East or west, north or south, we move away from the center of this science-impregnated life.

In our universities, science and the freedom to study all subjects by the scientific method are assured without question. Here are welded more effective tools for the understanding, interpretation, and guidance of life. Where, then, if not toward America and especially toward her universities, can a scientifically minded world look for leadership? The application of the scientific method to basic human problems thus becomes our proper concern. It is one of the primary social responsibilities of our universities to find the fields where the search for truth will give returns of greatest human value. Where the scientific method is fruitful we must see that society is given full opportunity to gain and use such knowledge.

Would it be too much to suggest that each department of the government should have associated with it a permanent, nonpolitical group of investigators, who, acting in an advisory capacity, would keep the department administrators informed regarding possible and desirable courses of action? The effectiveness of organized research in opening the world to our understanding, in guiding the development of our great industries, and in shaping the attack on disease can leave no doubt about the value of such a measure. Industry cannot afford to operate without the advice of its research laboratories. Why not permanent institutes of government research?

The power of the scientific method is established. The procedure for its effective application is well understood. Utopia, as seen by Plato, was a world led by rulers guided by reliable knowledge. May we not find in a more adequate extension of the scientific study of human problems the way to approach that goal?

THE MYSTERY OF MATTER[1]

J. W. N. Sullivan

THE doctrine of Materialism, although often regarded as incredible, was not considered to be ambiguous. The statement that mind is a product of matter, although objected to as unlikely, was not objected to as indefinite. The two terms, mind and matter, were accepted as referring to two distinct entities. Indeed, it was the great distinction between the two entities which made the doctrine that one is a form of the other seem so very unlikely. We knew mind and we knew matter, and it is precisely because we knew them so well that we had the greatest difficulty in seeing any connection between them.

Nowadays the position is rather different. Mind is still, of course, the thing of which we have the most direct and intimate knowledge, but matter has become mysterious. The statement that mind is a product of matter is not the clear statement it once was. It may be true, but it is also very obscure. To say that something is 'material' is to say very little about it—it is not to explain it in terms of something more familiar than itself. For what, in the light of modern science, do we mean by 'material'? When we have explained everything in terms of matter, what precisely have we done? What is matter?

The scientific answer to this question is of very great interest, not only for what it tells us about matter, but for what it tells us about science.

It has always been recognized, of course, that there are different kinds of matter. The most cursory survey of the external world is sufficient to convince us of this. But the first step toward the modern scientific analysis of matter came with the discovery that all matter, of every kind, is atomic in constitution.

[1]From *The Atlantic Monthly*, May, 1936.

A piece of matter is not continuous; it cannot be divided indefinitely. It is composed of a host of separate little ultimate particles. This fact about matter is curious and interesting, but it is not in the least disturbing. It does nothing to alter our fundamental conception of that substantial familiar thing called matter. For the tiny ultimate particles were supposed to be, in all essentials, just like the pieces of matter we know. They were very much smaller, that is all. It is true that some scientific men surmised that this analysis was not final. It was surmised that atoms themselves were complicated bodies, composed, probably, of still smaller bodies. But there was nothing at all revolutionary in this speculation. The new idea was on exactly the same lines as the old one.

The experimental confirmation of this idea did, however, introduce a disturbing factor. The constituents of the atom, when discovered, were found to be electrified. They were very small and light—about two thousand times lighter than the lightest known atom—and they carried an electric charge. This was somewhat unexpected, but further investigation led to a far more unexpected result. These little particles were found to consist of nothing but electricity! Since all atoms are constituted of these electric charges, it follows that all matter is electricity. This discovery was a real shock to one's habitual conception of matter. For one thing, the cardinal property of matter, its substantiality, seemed to be dissolved away. Electricity had been classed as one of the 'imponderables,' like light and heat. How could such an entity form the familiar hard, resistant matter of experience? If it was indeed true that matter is merely electricity, then it would seem that there must be something illusory about our ordinary perceptions of matter. Thus our common-sense notions of matter received their first shock. It became evident that matter is not the simple, straightforward thing we had always supposed it to be. We saw that it was something more mysterious, more elusive, and we could only accommodate these new ideas by making our notion of matter more abstract.

The ordinary human mind advances only very slowly along the path of abstraction. It always dowers the new abstraction with as many concrete elements as it can possibly preserve. Thus the electric constituents of matter, which experiment had revealed, were conceived, as far as possible, in terms of familiar things. They were conceived, for instance, as particles—that is to say, they were supposed to occupy definite positions in space and to move from one definite position to another by definite paths. The mathematicians had shown that such particles, although composed purely of electricity, would be able to play the part of material particles in a sufficiently convincing way. Thus it was still possible to 'picture,' more or less, these ultimate constituents.

433

No intolerable strain had yet been placed on the pictorial imagination, so that the theory was still what is called 'intelligible.'

When the mathematicians came to work out this theory in more detail, however, the strain on the pictorial imagination was greatly increased. For it was found that every now and again these electric particles moved from one point to another without passing over the intermediate space. We could not suppose that they were annihilated at one point and re-created at another. We had to admit that these electric particles did not quite fit into the conceptions of space and time which man had hitherto developed. This meant, of course, that they were strictly non-picturable, since we can form no picture of anything except within a space-time framework. Certain picturable elements still remained, however. The two kinds of electric constituents of the atom (electrons and protons) were still conceived as particles. They were still supposed to have definite locations and to describe definite paths, although their singular manner of vanishing from one path and immediately appearing on another was admitted to be baffling. This picture of the atom—Bohr's picture—was not a perfectly clear and definite thing. Nevertheless, a good deal of successful work was done on the basis of it. It evidently corresponded, in certain important respects, to reality.

About ten years ago, however, the defects of this way of picturing the atom became very apparent. The experimentalists had obtained certain results which could not be accommodated, as it were, by the atomic model that Bohr had imagined. Now when a scientific theory, which has had a successful career, encounters recalcitrant facts, scientific men do not, as a rule, immediately abandon the theory, lock, stock, and barrel. They proceed to modify the theory, preserving its main lines as far as possible. That procedure was followed in this case. The effect was tried of complicating the Bohr theory, while still preserving the main conception of the atom as a collection of particles. Singularly enough, this procedure is hardly ever successful. No amount of tinkering with Newton's law of gravitation will give us Einstein's law. The ether theory of light, after its first brilliant successes, encountered difficulties. It was modified and complicated for generations, but it never became successful and is now abandoned. In these cases, as in others, it was found that the fundamental assumptions on which the theory rested were inadequate. No amount of tinkering with the superstructure was of any avail; it was the foundations that were at fault. And in this case of the atom we now realize that the pure particle conception will not do.

The new theory is described by the title, 'The Wave Theory of Matter.' The ultimate constituents of matter can, it appears, be represented as groups of waves. It might be thought that this change, although doubtless of great importance scientifically, does nothing to lessen the *picturability* of these ultimate constituents. We are familiar with waves as we are familiar with particles. Our pictorial imagination can form images of both these things. But can we unite these images? Can we picture an entity which is both a wave and a particle? It is here that the new experimental analysis of matter becomes so baffling.

If we take a sheet of glass and lightly powder it with zinc sulphide crystals and then bombard it with electrons, we shall find that scintillations appear irregularly all over it. Each electron, on striking the screen, causes a faint spark which can be seen in the dark by the help of a magnifying lens. The stream of electrons behaves like a shower of rain falling on the screen, each impact giving a tiny spark. Here electrons quite certainly behave as if they were little particles. Now consider another experiment. We know that X-rays are waves. They are of the same nature as light waves except that they are very much smaller. This fact is proved by passing X-rays through crystals and examining the patterns produced on a photographic plate. We get alternate dark and bright bands, the dark bands being produced by the crest of one wave coinciding with the trough of another, and the bright bands by the coincidence of two crests. Nothing but a wave motion can produce this phenomenon. It occurred to Professor G. P. Thomson to perform a similar experiment with electrons. Electrons have nothing like the penetrating power of X-rays, but Thomson succeeded in preparing sheets of gold leaf only about one millionth of an inch thick, and the electrons were fired through these. Circular bright and dark bands were produced, just as in the X-ray experiments. Here is a conclusive proof, therefore, that electrons are waves.

The fact that an electron behaves both as a particle and as a group of waves takes it right outside the pictorial imagination. We have seen that matter has shown a baffling, elusive tendency ever since the atom was first disintegrated. The electrons and protons that constitute it have never been really domesticated, as it were, by the scientific imagination. There has always been something odd and paradoxical about them. But for the purpose of forming a picture these oddities could be ignored, and they could be likened, more or less, to objects of our ordinary experience. We can do that no longer. The new discoveries show that the ultimate constituents of matter are like nothing we have ever known. As Eddington says, we can combine the words 'wave' and 'particle' in a word,—say, 'wavicle,'—but we cannot combine the ideas corresponding to them.

We have encountered similar difficulties in the phenomena of light. The wave theory of light has been very successful, and it is quite true that light does sometimes indubitably behave as a system of waves. At other times it as indubitably behaves as a flight of little bullets. We cannot picture to ourselves the sort of entity that can behave in this way. The theory that light exists in atomic form explains many things, yet here again questions arise which have no satisfactory answer. If we make experiments to determine the size of an atom of light,—its spatial dimensions,—we find that it is both big enough to fill the lens of the great Mount Wilson telescope and small enough to enter an atom. We can only conclude that the notion of spatial size does not apply to such an entity. It somehow transcends space. If this is so, then it follows, of course, that it is forever unpicturable.

Scientific men are pragmatists in practice, whatever they may think they are in theory, and they are quite prepared to work with conceptions they know to be partial provided they get results. Recently some very interesting and important experimental work has been done on the atom, although the precise nature of the natural processes involved is not yet fully understood. But whatever it may be that is really going on in the atom, these experimental results can be fairly well described on the basis of the 'particle' conception.

Until quite recently the atom was supposed to consist of two kinds of electric particles—the 'proton' and the 'electron.' The proton is a charge of what is called positive electricity and the electron is a charge of negative electricity. In any atom these charges are so arranged that they balance, which is why an atom normally seems to have no electric charge. All the protons of an atom are concentrated in its 'nucleus,' together with a smaller number of electrons. Thus the nucleus of an atom always has a resultant positive charge of electricity, since it contains more protons than electrons. This resultant charge is compensated for by electrons which circulate round the nucleus, very much as the planets circulate round the sun. This is the celebrated 'solar system' model of the atom. As we see, it assumes the 'particle' conception of the electron and proton. This picture is inadequate and if taken too seriously, can land us in difficulties. But, if we are not content merely with mathematical symbols, it is perhaps as good a picture as we can form. In its main lines it certainly accounts for a large number of experimental results. The main features of radium disintegration, for example, can be explained by it.

In a radium atom the nucleus is actually breaking up. It shoots out electrons and also a much heavier kind of particle called the Alpha particle. This particle consists of a combination of four protons and two electrons, bound together in some exceptionally stable way. As a proton weighs nearly two thousand times as much as an electron, we see that an Alpha particle is, comparatively speaking, a very massive affair. It occurred to Lord Rutherford, some years ago, to use these particles to bombard atoms. The idea was that every now and then an Alpha particle might score a direct hit on the nucleus of an atom and possibly disrupt it. Since all the chemical properties of an atom depend on the constitution of its nucleus, we should thus be able to change an atom of one substance into an atom of another substance. We should have achieved, in fact, the transmutation of the elements. The experiments were successful. Certain elements were transmuted into others.

Nowadays we are not confined, for our projectiles, to the Alpha particles shot out by radium. A hydrogen atom consists of one proton with one electron circulating round it. It is a comparatively easy matter, by passing an electric discharge through hydrogen gas at low pressure, to strip the hydrogen atoms of their circulating electrons, and thus to obtain a supply of protons. If these protons are now subjected to an intense electric field,—something on the order of a million volts,—they can be made to acquire very great velocities. They can thus be used as artificially produced projectiles for atom bombardment. It is found that these projectiles disrupt atoms on which Alpha particles have no effect. It is a usual rule that, under Alpha particle bombardment, atoms release protons, whereas under proton bombardment they release Alpha particles. It is not a question of the bombarding particle *knocking* something out of the atom. It is rather that it sets up a disturbance in the atom and releases intense innate forces, for the energy of the particle emitted by the atom is altogether greater than the energy of the bombarding particle.

This is, in fact, a way of tapping the huge inner stores of atomic energy. But it is not in the least a practical method at present. In these bombardment experiments only one particle in many thousands, or millions, scores a direct hit. The energy obtained in this way is only a very minute percentage of the energy expended. Nevertheless, the point has been made that the atom can be artificially disintegrated and its inner store of energy partially released.

These results by no means exhaust the experimental discoveries which have been recently made in this field. We have said that an atom is built up of two sorts of entities, protons and electrons. We now know that these are not the only entities concerned. A positively charged electric particle has been found which is altogether different from the proton. It has the same electric charge as a proton, but it is very much lighter, being, in fact, of the same weight as an electron. It is called a 'positron.' It is a very evanescent entity, for its life is about one thousand-millionth of a second. At the end of that time it combines with an electron and the two vanish in a flash of radiation.

In modern experiments a positron has been caused to travel about a yard during its short life and to register its passage on a photographic plate. Years before its discovery, mathematical reasoning indicated its existence, but on such queer grounds that very few people could take it quite seriously. The mathematical researches of Dirac, who is the greatest of the British mathematical physicists, led to the conception that there are 'holes' in the universe destined for the reception of electrons. Most of such holes are already occupied, and the electrons occupying them cannot reveal their presence in any way. In time all the holes will be occupied, and that will mean the end of the material universe. In the meantime the unoccupied holes, surrounded by electrons already placed, manifest as positive charges, since they attract electrons. And these positive charges could not be of the dimensions of a proton, the only elementary positive charge known to exist; they must be of the dimensions of an electron.

It might have been supposed that this queer theory was merely a wild flight of fancy. But the actual discovery of the positron shows that it must be taken seriously. Indeed, the scientific analysis of matter has revealed it as so mysterious an entity that only the greatest efforts of the creative imagination, the greatest feats of abstraction, are now able to deal with it.

Another entity which has recently been discovered is the 'neutron.' When the element beryllium was bombarded by Alpha particles it was found to shoot out extremely penetrating rays. It was at first thought that these rays must be a sort of wave motion, like X-rays, as their penetrating power was much greater than that of any known type of particle. But calculations made on this supposition led to very unsatisfactory results. The nature of these rays was finally elucidated by Dr. James Chadwick, at Cambridge. He showed that they consist of a stream of 'neutrons,' each neutron being formed by a proton and an electron in very close combination. The electron and the proton are sufficiently close together to mask one another's electrical charge, so that the neutron does not appear to be electrically charged at all. From this fact comes its great penetrating power. It can pass through the atoms of matter without being deflected by their electric charges. This is not possible for such electric bodies as protons, for example, which can only penetrate a mere film of lead or a few centimetres of air. The neutrons from beryllium can penetrate several feet of lead and a mile of air.

The existence of these bodies raises various interesting speculations. Since they manifest no electric charge, it would be possible for them to come in actual contact with one another. Now the diameter of a neutron is only one hundred-thousandth part of that of an atom, and its mass is the same as that of hydrogen. Thus the density of a compact mass of neutrons would be enormous. A quart pot full of the stuff would weigh about one million million tons. We know of no material as dense as this anywhere in the universe. There are certain stars whose density is estimated to be one hundred thousand times that of water, and it may be that they contain some neutron material.

The existence of neutrons also makes it easier to conceive how complex atoms may have been built up from simpler ones. The nucleus of any complex atom contains many protons, and it is difficult to understand how random encounters could ever have brought them into such close proximity, considering the intense repulsive forces between them. But we can more easily imagine a number of neutrons collecting together, and their constituent protons and electrons, under the influence of some shock, forming the sort of combination we find in the nuclei of atoms. The existence of the neutron also throws light on the now well-known fact that a chemical element may have atoms of different weights. We used to be taught that the atoms of any chemical element were all of the same weight. That has been experimentally demonstrated to be untrue. In fact, the atoms of one and the same element may have quite a large range of different weights. Now the chemical properties of an atom, as we have said, depend on the electrical charge of its nucleus. Evidently the addition of a neutron to the nucleus does not affect the electric charge, since the neutron is electrically neutral. But it affects its weight. Thus those atoms which have the same chemical properties but are of different weights probably differ in the number of neutrons they contain.

Still another entity that has been recently discovered is 'heavy hydrogen,' or 'diplogen.' This is a form of hydrogen whose atoms are twice the weight of those of ordinary hydrogen. This discovery has been called the greatest American contribution to physical science since the Michelson-Morley experiment—the basis of the Theory of Relativity—of fifty years ago. The nucleus of an atom of this heavy hydrogen consists, not of one proton, as is the case with ordinary hydrogen, but of two protons and one electron. In any average specimen of hydrogen it is estimated that one atom out of every four or five thousand is of this heavy kind.

These heavy hydrogen atoms combine with oxygen, just as ordinary hydrogen atoms do, to form water. But the water so formed is rather heavier than ordinary water and has a higher freezing point and a higher boiling point. Also, it seems to be fatal to some forms of life that flourish in ordinary water. Seeds of the tobacco plant will not germinate in it, for example, although they develop well enough in ordinary water. Tadpoles of the green frog cannot live in it for more than an hour, and it kills the common aquarium fish in two hours. Researches on its influence on various forms of life are now being actively prosecuted. Various 'natural waters' are being analyzed to see if their properties depend at all on the amount of heavy water they may happen to contain. By the discovery of heavy hydrogen, therefore, a new field of inquiry has been opened up for the science of living things.

An even heavier form of hydrogen has been recently discovered, its atom having three protons and two electrons in its nucleus. It is possible, also, that there exist still other atomic entities. It seems likely, for instance, that there is an 'opposite' of the proton, just as the electron is the opposite of the positron.

So far we have been dealing with the experimental work that has been recently done on the atom, but the theoretical developments are not less interesting. In fact, they are even more interesting, for they seem to indicate a fundamental change in the attitude of science toward the problem of the external world. Our scientific knowledge, it is now realized, is subjective to an extent that we had not before suspected. We have already said that the 'particle' conception of matter is inadequate. It used to be thought that scientific analysis had shown that the material universe consisted of waves of radiation and of vast multitudes of electric particles. But we now know that to say the world is constituted in this way is to go beyond the evidence. This hypothesis does not enable us to account for the actual phenomena we observe. We should only be justified in saying that the world is constituted in this way if we could show that these particles, by obeying certain laws, would produce the facts of experience. And this is just what we cannot do. We have not succeeded in formulating a satisfactory set of laws on the basis of the particle conception. Our knowledge is not sufficiently definite, and there is good reason to suppose that it never can be sufficiently definite.

An electron, if it is conceived as a particle, must have at every moment a definite position and a definite velocity. But it appears to be impossible, in the nature of things, for us ever to have precise knowledge on these points. This is not due to the defects of our measuring apparatus. It is not an inability that could conceivably be overcome by technical improvements. It is due to the fact that nature is not the kind of thing that can be analyzed in that way. This doctrine, perhaps the most remarkable and far-reaching of all scientific doctrines, is called the Principle of Indeterminacy, or, sometimes, the Principle of Uncertainty. It states, in effect, that *exact* prediction in science is impossible. All our knowledge is knowledge of probabilities. We cannot say what *must* be, but only what the chances are that any one thing rather than any other shall happen.

What, then, becomes of the doctrine of strict cause and effect? Science has always assumed that all material processes are strictly determined, that all natural—or, at any rate, material—phenomena exemplify unambiguously the Reign of Law. We may not always know these laws, but it has not been doubted that the laws exist. The future, it has always been supposed, is the inevitable outcome of the present.

> Yea, the first Morning of Creation wrote
> What the Last Dawn of Reckoning shall read.

What is now the status of that belief? There is at present a great difference of opinion in the scientific world on this point. All are agreed that our present scientific knowledge is, in fact, a knowledge only of probabilities. But whether this is due to the limitations of science, or whether it is due to the fact that nature itself does not obey the law of strict cause and effect, is a question that is being hotly debated. Those who oppose the principle of determinism ask what reason, other than scientific evidence, we have for believing in it. We have no intuitive knowledge of it. Indeed, the thing we know most intimately, ourself, leads us to believe in the existence of free will. The idea that all our actions are strictly fated from the cradle to the grave has never been acceptable to the great bulk of mankind. We gave a grudging assent to its possibility because we thought that science had proved that determinism was triumphant in the external world, and we thought that what applied to matter might conceivably apply to man. But now that we know that science does not use the principle, and finds no evidence for it, why should we continue to believe in it? If we are to continue to believe in it, it must be on purely philosophical grounds. It may be that the purely philosophical arguments in its favor are convincing, but they can no longer invoke the prestige of science in their support.

Our scientific knowledge of the ultimate constituents of matter is partial knowledge. In tracing the position of an electron, for instance, we can say what the probabilities are that it is in one place rather than in some other place, and our knowledge of its motion can be represented by waves of probability. Sometimes the probability may be, as it were, diffused, so that the electron might be anywhere in a comparatively large volume. At other times the probability may be condensed, so that we can say definitely where the electron is. But in all cases our knowledge is probable knowledge. Whatever the objective reality may be, our knowledge of it is partial. In this sense, matter will always be mysterious.

CHEMISTRY ADVANCING[1]

George W. Gray

Ten thousand chemists gathered in New York in 1935 to celebrate the three-hundredth anniversary of the establishment of chemical industries on the American continent. It was, so statisticians said, the largest gathering of scientific workers ever assembled in the United States—and appropriately so, for chemistry is basic to our industrial civilization and the chemists constitute our largest group of technicians.

They are more than technicians. They are what some of us, more apt in phrase making than in quantitative analysis, are inclined to call doers of the impossible. For it is of the practical applications of chemistry, rather than of its theoretical principles and fundamental discoveries, that our thoughts first turn. We are still of a mind akin to that of old John Adams, in his address to practitioners of his day: "Chymists! Pursue your experiments with indefatigable ardour and perseverence. Give us the best possible Bread, Butter, and Cheese, Wine, Beer, and Cider, Houses, Ships and Steamboats, Gardens, Orchards, Fields, not to mention clothiers or cooks. If your investigations lead accidentally to any deep discovery, rejoice and cry 'Eureka!' But never institute any experiment with a view or hope of discovering the first and smallest particles of matter." One cannot say that the chemists have taken President Adams's oracular warning seriously. For while it is true that many of their deep discoveries have been hit upon by accident, it is also true that many more, and perhaps the most important discoveries, have been the rewards of planned expeditions into the realm of the first and smallest particles of matter. The three American scientists whose work has been recognized with a Nobel Prize in Chemistry each deliberately blazed a trail into the micro-cosmos: Theodore W. Richards, by his careful atomic weighing of elements; Irving Langmuir, by his exploration of the invisible flatland of monomolecular films; and Harold C. Urey, by his discovery of the double-weight hydrogen atom. Even so, it is the mundane tendency of the lay mind to evaluate the chemists for their practical achievements. We too subconsciously bracket them with clothiers and cooks. And also we are inclined to rate their bread, butter, and cheese above their protons, neutrons, and deuterons.

Perhaps this utilitarian attitude is the most instinctive approach to modern chemistry, even to its borderlands. The alchemy which fathered our science was a very utilitarian pursuit of two practical desires of mankind: first, the almagest, by which wealth might be attained from baser materials; and

[1]From *The Advancing Front of Science* by George W. Gray. McGraw-Hill Book Co., Inc., 1937.

second, the elixir of life, by which age and death might be defeated. In a certain sense these two pursuits are still dominant objectives of chemistry. In later chapters mention will be made of current work of the biochemists, and some accounting given of the modern search of the mystery of life, of aging, and of death. Here we shall dwell more particularly on the wealth winners; such realists as those who have snatched unwilling nitrogen out of the air to fertilize agricultural fields, those who have spun forests into fabrics finer than silk, those who have made rubber in a test tube without benefit of Brazil or the East Indies—to mention but three of the long roster of alchemical retrievers.

There is, for example, the incident of the floating laboratory. This was an old ship equipped with the necessary apparatus, manned with a staff of chemical engineers, and sent to prospect the ocean. For months at a time it was out there, pumping water through an ingenious chemical sieve, picking off certain preferred molecules from each gallon, and pouring the residue back into the ocean. At the end of their prospecting the sea miners had extracted a few hundred pounds of bromine at a cost of $500,000—which would seem to imply that bromine might be rated as a new substitute for gold.

But not so. Bromine is indispensable to the manufacture and use of no-knock gasoline; and because of the mounting demand of motorists for the improved fuel, it was necessary to look for new sources of supply. The old brine wells were failing, new ones were not being discovered, and in this dilemma the industrialists turned to that universal treasure trove, the sea, which contains all things in solution. Analysis shows that about seven millionths of each drop of sea water is bromine. But was chemistry able to extract so minute a fraction at a reasonable cost?

The floating laboratory and its prolonged experiment answered that question. Today a commercial plant for extracting bromine from the Atlantic Ocean is in operation on the North Carolina coast. It is turning out thousands of pounds a day. And since each cubic mile of sea water contains some 600,000 tons of the element, there is no danger of the factory ever being short of raw material.

This success suggests another question. Since the sea contains all things in solution, why not mine other substances too? Gold, for example, is selling for $35 an ounce, whereas bromine is quoted at less than 2 cents an ounce. Is there any gold in the sea?

Yes, and this North Carolina bromine plant has already extracted minute quantities of it and other precious metals. At a recent meeting of the American Chemical Society one of the engineers exhibited particles of pure gold and pure silver which had been taken from the flood of Atlantic water sluicing through the bromine extractors. The sea gold is dilute. A gallon of Atlantic water contains only one thirty-thousandth as much gold as it contains bromine, and of course the gold did not drop out of the water obligingly. It had to be captured by delicate processes which cost ten times the present market value of the gold. But the point is that the thing has been done—and what is done at great effort and expense now may be accomplished more easily and economically next time. Indeed, the chemist who attained this sea gold predicts that within our century we shall be mining the ocean for it on a commercial scale.

Getting a scarce product from a difficult source is one thing. Improving the product or making an entirely new one is another—and these doers of the impossible are versatile.

Take glass, for example. The very first characteristic of glass that occurs to you is its fragility. It is, traditionally, something to be handled with care. But in a research laboratory I saw a man tossing a glass lens into the air and allowing it to fall on a concrete floor. Indeed, the performance seemed to be a game to see how hard he could drop the glass. Repeatedly the lens fell from a height of 10 feet without even chipping. And this lens was not fabricated of thin laminated sections like an automobile windshield; nor was it reinforced by wires or any other mechanical aids. It was a solid piece of clear optical glass—tough glass that can be broken if you insist on it, but your blow must be thirteen times as great as that required to break a similar lens of ordinary glass.

The chemists make this tough glass by violating a long established rule of factory practice. The conventional idea is that after a piece of glass is poured or cast, it must be cooled slowly. But this tough glass gets no such babying. It is plunged from a heat of 1500° into a bath of oil at 400°, and by that sudden change of temperature the toughness is imparted. The exterior layer solidifies before the interior does; and in the slow contraction of the interior, tensions are set up which oppose and counterbalance exterior blows.

By another new process, glass is being spun into fibers soft as eider down. "Glass wool" is an old story, and has been used for many years as a packing for heat insulation and even woven into fabrics for hats, dresses, and scarfs; but this new fiber is glass in a new physical form, so fine that it is almost all surface, and yet so strong that it possesses a tensile strength approaching that of steel. The fibers are obtained by a process somewhat similar to that used in rayon manufacture—the molten glass is forced from tanks in fine filaments, the pressure being so great that the glass spurts out at a speed comparable to that of a rifle bullet. In addition to the customary uses of glass wool, many novel and indeed amazing applications of the new fiber are in process of development. It gives every promise of being a material with a future.

Glass suggests building materials. Glass brick and glass paneling and glass columns are now on the market, and houses with a wall or a roof of glass have been constructed. Chemists have added to glass the ability to filter the solar heat rays and transmit only the rays of light; so a glass house may be cool. And it may be proof against the stone thrower too, for toughness is not confined to optical glass. As a test a 3-ton truck was driven upon a 1-inch-thick sheet of this glass, a cable was passed about both, and the whole lifted high by a crane. The glass bent, but did not break.

Also just out of the laboratory are artificial stones and artificial woods made of waste, stainless metals made of new alloys, synthetic resins fashioned out of new chemical combinations. A typical example of the last named, and also of the skill of modern synthetic chemistry, is vinylite, developed at the Mellon Institute in Pittsburgh.

Visitors to the Century of Progress Exposition will remember the three-room apartment molded entirely of this new stuff out of a test tube: the floors of vinylite tiles, the walls of vinylite panels, the baseboards, sills, ceiling, all of the same; each door a single piece of vinylite, cast and pressed into shape; even the windows a translucent vinylite. More recently the applications of this material have been widely extended. It is possible to have whole tables, desks, chairs, chests, and other articles of furniture molded of one piece. And there are other plastics—some remarkably transparent like glass. The transparency of the new lucite, reports a chemist, "puts it on the same plane as quartz or the finest crystal." Some of these clear unbreakable glass-like plastics are lightweight, suggesting their adaptability for airplanes, automobiles, railway coaches, and other places where ruggedness and light weight are esteemed.

One of the objectives of modern chemical research is a cheap method of processing common clay for aluminum. Our present source of supply for this metal is bauxite ore, the deposits of which are closely held. But aluminum is one of the most abundant elements in the Earth; it is found in ordinary clay, which is widely distributed; and the unlocking of that plenteous source should make the metal cheaper. Then we may expect a rapid multiplication of its uses, which already are legion.

Aluminum of itself is relatively soft, but when alloyed with small proportions of other metals it becomes extremely hard and durable. These alloys, which received their first substantial encouragement from the aeronautical

445

designers, are now stepping over the lines into all sorts of industries. Factories have discovered that the heavier a crane is in proportion to its strength, the less load it can carry—so they are making giant cranes of aluminum alloy. And those swift streamlined passenger trains! They can be credited to the chemist's crucible quite as much as to the engineer's slide rule, for there is hardly a material in the new trains which did not come out of recent research. Locomotive parts are being built of lightweight alloys. One train of three cars weighs no more than a single Pullman car of the old all-steel construction.

Alloys in bewildering variety are on the horizon, and metals that were laboratory curiosities a few years ago are rapidly coming into useful service. Cadmium is threatening the supremacy of zinc. And also titanium—its pigments are taking the place of the familiar zinc in paints and rubber. The little known metal indium is substituting for silver as a mirror material. Tantalum, gallium, and germanium are making important beginnings in industrial applications, and in another 10 years these rarities will be commonplaces. The metal sodium (an ingredient of common salt) is a better conductor of electricity than copper—and the electrochemists are playing with that fact in researches that may prove revolutionary. Recent discoveries of the properties of skins of metals have given the chemist new and powerful means of adding durability, protecting against corrosion, and testing for invisible flaws. Surface effects of magnetism, X-ray reflections, and spectroscopic analysis have become tools of the metallurgist in applying the chemistry of metals to the multiplying uses of our age of speed.

But our age of speed glides forward not only on the new alloys, but also on the new fuels which chemists are obtaining from coal, petroleum, and wood. The process of cracking the heavy oils and other residue of petroleum, after the normal stores of gas and gasoline are extracted, is adding many millions of barrels of fuel to our use. In the cracking stills, the heavy residue (material that in other days had to be disposed of as waste) is subjected to high temperature and enormous pressure. The combined effect is to "crack" the large molecules into smaller ones, and some of the small molecules turn out to be gasoline, others to be a fine grade of furnace oil, others to be gas. By distillation each of these products is separated out, including not only fuels but other molecular structures which form the raw material for synthetic processes of making alcohol, lacquers, plastics, and rubber substitutes.

By another process or series of processes, which the chemists call polymerization, combustible gases are caused to combine into molecules of gasoline. And this synthetic gasoline is so uniform chemically, its molecules are so nearly the same throughout in structure and energy content, that the control of combustion in engine cylinders is greatly enhanced over that of the old natural gasolines. This enhanced control makes possible important improvements in power output and fuel economy. Since the raw materials of the polymerization processes are the gases which are yielded up as by-products of the cracking process and the dissolved gases derived from crude oil, natural gasoline, and natural gas industries, the new techniques of the polymerizers are powerful factors in getting more and more gasoline from our present raw materials. Recent estimates by Gustav Egloff suggest that 9000 million additional gallons of American gasoline can be obtained annually through these means. Therefore the new techniques are to be hailed as agencies of conservation.

The transformation of coal into gasoline—a process which is now operated on an industrial basis in Germany—was demonstrated in the United States in 1936 at the Bureau of Mines in Pittsburgh. Here, in a small experimental plant, powdered coal is treated to high pressures and high temperatures and exposed to hydrogen gas. In the mauling and mixing of the molecules some of the hydrogen atoms combine with the hydrocarbons of the coal to form the larger molecules of fuel oil, gasoline, or gas—for it is possible, by varying the treatment to transmute the coal into any selected one or more of several products. Hydrogenation, as the process is called, is more costly than our present processes of refining crude oil and cracking its residues; and there is no call for coal hydrogenation in the present stage of American economy. But the Bureau of Mines looks ahead to the approaching exhaustion of the petroleum reserves. Some authorities estimate that by the early 1950's the underground pools, which made North America the greatest petroleum producer, will have been exploited to the limit of economical extraction. Then the automobiles, airplanes, and other vehicles and utilities powered by explosive motors will have to look to other sources for fuel. The coal fields of the United States are many times more prolific than the petroleum fields. A. C. Fielder recently computed that if all the present proved petroleum supplies of the United States were spread over the state of Ohio they would cover its 41,000 square miles to a depth of $\frac{3}{4}$ inch; but if all the coal deposits were similarly distributed over the same area they would make a layer 76 feet deep. There is fuel here for hundreds of years of accelerating industrialism.

Frederich Bergius, the German chemist who developed the hydrogenation process of converting coal into oil, is also author of a process of converting wood into food. Dr. Bergius's method rests on an earlier discovery by two other German experimenters, Willstätter and Zechmeister, who found that the cellulose extracted from wood will completely dissolve if submerged in a strong solution of hydrochloric acid, and that while in this solution the cellulose "transforms" 100 per cent into glucose sugar. What happens in the

447

fluid is the merging of one molecule of water with one molecule of cellulose, the sum of the two being sugar; and because of this the process is called wood hydrolysis. But cellulose is only one ingredient of wood, and to separate it from the hemicelluloses, lignin, and other constituents of raw timber involves a costly preliminary process. The great achievement of Bergius is the application of the process to raw timber. The log ends and other refuse of logging, the sawdust, slabs, shavings, and other wastes of the lumber mill, whole trees or parts of trees as may be available, all are grist for Bergius's chemical mill. It converts the wood into digestible carbohydrates of the sugar type, to the extent of from 60 to 65 per cent, and even the fibrous residue is material for charcoal, wallboard, and other by-products. But the food derivatives are the prime objective, of course, and from the simple sugarlike products other foodstuffs may be obtained.

Thus, "the carbohydrates consumed by pigs will form fat," points out Dr. Bergius. "With a suitable yeast, protein can be produced from hydrolized wood solution. Crystallized glucose produced from the wood can supply a considerable amount of edible carbohydrates necessary for nutrition. In other words, it is possible to produce practically all the fundamental elements of nutrition from waste wood. This can be done without reducing the forest reserves, because the waste of the lumber production can supply enormous quantities of raw material for wood hydrolization. The process is not only suited to supply foodstuffs to countries lacking such, but also gives an opportunity to turn a waste product into something useful."

Here is an even more adept chemistry than that of the Brobdingnagians who made two blades of grass to grow where only one grew before. Nor is it only a project, a prospectus of possibilities: it has been done, and is in practical use today.

The achievements in fundamental chemical research are not so obvious as are the applications wrought in the industrial laboratories; they are not expressible in terms of added conveniences or lowered costs or utilized wastes, but I assure you they are pre-eminently important to the future of mankind—that is, if we may judge the future by the past. The very foundations of thought are in process of change. America is contributing to this revolution. The fact that twice within the 1930's the Nobel Prize in Chemistry has been awarded to a citizen of the United States is fairly circumstantial evidence that the science is alive and fructifying on these shores. Science is international, and planetary rather than continental, and I would not inject into this account any specious parochialism. But too long the chemical researchers within the United States have appeared to be preoccupied with profitable applications, and it is worth noting that fundamental discoveries are now increasingly rewarding seekers who "have no time to make money." Nor do the fundamental finds remain merely interesting curiosities very long. A recent *Industrial Bulletin* of Arthur D. Little, Inc., calls attention to the fact that heavy hydrogen, a discovery of 1931, has already shown a quality foreshadowing important industrial uses. The energy density of this rare variety of hydrogen, it seems, is enormously great. With this gas, jets of such high velocity are produced that the energy available in 1 pound of heavy hydrogen, and attributable to the speed alone, is equal to that obtainable from the combustion of 5 million pounds of coal.

Heavy hydrogen and its consequence, heavy water, are only the headliners among a horde of isotopes and compounds recently turned up in the pursuit of knowledge for its own sake. And these pioneering chemists—many of them mere youths in their twenties and thirties—are pressing the merger of physics and chemistry closer and ever closer with their applications of the new-found principles to chemical practice. We are coming into a new technique, the so-called quantum chemistry. Here chemistry emerges from the hit-or-miss of an empirical science to the attainment of a reasoned logic in which properties and behaviors are calculated and predicted. This new chemical competence rests on the surer knowledge of atomic structures and forces which recent research has brought, enabling the chemist to foresee not only the possible combinations, but also the speed and order with which the reactions will occur.

Let us consider the item of speed. Life itself is one phase of this engaging question, as the Princeton chemist Henry Eyring has pointed out, and I am quoting from a recent paper of his to illuminate our curiosity about chemical speed. "For molecules to combine to form new ones, they must collide with catastrophic violence," says Dr. Eyring. "The atoms in the two colliding molecules must approach so closely that they no longer know whether they are bound to the new or the old atoms. For convenience, this is known as the activated state. If these violent encounters occur once in every million million collisions, an experimental chemist will be unable to distinguish between this rate and reaction on every collision. He will simply say in either case that the reaction goes immeasurably fast. By cooling his vessel he slows down all the molecules and can so cut down his rate to something measurable. Thus, simply by observing how a chemical reaction changes with temperature, he can tell you how violent a collision must be in a particular case to cause reaction; but, until the last 3 or 4 years, he could not even guess how violent a new type of collision must be to bring about a reaction. This the quantum mechanics has completely changed. He can now calculate, as accurately as he pleases, how energetic a collision must be to cause chemical change, and, therefore, at what temperature it has a measurable rate. Moreover, approximate calculations, which are simply made, frequently tell him which of two reactions will go the faster. This is a type of question which to answer experimentally frequently requires a great amount of time and great expenditures of money. For the exact calculations one needs no other data than the laws of quantum mechanics and the fact that one is dealing with a certain set of charged particles, and all the physical and chemical properties emerge as a matter of course."

This new precision seems very far removed from that chemical pioneering of 300 years ago. It was in 1635 that the science obtained its first foothold in the New World. In that year John Winthrop, Jr., a young alchemist of the Massachusetts Bay Colony, visited England and obtained from the Crown a commission to develop certain native mineral resources. He was interested in the production of copper, glass, iron, lead, tar, and other "chymicals" including medicines—no mere dreamer, this alchemist! The Royal Society later asked him to see if the grain, American maize, would produce beer. Winthrop tried it and brewed a "pale, well-tasted middle beer." He even did research on cornstalks and found that they yielded "syrup sweet as sugar"—a foretaste of the extensive corn-syrup industry of today.

Winthrop's projects were primitive, his incentives appear to have been wholly commercial, his research strictly industrial. There was, in the year of his commission, not a college or university, not a laboratory or other scientific institution of any kind, in the Colonies, and indeed only the most fragmentary approaches to science in Europe. But out of these practical seekings chemistry grew, in knowledge and stature and wealth. It is interesting to reflect that the two American fortunes which have contributed most largely to the equipment and support of scientific research are founded on chemical industries— the Carnegie fortune on the steel industry, which received its greatest acceleration from Bessemer's process of promoting the chemisms of steelmaking, and the Rockefeller fortune on the petroleum industry, which is so directly indebted to Willard Gibbs's discovery of the phase rule as the foundation of physical chemistry. The Mellon fortune derived much from Charles M. Hall's application of electrochemistry to the extraction of aluminum, and in turn it has fostered many industrial researches to useful and successful fruition. Chemistry has been described as creative, but more aptly it may be characterized as a catalytic agency, activating industry, wealth, the other sciences— civilization.

THIS UNSCIENTIFIC AGE[1]

Robert L. Duffus

At least nine out of every ten educated persons if asked to characterize instantly and in a word the basic element in present-day civilization would certainly say "science." If they thought twice, or perhaps three times, before replying, or if they had the opportunity, as I recently had, to look at the situation through the eyes of a group of desperately earnest scientists and educators, they would realize that they were wrong.

Not only is our generation not scientific; it is less scientific than the generation which preceded it. In many ways it is less scientific than the generation which produced *The Origin of Species*; in some ways it is less rational than the late eighteenth century.

Look at the picture of our modern Age of Reason: widespread applications of censorship, which frustrate and deny the right of private judgment; educational systems which have grown into mere schemes for mass indoctrination; irrational impulses, emotions, and superstitions breaking down the machinery of distribution; continued and almost universal preparations for wars by which it can be mathematically demonstrated that no participant can possibly gain; the reversion of whole nations to a studied barbarism.

Some of these imbecilic objectives are achieved by means of new technics (the radio, psychological "conditioning," airplanes, poison gas, etc.), but that does not make them scientific. Science may be defined as a process of experimentation and rationalization, with the aid of which natural laws are formulated, tested, and utilized. By no stretch of the imagination can such a process be regarded as dominating the course of civilization in the year 1934. Science and scientific thinking are the attributes of a pitifully small minority, and not of that minority which is at present directing the affairs of mankind. Science on the one hand, and common use and wont on the other, are like the "Siamese twins" exhibited in a New York revue some years ago, who differed from other Siamese twins in that they were not Siamese, were not physically linked together, were not twins, and didn't even look like each other.

It is easy to deceive ourselves on this score because all of us unavoidably make use of a great number of scientific tools and playthings. Yet it is folly to believe that because a spiritual descendant of Attila avails himself of the discoveries of chemists and physicists to make his armies more terrible, he is assuming a scientific attitude; or that a cotton mill owner is scientific because he introduces new looms and cuts his labor costs; or that a man who operates a motor car or twiddles the dials on a radio set is on that account any closer to

[1]From *Harper's Magazine*, December, 1934.

451

an understanding of cause and effect than was his ancestor who drove a horse and played the fiddle.

Scientific information has entered into every literate person's life to a greater or lesser extent. The scientific mode of thought obviously has not. Actually—and this is the point of the argument—there is almost no connection between these two factors. Individually and collectively we may stuff ourselves with so-called scientific data from childhood to old age, and never be a whit the wiser. On the whole, our civilization has done precisely that.

Let us consider the case of the average American who, we like to believe, is the most enlightened of God's creatures. What opportunity does he have, after forgetting the rudiments learned in school, to come in contact with the workings of the scientific mind?

He does, or can, expose himself to a vast flood of facts *about* science. The agencies for the dissemination of these facts are of many kinds. They range from the carefully written but not too technical book of a man who is himself an investigator (and who is lucky if he can count his circulation by thousands instead of hundreds) to the flashy "freaks" which may be found in the Sunday or daily editions of the more sensational newspapers. Lectures, radio talks, motion pictures, and museums, each in a different way, add to the store of information available to at least a part of the public. There are popular magazines nominally devoted to "science." One or two scientific feature services are intelligently edited. On the whole, scientific data receive far more extensive and somewhat more enlightened treatment in the press and in other popular vehicles of communication than they did a few years ago.

Unfortunately there is every reason to believe that millions of our fellow-citizens open their eyes or ears to this factual flood in the same uncritical spirit with which their great-grandparents listened to old wives' tales or their remoter ancestors accepted the priestly interpretations of the utterances of the tribal gods.

Clever advertisers long ago learned the efficacy of the charmed phrase, "Science says," accompanied by the photograph of a learned-looking gentleman with a microscope, a white coat, and a neatly trimmed beard. For a large portion of the public science is in danger of becoming merely a new kind of magic. That is, it is in danger of being transmuted into something that is not science at all. Its facts may easily become as pretty and meaningless as so many sea shells picked up by someone who knows nothing about life in the sea. They may even lack the kind of system and logic that a traditional set of superstitions has.

This state of affairs would not be so menacing if science, regardless of whether we understand it or not, were not doing so many things to us. But the fact notoriously is that, without infecting more than an infinitesimal fraction of the population with its ideas and its intellectual habits, science has actually created a new human environment. So far as most of us are concerned, this vast change has been imposed and accepted rather than created and understood.

The folkways have thus been transformed much as they would be if there were an abrupt alteration in the climate and new species of plants and animals and new living conditions were spontaneously produced. Unfortunately, though science brought about this change in folkways, the change itself has not been scientifically guided. Despite certain social inventions (to borrow a concept of Prof. W. F. Ogburn) such as labor unions, workmen's compensation, direct primaries, holding companies, and so on, inventiveness has hardly been applied at all to human institutions. Nor is there likelihood that it will be until an appreciable percentage of the human race has learned to think scientifically. Until that time we shall be creatures of chance almost as much as were our ancestors who lived in trees and caves and never dreamed of controlling (unless by sacrifices and incantations) the forces of nature.

Indeed, our situation is more precarious than that of our ancestors, for we have subjugated Nature without collectively understanding her and use forces whose total effects we are not at present able to delimit. Without a general penetration of the scientific spirit into our consciousness we are just as likely to destroy ourselves as to benefit ourselves by our new powers.

Our failure to keep step with science may be thought of as having three phases: (1) we have not made adequate use of the scientific means at our disposal; (2) we have used scientific means to bring about what seemed to be a specific good, without taking account of other effects which may be positively harmful; (3) we have diverted science to purely destructive uses. Let us examine our predicament under these three heads.

The progress of medicine is a shining example of what applied science can do for the human race and also of the extreme reluctance of the human race to accept what science has to offer. It is true that for many years the American death rate has been falling: in 1880 it was nearly 20 for each thousand of population annually; at the present time it is only about 11 for each thousand. This reduction has been accomplished in large measure by an enormous drop in the mortality rates for infants and children, in lesser degree by increased control of such diseases as yellow fever, typhoid fever, tuberculosis, and hookworm disease.

Yet consider this passage from the report of the Committee on the Costs of Medical Care: "The death rates from cancer, diabetes, and appendicitis are rising threateningly. More babies are dying each year, many of them need-lessly, than there were American soldiers killed in the World War. Every year tuberculosis kills its thousands and costs the country more than half a billion dollars. By early application of our knowledge we could double the cured cases of cancer. The venereal diseases still levy a heavy toll of blindness and mental disorders upon the nation. A great army of rheumatics remains untreated without hope of alleviation or cure. Many diabetics still remain without insulin or receive it too late. Human life in the United States is being wasted, as recklessly, as surely, in times of peace as in times of war. Thousands of people are sick and dying daily in this country because the knowledge and facilities that we have are inadequately applied."

An analysis of these facts would reveal a number of causes for them. Poverty is one of them: we can seemingly afford more than twice as much for automobiles as for medical care. Ignorance is another: we spend nearly half a billion dollars in a normal year on patent medicines and the services of various quacks. Governmental parsimony is a third: we spend three times as much on our navy as we do on all tax-supported public health work. A fourth cause is the resistance of conservative medical men to the use of the social agencies necessary to bring the benefits of medical science to all the people. Ask your doctor what he thinks of health insurance or "state medicine."

All these causes are institutional, traditional, emotional. They reflect our inability to apply medical knowledge with the same relentless precision which produces it. We are scientific in the laboratory and hospital, credulous, super-stitious, and careless once we are outside their doors.

One more instance may be given of the inadequate use of existing scientific knowledge—an instance all too familiar to everyone who reads these words. An economic depression is nothing more than a clash between the technology of production and distribution on the one hand and certain obstructing folk-ways on the other. It is a commonplace, too banal to repeat here if it did not fit so perfectly into the argument, that poverty has become technologically unnecessary. It is not necessary to labor the point. Idle factories and un-employment at a time when human needs are tragically unsatisfied are a proof of it. So was the ability of the contending nations during the World War to withdraw millions of men from production and to spend billions of dollars for military purposes and still maintain the civilian populations. No one can deny the potential existence of a huge social surplus.

I am not leading up to a suggestion that we adopt Communism, Socialism, Fascism, or even the Douglas Social Credit plan, although all of these systems are more or less blundering methods of breaking down the deadlock between technology and the folkways. But let the reader ask himself what kind of reaction these names produce in him. Unless he is a very unusual person, the reaction will be emotional. Some people are even emotional about the New Deal. Now, emotion is very well in its place, and there is not the slightest danger that it will disappear from human life. But the very fact that we approach reforms in our social system emotionally shows that we are not approaching them scientifically. We are not treating the deadlock of distribution as an obstacle to be overcome by disinterested experiment. We go at it in the atavistic spirit of conflict, even of hate. But even brotherly love is not enough. The problem is one to be solved by instruments of precision, like a surgeon's, in hands that do not shake with fear, with anger or with love. The Golden Rule may emerge from that operation, but if so it will be because the scientists and technologists in charge took nothing, not even the Golden Rule, for granted.

But we have applied science, if not to our whole lives at least to a part of them. To be sure we have. We have built cities which are a marvel to behold. The largest of them is fairly honeycombed with subways, through which run trains drawn by an invisible power that no one understands. The trains, the motors, the signal lights, the tunnels themselves are products of an appalling ingenuity, of a prodigious body of knowledge. Above them are buildings hundreds of feet high, framing streets jammed with vehicles which are moved by never-ending millions of explosions taking place inside of exquisitely timed machinery.

The city itself, however, is not exquisitely timed. The subway is not a pleasant place at any time. During the rush hours it is as barbarous as any camp of Stone Age men. The speed of the motor car is reduced to a crawl by congestion. Fifty years ago one could drive with a horse and buggy from Thirty-fourth Street to Fifty-ninth Street along Fifth Avenue faster than he could now make the distance at most times of the day in an automobile.

From store doors, from apartment windows, and—worst horror of all— from moving cabs, the radio blares. We all know what imbecilities it gives voice to during at least nine-tenths of its operating time. Yet the radio too is a triumph of science, a dream of the ages come true. Overhead moves another triumph, droning heavily, perhaps emitting a huge advertising yowl. Over on Broadway the picture theaters are in full career, and they too would out-pace the maddest dreams of any builder of mechanical utopias in ages past. Or take off your hat and walk with reverent steps into Rockefeller Center. A whirl of feminine legs, like a great daisy, on a revolving stage, a full orchestra suddenly rising out of the depths and sliding smoothly backward, figures on a curtain going through a vulgarized version of a story as old as the hills.

People moving in unhappy throngs to and from their work, to and from their play; people crowded into rabbit-warrens, nerves made ragged by un-necessary noise and confusion; the constant roar of traffic in the streets. A city almost every detail of which is a product of modern science. A city put together almost without science.

What has happened is clear to anyone who will pause to consider how cities and civilizations grow in an unscientific age. Neither the city nor the civilization of which it is a part was planned. No pains were taken to see that any two things placed in juxta-position really belonged that way. The subways were built to relieve congestion, with no thought that they would also produce it. The big buildings were erected with the idea that they would prove convenient; no one foresaw that too many of them would be hideously inconvenient. "Improvements," each one commending itself to common sense, accumulated one after the other, with no care taken as to their inter-relations, until it is now a question whether the city, as a machine for living, is as satisfactory as it was a hundred years ago. And there are cities less happy than the one we have been picturing. The happiest cities, if all were well with science, should be those where the most science has been applied to the square inch. But they are not. The happiest cities of this modern world are the most shiftless ones, the ones least blighted with the products of our mis-directed ingenuity. I have two or three in mind. The reader, if he has traveled a little, may think of several.

Yet it is not science that has been to blame; it is the absence of science. We have not built cities as we have built bridges and buildings, with a previous calculation of stresses and strains. We have built them with less than the fore-sight of a child playing with blocks. There have been certain obstacles in the way. Quite true. But those obstacles have not been material conditions but an obsolete set of tribal mores. Human selfishness, embedded in moth-eaten institutions, has played, and continues to play, its part. But the mere refusal to consider things carefully, precisely, and intelligently in their relation to one another has played a larger part.

Certainly a very small minority of us would build exactly the kind of cities or exactly the kind of civilization we have if the choice were open. The sum total is decidedly too messy. That sum total was not deliberately willed by anybody. It happened into being because a large number of diverse and irreconcilable things were willed by a great many people. It was a product of acute specialization, the effect of which on society has been a kind of acute indigestion.

It is customary in these times to speak of "trends" and to defer to them as though they were natural laws. The "rush to the cities" was a trend, and we were urged to adapt ourselves to it. Congestion is a trend, and we are advised to make the best of it. Steel houses, double-decked streets, cellophane, the minute subdivision of labor until craftsmanship is in danger of disappearing, mechanization, centralization, chauvinism, militarism—all are, or may soon be, trends, and it is suggested that we learn how to adapt ourselves to them.

Some of them—let us not bother to decide which—may be good and acceptable. But there is no sound reason why we should accept any of them if they are not. We should stand up on our scientific hind legs and accept only those which can be demonstrated as good by a painstaking study of their present and probable effects. To submit blindly to a trend is to submit to the rule of superstition and unreason.

Reflect, for example, on the trend toward war, which falls into the third of our categories—the diversion of science to purely destructive uses. No one who can add up figures can possibly regard war as a paying enterprise. The last great war demonstrably was not, and warlike machinery has now been so much improved that the next one will be even less so. Now science has contributed enormously to the destructiveness of war. Science has taught us how to mutilate, disembowel, and strangle, at vast distances, and with the utmost precision. Yet war itself, all considerations of humanity set aside, is the negation of science, for it creates and perpetuates an atmosphere in which the spirit of free inquiry cannot survive.

It should be evident by this time that much of what is called science is not science at all but a misuse of applied science and a misunderstanding of science itself. The visual and auditory hideousness of cities, the dreadful monotony of factory work, "over-production," class conflict, war—all are due to partial and distorted applications of the existing body of knowledge. Science uninhibited and unrestrained could give our civilization health, leisure, beauty, peace, and even the brotherhood of man. It has failed to do so because we have refused to permit it to do so. We are like the barbarians who marched into Rome during the last days of the Empire. We are in the midst of riches which we are incapable of utilizing.

How shall we escape from the domination of instinct and emotion, which at present really determine our collective life? Manifestly by a process of education, the means for which must be far more ambitious than any the world has yet seen. Education must be continuous, from childhood to old age. Science must be made a whole, an entity, instead of a fraction. It must be so thoroughly embedded in the normal culture that it will displace superstition, magic, and unreasoning prejudice. The average man must possess the rudiments of scientific thought.

There need be no fear that anything precious will be lost by this process. Science is simply a quest for truth. Whatever truth there may be in the arts, in religion, in cherished observances will be preserved, not sacrificed, by the scientific approach. We do not need new doctrines, but rather a new attitude toward doctrines. The experience of vast populations with communism, fascism, and even democracy indicates that this should be a skeptical, experimental attitude. Skepticism is in one sense the fundamental of science, just as irrational acceptance is a fundamental of mobs, of armies, and of political parties.

Let us proceed on the assumption that we have a public which has to be educated out of the habit of accepting the unproven hypothesis. In that habit we have the key to many, though not all, of the world's present difficulties. We see it enforced by the police power in at least three countries—Russia, Germany, and Italy. We see it stimulated by ingenious advertising and by carefully planned propaganda in such qualified democracies as France, Great Britain, and the United States.

We can break it down only by a persistent, long-continued scientific counter-attack: scientific not because its subject matter is limited by laboratory technics, but because the scientific method—that is, the careful, logical, and unbiased weighing of evidence—must, if it is to continue in any field of knowledge, be applied to all fields.

I am irresistibly reminded of James Harvey Robinson's magnificent essay on "The Humanizing of Knowledge," and especially of that famous concluding passage in which he quotes Dr. T. V. Smith of the University of Chicago:

Many researchers think the popularization of science either hopeless or needless. In their sense of the term it is probably both. But if no precautions are taken to bridge the gap between scientific knowledge and popular prejudice it may grow so wide that the researcher will find himself engulfed. A man of science has recently declared boldly and rightly that "the emotional life of man is primary." In the development of both the race and the individual "the human heart has the right of way. . . . Science must humbly reinstate itself as the instrument of humanity's desires. The needs of humanity render this no more imperative than does the perpetuation of science itself. And since intelligence does exist as the instrument of human need, intelligence must save its life by losing its pride."

Events since these words were written have emphasized the frightful possibilities in giving scientific tools and weapons to a non-scientific society. Civilization cannot continue to exist half scientific and half committed to Stone Age prejudices and superstitions. There cannot long be one law of laboratory thinking and another of social, economic, and political thinking. That "careful and critical knowledge" (to quote Dr. Robinson again) which is called science must be applied to all fields of human activity or we shall eventually find it applied to none.

CATCHING UP WITH THE INVENTORS[1]

Arthur Train, Jr.

Have you an "electric pig" in your kitchen to grind up the garbage? Do you eat strawberries out of season grown in a chemical solution? Is your house guarded by an "electric eye"? Has your radio a facsimile print-ing attachment? Are your clocks electrically timed? Does your car have a continuous gear ratio? Do you receive your milk in a paper container? Do you use the kind of film in your camera that makes it possible to take difficult indoor pictures with an ordinary lens? Have you seen any stereoscopic or three-dimensional movies? Have you air-conditioning in your home? How many prefabricated houses are there in your neighborhood? How many "modern" houses? How often do you take the *Normandie* or the *Queen Mary* or Diesel electric streamlined trains or sleeper planes? Do you pick up the telephone at your elbow and call Hobart, Tasmania? If not, why not?

All these things are possible. The mere enumeration of them gives the characteristic atmosphere of the times in which we live. But if these things are characteristic of to-day, a majority of us are living twenty or thirty years in the past. For the introduction of technological developments is unfortu-nately not limited by time alone; it is limited by a number of other factors. The most important of these in the battle for survival is cost. Then there is the constitutional inability of most persons to grasp the implications of something that differs from what they have been accustomed to; it is hard to put new wine into old bottles. Then there is organized labor which disputes the right of the machine to take jobs away on the one hand, and on the other, capital, which has invested in expensive tools and hesitates to see them rendered ob-solete. All of these impediments can be reduced to one main underlying difficulty, which is that the course of technological progress, instead of being steady, is highly irregular.

According to a careful survey made a few years ago of a typical American locality, half the families whose total incomes are under $2000 a year have

[1]From *Harper's Magazine*, March, 1938.

radios, while all the families with incomes of $10,000 and over have them. Half the families in the under $2000 group own cars, but at $5000 and beyond they all do. Only 14 families per thousand under $5000 a year own a high-priced car, and only 114 above $5000 own two cars. Only 55 families per thousand in the under $2000 a year group own automatic refrigerators and at $10,000 and over there are still only 302. One hundred and seventy-one of these own refrigerators costing over $300. In the under $2000 group there are 24 families who occasionally visit Europe; there are 140 in the $10,000 and over group. The Department of Commerce Survey on the consumer use of selected goods and services by income classes in the main substantiates these findings, except that in the cities that were investigated more people in the higher-income brackets had refrigerators.

As for air-conditioning, it will have to become considerably cheaper before more than a few thousand families in the United States can afford to have it in their homes. A facsimile recorder, if anyone wanted it, would cost about $100; but of course there would have to be a service to supply the necessary copy. At the present time two newspaper stations are supplying such a service to 100 sets. A television receiving set in its present stage of development would cost in the neighborhood of $300. There are few private individuals in the country who could afford the luxury of a television transmitting set, which to-day costs around $300,000.

On the other hand, in 1922 a superheterodyne receiving set with only four tubes, and still battery operated, cost as much as $350. The merest $20 set to-day is far superior to it in tone and selectivity. Until recently the cost of the family automobile went down as steadily as its quality increased. From a luxury it has become a necessity, and the same is rapidly becoming true of the electric refrigerator.

On this basis, it may be fair to assume that the far more complicated television receiving apparatus might drop in the next 30 or 40 years to from one-half to one-quarter of its present price, and without auditory or visual perspective or color, might well cost around $50. Manufacturers, basing their estimates on the progress of television in England, expect to see about 20,000 sets the first year. Thus it will probably be a long time before every home has a television receiving set, and two-way point-to-point television for individuals belongs to the more distant rather than to the immediate future.

Moreover, it is not the actual cost of a new appliance that determines its adoption, but, unless it provides an entirely new service, its comparative cost—it has to be nearly as cheap as the next best thing in its line. Cost of course did not stop thousands of persons from buying expensive Leicas and those nice little movie cameras, and we also know that there is no way of telling when a process which now seems expensive may suddenly become cheap. Nevertheless, how many persons would buy a facsimile recorder for $100 when the current to run it alone would cost as much as the newspaper you can buy on the corner? How many persons who already had a television set would pay an additional $100 for visual and auditory perspective and another $100 for color provided no way were discovered to lessen the cost of these additional effects?

In the Report on Technological Trends and National Policy of the National Resources Committee, S. C. Gilfillan, formerly Curator of Social Sciences at the Museum of Science and Industry in Chicago, implies that in the past scientific writers have demonstrated their ability to predict the technological aspects of the future with a considerable degree of accuracy. We all know of course that, in addition to studying the art of flying, Leonardo da Vinci toyed with the idea of tanks and submarines, but gave them up as too pernicious. As a prophet Jules Verne did well. In *Looking Backward*, written in 1888, Edward Bellamy painted a fair picture of many technological developments of to-day. Even the old Hippodrome shows of our childhood were not as fantastic as they evidently were intended to be. But the report goes on to point out that of 65 predictions made in an article in the *Scientific American* in 1920, 78 per cent have been or will be proved right and 22 per cent wrong. Of 25 predictions made by Steinmetz in an article twenty-one years ago, 76 per cent have been or will shortly be realized, 24 per cent are doubtful, and there are no real errors. Unless there were also many other science writers whose predictions have been overlooked or forgotten because they were wrong, this would seem to imply that the prediction of future technological developments might be put on a scientific basis.

Well, it is a great temptation to try one's hand at this sort of thing because it almost always makes good reading. The less conscientious writers almost inevitably succumb to the temptation to make such copy saleable by sensationalizing it, so that the Sunday supplements are full of lurid descriptions of death rays, rocket planes, germ warfare, trips to the moon, the conquest of death, the production of human beings in the laboratory, and so on. These descriptions are all right as far as they go, except that the last line is always omitted, and that line is, "and then Johnny woke up." No one has yet attempted the far more difficult and less ingratiating task of picturing what the world will be like fifty years from now, taking into account the factors which impede technological progress and to which I have already summarily referred, such as (in addition to the comparative cost of the appliances themselves) the psychological resistance of the public to innovation, the danger of increased unemployment, the relation of wages to the cost of living, investment in obsolete plants, and the suppression of patents. To paint such a picture with anywhere near the accuracy of, shall we say, the luckier ones among the earlier prophets, one would have to have a notion of the form of government and kind of economic system we are likely to have. Lacking this foreknowledge, the best one can do is attempt to describe the kind of future world the technologists could make for us, and then enumerate and analyze the obstructing factors.

The relationship between scientists, engineers, and the ultimate consumer may be graphically expressed by three concentric circles. The innermost circle or core represents the scientists who, generally speaking, are working at pure theory. It is here that you will find men exploring the possibilities of the cathode ray, the breakup of the atom, and the immortality of flesh tissues, and making other inquiries which may not affect our environment for the next century or more. The next circle represents the men who translate the theories that have a contemporary application into living things of steel and magnesium and resin and concrete. Finally, the outermost circle represents us humble mortals who may or may not buy and use what the engineers have built for us, according to our psychological limitations. In the past it has generally taken about thirty-three years for an invention to travel from the inner core to the outer rim, although to-day the gap is decreasing. To paint a sensational picture of the future you need only dip your brush into the cosmic pigments with which the men of the innermost circle are working; to paint an exciting one you need only describe the materials in the hands of the engineers; but the true picture, considerably less dramatic, concerns itself with the everyday things with which common men and women surround themselves.

The temptation is all the greater to overlook the effect of the various resistances in painting a picture of the future, because it is undeniable that to-day we are in the midst of sensational developments whose implications are ignored by the average man. We are impressed by the great winged birds that span the oceans, but when we look at the caps on bottles of beer or the glass in our car windows it does not occur to us that a silent revolution is taking place. Recent developments in organic chemistry, metallurgy, and electronics are not only as startling as those of transportation and communication, but in many instances have made the latter possible.

Since this is a game that anyone can play, one guess being as good as another, let's see what we can do with it. If we confine ourselves to inventions that are either born or in the laboratory stage, we shall not fall into the error of producing apocalyptic visions after the manner of the Sunday supplements. Moreover, we can check our statements against those of the National Resources Committee's report which was compiled in good faith by a group of experts.

It is unfortunately impossible within the confines of one article to make a study of probable future trends in the various technological fields. About all one can do is to uncover a little peephole and look through it for an instant. If we are so rash as to say what we see, half the scientists in the country will rise up to tell us that there is absolutely no reason why the picture should not be entirely different, although there may be comfort in the fact that by the time anybody is actually in a position to prove us wrong we shall probably be either dead or senile.

Our hero, then, John Doe, born in the year of grace 1938, was in bed and asleep at the time our story begins in 1988. (No synthetic substitute for sleep had then been discovered.) Progress in biology, biochemistry, food technology, and related sciences was responsible for the fact that he was considerably heavier and taller than his forefathers, and also that, although half a century old, he was neither too fat nor too thin, and like Uncle Ned had "plenty of wool on the top of his head, the place where the wool ought to be."

The sounds of the city were filtered at the intake-ducts of the air-conditioning apparatus, and such few persistent discords and jangles as did penetrate into the room were deflected toward the ceiling by the walls which slanted gently upward, like the glass windows of radio broadcasting control rooms, where they were absorbed by special insulation. The entering air passed through a dust filter and was freed from other germs by ultra-violet rays. Research into the effects of ionization, barometric pressure, condensation nuclei, and the existence of a metastable state of oxygen had made it possible to supply Mr. Doe's room with air as invigorating as that of the seashore or the mountains. Its chemical composition was nicely calculated to give him a maximum of refreshment at night, while during the day its temperature, humidity, and degree of ionization were automatically varied from time to time in order to avoid the soporific effect of monotony. Incidentally, synthetic air, long considered fantastic, was well on the way toward becoming a reality.

Presently, as the radio-controlled clock proclaimed in a soothing voice that it was time to get up (for its direct reading dial showed the hour of seven), the air became sensibly warmer. Heating was provided by the simple process of running the refrigerator mechanism in reverse, although some architects recommended heating coils in the walls or radiant wires in the ceiling.

Although it was dark and rainy outside, the room was gradually flooded with a diffused light. The quantity required was measured out with nice accuracy by the ever-watchful photocell, and on sunny days when clouds

463

passed over the sun, the light in the room would remain constant. This light was provided by a type of gaseous discharge lamp, perhaps employing carbon dioxide, infinitely more efficient than the old-fashioned incandescent filament bulbs, and containing as good a proportion of infra-red and ultra-violet rays as that of the brighest summer sun, which were automatically turned on at intervals.

Meanwhile—the first item in a preselected program from different stations —the television screen faded in on an energetic man in a football sweater who beckoned to Mr. Doe to arise and begin his setting-up exercises. In apartment houses these television images were usually "piped" along a coaxial cable (an invention which the public of the '30s had failed to realize was as revolutionary as the telephone itself); but for private homes and for general purposes the old-fashioned system of coaxial cable and linked radio stations had been superseded by the "Yale lock" style of multiple wave-lengths using various permutations and combinations to give broader wave-band availability of an unlimited number of channels.

The bathroom into which Mr. Doe stepped for his matutinal shower was a prefabricated affair made like an automobile, all the various appliances such as tub, shower, basin, and toilet forming one integrated unit, with special metallic walls for the outer casing. Three identical bathrooms were grouped with it to form a square in the center of the house, so that a minimum of plumbing was required. The old-fashioned system of using thousands of gallons of water to dilute and remove waste, thereby sacrificing its valuable chemical properties, had long ago been superseded by chemical disposal of sewage. The development of new detergents also made it possible to "wash" without water if anyone so desired.

While Doe was slipping into a pair of shorts and a light, three-quarter length rayon fabric smock, which, after all, is all that anyone would need in an air-conditioned home, he haphazardly pushed in various buttons controlling the automatic tuning of his television set so that he might see with his own eyes what was going on in the different parts of the world. He was a man who liked to spend money on gadgets, and the morning paper had been printed out for him by the facsimile recorder while he slept. It was his habit to leave it on just as people in the old days left the radio on, and from the reams of stuff it printed out he would pick what he wanted and throw the rest away. Most of the time, however, he preferred to hear the news rather than read it.

The vegetables and fruit that graced the Doe table out of season had never known the rich soil of a truck garden. Some—possibly the more expensive ones—had been grown in a vegetable factory in the heart of the community center, in a heated tray containing various salts. Others had come in black iron, plastic-coated cans, flash-heated to preserve the natural flavor of the contents, while others, at the other end of the scale, reached his kitchen in a frozen state. Mr. Doe habitually reflected with satisfaction that he never had any trouble getting whatever he wanted whenever he wanted it, and that the real significance of chemically produced crops and other mechanical aids to agriculture was that they permitted an efficient control of the food supply.

His house was situated at a considerable distance from the city, in an "integrated" neighborhood which had been carefully planned by a city planning board. The houses were grouped about a park, and in addition to the school and library there was a central air-conditioning plant and a community center with a television transmission set, an auditorium whose television receiving set boasted color and three-dimensional sound and sight, a trailer camp, all kinds of recreational facilities, the vegetable factory, the poultry factory, and the plant where garbage was converted into fertilizer.

The house itself was somewhat smaller and had smaller rooms than one would have expected of a man with Mr. Doe's means. The large custom-built house had long ago gone the way of the large custom-built automobile. It was a long, low, flat-roofed building made up of a cluster of prefabricated units whose irregular arrangement prevented it from looking monotonous. Unlike the houses of the early part of the century and all preceding eras, whose aim was to give an impression of volume, the whole building was so translucent, neutral, and fragile-looking, so broken into planes by terraces and porches, that it gave the impression of being no more than a part of the out-of-doors which had been etched into the frame with a few strokes of a sharp pointed pencil.

In the construction of the house the use of wood, bricks, and plaster had practically been superseded by panels of beryllium and magnesium alloys; low-grade silicas, or glasslike materials; sheet materials such as asbestos cement, and occasionally plastic which had been developed to a point where its resistance to atmosphere was known. A considerable use was made of moving partitions which made it possible to enclose a small space when privacy was required, and still provide a large space when it was not. The insulation, of "mineral fluff," was of course built into the prefabricated panels.

In the various rooms many of the pieces of furniture were made of plastic molded as a unit, while others were made of magnesium alloy. In place of cushions, spongelike synthetic upholstery was used. Some of the most beautiful hangings were of translucent glass fabric.

Outside of a few first editions and beautifully bound volumes with handsome illustrations, Mr. Doe's library contained few books. It consisted chiefly of little drawers filled with thousands of tiny reels of film a few millimeters in width. On his table was a reading machine about the size of a portable typewriter, which projected the tiny photographed pages onto a small screen. Each of these tiny films also carried a sound track, and at his own discretion he could play them on a talking book. Wherever he went Mr. Doe carried a camera hardly bigger than a watch and also a tiny sound-recording device, so that anything he saw or heard during the day he could conveniently remember by mechanical means. The day had not arrived (predicted by Sarnoff back in 1936) when each individual would have his own wave-length and by means of a pocket radio could communicate with anybody anywhere. In Doe's office the principle of mechanical aids to memory was developed to a high state of efficiency. All of his records were "remembered," selected, and analyzed on photoelectric tabulating machines with far greater efficiency than the human brain could achieve and in much less time.

An inventory of the various objects and materials used in Mr. Doe's house would show that the strawboard and fiberboard that lined the walls, the insulating material between them and the outer wall, sometimes the outer wall itself, the synthetic textiles which comprised the clothing of much of the family, and the waterproof materials which protected them if they ever went out in the rain, and all small knick-knacks from ash trays to bottle caps, were made of various types of thermo-plastic resin derived from such inexpensive raw materials as soy bean, bagasse, sugar cane, straw, wood pulp, sorghum, linseed, flaxseed, cottonseed hulls, oat hulls, nut shells, Jerusalem artichokes, fruit pits, and skim milk.

We have seen how in Mr. Doe's house the electric eye, or photoelectric tube, coupled with the thyratron tube which enables it to act on what it sees, automatically measured the amount of illumination necessary to replace the waning light of day. It also performed the functions of a whole corps of servants. It opened the garage door as you drove up, opened the door between the kitchen and the dining room when someone advanced with a tray, opened the door of the refrigerator, and opened and closed windows. But its duties did not end with the fall of day. All night long it was on guard as night watchman, ready to give warning by ringing bells, turning on floodlights, photographing the intruder, paralyzing him with tear gas, and sending for the police.

The roof of the house, as in all houses at that time, was used as a landing field for the family's collection of steep-flight airplanes of assorted sizes, the top story being used as a garage. Doe didn't bother to use his car very often, and in general it was relegated to trips to the community center and to use by the children, playing the role of the station wagon of the late '30s. Its two-cycle motor, smaller, lighter, and more efficient than the old fashioned four-cycle one, could easily drive it along at an average speed of seventy miles an hour on the highly efficient fuels of those days. Such speeds, however, seemed like crawling to Mr. Doe and his friends, who used small steep-flight planes for short hops and giant stratosphere planes for distance flying.

This, then, is an attempt to describe a part—a fragment—of what we might reasonably expect the engineers to give us, although, in all honesty, it should be pointed out that it might be entirely different. Ideally, however, the engineers could probably make available, to most of us, most of the things I have described here, plus a number of essentials which are not novel enough to figure in the description. The productivity of existing plants, especially if some way could be found to replace the obsolete ones, is more than enough to care for our needs, and also, although this is more delicate, at prices that we could afford, as is in the main borne out by the report of the Brookings Institution and the report of the National Survey of Potential Product Capacity.

Most people find it hard to believe what they hear about the country's potential productivity. The reason for this is that such statements usually presuppose ideal conditions, just as did the picture of Mr. Doe's environment. Let us now take that picture and turn it into reality.

We gave Mr. Doe a prefabricated house, that is to say, made of prefabricated units. But many architects think that the one thing they can be reasonably sure a man of his means would not want would be a prefabricated house. A man of means is likely to want a house that demonstrates his financial ability to build himself something that expresses his own taste and his own individuality. As good taste becomes more widespread, such persons will be more and more likely to build houses that harmonize with the locality and with the landscape of their own particular acres.

We gave Mr. Doe a modern house, which would presumably be furnished in the modern style; but what happened to the o.iginal French expression of the "modern" style in furniture when it came over from Paris fifteen years ago? At first it was taken up by persons of taste and means, but when the department stores got hold of it and spread it among the crowd, the people of taste and means dropped it like a hot penny and went rushing headlong into a Victorian revival. Perhaps they were disturbed by the enthusiastic adoption of the "modern" style by hotels, bars, and restaurants.

The prefabricated house is more suited to persons with low incomes. But prefabricated houses are already on the market and the working man has not got them. This is partly because they are still too expensive. There is actually no prefabricated house quoted to-day that could not be built more cheaply in the usual way under favorable conditions. And to anticipate a future difficulty rather than a present one, there is a possibility of obstruction on the part of local and regional real-estate interests and plasterers' and woodworkers' organizations. It is a fact that to-day in some localities union painters will not handle a spray gun and that the union specifies the maximum width of brush a man may use on a particular job.

It is all very well to speak of a plastic chair, or even of a plastic room, molded as a unit; but there is no use on earth for a plastic chair unless it is cheaper and more durable than any other kind. Chairs can be made more cheaply of plastic to-day than of wood or steel tubing, but the die is very expensive and it would be necessary for manufacturers to order large quantities of the same type of chair. Of course new synthetic combinations are continually being discovered, plastics are becoming cheaper, and continuous instead of intermittent production is already possible. If the time ever comes when tables and chairs can be sold at really low prices, plastic furniture will be in considerable demand.

When we come to the moot question of television we get what is perhaps the best example of how little the public is able to grasp the problems of technology and how far they may sometimes get ahead even of the scientists. The people who are demanding television have no conception of the difficulties involved which translate themselves into terms of cost.

In order to see a picture in black and white, without visual or auditory perspective, just as you see it in the movies to-day, it is only necessary to transmit one picture along one channel of certain band width. This, however, is a difficult enough feat in itself, inasmuch as each picture must consist of no less than 200,000 separate elements of light and shade, and 30 pictures are transmitted a second, making in all 6,000,000 picture elements a second.

Now if you want to transmit auditory perspective you need a second sound-pick-up apparatus. If you want to transmit color you have to "trip" or switch in a relay to actuate a red screen alternating with a blue screen, but still on one channel, for every one you sent without it. And for this a "video" channel, twice as wide, would be necessary. Again, if you want visual perspective or stereoscopic effect, you might have to multiply the band width by three to accommodate the three additional channels. In all, you might have to be equipped to transmit three pictures in the time it now takes to transmit one, unless of course someone finds a simplifying principle of which we are unaware at present. Engineers are now working on the substitution of color elements for some of the elements which give the outline; but for the time being, if you were to try to get all these on the same channel, it would require the transmission of 18,000,000 elements a second. Moreover, in the present usable radio spectrum there is no place to accommodate the band widths which this kind of thing would demand. And we haven't yet enough practical experience in the use of such waves. Enough has been said to show that a television set cannot be improvised out of an old cigar box and a couple of coils of wire. There are some engineers who argue that the problem is so complex that even the desirability of solving it is open to question.

Taking television as an example, it can be argued that to-day we are gadget-conscious, like a child with new toys or a materially ambitious man who has for the first time acquired enough money to surround himself with the things he wants. But it is quite possible that before very long man will be bored with his new toys and will begin to work in the direction of originality, individuality, taste, and imagination. An interesting example is the imported "Bauhaus" idea being applied at Harvard and in Chicago, which represents an attempt at a synthesis of technology, artisanship, and aesthetics in design. The Bauhaus produced the first welded tubular chair in the modern style and some of the first modern houses. It represents a mile post along the road to integration.

We have seen that the life of an invention, as such, used to average about thirty-three years from the time it was conceived in the mind of the inventor until the time when, having overcome the successive difficulties in its path, it finally achieved commercial adoption. The lag between invention and application is as old as history. Queen Elizabeth considered the use of carriages effeminate. In America in the last century it was thought that the sight of trains rushing across the country under their own power would drive people mad, and in Germany it was contended that at fifteen miles an hour blood would spurt from the passengers' noses, mouths, and ears. Napoleon called gas lighting *une grande folie*. Faraday was contemptuously referred to as "the frogs' dancing master." The steamboat was known as "Fulton's Folly." The first automobile was required by law to be preceded by a man carrying a red flag by day and a red lantern by night. When the typewriter was introduced it was thought that women would break down under the strain of a six months' training course. Historical examples are plentiful enough to suggest that in the past all new ideas were at one time considered impractical.

Throughout history, workers have fought bitterly and sometimes with violence their displacement by the machine. To-day the worker is less vociferous, and it is generally agreed that new machines create new jobs, both for their own construction and repair, as in the case of dial telephones, but also through the creation of new wants, as in the case of the automobile and the radio. And we are becoming cautious—for example, although the Rust cotton-picker is being tried out in Russia, where there is no unemployment, we still hesitate to use it.

Now a great many people argue that the strongest resistance of all comes from invested capital, which naturally does not like to see plants rendered obsolete and profitable operations turned into losing ones. C. F. Kettering pointed out that the research worker was a man employed to keep people dissatisfied with what they have. And one banker described research as an activity which only served to make banking hazardous. There is little that illuminating gas can do, for instance, that electricity cannot, yet the utilities are too heavily committed to make the change. The newspapers are reluctant to take up radio activities which may make their plants unnecessary. A still better example is the development of what are called "grandeur" movies, using a film and a screen both much larger than at present, and giving greater clarity of detail; this has been held up by the difficulty of re-equipping all the theaters.

On the other hand, so much good work has come and is coming out of the research laboratories of the great corporations that it would be unfair to fail to credit private initiative with its share in the onward march of technical progress. Certainly the chemical industry cannot be charged with failing to look ahead and act upon its prognostications. Perhaps the most that can be said is that bankers and executives have a tendency to think in terms of equipment and to be over-reluctant to make changes. The engineer, who is the best qualified to perceive the advent of what may later necessitate fundamental changes of policy, is not often enough called into consultation.

With industrial enterprises everywhere at the mercy of the irregularity of technological progress, which shoots out in various directions at different rates of speed, only to curl up here and deflate there, like some subaqueous plant in a speeded-up motion picture, the credit structure is subjected to undue strain. Bankers are understandably afraid of waking up over-night and finding themselves hanging onto the coattails of a hitherto respectable business which through no fault of its own finds itself headed for the rocks.

Perhaps it would be possible to remove the resistance to technological progress by insuring organizations against obsolescence just as individuals are insured against old age, disease, and death. This might be done by a government agency operating along the principles of Social Security, for otherwise the insurance companies would find themselves in the position of betting against progress.

But could even a dictator with a galaxy of intelligences at his disposal shorten the process of psychological re-orientation, physiological re-education, physical re-equipment, and economic adjustment in such a way as to enable a people to enjoy the fruits of its own creative ability and enterprise? Would a democratic government be willing to go to the trouble and expense of reviving the ancient and hitherto dubious calling of soothsayer or prophet, and making it respectable? Could the art of prophecy, at least as far as technological evolution is concerned, be made as scientific as long-range weather-forecasting promises to become?

Critics of the Report on Technological Trends say that if this Report is an example of what happens when a commission attempts to unravel the intricate skein of our continuing development, it disproves its own case, and that the self-perpetuation of any such group would be undesirable. Needless to say, much of this criticism comes from experts who were not invited to be on the Commission. You can solve almost any problem in the world provided you choose the right man to cope with it, but somebody has to be able to select the man.

If there is any one prediction that can be safely ventured upon, it is that we shall increasingly be obliged to turn to the scientist and to his way of thinking. Our future is in the hands of the technologists. But to-day we still hold them back and delay the fulfillment of their prophecies.

Research Papers

OF THE ELEPHANT[1]

Sir Thomas Browne

THE first shall be of the Elephant, whereof there generally passeth an opinion it hath no joints; and this absurdity is seconded with another, that being unable to lie down, it sleepeth against a Tree; which the Hunters observing, do saw it almost asunder; whereon the Beast relying, by the fall of the Tree, falls also down it self, and is able to rise no more. Which conceit is not the daughter of later times, but an old and gray-headed error, even in the days of Aristotle, as he delivereth in his Book, *De incessu Animalium*, and stands successively related by several other Authors: by Diodorus Siculus, Strabo, Ambrose, Cassiodore, Solinus, and many more. Now herein methinks men much forget themselves, not well considering the absurdity of such assertions.

For first, they affirm it hath no joints, and yet concede it walks and moves about; whereby they conceive there may be a progression or advancement made in Motion without inflexion of parts. Now all progression or Animals' locomotion being (as Aristotle teacheth) performed *tractu & pulsu*; that is, by drawing on, or impelling forward some part which was before in station, or at quiet; where there are no joints or flexures, neither can there be these actions. And this is true, not onely in Quadrupedes, Volatils, and Fishes, which have distinct and prominent Organs of Motion, Legs, Wings, and Fins; but in such also as perform their progression by the Trunk, as Serpents, Worms, and Leeches. Whereof though some want bones, and all extended articulations, yet have they arthritical Analogies, and by the motion of fibrous and musculous parts, are able to make progression. Which to conceive in bodies inflexible, and without all protrusion of parts, were to expect a Race from Hercules his pillars; or hope to behold the effects of Orpheus his Harp, when trees found joints, and danced after his Musick.

Again, While men conceive they never lie down, and enjoy not the position of rest, ordained unto all pedestrious Animals, hereby they imagine (what Reason cannot conceive) that an Animal of the vastest dimension and longest duration, should live in continual motion, without that alternity and vicissitude of rest whereby all others continue; and yet must thus much come to pass, if we opinion they lye not down and enjoy no decumbence at all. For station is properly no rest, but one kind of motion, relating unto that which Physitians (from Galen) do name extensive or tonical; that is, an extension

[1]From *Pseudodoxia Epidemica* by Sir Thomas Browne. Book III, Chapter 1. Published in 1646.

of the muscles and organs of motion maintaining the body at length or in its proper figure.

Wherein although it seem to be unmoved, it is not without all Motion; for in this position the muscles are sensibly extended, and labour to support the body; which permitted unto its proper gravity, would suddenly subside and fall unto the earth; as it happeneth in sleep, diseases, and death. From which occult action and invisible motion of the muscles in station (as Galen declareth) proceed more offensive lassitudes then from ambulation. And therefore the Tyranny of some have tormented men with long and enforced station, and though Ixion and Sisiphus which always moved, do seem to have the hardest measure; yet was not Titius favored, that lay extended upon Caucasus; and Tantalus suffered somewhat more then thirst, that stood perpetually in Hell. Thus Mercurialis in his *Gymnasticks* justly makes standing one kind of exercise: and Galen when we lie down, commends unto us middle figures, that is, not to lie directly, or at length, but somewhat inflected, that the muscles may be at rest; for such as he termeth *Hypobolemaioi* or figures of excess, either shrinking up or stretching out, are wearisome positions, and such as perturb the quiet of those parts. Now various parts do variously discover these indolent and quiet positions, some in right lines, as the wrists: some at right angles, as the cubit: others at oblique angles, as the fingers and the knees: all resting satisfied in postures of moderation, and none enduring the extremity of flexure or extension.

Moreover men herein do strangely forget the obvious relations of history, affirming they have no joints, whereas they dayly read of several actions which are not performable without them. They forget what is delivered by Xiphilinus, and also by Suetonius in the lives of Nero and Galba, that Elephants have been instructed to walk on ropes, in publick shews before the people. Which is not easily performed by man, and requireth not only a broad foot, but a pliable flexure of joints, and commandible disposure of all parts of progression . . . But above all, they call not to mind that memorable shew of Germanicus, wherein twelve Elephants danced unto the sound of Musick, and after laid them down in the Tricliniums, or places of festival Recumbency.

They forget the Etymologie of the Knee, approved by some Grammarians. They disturb the position of the young ones in the womb: which upon extension of legs is not easily conceivable; and contrary unto the general contrivance of Nature. Nor do they consider the impossible exclusion thereof, upon extension and rigour of the legs.

Lastly, they forget or consult not experience, whereof not many years past, we have had the advantage in England, by an Elephant shewn in many parts thereof, not only in the posture of standing, but kneeling and lying down.

Whereby although the opinion at present be well suppressed, yet from some strings of tradition, and fruitful recurrence of errour, it is not improbable, it may revive in the next generation again. This being not the first that hath been seen in England; for (besides some others) as Polydore Virgil relateth, Lewis the French King sent one to Henry the third, and Emanuel of Portugal another to Leo the tenth into Italy, where notwithstanding the errour is still alive and epidemical, as with us.

The hint and ground of this opinion might be the gross and somewhat Cylindrical composure of the legs, the equality and less perceptible disposure of the joints, especially in the former legs of this Animal; they appearing when he standeth, like Pillars of flesh, without any evidence of articulation. The different flexure and order of the joints might also countenance the same, being not disposed in the Elephant, as they are in other quadrupedes, but carry a nearer conformity unto those of Man; that is, the boughts of the fore-legs, not directly backward, but laterally and somewhat inward; but the hough or suffraginous flexure behind rather outward. Somewhat different unto many other quadrupedes, as Horses, Camels, Deer, Sheep, and Dogs; for their fore-legs bend like our legs, and their hinder legs like our arms, when we move them to our shoulders. But quadrupedes oviparous, as Frogs, Lizards, Crocadiles, have their joints and motive flexures more analogously framed unto ours: and some among viviparous, that is, such thereof as can bring their fore-feet and meat therein unto their mouths, as most can do that have the clavicles or coller-bones: whereby their brests are broader, and their shoulders more asunder, as the Ape, the Monkey, the Squirrel and some others. If therefore any shall affirm the joints of Elephants are differently framed from most of other quadrupedes, and more obscurely and grosly almost then any, he doth herein no injury unto truth. But if *a dicto secundum quid ad dictum simpliciter*, he affirmeth also they have no articulations at all, he incurs the controulment of reason, and cannot avoid the contradiction also of sense.

NEUTRONS[1]

Karl K. Darrow

THE discovery of what may prove to be the third and last
of the fundamental corpuscles of matter, and what at any rate is a distinctive
kind of ionizing ray, was carried from start to completion in three stages
which followed quickly one on another in time but were far apart in space,
in three entirely separate institutes, of three different nations. Such histories
have not been rare in physics, yet this one seems abnormal. It is natural to
expect that when a physicist has made and published the first advances in a
field till then untrodden, those who wish to follow will have to spend so long
a time in gathering resources like to his, in imitating his equipment and in
learning his technique, that in the meantime he will go the rest of the way.
In the case which is my present topic there would have been good reason
to expect it, since in the closely-allied field of transmutation all research was
confined to a single laboratory for full three years after the first announcement, and to that laboratory and one other for fully another five,—this despite
the fact that controversy soon flared up between the two, so that decisive word
from some third institute was ardently desired. Yet, when from the Reichsanstalt in the last month of 1930 it was made known that alpha-particles
elicit penetrating rays from such elements as lithium, beryllium and boron,
the Institut du Radium and the Cavendish Laboratory were equipped and
were alert. Their contributions came with intervals of months, not years;
and progress could scarcely have been swifter, had all the work been ordered
by a sole far-seeing mind.

Bothe and H. Becker were the authors of the work at the Reichsanstalt,
with which the tale commences.[2] They bombarded various elements with
alpha-particles from polonium (whereof the range is 3.9 cm in air at 15° C
and 760 mm. Hg, the initial kinetic energy $5.25 \cdot 10^6$ electron-volts) and used a
Geiger point-counter for observing such rays as were able to come out from
the bombarded substance through a barrier of two millimetres of zinc and

---

[1] From *The Review of Scientific Instruments*, February, 1933.

[2] It should perhaps commence with mention of the observations which F. P. Slater
made in 1921 at Cambridge (England) of penetrating rays sent forth from tin and lead
subjected to alpha-particle bombardment. The status of these observations is peculiar;
they have never been confirmed or disproved, so far as I know; H. C. Webster of the
same laboratory, writing in 1932, speaks of unpublished vain attempts to produce such
rays with the alpha-particles from polonium, but does not distrust Slater's data; another
vain attempt was made by Bothe and Becker. Slater used alpha-rays from radon, having
energy about 3 percent greater than that of the polonium rays which are now chiefly employed; the difference is slight, but possibly great enough to bring into play a phenomenon
of "resonance."

brass. (A barrier such as this is amply sufficient for stopping alpha-particles, and such electrons as they may set free by ionizing atoms, and even practically the whole of the X-rays which may be emitted by atoms so ionized.) Lead and silver and calcium, and several lighter elements (N, C, O, Ne) were disappointing; there was no certainty of radiation. Magnesium and aluminum gave just a trace of a result; lithium and boron and fluorine, notable amounts of rays able to penetrate to the counter and affect it; and beryllium a *relatively* tremendous amount, towering up above all the others on Bothe and Becker's chart.

I will speak of these for a while as "penetrating rays," borrowing the term which used to be applied to what are now called "cosmic rays." It is useful here to be reminded of the cosmic rays, for there is indeed a very great resemblance, not so much between the two varieties of radiation (the cosmic rays being mostly much more penetrating than are these) as between the methods of observing them, the alternative theories of their nature, the schemes for making the decision-by-experiment between one theory and another. Here, as there, it is ionization of gas which is observed—ionization coming in spurts, which may be separately observed and counted by use of a Geiger counter or a quick-acting electroscope with proper amplifiers or an expansion-chamber, or may be summed up by the accumulation of charge in a slow-acting electrometer. Here, as there, the spurts of ionization are due to the transits of corpuscles across the gas, corpuscles which sometimes at least are recognizably electrons or atom-nuclei. But here, as there, it is not to be taken for granted that these directly-ionizing corpuscles spring from the source of the phenomena, the element bombarded by the alpha-particles. Here, at least, they start their flights in the matter environing the source, being launched on their courses by invisible agents which are presumably the true primary rays coming from the source. The problem thus falls into two, that of the nature of the secondary corpuscles which produce the ionization directly, that of the nature of the ultimate rays which release and impel the secondaries; it is the former problem which is the easier to solve, but the latter which is fundamental.

Another resemblance to the story of cosmic rays: here, as there, it was at first assumed that the rays are electromagnetic. It was assumed, that is to say, that the primary rays proceeding from the source are of the nature of gamma-rays, that they consist of photons of great energy; and that the corpuscles which effect the ionization are electrons which these photons have detached from atoms and endowed with great velocities. No other theory was entertained by the early observers, German as well as French; the assumption seemed so inevitable that they did not even bother to state it explicitly, much less to justify it; it enters undefended into the titles of their papers, "Artificial Excitation of Nuclear Gamma-Rays" and the like. The tacit argument must have been, that of all the previously-known types of radiation (cosmic rays alone excepted) the gamma-rays approach nearest in penetrating power to these, and are therefore the natural analogue. The conclusion was largely right; it is still believed that photons are abundant among these penetrating rays. Nevertheless there are also particles of quite another character, as we shall see.

The next work to be chronicled is that of Joliot and Irene Curie-Joliot, who undertook to continue Bothe's work (Bothe was meanwhile moving to Giessen) with the three elements for which he had proved the rays to be strongest. To bombard these elements with alpha-particles they had available *une source extrêmement forte*, 100 millicuries of polonium, a figure which speaks eloquently of the resources of the Institut du Radium when it is compared with the 3 to 7 millicuries which were all that Bothe and Becker had. They were thus able to detect the radiation from beryllium on the farther side of several cm of lead (later on, Thibaud and Dupré la Tour were to detect it beyond no fewer than 30 cm of this ponderous metal) and to trace the curve of its intensity—which is to say, of the current in the ionization-chamber—as function of the thickness of intervening metal. The intensity fell off with an exponential decline,[3] the exponent being 0.15 cm^{-1} (for the rays from B it was 0.22, for those from Li it was 1.7); this suggests electromagnetic rays of uniform wave-length and energy, and of penetrating-power far superior to that of ordinary gamma-rays. But such a suggestion implies a parallel beam of photons all alike, unmixed with any other kind of ray, and producing secondary electrons which at any place form ions at a rate proportional to the number of the photons at that place (in the technical phrase, a parallel beam of homogeneous gamma-rays in equilibrium with its secondaries); and in these and all other experiments the conditions were certainly far removed from that ideal state, both because the beam of rays divergent,[4] and for other reasons which will presently appear. All such values as the foregoing, all the curves of transmitted intensity *vs.* thickness of absorbing screen, are best taken as applying only to the particular detector, to the particular arrangement of absorbers and to the particular disposition of nearby solids, wherewith they were obtained.

Nothing, so far, to suggest that the primary rays are other than electro-

---

[3]So at least I infer from the article, which is laconic as is the custom in the *Comptes Rendus*. "On ne constate aucun effet de filtration; le rayonnement semble homogène."

[4]Owing to the feebleness of the rays the detector and its absorbing screens usually have to be close to the source—a difficulty frequently occurring in the study of transmutation.

magnetic! but in the first weeks of 1932 (the report appeared on 18th January) Curie and Joliot put various thin screens over the window through which the rays were entering the ionization chamber, and found that if these screens were of metal nothing sensational happened, but *if they were of paraffin, water or cellophane*—materials containing *hydrogen—the ionization-current went up instead of down*. This was not the first time that a screen had been observed to enhance the effect of what supposedly were gamma-rays, but in the previous cases it was permissible to infer that the rays were expelling electrons from the substance of the screen.[5] Here the substances were distinguished not by abundance of electrons, but by abundance of hydrogen atoms in their structure; and Curie and Joliot conceived the idea that the primary rays were ejecting protons from the screen, which entered the chamber and in it ionized abundantly. This theory they fortified at once by applying magnetic fields, and finding that the ionization persisted (electrons issuing from the paraffin would have been twisted back, unless extremely fast); by interposing 0.2 mm of aluminium, and finding that the extra ionization ceased (electrons, if extremely fast, might have got through); and by taking cloud-chamber photographs, and observing tracks of the aspect of proton-tracks springing out of the paraffin and traversing the ionization-chamber partly or altogether.

At once it was guessed by Curie and Joliot that these protons were recoiling from elastic impacts of the high-energy photons which the primary rays were still supposed to be—that they had suffered, in fact, the very same sort of blow as electrons suffer in the well-known "Compton effect." So great however was the energy of the protons (as evinced by their range) that photons of energy almost incredibly great had to be postulated; such would probably have an even greater penetrating power than that of the primary rays, and there were other objections more or less solidly founded on theory, which now it would be scarcely worth while to discuss. The French physicists were aware of these difficulties, and published them; but it was reserved for one of the Cavendish group to reject the idea altogether, and supplant it with the one which at present is accepted. Chadwick seized upon the revelations from the Institut du Radium with such alacrity that by February 27th he was reporting data obtained by counters and by cloud-chambers—data which confirmed that the rays emitted from beryllium when bombarded by alpha-particles are

[5]This has been observed in the study of cosmic rays: (cf. E. Steinke, Phys. Zeits. **31**, 1019–1022 (1930); T. H. Johnson, Phys. Rev. **41**, 545–551 (1932); J. M. Benade, Nature **130**, 699 (1932)). Piccard however found on his latest high-altitude flight that the effect of cosmic rays is not enhanced by a sheet of paraffin (A. Piccard and M. Cosyns, C.R. **195**, 604–606 (1932)).

481

able to confer great speeds not only upon protons, but on nuclei of other elements of low mass (a later list comprises Li, He, Be, B, C, N, O, A). Out of these data emerges the fact which speaks most clearly for his theory that the corpuscles which impel the protons and other nuclei are material particles of nearly the mass of a proton, instead of being corpuscles of light.

The argument is as follows. For simplicity let us consider solely the nuclei which are projected in directions pointing straight away from the source of the primary rays, and therefore must have suffered central impacts. Specially, let us take the cases of hydrogen and nitrogen nuclei thus projected. The ranges of these have been measured (of N by Feather, of H by various physicists) and their maximum speeds deduced by means of knowledge earlier acquired of the range-*vs.*-speed relations of charged particles. The values of speed accepted by Chadwick are $3.3 \cdot 10^9$ and $4.72 \cdot 10^8$, respectively. Now if the corpuscles which in central impacts gave to these nuclei these speeds were photons, it is easy to compute by the Compton-effect equations the energy U of the photons; if the impinging corpuscles were material particles of mass M and speed v, it is easy to compute both v and M. It turns out that by the first procedure, one gets different values of U from the two cases (55 and 90 million electron-volts, respectively); by the second, one gets compatible values of M and v. With the first theory, then, one would have to say that nuclei of different kinds were struck by different photons. This is not quite inconceivable, as there *might* be a mixture of gamma-rays of different energies, and a greater likelihood of the higher-energy photons interacting with the more massive nuclei. But it seems less acceptable than the other theory, which permits one to postulate a single kind of corpuscle to explain the impacts against both kinds of nucleus. This corpuscle must be neutral, as a particle of charge e and the computed mass and speed could never penetrate nearly as thick a layer of matter as it can traverse; it is therefore called the "neutron."

The value of M deduced from the foregoing data is given as 1.15 times that of the hydrogen nucleus; the possible error in the estimate of the speed of the recoiling nitrogen nuclei is such that Chadwick says, "it is legitimate to conclude that the mass of the neutron is very nearly the same as the mass of the proton."

Such is the history of the entry of the neutron into experimental physics; for, though such a corpuscle had earlier been thought of and even sought for, no simple phenomena had yet been observed for which it could provide an uniquely apt explanation. Almost exactly a year has now elapsed since that entry, and research has been active in the laboratories which I have mentioned, and in those of de Broglie and of Meitner; I quote a few of the results.

Distribution-in-speed of Neutrons. It is somewhat disappointing to have to say that the neutrons from (say) beryllium bombarded by alpha-particles do not all have the same speed; there is certainly a distribution over a wide interval of velocities and energies, which must complicate all the phenomena into which these corpuscles enter. This distribution-in-speed is of course inferred from that of the nuclei which the neutrons set into motion. The cloud-chamber method makes it possible to measure two qualities of the path of such a "projected" nucleus: its length, and the angle which it makes with the direction from the source to its starting-point. If the range-*vs.*-speed relation for the kind of nucleus in question is considered as certain, and if it be assumed that the neutron came straight from the source to the point of impact, these data suffice for computing (by the ordinary equations of elastic impact) the velocity of the neutron. Feather observed 105 tracks of recoiling nitrogen nuclei, and deduced for the speeds of the neutrons a distribution extending from 16 to $35 \cdot 10^8$ cm/sec.; Meitner and Philipp observed 42 tracks of recoiling protons, and deduced for the neutrons a distribution-in-speed from 7 to $35 \cdot 10^8$ cm/sec. In these cases, the impacts of neutrons against nuclei occurred in the gas of the expansion-chamber; when they occur (for instance) in paraffin, the maximum speeds of the forward-projected nuclei can be estimated from the thickness of aluminum foil which just stops them, though again the estimate involves presumptions as to range-*vs.*-speed relations; Curie and Joliot thus inferred the existence of two "groups" of neutrons, of speeds estimated as 29 and $38 \cdot 10^8$ cm/sec.

Particles of such speeds as these just cited have energy-values of the order of several millions of electron-volts, and protons against which they make central impacts will have ranges of several cm or tens of cm in air under standard conditions. Auger and others have noticed many much shorter tracks, identified as due to protons by their curvature in a magnetic field; these suggest a large proportion of very much slower neutrons.

The neutrons emitted from the source in the same direction as that in which the alpha-particles are going when they hit the beryllium nuclei are moving faster, on the whole—or at any rate, the maximum speed represented among them is greater—than those which are emitted in other directions.— They also are faster, the faster the alpha-particles; or (to describe the experiment better) they shift to lesser speeds, when retarding screens are inserted into the path of the alpha-particles from polonium to beryllium.

Deflection of Neutrons. Large blocks of lead placed beside an ionization-chamber (*not* between it and the source) doubled the number of neutrons entering the chamber and disclosing themselves by impelling nuclei. An

483

envelope of copper several cm thick, completely surrounding both the source and the expansion-chamber, caused a considerable increase in the number of proton-tracks registered in the latter. These results (the former reported by de Broglie and Leprince-Ringuet, the latter by Auger) and others, indicate that neutrons are subject to great deflections when they pass through matter—deflections apparently not attended by great energy-losses.

Interception of Neutrons. When screens of lead (or any other substance) of increasing thickness are placed successively between source and detector, the number of neutrons reaching the latter goes down; but (as I have stressed already) the law of decline depends on the transverse area of the screens and on the presence of neighboring solids, and the phenomena mentioned above show one reason why this must be so. The most thorough measurements yet reported are those of Thibaud and Dupré la Tour. A startling result has been published by de Broglie: it is found that neutrons from boron traverse 5 cm of lead(!) without more than the least appreciable diminution in number, though equal thickness of copper or of paraffin cuts them down by half.

Excitation-function of Neutrons. Rasetti lowered the speed of alpha-particles impinging on beryllium, and found that the number of neutrons reaching his detector fell off steadily, reaching zero when the residual range of the alpha-particles amounted to 9 mm.

Discrimination between Neutrons and Photons Emitted by Bombarded Beryllium. Of these two types of corpuscles, the former ionize through the intermediary of recoiling nuclei, the latter through that of recoiling electrons.[6] The tracks of electrons and of nuclei can often be discriminated by their appearance in a cloud-chamber. Nuclei produce as a rule a great many more ion-pairs than electrons. It is thus possible to set up a system consisting of ionization-chamber, electroscope and amplifier, which gives for each traversing nucleus a sudden kick proportional to the number of ion-pairs it produces, for an electron a correspondingly smaller kick which may be so small that it is not observed. If the electroscope simply indicates the total number of ions produced over a long period, this is likely to be chiefly a measure of the number

[6]Tracks due to electrons recoiling from impacts of neutrons have been sought for in vain by Dee. They should be short and should comprise only a relatively few (less than 400) ion-pairs, as against the tens of thousands produced by projected nuclei; for owing to the relatively small mass of the electron, it cannot receive much energy in an elastic impact from a neutron. It appears from Dee's experiments that the "collision cross section" for an electron exposed to oncoming neutrons must be much smaller than it is for a nucleus.

of nuclei and therefore of the number of neutrons traversing the chamber during that period; and the proportionate share of the neutrons in the total ionization can be raised by walling the ionization-chamber with paraffin. The Geiger counter on the other hand may be adjusted to respond alike to the secondary electrons impelled by photons or to the nuclei impelled by neutrons, or it may be adjusted to respond to the latter and not to the former. Becker and Bothe, experimenting lately in this manner, find that beryllium bombarded by alpha-particles from polonium ejects nineteen photons to every neutron.

Transmutation by Neutrons. Feather, in the course of his cloud-chamber experiments in which he observed 105 single tracks due to nuclei set into motion by impinging neutrons, observed also thirty-two examples of "paired tracks"—two paths springing from a single point. In some of these cases both of the visible tracks lie in a single plane with the invisible track of the neutron (i.e., the direction from the source); it is inferred that the neutron has expelled some particle or other from the nucleus and has itself coalesced with the residue. Several of the examples, when carefully analyzed with due regard to the directions of motion and the apparent speeds of the particles (deduced from their ranges) turn out to be compatible with the idea that the union of neutron and nitrogen nucleus divides itself into a boron and a helium nucleus—a "reaction" which can be written thus:

$$N^{14} + n^1 = B^{11} + He^4.$$

This is probably a reversible reaction, for when alpha-particles impinge on boron, neutrons are given forth, and nothing could be more natural than to assume that they result from the converse process.—In other cases observed by Feather, the paired tracks and the direction from the source to their starting-point do not all lie in a single plane.—Meitner and Philipp have observed apparent transmutations in nitrogen, oxygen and argon.

Mass of the Neutron. If the reactions described by the equation just above do actually occur, then the mass of the neutron can be found by treating the equation as an algebraic one: it is the sum of the masses of the B^{11} and He^4 nuclei, diminished by the mass of the N^{14} nucleus. It happens that all three of these last have been determined accurately by Aston; the value of $(B^{11} + He^4 - N^{14})$ is $1.0051 + 0.005$, in terms of the customary scale in which the mass of the oxygen nucleus is 16. The kinetic energies of the particles before and after the process should perhaps be translated into units of mass according to Einstein's equation $(E/m = c^2)$, and inserted into the equation;

this was done by Chadwick, but the alteration (it is upward, and amounts to 0.0017) is much smaller than the uncertainty in the figure just given; and anyway, we do not know but that some energy is given out in the form of radiation.

LITERATURE

Bothe's Laboratory. W. Bothe and H. Becker, Zeits. f. Physik 66, 298–306 (1930); Becker and Bothe, ibid. 76, 421–438 (1932); Naturwiss. 20, 757–758 (1932).

Institut du Radium. I. Curie and F. Joliot, C.R. 193, 1412–1417 (1931); 194, 273–275, 708–711, 876–877, 1229–1232 (with P. Savel), 2208–2211 (1932).

Other French Laboratories. P. Auger, C.R. 194, 877–879; 195, 234–236 (1932). M. de Broglie, C.R. 194, 879–880 (1932); de Broglie and L. Leprince-Ringuet, ibid. 194, 1616–1617 (1932); 195, 88–89 (1932). J. Thibaud and F. Dupré la Tour, C.R. 194, 1647–1648 (1932); C.R. 195, 655–657 (1932).

Cavendish Laboratory. J. Chadwick, Nature 129, 3129 (27th February, 1932); Proc. Roy. Soc. A136, 692–708 (1932). N. Feather, Proc. Roy. Soc. A136, 703–727 (1932). P. I. Dee, Proc. Roy. Soc. A136, 727–734 (1932). H. C. Webster, Proc. Roy. Soc. A136, 428–453 (1932).

Other Laboratories. F. Rasetti, Naturwiss. 20, 252–253 (1932); Zeits. f. Physik 78, 165–168 (1932). L. Meitner and L. Philipp, Naturwiss. 20, 929–932 (1932).

BYRON AND ENGLISH INTEREST IN THE NEAR EAST[1]

Wallace Cable Brown

ONE of the most important causes for the immediate popularity of Byron's Near East poetry "was the fascination which 'orientalism' in literature exercised, and for many years had exercised, over many readers."[2] The relationship of Byron to the one aspect of orientalism with which he is commonly associated—English interest in the Near East—is the subject of the present paper. This relationship, although tacitly assumed by Byron students, has never been examined in the light of the popular contemporary attitude toward that region.

By 1810, when Byron returned from his own trip to Greece and the Levant, two significant changes had occurred to bring the Near East, in all

[1]From *Studies in Philology*, XXIV, No. 1 (January, 1937).
[2]Samuel C. Chew, *Byron in England* (London, 1924), p. 9; see also E. H. Coleridge, ed., *The Works of Lord Byron, Poetry* (London, 1904), III, vii–viii.

its glamorous reality, nearer to Englishmen than ever before.[3] One was the development of oriental scholarship, under the guidance of Sir William Jones (1746–94), which made available, for the first time, a considerable body of direct translation from Arabic and Persian literature;[4] the other was the popularization, to an extent greater than ever before, of a large group of Near East travel books.[5]

Byron's relationship with English Near East travellers, both personally and through their travel books, was broad and intimate. In his Near East poetry, therefore, he would be likely to give his English readers just what they had come to expect from the travel books, despite the fact that he sometimes tended characteristically to belittle the work of his fellow-travellers. Thus he remarks in his journal:

> The relations of passing travellers are as little to be depended on as the invectives of angry factors; but till something more can be attained, we must be content with the little to be acquired from similar sources.[6]

And later, writing to his publisher John Murray from Italy, he exclaims peevishly: "Books of *travels* are expensive, and I don't want them, having travelled already; besides, they lie."[7] And to another correspondent: "Murray

[3]See Martha P. Conant, *The Oriental Tale in England in the Eighteenth Century* (New York, 1908), pp. 255–6.

[4]Important among these direct translations were: Sir William Jones, translation of the Arabic *Moallakat* (1783); J. D. Carlyle, *Specimens of Arabic Poetry* (1796); Sir William Ouseley, *Persian Miscellanies* (1796); Jonathan Scott, *Bahar-Danush, or the Garden of Knowledge*, "an oriental romance, translated from the Persian of Einauit Oolah" (1799); and James Atkinson, *Selections from the Shah Nameh of Firdausi*, "translated from the Persian" (1814). These early efforts led eventually to the complete translation of the *Arabian Nights* by Edward William Lane (1838–40). In the eighteenth century, English writers and their public had access to oriental literature mainly through the second-hand medium of French translations, in which the originals were often greatly gallicized and expurgated: "When Galland prepared his version of the *Arabian Nights* for European readers [1704–12], he omitted not only the coarseness of the original, but also many of its interesting minutiae, details which give to our later versions—Burton's and Payne's, for instance—the charm of good tales of travel and produce in the reader the vivid sense of actually being in the picturesque Orient. . . . Hardly any English writers until past the middle of the century knew or apparently cared to know the East well, either through travel or through books; hence the pale and colourless quality of their oriental fiction. Beckford was the first to introduce much picturesque detail, and in so doing anticipated the methods of Moore, Southey, Byron, and their successors." Conant, *op. cit.*, pp. 235–6. All the well known and frequently imitated 'tales'—the *Arabian Nights*, the *Persian Tales*, the *Turkish Tales*, etc.—came to England through the French: *Ibid.*, 1–72.

[5]See my article, "The Popularity of English Travel Books about the Near East, 1775–1825," *PQ*, XV (1936), 70–80.

[6]*Works, Poetry*, II, 195.

[7]*The Works of Lord Byron, Letters and Journals*, ed., R. E. Prothero (London, 1904), V, 94.

sends me books of travel—I do not know why; for I have travelled enough myself to know that such books are *full of lies*."[8] Byron, in these petulant remarks, should not be taken too seriously: in addition to his well-known ego-centricity, he possessed his full share of the traveller's natural inclination to disagree, particularly if he has been contradicted first, as Byron sometimes was (by William Turner in his *Journal of a Tour in the Levant*, for example[9]). A more reasoned and reasonable explanation of Byron's impatience with travel books appears in the following note to Murray:

Voyages and *travels*, provided that they are *neither in Greece, Spain, Asia Minor, Albania, nor Italy*, will be welcome: having travelled the countries mentioned, I know that what is said of them can convey nothing further which I desire to know about them.[10]

The predominant attitude of Byron toward travellers and travel books shows him far more sympathetic. Thus, in his advice to Moore about oriental description in *Lalla Rookh*, he says:

The only advantage I have is being on the spot; and that merely amounts to saving me the trouble of turning over books which I had better read again. If *your chamber* was furnished in the same way, you have no need to *go there* to describe—I mean only as to *accuracy*—because I drew it from recollection.[11]

And in a review of Sir William Gell's *Geography of Ithaca* and *Itinerary of Greece*, Byron remarks:

In his [Gell's] first sentence, he makes an assertion which is by no means correct. He says, "*We* are at present as ignorant of Greece, as of the interior of Africa." Surely not quite so ignorant; or several of our Grecian *Mungo Parks* have travelled in vain, and some very sumptuous works have been published to no purpose![12]

Finally, in the following letter to the Near East traveller, Edward D. Clarke, Byron exhibits a cordiality and respect that is far removed from his deprecations noted above:

Your very kind letter is the more agreeable, because, setting aside talents, judgment, and the *laudari a laudato*, etc., you have been on the spot; you have seen and described more of the East than any of your predecessors—I need not say how ably and successfully; and (excuse the bathos) you are one of the very few men who can

[8] *The Works of Lord Byron, Letters and Journals*, ed., R. E. Prothero (London, 1904), V, 307.
[9] For the account of Byron's reactions to Turner, who questioned his swimming the Hellespont, see *Ibid.*, V, 246–51.
[10] *Ibid.*, V, 373.
[11] *Ibid.*, II, 303.
[12] *Ibid.*, I, 361–2.

pronounce how far my costume (to use an affected but expressive word) is correct. As to poesy, that is, as "men, gods, and columns" please to decide upon it; but I am sure that I am anxious to have an observer's, particularly a famous observer's testimony on the fidelity of my manners and dresses; and, as far as memory and an oriental twist in my imagination have permitted, it has been my endeavour to present to the Franks, a sketch of that of which you have and will present them a complete picture.[13]

In the footnotes to his Near East poems (particularly Canto II of *Childe Harold*, *The Giaour*, *The Bride of Abydos*, and *The Corsair*) and in his letters and journals Byron often speaks with approbation of his fellow-travellers. Among those to whom he refers as though he knew them and their works well, may be mentioned: Richard Chandler, William R. Hamilton, Edward D. Clarke, Sir William Gell, William M. Leake, John Galt, William Bankes, J. L. Burckhardt, Lord Valentia, Henry Holland, W. G. Browne, and of course his own travelling companion, J. C. Hobhouse.[14] We know that Byron corresponded with Clarke and Bankes about the Near East,[15] and that, in an essay on the degradation of the modern Greeks, he wrote: "Mr. Hamilton, Lord Aberdeen, Dr. Clarke, Captain Leake, Mr. Gell, Mr. Walpole, and many others now in England, have all the requisites to furnish details of this fallen people."[16] Elsewhere he refers to Leake, a well known Near East traveller, as one of "my principal friends."[17] Byron reviewed two of Gell's books on Greece in the *Monthly Review* for August, 1811;[18] and asked his friend Francis Hodgson to review Galt's *Travels and Voyages* to the Near East for the same magazine in 1812.[19] He knew Valentia personally,[20] and by Holland, on his return from Greece and the Levant, was

---

[13]*Ibid.*, II, 308–9.

[14]In this list, the following were authors of some of the most popular Near East travel books of the period: Richard Chandler, *Travels in Asia Minor* and *Travels in Greece*, 1775–6; E. D. Clarke, *Travels in Various Countries of Europe, Asia, and Africa*, 1810–21; Sir William Gell, *Argolis: The Itinerary of Greece*, 1810; W. G. Browne, *Travels in Africa, Egypt, and Syria*, 1799; J. L. Burckhardt, *Travels in Nubia* and *Travels in Syria and the Holy Land*, 1819, 1822; Lord Valentia, *Voyages and Travels to India, Ceylon, the Red Sea, Abyssinia, and Egypt*, 1809; Henry Holland, *Travels in the Ionian Isles, Albania, Thessaly, Macedonia*, etc., 1815; and J. C. Hobhouse, *A Journey through Albania and other Provinces of Turkey in Europe and Asia*, 1813. See my dissertation, "The Near East as Theme and Background in English Literature, 1775–1825, with Special Emphasis on the Literature of Travel" (University of Michigan, 1934), I, 112–84.

[15]See *Works, Letters and Journals*, II, 308–11 and II, 185.

[16]*Works, Poetry*, II, 204.

[17]*Works, Letters and Journals*, II, 184.

[18]*Ibid.*, I, 350–65.

[19]*Ibid.*, II, 101–2.

[20]*Ibid.*, V, 424.

given a letter from Ali Pasha, the despotic leader of the Albanians.[21] The travel books of Browne, Burckhardt, and Chandler are also referred to by Byron with familiarity.[22]

Close parallels between descriptions and incidents in Byron's poetry and those in contemporary travel books are legion, and have been pointed out by editors and biographers of the poet from Galt and Tom Moore to E. H. Coleridge.[23] Such parallels show that Byron, consciously or not, was actually conforming closely in his poetry to the materials and points of view emphasized in the travel books. The following statement by Galt indicates the attitude of a contemporary and a traveller, and has not been substantially changed by later investigation:

The minute details in the pilgrimage of Childe Harold are the observations of an actual traveller. Had they been given in prose, they could not have been less imbued with fiction. From this fidelity they possess a value equal to the excellence of the poetry, and ensure for themselves an interest as lasting as it is intense.[24]

The use of Byron's poetry by subsequent travellers to the Near East in the early nineteenth century provides a further estimate of the general contemporary attitude toward his work. Clarke, for example, when introducing the account of his travels in Egypt and Greece quotes from Canto II of *Childe Harold*:

> "Wher'er we tread, 'tis haunted, holy ground,
> And one vast realm of wonder spreads around."[25]

In describing his approach to Prevesa, the southern port of Albania, Thomas S. Hughes could say nothing more suitable than to quote from Stanza xlii of Canto II:

Having passed the castle and a small island nearly opposite its northern extremity, where we were challenged by an English sentinel, the towers and forts of Prevesa were dimly seen peering above the distant waves:

> "—and with them stern Albania's hills,
> Dark Suli's rocks, and Pindus' inland peak," etc.[26]

[21]*Works, Letters and Journals*, II, 262–3.
[22]*Ibid.*, IV, 378–9; and *Works, Poetry*, II, 189.
[23]See, for example, Thomas Moore, ed., *The Works of Lord Byron* (London, 1835), II, *passim*; and *Works, Poetry*, II, *passim*.
[24]John Galt, *Life of Lord Byron* (London, 1832), p. 80; see also E. H. Coleridge's remarks about the Turkish tales, *Works, Poetry*, III, vii–ix and 150.
[25]Clarke, *op. cit.* (second edition), III, ii, footnote.
[26]T. S. Hughes, *Travels in Sicily, Greece, and Albania* (London, 1820), I, 406.

And later, on obtaining his first view of Berat in north-central Albania, Hughes refers to Byron's Stanza xlvi, because,

Such scenes as these will justify the bard, who thus describes them after his inspection of the most classic regions that have been celebrated in the songs of the poets.[27]

That Byron's work was looked upon as arising out of a travel-book milieu, is implied by the following comment in the *Eclectic Review*:

. . . his poetry is the essence of a score or two of travellers' journals, and while it often possesses the minute accuracy of an Itinerary, conveys to us at once not only the graphical truth but the moral feeling of the scene.[28]

And the general nature of this milieu, with emphasis on the pre-existent popularity of the materials which Byron fashioned into poetry, is unmistakably pointed out in the *Edinburgh Review*:

The objects he presents are marked out to him by men's present regards. . . . The whole substance and basis of his poem is, therefore, popular. All the scenes through which he has travelled, were, at the very moment, of strong interest to the public mind, and that interest still hangs over them. His travels were not, at first, the self-impelled act of a mind severing itself in lonely roaming from all participation with the society to which it belonged, but rather obeying the general motion of the mind of that society . . . all the Italian, Grecian, Peninsular, Ionian and Ottoman feeling which pervades Childe Harold, singularly suited as it is to the genius of Byron, was not first brought upon the English mind by the power of that genius, but was there already in great force and activity.[29]

The nature of Byron's relationship to English interest in the Near East thus becomes clear: he did not create that interest, for it "was there already in great force and activity"; he therefore capitalized it, and owed to it a considerable measure of the acclaim which made him famous overnight. Had he written about any region other than Greece and the Levant, his genius would have won him fame; but, in all probability, he would not have attained that degree of popularity which sold ten thousand copies of *The Corsair* on the first day of publication. A traveller himself, and intimate with other travellers and travel books, Byron caught the precise spirit of English interest in the Near East; and, with his eye on the romantic realities of that region, provided his readers with "the best possible substitute for the actual sight of the scenes themselves."

[27]*Ibid.*, II, 255.
[28]*Eclectic Review*, XIV, N.S. (Nov., 1820), 301.
[29]*Edinburgh Review*, XXX (June, 1818), 99.

THE STORY OF THE CHRISTMAS SEAL[1]

Carolyn Burwell

IN THE city of Copenhagen, the annual Christmas mail rush was in full swing. The regular and extra postal employees were working day and night so that the thousands of letters and packages would reach their destinations before the great day. Among the mail sorters was one Einar Holboll. He was thinking about the great number of wishes for health, happiness, and good cheer that were being sent upon their way. Suddenly, a wonderful idea came to him. Why could these letters and packages not bear more than just good wishes? Why could they not carry special stamps which had been bought for a small amount in order to secure good health and happiness for every one in Denmark? Thus, in 1903, the idea of a Christmas seal for charity was born.[2]

During the following year, Holboll worked to make his dream come true; and at Christmas time a small half-penny stamp was offered for sale. It was much the same size and shape as our Christmas Seals and bore the picture of Louise, the queen of Denmark, who had died six years before.[3] Because the post offices and mail carriers made the cause their own special one, three and three-fourth million seals were sold the first year, an average of one and a fourth seals for every man, woman, and child in Denmark. Each year since, the receipts have increased in spite of war and hard times; for the Danes feel that a letter is not a real Christmas letter unless it bears one of the little seals.[4]

In 1904, the first Christmas Seal Committee, consisting of Holboll and fourteen others, was formed. It decided that the money which was raised would be used to build sanitoriums. In 1912, the first institution was built with the seal money. This institution at Kolding Fjord, Denmark, was the first in the world exclusively for children.[5] Many other sanitoriums have been built since which have helped to give that health and happiness which Einar Holboll wanted for the people of Denmark.

Holboll died in 1927; but "his great idea, the Christmas Seal, has made its victorious progress all over the world."[6] "All kinds of people buy Christmas

---

[1]A paper submitted in Freshman English at the University of Minnesota in 1940.

[2]Leigh Mitchell Hodges, "The Seal Against Fate," *The Reader's Digest*, Vol. 29, No. 176 (Dec., 1936), p. 19.

[3]*Thanks for Health Day Newspaper*, p. 12.

[4]J. B. Nikolaisen, "Holboll and the Christmas Seal," *The American-Scandinavian Review*, Vol. XXVII, No. 4 (Dec., 1939), p. 297.

[5]*Ibid.*, pp. 298–299.

[6]*Ibid.*, p. 302.

Seals, the white man, the Negro, the yellow man, the rich, the poor, kings and queens and presidents, boys and girls from lands besides . . . [Holboll's] own."[7]

The United States was among the first countries to adopt the Christmas Seal. It was brought about mainly through the work of Emily P. Bissell of Wilmington, Delaware.[8] Jacob Riis, who received a Danish Christmas Seal on one of his letters, wrote an enthusiastic article in *The Outlook* proposing the use of Christmas Seals in the United States. Miss Bissell was inspired by this story to design a similar seal, in 1907, to raise money for a tuberculosis sanitorium of eight beds.[9]

The seals did not sell well at first; therefore, Miss Bissell went to Philadelphia, hoping to get aid from the *North American*, a widely read newspaper in that part of the country. The Sunday editor could not see much sense in the seals, but a columnist, Leigh M. Hodges, saw a great deal of sense in them. He took them to the publisher, E. A. Van Valkenburg, shouting, "Here's a way to wipe out tuberculosis!"[10] After a brief explanation, the elder man agreed to give Miss Bissell all the space she needed in the paper.

"The *North American* bought 50,000 stamps. When they first went on sale in its street-floor office, a ragged newsboy came in. Reaching up to a marble counter higher than his head, he laid down a copper and said, 'Gi' me one. Me sister's got it.' Those seven words settled it. If a street kid could get the message, the messenger was the kind needed. Next day the whole editorial space carried a plea for people to 'buy these bullets in the battle against our worst foe.' "[11]

Because the first seal sale was a great success, the American Red Cross sponsored the sale in 1908 and 1909.[12] The following year, the National Tuberculosis Association, which had been established in 1904, formed a partnership with the Red Cross. The Red Cross put its name, emblem, prestige and financial backing into the partnership. The National Tuberculosis Association organized and promoted the actual sale. It was also given supervision over the spending of the funds.[13] This partnership was dissolved in 1920, when the National Tuberculosis Association was given exclusive use of the seals for its support.

[7]P. P. Jacobs, *Christmas Seals Around the World*, p. 5.
[8]"Two Stamps on Christmas Cards," *Public Health Nursing*, Vol. 31, No. 12 (Dec., 1939), p. 660.
[9]H. E. Kleinschmidt M.D., *Tuberculosis*, pp. 70–71.
[10]Leigh Mitchell Hodges, "The Seal Against Fate," *The Reader's Digest*, Vol. 29, No. 176 (Dec., 1936), p. 20.
[11]*Ibid.*
[12]H. E. Kleinschmidt M.D., *Tuberculosis*, p. 71.
[13]*Talking Points About Tuberculosis*, p. 10.

The National Tuberculosis Association then automatically took over the designing and printing of the seals. At this time, the Association adapted the double-barred cross, which already was the emblem of the world-wide tuberculosis movement, as its symbol.[14] Each year a different Christmas Seal is printed, but the double-barred cross always appears in the design.[15] Each year millions of people express the wish of "Good will to men" by buying these penny seals.[16]

In 1938, a new custom was established in printing the seals. Each sheet of one hundred honored the four leaders in the fight against tuberculosis by a special seal in each corner bearing their portraits. They were: Laennec, who invented the stethoscope; Koch, who discovered the tuberculosis germ; Trudeau, who opened the first sanitorium in the United States; and Holboll, who conceived the idea of the Christmas Seal.[17] Every year since, four seals in each sheet have been set aside for a similar purpose.

These seals, which are the chief means of support of tuberculosis associations, are now sold by the local associations which are continually being established in counties, cities, and villages. The last of the forty-eight state societies was organized in 1917.[18] Now the same seal is sold in every state and section of the United States and in the outlying territories and possessions.[19]

The fair way in which the funds have been divided among the local, state, and national associations has been largely responsible for the steady growth of the movement.[20] Of the annual proceeds from the sales conducted by the local associations five per cent goes to the National Association; and a certain percentage, depending upon the needs of the local association, goes to the state.[21]

Among the hundreds of local associations, the Hennepin County Tuberculosis Association has maintained one of the most excellent records in the promotion of the Christmas Seal sales. The association was started in 1903 by the late Mrs. George H. Christian of Minneapolis, who had lost a brilliant young son because of tuberculosis. After his death she took up work which would help to prevent further loss of life from the disease.[22]

[14]*Talking Points About Tuberculosis*, p. 10.

[15]W. W. Charters, *The Message of the Double-Barred Cross*, p. 2.

[16]"How the Pennies Are Put to Work," *Hygeia*, Vol. 10 (Dec., 1932), p. 1117.

[17]"Christmas in the Home," *Journal of Home Economics*, Vol. 30, No. 7 (Sept., 1938), p. 477.

[18]*The Christmas Seal*, p. 5.

[19]P. P. Jacobs, *Christmas Seals Around the World*, Intro.

[20]*The Christmas Seal*, p. 6.

[21]H. E. Kleinschmidt M.D., *Tuberculosis*, p. 71.

[22]*Thanks for Health Day Newspaper*, p. 8.

In 1909, as president of the Hennepin County Tuberculosis Association, Mrs. Christian sold the first seals to be sold in the county. She and a friend, Mrs. Thomas F. Kinney, were driven around Minneapolis by Mrs. Kinney's daughter. At almost every small drug store and grocery store in Minneapolis, a small package of seals was left; and the store keepers were asked to try to sell the seals to their customers. After Christmas the small amounts of money and any unsold seals were collected from each little store by these women. Although the money raised in this way was not a very large sum, the Christmas Seal and the meaning behind it had become familiar to most of the citizens of Minneapolis, who have gradually made the buying of these seals an annual custom.

The proceeds from the sale of seals, besides supporting the tuberculosis associations, have promoted many lines of defense against tuberculosis. The most important of these is the education of the public in basic facts about tuberculosis so that they can protect themselves against it.[23] This is done mainly through literature, posters, lectures, radio broadcasts, motion pictures, slides, and exhibits.[24]

The early discovery of all unknown cases of tuberculosis forms another important line of defense.[25] Over a thousand clinics for the diagnosis and discovery of the disease are supported entirely or partly by seal funds.[26] With the Tuberculin Test of today, anyone who goes to these clinics for examination can know within forty-eight hours whether tuberculosis germs are at work in his body.[27] This early discovery not only prevents the spread of the disease to other persons but also gives the infected person a better chance to be completely cured.

The Christmas Seal funds are also spent to treat tubercular people.[28] The only known cure was discovered by Dr. Edward Livingston Trudeau. It consists of rest, fresh air, and good food.[29] Twelve hundred sanitoriums and hospitals, twelve hundred summer camps and open air schools for children,

[23]"The Christmas Seals," *Journal of Home Economics*, Vol. 27, No. 10 (Dec., 1935), p. 656.

[24]"Buy Christmas Seals," *Hygeia*, Vol. 13 (Dec., 1935), p. 1141.

[25]"The Christmas Seals," *Journal of Home Economics*, Vol. 27, No. 10 (Dec., 1935), p. 656.

[26]"The Christmas Seal Makes Its Annual Appearance," *Hygeia*, Vol. 14 (Dec., 1936), p. 1144.

[27]Leigh Mitchell Hodges, "The Seal Against Fate," *The Reader's Digest*, Vol. 29, No. 176 (Dec., 1936), p. 22.

[28]"The Christmas Seals," *Journal of Home Economics*, Vol. 27, No. 10 (Dec., 1935), p. 656.

[29]"Buy Christmas Seals," *Hygeia*, Vol. 13 (Dec., 1935), p. 1142.

and ten thousand public health nurses are able to apply Trudeau's remedy because of the support which is given to them by the seal.[30]

The Christmas Seal organization has already planned its 1940 fight against tuberculosis. "Intensified efforts towards early discovery and prevention of tuberculosis are planned by the Christmas Seal organization to include tuberculin testing and X-raying of school children, promotion of hot lunch projects, and instruction in good health habits."[31] "As long as this fundamental institution, the Christmas Seal, is preserved and advanced, so long will the tuberculosis movement receive renewed impetus for further conquests of the disease and the promotion of public health."[32]

BIBLIOGRAPHY

Books

CHARTERS, W. W. *The Message of the Double-Barred Cross.* New York: National Tuberculosis Association, 1939.

JACOBS, P. P. *Christmas Seals Around the World.* New York: National Tuberculosis Association, 1939.

KLEINSCHMIDT, H. E., M.D. *Tuberculosis.* New York and London: Funk and Wagnalls Co., 1937.

Talking Points About Tuberculosis. Minneapolis: Hennepin County Tuberculosis Association, 1939.

Thanks for Health Day Newspaper. Minneapolis: Hennepin County Tuberculosis Association, 1937.

The Christmas Seal. New York: National Tuberculosis Association, 1936.

Up-to-Date Facts About the Campaign Against Tuberculosis. Minneapolis: Hennepin County Tuberculosis Association, 1936.

Periodicals

"Banner Health Year Seen for Minnesota in 1940." *The Minneapolis Star-Journal* (Jan. 18, 1940), p. 15.

"Buy Christmas Seals." *Hygeia*, Vol. 13 (Dec., 1935), pp. 1141–2.

"Christmas in the Home." *Journal of Home Economics*, Vol. 30, No. 7 (Sept., 1938), pp. 476–7.

Hodges, Leigh Mitchell. "The Seal Against Fate." *The Reader's Digest*, Vol. 29, No. 176 (Dec., 1936), pp. 19–22.

[30]"The Christmas Seal Makes Its Annual Appearance," *Hygeia*, Vol. 14 (Dec., 1936), p. 1144.

[31]"Banner Health Year Seen for Minnesota in 1940," *The Minneapolis Star-Journal* (Jan. 18, 1940), p. 15.

[32]*The Christmas Seal*, p. 6.

"How the Pennies Are Put to Work." *Hygeia*, Vol. 10 (Dec., 1932), p. 1117.

Nikolaisen, J. B. "Holboll and the Christmas Seal." *The American-Scandinavian Review*, Vol. XXVII, No. 4 (Dec., 1939), pp. 295–302.

"The Christmas Seal Makes Its Annual Appearance." *Hygeia*, Vol. 14 (Dec., 1936), p. 1144.

"The Christmas Seals." *Journal of Home Economics*, Vol. 27, No. 10 (Dec., 1935), p. 656.

"Two Stamps on Christmas Cards." *Public Health Nursing*, Vol. 31, No. 12 (Dec., 1939), p. 660.

Reviews

KEATS'S ENDYMION[1]

John Wilson Croker

REVIEWERS have been sometimes accused of not reading the works which they affected to criticize. On the present occasion we shall anticipate the author's complaint, and honestly confess that we have not read his work. Not that we have been wanting in our duty—far from it; indeed, we have made efforts almost as superhuman as the story itself appears to be, to get through it; but with the fullest stretch of our perseverance, we are forced to confess that we have not been able to struggle beyond the first of the four books of which this "Poetic Romance" consists. We should extremely lament this want of energy, or whatever it may be, on our part, were it not for one consolation—namely, that we are no better acquainted with the meaning of the book through which we have so painfully toiled, than we are with that of the three which we have not looked into.

It is not that Mr. Keats (if that be his real name, for we almost doubt that any man in his senses would put his real name to such a rhapsody), it is not, we say, that the author has not powers of language, rays of fancy, and gleams of genius—he has all these; but he is unhappily a disciple of the new school of what has been somewhere called Cockney poetry,[2] which may be defined to consist of the most incongruous ideas in the most uncouth language.

Of this school, Mr. Leigh Hunt, as we observed in a former Number, aspires to be the hierophant. Our readers will recollect the pleasant recipes for harmonious and sublime poetry which he gave us in his Preface to *Rimini*, and the still more facetious instances of his harmony and sublimity in the verses themselves; and they will recollect above all the contempt of Pope, Johnson, and such poetasters and pseudo-critics, which so forcibly contrasted itself with Mr. Leigh Hunt's self-complacent approbation of

> —all the things itself had wrote,
> Of special merit though of little note.

This author is a copyist of Mr. Hunt; but he is more unintelligible, almost as rugged, twice as diffuse, and ten times more tiresome and absurd than his prototype, who, though he impudently presumed to seat himself in the chair of criticism, and to measure his own poetry by his own standard, yet generally had a meaning. But Mr. Keats had advanced no dogmas which he was bound

[1]The review of "Endymion: A Poetic Romance," published in *The Quarterly Review*, 1818.

[2]A nickname applied by Lockhart and other English critics to the poetry of Leigh Hunt, Shelley, Keats, and others.

to support by examples; his nonsense, therefore, is quite gratuitous; he writes it for its own sake; and, being bitten by Mr. Leigh Hunt's insane criticism, more than rivals the insanity of his poetry.

Mr. Keats's Preface hints that his poem was produced under peculiar circumstances.

"Knowing within myself (he says) the manner in which this poem has been produced, it is not without a feeling of regret that I make it public.—What manner I mean, will be *quite clear* to the reader, who must soon perceive great inexperience, immaturity, and every error denoting a feverish attempt, rather than a deed accomplished."—*Preface*, p. vii.

We humbly beg his pardon, but this does not appear to us to be *quite so clear*—we really do not know what he means—but the next passage is more intelligible.

"The two first books, and indeed the two last, I feel sensible are not of such completion as to warrant their passing the press."—*Preface*, p. vii.

Thus "the two first books" are, even in his own judgment, unfit to appear, and "the two last" are, it seems, in the same condition— and as two and two make four, and as that is the whole number of books, we have a clear and, we believe, a very just estimate of the entire work.

Mr. Keats, however, deprecates criticism on this "immature and feverish work" in terms which are themselves sufficiently feverish; and we confess that we should have abstained from inflicting upon him any of the tortures of the "*fierce hell*" of criticism, which terrify his imagination, if he had not begged to be spared in order that he might write more; if we had not observed in him a certain degree of talent which deserves to be put in the right way, or which, at least, ought to be warned of the wrong; and if, finally, he had not told us that he is of an age and temper which imperiously require mental discipline.

Of the story we have been able to make out but little; it seems to be mythological, and probably relates to the loves of Diana and Endymion; but of this, as the scope of the work has altogether escaped us, we cannot speak with any degree of certainty; and must therefore content ourselves with giving some instances of its diction and versification; and here again we are perplexed and puzzled. At first it appeared to us that Mr. Keats had been amusing himself and wearying his readers with an immeasurable game at *bouts-rimés*³; but, if we recollect rightly, it is an indispensable condition at this play, that the rhymes when filled up shall have a meaning; and our author, as we have

³Riming words proposed to fill out verses.

already hinted, has no meaning. He seems to us to write a line at random, and then he follows not the thought excited by this line, but that suggested by the *rhyme* with which it concludes. There is hardly a complete couplet inclosing a complete idea in the whole book. He wanders from one subject to another, from the association, not of ideas but of sounds, and the work is composed of hemistichs⁴ which, it is quite evident, have forced themselves upon the author by the mere force of the catch-words on which they turn.

We shall select, not as the most striking instance, but as that least liable to suspicion, a passage from the opening of the poem.

> —Such the sun, the moon,
> Trees old and young, sprouting a shady boon
> For simple sheep; and such are daffodils
> With the green world they live in; and clear rills
> That for themselves a cooling covert make
> 'Gainst the hot season; the mid-forest brake,
> Rich with a sprinkling of fair musk-rose blooms;
> And such, too, is the grandeur of the dooms
> We have imagined for the mighty dead; etc., etc.
>
> —[ll. 13–21]

Here it is clear that the word, and not the idea, *moon* produces the simple sheep and their shady *boon*, and that "the *dooms* of the mighty dead" would never have intruded themselves but for the "*fair musk-rose blooms.*"
Again.

> For 'twas the morn: Apollo's upward fire
> Made every eastern cloud a silvery pyre
> Of brightness so unsullied, that therein
> A melancholy spirit well might win
> Oblivion, and melt out his essence fine
> Into the winds: rain-scented eglantine
> Gave temperate sweets to the well-wooing sun;
> The lark was lost in him; cold springs had run
> To warm their chilliest bubbles in the grass;
> Man's voice was on the mountains; and the mass
> Of nature's lives and wonders puls'd tenfold,
> To feel this sun-rise and its glories old.
>
> —[ll. 95–106]

Here Apollo's *fire* produces a *pyre*, a silvery pyre of clouds, *wherein* a spirit might *win* oblivion and melt his essence *fine*, and scented *eglantine* gives

⁴Incomplete lines.

503

sweets to the *sun*, and cold springs had *run* into the *grass*, and then the pulse
of the *mass* pulsed *tenfold* to feel the glories *old* of the new-born day, etc.

One example more.

> Be still the unimaginable lodge
> For solitary thinkings, such as dodge
> Conception to the very bourne of heaven,
> Then leave the naked brain: be still the leaven,
> That spreading in this dull and clodded earth
> Gives it a touch ethereal—a new birth.
>
> [ll. 293–298]

Lodge, dodge—heaven, leaven—earth, birth; such, in six words, is the sum
and substance of six lines.

We come now to the author's taste in versification. He cannot indeed
write a sentence, but perhaps he may be able to spin a line. Let us see. The
following are specimens of his prosodial notions of our English heroic metre.

> Dear as the temple's self, so does the moon,
> The passion poesy, glories infinite.—[ll. 28, 29]

> So plenteously all weed-hidden roots.—[l. 65]

> Of some strange history, potent to send.—[l. 324]

> Before the deep intoxication.—[l. 502]

> Her scarf into a fluttering pavilion.—[l. 628]

> The stubborn canvas for my voyage prepared.—[l. 772]

> "Endymion! the cave is secreter
> Than the isle of Delos. Echo hence shall stir
> No sighs but sigh-warm kisses, or light noise
> Of thy combing hand, the while it travelling cloys
> And trembles through my labyrinthine hair."
>
> —[ll. 965–969]

By this time our readers must be pretty well satisfied as to the meaning of
his sentences and the structure of his lines. We now present them with some
of the new words with which, in imitation of Mr. Leigh Hunt, he adorns our
language.

We are told that "turtles *passion* their voices" [l. 248]; that an "arbor was
nested" [l. 431]; and a lady's locks "*gordian'd up*" [l. 614]; and to supply the
place of the nouns thus verbalized, Mr. Keats, with great fecundity, spawns

new ones; such as "men-slugs and human *serpentry*" [1.821]; the *"honey-feel of bliss"* [1.903]; "wives prepare *needments*" [1.208]—and so forth.

Then he has formed new verbs by the process of cutting off their natural tails, the adverbs, and affixing them to their foreheads; thus, "the wine out-sparkled" [1.154]; the "multitude up-followed" [1.164]; and "night up-took" [1.561]. "The wind up-blows" [1.627]; and the "hours are down-sunken" [1.708].

But if he sinks some adverbs in the verbs, he compensates the language with adverbs and adjectives which he separates from the parent stock. Thus, a lady "whispers *pantingly* and close" [1.407], makes *"hushing* signs" [1.409]; and steers her skiff into a *"ripply* cove" [1.403]; a shower falls *"refreshingly"* [1.898]; and a vulture has a *"spreaded* tail" [1.867].

But enough of Mr. Leigh Hunt and his simple neophyte. If any one should be bold enough to purchase this "Poetic Romance," and so much more patient than ourselves as to get beyond the first book, and so much more fortunate as to find a meaning, we entreat him to make us acquainted with his success; we shall then return to the task which we now abandon in despair, and endeavor to make all due amends to Mr. Keats and to our readers.

FREE LAND[1]

[By ROSE WILDER LANE. New York: Longmans, Green & Co., 1938][1]

Howard Mumford Jones

THIS might be described as a novel of the weather. I do not recall any recent book of my reading which is so full of blizzards and general climatic cussedness, and having dug myself out of the snow for the nth time, lived through a tornado, endured two or three hot spells, twisted hay to burn in the stove, gone on rescuing parties to dig up the frozen, and shovelled snow off the railway track for miles to let the dad-burned train through with supplies, I arrived at page 332 in a state of physical toughness which led me to imagine I was one of the original settlers in Dakota. And then I was considerably worried about debt. I went in one deceptive summer worth something over a thousand dollars, but by page 319 I was carrying a hundred dollars a year in interest on my debts, and if father hadn't advanced me two thousand on the last page, I don't know what I would have done.

[1]This review and the four which follow are from *The Saturday Review of Literature.*

"Free Land" is a novel of weather and the farm, of things and events rather than of persons. The hero and heroine are sufficient for the purpose of the tale, which is to show the heroism and suffering with which the Dakota plains were broken to the plough. The theme song is the once popular ditty:

> O Dakota land, sweet Dakota land!
> As on thy burning soil I stand
> And look away across the plains
> I wonder why it never rains.

Wisely or unwisely, David Beaton will not be licked by heat or blizzards, horse thieves or borrowed money, but clings to his soddy, improves it, rears a couple of children, plants turnips, buys oxen, and heroically—and cheerfully —works on to the end of the book, aided by his wife and helped by (and helping) his neighbors.

There is a refreshing absence of physical violence, cruelty, and bucolic despair in the book. This does not mean that violent events do not occur, but they are not played up for the sake of ferocity. Attention is centered rather on the quiet heroism of human nature, on its ability cheerfully to endure sorrow and catastrophe. Possibly because Mrs. Lane seems to be more interested in creating an authentic picture of farm life during the early days of the Dakota land boom, David and Mary persistently remain a little thin; they have almost no internal life because they are forever shown struggling with the elements. The minor characters suffer from the same cause.

The writing is simple, honest, and direct. The quiet heroism of the Dakota settlers is, of course, appealing, but the novel seems more important as document than as work of art. As a document it is an interesting fictional chapter in American history. Thus, indeed, one says to himself, did they toil to create another American state. Mrs. Lane steers a middle course between the heroic-pioneer school of writing and the dreadful-life-on-the-farm school of writing; the result is a pleasantly written book which restores one's faith in ordinary men and women.

MY AMERICA

[1928–1938. By Louis Adamic. New York: Harper & Brothers. 1938]

William Allen White

A CURIOUS but significant book is this. It might be well entitled "A Potpourri of America." It is not cast as autobiography, according to the formal rules of the autobiographical art. It is something more than an unrelated collection of essays, sketches, magazine articles, diary entries, and incidental philosophy. Yet because the incidental philosophy permeates all the contents of the book, it has unity. And when the reader has reached page 662, he knows what Louis Adamic thinks of America. Moreover, the reader knows that Louis Adamic's opinion is worth considering. For in this book he reaches such a wide scope of American areas, both geographically (from coast to coast and from the lakes to the south) and socially (from Rupert Hughes, "a sort of Doctor Johnson from Hollywood," to the coal bootleggers of Pennsylvania), that his evidence may well be accepted as the views of an expert.

He proves further that he is an expert by rendering a balanced judgment. In his America, he takes account of the unrest of labor. He has set down the real and cruel grievances of the underprivileged. He has a keen sense of the inertia of the middle class and of middle-class idealism and unconscious middle-class class-consciousness. He knows the road-side Americans, the girl at the lunch counter, the filling station boy who wipes your windshield and hopes next year to own a filling station down the road. And he knows the labor agitator and the labor dynamiter, and the boss's spy. You also meet the boss, who is harried, tempted, rather mean, sometimes gentle, occasionally, even generally, decent according to his lights and standards. Here in these pages one sees the mill town and the mining town; and the little country town with elm shaded streets and wide lawns where a good two-fifths of our population live; the towns between five hundred and fifty thousand, the homes and fortresses of the middle class. And one sees also here in these pages, the great magnificent cities, the wide harbors with gull-like ships and the rich black plowing land of the farms, and the desert with swirling dust. And when the reader comes to the last paragraph, which declares, "I want America to have a chance to think and debate about the methods of progress most suited to her, and gradually—not via any shortcuts—to deal with her internal discords and incongruities which are dislocating her life, throwing it out of focus. I want America to remain America. I want America eventually to become a work of art,"—when one reads that paragraph of this book, over the long winding way of this book, the general impression the reader gets is that he has been looking at a picture of democracy by a laughing idealist. The artist who paints this picture gives the impression that he has a potent passion for democracy even though he knows she has a wart on her neck and a wen on her chin, eats too many calories, and bulges in the wrong places, has a mad strain in her ancestry and goofey children, but still the passion persists and glorifies the picture.

- That is about what the book is—a beautiful book, as American as "Roughing It," brought up to date. It is as though Mr. Adamic had taken the song "America the Beautiful" and had played it on every kind of a musical instrument from a horse fiddle to a celestial harp, and by some magic had harmonized it all into a vast choral symphony. Which is to say that "My America" is well worth reading, rereading, pondering, and engraving upon the heart of America. In short it is a swell book!

I'M A STRANGER HERE MYSELF

[By Ogden Nash. Boston: Little, Brown and Company. 1938]

Louis Untermeyer

Ogden Nash has been both overpraised and underrated; his stock has gone up and down and up again; his highs are often confused with his lows. Nevertheless, in a rapidly changing world and a nervously fluctuating market, he has always had more orders than he could fill. Although highly salable, his work is interesting to brows of all altitudes; it is intelligent and always unpredictable. Nash is, therefore, something of a phenomenon as poet and producer, and he merits a more detailed stocktaking than he has received.

There are, first of all, Nash's two most obvious characteristics. Both of them are curiosities in technique: the long, asymmetrical lines, and the elaborately inexact rhymes. One or two fanatical source-hunters have found the origin of Nash's lengthy eccentricities in Gilbert's "Lost Mr. Blake." But an unprejudiced comparison will show that the two styles have nothing in common. Apart from the almost opposite idioms, Gilbert's lines are consistently long and fairly regular, while Nash's line-lengths vary from two to sixty-two syllables; Nash's unmatched and unscannable lines are his own, a distinct technical departure. Nevertheless, I do not think they are particularly effective. Their charm is the frail charm of the unexpected; with each repetition the surprise is a little less surprising—so much so that when Nash, after hundreds of purposefully shapeless verses, printed a few poems in traditional meters, his readers were really surprised. In the present volume, as in the preceding, "The Bad Parents' Garden of Verse," the keenest as well as the most comical verses are those in which the rhythm is regular and the lines quite orthodox in shape. I would be disposed to put the "invention" of the irregular line on the debit side.

The rhymes are another matter. Here the reader is constantly and incredibly assaulted by a shock which is partly esthetic and partly galvanic. A rhyming word is usually a preparation for another rhyming word; Nash delights the reader with the pleasure of inexactitude, with words that rhyme reluctantly, with words that nearly-but-do-not-quite rhyme, with words which never before had any relation with each other and which never again will be on rhyming terms. These distortions are at their best when they are their worst. What reader can fail to be startled when confronted with a poem which begins:

> Oh, sometimes I sit around and think,
>   what would you do if you were up
>   a dark alley and there was Caesar
> Borgia,
> And he was coming torgia,
> And brandished a poisoned poniard,
> And looked at you like an angry fox
>   looking at the plumpest rooster in
>   a boniard?

Such rhymes are as delightful as they are astonishing; they are like apparently improvised speeches in which the errors are more lively—and more likable—than the prepared accuracies. I should say that Nash's calculated recklessness in rhyme belongs definitely on the credit side.

Nash has been applauded for his industry and his verbal ingenuities. Both are virtues, but they become vices with Nash. For one thing, he writes too much. At first his work seems amazing; then it becomes amusing; after too many repetitions of the same effects, it descends to the mechanical. The present volume contains almost three hundred pages; were it half as long it would be twice as good. Productiveness not only compels Nash to pad but to pretend. He has to pretend to be funnier than he really is, or to be funny when he wants to be serious, or to give a "snap" to a title which might better have been casual or noncommittal. I feel he is working too hard when he forces himself to such titles as "To Bargain, Toboggan, To-Woo!" "Boop-Boop-Adieup, Little Group!" "Man Bites Dog-Days," "Where There's a Will, There's Velleity," "Little Miss Muffet Sat on a Prophet," "Barmaids Are

Diviner than Mermaids." Working overtime and straining too often puts much of Nash's output on the debit side.

But the rest of Nash belongs on the sunny side of the ledger. His verse always makes good reading; often it is the best light verse written in America today. The territory might be extended to include England, for, with the possible exception of A. P. Herbert, there is no one here or abroad who can surpass the straight-faced absurdity of "Adventures of Isabel," the sensible nonsense of "Curl Up and Diet," the clipped but devastating disposals of "Fellow Creatures." Nash's "The Bad Parents' Garden of Verse," and in particular "The Tale of Custard the Dragon," proved he could be as nimble and original as A. A. Milne; page after page in the present volume proves he can take the leap from childlike fancy to social satire in one effortless stride. It is hard for me to understand why no musician, manager, or theatrical producer has made Nash supply book and lyrics for a series of native comic operas, especially since there seems to be an almost hopeless search for librettists with imagination.

It is in this realm, the realm of incalculable imagination, that Nash is happiest and at his highest. Time and again he begins inconsequentially, with a wisp of an idea, or with no thought at all. Once upon a time, he mumbles to himself, there was a man named Mr. Strawbridge. Strawbridge rhymes with drawbridge, and so the poem not only is about Mr. Strawbridge who wanted a drawbridge, but about what kind of a drawbridge would please him best. He wanted it because he wanted to interfere with traffic; on his house he had a veranda built (rhyming with Vanderbilt) so that he could look at the Atlantic Ocean,

> But he said sometimes on Sundays and
> holidays he couldn't see the Atlantic
> for the motorists,
> And he said he'd rather see the former
> than the latter even though they were
> handsome and respectable Kiwanians
> and Lions and Rotarists,

And so the poem goes wildly on from one mad fantasy to another—and all because the name of Strawbridge popped into Nash's oddly proportioned mind.

Nonsense and criticism elbow each other in Nash; he is crazy storyteller one moment, a satirist the next, a wit who takes to clowning to correct pretense and expose hypocrisy. Playfully but incisively he makes his summaries with the deceptive calm of the following "tribute":

How courteous is the Japanese;
He always says, "Excuse it, please."
He climbs into his neighbor's garden,
And smiles, and says, "I beg your pardon";
He bows and grins a friendly grin,
And calls his hungry family in;
He grins, and bows a friendly bow:
"So sorry, this my garden now."

Such moments occur frequently enough to lift Nash above his own pleasant insanities; they are funny, but they are wryly, seriously humorous. Some day the committee which gratifyingly awarded a Pulitzer Prize to Morrie Ryskind, George S. Kaufman, and the Gershwins for "Of Thee I Sing" will give Nash that honor for adding a new approach, a new style, and a new meaning to American social verse. This will be as much a surprise to the committee as it will be to Mr. Nash.

REBECCA

[By DAPHNE DU MAURIER. New York: Doubleday, Doran & Co. 1938]

Basil Davenport

So CINDERELLA married the prince, and then her story began. Cinderella was hardly more than a school-girl, and the overworked companion of a snobbish woman of wealth; the prince was Maximilian de Winter, whom she had heard of as the owner of Manderley in Cornwall, one of the most magnificent show places in England, who had come to the Riviera to forget the tragic death of his wife Rebecca. He was twice the little companion's age, but she conceived a starved girl's adoration for him when he was kind to her, and there was something about her freshness that seemed to please him. Then to her astonished rapture, he proposed marriage to her, and carried her off to the splendors of Manderley, in its forest of azaleas, sloping down to the sea that had drowned Rebecca, the first Mrs. de Winter—"Mrs. de Winter," simply, as everyone still calls her. For slowly and subtly the girl's dream changes to a nightmare. The great house where she cannot find her way, the first wife's shuttered bedroom, the servants who say that in Mrs. de Winter's time there were no complaints, and above all the old housekeeper, who keeps for the first Mrs. de Winter the ghoulish devotion of Phaedra's nurse or Electra's old slave—they all close in on her, like the monstrous azaleas. There was some mystery about Rebecca's death, too, as the village idiot knows; but the book is skillfully contrived so that it does not depend only on knowledge of it for its thrill; it can afford to give no hint of it till two-thirds of the way through. But the revelation, when it comes, leads to one of the most prolonged, deadly, and breathless fencing-matches that one can find in fiction, a battle of wits that would by itself make the fortune of a melodrama on the stage.

For this is a melodrama, unashamed, glorying in its own quality, such as we have hardly had since that other dependent, Jane Eyre, found that her house too had a first wife. It has the weaknesses of melodrama; in particular, the heroine is at times quite unbelievably stupid, as when she takes the advice of the housekeeper whom she knows to hate her. But if the second Mrs. de Winter had consulted with anyone before trusting the housekeeper, we should miss one of the best scenes in the book. There is also, as is almost inseparable from a melodrama, a forced heightening of the emotional values; the tragedy announced in the opening chapter is out of proportion to the final outcome of the long battle of wits that ends the book. But it is as absorbing a tale as the season is likely to bring.

MARLBOROUGH, HIS LIFE AND TIMES

[*Vol. VI: 1708–1722*. By the Right Honourable WINSTON S. CHURCHILL. New York: Charles Scribner's Sons. 1938]

Arthur Lyon Cross

READERS who have been enchanted by Mr. Churchill's vivid and majestic epic will regret to have it brought to a close with this sixth volume. It deals with a titanic figure playing a dominant part in notable events. It overlaps, to a considerable degree, the "Age of Anne" by Professor George Macaulay Trevelyan, another historian of foremost rank and also a master of English style. Mr. Trevelyan's more restrained interpretation of the period has been appraised elsewhere, and it is sufficient to point out what a rare opportunity those specially interested in the men and the period have for comparing these two masterly accounts which have appeared within the same decade.

As we might expect from his preceding volumes, Mr. Churchill has sought widely and thoroughly for manuscript and printed materials on which to base his conclusions. Although he is qualified to speak with authority on naval and military matters, he has again taken the precaution to consult technical experts, to whom he pays an adequate tribute. The course of the campaigns, battles, and sieges are rendered crystal-clear by the aid of numerous maps and plans.

The military interest of the volume centers and culminates in the battle of Malplaquet, 11 September, 1709, "the bloodiest and best contested for a hundred years," in which, although Marlborough "snatched victory from the jaws of defeat," he failed to destroy the enemy. While he had two more years, he was being continuously undermined, and his vigor and achievements steadily declined. His active military career ended with the forcing of the *ne plus ultra* lines in 1711 and the capture of Bouchain. Then he was superseded by Ormonde, who was forced in 1712, by the notorious "restraining orders" to desert his allies. Prince Eugene, driven to taking desperate chances with his diminished forces, was obliged to yield one stronghold after another until he had lost in three months the gains of the three preceding years. It was a dismal termination of what he and Marlborough had accomplished by their combined genius.

Meantime, the strategic center had shifted to party politics in England. In his treatment of this lamentable series of maneuvers, Mr. Churchill shows the influence of his years of active participation in public affairs. While painstaking in pursuit of his evidence and particular in presenting it, he scorns impartiality when, in his opinion, a policy or a person deserves condemnation. He pays generous tribute to the dignity with which Harley, new Earl of Oxford, faced his downfall; but pours the vials of his wrath on St. John— or Viscount Bolingbroke—for his treacherous desertion of the allies and his black ingratitude toward his benefactor Marlborough. It is interesting to contrast the author's verdict with that of Professor Trevelyan, who, not oblivious of those faults and vices that justly brought Bolingbroke obscurity and misery, can conclude: "But he stands in history as the man who, by courses however devious and questionable, negotiated a Peace which proved in the working more satisfactory than any other that has ended a European conflict in modern times."

It would be interesting, did space allow, to comment on the lifelike portraits of the men who guided the complicated and sinister politics of the day. Suffice it to say that those who supported Marlborough are painted—and perhaps justly—in pleasanter colors than those who worked against him; even Macaulay's paragon, Somers, comes in for deserved castigation. Not infrequently the narrative is brightened by touches of humor and deft bits of sarcasm which throw into relief other passages of lofty eloquence. The illustrations, mostly reproductions of paintings, are a welcome addition, and the volume is a fine piece of book-making. Altogether, whether or no one agrees with all its findings, it is a scholarly as well as a brilliant achievement.

I MARRIED ADVENTURE[1]

[By OSA JOHNSON. Philadelphia: Lippincott. 1940]

Clifton Fadiman

THEY were Kansas products, both of them: the watchmaker's son who wasn't any too bright at school and the locomotive engineer's snub-nosed daughter. A couple of healthy and apparently almost dismally normal small-town kids, they married each other without any very solemn preliminaries and forthwith proceeded, with the aid of cameras, pygmies, head-hunters, cannibals, gazelles, lions, gorillas, and their own unusual qualities, to become Mr. and Mrs. Martin Johnson. The story of how this came about is now told in "I Married Adventure," a pleasant, forthright, occasionally exciting book by Osa Johnson, Martin's widow. It makes a canny bid for a number of audiences: camera fans, fireside explorers, animal lovers, and embattled feminist ladies, who will take vicarious satisfaction in Osa's ability to stand the gaff of hardship and danger as well as, or better than, the next man.

Martin, it seems, was a sort of Peck's Bad Boy, built by nature to run away from home. He liked cameras, animals, and geography, and it took him only a few years to fit these interests together and become the world's most famous photographer of the wild life, both feral and human, of the jungles of Borneo and Africa. Of course, as Osa affectionately makes clear, he had a few other qualities besides a liking for beasts and lenses. He was brave, resourceful, and had the kind of forceful simplicity that enabled him to sell his schemes for film-making to industrialists like George Eastman.

One other quality he possessed, which Osa doesn't mention—the sure touch of the born showman. He had the touch when, as a lanky kid, he started a small chain of nickelodeons, and exhibited the motion pictures of the trip he took with Jack and Charmian London in the *Snark*. He had the touch toward the end of his all too short life when, deciding that aerial photography would give the animal-and-exploring business a much-needed new twist, he and Osa learned to pilot a plane. Nor can it be denied that the Johnsons worked for all it was worth—and never for more than it was worth—the natural audience appeal that lay in the Mr.-and-Mrs. set-up. But for all the amiable kidding that the Johnsons inevitably got, there was never a suspicion of Barnum about their doings. Showmen? Certainly—but honest showmen. Never pretending to be anthropologists or trained naturalists, they took sound and often extraordinary pictures whose appeal was frankly dramatic, with a reasonable infusion of educational value.

[1]Reprinted from *The New Yorker*.

"I Married Adventure" is about adventure, but it's also about a marriage. When Osa became Mrs. Martin Johnson, she had not the remotest notion that she was going to spend the next twenty years of her life inducing testy cannibals to perform antics before the camera, shooting elephants in the nick of time, eating monkey meat, and helping to boss two hundred natives in the middle of nowhere in Africa. Apparently, Martin picked a wife out of air, and she was, by a miracle, precisely the one he needed. There never was any problem of adaptation. The little girl from Chanute, Kansas, took to head-hunters and rhinoceroses with as much untroubled ease as most of her schoolmates took to double boilers and the Thursday-afternoon bridge club. Whenever the Johnsons set about planning an expedition, some well-meaning old professional was bound to say, "That's no trip for a woman." That was all Osa needed to hear.

The style of "I Married Adventure" does not exist. It might be described as homespun had Osa ever had any settled home. She writes about as her husband talked when he lectured—with complete simplicity and lack of affectation better than the subtlest of platform tricks. Several times the story works in episodes that are genuinely thrilling, and once or twice—I think of Martin's lecture to the nine thousand Salt Lake City school children just before his tragic death—it touches the heart.

The eighty-three aquatone illustrations, many of them from stills, present the Johnsons, George Eastman, Jack London, native chiefs, gorillas, zebras, leopards, giraffes, hyenas, elephants, the then Duke and Duchess of York, and honey bears in a variety of graphic and appealing attitudes.

BIOGRAPHICAL NOTES

Louis Adamic (1899–   ) was born in Yugoslavia and came to America at the age of 14. He served with the United States army in France during the World War, and after his return worked as a laborer in restaurants, cabinet shops, shoe factories, and textile mills. Two of his well-known works are *Laughing in the Jungle* (1932), the story of his experiences in America as an immigrant, and *The Native's Return* (1934), an account of a visit to his native home.

Joseph Addison (1672–1719) is famous for his editorship, with Richard Steele, of the *Tatler* and the *Spectator*. Courthope, his biographer, declared him to be "the chief architect of Public Opinion in the eighteenth century." In many of his informal essays he treats with kindly humor the follies and affectations of his day in a style which Samuel Johnson declared to be "familiar but not coarse, and elegant but not ostentatious."

John Aubrey (1626–1697) was the son of a country gentleman. Through consistent effort he contrived to make the acquaintance of many of the prominent people of his day. In 1667 he met Anthony à Wood and, when Wood began assembling material for his famous *Athenae Oxonienses*, Aubrey offered to help collect data for him. From time to time Aubrey forwarded memoranda to Wood and in 1680 began the "Minutes for Lives" which Wood was to expand and use at his discretion. Aubrey left the verification of facts largely to Wood. Since Aubrey was merely a hanger-on in the houses of the great, he had little time for systematic research and the "Lives" are said to have been written early mornings while his hosts were recovering from their own entertainment. Aubrey and Wood eventually quarreled, probably because material furnished by Aubrey on the Earl of Clarendon led to a lawsuit against Wood for libel. In his "Minutes of the Life of Mr. John Milton" Aubrey collected some firsthand data. The reference to Milton's height as that of Aubrey's own implies that he had met Milton, and we know that Aubrey obtained some of his facts from Milton's son-in-law.

Francis Bacon (1561–1626) became Lord Chancellor of England in the reign of James I. He was deeply interested in scientific and philosophic studies and championed the experimental attitude toward knowledge. His place in English literature is secure by virtue of his authorship of the *Essays*, which are condensed and pithy comments upon life and the ways of adjusting oneself to a practical world.

517

ARNOLD BENNETT (1867–1931) was an English essayist, novelist, dramatist, and short-story writer whose most famous work is *The Old Wives' Tale* (1908). His last novel, *Imperial Palace*, was published in 1930, the year before his death. He engaged in writing as a profession frankly because he found it a profitable career. He interpreted life sincerely as he saw it, and he was able by mastery of a prodigious amount of detail to give zest and interest even to the lives of the dull and commonplace.

GEORGE BOAS (1891–   ) is associate professor of philosophy at Johns Hopkins University. His articles have appeared in the *Atlantic Monthly*, *Harper's Magazine*, the *Journal of Philosophy*, and the *Philosophical Review*. He is the author of *The Major Traditions of European Philosophy*, *Our New Ways of Thinking*, and *Philosophy and Poetry*.

CATHERINE DRINKER BOWEN (1897–   ) author, with Mme. B. Von Beck, of *Beloved Friend*, a biography of Tchaikovsky, contributed numerous articles and stories to *Harper's Magazine*, *Current History*, and other periodicals. Her collection of essays entitled *Friends and Fiddlers* was published in 1935.

WALLACE CABLE BROWN (1902–   ), a graduate of the University of Idaho, Oxford University (Rhodes Scholar), and the University of Michigan (Ph.D.), is an associate professor of English at the University of Kansas City. The research paper here printed is part of a monograph on the general subject of *The Near East in English Literature, 1775–1825*.

SIR THOMAS BROWNE (1605–1682) was a graduate of Oxford. He studied medicine and practiced for some time in Oxfordshire. Between 1630–1633 he left England and traveled widely on the Continent, receiving his M.D. from the University of Leyden before his return. He settled in Norwich and in 1642 gained fame with the publication of his *Religio Medici*. His inquiring mind led him to experiment in a variety of fields when not occupied with his medical practice, and in 1646 he published the *Pseudodoxia Epidemica*: "Enquiries into very many commonly received Tenents and commonly preserved Truths." The *Pseudodoxia* is a wonderful collection of out-of-the-way facts and scraps of erudition combined with some of the basic scientific misapprehensions of the day. These discussions of scientific evidence on every conceivable subject, often containing records of Sir Thomas's own experiments, are amusing and rather striking forerunners of the scholarly research papers of the present. Sir Thomas was also the author of "Hydrotaphia," a paper on urn burial, inspired by his interest in archeology.

THOMAS CARLYLE (1795–1881) was an eloquent spokesman against the spiritual torpor of his day. With intense moral indignation he attacked whatever he considered weak and false in social institutions. The idea of leadership by the best minds is inherent in all his work, and he declared the history of the world to be "but the Biography of greatness." In *Latter-Day Pamphlets* he gives expression to his political dogma of "government by the best" instead of "government by the worst" which he held democracy to be.

SAMUEL LANGHORNE CLEMENS (1835–1910), who wrote under the nom de plume Mark Twain, is one of the great comic storytellers of America. Many of his books, such as *Life on the Mississippi, Roughing It, Innocents Abroad, The Gilded Age,* and *A Connecticut Yankee in King Arthur's Court* expose with penetrating wit the foibles of human nature and the fallibility of American institutions. *Tom Sawyer* and *Huckleberry Finn* depict the kind of life Twain knew as a boy. In *Mark Twain's Autobiography*, not published until fourteen years after his death, are to be found the same buoyant spirit and keen observation on the ways of the world which characterize his other work.

ARTHUR COMPTON (1892–   ) is the Charles H. Swift Distinguished Service Professor of Physics at the University of Chicago. He was awarded the Nobel prize for physics in 1927. From 1931 to 1933 he directed the world cosmic-ray survey. He engaged in an effort to establish permanent cosmic-ray stations at seven widely separated places in the world.

JOSEPH CONRAD (1857–1924) was born in Russian Poland but became a British subject in 1884. He held a master mariner's license and for ten years was in command of English vessels at sea. He rapidly mastered the English language so well that his tales of the sea, with their penetrating analysis of character, became classics in English fiction.

JOHN WILSON CROKER (1780–1857) graduated from Trinity College, Dublin, in 1800. After two years of study he was called to the Irish bar. In 1807 he entered Parliament and in 1810 became Secretary to the Admiralty, a post which he held for twenty years under several political administrations. One of his first acts as secretary was to expose a fellow official who had misappropriated a million dollars. Croker combined literary interests with politics and his duties as secretary. He was associated with the *Quarterly Review* from its foundation, and for many years was a leading contributor. The rancorous tone of his articles engendered a great deal of party discord and bitterness. Croker was a staunch supporter in literature of the artificial methods of the eighteenth century and did all in his power to discredit the younger generation of poets. After 1834 he retired from his post at the Admiralty on a pension of £1500.

ARTHUR LYON CROSS (1873–1940), a native of Portland, Maine, graduated from Harvard and was long a professor of history at the University of Michigan. He was the author of numerous books, the most widely known being *A History of England and Great Britain*.

EVE CURIE (1904–   ) is the daughter of Madame Marie Curie, the famous scientist. Her biography *Madame Curie*, translated by Vincent Sheean, won instant recognition for its warm human and literary qualities. Eve Curie wrote regularly for Parisian journals on music, the theater, and motion pictures. She is an accomplished linguist and a music critic of some renown.

BERTHA LOUISE (CLARK) DAMON was born in the Connecticut village she calls North Stonefield. She graduated from college in New England but later moved to California, where she has spent about half her life. Although she had no formal training in architecture, Mrs. Damon became a successful builder of houses.

KARL K. DARROW (1891–   ) obtained B.S. and Ph.D. degrees at the University of Chicago and studied at the universities of Paris and Berlin. From 1917 he was a member of the technical staff of the Bell Telephone Laboratories. He served as acting professor of physics at Stanford, Chicago, and Columbia. He devoted much time to writing and lecturing about physics and the sciences closely allied to it.

BASIL DAVENPORT (1905–   ), a graduate of Yale and Oxford, is editor with the Book of the Month Club and author of a translation of *L'Aiglon*, by Edmond Rostand.

CLARENCE DAY (1874–1935) was the son of a Wall Street broker and grandson of Benjamin Day, founder of the *New York Sun*. When Clarence Day graduated from Yale in 1896, his father made him a present of a seat on the New York Stock Exchange, but the young man rebelled against becoming a businessman and joined the navy. In 1899, while stationed on a training ship in New York harbor, he was stricken with arthritis. He spent the next twelve years on crutches or in a wheel chair. He bought a ranch in Colorado and, although unable to walk a step, wedged himself in a saddle and rode horseback. Returning to New York he dabbled in stocks, making and losing a fortune. His health steadily declined and eventually he was confined to his bed. Turning then to writing, he won fame at the close of his life with his recollections of *Life with Father* and as the author of humorous essays.

ROBERT L. DUFFUS (1888–   ), author of many books and magazine articles on a variety of subjects, is also a regular contributor to the *New York*

Times. Two of his books are *Democracy Enters College* and *Night Between the Rivers.*

WILL DURANT (1885–) was born in North Adams, Massachusetts. He studied at St. Peter's College and obtained a Ph.D. degree at Columbia University. He taught at Columbia and at the University of California at Los Angeles. He is the author of numerous books on philosophy.

MAX EASTMAN (1883–) taught philosophy at Columbia until 1911. His first literary publication was *Enjoyment of Poetry.* In 1913 he founded *The Masses* and for five years was the editor and manager of this journal. Later Eastman founded *The Liberator,* which he edited until 1922. Then he went to Russia, where he studied the Russian language and the Soviet civilization. He translated a number of books from the Russian, including Trotsky's *History of the Russian Revolution.* He wrote books and magazine articles in the fields of fiction, literary criticism, and political philosophy.

ALBERT EINSTEIN (1879–), a physicist, was born in Württemberg, Germany, of Jewish parents. He became a professor of mathematics and physics at Zürich and at Prague, and in 1913 was made director of the Kaiser-Wilhelm Physical Institute in Berlin. He won the Nobel prize in 1921, and many honorary degrees and medals in recognition of his theory of relativity. Deprived by Hitler of his post in Berlin, Einstein became professor of mathematics at the Institute for Advanced Study at Princeton, New Jersey.

CLIFTON FADIMAN (1904–), a native of New York, graduated from Columbia in 1925, taught English at the Ethical Culture High School in New York for two years, and contributed to various newspapers and magazines. In 1929 he became editor with Simon and Schuster, holding this post until 1935. In 1933 he became book editor of *The New Yorker* and from 1938 he was even more widely known as master of ceremonies of the "Information Please" radio program.

CHARLES FERGUSON (1863–) was a minister, an editorial writer, a special representative of the government abroad, and an agent of the state department in the Far East. At the time of writing "Art For Our Sake," Mr. Ferguson was a member of the editorial department of the *Reader's Digest.*

BENJAMIN FRANKLIN (1706–1790) is generally considered the most remarkable American of his time. He was a successful printer and publisher, a shrewd businessman, an inventor, the founder of a library, a journal, a university. His studies of electricity gave him honors from France and England, and the universities of Harvard, Yale, Edinburgh, and Oxford granted him honorary degrees. He spent eighteen years in England as an agent of America, and in the Revolutionary War he was sent to France to secure aid for America. His *Autobiography* and *Poor Richard's Almanac* are his two best-known literary works. *Poor Richard's Almanac*, published as a pamphlet every autumn for twenty-five years, was extremely popular for its shrewd, practical advice upon how to become rich and respected. The sayings of Richard were put in the form of proverbs.

GEORGE W. GRAY (1886–   ) was born in Texas, graduated from Harvard, and became a writer of articles popularizing science. His first book, *New World Picture*, won the approval of the Massachusetts Institute of Technology *Review*. In gathering material for *The Advancing Front of Science*, Gray visited many laboratories and rechecked the material he had gathered with the scientists before publication.

JOHN HOLMES (1904–   ) is a poet and critic, assistant professor of English at Tufts College, and poetry critic for the *Boston Evening Transcript*. His first volume of poems, *Address to the Living*, was published in 1937. A collection of essays and illustrative quotations, entitled *The Poet's Work*, appeared in 1939.

OLIVER WENDELL HOLMES (1809–1894), an American poet and essayist, was professor of anatomy at Harvard from 1847 to 1888. Both his poems and his prose works reveal spontaneous humor and the genial power of satire. *The Autocrat of the Breakfast Table*, which Holmes called a "dramatized essay," appeared originally in the *Atlantic Monthly*, to which Holmes was a regular contributor. It is written in the form of a monologue which takes place at the table of a boardinghouse, frequently interrupted by a word from one of the other boarders, from the old gentleman, the theological student, the young man John, or the landlady. These papers and the series which later appeared in *The Professor of the Breakfast Table*, *The Poet of the Breakfast Table*, and *Over the Teacups* have been compared with Addison's *Spectator* in their wisdom and the pleasantly humorous manner in which they deal with the daily affairs of conduct.

THOMAS HENRY HUXLEY (1825–1895) was professor of natural history in the Royal School of Mines from 1854 to 1885. After the publication of *The Origin of Species* by Darwin in 1859, Huxley became an outstanding defender of evolution. He is best known as a writer and lecturer in the field of biology and paleontology and in the subjects of education, religion, and government as they are affected by scientific development.

HOWARD MUMFORD JONES (1892-   ), a native of Saginaw, Michigan, graduated from the University of Wisconsin. He taught at the University of Texas 1919–1925, at the University of North Carolina 1927–1930, and at the University of Michigan from 1930 to 1936. From 1936 he was a professor of English at Harvard. He is the author of poems and plays as well as of numerous scholarly works.

CHARLES LAMB (1775–1834) was employed as a clerk in the East India House until his retirement at the age of fifty. He spent his leisure time in writing, his *Essays of Elia* giving him a place as one of the most beloved of English essayists. One critic said of him, "There is more imagination to the square inch in Lamb's writing than in almost any other modern prose."

CEDRIC LARSON (1910-   ), A.B. Stanford University (Phi Beta Kappa), A.M. The George Washington University, worked in the Labor Department, Library of Congress, and taught in high school before entering the office of the Adjutant General of the United States. He is the author of a number of magazine articles.

HAROLD J. LASKI (1893-   ), professor of political science in the University of London, was also a frequent lecturer at Yale and Harvard. He has an international reputation in his field, is the author of many books, and a frequent contributor to the *New Republic, Nation*, and *Manchester Guardian*.

ERIKA MANN (1905-   ), the oldest child of Thomas Mann, was born in Munich and studied for the stage under Max Reinhardt in Berlin. She is the author of *Peppermill*, an anti-Nazi production for the stage, and *School for Barbarians*, which exposes education under the Nazis. She and her brother, Klaus Mann, are authors of the book *Escape to Life*.

THOMAS MANN (1875-   ) was born in Lubeck, Germany. In 1929 he received the Nobel prize for literature "without any great mental excitement." His best-known works of fiction are *Buddenbrooks, The Magic Mountain, Death in Venice and Other Stories*, and *Joseph and His Brothers*. Deeply interested in international relations, he wrote many essays on political, social, and literary subjects. After his "voluntary" exile from Germany in 1933, he lived in France and Switzerland, and then made his home in the United States, where in 1938 he applied for citizenship. *The Coming Victory of Democracy* is a lecture delivered on a coast to coast tour of the United States.

CLYDE R. MILLER (1888-   ), a graduate of Ohio State University, had a varied career as paleontologist, advertising writer, editorial staff writer, and lecturer in school administration. From 1928 he was an associate professor of education at Teachers College, Columbia. He became director of the Institute for Propaganda Analysis in 1937.

JOHN MILTON (1608-1674) was educated at Christ's College, Cambridge, and early consecrated himself to a poet's calling, believing that "he who would not be frustrate of his hope to write well hereafter in laudable things ought himself to be a true poem." While known as the greatest poet of Puritanism, he also wrote many prose tracts in defense of liberty—civil, social, political, and religious. The essay "Of Education" was written in the form of a letter to Master Samuel Hartlib, who later became a well-known merchant in London, interested in many projects for public reform.

JAMES R. MOCK (1903-   ), A.B. Depauw University, Ph.D. University of Wisconsin, was professor of history in Findlay College, Ohio, and then became a member of the staff of the National Archives in Washington, D. C.

DONALD MOFFAT (1894-   ) was born at St. Huberts, New York. A Harvard graduate, he wrote the "Mr. Pennyfeather" series of articles which appeared in the *Atlantic Monthly* in 1936 and 1937.

SIR THOMAS MORE (1478-1535) was Lord Chancellor of England under Henry the Eighth, but was indicted for high treason and beheaded when he opposed the king's defiance of the papacy. In *Utopia* More gives an account of an imaginary land beyond the sea called Utopia (Nowhere) where poverty and injustice have been abolished.

LEWIS MUMFORD (1895-   ) is an author and lecturer on American civilization and culture, also a contributing editor to the *New Republic* and an authority on architecture, city planning, and the arts. He received a Guggenheim fellowship in 1938. A few of his well-known works are *Golden Day*, *Technics and Civilization*, and *The Culture of Cities*.

JOHN HENRY NEWMAN (1801-1890) was a graduate of Oxford University and a fellow at Oriel College. For many years a clergyman in the Anglican church, he played an important part in the Oxford Movement, but became a member of the Catholic church in 1845 and served for four years as rector of the Catholic university at Dublin. While rector of the university, he delivered a series of lectures in defense of liberal education which was later published in *Idea of a University*. He was created a cardinal in 1879.

524

JOHNSON O'CONNOR (1891–   ) organized the Human Engineering Laboratory at the Stevens Institute of Technology and from 1930 was director of psychological studies at the Stevens Institute, and also assistant professor of industrial research at the Massachusetts Institute of Technology. He is the author of numerous articles describing measurable occupational characteristics.

THOMAS PAINE (1737–1809) was born in Norfolk, England, of a Quaker family. He supplemented a meager grammar-school education by attending science lectures. Encouraged by Benjamin Franklin, he came to America in November, 1774. In January, 1776, he published *Common Sense*, a remarkable republican pamphlet. George Washington said that it "worked a powerful change in the minds of many men." At the outbreak of the Revolutionary War, Paine served as volunteer aide-de-camp to General Greene. It was while serving in this capacity that he wrote the papers called *The Crisis*. The great service which he did through these papers for the American cause was recognized by various appointments to office and gifts of money from Congress. In 1787 Paine left America for Europe and interested himself in the cause of the French Revolution. He became a member of the French Assembly but, incurring the enmity of Robespierre, narrowly escaped death on the guillotine. On his release from prison he returned to America and died in New York City.

BLISS PERRY (1860–   ) graduated from Williams in 1881 and studied at Berlin and Strassburg. He taught first at Williams and later at Princeton. In 1899 he became editor of the *Atlantic Monthly*, a position which he held for the next ten years. In 1907 he accepted a professorship of English literature at Harvard, retiring in 1930. He was general editor of the Cambridge Edition of the Poets and the author of many scholarly studies.

FRANKLIN DELANO ROOSEVELT (1882–   ), born at Hyde Park, New York, graduated from Harvard, 1904; studied at Columbia University Law School. He was Assistant Secretary of the Navy, 1913–1920; Governor of New York, 1929–1933; thirty-second President of the United States.

JOHN RUSKIN (1819–1900), professor of fine arts at Oxford for many years, was considered the foremost art critic of his day. He believed that art reflected social conditions and that all human work depended "for its beauty on the happy life of the workmen." As a result he became active in various schemes of reform, being one of the first to advocate old-age pensions, better housing for workmen, and aid for the unemployed.

BERTRAND RUSSELL (1872–   ) was born in England where he was identified with liberal thought. Widely known as a mathematician, philosopher, and critic of modern social institutions, at one time he was a lecturer at Trinity College, Cambridge. During the war he was imprisoned for a time because of his pacifist activities. Some of his best-known works are *Why Men Fight, Mysticism and Logic, What I Believe, Religion and Science,* and *Power*.

GEORGE SANTAYANA (1863-   ), an American poet and philosopher, was born in Spain and educated at Harvard, where for some years he was a professor of philosophy. After 1912 he lived chiefly in England and Italy. His first essay, "The Sense of Beauty," brought him fame in the field of aesthetics, and from that time he became widely known as a philosopher and man of letters. Typical works are *The Life of Reason, Character and Opinion in the United States, Scepticism and Animal Faith,* and *The Last Puritan*.

SAMUEL H. SCUDDER (1837-1911) studied at Williams and at Harvard. In 1864 he was appointed custodian of the Boston Society of Natural History and in 1880 was chosen president of that organization. From 1886 to 1892 he served as paleontologist on the United States Geographic Survey. He was the author of numerous scientific studies on the fossils of North America.

WILLIAM SEABROOK (1886-   ), a reporter, feature writer, and free-lance writer, was also an extensive traveler, having spent considerable time in Arabia, Tripoli, Kurdistan, Haiti, and West Africa. Among his books are *Jungle Ways, Asylum,* and *These Foreigners*.

ROBERT LOUIS STEVENSON (1850-1894) was born in Edinburgh and studied engineering and law at the University of Edinburgh. He was admitted to the bar but never practiced law. He is best known as a short-story writer, essayist, and novelist.

FRANK SULLIVAN (1892-   ), a humorist who attained prominence as the conductor of a column in the New York *World,* is the author of *Innocent Bystanding* and *In One Ear*.

J. W. N. SULLIVAN (1886-1937) was educated at London University, and at the time of his death was considered one of the few brilliant interpreters of modern science, ranking with Sir James Jeans and Sir Arthur Eddington. His gifts were versatile. He was an outstanding mathematician as well as a novelist, musician, and philosopher, and was the author of a book on Beethoven and an autobiographical novel.

JONATHAN SWIFT (1667-1745) was the author of many satirical works which exposed the evils of his day. *Gulliver's Travels,* first published in 1726, is an attack upon the follies of mankind and the imperfections of social institutions and government. In "A Voyage to Brobdingnag" (part two of *Gulliver's Travels*), Gulliver visits a land of giants and in conversation with their king he describes conditions in his own country, England. By depicting the amazement of the king when he hears Gulliver's account of the land from which he has come, Swift delivers a telling satire upon the conditions of government in England. In the fourth voyage Gulliver visits the Land of the Houyhnhnms, the name Swift uses for the intelligent and superior horses who are the ruling animals.

JAMES THURBER (1894–   ) attended Ohio State University. In 1918 he was employed as code clerk in the State Department, serving in the Paris Embassy until 1920. After that he engaged in journalism. He was a reporter on the *Columbus Dispatch*, the Paris edition of the *Chicago Tribune*, and the New York *Evening Post*. In 1926 he joined the staff of *The New Yorker Magazine*. After leaving the staff of *The New Yorker* he was still a frequent contributor.

ARTHUR TRAIN, JR. (1901–   ) was a newspaper reporter, writer for the movies, and actor in summer stock companies. For two years he served as assistant naval attaché at the United States Embassy at Brussels. Returning to the United States he became a free-lance writer.

MARK TWAIN. See SAMUEL LANGHORNE CLEMENS.

LOUIS UNTERMEYER (1885–   ) resigned from his family's business house in 1923 to devote all his time to study and writing. From 1934 to 1937 he was poetry editor of the *American Mercury*. The author of poems, parodies, and fiction, he is best known perhaps for his excellent essays on American poetry and poets since 1900.

HERBERT GEORGE WELLS (1866–   ) was born in a suburb of London in the lower middle class. He received the B.S. degree from London University with first-class honors. After teaching science for some years, he turned to writing. He considered himself an educator-journalist rather than a literary artist, and is the author of many essays, scientific articles, scientific speculations in novel form, and romantic and realistic novels. He championed the creation of a world state in which the intellectual aristocrats would govern for the benefit of the majority. Later he declared that he saw signs of decadence in modern civilization, prophesying "a complete readjustment of the political systems of Europe . . . arising from an equally complete moral and intellectual revolution."

527

BIOGRAPHICAL NOTES

WILLIAM ALLEN WHITE (1868-   ) was born in Emporia, Kansas. He was proprietor and editor of the *Emporia Daily and Weekly Gazette* from 1895. His editorials won him international reputation. He was sent to France as an observer for the American Red Cross, and is a trustee of the Rockefeller Foundation and a member of the Pulitzer Awards Committee.

PHILIP YOUTZ (1895-   ), assistant director of the Brooklyn Museum, was at one time instructor in architecture at Teachers College, Columbia, and instructor in philosophy at Columbia. He served for some years as supervisor of adult education and art courses at the Peoples Institute of New York. From 1936 he was president of the American Federation of Arts.

STEFAN ZWEIG (1880-   ), a Viennese author of Jewish parentage, moved to London, where he writes fiction and biography. Among his works are *The Buried Candelabrum* and *Conqueror of the Seas: The Story of Magellan*.

528

STUDENT HELPS AND THEME
SUGGESTIONS

THOMAS HENRY HUXLEY · AUTOBIOGRAPHY

Which should you prefer, to have someone write an account of your life or to write it yourself? Do you think Huxley really regretted not having that "mellifluous eloquence which . . . leads far more surely than worth, capacity, or honest work, to the highest places in Church and State"? Which inherited trait do you think was the greatest influence in Huxley's career? In your opinion, is living under sharp discipline on bare necessities beneficial to the development of character? Huxley took up the post of paleontologist and lecturer on natural history with the intention of giving it up as soon as he could get a physiological post, but he held the office for thirty-one years. Do you think this situation common to the lives of most men? Considering Huxley's objective in life and his accomplishments, do you believe he lived his life to the fullest? Compare this short autobiography with a biographic sketch of Huxley in some good encyclopedia. What is the difference in emphasis? What are the essential differences in approach? What do you learn about Huxley's character by studying the facts he included and the facts he omitted?

Suggestions for Themes

The Day I Came Home with a Black Eye. The Highest Position I Hope to Attain in Life. My Job on a Boat. A Friend Whom I Saw after a Separation of Many Years. The Fun of Imitating People. My Mother's Influence upon Me. Being an Only Child. My Autobiography.

MARK TWAIN · EARLY DAYS

By what methods does Mark Twain get his humorous effects? Do you think his humor is, or will become, passé? Does the picture of his boyhood seem authentic, alive? How does emphasis upon his environment add to the effectiveness of the autobiography? Do you think his treatment of his mother is realistic or sentimental? What examples should you select to show how Mark Twain's writing reflects his time? Do you believe the writer's awareness of his period and his revelation of it to be an integral part of good autobiography? Examine his use of small detail.

Suggestions for Themes

My First Acquaintance with Tom Sawyer. Why I Liked the Rover Boys Series. Keeping Up with the Ruth Fielding Sequels. The Glamourous Vocabulary of Southern Cookery. My First Visit to a Plantation. If I Lived on a Houseboat. My "Early Days." Childhood Pranks. Family Gatherings When I Was Young.

BLISS PERRY · THESE CRUDE YOUNG MEN

Do you think "half the advantage of going to college lies in going away to college"? Why? Do you think it is unfortunate that Latin and Greek have largely disappeared from the average student's studies today? How should you explain the broadening and liberalizing of the curriculum during the past fifty years? What is the point of the incident concerning the boxing of the compass? Why was dormitory life at that time "primitive enough to have satisfied Rousseau"? Do you think students in your college today form their "own social groups with entire freedom"? Can you think of any organizations in your college comparable with the L.N.H. and the Philologian Society? Do you think the organization of athletics at that time more desirable than our own today? State in your own words the total impression you gain of Professor Bliss Perry's father. Do you think that "the best teaching may actually be done in courses that do not catch the public eye"? What mental picture do you gain of the famous Mark Hopkins? Do you think he would be equally successful today? Comment on the statement: "Not interested in right or wrong? Why, at bottom, young fellows aren't interested in anything else!"

Suggestions for Themes

Dormitory Life Today. One Adventure of My Own in a Classroom. Fraternities vs. Neutrals. A Great Teacher. On Choosing Electives. Disagreeing with the Teacher. My Own Experiences in Debating. Reading without Plan or Purpose. Getting a Hit the Last Time at Bat. Working on the School Paper. Today's "Crude Young Men."

CLARENCE DAY · A HOLIDAY WITH FATHER

How does the detail of Father's choice of hat immediately suggest his character? Can you think of some characteristic act of an acquaintance which is equally revealing? How is the local color of New York City during Clarence Day's childhood carefully sketched in as a background? The author skillfully recaptures the small boy's point of view. Can you discover by what means he does it? As you read, were you reminded of scenes from your own childhood? Should you say the author's chief interest is in autobiography, biography of his father, or recreating a vanished scene? Mark Twain and Clarence Day are both famous humorists. Is there a fundamental difference in their methods? Which do you prefer? Is the simplicity of Clarence Day's style deceptive?

Suggestions for Themes

Visiting My Father's Office. My First Adventure in a Restaurant. Father's (or Mother's) Clothes When I Was Young. My Earliest Ambition. Automobiles of Yesterday. Father Takes Me in Hand. On Having to Be Dressed Up. A Holiday with Father.

530

BERTHA DAMON · SEA CHANGE

What examples do you find of Grandma's "superior purposefulness"? Are there any similarities between Grandma and Clarence Day's Father? Do you think the writer has set down the literal truth, or do you think she has exaggerated details for their humorous effect? Compare the use of local color in this sketch with the picture of New York drawn by Clarence Day. Are the methods of presentation fundamentally alike? Without rereading the sketch, what details of a vacation at the seashore can you list? Would this list of details which made an impression on you as a reader help you to select vivid material for your own autobiography? By what device is the sketch given structural unity? Are the incidents of Grandma's daily dip and her battle with Great-Aunt Charity included simply because the writer thought them funny, or are they fundamental material in the development of the character study of Grandma?

Suggestions for Themes

Holiday at the Seashore. Our Camp at the Lake. Maiden Aunts. Cottage Furnishings. My Grandmother. Changing Styles in Sports Attire. Memories of Our Attic. Living the "Simple Life." "Accessories Are Important." On Being Little.

JOHN AUBREY · MINUTES OF THE LIFE OF MR. JOHN MILTON

Do you think John Aubrey's curiosity resembles that of a modern reporter? What passages indicate his fondness for anecdote? Could a vivid, although somewhat warped, biographic sketch of John Milton be written from these notes alone? What indications of unscholarly haste do you find in these "Minutes"? Do you have reason to distrust any of Aubrey's assertions? What conventional biographic material is included? Can you find any unconventional biographic material? What is a scrivener? an amanuensis? Point out passages of pure gossip. Do you find them revealing Milton's or Aubrey's mind? Do you think the humor in these "Minutes" is intentional or mainly unintentional?

Suggestions for Themes

Outline Notes for a Biography. Where Emphasis in Biography Should Be Placed. A Short Biography of Milton Based on Aubrey's "Minutes." My Impression of John Aubrey. Character Revealed in Anecdote.

531

SAMUEL H. SCUDDER · IN THE LABORATORY
WITH AGASSIZ

What is the basic reason for the use of some autobiography in this biographic sketch of Louis Agassiz? Have you ever known a teacher who used Agassiz's methods? What do you think of them? What would be your reaction if you had been in young Scudder's place? Have you on your own initiative ever looked at some object really carefully? What are the central character traits of Professor Agassiz which emerge from this sketch? As you read, did you look up "haemulons" in your dictionary to see what they were like? If not, did you really miss the point of the whole sketch? Do you think famous teachers today should spend part of their time instructing beginners, or do you think they should reserve all their time for advanced students? Weigh the problem carefully.

Suggestions for Themes

"Look at Your Fish." The Importance of Small Details. Why I Like Natural History. Scudder's First Day in the Laboratory Compared with Mine. Details about My Room I Had Never Noticed. The Career of Louis Agassiz. A Teacher Who Has Influenced Me.

STEFAN ZWEIG · TOSCANINI

Do you think perfection is attainable? Do you believe achievements come easily to the genius, or do you think the greater genius a man possesses the harder he must work to attain his desired end? Do you believe people exist who possess a kind of "electrical energy" which passes into "every muscle and nerve" of those who come near them? How do you interpret Zweig's statement that Toscanini's work is "ethical as well as artistic"? Do you think Toscanini's name is "writ in water"? What is your opinion of Zweig's portrait of the conductor? Do you think Zweig sacrifices detail for a single effect? Do you think his approach to his subject is sufficiently detached?

Suggestions for Themes

The Greatest Conductor I Have Heard. Attending the Rehearsal of a Symphony Orchestra. How I Learned to Enjoy Classical Music. A Person with "Electrical Energy." Visiting a Broadcasting Studio. My Opinion of Our Symphony Orchestra. Why I Like Salon Music. Music Out of Doors. Music on the Radio.

EVE CURIE · FORTY RUBLES A MONTH

Would you suffer the hardships which Madame Curie endured for the sake of education, or should you prefer to remain uneducated? How did her "immense enthusiasm . . . magnify her sordid existence into magic"? Do you think the poor student today endures as many trials and privations as the poor student forty or fifty years ago? If Madame Curie had made no important discovery nor attained any prominence in the field of science, do you think her laborious, studious life would have been in vain? In your opinion, is Eve Curie's emphasis upon the great scientist's enthusiasm, hope, and perseverance during her hardships too strong for the picture to remain convincing? Do you think this portrait is biased by the fact it was written by the scientist's daughter? Or do you think it is remarkably objective?

Suggestions for Themes

On Being Broke. Working My Way through College. Why I Choose to Be an Idler Rather than a Great Scholar. Why I Get Enjoyment from My Studies. When a College Grind Is Not a Grind. My Ambition. A Scientist I Know.

JAMES THURBER · E. B. W.

Humorists are frequently penetrating biographers. Why do you think this should be so? How large a part do anecdotes play in this sketch? Do you get a clearly focused picture of Mr. White? Study the economy of expression in the relation of some incident. Is there anything which could be left out? Why is the material presented in the order in which it is? Do you enjoy Thurber's nonsense? Try imitating his methods to see how he achieves his effects. Do you see how fine a border line there is between genuine humor and a heavy-handed attempt to be smart? Examine Thurber's use of parenthesis, parallel structure, and lists. What use does he make of the element of surprise? Why should informal biography of this type be worth your careful study?

Suggestions for Themes

James Thurber. On Reading *The New Yorker*. The Difference Between "It's Her" and "It Is She." A Thoroughly Informal Sketch of a Friend. On Being Shy. "The Wholesome Wants of Man Are Few." Party Bores. My "Ordinary, Normal Childhood." The Advantages of Informality in Prose. My Favorite Humorist.

JOHN MILTON · OF EDUCATION

To what does Milton refer in the statement: "These are not matters to be wrung from poor striplings, like blood out of the nose or the plucking of untimely fruit"? What practice does he believe breeds contempt of learning in the student? Do you agree that a complete education is that which "fits a man to perform justly, skill-fully, and magnanimously all the offices, both private and public, of peace and war"? Should you describe the tone and content of this letter as sublime or practical? It has been said that Milton's program of education calls for a race of young Miltons. Does this lessen the value of its principles? What is there about Milton's style that you like or dislike?

Suggestions for Themes

Additional Requirements for Milton's Academy in the Twentieth Century. The "Beginning, End, and Reasons of Political Societies," as Studied in Universities Today. The Difference between Exercise and Athletics. The Ideal Path of Educa-tion—"So Smooth, So Green. . . ." My Idea of Education. Education Out of Doors.

PHILIP N. YOUTZ · EDUCATION FOR LIVING

In what way may a college be a "racket operating entirely within the law"? Do you think the program advocated by Youtz would achieve a greater unification of education? How does his plan solve the problem of overtraining a minority in athletics? The author points out that the aim of the college must be "students who are self-disciplined, not students who are faculty-disciplined." Explain the differ-ence on the basis of your own experience. Do you agree that in a well-balanced edu-cation there should be no need of extracurricular activities? Point out what you consider would be the greatest benefits derived from the program Youtz proposes.

Suggestions for Themes

Luxurious Dormitories or Simple Barracks? My Visit to a Cement Plant (the State Senate, a Newspaper Office, a Mill, an Agricultural Experiment Station). Should Textbooks Be Discarded? How I Learned (or Why I Never Learned) to Swim. Pleasure on Skis. Professors Who Play Golf. My Definition of Culture.

LOUIS ADAMIC · EDUCATION ON A MOUNTAIN

How does Black Mountain College differ from Milton's academy? The BMC theory of education, Adamic points out, is that a student does not get education, he experiences it. Explain the difference. How is this a "qualitative method" rather than a quantitative one? How important do you think is the "capacity for deep de-jection and a tendency to say every once in a while 'I'm no good!'"? Do you agree that the privilege of students to criticize their teachers is a wholesome and ad-vantageous policy? What benefits does the college derive from its being a kind of village? Why is this psychological approach to education, this emphasis upon "group influence," a significant step in college development? Does this essay make you want to attend BMC?

534

Suggestions for Themes

My Favorite Class. My First Dramatic Role. Experiencing Art. Having a Sense of Humor. Being Self-conscious. My Greatest Humiliation at College. If I Were Allowed to Criticize My Professors. Ideal Classes Are Places for Relaxation. What Might Happen if BMC Had a Million Dollars Bestowed on It. My College Compared with BMC. My Ideal College.

ERIKA MANN · SCHOOL FOR BARBARIANS

The purpose of education, according to Hitler, is to "create the political soldier." Do you believe the ideals of truth and beauty can exist in such an education? How does the treatment of the subject account for the authentic tone which Miss Mann achieves? Compare the educational ideals in a "School for Barbarians" with those in Black Mountain College.

Suggestions for Themes

My Primer as I Remember It. My Favorite Textbook. A War Story My Father Told Me. My First Drawing Lesson. An Example of Propaganda (Good or Bad) in an American Classroom. A Political Science Student and a Business Major Have a Talk. The Book That Made the Greatest Impression on Me in Childhood. A Black Mountain College Student Writes to a Nazi Youth.

GEORGE BOAS · FRESHMAN ADVISER

Have you met students who are like Mr. Van Stiew, Mr. Hogarth, Mr. Wilkinson? Do you think the writer's characterizations are real? Explain the significance underlying the humor in this essay. Do you enjoy this type of essay more or less than one which has no narrative element? Give reasons.

Suggestions for Themes

What's Wrong with the Van Stiews? My First Day of College. How I Happened to Take Art Appreciation (or ——). Going Through the Ordeal of a Physical Examination. The Complexities of Registration. What I Thought of My Freshman Adviser. My Favorite Course in College. The Course I Dislike the Most. What Makes a Good Teacher.

FRANK SULLIVAN · FOOTBALL IS KING

Do you like an essay that attempts to amuse as well as to instruct the reader? Does this essay succeed in doing both? Define a cliché in your own words, giving several examples. Can you add any clichés used in football to those included by

535

Sullivan? Which of those he mentions have you heard most often? Why has this sport been surrounded with so many clichés? Why do you think there are comparatively so few clichés concerning bowling and tennis?

Suggestions for Themes

Clichés in Advertising. Clichés in Popular Music. An Imaginary Interview with a Movie Star's Press Agent. An Imaginary Interview with an Announcer of a Breakfast-Food Program. A Detective's Jargon. Applying for a Job According to Formula. The Verse of Edgar Guest.

BENJAMIN FRANKLIN · THE WAY TO WEALTH

Do you think Poor Richard had any fun? Do you believe sloth or overwork more destructive of health? Do you agree that "time be of all things the most precious"? Poor Richard says, ". . . industry gives comfort and plenty and respect." Is this always true? In your opinion is the man who always "bewares of little expenses" able to enjoy a pleasant life? Should you "rather go to bed supperless than rise in debt"? How should you describe Benjamin Franklin's style? Do you enjoy reading the maxims of Poor Richard? Why do you think they were especially popular in their own time?

Suggestions for Themes

My Savings Account and How It Grew (or Failed to Grow). Maxims Which I Remember from Childhood. My Opinion of the Budget-Keeper. A Poor Richard Whom I Know. How My Father Started in Business. Summer Work. On Borrowing Money. Robbing My Dime Bank.

THOMAS CARLYLE · HAPPY; LABOUR

Carlyle condemns the "Greatest-Happiness Principle" of mankind. How do you explain the term? Do you think happiness can be attained by searching for it? Do you agree that it makes little difference whether we are happy or not, considering that "Today becomes Yesterday so fast," and "all Tomorrows become Yesterdays"? Carlyle believed there was "a perennial nobleness, and even sacredness, in Work." Can you give examples of types of work in which there is not a "perennial nobleness"? Do you agree that the future of every idle man is hopeless? Should you rather be idle all the rest of your life or have the permanent position of scrubbing the floors of the city hall? What proportion of the people you know do you think are happy in their work? Should you have called Carlyle a realistic or idealistic writer in his own day?

536

Suggestions for Themes

Money and Happiness. Why I Think We "Should Cease Babbling about 'Happiness.'" People Who Pretend to Be Happy. A Truly Happy Person. The Kind of Work Which Is Noble. Why I Should Like to Have Lived in Pioneer Days. Work My Father Did When He Was My Age. My First Business Experience. On Being Happy While at Work.

WILLIAM SEABROOK · WHAT ARE YOU FIT FOR?

Should you like to be tested in Dr. O'Connor's laboratory? Rather than to give vocational guidance to a person, the laboratory attempts to give him a "conscious inventory of his natural aptitudes and potential capabilities." What is the difference? What particular case history interested you most in the article? How do you explain the difference between the objective and the subjective personality? Do you believe scientific testing of the kind described in this article should be made available to everyone, in all parts of the country? How early in life do you think a person should be tested? Do you think there are important imponderables in each person's personality which cannot be measured by any laboratory? Explain your reaction to this essay.

Suggestions for Themes

Why I Think I Have a Subjective Personality. Why I Think I Have an Objective Personality. On Being Unable to Remember Names and Faces. A Person with Eidetic Imagery. The Most Absentminded Person I Know. Feeling That "This Thing Has Happened Before." What I Think I Am Fit For. On Being Interviewed. My Opinion of Aptitude Tests.

HAROLD J. LASKI · THE DECLINE OF THE PROFESSIONS

Why must we not judge a profession by its men of genius? What is your opinion of the corporation lawyer? Do you think Laski's criticisms of the bench and the bar are just? Do you believe the lawyer himself is responsible for these evils rather than the competitive nature of his profession? Does it seem to you that the professions are declining? Are you in favor of socialized medicine? To what factors do you attribute the opposition on the part of the medical profession to socialized medicine? Do you think that if professions were organized as public services, competition would be eliminated? Do you think it should be? How does Carlyle's idea "We plead and speak, in our Parliaments and elsewhere, not as from the Soul, but from the Stomach" fit in with Laski's theme? What is your opinion of this essay?

Suggestions for Themes

Why I Dislike Visiting Sick People. On Seeing the Doctor. Fear of the Dentist's Chair. Why I Want to Be a Doctor. An Interesting Case in Court. A Judge Whom I Know. A Popular Lawyer in Our Town. Are the Professions Declining? On Choosing a Profession.

JOHNSON O'CONNOR · VOCABULARY AND SUCCESS

In scientific testing O'Connor has shown the high correlation between vocabulary and success. Do you think that the success is the result of a wide vocabulary or that a wide vocabulary is the result of the variety of experience which success affords? Do you know the meaning of all the words used as examples in this article? Do you know the reading habits of any of the successful men of your acquaintance? How do you account for the high score which major executives make in the vocabulary test? Do you think that the scope of one's vocabulary depends upon one's intelligence? Do you like to read the dictionary? In what ways may vocabulary influence one's life outside of business?

Suggestions for Themes

A Half Hour with the Dictionary. My Opinion of Vocabulary Tests. The Course Which Has Helped Me Most in Improving My Vocabulary. On Using Big Words. Vocabulary and the Art of Letter-Writing. What Is Success? The Jargon Used in Professions.

THOMAS MORE · LIFE IN UTOPIA

Consider More's statement that "the felicity of this life" consists in devoting whatever time may be spared from necessary occupation to the "free liberty of the mind and garnishing of the same." Are any modern trends in accord with this philosophy? Do you think it would be a good thing for all people to wear the same fashion in garments? What progress has been made in this century toward the six-hour day idealized by More? Do you believe that many people today are "wearied from early in the morning to late in the evening with continual work, like labouring and toiling beasts"? In choosing a career, should one regard the particular craft or profession of one's father with greater interest? Do the games of the Utopians appeal to you? More asks his reader to consider, of those who labor, "how few be occupied in necessary works." What should you consider examples of unnecessary works today? Do you disagree with More's concept of Utopia in this essay? Why do men dream of Utopia?

538

Suggestions for Themes

Fashions in Dress (desirable or undesirable). If I Were a Fashion Designer. The Most Interesting Lecture I Have Heard. Employment Created by Unnecessary Works. Rebuilding Our Home. My Requirements for an Ideal Ruler. A Prosperous Ploughman Today. A Sharecropper. My Utopia.

JONATHAN SWIFT · IN BROBDINGNAG

What is Swift's attitude toward suffrage? Do you agree with it? What is his criticism of the parliament? Do you agree with the king's statement that "ignorance, idleness, and vice, may be sometimes the only ingredients for qualifying for legislator"? How do you interpret his statement that "laws are best explained, interpreted, and applied by those whose interest and abilities lie in perverting, confounding, and eluding them"? Can you give examples from the present day illustrative of his point?

Suggestions for Themes

A Lawyer I Know. Why I Go to Church. Hearing a Court Trial. The Church Deacon. The Last School Board Election. Our City Council. A Scholarly Politician. A Feud in Our Neighborhood. Why I Like People. Why I Dislike People. Why I Like (or Dislike) Swift. The Influence of Swift's Own Life on His Ideas.

THOMAS CARLYLE · ON DEMOCRACY

To what does Carlyle refer in the phrase "this multitudinous efflux of oratory and psalmody, from the universal foolish human throat"? Do you agree with his opinion regarding the United States—that it could not be looked upon as a model for democracy (at that time) because it had not yet fought its battle? On what grounds does he object to suffrage? Do you agree with Carlyle that the number of "the wise and noble-minded" is not the majority? Explain what you think Carlyle means by the statement "The Universe itself is a Monarchy and Hierarchy . . . this is the model of 'constitutions.'" Do you think the ballot-box "raises the Noblest to the chief place"? On the other hand, do you think that monarchy or dictatorship guarantees a government by the wise of the "foolish"? In your opinion, does democratic government today prove Carlyle's predictions true or untrue? At first reading, why does Carlyle's essay seem to resemble so closely the speech of a totalitarian spell-binder? What adjectives would you use to describe Carlyle's style? Is Carlyle here really a propagandist against democracy? Study the essay to find the basic outlook on mankind which prompted Carlyle to write this piece.

Suggestions for Themes

A Political Session at Home. Memories of an Election. The Influence of Religion and Race in Casting Ballots. Democracy in College. Why History Is My Favorite Subject. Arguments with a Republican (*or* Democrat). What Living in a Democracy Means to Me. What Democracy Implies.

H. G. WELLS · THE UTOPIANS

Do you think it possible that the "mind doctor" will ever replace the policeman in our own civilization? Do you agree with Wells that this "mind doctor" type of government is more desirable than our own? Wells describes Burleigh as having ". . . his long legs crossed in front of him and the thumb and fingers of one hand placed with meticulous exactness against those of the other." What is the significance of this detail? In Wells's Utopia psychological science is encouraged and developed as vigorously as physical science. In our world what progress has psychology made toward developing into a science? Do you think private property is an intolerable nuisance of mankind? Wells believes that Utopia is not simply a creation of "exalted idealism" but that his Utopia points toward practical psychological truth. Do you believe, as he does, that there is a possibility of mankind's someday attaining this Utopia?

Suggestions for Themes

My Opinion of Wells's Utopia. The Burleighs and the Barnstaples. A World in Which "There Is Nothing for the Mere Looker-on." Why I Think Psychology Is Important in the Development of Mankind. "The Last Age of Confusion" as I Should Imagine It. Creative Service Today. A Great Modern Leader. More's Utopia Compared with Wells's.

THOMAS MANN · THE COMING VICTORY OF DEMOCRACY

What is democracy's aim with regard to education and culture? How does this aim differ from that of fascism? Do you believe that effective propaganda and strict discipline can "stultify, stupefy, level, and regiment" a whole race for the purpose of war? Explain the significance of the statement "Act as men of thought, think as men of action." Do you agree that it is a "thoroughly democratic slogan"? Mann believes that the essence of democracy is the "appreciation of the dignity of man." How do you interpret this definition? How is fascism "contemptuous" of man? Mann states that real democracy "can never dispense with aristocratic attributes." In what sense does he use the word "aristocratic"? Do you think Thomas Mann is a realist as well as a philosopher?

540

STUDENT HELPS AND THEME SUGGESTIONS

Suggestions for Themes

An Imaginary Conversation with a Fascist. How Mann Might Change His Essay if He Wrote It Today. Why I Think Europe Will Eventually Return to the Democratic Way of Life. The True Aristocrat. A Letter from Thomas Mann to Herr Hitler. Hitler Replies to Thomas Mann.

BERTRAND RUSSELL · THE TAMING OF POWER

Explain what Russell means by "The merits of democracy are negative." How is tyranny possible within a democracy? Do you think the government of the United States safeguards its minorities? Do you agree that in order to remain democratic a government may have to restrict minorities that wish to alter it? Why must economic as well as political power be "tamed" in a democracy? Give examples illustrating the difference between "ownership" and "control." Do you agree that "public ownership and control of all large-scale industry and finance is a necessary condition for the taming of power"? Do you think Russell's plan for educating children would be effective? He points out that wisdom consists in "independence of mind, somewhat skeptical and wholly scientific." Can you interpret this definition? Do you think Russell's essay reflects this wisdom?

Suggestions for Themes

Things I Own as a Citizen. A Teacher "Somewhat Skeptical and Wholly Scientific." On Being in the Minority. My Opinion of Government-Owned Enterprises. Why I Believe Large-Scale Industry Should Not (or Should) Be Owned and Controlled by the Public. Propaganda in College.

MAX EASTMAN · RUSSIA AND THE SOCIALIST IDEAL

The Marxian ideal was the "simple conception of men living together reasonably, generously and justly, without class exploitation, without war, and with freedom for everybody and a fair chance to grow." Is this your ideal? Why, according to Eastman, will Marxism be "laid away with Thomism, Calvinism, and the rest"? How does the substitution of "possibilities" for "destiny" differentiate the Marxian and the socialist programs? Explain the significance of Eastman's point that "'socialization' was accomplished in Russia on paper." How are the peasants and workers in Russia now more fully enslaved than they were before this "socialization"? Why are Trotsky's attacks upon the Russian government particularly impressive? Do you agree that the "opposition between manual and intellectual labor will never dis-

541

appear"? Why are the books of Andrew Smith, Fred E. Beal and Boris Souvarine, and this essay by Max Eastman, especially convincing? Why are the "ideals of initiative, variety, daring creativeness," necessary to the culture of a people?

Suggestions for Themes

Building Bridges and Pushing Barrows. Why I Believe (*or* Do Not Believe) in Socialism. The Increasing Power of the Proletariat in Democratic Nations. My Russian Friend. An Immigrant Family I Know. Why Russia and Germany Finally Became Allies. Why We Should (*or* Should Not) Oppose the Spread of Communist Doctrine in the United States. Communism on Paper and Communism in Practice.

FRANKLIN DELANO ROOSEVELT · THIRD INAUGURAL ADDRESS, JANUARY 20, 1941

Suggestions for Themes

An Inaugural Ceremony I Witnessed. The Third-Term Tradition in American History. Mr. Roosevelt Charms the Crowd. My Definition of Democracy. The First Inaugural of Washington. If I Were President. Looking Backward on the Third Inaugural Address.

THOMAS PAINE · THE CRISIS

Has the word "propaganda" always had its present unpleasant connotations? Do you recognize that there is good propaganda as well as bad, and that propaganda, indeed, is necessary to our national life? Give as many examples as you can of propaganda which has benefited the general public. Why has the whole subject of propaganda assumed great importance in recent years? List as many stock devices of war propaganda used by Thomas Paine as you can recognize as such. Do not expect to detect all of them; the next essay will help you to become wiser. Thomas Paine here has raised war propaganda to the level of literature. The piece is a classic of its kind. Can you name any writer or public figure today whose writing or speeches compare with it in eloquence? The American Revolutionary cause at the time Paine wrote was indeed a "crisis." Can you recall the essential facts of the situation?

Suggestions for Themes

Propaganda in the World of Sports. Necessary Propaganda in Our National Life. Thomas Paine—Patriot. Propaganda in This Morning's Newspaper. A Propaganda Novel. Propaganda in the Movies. When Thomas Paine Wrote *The Crisis*.

JAMES R. MOCK AND CEDRIC LARSON · THE AMERICAN MIND IN WARTIME

This chapter recounts one phase of America's war activity in the months which followed America's declaration of war on Germany in 1917. Had you any previous knowledge of the work of the Committee on Public Information? Have the authors convinced you of the importance of this aspect of war organization? Do you think the work of the Committee on Public Information was rather too successful? Do you think that "expression not repression" leads to more successful propaganda? Do you agree that "uniformity in testimony is convincing"? Do you think that some form of voluntary censorship is necessary in a democracy in time of war? Do you think this factual account is an inspiring demonstration of American capacity for unity in time of danger, or did you find it disillusioning? Do you think the same methods would be, or could be, used again in time of war? Do you think Mr. Pinchot's letter was naïve under the circumstances, or do you agree with him?

Suggestions for Themes

Voluntary Censorship in the College Press. Is Propaganda Necessary in Wartime? Mob Hysteria. Propaganda Technique Today. Why I Am (or Am Not) a Good Hater. The Problem of Minorities. America's Rediscovery of Patriotism.

CLYDE R. MILLER · HOW TO DETECT AND ANALYZE PROPAGANDA

Were you aware of the variety of techniques used in propaganda? Which ones do you think would be the most effective in reaching and influencing you? Why? On what issues do you feel strongly right now? What channels of information helped you to form your opinions? Do you think the unthinking student of the whole subject of propaganda might become suspicious of everyone and everything? Why would such an attitude be ridiculous? What do you think are the real benefits to be derived from the study of propaganda? Explain in your own words the significance in the difference between competition and monopoly of propagandas. Why should "students and teachers especially" know how to deal with propaganda unemotionally?

Suggestions for Themes

An Occasion on Which I Was Deceived. Dangers of Propaganda. Testimonials in Advertising. The Band Wagon in Politics. On Calling Bad Names. Glittering Generalities in the Pulpit. Propaganda Devices Used by Greek-Letter Societies. On Making Up My Mind.

STUDENT HELPS AND THEME SUGGESTIONS

INSTITUTE FOR PROPAGANDA ANALYSIS · THE FIFTH COLUMN

This paper should bring forcibly to your attention the dangers to be found in uncritical acceptance of propaganda. Can you name any innocent victims of mass "witch hunts"? How can the ordinary citizen distinguish between a person who is a dangerous enemy agent and one who is a victim of malicious gossip? How could you defend yourself if you were unexpectedly accused of fifth-column sympathies? Explain why the author labels the fifth column "the newest and most effective form of Name Calling." Do you think Jehovah's Witnesses deserve the attacks made upon them? Where should freedom in a democracy end? Do you think propaganda such as is discussed in this essay is dangerous to democracy itself? Can you point to any examples of the exploiting of public fear by private groups? What is the central fact you have learned from your examination of this essay?

Suggestions for Themes

A Practical Way to Safeguard against Treason. A Hoax Which Scared the Public. The Real Fifth Column in Any Period. My American Ideals. What I Have Learned from a Study of Propaganda. How Stories Grow in Telling. Keeping a Level Head in a Crisis. How to Help a Foreigner to Become a True Citizen.

JONATHAN SWIFT · THE ARMY IN BROBDINGNAG AND IN THE LAND OF THE HOUYHNHNMS

Point out the satirical passages in Swift which could be applied today with equal force to the fascist ideology. Do you think that confining the knowledge of governing "to common sense and reason, to justice and lenity to the speedy determination of civil and criminal causes" is possible in the present world? What is the significance of the phrase "whether it be better to kiss a post or throw it into the fire"? Do you believe the king's statement that, in time, reason must become corrupt under continued warfare? Why is the "gnnayh" particularly apt as a symbol? How should you characterize Swift's style? What contemporary qualities has it?

Suggestions for Themes

A Voyage to Brobdingnag in the Twentieth Century. The Loss of Lives through Differences of Opinion Today. Modern Warcraft. What Wars Are Really Justifiable. Past Wars That Were Justified. The "Gnnayhs" of Our Time. Swift Writes to Mussolini. The President of the United States Talks with the King of the Brobdingnags.

544

DONALD MOFFAT · WAR AND FOOTBALL

Of what value is the character of Mr. Pennyfeather in conveying the author's ideas? How does this piece of writing differ from your conception of the essay form? Do you think the writer succeeds in his endeavor to present both sides of the question? Mr. Pennyfeather emphasizes the importance of mob opinion and hysteria. Point out from your own experience evidence of public susceptibility to hysteria. Do you agree with Moffat that the instinct for war may "run its course" or are you inclined to hold that men like war and always will?

Suggestions for Themes

The First Football Game I Attended. How Football Is Glorified by Mob Opinion. Savagery in Football. Heroism in Football. The Emotional Appeal of a Uniform on Gridiron or Battlefield. The Press as a National Cheerleader. Mr. Pennyfeather Talks to Our Team.

THE EDITORS OF *TIME* MAGAZINE · BACKGROUND FOR WAR

This essay is a collection of facts and figures: how is this material made interesting? Point out any parts of this article which you think are especially well done. What do you think were the reasons for the renewed outbreak of the conflict in 1939? Do you think that the second World War was a continuation of the first, with only an armed truce intervening? Give reasons for your answer. How do you explain the fact that this essay contains numerous short paragraphs? List the principal facts which you have learned from your study of this selection. What connection do you see between the events of these 1063 weeks and the happenings of recent months; in other words, try in your own way to continue the story told in this selection.

Suggestions for Themes

The Last Fifty-Two Weeks. When the Post-War World Became a Pre-War World. The Fall of France. The Costs of War. Why the League of Nations Failed to Prevent War.

WILL DURANT · WHY MEN FIGHT

What are the reasons presented by the author to explain why men fight? What do you consider the best points in his discussion? Are there any statements with which you disagree? Do you think that war "will always be"? What is the contribution of the "business cycle" to the causes of modern war? What do you think are the most important effects of war? What does the word "nostrums" mean? Do you believe that future hope for peace lies in a federation of the English-speaking peoples of the world? Is the birth rate in the United States rising or falling? Why is the birth rate closely related to the problems of war and peace?

Suggestions for Themes

My Explanation of Why Men Fight. Why I Am a "Conscientious Objector." Group Hunger. Ancient Provocations to Conquest. The First Law of Governments Is Self-Preservation. Good Generals and Bad Statesmen. Why I Believe in War.

FRANCIS BACON · OF LOVE

How do you interpret Bacon's statement "The stage is more beholding to Love than the life of man"? Do you agree? Do you think that "it is impossible to love and to be wise"? How do you account for the "inward and secret contempt" held by one who does not respond to another's love? Do you agree that love should be wholly severed from "serious affairs and actions of life," or do you believe love should share all great problems? Do you think Bacon's attitude toward love is appropriate to this age, or does it seem to reflect the age in which he lived?

Suggestions for Themes

Why I Agree (or Disagree) with Bacon. Marrying for Companionship. Love and the Ability to Study. The Greatest Idealization of My Childhood. A Golden Wedding. On Being Disillusioned. Romantic Illusions Fostered by the Movies.

FRANCIS BACON · OF FRIENDSHIP

Do you agree that "a crowd is not company"? In your opinion is it possible for a human being to be a true friend, spiritually, intellectually, instinctively, at all times? In his own life, Bacon cultivated the friendship of the very great for his own benefit. Does this fact lessen the power of his ideas in this essay, in your opinion? Do you think it would be advisable for a heretic to preach a beautiful sermon on the strength of Christianity? Do you agree that the greatest fruit of friendship is that it redoubles one's joys and lessens one's griefs? Does this seem a selfish conception? How is it that a man "waxeth wiser than himself—more by an hour's discourse than by a day's meditation"? Do you think a friend's counsel is "drier and purer" than a decision you might make yourself? How would you illustrate Bacon's meaning of "these things are graceful in a friend's mouth, which are blushing in a man's own"?

Suggestions for Themes

My Most Intimate Friend. My Ideal of Friendship. The Value of Talking a Problem Through. An Unusual Beginning of a Friendship. Interesting Faces of Strangers. Why I Should Rather Be Independent than Rely on Friends. The Fun of Having a Roommate. The Annoyances of Having a Roommate.

FRANCIS BACON · OF MARRIAGE AND SINGLE LIFE

Does your observation of life make you agree with Bacon's statement that a wife and children are "impediments to great enterprises"? What do you understand "enterprises" to include? Do you think an artist's work is hampered by a family? a businessman's? Do you agree that single persons are more cruel and hardhearted "because their tenderness is not so oft called upon," or do you think married persons may just as easily become cruel and hardhearted because their devotion and concern tend to center about the family? Do you believe marriage more desirable than liberty? Is this essay as applicable today as it was in Bacon's time?

Suggestions for Themes

Why I Should Like to Marry (*or* Remain Single). Companionate Marriage. Marriage for Money. An Enviable Married Couple I Know. Marriage or a Career? The Ideal Marriage. The Home I Like Best to Visit.

JOSEPH ADDISON · A BUSY LIFE

Should you rather be remembered as a hearty eater or a lusty drinker than not be remembered at all? Why is "rubbing smooth stones upon one another" from morning to night not a suitable occupation for a human being? How should you characterize a man who wrote in his journal: "Nine o'clock. Tied my knee-strings and washed my hands"? What was your reaction to his entry: "From four to six. Walked into the fields. Wind, S.S.E."? How should you interpret Addison's meaning of "a *busy* life"?

547

SUGGESTIONS FOR THEMES

On Keeping a Journal. Reading Over an Old Diary. Memoirs of My Grandmother. Why I Enjoyed Reading the Journal of Katherine Mansfield (*or* the Diary of Pepys; *or* the Journal of Gamaliel Bradford). Why I Dislike Reading Memoirs. A "Busy" Person I Know. My Definition of Happiness. A Diary of the Last Twenty-four Hours.

JOSEPH ADDISON · THE BEAU'S HEAD

In describing the beau's head, Addison points out that the "pineal gland . . . smelt very strong of essence and orange-flower water." What picture does this create in the mind of the reader? What is the point of the satire concerning the "large cavity on the right side" of every beau's head? How do you interpret the meaning of Addison's statement that the "elevator muscle" of the beau's eye did not seem to have been used? Ordinarily the thought of a man's being killed by the "blow of a paving shovel" is depressing. Why is it amusing in this essay? How should you describe Addison's style?

Suggestions for Themes

A Twentieth Century "Beau's Head." Masculine Vanity. Why a Beau Is Not a Jolly Good Fellow. Why the Word "Beau" Has Disappeared from Our Vocabulary. Why I Like (*or* Dislike) Attending Balls. The Ideal College Man. A Motion-Picture "Beau." A Comparison between the Beau's Head and That of the Scholar.

JOSEPH ADDISON · THE COQUETTE'S HEART

Do you think Addison's description of the coquette's heart an accurate one? Might some of his discoveries in this anatomical dissection have been made in hearts other than that of the coquette? What is Addison's point in the use of the "weather-glass"? Do you agree, in general, with his theory that the man who laughs loudly is a coxcomb and that he who looks serious is a man of sense? In how many feminine hearts do you think the "flame-colored hood" lies "first and uppermost"? Do you believe that women so unfeeling as this type described by Addison exist? Should you like to meet and talk with a man like Addison?

Suggestions for Themes

The Ideal College Woman. On Coyness. Women's Fashions. The Pleasure in Feeling Well-Dressed. If Addison Were to Dissect a Coquette's Heart Today.

Judging a Woman by Her Taste in Clothes. The Elements of Charm in a Coquette's Heart. The Greatest Coquette in History. Feminine Vanity.

JOHN HENRY NEWMAN · PORTRAIT OF A GENTLEMAN

Do you think the definition of a gentleman as "one who never inflicts pain" a good one? Do you believe a man who "carefully avoids whatever may cause a jar or a jolt in the minds of those with whom he is cast" develops or weakens his own personality? Which do you think has actually been exalted by the world, the vivid and dynamic temperament or that of modest nobility? Newman condemns those who, in an argument, "like blunt weapons, tear and hack instead of cutting clean. . . ." How do you interpret his meaning? How could a true gentleman, although he may hold no religion, "seem like a disciple of Christianity itself"? Could this essay have been written by a man who was not a gentleman? In your opinion is the essay a portrait of an impossibility or of a true ideal which is to be striven for?

Suggestions for Themes

A True Gentleman Whom I Know. Why I Agree (or Disagree) with Newman's Definition. Earliest Recollections of My Grandfather. Need a Gentleman Be a Fop? The Average College Man as Compared with Newman's Gentleman. Faculty Manners. Student Manners. Manners of Motorists. A Workman Who Is a Gentleman.

OLIVER WENDELL HOLMES · ON TALK

Do you think that the average person feels greater resentment at criticism from a friend than at criticism from a casual acquaintance? What examples can you give of what Holmes means by "flourishes" in conversation? Do you agree that conversation would be dull if everyone held tenaciously to literal truth? Explain what Holmes means in his statement that usually there are at least six people engaged in a dialogue between two. What qualities do you think make a good conversationalist?

Suggestions for Themes

People Who Always Qualify Their Statements. Having Falstaff for a Companion. Why I Think Absolute Truth More Important than Brilliant Witticism. The Fun of Making Generalizations. The Art of Understatement. Humor on the Radio. Broadcasts of Round-Table Discussions. The Lost Art of Conversation. A Dinner Discussion at Home. Conversation at the College Soda Bar.

549

ROBERT LOUIS STEVENSON · ON MARRIAGE

Is it your opinion that matrimony is a shadow which "waits, resolute and awful, at the cross-roads"? Do you agree that friendships of men are vastly agreeable, but they are insecure? Does it seem to you that marriage narrows rather than broadens a man's life? Stevenson says there is less of this danger for a woman. Do you think his statement as true now as it was in the beginning of this century? If you had made up your mind to marry and "once talked yourself fairly over," do you think you could "pull it through" with almost anybody? If you thought Shakespeare wearisome, would you say so in the presence of a dozen college professors? Stevenson says it is more important that a wife be able to share a joke with her husband than that she have an intellect equal to his. Do you prefer to see a woman intellectually inferior to her husband? Do you agree with Stevenson's opinion that "marriage, if comfortable, is not at all heroic. . . . In marriage, a man becomes slack and selfish, and undergoes a fatty degeneration of his moral being"? Whose philosophy of marriage do you prefer, Bacon's or Stevenson's? Why?

Suggestions for Themes

Why I Like Robert Louis Stevenson. The Difficulties of Expressing One's Frank Opinion at All Times. A Person Who Made an Unusual Marriage. On Swapping Stories. My Philosophy of Marriage. The Right Age to Marry. ". . . Spring Winds Will Sow Disquietude . . . And the Whole World Keep Calling and Calling."

ARNOLD BENNETT · THE DAILY MIRACLE

Do you think the theme of this selection is that *time* is important? Would you exchange the next ten years of your life for ten thousand dollars? Do you believe that in these days, "If you have time you can obtain money . . ."? Are you of Bennett's opinion that "the minute practical examination of daily time-expenditure" is a wise habit? Has reading this essay led you to inventory your own expenditure of time? What is the central idea of the essay?

Suggestions for Themes

Why I Wish the Day Were Shorter. How to Live on Ten Cents a Day. Apology for Spendthrifts. A Few of My White Elephants. If the Day Were Twenty-four Minutes Longer. A Loafer Whom I Dislike. Why I Like (*or Dislike*) Busy People. On Getting Up in the Morning. From Alarm Clock to Class in —— Minutes. The Tyranny of Time.

GEORGE SANTAYANA · FRIENDSHIPS

Compare Santayana's conception of friendship with that of Bacon. Which type of friendship would prove more lasting, in your opinion? How do you interpret Santayana's statement "people are friends in spots"? Explain in your own words Santayana's conception of true friendship. Do you agree with it? Do you think friendship can "even bear not to be mutual"? How many true friends does the average person have? Santayana points out that we should not be jealous if we were simply merry. Do your observations support his statement? Should you rather have innumerable casual friends or a single true one? Do you think this essay depressing or uplifting? What is your opinion of Santayana's style?

Suggestions for Themes

On Being Independent. Why I Like (or Dislike) Being Alone. A Friendship Which Is Not Mutual. On Being Truly Merry. An Apology for Gregariousness. How I Lost a Good Friend. Santayana's Conception of Friendship as Compared with That of Bacon. Good Friends I Have Made While on a Vacation.

ALBERT EINSTEIN · LIVING PHILOSOPHY

Einstein says, "To make a goal of comfort or happiness has never appealed to me." Do you think most people share his feeling? Should you like never to "belong wholeheartedly" to country or state, to a circle of friends, or to your family? Do you think anyone can be entirely independent of "the customs, opinions, and prejudices of others"? How do you interpret his statement that "those who are led should not be driven"? Do you agree with Einstein's conception of religion? Do you believe with him that merely trying "humbly to comprehend even an infinitesimal part of the intelligence manifested in nature" is enough to live for?

Suggestions for Themes

My Own Living Philosophy. "A Horse of Single Harness." The Desire for Publicity. What I Owe to My Friends. On Taking Oneself Seriously. Why I Desire Luxury. Why I Agree (or Disagree) with Einstein.

GEORGE BOAS · THREE BLIND MICE

What is your opinion of the young woman who described her friend's disloyalty as being "ugly"? Do you think the person who "hates to be moral" an example of tolerance or of affectation? Do you agree that a person who hates to be intelligent for fear of seeming highbrow is a blind mouse? Should you rather be lauded for three or four years as a star football player or respected all your life as an intelligent man? Do you think it possible for a truly intelligent person to be highbrow? Have you known people who were afraid of being themselves? Which of the three blind mice do you think is most disgusting? In your opinion is this a good essay for college students to read?

Suggestions for Themes

More Blind Mice. Blind Mice I Have Known. My Definition of a Highbrow. Why I Should Like to Be a Football Star. The Influence of My Relatives upon My Choice of a Career. The Care and Cure of Blind Mice. Good Sports I Have Known. Virtues Which I Think Are Changing. My Moral Code.

CHARLES LAMB · A CHAPTER ON EARS

What is particularly modern about the opening of this essay? Lamb remarks that after sitting through an Italian opera he rushed out into the streets "to solace myself with sounds which I was not obliged to follow." What does he mean? Do you sympathize with his objection to music? What criticism does he make of his friend the organist? Which passage in the essay do you think most amusing? Do you think the essay capable of appealing to music lovers as well as to those with "no ear"? Give reasons for your answer.

Suggestions for Themes

My Musical Friend. The First Symphony Concert I Attended. Description of a Musical Audience. Listening to One Who Is Practicing on the Piano. Opera (*or* Symphony Orchestra) on the Radio. My Phonograph. The Kind of Music I Enjoy.

JOHN RUSKIN · GREATNESS IN ART

What is meant by the "language" of painting or poetry? What besides perfection in language is the aim of true art? Ruskin emphasizes the fact that it is "not by the mode of representing and saying, but by what is represented and said" that greatness in art must be determined. Do you think that this is a Victorian notion, or is it valid criticism? What criticism is made in the essay of the Dutch school? Do you agree with Ruskin's definition of the greatest picture, "that which conveys to the mind of the spectator the greatest number of the greatest ideas"? What does the word "ideas" mean? State in simple language your own opinion of what constitutes greatness in art.

552

Suggestions for Themes

Afternoon in a Museum. A Painting Which Has "Language" but No Thought. Victorian Fondness for Pictures Which Told Stories. Pictures Should Be Kept in Folders, Not on Walls. The History of the Painting I Like Best. On Greatness in Art.

JOSEPH CONRAD · PREFACE TO *THE NIGGER OF THE NARCISSUS*

Conrad defines art as "a single-minded attempt to render the highest kind of justice to the visible universe, by bringing to light the truth. . . ." How do you interpret the meaning of the word "truth"? Have you discovered any simple truth about the world around you through the medium of art? What is meant by "realism," "romanticism," and "naturalism"? Conrad distinguishes between the scientist and the artist. Do you think his distinction is sound? Do you agree that "all art . . . appeals primarily to the senses"? Would you call a beautiful painting art, if it had "perfect blending of form and substance" but did not appeal to the emotions? Why does Conrad wish "to make men pause to look"? What does he want to make them see? Does Conrad think that the real purpose of art is not to please but to teach?

Suggestions for Themes

A Story by Conrad Viewed in the Light of His "Preface." Sentimentalism in Music (*or* Poetry; *or* Pictures). Conrad and Whistler Compared. A Great Book. The Use of Description in *The Grapes of Wrath*. Why I Prefer Science. Writing for Pleasure. Why I Like Hemingway.

JOHN HOLMES · THE GREAT RICH VINE

Do you agree with Holmes's definition of a poet? What is meant by the statement that a poet's "borders are forever shifting"? Holmes quotes Keats's statement that the poetic character "has as much delight in conceiving an Iago as an Imogen." Explain the meaning of this as you understand it. Do you agree that great poets are "physically and temperamentally the toughest" people in the world? Why must a poet's style be "his own or nothing"? How do you interpret Whitman's statement that "the acting is to the actor and actress, not to the audience"? Holmes says that the poet wants his poetry to be "an exact representation of his one peculiar inner rhythm." What does he mean by "inner rhythm"? How does Holmes's style add to the effectiveness of his critical observations?

553

Suggestions for Themes

Masefield's "Sea-Fever." The "Inner Rhythm" of Carl Sandburg. Why I Like (*or* Dislike) Free Verse. The Poetry of Children in Conversation. My Definition of Poetry. My Favorite Sonnet. Why I Like Robert Frost. Experiments in Verse-Writing. On Popular Ballads. Rhyme in Popular Songs.

CATHERINE D. BOWEN · THE ROAD TO MUSIC

With which attitude toward music do you agree, that of Charles Lamb or that of Catherine Bowen? Do you agree that in teaching children music one should "keep 'em at it, whether they like it or no"? Do you think that music interferes with social amusements? The writer points out that if one waited for a child to grow to love music, his muscles would become too old to benefit by training. Do you think that this is a sound argument? What method of interesting children in music does the writer suggest in preference to verbal persuasion? Do you agree that "Hello, Beautiful" is just "soda pop"? Do you agree that the radio belongs in the kitchen? Do you believe in the school "which lets go, which roars its enthusiasm, turns red in the face, and pounds its feet when pleased"? How should you describe the style of Catherine Bowen?

Suggestions for Themes

My First Recital. Playing in a Jazz Orchestra. Memories of Music in Childhood. The Instrument I Should Most Like to Play. Listening to Toscanini. Having to Entertain Guests by Playing the Violin or Piano. My Road to Music.

LEWIS MUMFORD · SOCIAL SIGNIFICANCE OF CONTEMPORARY ART

What is the explanation given by Mumford for the antagonism of totalitarian governments toward the artist? How has public art helped to reëstablish the position of the artist? Do you agree that the habit of drawing upon the symbols of his own country narrows the artist's view? Which do you think the more liberal purpose of art, that of the proletarian or that of the "patriotic" painter? By what argument does Mumford discount the importance of "immediate intelligibility" in art? Do you agree with him that art "is by its very nature propaganda"? Differentiate between a "sign," a "symbol," and an "emblem." Explain Mumford's statement that art aims "not so much at rational acceptance as at providing a common background in emotions and feelings."

554

Suggestions for Themes

"Emblems" of the Communists (or the American Legion; or the Fascists). The Art Center in Our Town. Why I Like "Easy Reading." Paintings Which Impressed Me in Childhood. My Patriotic Friend. The Meaning of Nationalism. The Federal Theater. Why I Studied Music (or Painting; or Wood Carving). A Book I Enjoyed although It Was Not "Immediately Intelligible." Art in Popular Advertisements. Examples of Propaganda from One Issue of a Current Magazine.

CHARLES W. FERGUSON · ART FOR OUR SAKE

Ferguson points out that even capable artists admit that surrealist painting is "beyond their depth." How do you explain this situation? Do you agree that surrealist and dada art are merely a reflection of the mental and emotional confusion of people today? Do you think it deserves to be called art? What is your reaction to Gertrude Stein's poem beginning "Sweet, sweet, sweet . . ."? How is this trend, which emphasizes confusion, reflected in music, in novels? How may the age be considered responsible for this trend? Do you believe that art is still going in that direction, or that it is turning away? Ferguson quotes Schiller as having said that you could tell an artist by what he leaves out. Explain what is meant.

Suggestions for Themes

On a Surrealist Painting. Freezing Your Thoughts at Any One Instant during the Day. The Jumbling of Words in Popular Music. Definition of Surrealism. The Follow-Up of Surrealism: the Quiz Age. Reading Gertrude Stein. The Influence of Surrealism on Commercial Art. Photomontage. America's Weakness for Fads.

FRANCIS BACON · SALOMON'S HOUSE

How do you interpret Bacon's statement that the "end of our foundation is the knowledge of causes and secret motions of things"? Do you agree that this is the "end of our foundation"? How has modern science made use of the "violent streams and cataracts" which Bacon said could "serve us for many motions"? What, in the present age, is comparable to the "chambers of health" described in the essay? Do you agree that the "dissection and trials" of beasts is of great benefit to mankind? Bacon spoke of "heats in imitation of the sun's." How has modern science nearly realized this vision, and to what uses has the discovery been put? What parts of Bacon's imaginary picture have not yet been achieved by man? Do you think Bacon deserves to be called a prophet of modern science, or do you think that others in his day could have made the same prophecies? Try to make your own prophecies concerning the world three centuries from now. Does the attempt increase your admiration for Bacon's vision?

Suggestions for Themes

Why I Should Like to Be an Aviator. My Meeting with a Scientist. Visiting a Fish Hatchery. A Day at the Fox Farm. Reflections While under an Ultraviolet Lamp. My First Experience with a Microscope. Why I Should Like to Own a Greenhouse. Going through a Coal Mine (*or* a Blast Furnace; *or* a Cold-Storage Plant). Comic Strips Which Picture the Future.

THOMAS HENRY HUXLEY · THE METHOD OF SCIENTIFIC INVESTIGATION

Does this essay strengthen your interest in science? How should you explain the difference between induction and deduction to a high-school student? Describe the train of reasoning known as a syllogism. Huxley says, "You may have hypotheses, and hypotheses." What is his implication? In facing personal problems, one is often forced to make a decision which will affect one's whole life. Do you think scientific reasoning in such a case is possible? Do you think it desirable? What devices does Huxley use to make his exposition of his subject interesting?

Suggestions for Themes

The Only Mystery I Ever Solved. How I Found My Watch. Why I Should Like to Be a Scientist. Inductive and Deductive Reasoning in Buying a Suit. A Person I Know Who Is Consistently Unscientific in His Reasoning. Why I Like to Make Rash Generalizations. On Dissecting a Frog. On Falling in Love. Why I Go to Church (*or* Do Not Go). Emotional Decisions I Have Made.

ARTHUR H. COMPTON · CAN SCIENCE POINT THE WAY?

Concerning the question "of the means of living," how do science and religion differ in your opinion? Do you agree that the welfare of mankind is the fundamental concern of both? By the use of examples, explain the difference between the scientific and the philosophical approach. Do you think there should be permanent institutes of government research? With which attitude do you sympathize most, that of the religionist, the philosopher, or the scientist? After reading this essay, do you think that science *can* point the way? How does Compton's ideal of scientific method and scientific knowledge compare with Huxley's?

Suggestions for Themes

What a Train Ride Meant to Me in My Childhood. My First Trip in an Airplane. How I Could Amuse Myself if Deprived of All the Benefits of Science. Why I Believe in Both Science and Religion. On Reading the Bible. Why I Should Like to Be a Geologist.

J. W. N. SULLIVAN · THE MYSTERY OF MATTER

In his explanation of the atom and its constituents, do you think Sullivan has presented as clear a picture as possible? What new things did you learn about matter in reading this essay? Is it difficult for you to conceive of all matter as being electricity? In what courses or previous reading have you studied the behavior of protons, electrons, and positrons? Is it inconceivable to you that an atom of light is "both big enough to fill the lens of the great Mount Wilson telescope and small enough to enter an atom"? Can you explain what is taking place in a radium atom? What is the purpose of atom "bombardment"? Do you think that because "matter will always be mysterious" science can gain no further knowledge of it? Do you believe in the doctrine of strict cause and effect in nature? Does the style of the author add to your enjoyment of the essay? Do you think this essay fascinating or tedious? Why?

Suggestions for Themes

Why I Should Like to Experiment with Heavy Hydrogen. An Experiment with Laughing Gas. Argument on Religion in a Science Class. Why I Liked My Physics Instructor. Why I Liked (or Disliked) Sullivan's Essay. My First Lesson in Science. Why I Should Like to Study Astronomy.

GEORGE W. GRAY · CHEMISTRY ADVANCING

Are you in the habit of evaluating science in terms of bread, butter, and cheese, rather than in terms of protons, neutrons, and deutrons? Which of the scientific processes described in this essay do you find most interesting? How does science help to make nations self-sufficient? Do you think this trend toward self-sufficiency desirable? Why, in your opinion, are the achievements of fundamental chemical research less obvious than those of the industrial laboratories? How is the discovery of heavy water an example of "knowledge pursued for its own sake"? Do you think chemical research should preoccupy itself with "profitable applications"? How great a part of its development do you think chemistry owes to industrial inspiration?

Suggestions for Themes

Living in a Glass House. Why I Am Interested in Forestry. Why I Like (*or* Dislike) Laboratory Experiments. A Research Laboratory I Have Visited. The Scientist and His Laboratory as Portrayed by the Movies. Why I Prefer the World of Art to the World of Science. Why I Prefer the World of Science to the World of Art. What I Consider the Most Interesting Branch of Science. The Scientist and My Daily Life.

ROBERT L. DUFFUS · THIS UNSCIENTIFIC AGE

Duffus states in the beginning of the essay: "Not only is our generation not scientific; it is less scientific than the generation which preceded it." How do you explain his meaning? Do you agree with the statement? Do you think that the man "who operates a motor car or twiddles the dials on a radio set" is more scientific than his ancestor "who drove a horse and played the fiddle"? What criticism does Duffus make of the modern city? Explain his statement that we are like the "barbarians who marched into Rome during the last day of the Empire." Do you agree that war is the "negation of science"? What reasons do you have for your opinion? After reading this essay, do you believe that this is a scientific age?

Suggestions for Themes

This Emotional Age. A Barbarian in Rome. Visiting the World's Fair. If I Were a Yankee in King Arthur's Court. My Definition of Scientific Reasoning. The Place Where I Should Like Best to Live. The Best Book on Science That I Have Read.

ARTHUR TRAIN, JR. · CATCHING UP WITH THE INVENTORS

Should you enjoy living as John Doe in 1988 does in this essay? Do any of the conveniences of such a life seem utterly impossible to you? Should you like to live in a house that appeared "no more than a part of the out-of-doors which had been etched into the frame with a few strokes of a sharp pointed pencil"? Which should you prefer, a book with printed pages or a talking book? Do you think that Train's prediction of the automobile—that it fills the role of the "station wagon of the late '30s" in children's play—is sound? What factors make it impossible for a people to enjoy all the fruits "of its own creative ability and enterprise"? Which essay did you enjoy more, "Salomon's House" or "Catching Up with the Inventors"?

558

Suggestions for Themes

Train's Predictions Compared with Those of Another Scientist. Science, as It Is Found in the Sunday-Paper Supplement. What I Consider the Greatest Invention of Mankind. Why I Enjoy Driving a Car. What I Should Like to Invent. Why I Believe (or Disbelieve) Train's Predictions.

SIR THOMAS BROWNE · OF THE ELEPHANT[1]

Is this paper an example of inductive or deductive reasoning? Do you think it is a serious discussion at all points, or do you think Sir Thomas is poking fun at the reader from time to time? Sir Thomas Browne's vocabulary is famous. Try to discover its main characteristics. What evidence of actual scientific experiment do you find in his record of his investigations? Name some errors commonly believed by the uneducated today. Does this paper help you to grasp more firmly the simple fact of the enormous progress in science since Sir Thomas Browne's day? In what ways is this essay a true research paper?

[1]Another example of the research paper is the article entitled "Fifth Column" which will be found on page 274.

Suggestions for Themes

Superstition in Baseball. Superstitions of the Sea. Why I Am (or Am Not) Superstitious. A Biographical Sketch of Sir Thomas Browne. Popular Belief in Astrology Today. Of Black Cats. Of the Number Thirteen.

KARL K. DARROW · NEUTRONS

For the student beginning college work, why is there probably no more immediately practical type of writing than training in the preparation of a research paper? How do the footnotes allow a rapid judgment of the thoroughness and impartiality of the work? What is the primary purpose of the research paper? How does it differ from other types of expository writing? Why do you think strict adherence to some established form of footnotes is most desirable?

This paper is an excellent model of the organization and documentation now in standard use in research papers on scientific subjects. Note the use of abbreviations in footnotes and bibliography. If you had even a general acquaintance with the literature of physics, would these abbreviations be quite clear? Do you consider this paper interesting? Do you think it was written solely for specialists in this field? What expository devices does the author use to keep his discussion clear at all times? What parts of the paper did you fail to understand? How many terms did you look up? Are any words used which cannot be found in a good dictionary?

Suggestions for Themes

A research paper, based on your own investigation, on some scientific topic which interests you.

The History of the Use of Ether. Recent Discoveries in the Use of Sulfanilamide. Vitamins and the Common Cold. The Cyclotron. Further Investigations of Solar Eclipses.

WALLACE CABLE BROWN · BYRON AND ENGLISH INTEREST IN THE NEAR EAST

Notice that Professor Brown uses footnotes not only to identify direct quotations but also for other purposes as well. What are these further uses for footnotes? Why do you think scholars use them? What is the purpose of the first paragraph? Make an outline of this paper, noting briefly the subject matter of each paragraph. Be prepared to describe the function of each step in the writer's development of his thesis. Why has the author placed some of his own discussion in the footnotes? What is the purpose of the supplementary bibliographies included in footnotes 4 and 14? Try to discover the meaning of all abbreviations used in the footnotes. What is the advantage to be gained in numbering the footnotes from 1 to 29 rather than in numbering page by page? When is it permissible to use *Op. cit.? Loc. cit.?*

Suggestions for Themes

American Interest in the Far East. Newspapers a Hundred Years Ago. Interest in Books of Travel Today.

A research paper, based on your own investigation, on early books of travel and exploration in America.

CAROLYN BURWELL · THE STORY OF THE CHRISTMAS SEAL

In the research papers by Professor Brown and Dr. Darrow the student has been supplied with models of professional papers which illustrate the correct handling of a variety of technical problems in the use of footnotes. These articles are by their nature somewhat technical in subject matter and have been presented in this volume in order that the student might study the differences in forms of documentation between the scientific and the literary research paper. The present paper is reprinted as an example of satisfactory student work in Freshman English. It is not, of course, professional work in either its background or its organization, but students should be encouraged to do painstaking research projects within the time

560

allotted by discovering that students in Freshman English everywhere are finding for themselves topics for investigation which are of universal interest. Almost any topic, from the story of the Christmas seal to the methods of manufacture of a lead pencil, can be developed into an informative research paper if the student will take the trouble to use to full advantage the research facilities of his college library. Note here that the student has consulted periodicals as well as books. Originally, since the paper was submitted in manuscript form, the footnotes were gathered together and placed at the end. This practice is followed in many professional research studies of book length and is a perfectly legitimate form of documentation.

JOHN WILSON CROKER · JOHN KEATS'S
ENDYMION

This single review from the distant past is reprinted both as an example of how *not* to write a review and for its historical interest to students of English literature. It is undoubtedly the most notorious review ever written. Keats at the time was an unknown and inexperienced young poet who had been befriended by the famous poet and journalist, Leigh Hunt. Unfortunately for Keats, Leigh Hunt and John Wilson Croker were enemies. Keats was the innocent victim of their quarrel, for this review was Croker's method of attacking Hunt indirectly. It is written in the approved reviewer's manner of that time; use of vulgar and humiliating personalities was then the rule rather than the exception. Keats at first was so discouraged that he declared he would write no more. He soon realized, however, that he must follow his chosen career with new vigor. In the next three years Keats produced work which has placed him in the very first rank of English poets. Keats's early death from tuberculosis gave rise to the tradition that hostile reviews had crushed his spirit, that at least indirectly they were responsible for his death. This notion is not only untrue but grossly unfair to Keats as a man.

Suggestions for Themes

Keats and Leigh Hunt. My Own Review of *Endymion*. A Review of a Contemporary Poet's Work. On Fitting the Review to the Book.

HOWARD MUMFORD JONES · ROSE WILDER
LANE'S *FREE LAND*

How does the first sentence establish the point of view of the entire review? Make a list of other points about the novel mentioned by the reviewer. How are these related to the central theme of the review? What is the implied tribute in the reviewer's comment that he dug himself "out of the snow for the nth time"? Study the use of topic sentences. How do they contribute to the clarity and vigor of this review? Does the reviewer make you want to read the book? Does he tell you all you need to know about the plot? Does this review give you a better idea of what the book is like than would a careful summary of the plot, no matter how complete? How much of the author's plot is it fair and sporting for the reviewer to reveal?

Suggestions for Themes

Write a review of a novel about your state.

WILLIAM ALLEN WHITE · LOUIS ADAMIC'S
MY AMERICA: 1928-1938

Why is this review much more factual than Howard Mumford Jones's review of *Free Land*? Why does the reviewer feel it necessary to assure us that the book has unity? How is the transition made between the first and second paragraphs? What do you consider the most interesting and stimulating sentence in the review? Note how sparingly Mr. White uses quotation from the book. How is the quotation beginning "I want America to have a chance . . ." made to serve as the central theme of the review? Do you think the review would have been stronger if it had included some adverse criticism? Do you think that the reviewer was too enthusiastic? Do you like the slang exclamation with which the review closes? Why is William Allen White particularly well qualified to review a book of this kind?

Suggestions for Themes

Write a review of a recent book about America or Americans.

LOUIS UNTERMEYER · OGDEN NASH'S
I'M A STRANGER HERE MYSELF

Who is Louis Untermeyer? Compare this review with Croker's review of Keats's *Endymion*. Do you think this review is on the whole friendly and constructive in its criticism? This review is a critical evaluation of Nash's work as a whole. Do you think Mr. Untermeyer has rather neglected the book he set out to review, or do you think an evaluation of a new book in terms of its author's former work is the fairest possible approach? Does Mr. Untermeyer tell you what the book is like, as Mr. White succeeded in telling you what Adamic's book was like? Note how carefully Mr. Untermeyer has organized his critical remarks under separate topics: line length, rhymes, etc. Do you think this strict organization in a review is helpful to the reader? The good reviewer never quotes for the mere sake of filling space, a principle the student will do well to adopt in his own work.

How does Mr. Untermeyer apply his quotations to the subject of the paragraph in which they appear? Mr. Untermeyer is famed for his caustic wit. Do you find evidence of it here? If the reviewer meant to be friendly, his review should make you want to read the book in spite of any adverse criticism included in the review. Do you now desire to read Mr. Nash's volume?

Suggestions for Themes

The Difference between Irony and Satire. A Review of a Volume of Humorous Verse. My Favorite Humorist. Types of American Humor.

BASIL DAVENPORT · DAPHNE DU MAURIER'S
REBECCA

Note that each book presents to the reviewer an individual problem. A review must be by its very nature a highly personal estimate of a book's worth. The student will certainly profit by a careful study of the kinds of things the professional reviewers single out to comment upon; but he must not suppose that the same topics would be important in criticizing all books. What is the purpose of the first sentence of this review? Does the long first paragraph seem to you well organized? Does the reviewer stop at exactly the right point in his summary of the plot? How is the second paragraph linked to the first? What idea is restated throughout the review? Do you prefer the measured praise here given to the enthusiasm displayed by William Allen White in his review of *My America*? Do you think that character and setting are given too little attention by the reviewer? Why do you think the reviewer begins so many sentences with the word "but"? Do you consider this an interesting and skillfully written review? Why?

Suggestions for Themes

Write a review of a current novel.

ARTHUR L. CROSS · WINSTON CHURCHILL'S
MARLBOROUGH

This is a scholar's review of a scholarly book. In what ways does the review differ from the others printed in this section? What parts of the review suggest that the writer has carefully weighed every word of praise and censure? Describe your exact impression of the book from your reading of the review. Make a brief outline of the structural organization of this review. To what points has the reviewer given particular emphasis?

Suggestions for Themes

Write a review of a biography.

CLIFTON FADIMAN · OSA JOHNSON'S
I MARRIED ADVENTURE

In what ways does this review differ in style from the other reviews you have examined? Do you think that Mr. Fadiman's emphasis on Mr. and Mrs. Martin Johnson themselves, rather than on their adventures, is a sound approach when reviewing a book of this type? Why? Mr. Fadiman neglects to tell us where the book begins and how it ends. Has he overlooked important points? Pick out the sentences in which the reviewer registers adverse criticism. What does Mr. Fadiman say in praise of the book? Restate in your own words the evaluation of the book given in this review. What does the word "feral" mean? How does Mr. Fadiman's use of unexpected words add to the reader's enjoyment of this selection?

Suggestions for Themes

Write a review of a book of travel or adventure. Write a review of an autobiography.

INDEX

INDEX

566

INDEX

PRINTED IN THE UNITED STATES OF AMERICA